integral theory in action

SUNY series in Integral Theory

Sean Esbjörn-Hargens, editor

integral theory in action

applied, theoretical,
and constructive perspectives
on the AQAL model

edited by
sean esbjörn-hargens

Published by State University of New York Press, Albany

©2010 State University of New York

For information, contact State University of New York Press, Albany, NY
www.sunypress.edu

Production by Ryan Morris
Marketing by Michael Campochiaro

Library of Congress Cataloging-in-Publication Data

Integral theory in action : applied, theoretical, and constructive perspectives on the AQAL
   model / edited by Sean Esbjörn-Hargens.
   p. cm.—(SUNY series in integral theory)
Includes bibliographical references and index.
ISBN 978-1-4384-3385-1 (hardcover : alk. paper)—ISBN 978-1-4384-3384-4
   (pbk. : alk. paper)   1. Social sciences—Research—Methodology.
   2. Interdisciplinary research.   I. Esbjörn-Hargens, Sean.
H62.I6523 2010
300.1—dc22

                                                          2010005118

10 9 8 7 6 5 4 3 2 1

This book is dedicated to my wife,
Vipassana Esbjörn-Hargens

Whom I first met at Ken Wilber's house at an early Integral Institute meeting and who has been right next to me as I have developed and contributed to the field of Integral Theory. My contribution would not be possible without her love, support, and patience.

Contents

List of Illustrations

Figures

Tables

Acknowledgments

In the summer of 2008, John F. Kennedy University (JFKU) hosted in partnership with Integral Institute (II) the first biennial Integral Theory Conference (ITC) in Pleasant Hill, California, August 7–10. All of the chapters in this book were originally written for and presented at this conference. As you can imagine, launching an ongoing academic conference for an emerging field is no small feat. Special appreciation goes out to all those who prepared for, attended, and presented at ITC 2008. By all accounts the event was a success and set in motion a trajectory of scholarship and practice that will serve the future ITCs well. The conference team at JFKU is already busy at work preparing for ITC 2010. Our sense is that this second conference stands to be even better than the first. Time will tell.

In particular, I would like to thank a number of key individuals whose contributions made the first conference and this volume possible. First of all, a deep gasho bow goes to Ken Wilber for his excitement and support for the aims of the conference, which in many ways are about going beyond him and allowing many scholar-practitioners to join the conversation and contribute to the development of Integral Theory. His capacity to see the value of this initiative for the development of the field speaks to his generous and visionary nature.

I owe my conference co-founder and co-organizer Mark Forman a huge acknowledgment. While I had mentioned to people at JFKU over the years, "Wouldn't it be great to host an integral conference here?" This event would *never* have happened had it not been for Mark's initiative and hard work. Ever since Mark approached me with the idea in the summer of 2007, he consistently was the engine pulling the conference train—leading us through all the terrain that comes with "figuring it out for the first time." It was such a joy to work (and play) alongside Mark in creating and producing the conference.

Mark and I were blessed to have an enormously competent and dynamic conference team. The core team consisted of David Zeitler, John Scheunhage, Jordan Luftig, Anne Marie Taylor, and Carissa Wieler. Each one of these individuals brought unique talents and vision to the process as we met weekly for most of a year and have contributed to the contents of this volume in numerous ways. Peter Rojcewicz, the Dean of the School of Holistic Studies (SHS), played a particularly valuable role in championing the conference from the beginning and ensuring that it was a success. Alongside Peter were the faculty members of the SHS who have consistently supported the development of JFKU as a global leader in the field of Integral Theory. Special mention goes to Ray Greenleaf, Vernice Solimar, Michele Chase, Theresa Silow, and Marilyn Fowler. Other key individuals at JFKU who played an important role include Alex Kramer and Susan Davi, both of whom provided much needed guidance in making sure the conference interfaced seamlessly with the university. At Integral Institute, Mark and I were supported by Robb Smith and Clint Fuhs, both of whom were quite instrumental in making the conference happen.

It has been a delight to work with Jane Bunker of State University of New York, who not only has supported the publication of this volume, but whose excitement for the emerging field of Integral Theory has made possible the SUNY book series in Integral Theory. Jane's commitment to transpersonal, holistic, and integral approaches to academics is inspiring and much needed in the academy. Lastly, I wish to thank Lynwood Lord, the managing editor of the *Journal of Integral Theory and Practice* (JITP), for his extensive formatting work on early versions of the manuscript as well as his helpful edits on the introduction and Brad Reynolds, the graphic artist who converted all the tables and figures in the volume into the art that now graces its pages. I have the pleasure of working with both Lynwood and Brad in the context of JITP, so I was quite pleased to have their talent supporting this project as well.

Four of the papers presented at the conference and contained in this volume were published in part or whole as earlier versions after the conference and before the publication of this volume. Chapter 1, "An Overview of Integral Theory: An All-inclusive Framework for the Twenty-First Century," originally appeared as a white paper for the Integral Institute: S. Esbjörn-Hargens, *An Overview of Integral Theory: An All-inclusive Framework for the 21st Century* (Resource Paper No. 1) (Boulder: Integral Institute. 2009). Chapter 2, "An Integral Perspective on Climate Change: Implications for Response Strategies," by Karen O'Brien, originally appeared as a white paper for the Integral Institute: K. O'Brien, *Responding to Climate Change: The Need for an Integral Approach* (Resource Paper No. 4) (Boulder: Integral Institute, 2009). Chapter 4, "Beauty and the Expansion of Women's Identity," by Vanessa Fisher, is based on an earlier version of the article that was published directly after the ITC: V. Fisher, "Beauty and the Expansion of Women's Identity," *Journal of Integral Theory and Practice* 3(3) (2008): 68–86. Chapter 16, "Of Elephants and Butterflies: An Integral Metatheory for Organizational Transformation," by Mark Edwards, is based on and includes material from M. G. Edwards, *Organisational Transformation For Sustainability: An Integral Metatheory* (New York: Routledge, 2010).

Foreword: The Integral Enterprise

Current Frontiers and Possible Futures

Roger Walsh

The integral enterprise, which focuses so centrally on development, is itself developing. The number of people using it is increasing, the range of applications expanding, and the sophistication of thinking deepening. What was initially the vision of one brilliant man, Ken Wilber, has expanded into a multinational, multidisciplinary, theoretical, and practical enterprise. In some ways this is surprising. For as Zachary Stein points out in his chapter, integral ideas are not necessarily simple or easy. Likewise, Susanne Cook-Greuter's chapter demonstrates that the higher developmental stages, which the integral vision points to and aspires to foster, are rare. Yet the desire for a vision, a synthesis, that encompasses and frames the avalanche of information now upon us seems to be attracting surprising numbers of people to Integral Theory and its application.

Of course, enormous—in fact, boundless—amounts of work remain to be done. The integral vision needs to expand, deepen, refine, and be more widely applied. We are looking at decades of exploration and work—work that will transform and mature the integral enterprise in currently inconceivable ways. Just as transhumanists suggest that future technologies may so transform humanity as to birth a new species of "transhumans," who are barely recognizable to us, so too, the integral enterprise will hopefully evolve into an ever more comprehensive and effective "transintegral" discipline beyond our current range of vision. Satprem, the biographer of the great Indian philosopher-sage, Aurobindo, described the difficulties of recognizing the higher potentials and possibilities of Aurobindo's integral vision in this way:

> This is why it is so difficult to explain the path to one who has not tried; he will see only his point of view of today or rather the loss of his point of view. And yet, if we only knew how each loss of one's viewpoint is a progress and how life changes when one passes from the stage of the closed truth to the stage of the open truth—a truth like life itself, too great to be trapped

by points of view, because it embraces every point of view and sees the utility of each thing at every stage of an infinite development; a truth great enough to deny itself and pass endlessly into a higher truth. (Satprem, 1968, 84)

This is an exquisite description of some of the challenges of integral maturation. Yet this maturation that is being asked of integral practitioners is necessary to effectively foster the further development of the integral enterprise. What will this development require? Answer: at least, two things—a lot of very careful work, and becoming *gnostic intermediaries*.

Requisites for Furthering the Integral Enterprise

To ensure a positive hearing for integral ideas, and to facilitate entry into the mainstream, will require considerable high-quality work. Conceptually, this will include rigorous thinking, precise analysis, and thoughtful criticism. Practically, it will involve careful experiments to test the theory, and successful applications of the theory. However, as noted above, integral effectiveness will also require something further. It will also involve that we develop into "gnostic intermediaries." So what is a gnostic intermediary?

The term was first used by Carl Jung to refer to Richard Wilhelm, the translator of the *I Ching*. Jung suggested that Wilhelm embodied the wisdom of the *I Ching* so fully, that he could communicate it directly from his own experience. More generally, a gnostic intermediary is a person who is able to directly transmit wisdom from one culture or community to another. In the case of integral, this means transmitting wisdom from the world's spiritual and contemplative disciplines, and from non–Western psychologies and philosophies. What does this demand?

It seems to require three tasks and capacities. First, one must imbibe, and even become, the wisdom oneself. This is no small task. In fact, imbibing spiritual wisdom can easily take a lifetime. Yet imbibing some of this wisdom is important for integral practitioners, since the upper reaches of the integral vision draw on the accumulated wisdom of the world's spiritual traditions. As such, this vision aspires to communicate and foster their second- and third-tier understandings. Comprehending and communicating these postconventional and transconventional understandings is one of the major challenges, and opportunities, for integral practitioners and contributors.

The second requirement of gnostic intermediaries is linguistic and conceptual competence. They must master the language and conceptual system of the people and culture to which they wish to communicate. For integral practitioners, this will mean mastering the terms and concepts of specific contemporary disciplines—such as psychology, philosophy, anthropology, psychotherapy, and more.

The third requirement involves translation. Gnostic intermediaries must be able to skillfully translate the wisdom from wisdom-bearing cultures into the language and conceptual system of the recipient culture and discipline, in such as way as to create an "Aha!" experience of understanding.

So to be an effective integral practitioner asks a lot. Yet fortunately, such people are coming forward in increasing numbers, and the book you hold in your hands demonstrates this well. The authors are committed scholars, contemplative practitioners, and effective contributors. Together, they are skillfully deepening, critiquing, refining, and applying the integral vision, and thereby pushing the integral vision into novel dimensions and depths. To read this book is to be inspired by the work of these authors, and to appreciate the innumerable potential facets of the integral enterprise.

Notes

Editor's note: For an expanded version of this foreword see R. Walsh, "The State of the Integral Enterprise, Part 1: Current Status and Potential Traps," *Journal of Integral Theory and Practice* 4(3) (2009): 1–12; and R. Walsh, "The State of the Integral Enterprise, Part 2: Key Ideas for a World at Risk," *Journal of Integral Theory and Practice* 4(3) (2009): 13–22. Both of these articles are based on the keynote address that Roger Walsh delivered at the first biennial Integral Theory Conference (August 7–10, 2008, Pleasant Hill, CA).

References

Satprem. 1968. *Sri Aurobindo or the adventure of consciousness*. Trans. L. Venet. New York: Harper and Row.

Introduction

Integral Theory in Action

Sean Esbjörn-Hargens

When 500 individuals from 30 countries gathered in Pleasant Hill, California, to listen to 100 individual talks, 12 panels, and 20 poster presentations, something extraordinary happened at the first biennial Integral Theory Conference (ITC) in 2008. Just as when the crew of the Apollo 17 mission took the famous "Blue Marble" picture of our Earth, and people could for the first time take the planet as an object of awareness, so could the integral community finally see its global face. It was the first international gathering of integral scholar-practitioners; transforming Integral Theory from "subject to object" (to borrow a phrase from Robert Kegan's model of transformation).

For the first time, the integral community could take Integral Theory as an object of critical reflection and exploratory dialogue. No longer was Integral Theory primarily a set of two dozen books written by one man and a series of blogosphere debates between that man and some of his critics. Rather, Integral Theory became, in the course of one weekend, an actively networked global community of scholar-practitioners from 50 distinct disciplines. Obviously, individuals have been applying Integral Theory for many years to their personal and professional contexts. The difference I am pointing to here is that most of those examples of Integral Theory in action occurred in isolated pockets, without the benefit of their pioneers being part of a larger community of praxis and discourse.

Thus, ITC 2008 brought together academics and practitioners from all over the world who are working within and helping to develop the field of Integral Theory. Conversations that had never occurred or been possible before were all of a sudden a reality. This experience reminded me of learning French and how at a certain point after learning lots of isolated new words, phrases, verb conjunctions, and rules of grammar there would come, in almost an instant, a new level of connectivity in my grasp of the language and whole new worlds of conversation—in French—were made available to me. Similarly, ITC 2008 supported an emergent level of discourse as it interlinked, placed into contact,

1

juxtaposed, and contrasted important perspectives on Integral Theory. Thus, this volume is the result of that historic global gathering and is both a testament to the current state of this exciting and emerging field and a contribution toward the further application, refinement, development, and critique of Integral Theory. Each contribution in this volume provides a glimpse into the new kinds of conversations that are now possible within Integral Theory.

In recent years, an increasing number of scholars have begun to use Integral Theory in their courses and published work, as well as graduate students using it for their research. For example, over the past 10 years, 100 theses and dissertations have been written using Integral Theory as their primary theoretical foundation—many of which have actually been written in the past five years.[1] This fact highlights that Integral Theory is increasingly gaining acceptance as an approach for conducting scholarly research in academic contexts. The primary areas of focus of these theses and dissertations are: religion and spirituality; psychology, psychiatry, and psychotherapy; ecology; education; art; and health and medicine.

Likewise, in the past decade there have been more than 150 articles published in minor and major peer-reviewed academic journals, including *Journal of Transpersonal Psychology, Constructivism in the Human Sciences, Journal of Consciousness Studies, Counseling and Values, Journal of Business Ethics, The Journal of Future Studies, Journal of Organizational Change Management, Advances in Nursing Science, Journal of Contemporary Criminal Justice,* and *Journal of Men's Studies.*[2] To date, the academic fields that have produced the largest amount of theoretical and applied material using Integral Theory include: psychotherapy and psychology; education; research; ecology and sustainability; future studies; and business and management.

In addition to these uses in academic contexts, there have been more systematic efforts to establish Integral Theory as a legitimate field of discourse and application. In particular, there are five main efforts that are currently contributing to this happening: a journal, an online master's program, a research center, an international conference, and an academic book series. In reviewing these projects and their affiliated efforts, we can gain a sense of how far Integral Theory has come as an academic discipline in just the past five years and obtain a sense of the trajectory this exciting new approach is on. Mentioning these developments here, as you will see, will set the stage for highlighting the significance and timeliness of this volume.

An Academic Journal

In 2003, I established the *Journal of Integral Theory and Practice* (JITP), an academic, peer-reviewed, theoretically vetted venue for content exploring the AQAL model.[3] After three years of establishing the formal structures and soliciting content and editing 40 articles simultaneously, the first two issues appeared in 2006. Over the past four years (2006–2009), JITP has published 140 articles (approximately 3,000 pages of applied integral content). And for the year ahead we already have enough articles to fill all four issues. So clearly there is a lot of academic material being generated by integral scholar-practitioners from around the world. In addition to JITP, there is *Integral Review* (IR), another academic journal that has emerged as an important voice on integral studies in general and has published valuable articles that focus on Integral Theory. In short, over the past few years an impressive amount of academic material has been published on Integral Theory. Michele Chase's chapter in this volume provides a wonderful analysis of the strengths and weaknesses of JITP and its content over the first two and one-half years of publication (i.e,, the first nine issues).

An Academic Program

In the summer of 2005, I began putting a proposal together at John F. Kennedy University to create an online Master of Arts degree solely devoted to Integral Theory. In 2006, we got approval to begin a one-year certificate (10 courses/25 units) in Integral Theory. This certificate was set up to double as the first year of the master's. The following fall (August 2007), we received full accreditation for the MA degree. We are now moving into our fifth year of the program. Each year since its inception we have received more applications for admissions than the previous year. Beginning this fall we will have around 100 students enrolled in the program and 20 faculty associated with it.

Also in the summer of 2005, at the same time that I was working with JFKU to create the Integral Theory program, Randy Martin and I began developing an Integral Theory certificate and an Integral Theory track in Organization Management and Development at Fielding Graduate University. As with JFKU, these integral programs were first offered in Fall 2006.

In fall of 2006 I approached Allan Combs, who had recently been hired by California Institute of Integral Studies, about setting up an Integral Theory track in their online PhD program in Transformative Studies. We explored various structures for the program and I encouraged him to investigate what might work best in his program. He continued to work toward developing this track in spite of various obstacles. In 2008, this track began and requires students to use Integral Theory as the basis for their dissertation research (e.g., honoring first-, second-, and third-person perspectives; recognizing the developmental dimension of individuals). In summary, since 2006 a number of academic programs at the graduate school level (certificates, tracks, and a full master's program) based on Integral Theory have been launched and are enjoying success. Thus, prospective Integral Theory students have an increasing number of choices for their Integral Education.

An Academic Research Center

For years I imagined supporting graduate students the world over who wanted to use the Integral model in their studies and use Integral Methodological Pluralism in their research. I recall all too painfully what it was like trying to incorporate the AQAL model in my graduate studies, going against the cultural grain of my alma mater. Consequently, when I developed the online program at JFKU I built into it funding for establishing an Integral Research Center (IRC). This center was launched in March 2008 in conjunction with the publication of two special issues of JITP devoted to Integral Research (Vol. 3, No. 1 and Vol. 3, No. 2).

The IRC is committed to the development and promotion of informal and formal mixed-method research that utilizes first-, second-, and third-person practices informed by the AQAL model. As a result, the IRC is a pioneer of developing and applying Integral Methodological Pluralism. The center accomplishes this through a variety of activities, including: providing $10,000 annually for scholarships, a $5,000 annual research grant for graduate students in the online MA in Integral Theory, and a $5,000 annual research grant for a non-JFKU graduate student conducting mixed methods research informed by Integral Theory; doing original research using six methodologies on the transformative effects of Integral Education; providing a discussion forum for graduate students interested in or doing Integral Research in their thesis or dissertation; promoting Integral Field Studies courses that provide individuals the opportunity to practice real-time applications of integral principles and methods and an opportunity to bear witness to grassroots organizations utilizing "folk" Integral approaches in the global South; publishing academic articles and original research through special issues of JITP; supporting scholar-practitioners through the provision of various resources (e.g., articles, charts, examples, case studies, lists of methods, ways to synthesize and integrate data); and sponsoring an Integral Research track at the biennial Integral Theory Conference, which provides researchers a chance to present their findings, methods, and ideas around Integral Research. Thus, the IRC is committed to supporting the global community of integral scholar-practitioners.

The establishment of Integral Research as a new approach to mixed methods is one of the most important contributions toward legitimizing Integral Theory. It accomplishes this by providing Integral Theory with the methodological means by which to critically and empirically explore its claims, refine its theoretical distinctions, and effectively apply itself to more disciplinary contexts.

As noted above, numerous master's theses and dissertations have drawn heavily or exclusively on Integral Theory. Yet none of these efforts have had the benefit of being able to use an established integral methodology. In most cases, these efforts use Integral Theory or some aspect of it (e.g., the four quadrants) as an interpretive framework within which they make sense of positions, worldviews, and data from various approaches. In some cases, scholars have used Integral Theory to help them organize and augment their own original research efforts. In spite of these pioneering efforts, I have often heard graduate students exclaim some version of, "I want to use Integral Theory but my committee doesn't know what it is and I don't know how to actually use it for research!" With this distress call echoing in my mind and resonating in my heart, I set about establishing a new form of research and began teaching courses in three graduate-level programs on Integral Research.

An Academic Biennial Conference

For many years I have envisioned the existence of a regular academic conference devoted to Integral Theory: a conference that would serve as a global gathering of integral scholar-practitioners. In fact, I recall the early meetings of Integral Institute, in 2000 and 2001, where this was a common suggestion made by participants: "Let's have a major conference!" While such suggestions were always greeted with head nodding and enthusiasm, no one stepped forward to organize such a major event. So, for more than eight years this idea was floating in the integral air. In 2007, I submitted to JFKU, as part of the five-year vision for the Integral Theory program, the idea of JFKU hosting an international conference by 2010. Thus, when my colleague and friend Mark Forman approached me in the summer of 2007 about doing a major conference on Integral Theory at JFKU, I jumped at the chance.

When Mark and I sent out the call for papers in September 2007, we hoped to receive 50 to 70 submissions. We were amazed at the overwhelming response! In total, we received more than 120 great submissions. As a result we restructured the conference to be able to showcase the top 100 individual presentations. In addition, we set up 12 panels on important topics relevant to the future of Integral Theory (e.g., "Does Integral = Ken Wilber?" "Integral Theory in Academia," "The Integral Body," and "Integral Education"). There were also around 20 poster presentations. Thus, over 120 academics from all over the world gathered to present at the conference either in individual presentations, poster sessions, or on panels. So clearly, the academic world was ready for such a conference and arguably it was several years overdue. JFKU and Integral Institute will host this conference every other year. Now there will be an ongoing venue for academics to showcase their integral applications, theoretical musings, and Integral Methodological Pluralism research.[4]

The title of the first biennial Integral Theory Conference was *Integral Theory in Action: Serving Self, Other, and Kosmos.* This event was the culmination of a remarkable year of planning and communication with the larger integral community. While we anticipated a solid turnout of presenters and attendees, we were surprised at the overwhelming interest generated by the event (e.g., selling out with 500 attendees nearly two months prior to the conference and generating a waiting list of nearly 300). We felt this level of interest was an indication of a new phase of Integral Theory, wherein a global network of scholar-practitioners can begin to have an academic conversation. We were deeply moved by the response since announcing this event, and inspired by the connections facilitated between presenters and attendees alike.

Our intention for the conference was to make Integral Theory the object of critical reflection and the subject of applied discussion. The goal was to provide an academic forum where we could ask pressing questions concerning the state and potential growth of the integral field: What types of research and scholarly analysis need to be engaged to carry the integral field forward? What works and does not work in terms of applying Integral Theory in our various professions? What are the strengths and limits of the AQAL model and what alternative views need to be considered and explored? We hoped that the conference would create a space for a diversity of perspectives expressed through free thought, respectful challenge, theoretical exploration, and shared celebration. We believed the ITC would help set the tone for the integral field for years to come, and we were guided by the premise that the deeper the exchange that happened at the conference, the greater the benefits would be for the larger integral community. The overview of chapters below will give you a sense of the kinds of content, issues, and debates that were present at the first ITC as well as illuminate some of the key issues facing the growing field of Integral Theory.

An Academic Book Series

Given the success of the conference and the amount of material it produced, I decided that an edited volume based on the conference would be a valuable resource for integral scholar-practitioners. I approached SUNY about this idea and Jane Bunker, editor-in-chief, was very excited and interested. I was also doing a co-edited volume on Integral Education with SUNY and I was aware that SUNY was also in the process of publishing Mark Forman's book on Integral Psychotherapy. As I realized that SUNY was in the process of simultaneously publishing three books on or related to Integral Theory, I had the idea of doing an entire academic book series on Integral Theory. Jane was enthusiastic about the idea and before I knew it, it was a reality. So over the past 18 months I have been busy clarifying the vision of the series and talking with potential authors.

The SUNY Series in Integral Theory presents authored and edited volumes that are committed to improve and diversify integral thought and the application of the AQAL model. It purposes to do this by turning Integral Theory onto itself: as an act of theoretical-applied self-reflection. In so doing, the series will play an important role in setting the stage for the continual emergence of Integral Theory as a legitimate field of academic discourse within multiple disciplines. The series proposes to do this by bringing together the best academics in the field of Integral Theory and showcasing their work through applications, theoretical extension and clarification, and critical reflection. Integral Theory will flourish insofar as valuable contributions are made to it via direct criticism, theoretical clarification, and real-world application from many individuals working within its principles.

The series will publish three to five books each year, which aim to deepen the conversation around Integral Theory and its application. While the majority of these books will be grounded in the AQAL model, the series will also include alternative and complementary approaches to Integral Theory. In 2010 this volume and three others will be published (two on Integral Psychotherapy and one on Integral Education), with the entire series launched at ITC 2010.[5] Currently there are a number of manuscripts (e.g., on Integral Recovery, Integral Gender Studies, Integral Meta-Studies, and Integral Religious Studies) in process for publication in 2011, with another dozen being considered or written. Many of the scholar-practitioner's that presented at ITC 2008 and who will present at ITC 2010 will be featured as authors and editors within this series. Thus, this new book series will go a long way in helping to showcase the amazing integral work that is occurring around the planet.

In summary, these recent academic developments (quarterly journal, online graduate programs, research center, biennial conference, book series) signal a whole new phase of the integral movement: the development of a global community grounded in the tradition of academic discourse. This emerging academic community now has the support of traditional academic institutions such as peer-review journals, international conferences, and accredited graduate programs. Consequently, Integral Theory can now more than ever begin to increase its status as a legitimate academic and applied approach to the complex problems we face in our local communities and across the globe. Finally, there is an emergent network of academics and practitioners who are working together to share their integral insights and bring forward their critical observations. When one considers that each of these academic initiatives features prominently the term *Integral Theory*, it raises the issue of how exactly this term is being used. Is this use of Integral Theory primarily referring to Ken Wilber's approach, or is it a more generic use to refer to any and all integral approaches (e.g., Aurobindo, Gebser, László)? Since I have played a major role in the creation of each of these initiatives, I can clearly state that I hold them all in a "Wilberian" light. Since this an appropriately controversial topic, let me spend some time explaining why and what I mean by Wilberian.

Integral Theory and Integral Studies

It was around 2000 that Ken Wilber and scholar-practitioners using Wilber's Integral approach (i.e., Wilberians) began to refer to his body of work and secondary material as *Integral Theory*. Just to provide you a sense of the span and depth of this body of work, I currently estimate Wilber's corpus at approximately 10,000 pages of published material spanning three decades and I conservatively estimate the related Wilberian material also at approximately 10,000 pages of published material spanning mostly the past decade, with the latter figure growing rapidly each year.[6] The point I am making in providing these page estimates is to demonstrate that there is a substantial body of material (mostly academic) that is based directly on or inspired by Wilber's integral vision and its AQAL model. This body of work is officially called by Wilber and his students Integral Theory. In other words, it is the name they have assigned to this corpus.[7]

The use by Wilber and others to refer to his Integral approach as Integral Theory (i.e., as a proper noun) was formalized in 2003 when I founded the *Journal of Integral Theory and Practice*, which is and has always been explicitly a Wilberian venue. This usage of Integral Theory was reinforced in 2005 when I began to establish the Department of Integral Theory at JFKU, which is primarily based on Wilber's Integral approach. Then in 2007, Mark Forman and I set about creating the biennial Integral Theory Conference. As with the previous initiatives, this too was conceived of as primarily a Wilberian enterprise. The following quote from Mark and myself illustrates how "Wilberian" is to be understood (i.e., not as "Wilbercentric" or Wilber exclusive, but rather as Wilber-based, that is, built upon the foundation provided by Wilber and his proponents and critics):

> One of the major aims of the conference in general . . . is to decouple Ken Wilber and Integral Theory. We bring a deep honoring of what Wilber has enacted through his writings and activities and an excited anticipation of any new writings he generates. He is without a doubt the most important

theorist associated with Integral Theory and there is no reason to assume this will change anytime soon. But to this orientation we also bring a desire to make sure Integral Theory receives the benefit of many contributors. In other words, we do not want Integral Theory to be a "one man show." *We are fine with "Wilberian Theory" being synonymous with "Integral Theory" as long as "Wilberian Theory" is understood to mean "AQAL Theory" and not meant as "Ken's Theory."* So while Wilber might be the originator of Integral Theory, as Freud is the originator of psychoanalysis, he does not own Integral Theory. In our view, Integral Theory will only thrive insofar as valuable contributions to its criticism, clarification, application, and expansion come from many individuals working within its context and not just taking aim from the outside (e.g., by people who have never really tried applying the AQAL model to some contemporary issue). While we welcome insights from the "outside," it is our experience that they are of less value than those that come from a committed place to improve Integral Theory by turning Integral Theory onto itself: an act of theoretical-applied self-reflection.

For us, Integral Theory is bigger than Wilber, even though Wilber is a big, important, and valuable figure within Integral Theory. (Forman and Esbjörn-Hargens, this volume, 23–31; emphasis added)

Consequently, in this volume, and in the context of the other initiatives outlined above, I make a distinction between *Integral Theory* and *integral studies*. Integral Theory is used to refer to Ken Wilber's writings and those scholar-practitioners who are contributing to the development of the AQAL model through application, theoretical extension, and constructive critique. In contrast, integral studies is the wider category and is used more generally to include the writings of Wilber (and Wilberians) as well as individuals with their integrative visions, such as Rudolph Steiner's esoteric cosmology, Jean Gebser's sociocultural analysis of worldviews, Sri Aurobindo's integral yoga psychology, Ervin Lász-ló's TOE based in physics and systems thinking, William Torbert's Developmental Action Inquiry, and Don Beck's Spiral Dynamics Integral model of value systems. Also, integral studies can be broadly construed to also include metatheory (e.g., George Ritzer's work in sociology), critical realism (e.g., Roy Bhaskar's work in philosophy of science), and science and technology studies (e.g., Bruno Latour's work in the sociology of scientific knowledge).

I find that this distinction between Integral Theory and integral studies is justified for a number of reasons. First, Wilber himself (and his proponents) calls his integral approach Integral Theory. They have done this for almost a decade. No other approach that I am aware of refers to itself in name as "integral theory." Clearly, many consider themselves to have an integral theory(e.g., Sorokin's "integral theory of truth and reality" or Lászlzó's "integral theory of everything"), but that is different than naming their theory "Integral Theory." Because Wilber calls his work Integral Theory, I feel he and others are justified in using a capitalized "Integral" when "Integral" is synonymous with Integral Theory or the AQAL model. Similarly, capitalization of terms such as "the Integral framework," "the Integral model," and "the Integral approach," or even of fields such as "Integral Ecology" or "Integral Psychotherapy," are all justified when the context is clear that such capitalizations are being used to communicate that "Integral = AQAL." This is the case in this volume. This use of capitalization is less of a colonizing "branding move" (which it is often accused of) and more commonly, I believe, an issue of grammar and common stylistic representation. While not currently a dominant practice it is academically acceptable to capitalize the names of single author theories (e.g., Fisher's Skill Theory, Torbert's Developmental Action Inquiry). I do not want to deny the politicized dimension of this, but I feel all too often the grammatical reasons for such capitalizations are ignored in favor of alleged sinister motives on behalf of Wilber's Sauronic plan to "rule them all." After all, it is totally acceptable for other integral traditions to capitalize "Integral" when referring to non-Wilberian approaches, as long as they make the context clear. Aurobindeans do this all the time with Integral Psychology and Integral Education. Just because Wilberians use capitalization to signify their approach does not mean that they think they now own "integral." Equating "Integral" with AQAL is no doubt provocative to many in the wider integral community. However, the point here is not that other integral approaches cannot capitalize integral in their own contexts. Thus, this is often less of a power-truth move (AQAL is the best and only approach to integral) and is more often a stylistic move (AQAL is synonymous with Integral when capitalized, given Integral Theory is a proper noun).

Second, as noted above, Wilber and his proponents have produced a massive amount of theoretical and applied material—enough material that it often surpasses in both quality (e.g., coherence, internal consistency, fecundity, and parsimony) and scope many so called integral theories. In other words, Integral Theory as a Wilberian enterprise is quite substantial. In fact, it is currently being used in more than three dozen distinct disciplines, which is more than any other current integral approach. Although Steiner's and Aurobindo's both have quite an impressive portfolio of applied examples across many disciplines neither of their integral approaches is used in as many fields as Wilber's. Nor is Bhaskar's critical realism or meta-Reality as widely applied at so many scales both in popular, professional, and academic contexts. One of the consequences of this range of application is that it signals an unprecedented momentum, scale, and accessibility to Integral Theory that has yet to be enjoyed by any non-Wilberian approaches to integral. This widespread accessibility of Integral Theory has made it quite common parlance to use "Integral Theory" in a Wilberian sense. In other words, the amount of individuals who use it in a non-Wilberian sense is relatively quite small, I believe, in both the literature and applied settings.

Third, Wilber has produced the AQAL framework, which is a metaframework that is arguably dare I say more integral (e.g., inclusive) than most other approaches that might aspire to the status of an integral theory. For example, Gebser's sociocultural theory of evolution is an integral theory of primarily one aspect of reality—cultural evolution. Gebser does not have a well-developed theory of subtle energies, the relationship between psychological stages and transpersonal states, the mind-body problem, the way major methodological families are related to each other (to name just a few areas where Wilber excels). This is not to assign fault to Gebser; I am simply pointing out that specific theories that contribute to an integral theory of reality often fall far short, in my view, from being complete. Besides, having a theory about the integral structure of consciousness in cultures (à la Gebser) or individuals does not in itself create an integral theory. Similarly, a theory that comes from integral awareness (e.g., the Autonomous level of Jane Loevinger's model of ego development) does not ensure you will have an integral theory. When I look around at all the possible contenders for a robust integral theory, I am struck by the inclusive dynamic architecture that Wilber and associates have crafted. Whether one likes or dislikes Wilber or his AQAL model, one is hard-pressed not to acknowledge the comprehensive nature and inclusive potential of his integral vision. Thus, Wilber's Integral Theory is arguably the most integral of all the integral theories.

Fourth, much of what passes for an "integral theory" is more of an approach than it is an actual theory. In contrast, Wilber is a serious theoretician and is quite skilled at what he does. I feel it is fair to say that he is the most sophisticated theory builder currently associated with integral studies. I would place Roy Bhaskar high on the list, but one of the things that I feel sets Wilber and Integral Theory apart is its accessibility to the average well-educated adult (in contrast to Bhaskar's critical realism, which remains largely associated with professional academics). Also, in my experience, many of the so-called integral theories actually are less of a theory than they are an approach. Thus, I feel there are many integral approaches out there, with Wilber's AQAL model being just one of them, but when it comes to integral theories, I would contend there are very few integral ones (and, as noted above, of those integral theories I feel Wilber's is currently the most integral in that it includes more than most and has the potential to include more than any other theory). Also, Wilber's Integral Theory is arguably the most theoretical of all the integral theories. Ironically, this theoretical maturity is in part what lends its self to being applied in so many different contexts.

Another issue related to these points is that it does not make sense to me to place Gebser, Beck, Steiner, Torbert, and so on into a big integral container and then label that a theory. This is a major reason why I opt to refer to that collection of theorists and their theories as integral studies. In other words, a heap of similar and complementary ideas does not add up to a theory, let alone an integral theory. Such a heap is eclecticism. The kind of eclecticism that Integral Theory is designed to avoid. It is for this reason I personally avoid using "integral theory" (lower case) as the generic expression of a non-Wilberian or even a "Wilberian plus many others" approach. Consequently, I prefer integral studies instead of integral theory—feeling that the former is a more accurate description of a large and growing group of theorists and theories, which often contradict as much as they overlap. My experience is that generic uses of "integral theory" tend to be either confusing (it is not clear what its relationship is to Wilber's work), almost meaningless (it is hard to talk about an integral theory without including Wilber, and once you include Wilber's approach it is so substantial that it tends to overshadow and undercut any generic usage), or inaccurate (it is not being used to represent a single or coherent theory).

In short, I feel it is justified and preferable to use Integral Theory to exclusively refer to a broadly Wilberian-based approach to reality. I have provided four distinct reasons for this above, which I summarize as: (1) Integral Theory as a proper noun, (2) Integral Theory as common parlance, (3) Integral Theory as more integral, and (4) Integral Theory as a real theory. This important issue (Integral Theory versus integral studies)—and the four points I have raised in support of defining Integral Theory in Wilberian terms—deserves more attention than space in this introduction allows. I am quite open to counterpoints to the positions I have presented above as well as the opportunity to unpack these brief comments. Also, I do not feel that this issue should be decided by a single person such as myself (or anyone for that matter). Rather, I feel that the integral community and our resulting practices of discourse will enact this over time. It may be the case that this issue is never neatly and easily resolved, and that is fine, too. What I have sought to do in this section is provide my own thoughts and considerations on the topic and give some important background context to this worthwhile discussion and debate. Now let us turn our attention to the contents of this volume.

In This Volume

From the 100 presenters at the conference, nearly 2,000 pages of academic content were produced. I have selected 16 exemplary essays and placed them into three categories of perspectives that I feel are essential to the development of Integral Theory: applied, theoretical, and constructive.[8] Eight of the chapters here were "Best Paper" award winners at the end of the conference in the following categories: one for each of the quadrant perspectives, theoretical contribution, research contribution, constructive criticism of Integral Theory, and alternatives to Integral Theory. Additional chapters were obtained from some of the Honorable Mentions in the above categories, with still other noteworthy pieces being chosen for this volumeto fill out important aspects of Integral Theory and making a contribution to deepening the academic conversation. In order to set the context for the content presented here, I have included the essay, "The Academic Emergence of Integral Theory," which Mark Forman and I wrote in response to an online essay posted by Frank Visser a few months before the conference. This essay was widely distributed on the Internet and we received a lot of positive feedback from all kinds of individuals. By including this here as a prologue, I aim to provide some context that people were walking into the conference with and the spirit of exchange that Mark and I are committed to engender through this and future conferences. Thus, I have left this piece in future tense, as it was originally written. A number of presenters (including several of the authors in this volume) cited this essay in their conference papers, which I feel highlights that Mark and I struck a resonant note in the academic community with our comments and vision. Following this prologue is the first chapter, "An Overview of Integral Theory: An All-inclusive Framework for the Twenty-First Century." This chapter was not a conference paper and was written for this volume, although an earlier version was posted on the Integral Institute website as a resource paper. This chapter serves to provide an up-to-date and comprehensive tour of Integral Theory and its AQAL model. I have written it in a way that will serve individuals new to Integral Theory as well as those who are seasoned scholar-practitioners.

Applied Perspectives

In the first section, *Applied Perspectives*, there are five chapters on various aspects of self, others, and the world. Karen O'Brien opens the volume with "Responding to Climate Change: The Need for an Integral Approach." O'Brien is a climate change researcher based in Olso, Norway, and was the lead author for the adaptation article in the Fourth Assessment Report for the Intergovernmental Panel on Climate Change (IPCC), which won the 2007 Nobel Peace Prize alongside Al Gore. In her chapter, she looks at the six key areas where an Integral approach makes a difference in approaching the global issue of climate change. Then she explores how these areas can be understood in the context of a climate change "hot spot"—the Artic.

Next, Theresa Silow, director of the somatic psychology track in the MFT counseling program at JFKU explores the role of Integral Theory in supporting the first-person cultivation of embodiment. In her "Embodiment, an Ascending and Descending Development," she identifies the points of contact between the transcendent (as represented by transpersonal psychology) and the immanent (as represented by somatic psychology). Silow shows how Integral Theory can facilitate a deeper integration of the insights of these two important orientations to our direct experience. In particular, she explores the paradoxical nature of embodiment as the integration of horizontal and vertical movements in Ascent and Descent.

In "Beauty and the Expansion of Women's Identity," Vanessa Fisher, an up-and-coming figure in Integral Theory, takes us on her journey through the worlds of art, individual beauty, and feminism. Her work weaves a wonderful tapestry between the personal and the philosophical and illustrates the power of an integral analysis for making sense of the existential relationship between self and world. She confronts the strained relationship between beauty and feminism and champions that they are not mutually exclusive. She uses Integral Theory to situate how feminism has historically addressed "the beauty question" and parallels this discourse with the evolutionary unfolding of female identity itself. Fisher uses performance artist Hannah Wilke as a case study of a pioneering feminist trying to reconcile beauty and her own identity as a woman. In addition, Fisher surveys the masculine and feminine polarity in the field of aesthetics itself and gives an eloquent account of her own struggle to transcend but include her beauty.

Michele Chase provides a delightful experience in "Writing to Effect: Textual Form as Realization in an Integral Community." Chase is chair of the Department of Holistic Health Education at JFKU, and received her doctorate in English. Thus, like many integral scholar-practitioners, she is a meeting point between different disciplinary perspectives. She makes the most of this confluence in this chapter. Here she embodies a playful and important inquiry into the nature and role of writing in serving the commitments of a knowledge community such as Integral Theory. In the process, she questions some of the expectations of academic writing in service of actually realizing the goals of a truly transformative discourse. I sincerely hope all authors within the integral community read her analysis of the first nine issues of the *Journal of Integral Theory and Practice* (JITP), as her insights go beyond this particular publication. Her analysis has helped me to be much more reflective with regard to my role as executive editor of JITP.

The final chapter in this section is from Elliott Ingersoll, a prominent integral psychotherapist and professor of counseling at Cleveland State University. In "An Integral Understanding of the Etiology of Depression," Ingersoll uses the four quadrants to explore the etiology of one of the most common issues clinicians face. Drawing and weaving together a dozen schools of thought and their theories, Ingersoll demonstrates how anything less than an Integral approach runs the risk of leaving out too much. This chapter provides a good template of how integral scholar-practitioners can use the four quadrants to organize a comprehensive view of any phenomena or topic.

Theoretical Perspectives

In the next section, *Theoretical Perspectives*, six chapters are provided that contribute something theoretically valuable to the development of Integral Theory. In some cases, this is accomplished by discussing areas currently underexplored within Integral Theory, and in other cases it results from clarifying current theoretical understandings within Integral Theory. Zachary Stein, a doctoral candidate at the Harvard Graduate School of Education and a senior analyst for Developmental Testing Service, made a strong impression on conference attendees. His combination of open heart and clear mind embodies important aspects of the integral ideal of scholar-practitioner. He has already begun to make important contributions to Integral Theory, especially in the philosophical, ethical, and empirical realms of psychological measurement. He continues this trajectory with his "Now You Get It, Now You Don't: Developmental Differences in the Understanding of Integral Theory and Practice." In this chapter, Stein provides a historical context for developmental thought and introduces us to Kurt Fisher's skill theory. In particular, he engages in the important process of applying developmental theory to the actual understanding and use of Integral Theory. In doing this and providing the outlines of a research program Stein initiates an important reflective move that has yet to be made by integral theorists and practitioners. Namely, Stein points out that the key distinctions within Integral Theory (e.g., quadrants and levels) will all be understood slightly (though importantly) differently depending on the level of psychological development of the user. This kind of understanding has important implications for the integral community as it tries to teach, learn, and apply these distinctions. Stein's suggestive analysis forms the basis of the Lectical Integral Model Assessment (LIMA), which is being developed as part of the iTEACH project at JFKU.

Next, Michael Zimmerman, a lifelong academic philosopher who has drawn on Integral Theory since the 1980s, introduces the integral community to the important work of evolutionary theorist Stanley N. Salthe. In "The Final Cause of Cosmic Development: Nondual Spirit or the Second Law of Thermodynamics?" Zimmerman provides an important comparison/contrast analysis between Salthe's use of thermodynamic equilibrium and Wilber's use of "Kosmic Eros" to explain the development of complexity in nature. One of the contributions Zimmerman makes in this chapter is in demonstrating the ways that Salthe has an integral philosophy very compatible with Integral Theory, but has a different set of assumptions and outcomes. In so doing, Zimmerman helps us become more capable of reflecting critically on Integral Theory and also identifies complementary and alternative perspectives that can enrich Integral Theory.

In "Frames of AQAL, Integral Critical Theory, and the Emerging Integral Arts," Michael Schwartz, a professor of History and Philosophy of Art at Augusta State University, accomplishes a number of things. First, he explores what happens to Integral Theory when it is framed from different angles such as philosophy or theory. Then, using historiography he gives us a sense of what a mature *integral critical theory* consists of and points to potential future developments of the AQAL model. Schwartz provides critical reflections on Integral Methodological Pluralism and the nature of Integral Art. Lastly, he begins an "integral-critical-historical" exploration of art. By weaving together these various trajectories of inquiry, Schwartz triangulates a vision of the future contributions Integral Theory can make to the integral arts.

Then, in "Integral Situational Ethical Pluralism: An Overview of a Second-Tier Ethic for the Twenty-First Century," Randy Martin addresses an area that is underaddressed in Integral Theory. This is especially the case given the prominent role of topics such as the moral line of psychological development and the *Basic Moral Intuition* (BMI). Martin is the chair of the criminology department at Indiana University of Pennsylvania, so his view of ethics is deeply informed by the consequences of unethical behaviors in our society. This chapter does much to start a conversation about what constitutes Integral Ethics. In particular, he highlights how the BMI and vision-logic are key concepts in Integral Theory for articulating a global ethic. Although Martin does not provide detailed examples of this ethic, he provides an important set of considerations for developing and applying such an ethic.

Next, in an "An Integral Map of Perspective-Taking," Clint Fuhs sheds some much needed light on one of the most interesting areas of Wilber's more recent work: a symbolic logic of perspectives. He begins by providing a historical context of previous research on perspective taking. This chapter will be invaluable to the integral community because it for the first time presents Integral Calculus in a straightforward and consistent way. In addition, Fuhs avoids many of the confusing pitfalls that have accompanied earlier uses of its fascinating equations of how first-, second-, and third-person perspectives interact to create reality. Fuhs is a long-time senior student of Ken Wilber and is currently a doctoral candidate at Fielding Graduate University, where he is further researching developmental perspectives and how to represent them symbolically.

The last chapter in this section comes from the world-renowned developmental psychologist Susanne Cook-Greuter. In her "Second-Tier Gains and Challenges in Ego Development," Cook-Greuter continues her life-long project of researching and measuring the higher stages of ego-identity. This chapter presents her most recent research findings as well as her current formulations of the top two stages of postconventional ego development: Autonomous and Construct-aware. In particular, she focuses on some of the "pitfalls" and shadow dynamics that besiege these higher stages. This exploration is important because there is much talk in the integral community about the value of establishing and embodying these higher stages, but there is not a thorough understanding of the ego traps and difficulties that individuals at these higher stages face. It will be important for proponents of Integral Theory to be better versed in the downside of the higher stages so as to avoid the hubris that can come with using developmental models to understand self and others.

Constructive Perspectives

In the last section, *Constructive Perspectives*, five chapters are provided that contribute toward a more reflective and sober embrace of Integral Theory. One of the key components of academic discourse is critical and constructive engagement. All of these chapters provide beneficial and alternative views that can help deepen and expand theory building and applications within Integral Theory. The first chapter is Sam Mickey's, "Rhizomatic Contributions to Integral Ecology in Gilles Deleuze and Félix Guattari." Mickey is a doctoral candidate at California Institute of Integral Studies, my alma mater and where I developed the Integral Ecology framework.[9] So it is great to have Mickey furthering this project by bringing Deleuze and Guattari's rhizomatic thought to bear on it. All too often, proponents of Integral Theory take a posture against postmodernism and its theorists. Thus, Mickey makes an important contribution by demonstrating how Integral Theory still has much to gain by interacting with postmodern theorists and their insights. In fact, Mickey makes a case for Deleuze and Guattari as post-postmodern theorists through their enactive concepts of rhizomes and geophilosophy. Thus, they are invited to join the growing list of key integral theorists.

Next, independent scholar-practitioner Tom Murray provides some guidance to the Integral Theory community's aspiration toward new forms of community and dialogue.[10] In "Exploring Epistemic Wisdom: Ethical and Practical Implications of Integral Studies and Methodological Pluralism for Collaboration and Knowledge Building," Murray outlines the practical and theoretical implications of integral approaches to discourse, validation, and the establishment of knowledge. In particular, Murray focuses on "methodological pluralism" and how it connects to issues of *epistemic indeterminacy* and various social vulnerabilities. In general, Murray's chapter serves as an important invitation toward our developing more postformal modes of building integral approaches both within Integral Theory and the broader field of integral studies.

In "Appropriation in Integral Theory: The Case of Sri Aurobindo and the Mother's 'Untold' Integral View," Charles Flores, a long-term practitioner of Integral Yoga himself, provides a cautionary tale. Flores details how "well-intended sympathizers" of Integral Yoga often fail to appreciate the complex nuances of Aurobindo's work and instead rely on Wilber's interpretations. Thus, Flores is reminding all of us the value of becoming familiar with the primary sources of key thinkers and theories. This is especially important for scholar-practitioners of a metatheory such as Integral Theory, which can often get lost in its own 50,000 foot view and fail to see with enough granularity how it is distorting or misappropriating other theories, positions, schools of thought, and authors for its own ends.

Following this chapter is Mark Edwards's "Of Elephants and Butterflies: An Integral Metatheory for Organizational Transformation." Edwards is one of the most important emerging voices in the field of Integral Theory. He has a deep appreciation for the work of Wilber but is also not afraid to point out its blind spots and limitations. In this chapter, Edwards brings his study of metatheory to bear on how organizations transform. In the process, he makes a number of poignant observations of Integral Theory—from both a metatheory perspective and an applied example—that we all should be very attentive to. In particular, he demonstrates that Integral Theory isn't the only metatheory game in town, and that many of what Integral Theory claims to be its unique distinctions are in fact shared by other metatheory approaches, such as those by Roy Bhaskar or George Ritzner. Furthermore, some of these other metatheories have distinctions, or what Edwards calls *integral lenses* (of which he identifies 24) that are undervalued or entirely absent within current Integral Theory formulations. Could it be that Integral Theory is not as integral as it considers itself to be? In any case, Edwards here and elsewhere is transforming the conversation around and practice of Integral Theory in important ways.

The last chapter is by the renowned Bill Torbert and his colleagues, Reut Livne-Tarandach, David McCallum, Aliki Nicolaides, and Elaine Herdman-Barker. In their chapter, "Developmental Action Inquiry: A Distinct Integral Theory That Actually Integrates Developmental Theory, Practice, and Research," they present an alternative to Wilber's Integral Theory. Developmental action inquiry combines first-, second-, and third-person perspectives and practices within a developmental framework. Thus, it can be said to be an alternative all quadrant (i.e., first-, second-, and third-person perspectives), all level (i.e., the Leadership Development Profile) approach to Integral Theory. In fact, Torbert is known to refer to Wilber's four quadrants as the "Flat Four" and his own four terrains of experience as the "Deep Four." This distinction is used by Torbert to highlight how his approach emphasizes action-inquiry in real time, whereas Wilber's approach can easily be and often is just used to theorize and abstract reality. Torbert's work in general, and this chapter in particular, serves as an important counterpoint to Wilber's work and is at the same time complementary to it. Through their juxtaposition and synergy, both approaches can benefit through their scholar-practitioners being familiar with the tenets of each other's method(s). This chapter also provides an important overview of the validity around the Leadership Development Profile (LDP) and some of the most recent research on action-logics.

Serving as a conclusion to this volume, Ken Wilber provides an afterword. In "The Dawn of an Integral Age," Wilber reflects on his own work over the past 30 years and looks ahead toward the future of Integral Theory as it continues to develop as an academic discourse. He points out that the next decade is going to be one of immense growth and diversification of Integral Theory. Pointing to sociologist Jeffrey Alexander's work, Wilber suggests that we are on the brink of a new major epoch where the view that "everyone is right" informs our efforts at addressing the major global issues of the twenty-first century, including the ecological, economic, and cultural crises that grab headlines each day. In concluding, Wilber invites everyone to get involved with ushering in the Integral Age.

Enacting an Integral Future

This volume serves in part as a historical snapshot of the Integral Theory Conference and the formative years of Integral Theory's emergence as a distinct academic field of discourse and practice. In addition, it serves in part as a foundation for building Integral Theory and setting in motion a number of trajectories of discourse for the future of the discipline. In closing, I want to highlight some of the key themes and salient issues that I feel surface in the course of the chapters in this volume. These integral arcs will, hopefully, be taken up and engaged with by the community of practice over the coming years. How we as a community choose to interface with these vibrant and complex issues will have an important influence on the long-term viability of Integral Theory and its application. In Roger Walsh's foreword, he spoke about the "current frontiers and possible futures" of Integral Theory. Below is a list of the most prominent issues facing Integral Theory as I currently see them. Feel free to add your own to this list as you traverse through the integral landscape of this volume. I have organized them by significant questions facing Integral Theory as an emerging field.

What Is Integral Theory?

- Clarify the relationship between Integral Theory, integral theories, and integral studies.
- Continue to decouple Wilber the man and Integral Theory the field, so that Integral Theory transcends and includes him.
- Explore the similarities and differences between Wilber and other key integral thinkers such as Edgar Morin and Stanley Salthe.
- Interface with other metatheory approaches such as George Ritzner and Roy Bhaskar.
- Explore the limits and blind spots of Integral Theory—what it is leaving out, how it is distorting what it includes, in what ways it overemphasizes certain distinctions over others.
- Develop Integral Calculus further and provide illustrative advantages to its use.
- Explore the lineage of and philosophical traditions that feed into and are expressed through Integral Theory, thereby situating Integral Theory in a historical arc.

What Is the Role of Developmental Theory?

- Expose the shadow aspects of working with developmental models.
- Articulate the ethics of working with developmental models.
- Apply developmental assessments to ourselves so that we know what it is like to be under their gaze and are more aware of the limits and strengths of these instruments of transformation.
- Expand our use of developmental models beyond Beck, Kegan, Cook-Greuter, and Torbert.
- Research the contours of the "higher stages" so we are more clear about what they are and are not.

What Is an Integral Community of Practice?

- Establish an international network of organizations and events that support and deepen the integral inquiry needed within the field.
- Deepen current applications within existing fields (e.g., Integral Ecology and Integral Psychotherapy).

- Apply Integral Theory to new domains and areas such as Integral Parenting, Integral Architecture, and Integral Biology.
- Explore how to be a community of integral discourse through the creation of structures and processes that support feedback, criticism, and reflection.
- Create new kinds of injunctions for shared practice and discourse.
- Develop new forms of integral data analysis from multiple sets and methods of practice.
- Apply Integral Theory to the leading issues of the twenty-first century (e.g., climate change, human trafficking, healthcare, international terrorism).

What Is the Relationship with Postmodernism?

- Clarify whether Integral Theory is a form of constructive postmodernism, or is it post-postmodernism.
- Identify the contributions of postmodernism that have not been fully incorporated.
- Bring the body, the intuitive, the soul, the feminine, the indigenous, and diversity more fully into dialogue with the principles of Integral Theory.

It is my hope that these questions will continue to be taken up by scholar-practitioners in the field of Integral Theory and that more will be added to this initial list. The authors in this volume offer us much in beginning to consider and respond to these issues. The Integral Theory Conference will continue to offer academics and practitioners a place to engage in these kinds of consider-ations. Together may we enact our integral future in a way that serves as many perspectives as possible. I hope to see you at one of the upcoming Integral Theory Conferences.

Notes

1. A downloadable document containing all the abstracts of these theses and dissertations is available at www.integralresearchcenter.org/source.
2. This list does not include those chapters published in the *Journal of Integral Theory and Practice* or *Integral Review*.
3. In 2008, the journal's title was shortened from *AQAL: Journal of Integral Theory and Practice* to simply, *Journal of Integral Theory and Practice*.
4. For more details, see www.integraltheoryconference.org.
5. See chapter 1, note 9 for a list of the titles being published in 2010.
6. The basis of estimation for these two figures is as follows: for Wilber's own work I included his collected works, the books published since the collected works came out,

the articles not yet included in the collected works, and the Excerpts posted on his Shambhala Web page; for the Wilberian material, I only included books, articles, and dissertations that draw heavily on Wilber's writings in a constructive spirit regardless of whether they are critical of or sympathetic to his Integral approach.

7. The Integral Theory corpus itself is situated in a lineage of philosophical examination and psychological inquiry that has roots in figures such as James Mark Baldwin, Charles Sanders Peirce, and Jürgen Habermas. In many ways Wilber's vision is just the most recent though admittedly unique articulation of the tradition of American pragmatism.

8. In addition to these 16 essays, the *Journal of Integral Theory and Practice* (Vol. 4, No. 3) published 10 additional essays that were presented at the conference. This collection covers a wide range of applications of the AQAL model, including politics, diversity issues, postsecondary education, music theory and pedagogy, recovery work, philosophy, paranormal phenomena, and thanatology. All of these chapters (in this volume) and articles (in the JITP issues) have accompanying MP3 recordings of the authors presenting their papers as part of the Integral Theory Conference. Visit www.integraltheoryconference.org for details on how to obtain these recordings as well as all the other recordings made of all other presenters at ITC 2008.

9. For a complete overview of this framework, see Esbjörn-Hargens and Zimmerman (2009).

10. In many ways this chapter by Murray builds on an earlier article he published in *Integral Review*. See Murray (2006). This previous work is a well-researched and extensive exploration (54 pages in length!) of "knowledge building" in the context of dialogue practices between and among integral authors. One of Murray's (2006) observations is that these authors "by and large exhibit the same limitations as traditional intellectual discourses" (210). In response to this situation Murray (2006) offers many worthwhile insights and injunctions about the process of enacting "collaborative knowledge." I feel this article is essential reading for the integral community as it outlines a number of issues we need to consider and engage in.

References

Esbjörn-Hargens, S., and M. E. Zimmerman. 2009. *Integral ecology: Uniting multiple perspectives on the natural world.* Boston: Integral Books.

Martin, J. 2008. Integral research as a practical mixed-methods framework. *Journal of Integral Theory and Practice* 3(2): 155–64.

Murray, T. 2006. Collaborative knowledge building and integral theory: On perspectives, uncertainty, and mutual regard. *Integral Review* 2: 210–64.

Wilber, K. 1977. *The spectrum of consciousness.* Wheaton, IL: Quest Books.

———. 1995. *Sex, ecology, spirituality: The spirit of evolution.* Boston: Shambhala.

The Academic Emergence of Integral Theory

Reflections on and Clarifications of the
1st Biennial Integral Theory Conference

Mark D. Forman and Sean Esbjörn-Hargens

Introduction

As founders and organizers of the first biennial Integral Theory Conference, we feel moved to respond to Frank Visser's latest posting ("Assessing Integral Theory"). We do this in the spirit of dialogue and out of a sense that his characterization of our event was misleading and inaccurate in important ways. To be fair, Visser's essay is less about the conference and more about what constitutes theory building and the checking of its validity. His main focus is on how Wilber has failed to build theory and have it validated in a scientific or academic fashion. We would like to raise several points relevant to this.

First, however, we would like to underscore that we agree with elements of Visser's essay. We agree that Integral Theory (broadly defined or defined simply as Wilber's corpus) has not yet made strong enough inroads into the academic world. We recognize that the burden is on those of us engaged in Integral Theory to help it conform more strongly to the norms of academic discourse, research, and critical analysis.

Likewise, we agree, as academics, that Wilber's writing has generally fallen in a place in between traditional academic discourse and more general popular philosophical discourse. While both of us feel greatly indebted to Ken Wilber for his obvious contribution to the integral movement and honor the extent to which he has indeed sought empirical support (narrow and broad) for many of his ideas, we think that Visser rightly points out the challenges Wilber's writing style presents from an academic point of view.

Finally, we also agree that much value could have come out of Wilber engaging with patience and curiosity the various critiques the Integral World Web site has housed. We would be among the first to read and study such dialogues closely were they to take place. And yet we recognize these squandered opportunities while simultaneously not being convinced that Wilber's silence has only been a matter of him being a self-referential "jerk." Nor are we sure that the general lack of response by Wilber's students and proponents of his work is simply the result of them sleeping with the devil. We will address this issue further at the end of this essay.

All this said—and we believe these are some substantial areas of agreement—we also feel that Visser's overall characterization of the relationship between Integral Theory and academia misses the mark in several places. More centrally, we believe that his characterization of our conference as a place where "a kind of Wilber celebration is staged"—which we take to mean it will be an unthinking, uncritical, or idol-worshipping look at his work—is both inaccurate and demonstrates the same kind of dismissive tone that he has so vehemently charged Wilber with using with his critics. This accusation appears especially cynical given that much of the conference has been explicitly and obviously designed to address the kind of critiques that Visser's Web site has showcased over the years. To us it was notable that he primarily highlighted the potential downsides of the conference (e.g., to be more of the same "self-referential discourse" he attributes to Wilber) without presenting much, if any, of its possible opportunities (e.g., the first open academic space that is beginning a much-needed and arguably far overdue process of critical reflection and application of Integral Theory).

We would therefore like to outline a few points that give a more accurate view of the conference and to provide what we feel is a more balanced impression—in the context of discussing the conference—of the relationship between Integral Theory and academia. We will end this response with some of our concerns with the quality and nature of the work found on the Integral World Web site itself.

Critics and Our Call for Papers

The conference's call for papers was open and disseminated widely. It was sent to all the major alternative schools, including those which house significant numbers of Wilber's critics (e.g., CIIS in San Francisco). It was sent out through all available integral e-mail lists and groups and it was posted, by direct request by us, on Visser's Web site. We were hoping to get between 50 and 70 submissions and were pleasantly surprised when nearly 120 came in from 11 different countries.

The call specifically stated we were open to critiques of Integral Theory and alternatives to Wilber's AQAL model. We simply did not hear anything—even in the form of a cautious inquiry—from many of those persons who are most identified as Wilber's critics as posted on Visser's site. We did not hear from Andrew Smith, Christian De Quincy, Alan Kazlev, Jeff Meyerhoff, Ray Harris, Gerry Goddard, Peter Collins, Michael Bauwens, John Heron, or Geoffrey Falk about the possibility of presenting or attending. We surely would have offered them a place had they contacted us.

Suffice it to say that given how much these individuals have highlighted the value of critical dialogue and academic standards it seemed somewhat ironic that none of them have chosen to participate in this venue, which took measures to ensure they would feel welcomed and not as though they were walking into the pro-Wilber lion's den. A missed opportunity, for sure. Furthermore, we personally contacted some of the persons we believe to be among the more articulate of Wilber's critics. These include Sean Kelly, Steve McIntosh, Bonnita Roy, and Mark Edwards (all of whom are attending and presenting) and Jorge Ferrer and Steven Taylor (both of whom declined). We also, as Visser knows, approached him and encouraged him to consider attending and would have been excited about him presenting. Visser's *Thought as Passion* is an amazing and uniquely valuable overview of Wilber's progression as a theorist and demonstrates his deep knowledge of Wilber's corpus.

Critical presentations will be featured at the event—we have not pushed them under the rug, as Visser's essay would likely mislead one to believe. For example, Bill Torbert, who is perhaps our most prominent presenter excepting our keynote speakers, has titled his presentation "Developmental Action Inquiry: A Distince Integral Theory That Actually Integrates Developmental Theory, Practice, and Research" [this volume]. Please note the phrase "actually integrates"—this is a direct and open challenge to the AQAL approach and we were more than happy to allow him the forum to express his ideas. We are not simply giving him one shot at it, either. In addition to their 90-minute presentation, Torbert and his team of co-presenters will be represented on one-third of our panel presentations.

Critical Panel Discussions

We have set up two important panels that are aimed at exploring many of Visser's concerns, which as noted above we share. The first one is "Does Integral = Ken Wilber?" This will be a provocative discussion. The majority of the persons on this panel (Torbert, Edwards, Roy, McIntosh) have been critical of Wilber, so we have weighted this discussion with people who are inclined to say "NO!" And since one of us is moderating the panel (Sean), we can guarantee that we will dig under the surface of a simple "no" and explore the deeper implications of Wilber's relationship to the field of Integral Theory.

One of the major aims of the conference in general and this panel in particular is to decouple Ken Wilber and Integral Theory. We bring a deep honoring of what Wilber has enacted through his writings and activities and an excited anticipation of any new writings he generates. He is without a doubt the most important theorist associated with Integral Theory and there is no reason to assume this will change anytime soon. But to this orientation we also bring a desire to make sure Integral Theory receives the benefit of many contributors. In other words, we do not want Integral Theory to be a "one man show." We are fine with "Wilberian Theory" being synonymous with "Integral Theory" as long as "Wilberian Theory" is understood to mean "AQAL Theory" and not meant as "Ken's Theory." So while Wilber might be the originator of Integral Theory, as Freud is the originator of psychoanalysis, he does not own Integral Theory. In our view Integral Theory will only thrive insofar as valuable contributions to its criticism, clarification, application, and expansion come from many individuals working within its context and not just taking aim from the outside (e.g., by people who have never really tried applying the AQAL model to some contemporary issue). While we welcome insights from "outside" it is our experience that they are of less value than those that come from a committed place to improve Integral Theory by turning Integral Theory onto itself: an act of theoretical-applied self-reflection.

For us, Integral Theory is bigger than Wilber, even though Wilber is a big, important, and valuable figure within Integral Theory. Our experience of the Integral World Web site is that it primarily focuses on Ken Wilber and less so on Integral Theory. In this sense the previous name "World of Ken Wilber" feels more appropriate than the new name of "Integral World." We find much of this Web site to be Wilber-centric and caught up in assigned failings and limits of Wilber's personality. This Web site serves an important function in the ecology of Integral Theory but in our assessment it is a narrow and limited contribution. Our conference is not about Ken Wilber. It is about Integral Theory. This makes it markedly different than the three-day gathering in San Francisco in 1997.

The second panel worth noting here is the one on "Integral Theory in Academia," which is filled with long-standing academics, six of whom have PhDs and one of whom is a doctoral candidate. The focus of this panel will be to explore the possibilities and pitfalls of Integral Theory building inroads to the academy. We hope to identify valuable next steps for Integral Theory in becoming a more established academic field of discourse.

Finally, it is worthwhile to mention that our two keynotes are exploring important topics that have been underaddressed in integral circles. Roger

Walsh will be talking in part about the forms integral shadow takes in individuals and the community [see his two-part article mentioned at the end of his foreword this volume]. Susanne Cook-Greuter will be talking about the spectrum of narcissism from birth up through the highest structure-stages (this volume). Both of these addresses are aimed at bringing a reflective quality to the emerging community of integral academics.

Integral Theory's Presence in Academia

While we agree Integral Theory has not yet achieved nearly the penetration into academic circles that it could—and, as a part of the integral community, we accept responsibility for this—we also feel that the gap Visser describes between academia and Integral Theory is neither as daunting nor as empirically real as he suggests. A quick look at our presenter biographies shows that a large number of them have current, academic affiliations and even more have come through mainstream academic graduate programs. Excluding the alternative programs (Institute of Transpersonal Psychology, the California Institute of Integral Studies, John F. Kennedy University, Fielding Graduate University), our presenters are currently affiliated with Harvard University, Stanford University, Columbia University, Penn State College of Medicine, Boston College, University of Rochester, Florida State University, University of California, California State University, Augusta State University, University of Pennsylvania, University at Albany, National University, and Cleveland State University. And this is just the U.S. contingent: the vast majority of our international presenters are also academically affiliated in their countries of origin.

Clearly, unless we want to be disingenuous or dismiss evidence we do not want to see, there is some real connection being made between academics and Integral Theory. It may be just a beginning—this remains to be seen—but it is demonstrably real. Our current estimate suggests that upward of 50 academic disciplines have individuals (many of them professors) within them now applying and using Integral Theory and the AQAL model to address issues in their fields.

Recently, one of us (Sean) wrote about the academic status of Integral Theory in the editorial for the last issue of the *Journal of Integral Theory and Practice* (Vol. 3, No. 1). In a section entitled "Integral Theory as Academic Contender" it was discussed how in the last few years Integral Theory has made significant steps toward becoming a viable academic field through the establishment of: peer-reviewed journals (*JITP* and *Integral Review*); accredited graduate level academic programs (five programs at John F. Kennedy University, two at Fielding Graduate University, and one at California Institute of Integral Studies—not to mention the many individual academics in various institutions teaching courses based in full or part on the AQAL model); a biennial academic conference—the first of which is a sold-out success with 100 presenters, 12 panels, 20 poster presentations, and almost 500 attendees (including presenters) from more than 30 countries; and an academic research center, the Integral Research Center, which is supporting the global community of integral scholar-practitioners engaged in research based on Integral Methodological Pluralism. Soon the IRC Web site will list nearly a dozen research projects occurring all over the world using Integral Theory as its framework.

The Importance of Real World Application for Academic Study and Research.

In his essay, Visser makes the suggestion that the conference's emphasis on application will result in "application [being] mistaken for validation." We feel that this is both highly dismissive and also demonstrates a significant misunderstanding on Visser's part concerning the relationship between application, academia, and critical discourse.

As persons who have actively worked to apply the model in practice (in education, research, ecology/sustainability, and psychotherapy) we have experienced that the realm of application is often exactly the context in which the flaws in theoretical models become obvious. In our call for papers, for example, we specifically asked that those presenting on application address alternatives to Integral Theory and its AQAL model and point out elements of the Integral approach that do not work or that need modification. This is our experience with any responsible group of practitioners who attempt to apply a model "on the ground"—they are often the first to spot the flaws. We dare even suggest that persons who focus on theoretical issues are often (ironically) less capable in their ability to think critically about the real limits of theory than those who are called to work and serve actual persons and communities.

It is worth noting in this context that most of the critics associated with www.integralworld.net are not scholar-practitioners of the AQAL model or Integral Methodological Pluralism (IMP). Rather, they mostly take issue with theoretical aspects of Wilber's work, often through a hermeneutics of suspicion with a deconstructionist tone. All of this is fine and valuable—our point is that the critics associated with Visser's Web site take up only one aspect of the project that we are engaged in. They do not address the issue of making Integral Theory more viable through peer-reviewed research or real-time real-world application.

In addition, Visser's mention of the idea of "validation" in the above quote misses the actual academic meaning of that word. To validate something in an academic context is primarily an empirical exercise—one cannot, by definition, validate something through anecdotal agreement. As academics we know this lesson well and would never presume that a gathering of practitioners proves anything definitively. One must show through some kind of research that a particular model "works" and that it accurately describes a particular issue. Hence, the recent establishment of the Integral Research Center, which was created to help address this aspect.

But we also feel that when Visser does correctly discuss the empirical nature of validation he is too narrowly focused on the "scientific" and falls short of an integral assessment of Integral Theory. In fact, Jorge Ferrer—one of Wilber's strongest critics—has highlighted the dangers of such a scientific colonization of validity criteria. We want to see and promote a multi-method assessment (e.g., something like IMP) of Integral Theory and its distinctions, claims, and positions. This of course would give "scientific theory" a prominent place at the validity table; but there are many other considerations as well, especially when dealing with metatheories such as Integral Theory. See the article by Mark Edwards in *JITP* (Vol. 3, No. 2) for a thoughtful and critical exploration of these issues in relationship to Integral Theory and the AQAL model [also see his chapter in this volume].

In this sense, then, we take the issue of validation seriously and have consciously sought to demonstrate this in our actions related to the conference. We are giving an award specifically for the best research contribution. A good portion of the conference proceeds will go to giving of grants to fund research projects related to Integral Theory (through the Integral Research Center). Also, one of our panels will be specifically on the topic of developmental research. Far from being a unitary chorus, we will have representatives of three different research lineages on this panel and plan to draw out their empirical and theoretical differences (with Mark as moderator). Our surveys suggest that this will be among our best-attended sessions.

Finally, anyone familiar with academic outcome research knows that one ultimately needs an active body of practitioners to begin to do significant research into a construct or set of interventions. To try and validate a particular approach to community development, sustainability, organizational development, business, medicine, or psychotherapy—to try and show in a meaningful way that it does what it claims to—requires that there be a large enough group of practitioners to attract grants, funds, and the interest to carry out research. There was not large-scale research on cognitive therapy before there were cognitive therapists or on meditation before there were meditators. Nor can one research a community intervention until it is up and running in communities. What does Visser suggest? As we see it we need to build a critical mass of practitioners and attract research funds through, in part, large gatherings at which to exchange ideas and encourage attempts at application. We are doing what is done in every other applied academic field. We see the application aspect of this conference as a part of the larger process of empirical research, not as an attempt to congratulate ourselves on how well we think this approach works.

Our Criticisms of www.IntegralWorld.net

One of the things that strikes us as most ironic about Visser's criticisms is that the very ones he applies to Wilber can be applied equally, or even more force-fully, to the content posted on his site. This is the reason that we do not place entire blame for a lack of critical debate at Wilber's feet. From an academic standpoint the Integral World Web site lacks peer review and as a result many of the critiques—while worthwhile—are presented in a way that would *never* be accepted in an academic context. So for many of us academics it is hard to discover the posted gems on this Web site because they are buried in rhetoric that all too often lacks the rigor, appropriate citation, self-reflectivity, and openness that they often accuse Wilber of lacking. On many occasions we have heard academic colleagues—and we resonate with their perspective—describe the material on this Web site as "toxic," "emotive," "narcissistic," "self-referen-tial," and so on—as we all know, all these characteristics have been assigned to Wilber on this very Web site. Our point here is simply that as academics we want a different kind of discourse than what either Wilber or the Integral World Web site offers. We find both unsatisfactory in many respects. The tone and approach of each "party" falls short in several ways of academic exchange and exploration. Our conference is intended specifically to provide a forum for a calmer and more sober debate to occur. At our conference we are excited to celebrate Wilber, there is so much to be joyful about, and equally jazzed to critique Integral Theory; there is much important improvement and clarifica-tion to be done, particularly with application.

Conclusion

It is our hope that this response makes clearer the intentions that the confer-ence has in terms of addressing the kinds of issues that are important for the continued growth, refinement, and expansion of Integral Theory. In whatever ways this first conference falls short of our desired goals, we will take those lessons into the next conference in 2010. We are committed to continual development of Integral Theory as an academic endeavor that is supported by a diverse chorus of scholar-practitioners involved in generating integral solutions to the complex problems we face in our communities and around the globe. If you are not joining us for this year's event, may you be inspired to join us at the next.

Note

Visser posted his article on his Web site (www.integralworld.net) on June 17, 2008. Mark and I e-mailed him the response above on June 26, 2008. His article, "Assessing Integral Theory: Opportunities and Impediments," can be found here: http://www.integralworld. net/visser26.html and his thoughtful reply to our posting "Rebuilding Integral Bridges: Response to Forman and Esbjörn-Hargens" can be found here: http://www.integralworld. net/visser27.html.

An Overview of Integral Theory

An All-Inclusive Framework for the Twenty-First Century

Sean Esbjörn-Hargens

The word integral means comprehensive, inclusive, non-marginalizing, embracing. Integral approaches to any field attempt to be exactly that: to include as many perspectives, styles, and methodologies as possible within a coherent view of the topic. In a certain sense, integral approaches are "meta-paradigms," or ways to draw together an already existing number of separate paradigms into an interrelated network of approaches that are mutually enriching.

—Ken Wilber

The world has never been so complex as it is right now—it is mind boggling and at times emotionally overwhelming. Not to mention, the world only seems to get more complex and cacophonous as we confront the major problems of our day: extreme religious fundamentalism, environmental degradation, failing education systems, existential alienation, and volatile financial markets. Never have there been so many disciplines and worldviews to consider and consult in addressing these issues: a cornucopia of perspectives. But without a way of linking, leveraging, correlating, and aligning these perspectives, their contribution to the problems we face are largely lost or compromised. We are now part of a global community and we need a framework—global in vision yet also anchored in the minutiae of our daily lives—that can hold the variety of valid perspectives that have something to offer our individual efforts and collective solution building.

In 1977 American philosopher Ken Wilber published his first book, *The Spectrum of Consciousness*. This groundbreaking book integrated the major schools of psychology along a continuum of increasing complexity, with different schools focused on various levels within that spectrum. Over the next 30 years he continued with this integrative impulse, writing books in areas such as cultural anthropology, philosophy, sociology of religion, physics,

33

healthcare, environmental studies, science and religion, and postmodernism. To date, Wilber has published more than two dozen books and in the process has created *Integral Theory*.[1] Wilber's books have been translated into more than 24 languages, which gives you an idea as to the global reach and utility of Integral Theory.[2] Since its inception by Wilber, Integral Theory has become one of the foremost approaches within the larger fields of integral studies and metatheory.[3] This prominent role is in large part the result of the wide range of applications that Integral Theory has proven itself efficacious in as well as the work of many scholar-practitioners who have and are contributing to the further development of Integral Theory.

Integral Theory is the comprehensive study of reality, which weaves together the significant insights from all the major human disciplines of knowledge acquisition, including the natural and social sciences as well as the arts and humanities. As a result of its comprehensive nature, Integral Theory is being used in over 35 distinct academic and professional fields such as art, healthcare, organizational management, ecology, congregational ministry, economics, psychotherapy, law, and feminism.[4] In addition, Integral Theory has been used to develop an approach to personal transformation and integration called Integral Life Practice (ILP). The ILP framework allows individuals to systematically explore and develop multiple aspects of themselves such as their physical body, emotional intelligence, cognitive awareness, interpersonal relationships, and spiritual wisdom. Because Integral Theory systematically includes more of reality and interrelates it more thoroughly than any other current approach to assessment and solution building, it has the potential to be more successful in dealing with the complex problems we face in the twenty-first century.

Integral Theory provides individuals and organizations with a powerful content-free framework that is suitable to virtually any context and can be used at any scale. Why? Because it has the capacity to organize and honor all existing approaches to and disciplines of analysis and action, and it allows a practitioner to select the most relevant and important tools, techniques, and insights. Consequently, Integral Theory is being used successfully in a wide range of contexts such as the intimate setting of one-on-one psychotherapy as well as in the United Nations "Leadership for Results" program, which is a global response to HIV/AIDS used in more than 30 countries. Toward the end of this chapter I provide additional examples of Integral Theory in action to illustrate the variety of contexts in which people are finding the Integral framework useful. Additional examples will be provided by subsequent chapters.

Wilber first began to use the word *integral* to refer to his approach after the publication of his seminal book *Sex, Ecology, Spirituality* in 1995. It was in this book that he introduced the quadrant model, which has since become iconic of his work in general and Integral Theory in particular. Wilber's quadrant model is often referred to as the *AQAL model,* with "AQAL" (pronounced *ah-qwal*) serving as an acronym for "all quadrants, all levels." Quadrants and levels are two of the five basic elements within Wilber's Integral approach. The others are *lines, states,* and *types*—all of these plus levels are some of the most basic repeating patterns of reality, which occur in each of the four quadrants. Thus, by including all of these patterns you "cover the bases" well, ensuring that no major part of any solution is left out or neglected.

These five elements provide the theoretical architecture for a content-free framework (i.e., the AQAL model). Each of these five elements can be used to "look at" reality and at the same time they represent the basic aspects of your own awareness in this and every moment. In this overview I will walk you through the essential features of each of these elements and provide examples of how they are used in various contexts, why they are useful for an integral practitioner, and how to identify these elements in your own awareness right now. By the end of this tour, you will have a solid grasp of one of the most versatile and dynamic approaches to integrating insights from multiple disciplines. So let us begin with the foundation of the AQAL model: the quadrants.

All Quadrants: The Basic Dimension-Perspectives

According to Integral Theory, there are at least four irreducible *perspectives* (subjective, intersubjective, objective, and interobjective) that must be consulted when attempting to fully understand any issue or aspect of reality. Thus, the quadrants express the simple recognition that everything can be viewed from two fundamental distinctions: (1) an inside and an outside perspective and (2) a singular and plural perspective. A quick example can help illustrate this: imagine trying to understand the components of a successful meeting at work. You would want to draw on psychological insights and cultural beliefs (the insides of individuals and groups) as well as behavioral observations and organizational dynamics (the outsides of individuals and groups) to fully appreciate what is involved in conducting worthwhile meetings.

These four quadrants also represent *dimensions* of reality. These dimensions are actual aspects of the world that are always present in each moment. For instance, all individuals (including animals) have some form of subjective experience and intentionality, or *interiors,* as well as various observable behaviors and physiological components, or *exteriors.* In addition, individuals are never just alone but are members of groups or collectives. The interiors of collectives are known generally as intersubjective cultural realities whereas their exteriors are known as ecological and social systems, which are characterized by interobjective dynamics. These four dimensions are represented by four basic pronouns: "I," "we," "it," and "its." Each pronoun represents one of the domains in the quadrant model: "I" represents the Upper Left (UL), "We" represents the Lower Left (LL), "It" represents the Upper Right (UR), and "Its" represents the Lower Right (LR) (see Fig. 1.1).

As both of the Right-Hand quadrants (UR and LR) are characterized by objectivity, the four quadrants are also referred to as the three value spheres of subjectivity (UL), intersubjectivity (LL), and objectivity (UR and LR). These three domains of reality are discernable in all major languages through pronouns that represent first-, second-, and third-person perspectives and are referred to by Wilber as "the Big Three:" I, We, and It/s. These three spheres can also be characterized as aesthetics, morals, and science or consciousness, culture, and nature (see Fig. 1.2).

Integral Theory insists that you cannot understand one of these realities (any of the quadrants or the Big Three) through the lens of any of the others. For example, viewing subjective psychological realities primarily through an objective empirical lens distorts much of what is valuable about those psychological dynamics. In fact, the irreducibility of these three spheres has been recognized throughout the history of Western philosophy, from Plato's True, Good, and Beautiful to Immanuel Kant's famous three critiques of pure reason, judgment, and practical reason to Jürgen Habermas's validity claims of truth, rightness, and truthfulness (Fig. 1.2). Wilber is a staunch advocate of avoiding reducing one of these spheres into the others. In particular, he cautions against what he calls *flatland:* the attempt to reduce interiors to their exterior correlates (i.e.,

INTERIOR   EXTERIOR

	UPPER LEFT	UPPER RIGHT
I N D I V I D U A L	I Intentional (subjective)	IT Behavioral (objective)
C O L L E C T I V E	WE Cultural (intersubjective)	ITS Social (interobjective)
	LOWER LEFT	LOWER RIGHT

Figure 1.1 The four quadrants

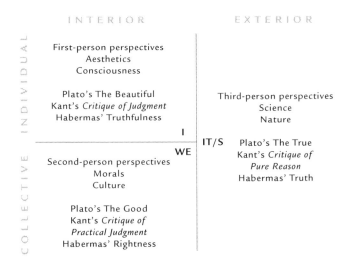

Figure 1.2 The Big Three

collapsing subjective and intersubjective realities into their objective aspects). This is often seen in systems approaches to the natural world, which represent consciousness through diagrams of feedback loops and in the process leave out the texture and felt-sense of first- and second-person experience.

One of the reasons Integral Theory is so illuminating and useful is that it embraces the complexity of reality in ways few other frameworks or models do. In contrast to approaches that explicitly or inadvertently reduce one quadrant to another, Integral Theory understands each quadrant as simultaneously arising. In order to illustrate the simultaneity of all quadrants I will provide a simple example with Figure 1.1 in mind. Let us say I decide I need to buy some flowers for the garden and I have the thought, "I want to go to the nursery." The Integral framework demonstrates that this thought and its associated action (e.g., driving to the garden store and purchasing roses) has at least four dimensions, none of which can be separated because they co-arise (or *tetra-mesh*) and inform each other. First, there is the individual thought and how I experience it (e.g., mentally calculating travel time, the experience of joy in shopping, or the financial anxiety over how I will pay for my purchase). These experiences are informed by psychological structures and somatic feelings associated with the UL quadrant. At the same time, there is the unique combination of neuronal activity, brain chemistry, and bodily states that accompany this thought, as well as any behavior that occurs (e.g., putting on a coat, getting in the car). These behaviors are associated with various activities of our brain and physiological activity of the body, which are associated with the UR quadrant. Likewise, there are ecological, economic, political, and social systems that supply the nursery with items to sell, determine the price of flowers, and so on. These systems are interconnected through global markets, national laws, and the ecologies associated with the LR quadrant. There is also a cultural context that determines whether I associate "nursery" with an open-air market, a big shopping mall, or a small stall in an alley, as well as determining the various meanings and culturally appropriate interactions that occur between people at the nursery. These cultural aspects are associated with worldviews in the LL quadrant.

Thus, to have a full understanding of and appreciation for the occurrence of the thought, "I'm going to the nursery," one cannot explain it fully through just the terms of *either* psychology (UL), *or* neurobiology and physiology (UR), *or* social and economic dynamics (LR), *or* cultural meaning (LL). For the most complete view, as we will see, one should take into consideration all of these domains (and their respective levels of complexity or depth). Why is this practical? Well if we tried to summarize this simple situation by leaving out one or more perspectives, a fundamental aspect of the integral whole would be lost and our ability to understand it and address it would be compromised. Thus, integral practitioners often use the quadrants as their first move to scan a situation or issue and bring multiple perspectives to bear on the inquiry or exploration at hand.

Quadrants and Quadrivia

As noted above, there are at least two ways to depict and use the quadrant model: as *dimensions* or as *perspectives*. The first, a *quadratic* approach, depicts an individual situated in the center of the quadrants (see Fig. 1.3). The arrows point from the individual toward the various realities that he can perceive as a result of his own embodied awareness. Through his use of different aspects of his own awareness, or through formal methods based on these dimensions of awareness, he is able to encounter these different realities in a direct and knowable fashion. In brief, he has direct access to experiential, behavioral, cultural, and social/systemic aspects of reality because these are actual dimensions of his own existence. This is useful to him because it empowers him to notice, acknowledge, and interact more effectively with his world. In short, the more of these "channels" he has open the more information he will be obtaining about what is happening around him, and he will be able to feel and act in ways that are timely and insightful. Notice right now how you are engaged in all three perspectives: first-person (e.g., noticing your own thoughts as you read this), second-person (e.g., reading my words and interpreting what I am trying to convey), and third-person (e.g., sitting there aware of the light, sounds, and air temperature around you). Do you see how

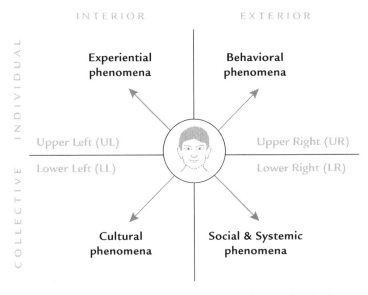

Figure 1.3 The four quadrants of an individual

you are always experiencing the world from all four quadrants—right here, right now? It is that simple.

Another way to represent the quadrant model is as a *quadrivia*. Quadrivia refers to four ways of seeing (*quadrivium* is singular). In this approach the different perspectives associated with each quadrant are directed at a particular reality, which is placed in the center of the diagram. Let us say hundreds of fish are dying in a lake. The death of these fish become the focus or object of investigation and analysis, with expertise from each of the quadratic domains evaluating the situation. The arrows pointing toward the center indicate the methodologies that different experts (associated with each quadrant) use to study the dying fish. In an Integral approach these include exploring the emotions, self-identities, and beliefs of individuals who live on the lake through *psychological and experiential inquiry*; exploring the empirical, chemical, and biological factors contributing to the dying fish through *behavioral and physio-logical analyses*; exploring the philosophical, ethical, and religious viewpoints of the community around the lake through *cultural and worldview investigations*; and exploring the environmental, political, educational, legal, and economic factors of the situation through *ecological and social assessments* (see Fig. 1.4).

In sum, the quadrants highlight four irreducible dimensions that all indi-viduals have and quadrivia refer to the four fundamental perspectives that can be taken on any phenomena. In either case, the four quadrants or quadrivia are co-nascent—literally "they are born together" and are mutually implicated in

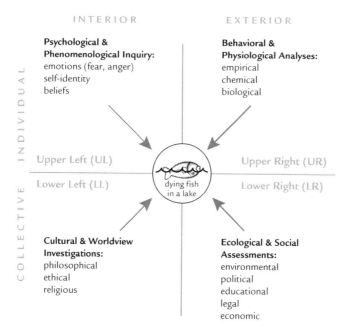

Figure 1.4 The four quadrivia of a lake

one another. In other words, they co-arise and tetra-mesh. This understanding is useful because it honors the complexity of reality in a way that allows the practitioner to address problems in a more skillful and nuanced way. Furthermore, the quadrants represent the native ways in which we experience reality in each moment ("looking as") and quadrivia represent the most common ways we can and often do look at reality to understand it ("looking at").

All Levels: Depth and Complexity

Within each quadrant there are levels of development. Within the interior, Left-Hand quadrants there are levels of *depth* and within the exterior, Right-Hand quadrants there are levels of *complexity*. The levels within each quadrant are best understood as probability waves that represent the dynamic nature of reality and the ways different realities show up under certain conditions. Additionally, each quadrant's levels are correlated with levels in the other quadrants. For example, a goal-driven executive (UL) who has high blood pressure (UR) will most likely be found in a scientific-rational culture or subculture (LL), which usually occurs in industrial corporate organizations (LR). In this example, all of these aspects of the situation are occurring at the same level of complexity and depth within their respective quadrants and are therefore correlated at level five in Figure 1.5. The inclusion of levels is important because they allow us to appreciate and better interface with the realities associated with each quadrant. Each quadrant serves as a map of different terrains of reality. The levels within each quadrant represent the topographical contour-lines of that terrain. This helps us to identify the unique features of that particular landscape, which enables us to travel through it more successfully and enjoy the amazing vistas along the way.

Levels or *waves* in each quadrant demonstrate *holarchy*, which is a kind of hierarchy wherein each new level transcends the limits of the previous levels but includes the essential aspects of those same levels. Thus, each wave inherits the wave of the past and adds a new level of organization or capacity. As a result, each level of complexity or depth is both a part of a larger structure and a whole structure in and of itself. In the subjective realm, sensations are transcended and included in impulses, which are transcended and included in emotions, which are transcended and included in symbols, which are transcended and included in concepts. Likewise, in the intersubjective realm this dynamic occurs from archaic interpretations to magical explanations, to mythical stories, to rational views, to integral understandings. In the objective realm this movement occurs from atoms to molecules, to cells, to

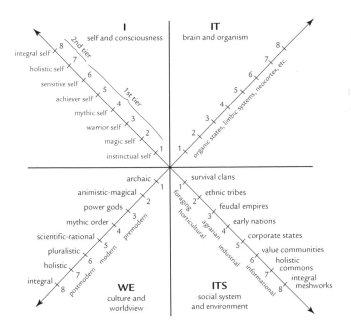

Figure 1.5 Some levels in the four quadrants

tissues, to organs. And in the interobjective realm this occurs in the movement from galaxies to planets, to ecosystems, to families, to villages (see Fig. 1.5 for another presentation of what is transcended and included in each quadrant).[5] Regardless of where different researchers might draw the line between levels, a general pattern of evolution or development occurs in each quadrant: depth enfolds (i.e., folds in on itself), complexity increases (i.e., expands out and includes more).

Levels of development are often represented by arrows bisecting each quadrant (as in Fig. 1.5). Integral Theory uses the notion of general *altitude* as a content-free way of comparing and contrasting development across different domains either within or between quadrants. This is akin to using a thermometer to gauge temperature in a variety of settings—a centigrade thermometer works at the Equator just as well as in the Arctic, and as a result allows us to compare the weather in those distant places in a meaningful way. Integral Theory uses the colors of the rainbow to represent each distinct level (e.g., red, amber, orange, green, teal, turquoise). This spectrum of color also represents the general movement of a widening identity: from "me" (egocentric) to "my group" (ethnocentric) to "my country" (sociocentric) to "all of us" (worldcentric) to "all beings" (planetcentric) to finally "all of reality" (Kosmoscentric) (see Fig. 1.6). This general trajectory of expanding awareness has correlates in each quadrant. Integral Theory also uses the image of concentric circles (often overlaid on the quadrants) to highlight the nested quality of levels transcending and including each other (see Fig. 1.6).

The inclusion of levels in an Integral approach is valuable because it recognizes the many potential layers of development within any domain of

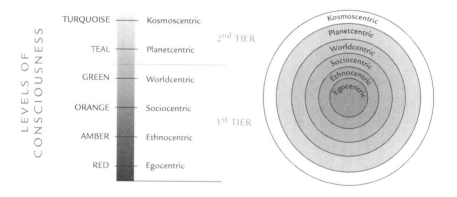

Figure 1.6 Widening identity (left) and the nested quality of levels as they transcend and include each other (right)

reality. Practitioners gain valuable traction by aiming their efforts at the appropriate scale and thereby finding the key leverage point—like an acupuncturist hitting the right spot for optimal health and well-being. This conserves energy and resources and focuses efforts optimally. For example, imagine working with a group of teachers on developing a new mission statement for their educational program. Clearly, working with the realities of the LL quadrant will be paramount—articulating shared vision and meaning, exploring via dialogue various phrases that might be used in the document, and so on. But you are going to be more effective in facilitating this collaborative process if you have a sense of the levels of shared meaning that are operative in this group and what they are trying to communicate in their statement. Are they operating primarily out of modern values, postmodern values, or a combination of both? Knowing this will greatly inform your capacity to serve their effort. Thus, it often is not enough to just be aware of the quadrants—you must also work with the depth and complexity within each domain.

Just as we can locate each quadrant in our own awareness through the use of first-, second-, and third-person perspectives, so too can we locate levels of depth and complexity in our direct experience. To illustrate this, all you have to do is notice how you tend to go through your day with a predictable amount of depth and complexity. For example, on good days you feel more depth and can handle more complexity and on other days you seem to be tripping over everything (diminished capacity to handle complexity) and find yourself getting irritated at the smallest thing (diminished capacity to experience depth). Thus, you often go through your day primarily expressing one altitude or level more than others, although you have a felt sense of what it is like to be "up leveling your game" (a level above) or "misfiring with each step" (a level below).

All Lines: Various Developmental Capacities

Lines of development are another way to describe the distinct capacities that develop through levels in each aspect of reality as represented by the quadrants. So if levels are contour-lines on a hiking map for reality, then lines of development represent the various trails you can take to transverse the vast wilderness of human potential and social complexity. For example, in the individual-interior quadrant of experience, the lines that develop include, but are not limited to, cognitive, emotional, interpersonal, and moral capacities. These capacities are often thought of as the multiple intelligences that each person has. The idea being that each of us is more developed in some areas than others. Integral Theory uses a *psychograph* to depict an individual's unique assortment of development in various individual lines (Fig. 1.7).

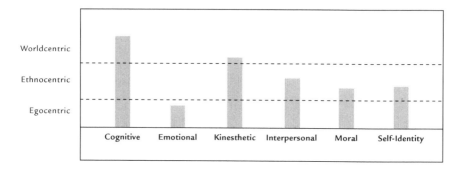

Figure 1.7 A psychograph

Similarly, a *sociograph* is used to represent the various lines of development within a family, group, culture, or society (Fig. 1.8). The kinds of lines found in cultures include things such as kinesthetic capacities, interpersonal maturity (e.g., absence of slaves, women's rights, civil liberties), artistic expression (e.g., forms of music, government funding for the arts), cognitive or technological capacities, physical longevity (e.g., healthcare systems, diet), and polyphasic maturity. *Polyphasic* refers to a culture's general access to different states of consciousness. For example, many indigenous cultures embrace access to and cultivation of different kinds of states of awareness while rational Western societies tend to emphasize rational waking consciousness at the exclusion of other modes of experiencing reality. An integral practitioner can use lines as a diagnostic tool to ensure these aspects of individuals or groups are acknowledged and effectively addressed. Below is an overview of the kinds of lines that can be included in an integral assessment.

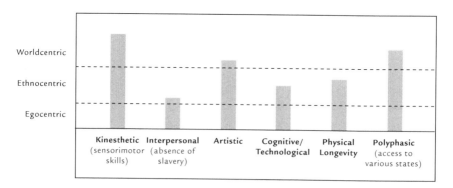

Figure 1.8 A sociograph

Each line within a quadrant has correlates in the other quadrants. For example, as the cognitive line develops in the UL quadrant there are corresponding behavioral and neurophysiological developments in the UR quadrant, corresponding intersubjective capacities in the LL quadrant, and grammatical structures in the LR quadrant. In fact, there are a variety of lines in each quadrant. Above I listed some of the common lines associated with the UL. Lines associated with the UR include the developmental pathways of things such as skeletal-muscular growth, brainwave patterns, the neuronal system, and other organic structures of the body. In the LL we find lines such as the sequence of worldviews and cultural values, various intersubjective dynamics, religious and philosophical viewpoints, and linguistic meaning. Lastly, in the LR specific lines include how ecosystems develop as well as evolutionary pathways of adaptation, geopolitical structures, and forces of production (Fig. 1.9).

What distinguishes a line from other patterns such as states or types is that a line demonstrates sequential development with increasing levels of complexity or depth that transcend and include the previous level. In other words, there has to be an identifiable series of stages that unfold in a particular order and any given stage cannot be skipped. For example, within the LR line of forces of production we see a societal path starting with foraging (e.g., hunting and gathering) giving way to horticulture (e.g., using a hoe) giving way to agrarian methods (e.g., using a plow), and so forth—each new development is dependent on what came before and is in part a response to the limits of that previous level.

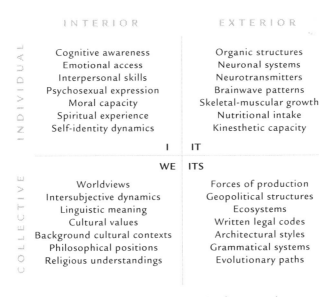

Figure 1.9 Some lines in the four quadrants

The lines element especially demonstrates how Integral Theory includes the contributions of many existing fields and organizes them in a useful way. Also, lines are important to integral practitioners because they identify distinct aspects of each quadrant that demonstrate development and evolution. By being aware of the specific dynamics of growth and the typical trajectory of such transformation, a practitioner can better support and make use of these streams of development. Consequently, integral assessments will often identify which lines are strong and which ones are in need of attention, leveraging the more developed ones to assist in addressing the limits of the less developed ones. Knowing the level of development within various lines provides integral practitioners with valuable information about the realities of a given situation and helps the practitioner align those realities for optimal improvement.

As with the other elements of the AQAL model, we do not have to go far to discover lines in our immediate awareness. Just recall a recent moment where you felt stretched or challenged, such as giving difficult feedback to a colleague or trying some new task that required a high level of hand-eye coordination. Now bring into your awareness an area where you are often more capable than your colleagues, such as seeing multiple perspectives at the same time on some complex situation or an ability to emotionally connect to your friends and describe—better than they can—what they are feeling. Drawing on personal examples of areas where you are less or more developed than people around you shows we all have a unique combination of lines at various levels of development. In fact, rarely a day goes by that we are not aware of the truth of this within ourselves and in our interactions with others. Besides, life would be significantly less interesting if everyone was equal in depth and complexity in most areas.

All States: Temporary Expressions

In addition to levels and lines there are also various kinds of states associated with each quadrant. States are temporary occurrences of aspects of reality (lasting anywhere from a few seconds to days, and in some cases even months or years). They also tend to be incompatible with each other. For example, you cannot be drunk and sober at the same time, a town cannot experience a blizzard and a heat wave on the same day. Below are a few examples of the kinds of states associated with each quadrant (Fig. 1.10). Thus, to continue with our hiking metaphor, states can be likened to the momentary glimpses of nature you get as you walk along the trail. For example, how a breathtaking vista keeps "popping" through the trees as you hike or your experience of a bird that grabs your attention as it makes a unique *click-clack-clack* sound and then is gone. Before you know it, these attention-grabbing experiences recede into the background and you are back on the trail pounding dirt with your hiking boots.

In the UL quadrant there are *phenomenal states* such as elevated and depressed emotional states, insights, intuitions, and moment-to-moment feeling states. There are also the *natural states* of waking, dreaming, and deep sleep as well as the Witness (the pure observing awareness of all the other states) and even non-duality, where the Witness dissolves into everything that is witnessed. Various religious traditions provide us with rich and sophisticated descriptions of these states and practices for cultivating them. In addition, there are *altered states* of consciousness that can be either externally induced (e.g., through the use of drugs, trauma, or a near-death experience) or internally induced or trained (e.g., meditative, holotropic, flow, lucid dreaming, peak experiences). When states are trained they often unfold and even stabilize in a sequential pattern, moving from gross to subtle to very subtle (i.e., causal) forms of experience and are thus referred to as *state-stages*. This is contrasted with the *structure-stages* of psychological development (discussed above in the levels and lines sections). Both states and structures of consciousness can occur in stages, with state-stages expanding horizontally and structure-stages growing vertically.

In the UR quadrant there are *brain states* (alpha, beta, theta, and delta) and *hormonal states* associated with the cycles of estrogen, progesterone, and

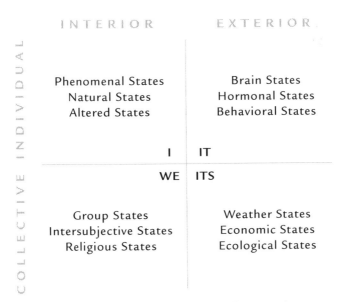

Figure 1.10 Some states in the four quadrants

testosterone. There are also *behavioral states* such as crying and smiling. In fact, states are often used to describe the ways natural phenomena morph from one thing into another (e.g., H_2O turning from solid ice to liquid water to gaseous steam).

In the LL quadrant we find *group states* such as mob mentality or mass hysteria, crowd excitement, and group-think. There are also *intersubjective states* such as the somatic states that occur between infants and their mothers or shared resonance between two people in an engaging dialogue. Similar to altered states in individuals, there are *religious states* within groups such as shared ecstasy and bliss or a communal experience of the divine.

In the LR quadrant there are *weather states* (drought, snow storms, torrential rain) and fluctuating room temperature indoors. Our financial markets go through a variety of *economic states* such as bear and bull markets, bubbles, recessions, and so forth. We also talk about old-growth forests representing a climax community—a steady-state of equilibrium. This notion of equilibrium is illustrative of various *ecological states* such as entropy (increased disorder) or eutrophy (being well-nourished).

The inclusion of states is useful for practitioners because our realities both internally and externally are always shifting—all kinds of state changes occur throughout our day within ourselves and our environments. Including states allows us to understand many of the ways these shifts occur and why. This in turns allows us to be attentive to these shifts and place them in service of our efforts instead of being knocked off center by their occurrence. For example, when we are aware of the many states a group of people go through in a full-day workshop, we can design our curriculum to honor these shifting "moods" and to even make use of them to facilitate learning.

As far as locating this element in our direct awareness, we only have to notice how many different emotions we experience in a short period of time. Most of us are aware of how quickly we can shift from feeling "on cloud nine" due to some really good news to getting frustrated because some "jerk" just cut us off on the freeway to feeling anxiety about having to speak in front of a group at work to getting hungry and wondering what are you going to have for dinner. . . . And to think that all of these states can occur within five minutes.

All Types: Various Styles

Types are the variety of consistent styles that arise in various domains and occur irrespective of developmental levels. Types can overlap or be incongruous. Drawing again on the hiking metaphor, we can think of types as the different kinds of hikers there are—those who like to go fast, those who meander, those who take lots of pictures, those who like to sing, and so on.

These kinds of people tend to hike like this regardless of what kinds of trails they are on or terrains they are moving through; they bring their unique style wherever they go. As with the other elements, types have expressions in all four quadrants (see Fig. 1.11).

In the UL quadrant there are *personality types*. There are numerous systems that map the number of different personalities, including Keirsey (4 types), Enneagram (9 types), and Myers-Briggs (16 types). In this quadrant there are also the *gender types* of masculine and feminine. In general, individuals have access to both masculine and feminine qualities and thus tend to have a unique combination of traits associated with each type. In the UR quadrant there are *blood types* (A, B, AB, O) and William Sheldon's well-known *body types* (ectomorph, endomorph, mesomorph). In the LR quadrant there are ecological *biome types* (e.g., steppe, tundra, islands) and governmental *regime types* (e.g., communist, democracy, dictatorship, monarchy, republic). In the LL quadrant there are types of *religious systems* (e.g., monotheism, polytheism, pantheism) and different types of *kinship systems* (e.g., Eskimo, Hawaiian, Iroquois, Omaha, Sudanese).

The usefulness of types has been acknowledged in multiple contexts, such as designing nutritional diets or building effective work teams. Being aware of types allows integral practitioners to adjust their craft to accommodate some of the most common and consistent styles associated with various contexts. Types

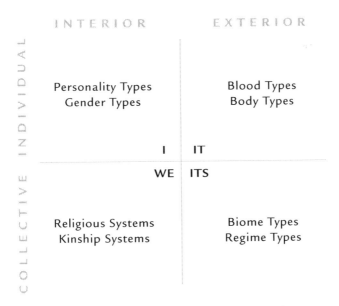

Figure 1.11 Some types in the four quadrants

are very stable and resilient patterns—after all, they are horizontal structures or *type-structures* (in contrast to vertical structure-stages). So by becoming more aware of them and their role in whatever you are attempting to do, you are more able to infuse sustainability into your efforts by linking to existing enduring patterns.

Within our own awareness, types are most obvious when we consider masculine and feminine expressions. We each have access to both, and know what it feels like to be solid and agentic—for example, going for the goal (one aspect of masculine) or enjoying the game for the game's sake (one aspect of feminine). We can even shift between these styles, although some of us are more identified with one side of this spectrum than others. You likely can think of men or women you consider more masculine or more feminine and what it feels like to be around them—do you find yourself being more masculine or feminine as a way of meeting them in that mode or by way of providing a contrast with their type? Another area where we have a direct experience of types is in terms of personality qualities such as introversion and extroversion. Thus, we are often aware of type dynamics in our experience of ourselves and others.

All Zones: Different Ways of Knowing

In addition to the five elements of Integral Theory, which comprise the basic foundation of the AQAL model, there is an another more advanced aspect that is important to mention. This aspect is less of a new element and more of a complexification of the first one (the quadrants). Each of the perspectives associated with the four quadrants can be studied through two major methodological families, namely from either the inside (i.e., a first-person perspective) or the outside (i.e., a third-person perspective). This results in eight distinct *zones* of human inquiry and research. These eight zones comprise what Integral Theory calls *Integral Methodological Pluralism* (IMP), which includes such approaches as phenomenology (an exploration of first-person subjective realities), ethnomethodology (an exploration of second-person intersubjective realities), and empiricism (an exploration of third-person empirical realities).[6] Figure 1.12 includes all eight zones and their respective labels. IMP represents one of the most pragmatic and inclusive theoretical formulations of any integral or metatheoretical approach. It gives the integral practitioner assurance that they are using tried and true methods of investigation that human ingenuity has produced over the last 2,000 years.

Integral Methodological Pluralism operates according to three principles: *inclusion* (consult multiple perspectives and methods impartially), *enfoldment* (prioritize the importance of findings generated from these perspectives),

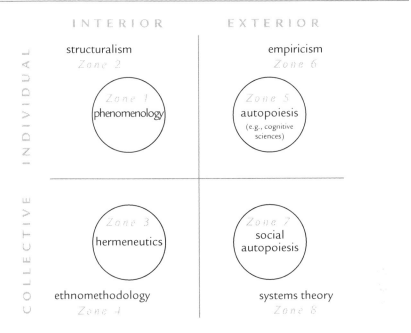

Figure 1.12 Eight methodological zones

and *enactment* (recognize that phenomena are disclosed to subjects through their activity of knowing them). As a result of these commitments, Integral Theory emphasizes the dynamic quality of realities as being *enacted* through a subject using a particular method to study an object. That object can be a first-, second-, or third-person reality. For example, we can study first-person psychological realities as an object of investigation just as easily as we can study third-person biological realities.

Because Integral Theory acknowledges and includes all the major insights from established forms of research, it emphasizes the importance of including all zones in its efforts to understand anything in a comprehensive way. It uses the IMP framework as a way to marshal, coordinate, and assess pertinent perspectives and their research findings. To return to our integral hiker, IMP provides her with multiple ways of interacting with and knowing the landscape she is traveling through. Her compass, binoculars, book of edible plants, early morning meditations, and previous wildlife encounters all provide her with different ways of knowing the wilderness in ways that are meaningful and valuable to her as a hiker and nature lover.

Among the many important perspectives on reality, there are schools of thought that specialize in using the methods, practices, and techniques associated with each zone. Consequently, in addition to the five elements presented above, an Integral approach must include all eight zones or it risks leaving out important aspects of reality that have a bearing on effective solutions to the problems facing our communities and our planet. In other words, the more of reality we acknowledge and include, the more sustainable our solutions will become, precisely because a project will respond more effectively to the complexity of that reality. We cannot exclude major dimensions of reality and expect comprehensive, sustainable results. Eventually those realities that have been excluded will demand recognition and incorporation as the design falters and is abandoned for more nuanced and comprehensive strategies. Hence the need for an Integral approach.

An integral practitioner is constantly combining first-, second-, and third-person methods, practices, and techniques in an effort to research the many essential aspects of a given situation. Performing such Integral Research, either through informal or formal means, the practitioner is engaged in Integral Methodological Pluralism. This kind of integral mixed methods orientation is extremely valuable because it allows practitioners to often discover surprising relationships between first-, second-, and third-person realities that later become essential links in their designs and solutions. Through IMP, integral practitioners are often able to identify valuable connections between distinct realities that have yet to be identified or leveraged in previous efforts. Thus, equipped with the eight major forms of knowledge acquisition developed by humanity, the integral practitioner is well positioned to know the complexity and depth of reality and to place that insight into service for self, culture, and nature. The reason an integral practitioner can use this wide assortment of formal methods in the first place is that they are actively engaged in using all of these methods informally in their own embodied awareness. In fact, each major methodological family (e.g., empiricism or hermeneutics) is simply a formalized version of something we do naturally all the time. For example, our ability to take a third-person perspective on the world around us (e.g., looking at the flowers growing along the sidewalk) is the basis for empiricism and our ability to take a second-person perspective with our friends (e.g., talking to them about why they want to quit their job) is the basis for hermeneutics. Consequently, the eight zones of IMP is simply a reminder of the many ways we know ourselves, others, and the world around us. The Integral framework allows us to coordinate these multiple ways of knowing and place them into orchestrated action in the world.

In summary, Integral Theory is characterized as being *perspectival, post-metaphysical,* and *postdisciplinary.* It is perspectival in that it includes first-, second-, and third-person perspectives in a nonreductive way—often through the use of the four quadrants, which represent subjective, intersubjective, objective, and interobjective realities. In addition, it draws on constructive developmental research to point out that individuals at different levels of psychological complexity hold different perspectives on the same phenomenon. It is postmetaphysical in that it uses the eight zones of Integral Methodological Pluralism to include the enduring truths and insights from all the major modes of investigating reality. As a result of this broad empiricism Integral Theory emphasizes the enactive nature of all phenomena and thus avoids postulating preexisting ontological structures.[7] It is postdisciplinary by virtue of its applicability within, between, and across disciplinary boundaries. In other words, Integral Theory is just as effective within a single discipline such as psychology as it is in supporting inter- or transdisciplinary efforts. Due to its content-free status Integral Theory is often used as a transcdisciplinary framework to bring insights from many divergent disciplines to bear on a single issue or aspect of reality.

Integral Theory in Action

As you can see by now, an all-quadrants, all-levels, all-lines, all-states, all-types, *and* all-zones approach is pretty comprehensive. Of course, you do not have to use all of these distinctions all the time. In fact, even using two of these elements can make your approach to analysis or solution building more integral than many others. However, having all six of them in your "toolbox" allows you more capacity to respond to the complexity of our world and provides a place for including the essential aspects of any given situation. In addition, it helps us understand the relationships between the various facets of reality that we come across. In fact, this is what sets Integral Theory apart from all other integrative and comprehensive approaches to solution generation and change facilitation. Arguably there is no metaframework as inclusive and theoretically sound as Integral Theory, which is what has made it such a useful approach in so many contexts. The AQAL model is a dynamic framework that does more than just cover the basic elements of reality—it interrelates them in a way that allows us to ensure that we are leveraging our efforts in an functional, aesthetic, accurate, and just way. In other words, an Integral approach allows for True, Good, and Beautiful solutions to the major problems we face as we travel into the twenty-first century.

In fact, the AQAL model is multivariant and can be understood in a number of ways. AQAL is a *map* because it is a series of third-person symbols and abstractions that can guide a person through the contours of their own awareness, as well as through some of the most important aspects of any situation. It is a *framework* because it creates a mental space where one can organize and index their and others' current activities in a clear and coherent manner. It is a *theory* because it offers an explanation for how the most time-tested methodologies and data they generate can fit together. It is a *practice* because it is not just a theory about inclusion but an actual series of practices of inclusion. It involves the metaparadigm of correlating humanity's most fundamental methodologies of knowledge generation. AQAL can also be practiced in a more personal setting, which results in Integral Life Practice (ILP). It is a set of *perspectives* because it brings together first-, second-, and third-person perspectives. It is a *catalyst* because it psychoactively scans your entire body-mind and activates or "lights up" any potentials (quadrant, level, line, state, or type) that are presently not fully being used. Lastly, it is a *matrix* because it combines all quadrants, levels, lines, states, and types in a way that generates a space of potential out of which more of reality can be enacted and be accounted for than any other model has ever included. In short, the AQAL model can be summarized as a *third-person map* of reality, a *second-person framework* for working within and across disciplines, and a *first-person practice* for engaging the development of our own embodied awareness. All three of these aspects of the AQAL model—map, framework, and practice—contribute to an increased experience of intimacy with reality by expanding and deepening our contact with more dimensions of ourselves, our communities, and our environments.

Now that you have a general overview of the AQAL model, I can highlight how approaches are using integral principles successfully in the field: in the classroom, in the board room, in the political arena, and in home offices. In addition to disciplinary uses of the AQAL model (e.g., Integral Ecology or Integral Psychotherapy), there have also been systematic efforts to advance Integral Theory as a specific field of meta-studies. Four main efforts currently contribute to this goal: (1) the peer-reviewed *Journal of Integral Theory and Practice*, which has published more than 150 academic articles and case studies to date; (2) John F. Kennedy University's Department of Integral Theory, with its online master of arts program and one-year certificate in Integral Theory (this program is doing much to train the next wave of integral leadership in application of the AQAL model); (3) the Integral Research Center, which is supporting graduate-level mixed methods research around the world, which is informed by Integral Theory; (4) the international biennial Integral Theory Conference, which recently brought together 500 academics and practitioners from all over the globe who are applying and refining Integral Theory; and (5) the SUNY Press series in Integral Theory, which is committed to publishing three to five volumes of the best academic material that advances the field each year.[8] This systemic effort is important because it allows discipline-specific practitioners (e.g., integral psychotherapists or integral educators) to know the model is sound, it educates integral practitioners to understand the model as a whole (independent of any discipline-specific application), and it creates a community of discourse and inquiry to further the development of the model in a way that invites critical thought and demonstrated practical efficacy.

In recent years a number of books have been published applying Integral Theory to various areas such as urban design (Marilyn Hamilton's [2008] *Integral City*), psychological assessment (Andre Marquis's [2007] *The Integral Intake*), organizational dynamics (Mark Edwards's [2010] *Organizational Transformation for Sustainability*), health (Elliott Dacher's [2006] *Integral Health*), ecology and environmental studies (my and Michael Zimmerman's [2009] *Integral Ecology*), psychopharmacology (Elliott Ingersoll and Carl Rank's [2006] *Psychopharmacology for Helping Professionals*), business (Daryl Paulson's [2002] *Competitive Business, Caring Business*), and international community development (Gail Hochachka's [2005] *Developing Sustainability, Developing the Self*). Numerous other titles are in press or in preparation. As noted above SUNY Press has recently established an academic book series in Integral Theory. In addition to this volume in the series, there are three others being published alongside it: two on Integral Psychotherapy and one on Integral Education.[9] Additional volumes will be coming out soon on Integral Recovery, Integral Gender Studies, Integral Leadership, and Integral Religious Studies. Numerous other manuscripts are in preparation. To date, the fields that have produced the largest amount of theoretical and applied material using Integral Theory include psychotherapy and psychology, education, mixed methods research, ecology and sustainability, international development, future studies, business, and organizational management.[10] Following are short descriptions of a number of current examples of Integral Theory in action.

Integral Education

The Integral Research Center (IRC) has recently designed and launched an ambitious longitudinal study using methods from all eight zones of Integral Methodological Pluralism to assess the transformative effects of Integral Education at John F. Kennedy University. The IRC is working with Theo Dawson of Developmental Testing Service and Susanne Cook-Greuter of Cook-Greuter and Associates to help with the research design, which includes the Lectical Assessment System (LAS) and the Sentence Completion Test (SCT). This study aims to discover, "In what ways do students transform within the online master of arts program in Integral Theory?" Do they, over the course of three years of coursework, demonstrate vertical stage development (e.g., exiting one level and beginning to stabilize the next one) and/or horizontal development (e.g., increased access to emotional content). If so, what aspects are developing? The results of this ongoing study will be used to improve the developmental potential of the curriculum, making it even more conducive to psychological transformation and growth.[11]

Integral International Development

One Sky–Canadian Institute for Sustainable Living in partnership with Drishti–Centre for Integral Action recently received a $500,000 grant from the Canadian International Development Agency for a three-year leadership development project entitled, "Integral Applications to Sustainability in the Niger Delta." Building on previous work it had done in Nigeria, One Sky was aware of the value of interventions associated with the Right-Hand quadrants that focused on "development, financial management, improved communications, and policy influence." While recognizing the essential role such efforts play, One Sky became increasingly aware of how these efforts could not be sustained without supportive interventions from the Left-Hand quadrants that focused on "personal leadership, self-awareness, moral intelligence, and interpersonal skills." Consequently, their project is working with 30 young Nigerians from nearly a dozen organizations in the Cross River region of the Niger Delta on environmental and economic sustainability. "The project essentially involves engaging a personal development process (I), held in place with learning communities and a new social discourse (We), and enacted in breakthrough initiatives in their home organizations (It/Its)."[12] In addition, this program will be evaluated through a pre/post assessment based on the principles of Integral Research.

Integral Forestry

Next Step Integral, an international nonprofit, was established in 2003 by Stephan Martineau. Soon he joined forces with Lisa Farr, the director of a local watershed association, to begin the arduous task of establishing an Integral approach to a community forest project in the Slocan Valley of British Columbia, Canada. This goal was particularly daunting given the historical tensions over a 35-year period between various worldviews within and outside of the community (e.g., loggers, miners, farmers, environmentalists, First Nations individuals, artists, practitioners of multiple religious faiths, government workers, and a multinational corporation). Also, there had already been *nine* failed attempts by the B.C. government to establish a workable solution to the divisions within the community between stakeholders connected to the forest. The guiding principles of their initiative included: recognizing and honoring the diverse perspectives about the forest of Slocan Valley residents; recognizing that these perspectives were informed by lenses associated with each of the quadrants (e.g., behavioral, cultural, psychological, historical); and recognizing that any viable long-term solution would have to integrate the many conflicting views within the community. In addition, Martineau identified a number of "main capacities" explicitly grounded in the AQAL model but used implicitly to support their initiative: holding and inhabiting multiple perspectives; an awareness of and an ability to work with the multiple lines of individuals; a commitment to personal growth and shadow work; creating shared motivations; balancing empathy, engagement, and impartiality; and cultivating qualities, attitudes, and capacities that supported mutual understanding.

On January 14, 2007, Next Step Integral submitted an application for a Community Forest Agreement to allow the local community to manage 35,000 acres of contested forest. In July of that same year their proposal was approved! Thus, three years of negotiations and grassroots work guided by the AQAL model resulted in the creation of a large-scale integral forestry cooperative—the first of its kind in the world. This community forest project has support of an impressive 95 percent of the inhabitants in the valley. Aptly named the Slocan Integral Forestry Cooperative (SIFCo), this project is a true testimony to the power of the Integral model—even as an implicit guide—in working with diverse perspectives to achieve a common goal that other approaches failed to manifest. Now that SIFCo has been granted tenure over the land, the coming years shall be an important testing ground and source of clarification of the tenets of Integral Ecology in general and of Integral Forestry in particular.[13]

Integral Coaching

Integral Coaching Canada (ICC), an Ottawa-based company, has developed an entire school and methodology for professional coaching based on the AQAL model. Over the past 10 years ICC has emerged as one of the premier schools in the world for professional coaching. They have a rigorous methodology that combines embodied perspective taking, presence, and powerful conceptual distinctions. Coaches use all five elements discussed above to support their own personal growth and to work with their clients' development. Typically it takes an individual two years to complete the certification process and become an Integral Coach®.[14] ICC has a strong reputation for demanding a great deal from their coaches-in-training, which includes each trainee committing to an Integral Life Practice that includes meditation, body work, journaling, and reading. They are one of the few coaching schools I am aware of that incorporates developmental psychology (e.g., Robert Kegan's subject-object theory) as the spine of their methodology.[15] This alone gives ICC a tremendous advantage over other schools because their approach is built on extensive psychological research about how and why humans transform and integrate new capacities. In fact, ICC's application of the Integral framework is one of if not the most sophisticated uses of integral principles in any context or field.

Integral Politics

The State of the World Forum (SOWF) was established in 1995 by Jim Garrison with Mikhail Gorbachev. SOWF began as a series of annual conferences that convened hundreds of international leaders (ranging from community organizers, Nobel laureates, social activists, heads of state, and business leaders) to explore key issues facing the globe. These gatherings established a Global Leadership Network committed to the guiding principle: "Transforming conversations that matter into actions that make a difference." Over the years, SOWF sponsored a variety of gatherings and "strategic initiatives" that resulted in a number of projects and nonprofit organizations.[16] In 2008, SOWF set its sights on the borderless problem of climate change and the global transition toward a "green economy," and in August 2009 initiated a 10-year cycle of international annual gatherings. The first gathering occurred in Brazil, subsequent ones will occur in various cities around the world. SOWF has adopted the AQAL model as the organizing framework for each event. Consequently, Integral Theory will be used for designing each conference and for guiding the development of policy recommendations to political leaders at all levels of government and civic responsibility. These gatherings will take place in different countries around the globe and build a coalition of multistake holders committed to developing innovative policy and effective action for confronting climate change and serving to guide the emergence of new sources of energy. The *Journal of Integral Theory and Practice* has recently published two special issues (4.4 and 5.1) with seven articles each on applying Integral Theory to climate change. Now, this is *Integral Theory in action*—working across the globe with diverse leadership to address humanity's first planetary crisis.

Conclusion

The above examples are wonderfully far-ranging in their focus and scale. This variety of Integral Theory in action speaks directly to the flexibility and coherence of its theoretical foundation: the AQAL model. By acknowledging the multifaceted nature of complex issues and problems, Integral Theory creates a space for multiple perspectives to contribute to the discovery of viable solutions. In our ever-evolving universe, Integral Theory issues to each of us a clarion call to strive toward inhabiting multiple perspectives—especially those that stand in contrast to our own habits of thinking and feeling. Only through developing such a worldcentric perspective can we adequately achieve the mutual understanding so desperately needed on a planet fragmented by conflicting worldviews and approaches. Practitioners of Integral Theory are committed to honoring and including the multidimensionality of reality as well as cultivating their own capacity for worldcentrism. It is this dual commitment of comprehensive acceptance and perspective taking that allows the individuals and organizations in the above examples to be so successful in their respective integral endeavors—each one of them serving as an exemplar of what a more integral world looks and feels like. The world is an amazing, mysterious, and complex place. Integral Theory's all-inclusive framework is particularly well suited for honoring the world in all its complexity and depth as well as shining a light on the path each of us can take to make a contribution and tackle the looming issues that will confront us in the twenty-first century.

Acknowledgments

I would like to thank Vipassana Esbjörn-Hargens, Lynwood Lord, Jordan Luftig, John Scheunhage, and David Zeitler for helpful comments that strengthened the quality of this chapter.

Notes

1. A complete listing of Ken Wilber's work can be found in Appendix 2 of Brad Reynolds's book, *Embracing Reality: The Integral Vision of Ken Wilber* (2004). Most of this material can be found in Wilber's *Collected Works*.

2. Frank Visser reports that 22 of Ken Wilber's books have been translated into more than 25 languages, thus making Wilber the most translated academic author in the United States. Visser reports: "Up till now his books have been translated into German, Dutch, French, Spanish, Portuguese, Italian, Russian, Czech, Hungarian, Turkish, Bulgarian, Latvian, Estonian, Slovenian, Slovakian, Serbian, Greek, Hindi, Chinese (China and Taiwan), Korean, Swazi, Japanese, Polish, Danish, Swedish, and Latvian. In addition to these, some illegal editions have appeared in African and Indian dialects." For a chart of all these translations, see www.integralworld.net/translations.html.

3. There is an important difference between integral studies and Integral Theory. Integral studies is the broader category and includes integral thinkers such as Jean Gebser, Sri Aurobindo, Ken Wilber, and Ervin Láslzó. In contrast, Integral Theory is a subset of integral studies, which focuses primarily on Ken Wilber's work and is committed to the critique, application, and theoretical development of the AQAL model. The field of metatheory includes the work of individuals such as Roy Bahskar and George Ritzer. For a more extensive discussion of these distinctions see the "Integral Theory versus Integral Studies" section (pages 1–22) of the introduction to this volume.

4. See the *Journal of Integral Theory and Practice* for chapters in these and many other disciplines.

5. Note that the examples given for each quadrant are not correlated between themselves; they only represent single examples for each quadrant.

6. For a discussion of the limits of Wilber's use of labels for each zone, see Martin (2008).

7. Although Integral Theory does make a distinction between involutionary and evolutionary pre-givens. See Wilber (2002).

8. For further information on these efforts, consult their respective Web sites: (1) *Journal of Integral Theory and Practice* (www.integraljournal.org); (2) John F. Kennedy University's Department of Integral Theory (www.jfku.edu/integraltheory); (3) The Integral Research Center (www.integralresearchcenter.org); (4) the international biennial Integral Theory Conference (www.integraltheoryconference.org); and (5) the SUNY Press series in Integral Theory (www.sunypress.edu/Searchadv.aspx?IsSub mit=true&CategoryID=7259).

9. Forman (2010), Ingersoll and Zeitler (2010), Esbjörn-Hargens, Reams, and Gunnlauson (2010).

10. See the resource page at www.integralresearchcenter.org for listings of all the published material in these areas.

11. A full description of this project can be found at www.integralresearchcenter.org. Also see Stein this volume.

12. All quotes in this paragraph come from www.onesky.ca, which can be visited for more information on this project.

13. Visit http://www.sifco.ca for more information on this project.

14. Integral Coach and Integral Coaching is a registered trademark in Canada and owned by Integral Coaching Canada, Inc. For information on their trainings see their Web site: www.integralcoachingcanada.com.

15. For an extensive overview and introduction to Integral Coaching Canada's approach, see issue 4(1) of the *Journal of Integral Theory and Practice*, which is devoted entirely to their work. For another approach to coaching that makes extensive use of Kegan's theory see Otto Laske's (1999) impressive *Developmental Coaching* or visit his website: www.interdevelopmentals.org.

16. Visit www.truthisnotenough.com for more information.

References

Bhaskar, R. 2002. *meta-Reality: The philosophy of meta-Reality, Volume 1 a philosophy for the present*. Thousand Oaks, CA: Sage.

Dacher, E. S. 2006. *Integral health: The path to human flourishing*. Laguna Beach, CA: Basic Health Publications.

Edwards, M. 2009. *Organizational transformation for sustainability: An integral metatheory*. New York: Routledge.

Esbjörn-Hargens, S., and M. E. Zimmerman. 2010. *Integral ecology: Uniting multiple perspectives on the natural world*. New York: Random House/Integral Books.

Esbjörn-Hargens, S., J. Reams, and O. Gunnlauson. (Eds.) 2010. *Integral education: New directions in higher learning*. Albany: State University of New York Press.

Forman, M. 2010. *A guide to integral psychotherapy: Complexity, integration, and spirituality in practice*. Albany: State University of New York Press.

Hamilton, M. 2008. *Integral city: Evolutionary intelligences for the human hive.* Gabriola Island, B.C.: New Society Publishers.

Hochachka, G. 2005. *Developing sustainability, developing the self: An integral approach to international and community development.* The Polis Project on Ecological Governance. Victoria, B.C.: University of Victoria, Canada.

Ingersoll, R. E., and C. F. Rank. 2006. *Psychopharmacology for helping professionals: An integral exploration.* Toronto: Thomson Brooks/Cole.

Ingersoll, E., and D. Zeitler. 2010. *Integral psychotherapy: Inside out/outside in.* Albany: State University of New York Press.

Laske, O. 1999. "An integrated model of developmental coaching." *Consulting Psychology Journal* 51(3): 139–59.

Marineau, S. 2007. Humanity, forest ecology, and the future in a British Columbia valley: A case study. *Integral Review* 4: 26–43.

Marquis, A. 2007. *The integral intake: A guide to comprehensive idiographic assessment in integral psychotherapy.* New York: Routledge.

Martin, J. 2008. "Integral research as a practical mixed-methods framework: Clarifying the role of Integral Methodological Pluralism." *Journal of Integral Theory and Practice* 3(2): 155–64.

Paulson, D. 2002. *Competitive business, caring business: An integral business perspective for the 21st century.* New York: Paraview Press.

Reynolds, B. 2004. *Embracing reality: The integral vision of Ken Wilber.* New York: Tarcher.

Ritzer, G. 2001. *Explorations in social theory: From metatheorizing to rationalization.* Thousand Oaks, CA: Sage.

Visser, F. 2003. *Ken Wilber: Thought as passion.* Albany: State University of New York Press.

Wilber, K. 1995. *Sex, ecology, spirituality: The spirit of evolution.* Boston: Shambhala.

———. 1999–2000. *The collected works of Ken Wilber.* Boston: Shambhala.

———. 2002. Excerpt A: An integral age at the leading edge. Retrieved March 4, 2004, from http://wilber.shambhala.com/html/books/kosmos/excerptA/intro.cfm.

———. (2003) Foreword. In F. Visser, *Ken Wilber: Thought as passion.* Albany: State University of New York Press.

———. 2006. Integral methodological pluralism. In *Integral spirituality: A startling new role for religion in the modern and postmodern world.* Boston: Integral Books.

———. 2008. *The Integral Vision.* Boston: Integral Books.

———, T. Patten, A. Leonard, and M. Morelli. 2008. *Integral life practice: A 21st-century blueprint for physical health, emotional balance, mental clarity, and spiritual awakening.* New York: Random House/Integral Books.

part 1

---

applied perspectives

2

Responding to Climate Change

The Need for an Integral Approach

Karen O'Brien

Climate change is now recognized as one of the most challenging and complex problems facing humanity—the problem is real, the stakes are high, and there is no single "solution." No measure will be met with the instant gratification that is often expected by people in modern, high-energy consumption societies. We are already committed to changes based on past emissions of greenhouse gases into the atmosphere, and it is the future that is being decided (Parry et al. 2008a). Actions taken over the next decade will have an enormous influence on the rate and magnitude of climate change that will take place over the next centuries, and both adaptation and mitigation are seen as necessary responses (Parry et al. 2008b; Schellnhuber 2008).

The consequences of increasing temperatures, changing precipitation patterns, and a rise in sea level will affect all aspects of the Earth system, from phytoplankton in the sea to mountain glaciers in the Himalayas (IPCC 2007a, 2007b). Social-ecological systems will undergo transformations that test their resilience, and many species are expected to disappear as the result of changes to habitats and food supplies (Steffen et al. 2004). Ecosystem services will be altered, for instance, the provisioning of food and water, the regulation and control of disease, and pollination processes, to name a few (MA 2006). The challenges faced by humans at the turn of the twenty-first century—poverty, disease, conflict, environmental degradation, and so on—may be exacerbated by climate change. In short, the implications of climate change are serious. Climate change can be considered as the biggest environmental threat in human history, and as the defining human development challenge for the twenty-first century (IPCC 2007b; UNDP 2007; Stern 2007).

Yet climate change is not simply an environmental problem that can be addressed by regulating greenhouse gas emissions. It is about human development, social justice, equity, and human rights (Adger et al. 2006). It is about human security and the capacity of individuals and communities to respond to threats to their social, environmental, and human rights (Barnett et al. 2008). As the United Nations Development Programme puts it, "It is about people developing the capabilities that empower them to make choices and to lead lives that they value" (UNDP 2007, 7). Climate change is closely related to how humans perceive themselves in the world and how they confront change. In fact, although it is certainly about the climate, at another level it is about how humans both create and respond to change.

In this chapter I discuss why an Integral approach is not only necessary for addressing climate change, but urgent. I argue that an emphasis on understanding climate change from an objective, systems perspective has downplayed the importance of subjective, interior dimensions of climate change, when in fact the integration of both aspects is needed. I then present six reasons why an Integral approach can be considered both useful and necessary for responding to climate change. Finally, I consider what Integral Theory might offer to current policy debates about one of the world's climate change "hot spots"—the Arctic region.

An Objective View of Climate Change

Most of the scientific research on climate change that has been presented in the four assessment reports of the Intergovernmental Panel on Climate Change (IPCC) has been carried out from a systems perspective. This research has contributed to a better understanding of complex, interacting systems, including the identification of important interactions and feedbacks. Earth-systems science in general has shown how changes in biogeochemical cycles, land cover changes, and other human activities have influenced the global climate and hydrological systems (Steffen et al. 2004). General circulation models of atmosphere-ocean-land-ice interactions have been used as a basis for assessing the physical and social impacts of climate change, and vulnerability approaches have provided insights on the underlying social, economic, political, and environmental contexts that contribute to negative outcomes. Integrated assessment models link knowledge from diverse disciplines and scales of analysis into a single framework, highlighting the connections and policy implications (Bouwman et al. 2006). Agent-based modeling simulates the actions and interactions of autonomous individuals, showing how they influence the system as a whole (Ziervogel et al. 2005). Research on coupled social-ecological systems shows that humans are having a profound effect on the planet, and there are increased calls for "resilience thinking" (Walker and Salt 2007). Together, these approaches have contributed to the emergence of sustainability science, which represents a new paradigm in scientific inquiry based around a normative call "to map the broad, inclusive, and contradictory currents that humankind will need to navigate toward a just and sustainable future" (Kates and Parriss 2003, 8067).

Although many useful frameworks, methodologies, and approaches have been developed to address the complexity of the Earth system, it is widely recognized that responses to climate change will require not only institutional changes, but also changes in human behavior. Studies of human behavior in relation to environmental change have generated new insights on how and why human actions do or do not occur (Stern 2000; Grothmann and Patt 2005). This research has provided a foundation for identifying both policy and practical responses to climate change. Although the contributions of these methodologies and approaches are impressive, the more that research on climate change progresses, the more it becomes clear that there is more to the climate change problem that must be included in analyses of the causes, consequences, and behavioral responses—including dimensions that cannot be adequately captured in objective, "systems" thinking. Some of this has been mentioned in postmodern critiques of climate change research that draw from social constructivism, critical realism, and other social theories to understand how and why climate change is a problem (Castree and Braun 2001; Forsyth 2003). For example, David Demeritt (2001) builds on some of the critiques of the reductionist formulation of climate change and argues in favor of a more reflexive understanding of science as a social practice. Similarly, Mike Hulme (2009) argues that culture and climate are intimately related, and that the contemporary discourse of climatic catastrophe can only be dissolved through cultural change.

In spite of these critiques, the models and frameworks most often used by the scientific community do not incorporate the subjective and interior "human" dimensions of climate change (Hulme 2009). When included, the interior aspects of humans are flattened out and simplified, ignoring the depth of human experiences and development. Human motivations and the various lines of psychological development in individuals have most often been disregarded, and the role of culture, values, and worldviews is only just beginning to receive attention in climate change research. Where interiors have been studied, they have not been well integrated with research on systems and behavior. As Integral Theory makes clear, however, all of these aspects *and* their integration are essential to understanding climate change.

Integral Theory and Climate Change

Integral Theory offers a framework that takes into account the bigger picture in which climate change is occurring, and thus it can offer insights on the types of responses and strategies that are necessary to confront the challenge—responses that address all quadrants, levels, lines, states, and types (i.e., the AQAL model) (Wilber 1996; Esbjörn-Hargens and Zimmerman 2009). Below, I discuss six reasons why Integral Theory may be both useful and necessary for responding to climate change.

1. *Integral Theory recognizes the interior and exterior dimensions of climate change—and of climate change research.* The problem of climate change can be studied from both subjective/intersubjective and objective/interobjective views, from the perspectives of I, we, and it(s). However, as described above, it has for the most part been studied from an (inter)objective perspective, or from within the Right-Hand quadrants of the Integral framework. Integral Theory draws attention to the role of cognition and consciousness, and to the importance of individual and collective values and beliefs as influences on behavior and systems. These subjective, interior dimensions represent an important part of the picture, and they need to be considered in discussions and debates about climate change.

The research itself on climate change must also take into account both interior and exterior dimensions of the issue. One of the interesting aspects of the climate change problem is that it is very difficult to study from an exclusively objective perspective. It is a problem that scientists are a part of and contribute to, and it is a problem that will affect them, as well as their children and grandchildren, in the future. In other words, scientists have a personal stake in the problem, as contributors both to the problem and to the solution. Climate skeptics often point to a very different stake (e.g., research funding) as driving the interest in climate change. However, many climate change researchers are personally and collectively concerned about the issue, and they are more often driven by interior motivations than the availability of funding. Although many scientists are concerned about the ability of society to respond rapidly and effectively to climate change, at the same time they are asked to continually fly around the world to meetings to discuss the problem. Such contradictions can create an interior dissonance for individuals and groups working on climate change research. Thus, although the science of climate change focuses largely on the exterior aspects of the problem, Integral Theory recognizes that the interior aspects also matter, not only in relation to the subjects of the research, but also in relation to the researchers themselves.

2. *Integral Theory emphasizes that the four quadrants (I, we, it, its) "tetra-arise."* All four quadrants are closely related, and cannot be seen as isolated or independent from each other. The systemic processes associated with climate change are linked to human development: the impacts of climate change can

influence human development, just as human development can influence the future climate system. It is, for example, clear that the impacts of climate change may create additional challenges in meeting the United Nations Millennium Development Goals, particularly if climate variability and extreme events increase (Schipper and Pelling 2006). Food, water, and shelter are basic human needs and if they are not satisfied, prioritized values and motivations may shift, setting some societies on a backward trajectory in terms of human development (Inglehart 1997). Climate change, which is often seen as an abstract and future problem, may not be prioritized in times of economic stagnation and political crisis (Inglehart 1997).

It is important to recognize that *responses* to climate change may also affect human development. Indeed, one person or group's adaptation to climate change may increase the vulnerability of others; mitigation efforts can likewise influence development trajectories, either positively or negatively. The recent experience with biofuels and its impact on global food availability and access illustrates the complex nature of responses (Runge and Senauer 2007). Climate change interacts with many other global processes, including trade liberalization and other manifestations of globalization, thus it is difficult to project the exact outcomes of any policy or strategy (Leichenko and O'Brien 2008). An Integral approach captures the way that relationships emerge synchronously and causally in all four quadrants.

3. Integral Theory recognizes stages of human development and "altitudes." Human beings are diverse, and individuals can be characterized by many different lines of development: cognitive, moral, interpersonal, emotional, psychosexual, kinesthetic, self, values, needs, and so on (Wilber 2006). Differences in the cognitive line of development alone have significant implications for responses to climate change. Indeed, climate change is a cognitively complex issue: it is a "big picture" problem, and to understand its full implications a worldcentric perspective is required as well as an ability to handle both complexity and paradox. Individuals, groups, and institutions need a well-developed capacity to be self-reflexive, or as Kegan (1982, 105) puts it, "to hear, and to seek out, information which might cause the self to alter its behavior, or share in a negative judgment of that behavior." This demands a high level of cognitive development, which may be demanding for many adults, leading to a situation that Kegan (1994) refers to as being "in over our heads" in relation to contemporary global problems.

The science and policy communities dealing with climate change often do not recognize or respect different stages of development, and instead insist that presenting rational arguments and complex graphics of climate model output should be enough to convince people to change their behavior. Rather than presenting information in an accessible manner that can be understood from diverse perspectives, there is a tendency to reiterate the complexity of the argument. Speaking louder and more often will not, however, persuade most people in the world that climate change is a real problem. In fact, the psychology literature suggests that many people need to have visceral experiences of climate change impacts before it matters to them (Weber 2006). In other words, people may need to subjectively experience and feel the exterior, objective manifestations of climate change. Otherwise climate change remains abstract and "unreal." Although scientists debate the extent to which current weather variability and extremes (e.g., hurricanes, floods, droughts) are linked to anthropogenic climate change, many of the observed changes and anomalies in climate conditions around the world may nonetheless be helping to convince people that climate change is an important issue, as much as or perhaps more than IPCC reports or Al Gore's film, *An Inconvenient Truth*. Rather than waiting until climate change is viscerally experienced or felt by many, which may occur after it is too late to prevent dangerous climate change, there are many ways that artists, museum curators, advertisers, and others can creatively present climate change to different audiences. Using an Integral approach, climate change can be translated to reach people with different beliefs, values, and worldviews.

4. Integral Theory recognizes that values and worldviews are changing. Human values are important to understanding the impacts and consequences of climate change, and for making the problem real and relevant to diverse groups (O'Brien 2009). Recognizing that climate change will mean different things to different individuals, communities, groups, or cultures is essential to providing ownership of the problem, which can be considered a prerequisite for responding to climate change. Values are often assumed by researchers to be random or culturally specific, and static, and until recently, more research attention has focused on explaining differences in values than on understanding changes in values (Rokeach 1979). It is, however, also important to recognize that values change as humans develop, both as individuals and through generations. There is a growing body of research that shows that values are structured in a coherent way and that they change over time as individuals and societies undergo processes of development (Schwartz 1994; Inglehart 1997). The future values of today's children and young adults—some of whom are likely to develop "post" postmodern worldviews—need to be taken into account in contemporary responses to climate change. Likewise, the values of future generations must be considered, and this includes the possibility that integral and holistic worldviews may be dominant. Integral Theory draws attention to the possibility that climate change may occur in the face of the values associated with integral stages of human development and beyond, and this has implications for the types of responses that are prioritized.

5. *Integral Theory recognizes a diversity of needs and motivations, and hence responses.* There is no single solution to climate change, and it is unlikely that a single solution will be found. New technologies and innovations (e.g., efficient carbon capture and storage, harvesting solar power from space, geo-engineering) may take years to develop, and they may create new risks and problems (Jamieson 1996). What is needed is not a "magic bullet," but a multitude of measures that transform energy systems, social systems, economic systems, and institutions at an unprecedented rate and scale. The most important solutions to climate change already exist. While there is still a need to focus research and development on, for example, plant breeding and improved renewable energy technologies, there are a tremendous number of changes that can be enacted immediately, and which may have positive social effects regardless of climate change. However, it is important to target these different responses to the existing diversity of needs and motivations.

A global consensus on climate change is unlikely to occur until after the effects become clearly visible, when thresholds or "tipping points" may have already been reached (Lenton et al. 2008). Yet many of the actions and responses needed to avoid dangerous climate change make good sense for other motivations, and thus can appeal to people with diverse and often conflicting perspectives. For example, the vision plan for the city of San Buenaventura in California draws attention to the urgent actions needed to prevent a *peak oil* crisis, but it focuses on improving the quality of life and leaving future generations with a healthy planet (Chen et al. 2007). Although the driving force behind the visionary plan is not concern about climate change, the plan supports many of the objectives of climate change mitigation and sustainable development. Integral Theory provides a map for understanding the diverse motivations from which climate change responses can be initiated.

6. *Integral Theory encourages Integral Methodological Pluralism.* Interdisciplinary research is considered essential to understanding coupled social-ecological systems and the implications of climate change for humanity. Yet interdisciplinary research has proven to be very difficult, particularly when research is based on differing conceptual or mental models (Newell et al. 2005). Although it is easy for scientists from diverse disciplines to collaborate when they share the same conceptual framework, such as a systems perspective, it becomes much harder when researchers hold different models of reality (e.g., social constructivism versus neoclassical economics). Yet it is becoming increasingly clear that fragmented research, as well as interdisciplinary research that

is limited to one particular paradigm, based on one worldview, or limited to one way of knowing, is unlikely to be sufficient to meet the challenges of climate change. Without a common framework, it is difficult for scholars from different disciplines to see how diverse fields, approaches, and methodologies relate and fit together. Integral Theory provides a framework for understanding climate change that accommodates methodological pluralism and can facilitate interdisciplinary research based on multiple perspectives.

To respond to climate change successfully and avoid disastrous outcomes for humanity requires both a map and a vision. Integral Theory offers such a map, and insights from the literature and debates on sustainable development, human development, and human security can contribute to a vision for a positive future under climate change. Nonetheless, some questions remain. How, in practice, might an Integral approach improve knowledge and understandings about responses to climate change? How can Integral Theory inform adaptation and mitigation strategies and policies? Unfortunately, there are not many examples of climate change research that is informed by Integral Theory. One exception is Christopher Riedy's research on the implications of Integral Theory for sustainable development and climate change responses in Australia (Riedy 2005). He presents an integral policy response to climate change that combines participatory integrated assessment, normative futures work, and other measures and strategies that emphasize both subjective and objective dimensions of sustainable development. Recently the *Journal of Integral Theory and Practice* ran two special issues (Vol. 4, No. 4 and Vol. 5, No.1) on climate change that contain 14 articles informed by Integral Theory. These articles explore philosophical, behavioral, cultural, economic, global, rhetorical, ideological, psychological, civic, organizational, and policy dimensions of climate change.

Thus, there are numerous areas, locations, and cases where Integral Theory can make valuable contributions to understanding or identifying appropriate responses to climate change. In particular, there is one "hot spot" where an Integral approach should be prioritized and tested—the Arctic region. The Arctic is undergoing dramatic changes, including the rapid melting of sea ice as the result of climate change, and it is a region where different geopolitical interests—particularly interests in oil, gas, and mineral resources—converge to create a number of obstacles to responding to climate change (Borgerson 2008). Below, I describe this case and pose some questions that might be addressed and answered through an Integral approach.

The Arctic: An Integral Hot Spot

Climate change is currently most visible in the Arctic (ACIA 2004). The obstacles to responding to climate change in a sustainable and equitable manner are great in this region, and the stakes are high. Different interests, combined with different economic and military capacities, have drawn attention to the role of the Arctic in international security debates (Solana 2008). Biodiversity protection, the rights of indigenous populations, exploitation of fisheries, expansion of tourism, and opportunities for economic development, military superiority, and oil, gas, and mineral exploitation all form parts of different discourses on the future of the Arctic (Kristiansen 2008). Indeed, multiple stressors interact in the Arctic, including the accumulation of heavy metals and persistent organic pollutants in species at the top of the food chain as well as the impacts of growing transport, trade, and tourism (ACIA 2004; Leichenko and O'Brien 2008).

The melting of sea ice will enhance transport and trade throughout the region, including through the northern sea route (NSR), which is a collection of sailing lanes north of Russia, extending from Novaya Zemlya in the west to the Bering Strait in the east (O'Brien and Leichenko 2008). The NSR includes the main part of the stretch known as the Northeast Passage, which connects the Atlantic and Pacific Oceans along the northern coast of Asia. The NSR represents a considerably shorter trade route connecting Europe and northeast Asia, and could potentially capture some of the shipping trade currently routed through the Suez and Panama canals. To date, the most significant limitation to the development of the NSR has been ice coverage, as well as political, financial, and institutional factors (O'Brien and Leichenko 2008).

Reduced sea ice, combined with the expansion of transport routes in the Arctic, may lead not only to increased international trade, but also to increased fossil fuel extraction and an increase in global greenhouse gas emissions (Leichenko and O'Brien 2008). An estimated 20 percent of the world's oil and gas resources are located in the Arctic—an estimate that has not escaped the attention of nations with Arctic land claims and multinational oil companies. The oil and gas resources located in the more accessible western regions of the Barents and Kara seas are already being explored and exploited, and a future without sea ice offers new opportunities for profit. Yet an increased extraction and consumption of Arctic oil and gas are expected to substantially increase global carbon dioxide emissions, which is likely to accelerate climate change.

The different interests in the Arctic are likely to create new opportunities for some, but at a large cost. As Robin Leichenko and I note (2008, 101), "The vision of a warmer Arctic, bustling with economic activity, represents paradise for some but catastrophe for others. Indeed, the pursuit of new opportunities in the Arctic strongly aligns with the interests and values of some individuals or groups, yet creates friction with those of others." Although there appears to be a clear pattern of winners and losers related to these changes, the pattern can be expected to be ephemeral as sea level rises and changing temperature and rainfall patterns influence coastal areas and ports: "Those with economic interests in the north who are rejoicing at the possibility of an open Arctic and the trade opportunities that it creates may fail to recognize that sea level rise and changing weather patterns represent a dire threat to many of the consumers and trading partners that these countries envision" (Leichenko and O'Brien 2008, 102). In the long run, there will be few or no winners with climate change, and scientific studies of Arctic ice melt show that the long run is getting closer and closer.

Why is an Integral approach needed in the Arctic? First and foremost, because powerful economic interests are intent on extracting and exploiting the enormous wealth of the Arctic region—climate change will facilitate this, yet will also be accelerated by such activities. Those with a modern worldview (i.e., those who focus on the vast possibilities of technology and economic growth) are not limited to oil and gas oligarchs in Russia, but also include the state-run oil company of Norway and many multinational energy corporations. The prevailing argument is that new technologies in carbon capture and storage, and eventually de-carbonization technologies, will allow fossil fuels with low emissions of greenhouse gases to be used in distributed sources, such as automobiles (Metz et al. 2005). However, this vision is not shared by many concerned with the ecological impacts of carbon capture and storage, or with the complexity of impacts of climate change and the consequences for humanity. Indigenous groups and Arctic residents hold different perspectives, which in some cases reflect traditional worldviews, and in other cases reflect a concern with equity and human rights (Krupnik and Jolly 2002). The conflict of values in the Arctic is not trivial, and has implications for all of humanity. An Integral approach that focuses on stages of human development can potentially help to identify new ways of discussing the issues to get to solutions that can reconcile prioritized values of modernism (e.g., concerns with developing the resources of the Arctic) with the values of postmodernism (e.g., concerns for environmental and human security).

Conclusion

I have argued that an Integral approach to climate change is both urgent and necessary. Climate change scientists can benefit from an Integral approach, as it provides an inclusive framework that can guide interdisciplinary research. Policymakers and practitioners who deal with the complex challenges of global warming, amidst many other processes of change, can also benefit from an Integral approach, which draws attention to human development and relationships to culture, values, and worldviews. Focusing on *change*, rather than on climate, allows one to see obstacles to and opportunities for responding successfully to climate change.

Currently, some in the climate change research and policy communities argue that increased scientific knowledge and reduced uncertainty is a prerequisite for actions to reduce the impacts of climate change (see Dessai et al. 2007). Other researchers and activists take it for granted that everyone is—or should be—concerned with climate equity and justice, that everyone places equal value on future generations, and that everyone understands the stakes and will respond rationally to avoid costly or dangerous outcomes. The focus has thus been on providing information and explaining the science of climate change and its impacts and significance to diverse groups. Yet this has not been a particularly effective strategy, and greenhouse gas emissions are rising faster than anticipated. Given that actions taken in the next decade may be decisive in influencing future rates and magnitudes of change, insights from Integral Theory may provide new ways to facilitate rapid transformation. At the least, it offers a framework for understanding change, including evolving perspectives on environment-society relationships. Recognizing the depth of the human dimensions of climate change may be essential to responding to the enormous challenges posed by climate change.

To conclude, it is important to note that climate change is almost always represented as bad news, except among skeptics who often argue that a warmer world may be more beneficial for human beings than a cold world. However, climate change can be viewed as good news from a nonskeptic perspective: never before in human history has there been such strong evidence that we live in an interconnected world, where actions taken in one place have consequences in another. The notion of winners and losers, which has been a driving force for competition among individuals and between groups and states, becomes an illusion as the process of climate change accelerates. Inequality and injustices that have persisted throughout history must be confronted in order to address climate change, and there is now a window of opportunity to recognize that human well-being and human security are really about the connections and relationships among different perspectives. In other words, climate change forces us to realize that the "I, we, and it(s)" are in this together.

References

ACIA (Arctic Climate Impact Assessment). 2004. *Impacts of a warming Arctic: Arctic climate impact assessment.* Cambridge: Cambridge University Press.

Barnett, J., R. A. Matthew, and K. O'Brien. 2008. Global environmental change and human security. In *Reconceptualizing security in the 21st century*, ed. H. G. Brauch et al. Berlin: Springer.

Borgerson, S. G. 2008. Arctic meltdown: The economic and security implications of global warming. *Foreign Affairs* 87(2). Retrieved February 11, 2009, from http://www. foreignaffairs.org/2008/2.html.

Bouwman, A. F., T. Kram, and K. K. Goldewijk. (Eds.) 2006. *Integrated modeling of global environmental change: An overview of IMAGE 2.4.* Bilthoven, The Netherlands: Netherlands Environmental Assessment Agency (MNP). Retrieved June 15, 2007, from http://www.mnp.nl/bibliotheek/rapporten/500110002.pdf.

Castree, N., and B. Braun. (Eds.) 2001. *Social nature: Theory, practice, and politics.* Malden, MA: Blackwell.

Chen, Y., M. Deines, H. Fleischman, K. McCown, S. Reed, I. Swick, and J. H. Woodward. 2007. *Transforming urban environments for a post-peak oil future: A vision plan for the city of San Buenaventura.* Poster presented at Resilience 2008, April 14–17, 2008; Stockholm, Sweden.

Demeritt, D. 2001. The construction of global warming and the politics of science. *Annals of the Association of American Geographers* 91(2): 307–37.

Dessai, S., K. L. O'Brien, and M. Hulme. 2007. On uncertainty and climate change. *Global Environmental Change* 17: 1–3.

Esbjörn-Hargens, S., and M. E. Zimmerman. 2009. *Integral ecology: Uniting multiple perspectives on the natural world.* New York: Random House/Integral Books.

Forsyth, T. 2003. *Critical political ecology: The politics of environmental science.* London: Routledge.

Grothmann, T., and A. Patt. 2005 Adaptive capacity and human cognition: The process of individual adaptation to climate change. *Global Environmental Change* 15: 199–213.

Hulme, M. 2009. *Why we disagree about climate change: Understanding controversy, inaction, and opportunity.* Cambridge: Cambridge University Press.

Inglehart, R. 1997. *Modernization and postmodernization: Cultural, economic, and political change in 43 societies.* Princeton: Princeton University Press.

IPCC (Intergovernmental Panel on Climate Change). 2007a. *Climate change 2007: Impacts, adaptation, and vulnerability. Summary for policymakers.* Contribution of Working Group II to the Fourth Assessment Report of the Intergovernmental Panel on Climate Change.

IPCC (Intergovernmental Panel on Climate Change). 2007b. *Climate Change 2007: The physical science basis. Summary for policymakers.* Contribution of Working Group I to the Fourth Assessment Report of the Intergovernmental Panel on Climate Change.

Jamieson, D. 1996. Ethics and intentional climate change. *Climatic Change* 33: 323–36.

Kates, R. W., W. C. Clark, R. Corell, J. Hall, J. Michael, C. Carlo C., I. Lowe et al. 2001. Sustainability science. *Science* 292: 641–42.

Kates, R. W., and T. M. Parriss. 2003. Long-term trends and a sustainability transition. *Proceedings of the National Academy of Science* 100(14): 8062–67.

Kegan, R. 1982. *The evolving self: Problem and process in human development.* Cambridge: Harvard University Press.

———. (1994). *In over our heads: The mental demands of modern life.* Cambridge: Harvard University Press.

Kristiansen, Ø. 2008. *The Arctic Express: An emerging transport route and its feedbacks to global environmental change.* Master's thesis in Human Geography, Department of Sociology and Human Geography, University of Oslo, Norway, 2008.

Krupnik, I., and D. Jolly. (Eds.) 2002. *The Earth is faster now: Indigenous observations of Arctic environmental change.* Fairbanks: Arctic Research Consortium of the United States.

Leichenko, R., and K. O'Brien. 2008. *Environmental change and globalization: Double exposures.* New York: Oxford University Press.

Lenton, T. M., H. Held, E. Kriegler, J. W. Hall, W. Lucht, S. Rahmstorf, and H. J. Schellnhuber. 2008. Tipping elements in the Earth's climate system. *Proceedings of the National Academy of Sciences* 105: 1786–93.

MA (Millennium Ecosystem Assessment) 2005. *Ecosystems and human well-being: Synthesis.* Washington, DC: Island Press.

Metz, B., O. Davidson, H. de Coninck, M. Loos, and L. Meyer. 2005. *Carbon dioxide capture and storage.* IPCC Special Report, Summary for Policymakers and Technical Summary. UNEP and WMO: Intergovernmental Panel on Climate Change.

Newell, B., C. L. Crumley, N. Hassan, E. F. Lambin, C. Pahl-Wostl, A. Underdal, A., and R. Watson. 2005. A conceptual template for integrative human–environment research. *Global Environmental Change* 15: 299–307.

O'Brien, K. (2009). Do values subjectively define the limits to climate change adaptation? In *Adapting to climate change: Thresholds, values, governance,* ed. W. N. Adger, I. Lorenzoni, and K. O'Brien, chapter 10, 164–80. Cambridge: Cambridge University Press.

Parry, M., J. Lowe, and C. Hanson. 2008a. *The consequences of delayed action on climate change.* Briefing for Poznan, Poland meeting on climate change.

Parry, M., J. Palutikof, C. Hanson, and J. Lowe. 2008b. Climate policy: Squaring up to reality. *Nature Reports Climate Change* 2: 68–70.

Ramanathan, V., and Y. Feng. 2008. On avoiding dangerous anthropogenic interference with the climate system: Formidable challenges ahead. *Proceedings of the National Academy of Sciences* 105: 14245–50.

Riedy, C. 2005. *The eye of the storm: An integral perspective on sustainable development and climate change response.* Doctoral dissertation, University of Technology, Sydney, Australia, 2005.

Rokeach, M. (Ed.) 1979. *Understanding human values: Individual and societal.* New York: The Free Press.

Runge , C. F., and B. Senauer. 2007. How biofuels could starve the poor. *Foreign Affairs* 86(3). Retrieved February 11, 2009, from http://www.foreignaffairs.org/2007/3.html.

Schellnhuber, H. J. 2008. Global warming: Stop worrying, start panicking? *PNAS* 105(38): 14238–40.

Schipper, L., and M. Pelling. 2006. Disaster risk, climate change, and international development: Scope for, and challenges to, integration. *Disasters* 30: 19–38.

Schwartz, S. H. 1994. Are there universal aspects in the structure and contents of human values? *Journal of Social Issues* 50: 19–45.

Solana, J. 2008. *Climate change and international security.* Paper presented to the High Representative and the European Commission to the European Council (S113/08). March 14, 2008.

Steffen, W., A. Sanderson, P. D. Tyson, J. Jäger, P. A. Matson, M. Moore III et al. 2004. *Global change and the Earth system: A planet under pressure.* Berlin: Springer.

Stern, N. 2006. *The economics of climate change: The Stern review.* Cambridge: Cambridge University Press.

Stern, P. 2000. Toward a coherent theory of environmentally significant behavior. *Journal of Social Issues* 56: 407–24.

UNDP (United Nations Development Programme). 2008. Fighting climate change: human solidarity in a divided world. 2007/2008 Human Development Report. Retrieved February 11, 2009, from http://hdr.undp.org/en/reports/global/hdr2007-2008/.

Walker, B., and D. Salt. 2006. *Resilience thinking: Sustaining ecosystems and people in a changing world.* Washington, DC: Island Press.

Weber, E. U. 2006. Experience-based and description-based perceptions of long-term risk: Why global warming does not scare us (yet). *Climatic Change* 77: 103–20.

Wilber, K. 1996. *A brief history of everything.* Boston: Shambhala.

———. (2006). *Integral spirituality: A startling new role for religion in the modern and postmodern world.* Boston: Integral Books.

Ziervogel, G., M. Bithell, R. Washington, and T. Downing. 2005. Agent-based social simulation: A method for assessing the impact of seasonal climate forecast applications among smallholder farmers. *Agricultural Systems* 83(1): 1–26.

3

Embodiment, an Ascending and Descending Development

Theresa Silow

Lying on my back in the quiet of my meditation room, my attention slowly enters into my body. My awareness begins to deepen into my interior from surface to depth: noticing the rhythm of my breath; the expanding and diminishing movement of my rib cage; the contact with the surface of the mat I am lying on; small wave-like movements in my intestinal tract; a sense of tingling behind my eyes; contraction and holding around my sacrum; currents of energy in my belly. The myriad of sensations go on and on. I am simply staying present to all of these experiences. "I" am witnessing my felt interior landscape.

As I am "hanging out" with these sensory currents, my relaxation begins to expand. The somewhat distinct sensations, although still present, are softening and becoming more blurred. The holding around my sacrum reveals vibration and quivering. A sense of fluidity begins to spread from my tailbone all throughout. The sensations become hazier, they no longer seem to be separate events, but part of a larger symphony of experience. Very gradually my entire body is breathing and humming in one rhythm and flow.

Dropping even deeper, my awareness shifts from focusing on sensory contours toward embracing the background of these experiences, like shifting from the lines and shapes of colors of a painting to the canvas itself. A sense of thickening around the midline of my body makes itself known. It feels potent, with a gravitational pull, like an elongated black hole. Ever so slowly, as my awareness hovers, "I" am being enveloped by this curious, vast, and compelling blackness. Slowly, yet inevitably, the black potency is wiping "me" out. There is only deep and utter abiding in the blackness. Shivering shades of light illuminate the darkness.

Experiences such as the above have a profound impact on me. They leave me with a sense of having touched eternity and the Mystery itself. Great curiosity about the nature and workings of my body and my personal process of embodiment arises. Questions like "What is body?" and "Are these experiences uniquely 'mine' or is there a general developmental process of embodiment at hand?" come up.

The developmental trajectory, which in the integral literature is described as a development from pre-personal, to personal, to transpersonal—the stages before, of, and beyond personality and ego—when discussed with regard to embodiment, seems to take on a particular course. An initial developmental ascent is the movement from deeply preconsciously embodied and sensory bound states toward a firm establishment of self and body (subject and object), the development of cognition, abstract thinking, toward transcendent consciousness with qualities of boundlessness and universality (Wilber 2000). Estrangement from the body, which is often considered to be the result of traumatic experiences, is presented here as a potentially normative process of development.

Based upon my experience and scholarly work, I further suggest that somewhere along this development a turn back toward bodily experience ushers in a descending developmental phase toward deep embodiment, the sensuousness of life, and the depth of matter. Similar to the ascending development toward unity—a turning toward bodily experience, at some point, seems to bring about the experience of nonduality and a dissolution of self and body. Yet, the descent opens up a direct participation with the creativity of matter and the force of life rather than carrying us away into transcendent realms.

Conventional discourse—even somewhat duplicated in the integral literature—is centered around an ascending development. While a focus on the ascent is viable, what remains largely unexplored is the experience along this development of turning back toward or integrating at a higher level the body. To counterbalance this gravitational pull toward the ascending aspect of development, I wish to invite curiosity and discussion about the particulars of the descent toward conscious embodiment.

I will present some viewpoints on early embodiment—mostly arising out of developmental psychology—and concepts addressing shifts in embodied consciousness, which are explored through somatic and contemplative practices. The discussion of the descent will touch on both the "what" of the process and give some insight into the "how" of its unfolding. I have explored the descent into the body through my own somatic and contemplative practice and through teaching and will include students' first-person accounts to describe some experiences of the descent. In conclusion I will offer reflections upon this developmental process in light of an integral orientation.

What Is Embodiment?

The term *embodiment* is currently a well-discussed concept in the literature across disciplines such as psychology, education, health sciences, philosophy, and spirituality. In spirituality, embodiment is often seen as pure experience of realization, not necessarily related to body per se. However, in a broader discussion the term is generally employed to describe a certain degree of contact with one's body or the process of deepening awareness of one's body. For the purpose of this discussion I will focus on this phenomenological perspective, which is in alignment with the Upper-Left subjective interior quadrant (especially zone 1) of the integral AQAL model. Yet, to widen as well as ground the discussion here, I also include the objective exterior perspective of the Upper-Right quadrant, which gives insight into what neural connections and networks are necessary and at work when a conscious subjective experience is present. Looking at early developmental stages of embodiment, which are deeply shaped by relational dynamics and experiences, I also touch on the Lower-Left intersubjective quadrant. As always, none of these quadrants can truly be separated, yet differentiating between the different perspectives will help us to paint a richer and more complete picture of the issue at hand.

Body Schema and Body Perception

To highlight the importance of felt experience, I will focus in this discussion about embodiment on the concept and experience of *body perception*. It is useful to introduce two different concepts of embodiment here. Sean Gallagher (2006), an interdisciplinary philosopher, uses *body schema* and *body image* to explain embodiment. "[A] *body schema* is a system of sensory-motor capacities that function without awareness or the necessity of perceptual monitoring" (24). Body schema describes the facility to move one's body consciously or unconsciously—such as being able to quickly and without conscious perception walk or run away from a possibly dangerous situation. Here the emphasis is on the Upper-Right quadrant (UR). In contrast "[A] *body image* consists of a system of perceptions, attitudes, and beliefs pertaining to one's own body (24). Body perception here describes the capacity to experience or perceive one's body and its movement—like being aware of the felt experience of walking— rather than attitudes and beliefs about one's body. Here the emphasis is on the Upper-Left quadrant (UL).

As may be apparent, these two systems of *body schema* and *body perception* are closely intertwined yet not identical. For one, the relationship between the two is similar to the relationship of movement and sensation. Movement, particularly non-habitual movement, inspires sensation and sensation guides movement (Silow 2002). Yet, when talking about body schema we are largely talking about movements performed without conscious awareness. These habitual movements seem to reinforce the lack of body perception or conscious embodiment. How can we move out of this habituated state and cultivate body perception? To begin answering this question, it is constructive to present some of its neurological underpinnings in more detail. Neurologically speaking, it is the somatosensory system, a broad and inclusive system that provides the capacity for sensing bodily experience and supplying the central nervous system with information about the interior landscape.

The Somatosensory System

The somatosensory system is made up of several subsystems: the musculo-skeletal division, the visceral division, the vestibular system, and fine touch. Antonio Damasio (1999), a behavior neurologist and neuroscientist, presents these subsystems in a very insightful and clear way. He describes the muscu-loskeletal aspect of the somatosensory division, also known as *proprioception* or kinesthesis, as the system that provides information about the state of the muscles and their ongoing movement, for example sensing the movement of muscles while dancing. The visceral division, often described as *interoception*, another equally important and elaborate subsystem with communication through both hormonal messengers in the bloodstream and neural pathways, provides information about our deep interior, such as a general sense of restfulness or vitality. The vestibular system, in coordination with the muscu-loskeletal division, maps the body in space and provides information about our relationship to gravity, for instance, by noticing the lean forward while hiking up a mountain. It thus complements the information of the two subsystems described above. Finally, there is the division of fine touch that conveys infor-mation received from sensors in the skin, activated when physical contact with another person or object, such as touching and sensing the softness of a baby's skin, is made. All of the above contribute to the perception and mapping of one's own bodily experience.

In discussing the somatosensory system, the vastness and richness of body perception becomes visible. Sensing one's body extends beyond awareness of one's own movement. It includes interoceptive sensations from organ and glandular tissue, vestibular feedback about the body's orientation in space, and the information received through fine touch. All these streams of information provided through the various neural pathways, when experienced consciously, contribute to a phenomenologically experienced sense of embodiment. The question of importance here is "when" and "how" do these embodied capacities come into existence?

Ascending Development—Leaving Our Senses

Bodily experience is the foundation of early stages of development. In an attempt to understand embodiment more fully, it is useful to veer our atten-tion here toward concepts about early movement development and theories about early stages of bodily organization, emergence of self, development of cognition, and the traversing of pre-personal and personal stages of development. With it we are exploring the ascending evolution from deeply embodied embeddedness toward a more or less pronounced distancing from direct and bodily experience.

Gallagher (2006) considers a basic body schema to be present right at birth and speculates that the prenatal period is the time when it begins to develop. The earliest body schemas are generated and facilitated through prenatal movement. Gallagher further speculates that somewhere along the process movement development is accompanied by proprioceptive development. Movement instigates sensory information, which gets transmitted to the brain, where eventually a proprioceptive sense of movement is registered. Thus, "movement precedes the awareness of movement but contributes to the generation of that awareness (in the form of proprioceptive awareness) when the system is sufficiently developed to allow for it." (97). Gallagher views the prenatal period as the time when *body schema* and *body perception* begin to develop and sees movement as the prerequisite for both. Therefore, embodiment begins in the womb with the emergence of movement and the preconscious experience of sensation in the wake of it.

Movement Development

Bonnie Bainbridge Cohen, a somatic pioneer and educator, looks at early human movement development in utero and after birth as the recapitulation of evolutionary movements across a range of species (Hartley 1995). The development unfolds from a basic cellular metabolic movement (movement of the amoeba); to naval radiation, movement initiated at the navel and sequencing through all extremities (starfish); to movement initiated by the mouth (tunicate); to soft sequential pre-spinal movement (lancelet amphioxus). With these basic movement patterns the embryo and fetus slowly grows an increasingly complex movement repertoire. Movement development continues outside the womb as even more elaborate neurological movement patterns come "online." Starting with movement initiated in the spine, such as the infant being able to lift the head (fish), to homologous movements, a pushing into or reaching with either both arms or both legs (frog); to homolateral movements exhibited in the low belly crawl with the arm and leg of one side coming into motion simultaneously (reptile); to contralateral movements that cross the midline, diagonally integrating upper and lower extremities, and both sides of the brain, as expressed in a fully developed crawl (mammal) (24–62).

These emerging patterns of movement, arising with the maturing of the nervous system, establish a complex body schema and instigate an elaborate sensory palate, which means embodiment as a whole becomes more differentiated. While these musculoskeletal capacities of the nervous system are developing, we have to look at how other aspects of embodiment concurrently come to the fore. Early movement capacities do not develop in a vacuum, nor is the developmental process a linear one. While movement and sensory capacities become elaborated, a sense of self and identity is being formed in the context of body experience, experience of the environment, and contact with others.

Bodily Organization of Self

In alignment with the discussion about early development being body-centered, Daniel Stern (1990), a developmental psychologist and researcher, describes the first two developmental stages, the emergent sense of self (0–2 months) and the core sense of self (2–6 months), as fundamentally body-based. During the first two months, the time of the *emergent sense of self,* an organization of self comes into being based on reoccurring organismic experiences, consisting of feeling tones, pleasure, discomfort, discrete affects, motor experiences, and perceptions across different sensory channels. Repeated vital experiences such as hunger, as depicted in Stern's fictitious first-person description of a baby's experience below, elicit an all-encompassing nervous system response:

> Uneasiness grows. It spreads from the center and turns into pain. . . . It is at the center that the storm breaks out. It is at the very center that it grows stronger and turns into pulsing waves. These waves push the pain out, then pull it back again. . . . The pulsing waves swell to dominate the whole weatherscape. The world is howling. Everything explodes and is blown out and then collapses and rushes back toward a knot of agony that cannot last—but does. (31–32)

Experiences like the above, when felt repeatedly, become elements of a basic organismic organization and essentially a rudimentary sense of self. Similar to Stern, Damasio (1999), describes this early emergent sense of self as a preconscious, biological construct. The *"proto-self"* as he calls this early organization "is a coherent collection of neural patterns which map, moment to moment, the state of the physical structure of the organism in its many dimensions" [italics omitted] (154). This conglomerate of neural patterns is registered in many different places and at different levels of the brain. It is a dynamic and continuously emerging network that, upon reoccurring sameness of bodily experiences and states, becomes the neurological wiring of our earliest sense of self.

According to Stern (1985), after this earliest embodied organization has been laid down, the infant gradually turns toward "other" as a reference point and experiential anchor, establishing a more solid *core self*. The self here is primarily congealed out of embodied experience arising out of the dyadic situation. The building blocks for the development of the core self are *self invariants*, experiences of coherence and continuity of bodily and affective states, and a sense of agency. These episodes of experience bundled together through representational memory allow the infant to identify repeated similarities within experiences and distinguish between "what is me" (self) and "not me" (other). As described by Stern (1990) in the speculated brief episode between mother and infant below, the infant begins to experience herself as impacted by the quality and particulars of the interaction:

> I enter the world of her face. Her face and its features are the sky, the clouds, and the water. Her vitality and spirit are the air and the light. It is usually a riot of light and air at play. But this time when I enter the world is still and dull. Neither the curving lines of her face nor its rounded volumes are moving. Where is she? Where has she gone? I am scared. I feel the dullness creeping into me. I search around for a point of life to escape to.
>
> I find it. All her life is concentrated into the softest and hardest points in the world—her eyes.
>
> They draw me in deeper and deeper. . . . And there I feel running strong the invisible currents of her excitement. They churn up from those depths and tug at me. I call after them. I want to see her face again, alive. (58)

In descriptive words, the above report speculates how the dyadic experience takes over the infant's inner state. States of arousal, such as excitement or dullness, are experienced as different from mother's behavior, whereabouts, and presence. Both a notion of "in here" and "out there" begin to establish a sense of "self" and "not self."

What is also apparent in the above description is that the quality of the interaction defines and dominates the infant's immediate world and her felt experience. Alan Schore (2000), a neuropsychoanalyst, provides more detail about the early relational dance by highlighting the powerful imprint these interactions have on bodily experience and the developing nervous system. He takes it even farther than Stern by describing these early exchanges as a *dyadic regulation of emotion*. In the best-case scenario, through imitating, mirroring, matching, or counterbalancing movements, sounds, gestures, and facial expressions in response to the infant's expressions, the caregiver helps the infant to down-regulate or dampen negative emotions and up-regulate or amplify positive emotions and affect. An important element here is that Schore sees the dyadic dance of affect attunement as essentially a brain-to-brain interaction, that—whether successful or not—becomes imprinted in the brain as a template for self-regulation and contact with an other. The quality of the relational experience has an effect on the individual's capacity to experience, tolerate, and regulate states of arousal and episodes of interaction (3–4).

Returning to our discussion about embodiment as a development, Stern, Damasio, and Schore propose that these early stages of development are very strongly rooted in direct and embodied experience. Sensing the state of one's organism, its particular movements, and perceiving self and other becomes the bedrock of identity. The wide spectrum of proprioceptive/kinesthetic, intero-ceptive, and exteroceptive information is engaged in developing these early stages of "self."

Discussing the following stages, Stern (1985) describes the development of self as essentially a movement away from direct experience. In his proposed third stage of development a *subjective sense of self* (7–9 months) is being formed. The infant's orientation shifts from evident behavior (physical gestures and facial expressions) to the mental state underneath the behavior (124–26). The infant discovers that she has her *mindscape* and other people have their mindscape. Mindscapes contain intentions, desires, feelings, atten-tion, thoughts, and memories that make up the private world of the infant and can be shared with others via sharing attention, intention, and affective states. This shift away from overt behavior to a subjective mental state has enormous consequences for the experience of embodiment. The attention of the devel-oping individual moves from basic movements, perceptions, and relational patterns to a meaning-making process. Concurrently, *direct felt experience begins to recede into the background.*

The fourth and last stage in Stern's (1985) developmental model is that of the *verbal sense of self* (second year). It is significant in our discussion here as this stage continues to widen the gap between meaning making and direct experi-ence. As language emerges, the toddler is able to describe and represent her own experience. New possibilities of sharing experience through description and naming, arise. Yet, this new developmental stage can be seen as a double-edged sword. Language, the more it becomes established, tends to have an alienating effect; it represents a movement away from direct experience and, eventually, a more pronounced estrangement. Thus, language not only creates a space between interpersonal experience as lived and as represented, it simultaneously tends to distance the infant from direct embodied awareness. Embodied experi-ence, even though not entirely abandoned, consequently fades even further into the background while a verbal sense of self becomes more pronounced.

In elaborating this pivotal shift from embodied experience to meaning making and cognition, it seems imperative to mention Piaget's developmental model (Cowan 1978). Similar to Stern, Piaget saw the early sensorimotor stage and exploration as the basis for later cognitive functioning. Concrete knowledge in his view is gained through an array of fundamental movements, such as grasping, reaching, holding, and other perceptual and sensory activities like visual explorations. The more complex the movement is, the more complex is the meaning making of the world. The subsequent preoperational, concrete operational, and formal operational stages are essentially all based on the initial direct sensory experience. Similar to Stern, Piaget saw body-based exploration as the foundation for meaning making and considered early sensory behavior to be eventually abandoned as more complex representations (symbolic, logic, abstract functioning) become firmly rooted. Implicitly, again alienation from direct embodied experience is considered inevitable in Piaget's model with the advent of language and abstraction—even though his proposed timeline for this process may differ.

Orienting Away from the Senses

To recap, early bodily organization, movement capacities, and dyadic experiences represent early states of embodiment, and early templates for a sense of self. While body organization, movement expression, and interactional patterns continue to be elaborated and refined over time, they no longer require full attention and participation. Attention shifts toward cognitive and abstract capacities. With the amplification of meaning making, language, and abstract faculties, the actual experience of body senses becomes less conscious to the point where it moves into the background of the perceptual field. Body schema and in particular body perception become but a mere backdrop to awareness.

Disconnection from embodied experience is often seen as the result of challenging and traumatic experiences. Not to minimize the validity of this viewpoint, since traumatic and overwhelming experiences often result in some form of dissociation (Levine 1997; Ogden 2005; Rothchild 2000), I propose that a certain degree of "disembodiment" or distance from the body may be part of a common developmental process. Thus, the ascending development, seen in the integral literature as a move from multiplicity or form to oneness (Wilber 2000), with regard to embodiment is a development from direct body perception toward loss of contact with the lived body, which may be reestablished in a new way as development further unfolds.

Descending Development—Coming to Our Senses

The degree to which a development away from direct experience happens will depend on many different factors. To go into detail about this would take us beyond the scope of this chapter. Yet, no matter if we are talking about a partial or a more complete abandonment of bodily experience, the state of fragmentation calls at some point for a "coming to our senses" (Johnson 1983, 152). It may be the pain caused by a sense of fragmentation that precipitates a turn toward the senses, it may be a crisis of sorts that brings about such a shift, or it may simply be the yearning for wholeness that pulls an individual in this direction. However, for many this means a 180 degree turn toward one's experience.

I would like to claim that the turn, no matter how drastic, essentially signifies the entry into a new developmental phase, represented by what might be seen as a downward direction toward bodily awareness and exploration. That which has been "forgotten" needs to come back into the perceptual field through some form of sensory cultivation. *Body schema* and *body perception* need to return to the foreground. With the knowledge about the importance of such an attentional shift the question arises whether the return or descent itself, similar to the ascent, unfolds according to a particular trajectory or course.

I would argue here that the development toward *conscious embodiment* is a nonlinear, but nevertheless, somewhat backward traversing of the ascending stages. The way up is the way down (Wilber 2000; Ray 2008). The developmental task is to consciously embrace and tolerate the various layers of experience and allow bodily experience to deliver us into deeper states. Before veering our attention further toward these different levels of experience, our discussion needs to take us into *how* can the descent be facilitated and supported? How can we bring felt experience and sensations back into consciousness?

Throughout *Sex, Ecology, Spirituality* Wilber discusses the Centaur, which he uses to symbolize the wider and deeper integration of the body and mind that accompanies postconventional psychological development. This return to/emergence of the body in consciousness can be traced all the way back to chapter 7 of *The Atman Project*. While much of the phenomenological literature emphasizes a *return to* narrative, a somatic and Integral approach recognizes that the task before us includes returning to lost or neglected sensory and somatic capacities and experiences as well as the *emergence of* new forms of embodied experience that are only available with the development of consciousness.

Movement and Sensation

As noted above, neurophysiology tells us that sensation and movement are two sides of the same coin. The constant interplay between movement and sensation is described by the term *sensory-motor feedback loop* (Hanna 1988). Similar to the events during uterine life, where movement instigates the capacity for sensation (Gallagher 2005; Blechschmidt 1982), movement continues to inspire sensation via activating the kinesthetic, proprioceptive, and interoceptive elements of the somatosenses. Movement in its potentially wide spectrum, from extrinsic, volitional, and high energy movement, to subtle and intrinsic movements, including pulsations and micromovements, is a fundamental element in the pursuit of cultivating body awareness. Particularly non-habitual and nonlinear movements, such as wave motions and micromovements, in concert with a rich array of breaths and subtle sounds, allow us to deeply touch ourselves (Gintis 2007). The more varied and textured the movement is, the more it provides stimulation to the nervous system, and sensitizes and opens the body.

The Importance of Attention

Sensation and movement are the main ingredients that move us toward fuller embodiment. Nevertheless, they must be coupled with deep attention in order to deliver us into the mystery of our bodies. Only when movement and sensation are consciously attended to can our somatosenses reach consciousness. What is it that the element of attention brings to this process? John Dewey (n/d), philosopher, psychologist, and educational reformer, had an interesting viewpoint here. He believed there is no sensation without consciousness. The stimulus within the nervous system, informing us of the current condition of our body's interior—be it movement, vibration, pulsation, pressure, heat, tension, pressure, and more—is the necessary prerequisite. For sensory impulse to be recognized as sensation or body perception, sensory stimuli need to be coupled with awareness. Otherwise, sensations, present below the threshold of awareness, are not experienced as body perception. How the emergence of conscious sensation might be experienced is recounted in the description below:

> As I stopped pulsing, images formed by sensations float up in my awareness from different parts of my body. Sometimes, even when I'm not paying attention. . . . There is a whole world inside my body that is going on all the time, whether I notice it or not. (Lana, S. personal communication, July 2006)

Lana, a student in one of my somatic classes, very fittingly speaks about a rich world going on inside, whether she perceives it or not. Only when her awareness is receptive to particular stimuli, are they experienced as sensations.

Going with or Going against the Current

In many somatic and some spiritual approaches sensations are considered the umbilical cord that connects us with deeper layers of experience. Yet, the intention of cultivating awareness of sensation can be realized through different methods. Within the field of somatic psychology what is often highlighted is the importance of giving unencumbered expression to sensory impulses. A full sequencing of sensory impulses through the body is regarded as the pathway to bringing the organism from a state of fragmentation back to wholeness (Aposhyan 2004). Health from this perspective is precipitated by allowing the body to complete its natural movements and unravel contractions and tension patterns. Tracking and expressing sensory impulses here can be described as *going with the current.*

On the other hand, a *going against the current,* a different way of cultivating sensory awareness, is more often described by Eastern spiritual traditions. Tantric practices in particular, work with what Eliade (1969) calls a *regressive process,* through which the practitioner learns to experience, tolerate, and witness sensation without reacting impulsively or expressing it freely. Sensations and tensions here become the very fabric of yogic cultivation. Containing and not reacting to sensation can be described as going against the current, which builds up energy to bring about a transformative shift

Both approaches, free expression of sensory impulses or going with the current, and not acting on sensations but rather witnessing them or going against the current, when practiced consciously, can take our awareness into deeper states of existence. The capacity to express sensory impulses more fully and freely, and the ability to contain and witness sensory experience become pathways to cultivating deeper states of embodiment.

From discussing the "how" of this process, even though in a very rudimentary fashion, it is important to turn back to looking at the "what" of this journey. Although, as mentioned above, this is not a linear process, as we turn toward our bodily experience, there seem to be particular layers of experience that we encounter. The process of the downward journey takes us from the surface to the depth (Ray 2008).

Reconnecting with the Personal Body

On this downward journey we often recognize *personal patterns* as one of the first layers we encounter. Tracking and exploring our sensations takes us back into the ways we have learned to somatically organize ourselves in relationship to our needs, to others, and to the overall environment. By becoming aware of tension patterns, habitual postures or gestures, habitual states of affect regulation, and states of numbness, we are confronted with the very organization of our personal and historical body. We come face to face with early or challenging experiences and the resolutions we found through particular somatic states of being, such as overcharge or undercharge (Keleman 1979). We begin to notice how these somatically based maneuvers have become braided into our character organization, as part and parcel of who we take ourselves to be. Thus, we are called back into our personal psychology and somatic organization.

Diving into the Fluid Body

As we touch underneath the habits and patterns of our personal body we may find ourselves in a very different terrain. Our awareness may shift from noticing volitional/muscular movements or habitual states of arousal to sensing ongoing rhythms and tides within our organism that seem to flow from here until eternity. We meet a layer of motion and waves that undulate in their own speed and rhythm, like the tides within the ocean. "Biomorphic" movements, as Emily Conrad, a somatic innovator, calls these undulating waves, pulsations, or infinitesimally small micro-movements (Gintis 2007), remind us of the watery origin of our organism. When our embodied awareness delivers us to this layer of experience, Conrad's notion (1998) that movement is not something we do, but something we are, becomes a felt reality. The watery atmosphere blurs sensate distinctions of individual movements or various bodily structures. We find ourselves part of an ongoing tide of internal motions with a sense of organismic wholeness, in resonance with life at large.

Cultivating the Quasi Subtle Body

When turning toward the body and cultivating embodied experience, we also may encounter elements of what is often referred to as the *subtle body,* the particulars of which in some traditions are described by chakras and nadis, meridians and acupuncture points, or through the lataif system (Almaas 1986; Eliade 1969; Saso 1997; Wangyal 2002), just to name a few. Without engaging a discussion of how these different maps may overlap, it is safe to say that a common element of subtle anatomy is a focus on three different body centers—the head center, the heart center, and the belly center. Cultivation practices are aimed at balancing and integrating these centers (Bennett 1994). Conscious attending brings to the forefront awareness of the subtle body or, as Yuasa (1987) calls it the *quasi body*—not a physical body, verifiable through anatomical investigation, but a body that reveals itself only in the course of cultivation.

The following report describes what happened for one of my students Melanie S. (personal communication, July 2006) while and after exploring eye movements:

In the dark with the music, my eyes moved quickly, darting randomly around, and I felt tension in my head, and the mind hanging on wanting to know what's happening. . . . Finally, I let the eyes stop moving and roll back to the center of my head. . . . Then, suddenly, following this movement, a space opened in my head and filled with blue light. Reaching upward, my gaze was drawn into a white column of light going up and out the top of my head. . . . It was quite exciting to understand, finally, what opening the crown of the head really meant. I get it now. Such a strong feeling of lightness and freedom.

Movement of the eyes and the very focus on the head area brought awareness of the subtlety and vastness of the head center to the forefront. It put Melanie in touch with nuances of Yuasa's (1987) quasi body, a level of experience that is not available through ordinary consciousness.

The Dissolution of Subject and Object

As we continue to deepen our exploration into our physical body, we may find ourselves experiencing an extraordinary shift in consciousness. Deep and prolonged attentiveness to our body, through movement, sensory tracking, inquiry, and presencing can precipitate a profound absorption that marks a pivotal change from a conventional perspective, where the experiencer is separate from the experience. Dōgen, a Japanese Zen monk of the thirteenth century, discusses this fundamental shift. As one undergoes deep meditative introspection and inquiry, the conventional perspective, in its distinction between subject and object—the subject being the "I" or self and the object being the body—falls away. When this occurs, a radical shift in awareness happens. Dōgen describes this shift as the *molting of the body-mind* (as cited in Yuasa 1987, 123). In ordinary consciousness, the body is experienced as separate from the mind, and the mind seems to control the body. Through continued practice, the self-consciousness of the mind becomes extinguished. The mind—the subject—no longer separates itself from the body—the object—but becomes completely one with it. This process of molting is the process by which the body is no longer a thing we have, but an experience we are (Yuasa 1987). Direct experience is no longer mediated by a particular identity.

This shift in perspective is very clearly demonstrated through Laura's (Laura P., personal communication, July 2006) experience. Laura was not only seeing or observing elements of her own body, but also became the very act of seeing:

The swirling of the energy into my head and the movement of my eyes brought me directly into my body . . . right into and within my skull where I became the fibers of my head, brain and eyeballs. I was myself seeing from myself. I could feel the largeness of my eyeballs moving around and could even sense my skull surrounding my eyes. Instead of just seeing, I was also the act of seeing. It was a feeling of awe. . . . There was no me and my body, we were one and the same.

The potent shift described above, the molting of the body-mind as Dogen calls it, allows us to experience ourselves/our bodies from a totally different vantage point. The distinction between subject and object falls away. Laura's sense of awe gives us a notion of how powerful and impactful this experience can be.

Dark Consciousness

From deep to deeper, continuing in this downward journey takes us even further into unknown layers of our body. Having touched on the layers of the personality, the fluid body, and the phenomena of the quasi subtle body, there is a mysterious layer that seems underneath all of these. From an alchemical perspective it would be described as the *primordial layer of the body.* (This is also called the *causal body* in Integral Theory). It is not a passive or empty state, but a state of potency of our deep nature, an endless, unconditioned existence [Ray 2008].) Kukai, a ninth century Japanese mystic and intellectual, coming from an earthbound tradition, highlighted the importance of exploring this realm, which he considered the body's deep darkness. The concept of darkness here does not mean that the body is bad or negative, it rather implies depth and mystery with qualities not readily apparent. (Yuasa 1987).

Similar to Kukai's notion of the dark mysterious consciousness hidden in the body, Ridley (2006), a contemporary Western biodynamic craniosacral practitioner and teacher, describes a quality to be found at the very bottom of experience. He portrays this quality not only as darkness, but also as stillness. This *dynamic stillness,* as he calls it, is no longer differentiated by waves or motion of some kind, but the place where everything ceases. "There is only infinite stillness, silence, and emptiness—a radiant blackness that is aware" (113). Ridley considers this to be the place where no experience exists, only awareness dropped into infinity, and nothingness remains. He considers it the background and source of all manifestation and form.

Even though the above concept of an underlying darkness and stillness is difficult to grasp in words, Anne's (Anne S., personal communication, July 2006) report below gives us a sense of how this might be experienced:

There was a quietness that I had not experienced before, a stillness. I had a sense of containment, a darkness, a void. I fell completely in my body and had a sense of a complete and undefinable safety. I tried to be more "aware" of how I was feeling, how my body's mind felt, what my mind was experiencing, but all I could sense, feel and be aware of was this darkness, so still, quiet, and serene. . . . I am filled with a sense of wonder, a sense of awe. This feeling has stayed with me since. . . . What I had experienced . . . was a "gentle holding." A gentle holding was the experience of a true and pure love, a love whose very fragility is its strength.

The description here documents the power and impact this dimension of dark stillness had on Anne's overall sense of being. She noted how it was not possible to be "aware" of it as outside of herself, but could only be felt in a very direct and immediate way.

Consciousness Inherent in Matter

In our discussion we have explored embodiment as an ascending and a descending process. The ascent is a movement from early and less differentiated states of embodiment into differentiation of movement, perceptual, and relational capacities, toward a gradual shift away from body experience. The descending process is a turn back to body experience and a deep exploration of the sensory landscape. This process often involves a state-training process of exploring gross sensations, subtle energies, and causal stillness in the body.

As soon as we pursue a descent into the body, we are implying a worldview that sees value in the material realm itself. Sri Aurobindo early on presented the notion of ascent and descent in his integral cosmology. He described matter as an expression of spirit and saw no matter as devoid of Spirit. Spirit is manifest as matter, and is "involved from the beginning in the whole of matter and in every knot, formation and particle of matter" (as cited in McDermott 1997, 73). Evolution, in his understanding, is a journey of consciousness. Before time as we know it, there is only primordial silence, a state of formless consciousness. It is out of this silence that the universe emerges. Beginning with undifferentiated primordial matter, consciousness, through the evolutionary process, evolves and participates in bringing forth complex forms. Evolution in Aurobindo's notion is the unfolding of spirit through matter.

The importance of this perspective is not just that he offers an evolutionary viewpoint; implicit in it is the recognition of the importance of matter. Matter is not just matter. Matter is the hiding place of Spirit. Seen through this paradigm "body" is not just a subservient medium but an intelligent form. Body is not just a vehicle that we are encumbered by and need to keep in good working condition so as not to interfere with the soul's development. In the contrary, implicitly and explicitly Aurobindo gives us an compelling reason why it is of utmost importance to inquire into and experience our physical body in a conscious, active, and focused way. Conscious attending to the body means participating with the intelligence inherent in all form.

Ascendence, Descendence and Trans-Descendence

In alignment with this worldview, which embraces both form and formlessness, Aurobindo (Satprem 1970) and Wilber (2000) promote human development as an ascending and a descending process. As already mentioned above, the ascending process is a movement from multiplicity or form toward oneness. It allows us to move beyond matter and cultivate more complex stages of consciousness and transcendent states of consciousness. Through the downward movement we encounter the individual and unique, the sensuousness of life, and the depth of matter. Descending into the body thus means deeply engaging with it and exploring it—bone not just as bone, skin not just as skin, and flesh not just as flesh—but all of it as intelligence in action. An intimate encounter with our physical form simultaneously delivers us into an underlying oneness that is deep to the particulars of bodily experience. Thus the descent is not simply a movement of descendence into form (returning to content associated with early-stage development), but also a movement of *trans-de-cendence* (Kasulis, personal communication, Fall 2000) accessing embodied states of consciousness. As the awareness of self joins with the processes of the body, the hidden consciousness within is unleashed as undifferentiated and primordial state of matter.

   In terms of Integral Theory, embodiment involves Descent into the forgotten somatic content of early stages of psychological development as well as the Ascent into the emergent somatic content of postrational stages of embodied awareness. However, in my view and experience this "Ascent" is actually another dimension of the Descent (e.g., trans-de-cendence). In addition, Integral Theory points out that states of embodiment and consciousness can be cultivated to recognize somatic realities associated with either the earliest or highest stages of development. Thus, integral embodiment involves going back to the body (reconnecting with aspects originally encountered in early development) and going "forward" to the body (making contact with new emergent layers and aspects of the body). Obviously, we are only now beginning to understand these fascinating relationships between these vertical and horizontal aspects. Thus, much important integral work remains to be done in this domain.[1]

Conclusion

Early human development, starting in utero, is a process of embodiment based on the growth and differentiation of the human organism that occurs in tandem with the development of identity. As the nervous system matures, our movements become more complex, our sensory and perceptual capacities become elaborated, and body schema and body perception are forming. A self is being formed as an internal coalescence of ongoing sensory, feeling, and perceptive processes. With the further unfolding of the ascending developmental process representation of experience and abstraction become more dominant, and body schema and body perception are gradually relegated to the subconscious or unconscious. An increased abandoning of bodily experience is discussed here not only as the result of traumatic and challenging experiences, but also as a necessary developmental process that firmly establishes the subject, the self, and the object, the body.

A fundamental turn toward direct experience is required to descend into bodily experience and develop consciousness of body perceptions. This is what can be regarded as the downward development, a movement away from objectification and disengagement from the body to a deeply subjective experience. The journey of descent into the body is greatly facilitated through coupling cultivation of movement, sensory abilities, and awareness.

Conscious exploration of sensation and movement brings us back in touch with our personal history and resulting somatic organization. Yet, bodily exploration also allows us to deeply touch vital and subtle (and causal) realms of experience. This can precipitate a radical shift in awareness that obliterates the division between subject and object, or self and body, and allow for the experience of a potent and undifferentiated state of awareness. The downward path can be regarded not only as descending into form, but also as trans-descending into primordial consciousness.

I am presenting a broad sweep of a developmental process in the above discussion, with the intention to inspire further exploration about the development of embodiment. Although the notion of the Ascent and the Descent is part of an integral paradigm, the discussions thus far strongly center around ascending developmental processes. Exploring the ascending development in relationship to the descent may help us to bring deeper understanding about the link between the two, the dynamic at hand, and allow us to uncover keys for facilitating the descending aspect of this journey more skillfully and artfully.

The developmental trajectory is presented in somewhat of a linear fashion for the sake of simplicity. The way up was described as the way down. Nevertheless, the question arises: To what degree is an ascending development the prerequisite for a descending development and conscious participation with matter? Exploring this question would have taken us into a depth and detail not permissible due to the length of this chapter. It is nevertheless a question that needs to be attended to in some other discussion.

On a collective scale, exploring an ascending and descending direction of embodiment may allow us to expose an overall dualistic viewpoint, separating body from mind/soul, as a developmental stage. A dualistic world view from this vantage point can be regarded as the ascending half of an incomplete collective development. It also allows us to question the often prevailing notion of spiritual development as solely a process of transcendence, and will encourage us to recognize the divine in all of body, form, and matter.

In closing, the descent into matter and the body per se is a process that is barely understood and difficult to undergo. Beyond meeting the personal layers of our conditioning, the Descent will allow us to encounter the sensuousness of our body, the dynamism of life, and the darkness of matter. An experience of oneness is available through both, the ascending and the descending development, yet, it is only through the descending journey that we may directly participate in the creative force of life and matter. It is a deeply mysterious journey!

Note

1. In conversation about this section of the chapter and the relationship between Ascent and Descent in the context of bodily experience Sean Esbjörn-Hargens commented: "Both Ascent and Descent dynamics can be seen—in this context—to have horizontal and vertical movements (i.e., your trans-descendence). So Ascent is not just a vertical escalade and Descent is not just a horizontal embrace. Rather, Descent into the body can include both descending into the body that *is* and ascending into the body that *will be*. So we can and should simultaneously ascend and descend into bodily experience. This, dual emphasis opens up some rich new embodied territories and is a unique offering of your analysis here. Also, integral embodiment can be understood as the multidimensional integration of vertical stages and horizontal states as related to bodily experience" (personal communication, December 8, 2009).

References

Almaas, A. H. 1986. *Essence*. York Beach, ME: Samuel Weiser.

Aposhyan, S. 2004. Body-mind psychotherapy in context. In S. Aposhyan, *Body-mind psychotherapy*, 3–19. New York: W. W. Norton.

Bennett, J. G. 1994. *Deeper man*. Santa Fe: Bennett Books.

Blechschmidt, E. 1982. *Sein und werden: Die menschliche freuhentwicklung* [Being and becoming: Early human development]. Stuttgart: Verlag Urachhaus.

Bruteau, B. 1971. *Worthy is the world: The Hindu philosophy of Sri Aurobindo*. Cranbury, NJ: Associated University Presses.

Conrad, E. 1998. *Life on land*. Santa Monica: Continuum.

Cowan, P. 1978. *Piaget: With feeling*. New York: Holt, Rinehart, and Winston.

Damasio, A. 1999. The organism and the object. In *The feeling of what happens*, 133–67. New York: Harcourt Brace.

Dewey, J. (n.d.). *The works of John Dewey*. Chicago: Illinois State University Press, 93–115.

Eliade, M. 1969. *Yoga: Immortality and freedom*. Princeton: Princeton University Press.

Gallagher, S. 2005. *How the body shapes the mind*. New York: Oxford University Press.

Gintis, B. 2007. *Engaging the movement of life*. Berkeley: North Atlantic Books.

Hanna, T. 1988. *Somatics: Reawakening the mind's control of movement, flexibility, and health*. New York: Addison-Wesley.

Hartley, L. 1995. *Wisdom of the body moving: Introduction to Body-Mind Centering*. Berkeley: North Atlantic Books.

Johnson, D. H. 1983. Coming to our senses. In *Body: Recovering our sensual wisdom*, 152–74). Berkeley: North Atlantic Books.

McDermott, R. A. (Ed.) 1987. *The essential Aurobindo*. Hudson, NY: Lindisfarne Press.

Keleman, S. 1979. Somatic organization: The how of behavior. In *Somatic reality: Bodily experience and embodied truth*. Berkeley: Center Press.

Levine, P. 1997. *Waking the tiger: Healing trauma*. Berkeley: North Atlantic Books.

Ogden, P., K. Minton, and Pain. 2005. *Trauma and the body: A sensorimotor approach*. New York: W. W. Norton.

Ray, R. 2008. *Touching enlightenment*. Boulder: Sounds True, Inc.

Ridley, C. 2006. *Stillness: Biodynamic cranial practice and the evolution of consciousness*. Berkeley: North Atlantic Books.

Rothchild, B. 2000. *The body remembers: The psychophysiology of trauma and trauma treatment*. New York: W. W. Norton.

Satprem. 1970. *Sri Aurobindo or The adventure of consciousness*. Mt. Vernon, WA: Institute for Evolutionary Research.

Schore, A. N. 2000. *Affect regulation and the origin of the self*. Presentation for Hakomi Integrative Somatics Center, Boulder, Colorado.

Silow, T. 2002. *The kinesthetic sense: Exploring sensation, self-emergence, awareness, and stress negotiation through somatic practice*. Columbus, OH: Unpublished Doctoral Dissertation.

Stern, D. N. 1985. The four senses of self. In *The interpersonal world of the infant*, 37–161. New York: Basic Books.

———. 1990. *Diary of a baby*. New York: Basic Books.

Tenzin Wangyal Rinpoche. 2002. *Healing with form, energy, and light*. Ithaca: Snow Lion Publications.

Wilber, K. 1980. *The Atman project: A transpersonal view of human development*. Wheaton, IL: Quest Books.

———. 2000. *Sex, ecology, spirituality*. Boston: Shambhala.

———. 2006. *Integral spirituality*. Boston: Integral Books.

Yuasa, Y. 1987. *The body: Toward an Eastern mind-body theory*. Albany: State University of New York Press.

## 4

Beauty and the Expansion of Women's Identity

Vanessa D. Fisher

The history of women's beauty is written in bodily gestures that express both the constraints of her culture as well as the unfolding desire of her interiority. Embracing the power of beauty has always been problematic for feminism, and for good reason. We have yet to create a language for our own yearning or find an expression for our own radiance that could embrace other women rather than attempt to outshine them. We have yet to realize that our expression of beauty itself has an evolution that continually expands our identity and embodiment over the course of development. This chapter therefore offers an AQAL analysis of some of the current views that dominate feminist discourse on women's beauty. It is also a personal story of my own ongoing journey as a young woman trying to reclaim my beauty, for the benefit of all beings.

A Personal Search for Beauty

In eleventh century China, there lived a Taoist woman named Sun Pu-erh who sought the path of enlightenment. Sun Pu-erh's dedication to truth caused her to search out one of the great enlightened masters of her time in hopes that he would take her as his student. The enlightened master soon came to recognize the passion and perseverance in Sun Pu-erh and told her that if she truly wished to attain immortality she would need to travel to Loyang, where she could cultivate the Tao. But when Sun Pu-erh revealed her face to her master he was taken aback by her beauty and told her that her appeaance would remain an obstacle to her enlightenment. He denied permission for Sun Pu-erh to travel to Loyang for he believed she would be the constant target of men wishing to overpower and take advantage of her.

Unwilling to let her appearance be an obstacle to her path, Sun Pu-erh immediately went home to her kitchen and heated a wok full of cooking oil.

When the oil began to boil, Sun Pu-erh picked up the wok, closed her eyes, and poured the oil over her face. With scars etched across her skin, Sun Pu-erh returned to her master, who, amazed by her sacrifice, gave her permission to travel to Loyang (Halprin 1995, 2).

When I came across this story and its powerful imagery, I remember it deeply resonating with my own struggle with beauty. As a young woman dedicated to the search for my Divine Identity, I had always considered my struggle with beauty to be the most superficial concern and ultimately the greatest obstacle on my spiritual path. Yet the more I attempted to deny my deepest yearning for beauty, the more beauty came to haunt me. I often had visions of blinding myself, a similar sacrifice to that of Sun Pu-erh, brought on by my own sense of desperation. Perhaps I felt that it was only in such a dramatic renunciation that I could finally unhook the pain of this unwanted desire. But deep within, I continued to wonder whether such an act would truly offer me the release that I was searching for.

It would take me many years before I realized that denying beauty only repressed it to the unconscious realms of my own shadow, along with the all the desires of my body and sexuality. And eventually my shadow would find its way back into consciousness, painfully forcing me to see that it was in my very yearning for beauty that I would discover my unique channel to the Divine.

Feminism and the Beauty Question

Sifting through the feminist literature, I realized that my confusion surrounding beauty was also a collective struggle and a topic that has, in many ways, been left largely unreconciled for women. Looking back, we see the seeds of feminism being sown within the newly emerging modern worldview (orange altitude) and its budding worldcentric awareness, which began to take root in the West during the late nineteenth century. For the first time, many women had growing access to educational and professional domains that had previously been exclusive to men. During this era, the majority of feminists agreed that in order to support their advancement and be seen as equal valued subjects to men, there was a need to reject societal ideals of beauty and the passive objectification of the female body. It was through this rejection of beauty that women felt they could redirect their energy and attention toward exploring the untapped potentials of their own minds. Mary Wollstonecraft was one of the earliest feminists to articulate the imprisonment of women in their own bodies:

> Taught from their infancy that beauty is a woman's scepter, the mind shapes itself to the body, and, roaming round in its gilt cage, only seeks to adorn its

prison. . . . If women do not resign the arbitrary power of beauty—they will prove that they have *less* mind than men. (Steiner 2001, 21)

The challenge for women became one of stepping out of their natural tendency toward subservience to male desire, which meant detaching from the power they had gained from their dependence on their bodies and physical beauty, so that they might build the important foundation for asserting their minds.

As feminism and feminist values grew in strength during the 1950s and 1960s, modernism was slowly giving way to postmodernism and awareness of the influence of culture (LL quadrant) on shaping and constructing our reality was at the cutting edge of intellectual inquiry. Within this new paradigm, feminists became increasingly aware of how much sociocultural systems (LL and LR) had continued to shape women's understanding of their own beauty. In the West, this understanding brought with it intensified feelings of imprisonment and resentment toward the limits and dictates of what came to be viewed as a massively oppressive sociocultural system (the patriarchy). Within the context of this growing awareness, beauty became increasingly problematic for the self-proclaimed feminist.

With the publication of books such as Naomi Wolff's *The Beauty Myth* in the early 1990s, beauty soon became regarded as a currency system (LR) built upon the values and discourses of the patriarchy (LL), which aimed to keep women separate from one another and subservient to male desire. The "beauty myth" was exposed and identified by many feminists as a creation of their sociocultural surroundings with which they felt they had no part in defining for themselves. Some came to regard beauty as a male problem, arguing that since men had the most control over the public sphere, then it was men alone who had constructed and controlled this elaborate deception called "beauty." Thus, feminists felt that the only proper response was to reject this construction for the purpose of freeing women's autonomy.

Within this important postmodern awakening to the influence of the LL and LR quadrants in shaping our understanding of beauty, there was also an unfortunate turn toward reductionism. Beauty was deconstructed and reduced to a purely sociocultural phenomenon (thus stripping the important influence of the UL and UR quadrants) and also flattened into the limits of one level of interpretation, namely, the postmodern worldview (green altitude). To reiterate this point: postmodernism, with all its gifts, painfully curtailed beauty's expansive expression by not only collapsing the UL and UR quadrants into the LL and LR, but also by simultaneously collapsing all levels of aesthetic development into a green flatland worldview (a crucial point that I will return to later).

Within this postmodern context, any woman who continued to enjoy exhibiting her beauty was easily regarded as a pawn in the patriarchal system, for there was no room in the green worldview for a woman to assert independence in her choice to express beauty nor was there an interpretive structure available that could see important qualifying distinctions (e.g., that there are many levels of interpretation and motivation that exist for expressing beauty). It was in this postmodern deconstruction that all beauty soon came to be regarded as morally suspect, and it is here where the evolving feminist consciousness still largely finds itself today.

Amidst the haze clouds arising from the deconstructive dust of our postmodern era, there has been a small number of feminists who have returned to the beauty question and struggled to address the issue of beauty as not merely a male or sociocultural construction but also a deeply rooted female yearning (e.g., Wendy Steiner, Nancy Etcoff, Linsa M. Scott, Luce Irigaray, and Ellen Zetzel Lambert). These feminists are attempting to speak to the desire for beauty that women seem to naturally harbor and are working to try to sort out what beauty might mean for us as women in today's world. Most of these women are doing so largely through the UL quadrant (namely, zone 1) by attempting to bring back the important reality of the subject; a subject that is not merely a construction of cultural networks but also an independent self with an inherent desire for beauty. Some are even attempting to overcome this LL/LR reductionism by utilizing the cognitive sciences, as well as research in evolutionary biology, to help reshape our understanding of beauty (mainly through UR methodologies) (Etcoff 1999). But there have been no feminists, at least that I can find, who are addressing the issue of beauty in relation to interior aesthetic stage development (zone 2 methodologies) and thus in my opinion one of the richest domains, namely the developmental aspect of beauty's unfolding, is still being largely left in the dark (again, a topic I will return to later).

Women's seeming lack of investigation into the issue of beauty could be seen as a residual side effect of the postmodern deconstruction that has often left us feeling uncomfortable to engage discussions about beauty that we have convinced ourselves are vain, self-indulgent, and ultimately unimportant. Ellen Zetzel Lambert, a feminist active throughout the 1960s who in the 1990s returned to recognize the deeper issue of beauty in her book, *The Face of Love: Feminism and the Beauty Question*, admits that it is an uncomfortable topic for her to speak about. She states, "As a committed feminist, I've felt embarrassed that the beauty question should still matter to me" (Lambert 1995, xi).

There seems to be a common acknowledgment among the few feminists returning to the beauty question that beauty has, oddly, become one of the greatest taboos in feminist discourse. These feminists see beauty as a topic that needs to come to the forefront in the twenty-first century in order to address what Lambert describes as the divided feeling of today's young women, who are highly informed of the importance of their minds over their physical appearance and thus have become all the more ashamed of their concern for their appearance. This split and shame is due to women seeing their bodies as separate from their "real" identity, thus adding to the sense of confusion and embarrassment that "liberated" young women are feeling about the beauty question (Lambert 1995, 28).

There is a distinct voice emerging from these few feminists that speaks to the need to reopen the forum and invite fresh perspectives on beauty. As Nancy Etcoff (1999) reiterates, "Beauty is not going anywhere. The idea that beauty is unimportant or a cultural construct is the real beauty myth. We have to understand beauty, or we will always be enslaved by it" (242). Redefining beauty from an Integral standpoint—one that situates beauty in an AQAL matrix of quadrants, levels, lines, states, and types—can help feminism disentangle from its attachment to the postmodern worldview and bring light and fresh air to an often painful and delicate subject for the emerging feminist to ponder.

Beauty As an Art Form

Perhaps the place to begin looking for an emerging language of beauty, one that can move us beyond the limits of our current postmodern discourse, resides in the realm of art making itself. In the 1960s, postmodernism had been a breakthrough in opening the art world back into the realm of beauty as aesthetic pleasure, as artists reacted against much of the restriction of modernism that had dominated the art world for so long (Steiner 2001, 125). At the same time, the second-wave feminist movement had been coming to the fore, and women themselves were entering more into the male-dominated art field. Because feminism championed that women assert their agency, there was resistance to return to old images of passive female subjects in art, thus keeping the door largely closed on the reconstitution of the female body as a symbol of beauty. As a woman artist during this era, the difficult issue revolved around how to represent the female body in a way that brought agency and dignity to the female subject and was in line with the current version of feminist values. Beauty and the representation of women in art became a highly controversial topic and opinions on women, and beauty still remain divided among feminists and artists today.

The difficult challenge for female artists became how to integrate their still problematic female bodies with their recently freed minds without falling into old roles of passive sexualized objects. Wendy Steiner recognizes that the dawning of the twenty-first century presents us with a turning point in which we realize that an aesthetic incompatible with femininity is impossible and yet we are not quite sure what the alternative will look like. She states, "Many are pointing us back to beauty as if it were the most compelling problem for anyone trying to make sense of twenty-first-century existence" (Steiner 2001, xvii).

Hannah Wilke: Reclaiming Female Objectivity

Through my investigation of feminists in the 1960s, I came across a less well-known artist, Hannah Wilke. What I found in the depths of Wilke's art and life was a courageous feminist who willingly worked on the edges of this emerging aesthetic struggle through her own art making in order to bridge this difficult integration of body and mind. At a time when there was great resistance against the provocative nature of her art and what others saw as an objectification of her "beautiful" female body, Wilke continued to struggle to reclaim her beauty and eroticism and bring its much needed transformative power back into feminist discourse.

Hannah Wilke has often been described as one of the most daring and versatile artists of the 1960s. Wilke started her art career trained in sculpture, using clay, gum, latex, and kneaded erasers to sculpt representations of female genitalia, manipulating all types of media into a variety of vulvic forms. Wilke realized that most women felt shame about their own sexuality and attempted to bring integrity to the flesh through her sculptural forms in order to develop love for that which many women hated most about themselves (Hansen et al. 1998, 6).

Wilke was always deeply engaged with philosophy, politics, literature, art history, and religion as well as her own autobiography. In the 1970s, Wilke extended her art practice to include the exhibition of her own body as a social, political, and sexual statement (Hansen et al. 1998, 10). As a self-proclaimed feminist, Wilke was focused on a reclaiming of the erotic in all spheres of life, and her art challenges the viewer to question their understanding of feminism and its relationship to beauty.

Wilke once stated, "I am a victim of my own beauty" (Frueh 1989, 52). This was her own recognition of the conflict that many women of her time faced surrounding the issue of their beauty: whether they had it or not, they always felt victimized by it and somehow always felt wrong. Wilke chose to display the inappropriateness of her beauty as a means of confronting its own wrongness (Frueh 1989, 52). She saw her art as a way to address the taboo of her own beauty and the conflicts and struggles she experienced with her body as a feminist. Her feminist contemporaries found Wilke's art to be vulgar and in contradistinction to the feminist movement that was attempting to bring sexual dignity to women, and so Wilke was often criticized for confusing her roles as feminist and flirt (Hansen et al. 1998, 26). But Wilke was very aware of the positioning she was taking with her body and beauty, and was critical of politics and theories surrounding feminism that excluded the erotic.

Intrigued by the art of word play and linguistics, Wilke continually used humor and puns in the titles of her exhibitions. She loved how meaning could transform through subtle shifts in language, allowing two or more interpretations to be present and never feeling the need to settle on one. She felt that this "ethics of ambiguity" conveyed the paradox she felt within herself as a female and the roles she was supposed to play in society, and felt the incorporation of paradox to be central to her artistic expression (Hansen et al. 1998, 26).

One such example comes out of Wilke's 1977 photographic series where she has laid herself naked across the grass with the title, "I Object: Memoirs of a Sugar Giver," written over her head. Depending on where one puts the emphasis and whether "Object" is read as a noun or verb, it could either mean "I am an Object" or "I Object to being objectified" (Hansen et al. 1998, 26). Through this play on words, Wilke was attempting to acknowledge the double bind of being an American woman in the late twentieth century. Despite a heightened feminist consciousness, Wilke still saw that women continued to be concerned with their appearance and desirability and her work attempted to expose the deepening split between feminism and femininity.

Wilke used her art as a space to explore the outside/inside dichotomy addressing the need for women to reclaim their objectness. "Why not be an object?" she asks, one who is aware of her I-ness, an "I-Object" (Frueh 1989, 52). Wilke saw the asserting of oneself as an object to be an equally essential act of female agency and was aware of the need for both assertions if one was to attempt to live freely and fully integrated as an embodied feminist. Joanna Frueh (1989) comments on this importance for women to claim their object-ness when she says,

> In contemporary usage, the word object applied to a woman is considered negative. She is solely a sex object, a thing perceived without empathy or compassion. However, an object, defined as something that is or is capable of being seen, touched, or otherwise sensed, exists; thus, respecting object hood can be an assertion of existence. Wilke knows that women are ashamed of nudity. To be female and sexual is forbidden. If you show your body and are proud of it, it frightens people, for then a woman exists, intensely. (44)

Wilke also saw the power latent in female beauty and its ability to engage and allure others, so she used her own body as an artistic canvas to evoke questions and discussion about gender roles, social structures, sex, economics, and religion. In a series she entitled *SOS Starification Object Series: An Adult Game of Mastication,* Wilke studied the poses and gestures out of top fashion and advertising magazines and mimicked the stylization of gender in the media by embodying similar poses (Hansen et al. 1998, 28). She scarred herself with vulvic shaped gums in an attempt to show the scarification of women through media as well as a way to laugh and make fun of it, for Wilke was well known for her sense of humor.

Wilke was diagnosed with lymphoma in June 1987. As her cancer progressed, she would continue to document her autobiography through drawings and photographs. Wilke posed her body as art well into the late stages of her disfiguring illness, often copying gestures that she had used in the '70s, humorously emphasizing the myth of eternal youth and conveying the need for reclaiming the body and beauty in all stages of life. For Wilke, life had always been impelled by the beauty and erotic power of the human gesture to create, which she articulated and embodied with grace until her death in 1993. Wilke truly stands out as an exemplar for an evolving feminist consciousness that is continually struggling to work through, discover, break out, and emerge into new levels of understanding in relation to beauty.

The Aesthetics of the Masculine and Feminine

In order to bridge a few important trends in aesthetic philosophy, as well as tie together some important concerns of feminist theory, I thought it would be useful to look at the issue of beauty through the lens of the masculine/feminine dynamic.[1] Asking how the masculine/feminine dance can be incorporated into our emerging Integral aesthetic can perhaps offer insight into the many different ways in which we experience, express, and respond to beauty. It also seems to bring clarity to some important distinctions that, when put together, complement one another and create a more expansive picture of the rich dimensions beauty has to offer.

There were two main figures that stood out during my research as representatives for what could be called masculine and feminine aesthetic orientations. The first was the well-known eighteenth-century German philosopher Immanuel Kant and the second was Luce Irigaray, a contemporary French feminist philosopher who both critiques and draws from the unique ethical philosophy of Immanuel Levinas, a twentieth-century philosopher and Talmudic commentator. These theorists seemed to hold a rich resource for beginning to honor the unique expressions of the masculine and feminine typologies and to help us form the beginnings of an Integral aesthetic that could include them both.

One of the central issues that I saw arising within aesthetic philosophy that could perhaps be resolved by bringing in the masculine/feminine typology was a conflict of how best to interact with the experience of beauty in an "other," and perhaps the struggle to articulate what the "superior" aesthetic experience truly is. Immanuel Kant was a major contributor to the evolution of aesthetic theory during the eighteenth century and played a significant role in asserting the independence of beauty from the domains of science and ethics. In my opinion, what was so unique about Immanuel Kant's contribution was both his belief in the possibility of a universal subjective validity when it came to aesthetic judgment, and even more importantly, his specific articulation of a rational set of injunctions that could be implemented and, if followed correctly, would lead to this kind of universal agreement. Kant definitely favored a level of freedom from the objects of beauty themselves, and thus it makes sense that his first injunction was a subjective one in which he asks us to internally reflect on our aesthetic response and separate out whatever is merely agreeable or good because it satisfies some pleasure in charm, emotion, sensation, or moral connotation (Kelly 1998, 33). Without this first essential step of rigorous self-reflection, our experience will often fail to have the quality of disinterested pleasure that Kant argued was necessary.

For me, this type of injunction reflects a very masculine practice for cultivating our capacity to Witness, which is essential to obtain a certain level of distance on our own subjective likes and dislikes when it comes to beauty and attraction. We again feel the contours of the Witness spoken through Kant's articulation of what he considered the highest experience of beauty, what he called the *sublime*. The sublime was a beauty that we confronted in vast landscapes, towering mountain ranges, and cascading views of starry skies, all of which acted as invitations by nature into the sublimity of our existence. In this sublime aesthetic moment, Kant believed that we were able to see past the mere objects in view and take in the transcendental and formless quality of the whole. It was a call to Infinity that surpassed the limited extension of our human senses. And for Kant, because the concept of Infinity as totality could never be exhibited through sensory experience, he saw it as supersensible or beyond any perceivable object (Kelly 1998, 37).

In this way, Kant's injunctions help us to practice inhabiting our own formless awareness as it holds the space for forms to arise and fall without being attached to the specific qualities that they take or the particular emotions that they stir within us in their momentary passing. Kant offers us a tool for witnessing without grasping at any specific location, which brings with it a greater appreciation of the transcendental aspect of beauty's expression. Thus, the masculine, in its highest form, can represent the essential freedom from attachment to the specific appearances of beauty because of its capacity to release forms in every moment as they arise out of emptiness.

The possible unhealthy side of the masculine is an extreme detachment from all forms, the result of a belief in beauty exclusively as a transcendental quality (the sublime), which causes the viewer to lose any felt connection to the relative forms that it witnesses arising; the ultimate observer that is only able to experience the formless but unable to be touched or participate in the movement of the forms that arise within it. The proper balance for this masculine freedom is an equal appreciation of the feminine fullness of beauty, a dynamic for which we can account by turning to the philosophy of Immanuel Levinas and Luce Irigaray.

The unique philosophy of Levinas offers us the starting point to delve into ideas of what part beauty and desire play when we turn our focus to the realms of feminine fullness and relational engagement. Here we are interested in how beauty and attraction both inform and impel us toward embodied sensitivity toward one another in honor of our unique individual expressions. Although Irigaray departs from Levinas in some significant ways, both philosophers consider beauty and desire to be intimately tied with conceptions of ethical relations and responsibility.

To begin with Levinas, he started with a philosophy that questioned the very foundations of Western ontology by arguing that things do not come into being already contained and structured within preexisting ontological realities, but rather life and humanity itself only come into existence through the interaction of relationships. Thus, for Levinas, ethics precedes ontology (Rose and Sanders n.d.). It was through this ultimate ethical situation that we rejoined the Infinite through the human face (Jantzen 1998, 237). In his desire to overcome the notion of God as a distinct ontological reality, which he felt caused us to turn away from the divine in the face of the Other, he attempted to put forth an understanding of God that was embedded in intersubjectivity and language. In contrast to Kant, a deep felt connection to our own desire and attraction are central to the ethical relationships we create with others. For Levinas,

> [D]esire itself is reshaped by the face of the Other, shaped into a response that goes far beyond myself. It is not the name of a lack, but the release from self-enclosure, a joy, therefore, that is always in excess, and a desire not diminished in its fulfillment. In all this, it bears the trace of the divine. (Jantzen 1998, 251)

Luce Irigaray shares in these values of relational and embodied ethics/aesthetics, and for both Levinas and Irigaray, embodied desire is not something to be fought or ignored but rather is seen as the very site of transcendence (Jantzen 1998, 252). But Irigaray uses Levinas's philosophy as a bridge to enter even more fully into the ideas and images of embodied desire and ethics. Irigaray brings an even more concrete and sensual language as well as a more feminist lens that offers greater attention to our own unique difference and the dynamics of our relations with other beings of unique difference. For Irigaray (2004), the attraction that leads to the caress is a gesture-word that penetrates into the realms of deep felt intimacy, both for the one who touches and the one who accepts (20). It is essential for Irigaray that in order to go beyond a limit, there must also be a boundary. She states, "To touch one another in intersubjectivity it is necessary that two subjects agree on the relationship . . . each must have the opportunity to be a concrete corporeal and sexuate object, rather than an abstract, neutral, fabricated or fictitious one" (Irigaray 2004, 20).

With Irigaray (2004), we gain access to the transcendental through the vehicle of a horizontal relationship with an individual, an individual whose differences are respected and invited within ourselves without destroying the other (176). For Irigaray (2004), attraction and desire can be neither rendered into one nor divided into two but always dance in the space of holding both. She writes,

> In my desire for you, in the love that I share with you, my body is animated by the wanting to be with you or to you, with me or to me, and it also longs for existence of a between-us. It wishes to love and to be loved, to leave itself and to re-enter itself. . . . I seek for a complex marriage between my interiority and that of a you which cannot be substituted for me, which is always outside of me, but thanks to my interiority exists . . . (22)

In the perspective of Levinas, and even more so in Irigaray, we see beauty and attraction as a passionate, embodied gesture that begs for interaction and collaborative creation. In respect for the mysterious dynamics of exchange that occur between two people, Irigaray points out more than once the danger of purely abstracting our relationships with each other into a realm of Absolute Singularity or Universal Subjectivity (and, of course, this warning echoes that of Levinas who felt the same weariness about strict singular ontological claims concerning God and reality). From this perspective, the dynamics of beauty and attraction cannot be fully accounted for by exclusive notions of an Ideal Platonic Form or a sublime formless reality that has the potential to divorce itself from the realm of bodies, words, and sensuous relationships. Rather, from this perspective, beauty is a movement, an ever-evolving dynamic of becoming that is continually manifested through creative tensions and energies arising between "separate" subjects and objects.

In this way, Levinas and Irigaray lean toward the feminine in their perspective on beauty and attraction as an interactive, embodied, and intersubjective process. We can look to Irigaray's writing as a manifestation of the more feminine typology and expression of beauty, an expression that favors a focus on the constant movement and flow between self and other and honors the particularities of each intersubjective exchange. The higher forms of this feminine expression would eventually become the act of a free dance of energetic engagement through the process of surrendering into the flow between self and other. These higher forms of feminine desire would arise from a realization of the single energetic flow that runs through the ground of emptiness and breathes itself gracefully through all forms. The desire to touch becomes the desire to dissolve into every object: completely surrendering and merging into beauty's vibration through all the transient manifestations it encounters through form.

The possible downside of the feminine type, when not incorporating a degree of masculine freedom, can manifest as a pathological attachment to the forms of beauty, something which Irigaray also works to avoid. This is to be contrasted with higher expressions of feminine fullness, which find their roots in the vibration that arises from and through emptiness. Thus, the healthiest expression of that radiance arises when there is an embodied awareness of emptiness so that its expression is not stifled by egoic contractions of needing to be seen or fear of being seen, nor will it get caught in the pain of attempting to fulfil its desire for fullness by seeking it in forms that are inherently empty.

Keeping these masculine and feminine aesthetic expressions in mind, I would like to shift my focus to women's unique developmental relationship with their own beauty. We can recognize two distinct patterns to this development. One is brought forth by focusing specifically on the unfolding feminine energy (Shakti) that is attempting to express its inherent desire for beauty and shine with greater degrees of fullness. This desire for Shakti expression (which predominantly manifests through state-stages) is simultaneously unfolding alongside the structure-stage development of an evolving feminist consciousness that is attempting to assert women's sociopolitical equality with men and emerge into ever-increasing levels of autonomy.

Beauty and States of Consciousness

Beauty unknowingly became the koan for my interior struggle with deep existential anguish. It was also through my own intimate confrontations with death, illness, ugliness, and disfigurement that beauty became a more rampant and dark shadow within my own being. The more I reached out to explore the expansive world of the mind and intellect as well as the mysterious realms of the soul and spirit, I came to find my struggle with my body and beauty to be greatly intensified. A growing obsession to understand the nature of beauty in the face of my own death and decay continually heightened a very painful alienation from my own female body. Throughout this period, I came to feel an even stronger desire to renounce the attention I had received for my physical appearance in order to uncover the deeper realms of beauty within my own being. But this desire to disengage from the merely gross forms of beauty conflicted with my fear of releasing something from which I had come to gain so many worldly benefits.

As I worked to unravel the mysteries of beauty through intellectual maps and tastes of the transcendental, I also lived out the struggle of this "beauty koan" on a very physical and emotional level. My body became the lived site for the struggle of my mind and soul as I fluctuated between periods of physical beauty and periods of what felt like unbearable ugliness. At times afflicted with all kinds of bodily ailments and visions of inner torment, it seemed that within this pain I was also given a wider expansion within my being that allowed me to be touched by chords of resonance of the deeper beauty that I truly longed for. In times when I would go through periods of noticeable physical beauty, I feared the praises of physical attractiveness, worrying that I would become attached to attention at the cost of my soul and the deeper desires of my Self. In times of noticeable physical ugliness, I would feel tortured in having lost the privilege of being considered a "beautiful woman" by our culture's standards, but it was also these times that afforded me the opportunity to explore the deeper aspects of my being and identity. The koan of beauty became my painful lesson in impermanence. My mind worked ferociously to understand the nature of beauty so that I might free myself from the illusion of surfaces, while my body continued to become an unbearable prison in constant shift between two extreme opposites.

It was during these times when nothing seemed able to comfort me that I found small openings of beauty in others could induce a kind of warm disorientation that momentarily broke me loose from the binds of this unrelentingly intense pain. When everything within me felt dark and ugly, it would be these simple moments of recognizing the beauty of a leaf or a human face that would fill me with overwhelming gratitude. And it was in these movements of beauty that my thoughts and preoccupations with my struggle seemed to be mysteriously suspended, and, without any will of my own, I was brought to deeper resonance with the beauty that I truly yearned for. I began to have more of these experiences with others that came unexpectedly, and my appreciation for their beauty began to grow even as I struggled to feel any sense of beauty within myself or how I was connected to the beauty I was perceiving.

As difficult as it was to surrender to beauty in an "other" when I felt consumed by ugliness, it seemed to offer such profound gifts to my soul in transition and its state of painful disorientation that I would muster all my courage at times to do so. Perhaps the most potent appreciations on my own journey, the ones that have offered the most healing to me as a female, have been in the act of appreciating the beauty of another woman and holding space for her expression of that beauty in whatever physical or artistic form it may take. To be able to appreciate and feel grateful for the beauty in another woman was, at times, the only thing that gave warmth and peace to my soul in this state and emptied its unbearable self-contraction.

The divine for me has always been connected to a recognition of beauty, and thus a sincere embrace of beauty in another held the very touch of divine release. Surrendering to the beauty of another woman became an act that continually brought me closer to my own beauty by reminding me of that single movement of feminine grace from which the bonds of jealousy, competition, and envy could gently and ecstatically be unwound.

We could identify this shift and transformation I am now articulating as a movement within states (the horizontal axis on the Wilber-Combs lattice) rather than necessarily a shift in structures (vertical axis on the Wilber-Combs lattice), which I looked at more through the example of Wilke and her struggle to evolve into an integral stage (teal altitude) of development.[2] The existential tipping point was for me the beginning of an opening where I could explore the territory of states in relation to beauty. As we train and evolve our identity through horizontal states, we become more receptive to the subtleties of beauty's numinous expressions and more openly in love with embracing the beauty of others. In my own interior journey, this process was experienced as a kind of painfully ecstatic emptying that allowed me to become a more clear and devoted receiver of beauty through others as well as a more open conduit for grace in the process. As we feel ourselves becoming a more subtle listener and perceiver, we find ourselves redirecting the attention and energy that had once been used to assert our own ownership of beauty to a place of inner stillness. In this stillness, it seems that our only desire is to be penetrated by the beauty of others, which is ultimately the desire to be touched by the divine. This could be described in third-person terms as the movement from gross to subtle to causal states.

On the soul's journey to causal absorption, we come to see that the practice of surrendering to another's beauty is in essence the very act of surrendering to our own higher Self, and this act in itself has the power to pour a channel of clarity through our being as beauty comes to contain within it the very energy of divine feminine vibration, expressed in a multitude of subtle energetic flavors. Irigaray (2004) offers a beautiful articulation of how we can approach the other with this sense of mystery:

> The other is the one towards whom we advance in darkness, the disclosure of their coming never being revealed in the light of day. . . . [I]t is in the

respect of a mystery that we preserve in us for them that the other might take shelter. (31)

As our soul continues to awaken into a nondual state (if we can name it as such), we no longer experience being seen in the same way. In our love for returning to our own utter transparency, beauty itself reclaims its breath and its gestures through our unique bodies, hearts, and minds. Performing our beauty then becomes an act of continual consent of surrender to that single energetic vibration that runs through the emptiness between us. It is within this performance of beauty that we learn how to dance freely in radiant fullness, a radiance that does not outshine the other but lovingly invites them forward into that same dance of intimate fullness.

In connecting this state-stage evolution with the masculine/feminine types that Kant and Irigary have illuminated so beautifully for us, we can perhaps bring more clarity to these two paths to Spirit. It seems that some are more inclined to travel to their natural state of inner equanimity through the process of greater freedom and emptiness. Thus, through a practice of witnessing, one gains the capacity to be unmoved and untouched by the objects that normally cause self grasping and limit the breadth of our view on beauty. This we could label as perhaps the more *masculine* path to Spirit. We could then say that the *feminine* path to expanded awareness tends to evolve more through a process of engagement. If this engagement is truly developing to higher state-stages of refinement, it is inherently going to be creating an increased degree of detachment from limited forms, as the energetic engagement with beauty becomes ever more subtle, refined, and inclusive. This expansion through movement seeks to empty itself and find its Higher Self through the process of surrender in its interactions, finding freedom through deeper experiences of fullness and falling more into intuitive harmony with the objects and energies that surround it. Irigaray (2004) writes, "Listening-to favors becoming fluid . . . a raising of energy without stopping it in fixed forms. An energy which also can circulate as breath between the inside and outside, and thus communicate with cosmic energies and the energy of other(s)" (101).

We can see that ultimately these two paths are not separate and that they must dance together as they evolve and eventually dissolve into the ever-present recognition that consciousness (freedom) and light (fullness) exist as the nondual formulation which brings forth every aspect of existence.

The Stunting of the Female Aesthetic Line of Development

Now that I have spent the time bringing to light the many possible dimensions of beauty in its process of unfolding through both the vertical axis (amber to orange to green to teal, etc.) and through the horizontal axis (gross to subtle to causal to non-dual), I want to spend some time focused on a couple of the most powerful blocks that I see are stunting women from fully realizing and occupying these different dimensions of their own beauty.

I want to start by reiterating a definition of the aesthetic line, which is a line that unfolds relatively independently through each vertical stage of development. The aesthetic line, as defined by Wilber (2006), is "the line of self-expression, beauty, art, and felt meaning" (60). The question that this line asks is: What is attractive? We can also look at the aesthetic line through both the masculine and feminine typologies, which leaves us with two central questions: What is attractive to me? (the aesthetic concern of the masculine), and What is attractive about me? (the aesthetic concern of the feminine).[3]

This understanding of the aesthetic line along with its masculine/feminine typologies plays a crucial role in the argument that I am going to make, and that is that the way a woman relates to her own beauty is the way that she relates to the Shakti force itself. And the health of the relationship between each woman and her Shakti energy also determines the health of her relationship to her own creativity and self-expression. Thus, a stunted aesthetic line would mean the very stunting of the Shakti force, which, as we will see, has profoundly devastating consequences for women, in particular.

Before I enter this last argument further, I want to fully illuminate what I see as the aesthetic disease of our postmodern era. First, we must understand why the extreme postmodern stance on beauty has taken such strong and seemingly unmovable roots in certain circles of feminism. I believe we can make sense of this stance by looking at it as one of two very distinct trends in the evolution of our understanding of beauty in today's Western world. If the postmodern feminist stance on beauty is dominated by green altitude values and interpretations, then there is also a second, powerful current when it comes to the expression of beauty, and that is, of course, the beauty fed to us by our dominant consumer culture. This second current is marked by a mixture of three distinct characteristics: the use of orange altitude cognition and modern technologies (e.g., mass media and advertising), an adherence to largely amber altitude gender roles (e.g., even pornography largely situates men and women in very traditional gender stereotypes), and a pathological red underbelly of narcissism, which largely drives the entire enterprise. And it is this second current of beauty's expression that postmodern feminists are so understandably reacting against.

The reason I see this as so important to bring up is that it shows how drastically feminism and dominant culture have split on the issue of beauty and how deeply it is affecting the hearts and minds of women who live under this split. Where extreme postmodern feminism has, in a sense, deconstructed and "banished" beauty for the purpose of gender equality and justice, the dominant discourse in the West has become fixated on physical beauty, within a very limited and pathological worldview. I would also argue that the consumer cultural phenomenon of elevating physical beauty has not been solely due to males constructing it, for I see a majority of the alliance/support for this elevation coming from women themselves. Access to careers in modeling, acting, and other aspects of the growing beauty industry originally offered women a way to get out of traditional roles and an easy way to gain economic independence. We can look to examples of this today in China and India where the movement from traditional (amber altitude) to modern (orange altitude) worldviews is presently in full effect and the beauty industry has all but exploded.

It was in reaction to this cultural elevation that the postmodern feminists were attempting to deconstruct beauty and unhinge the growing beauty obsession that they could see was spinning out of control. It soon became an emotional fight for feminists who were moving into a green altitude worldview while the larger culture around them only seemed to be solidifying its competitive stance. It was this reaction that created one of the major splits that Hannah Wilke was attempting to address in her own work and life, specifically the split between feminism and culture.

Postmodern feminism was rightly reacting against what was becoming a rampant, internalized "lookism" that was dividing women further from one another and creating an increasing culture of obsessive and superficially narcissistic females. The green worldview was attempting to bring women together rather than divide them, and provide a more inclusive paradigm that could hopefully correct what was becoming an increasingly toxic, competitive society filled with jealousy and self-interest.

So where did all this well intentioned care and inclusiveness go wrong? It starts with the inherent problem that postmodern feminism (and feminism in general) has largely refused to acknowledge zone 2 realities, namely, the existence of developmental levels. And due to this sometimes vehement refusal to acknowledge development (for the notion of "stages" resonates too closely to our memories of oppressive hierarchical systems), feminism would never truly be able to see the source of the real problem. It is because of this flatland view of reality that the best-intentioned approaches were bound to go terribly wrong.

Because green altitude has trouble seeing developmental complexity, it makes sense that postmodern feminists would look to beauty itself as the problem and thus see the need to "get rid of it," for it was this idea of beauty that was causing all the problems in the first place, right? If we take an integral perspective that willingly acknowledges and embraces stages of developmental unfolding (honors the validity of zone 2), we can begin to see the issue from a different angle. Through the eyes of a second-tier perspective, we begin to see that it is not beauty in itself that is the problem here but rather an orange stage of aesthetic development that has gone horribly awry. This unhealthy aesthetic stage is, as I mentioned earlier, characteristically marked by its red narcissistic underbelly which really only uses orange cognition and technologies to exploit its own limited understanding of the beautiful. This unhealthy orange interpretation of beauty thus continues to be increasingly solidified in our shared sociocultural sphere by both men and women as we co-create our own aesthetic prison. In this system, our interpretation of beauty has only exacerbated our separation and competition with one another and that is the real problem, not beauty in itself, which I believe actually has the power to heal this split.

Feminists were unaware of this complexity because they had no room in their paradigm to incorporate zone 2 realities and thus had no tools to spot the contours and complexities of both healthy and unhealthy development or to know how to correct them. Because of this lack of developmental sensitivity, beauty itself was often made into the enemy of the feminist movement rather than recognizing that the real enemy to the emergence of green altitude values was actually a deeply stuck and unhealthy stage of aesthetic development that only used beauty to support its own swelling pathology—increasing profits by stripping women of their own deepest potentials at as early an age as possible.

The postmodern feminist attempt to deconstruct beauty would only exacerbate this because they never addressed the real problem, which lies in a very stunted aesthetic line of development. And the pathological orange/red system would continue to gain tremendously from this deep misunderstanding. To get a better handle on what I am proposing, we can look at this misunderstanding in light of what Wilber (2006) calls a "Line/Level Fallacy (LLF)," the confusion of a level of development for the entire line itself (184). It is the LLF that the postmodern feminists have unknowingly committed and needs to be unwoven and seen for the harm that it is doing. It all started when feminists had recognized the no longer useful orange/red interpretation of beauty (although they would not use this language). This "commodified aesthetic" was having increasingly toxic consequences, as could be witnessed by the growing rates of eating disorders, suicides, and low self-esteem among young women. But because feminists could not recognize the real problem, which was an orange/red level pathology within the aesthetic line (a line also capable of green, teal, indigo, and violet expressions), it chose what seemed like the only proper solution, which was to throw out women's interior aesthetic line altogether, which became the exile of beauty in feminism. (I realize I am making a sweeping generalization here but I would argue that even if some feminists do not take this extreme stance, they are still unequipped to deal with this issue because most do not have a deep understanding of zone 2 development). At the same time, the dominant sociocultural sphere was becoming increasingly obsessed with its own orange/red fixation on the merely gross forms of beauty, and here is where we find the crux of the issue.

In an attempt to throw out the aesthetic line, feminism, perhaps unknowingly, took a swift turn into repressing all those fundamental human questions that only the aesthetic line can answer for women. At this point, any woman who now expressed beauty (i.e., Hannah Wilke) became the site for the feminist shadow, an anger and resentment projected onto their own deepest unrealized potentials and longing. This became the stunting of the aesthetic line from above through *repression*. Simultaneously, the dominant culture was also perpetuating the stunting of the aesthetic line from below through its *fixation* at the orange/red level(s). What Wilber has termed the "pressure cooker" can be applied here in relation to what is occurring in the aesthetic line of development of women today.[4] Beauty has been fixated from below and deconstructed and repressed from above, and the problem is that, unlike what some extreme postmodern feminists might like to believe, you cannot get rid of beauty; you cannot rid a human being of those fundamental questions and desires that only the aesthetic line can answer. And thus the aesthetic line for women remains severely stunted, with a growing temperature threatening to blow the lid off the pressure cooker as it leaves thousands of girls with severe physical and psychological damage in its wake. In this context, young women have one of two choices: to either identify with the feminists and repress their own deepest and highest expressions of beauty or identify with the dominant cultural images of beauty, which at least allows them to keep in touch with some form of their own beauty and aesthetic yearning but unfortunately at a very limited and pathological level.

So what is the role of feminism in the face of this toxic situation? I believe it starts with taking the lid off the pressure cooker from above by acknowledging developmental realities! This includes not only acknowledging vertical stage development but also horizontal state development. This additional acknowledgment of horizontal states would allow beauty to be seen and experienced not merely in the realm of gross surfaces, but also through subtle and causal apprehensions. Secondly, we need to stop reducing beauty to a pure construction of the LL and LR quadrants and honor the essential and unique role that beauty plays in every woman's life journey. By bringing in developmental sensitivity and a four-quadrant approach, we can allow young women free range to explore the contours of their own relationship to beauty. Through this act of permission we also begin to create space for the aesthetic line to breathe and blossom, unfurling into its own natural developmental unfolding through green, teal, and indigo stages as well as subtle, causal, and non-dual states where restrictive definitions of beauty that currently hold us no longer starve our deepest vision of the beautiful. And through the cultivation of deeper stages and states we find diverse new ways to express our own beauty, more expansive ways to appreciate each other's beauty as well as discover more rich avenues from which to contribute to the creation of beauty through our own unique artistic expressions.

3-2-1 Practice for Integrating the Shadow of Beauty

In order to deal with strong shadow elements that can often come up in my being surrounding issues of jealously and judgment of other women, I have found the cultivation of a specific 3-2-1 shadow practice to be especially useful.[5] I start by putting on a piece of soothing music. Then, lying on my bed, I attempt to release as much tension from my body as possible by connecting with the rhythm of my breath, first filling up my belly, then my solar plexus, and then my chest. With a relaxed body, I gently close my eyes and bring forward a visualization of a specific woman in my life that I am currently jealous of because of her beauty. I then stand her in front of me to the left and take a moment to silently scan her body and look into her eyes, thus taking in the third-person contours of my object of jealously. I then move into a second-person dialogue with my object of jealousy by letting all the emotions and voices arise that need to come to the surface as I look at her, and if I am in a good space, I can also allow her to speak back to me with any reactions I believe she might experience from my outburst.

With my object of jealousy situated to my left, I then bring forward a visualization of someone in my life whom I have categorized as ugly, someone who perhaps induces a kind of fear in me and unleashes my own insecurity. I then place that woman on my right and go through the same process with my object of insecurity that I previously went through in relation to my object of jealousy. After this initial confrontation and dialogue with my two shadows, I ask each of them to look at the other and then back at me as I breathe through and release the many voices, emotions, memories, and judgments that these two women have provoked in me. As all these distractions begin to wash into the background, I focus on looking directly into their eyes. It is important at this point that I initiate physical contact with these women by taking both of their hands before gesturing our flight up into the air. With one woman on each side we release into laughter and joy as we take in the beauty of the open scenery and the freedom of our flight away from worldly concerns. I usually imagine flying over an ocean, letting our bodies become lighter and more transparent as we scan the beauty of nature all around us and feel less attached to the limits of our physical form. In the last visualization, I again look them both in the eyes, all of us acknowledging the Divine Identity that streams equally within us and also the pain that exists in the relative separation we experience between us. I then invite them both into myself, giving full permission for both the beauty and the pain to enter my heart and allowing both these women to merge their souls into my body, letting my heart receive them equally before filling it with light.

After this visualization, I can often experience intense emotions of love and sadness, and I find it helpful to write in my journal immediately following the exercise so that I can remember the textures and qualities it evoked in me and let these women into my first-person experience. I have found this visualization helps me not only expand my compassion for others but also allows me to become the bridge for the many selves within my own being, reclaiming both the pain and beauty and finding the divine that resides within it all.

Expressing Beauty through Art

As I have mentioned throughout this chapter, a woman's relationship to her own beauty determines the health of her relationship to the Shakti force itself. And because Shakti is so intimately related to creativity, a healthy relationship to the development of our own aesthetic line is central for the fullest expression of our own unique gift of creativity. Finding an outlet for artistic expression was one of the major transformative tools that allowed me to express my own radiance without the normal chains that I often experienced on my own aesthetic perception. By connecting with our own creative talent, and expressing our gift of beauty back to the world, we also come to expand our definition of beauty and our unique relationship to beauty as women.

Art offers a way for us to find our own resonance with the deeper breath of beauty running through us and can empty us more and more as we participate in the offering of it to others. In this way, art connects us to our Infinity and offers a mode to see through the illusions of our own limitations, while also embracing them simultaneously. I believe artistic practice to be a key tool for exploring and touching the ever-present states that are available to us (gross, subtle, causal, and non-dual). Thus, art is a perfect practice for unsticking the pathological grasp that may be currently holding our aesthetic line in its stiff grip.

Through these expressions of beauty that tap us into higher states, we also create channels of connection through the apparent separation that we experience between one another. And depending on our degree of receptivity to these channels and the vibrations they carry, we can help each other to find our way Home in our ability to touch and be touched by the free gift of beauty that streams through all different forms of artistic expression. In One word, One sound, One touch brought forth by the flow of artistic expression, we can bring healing to others and ourselves as we momentarily become both the giver and the receiver of beauty and merge with that shared movement of mysteriously arising grace. As we become Shakti herself, as the Devi becomes manifest through us, we offer a touch of grace through our voices and hands that has the power to bring us as women to the center of our One shared Divine Identity, before finally extending itself outward in release beyond all limitations of gender and form.

Acknowledgments

I want to acknowledge the support and input of Willow Pearson who offered me the opportunity to write this chapter and has been a continual part of the editing and shaping of integral beauty as well as an invaluable friend. A big thank you to Sarah Nicholson, Michael Schwartz, and Matt Rentschler for their heartfelt feedback. Many thanks also to my father R. Michael Fisher, and stepmother Barbara Bickel for their support and ongoing talks about art and beauty. Special thanks to my older sister Leah and my friends Sophia Marten and Chloe Hunter as well as all the young women I lived with at Yasodhara ashram where my own will alone could not have pulled me through finishing the final draft of this chapter. Thank you all for being the living embodiment of radiance and for reflecting my own beauty back to me.

Notes

1. For further information on the masculine/feminine typologies, see Wilber (2006, 11–15).
2. For an explanation of the Wilber-Combs lattice, see Wilber (2006, 90).
3. This understanding of aesthetic line typologies came largely from personal communication with aesthetic philosopher, Michael Schwartz, who shared with me his art interpretation of Massacio's, "Expulsion" or "Fall," from the Brancacci Chapel. Schwartz understands this art piece as "an archetypal image of post-medieval Western views of the masculine and feminine, as embodied by Adam and Eve. A quick reading of the image in these terms: Adam covers his sight, Eve her breasts and genital region—these are the features of themselves that they have become self-conscious about and ashamed of as well. Adam is an ashamed Seer, the self as subject; Eve is the ashamed Seen, the self as embodied object. The tantric expansion of these more contracted moments are, following Deida and others, the masculine as the eternal witness that is Shiva and the feminine as the perpetual energetic-embodied dance that is Shakti—together uniting as Conscious Light. The masculine provides stillness, direction, freedom; the feminine provides energy, life-force, love" (Personal Communication, June 2006).
4. For more on this use of this metaphor, consult Wilber (2006, 181).
5. To learn more about the 3-2-1 shadow process, consult Wilber (2006, 136).

References

Armstrong, J. 2004. *The secret power of beauty: Why happiness is in the eye of the beholder*. London: Penguin Books.

Eco, U. 2004. *History of beauty*. New York: Rizzoli International.

Etcoff, N. 1999. *Survival of the prettiest: The science of beauty*. New York: Doubleday.

Frueh, J. 1989. *Hannah Wilke: A retrospective*. Columbia: University of Missouri Press.

Halprin, S. 1995. *"Look at my ugly face!": Myths and musings on beauty and other perilous obsessions with women's appearance*. New York: Viking Penguin.

Hansen, E. D., K. Dybbol, and D. Goddard. (Eds.) 1998. *Hannah Wilke: A retrospective*. Copenhagen: Contemporary Art Center Representing Artists and Exhibition Organizers.

Irigaray, L. 2004. *Key writings*. New York: Continuum.

Jantzen, M. G. 1998. *Becoming divine: Towards a feminist philosophy of religion*. Manchester, UK: Manchester University Press.

Kelly, M. (Ed.) 1998. *Encyclopedia of aesthetics* (Vol. 3). New York: Oxford University Press.

Lambert, E. Z. 1995. *The face of love: Feminism and the beauty question*. Boston: Beacon Press.

Plotinus. 1991. *The enneads*. London: Penguin Books.

Rose, D. B., and A. Sanders. n.d. A dialogue about the philosophy of Levinas. ABC Radio National: The Philosopher's Zone. Retrieved November 5, 2006, from http://www.abc.net.au/rn/philosopherzone/stories/2006/1672842.htm#.

Steiner, W. 2001. *Venus in exile: The rejection of beauty in 20th century art*. New York: The Free Press.

Wilber, K. 2006. *Integral spirituality: A startling new role for religion in the modern and postmodern world*. Boston: Integral Books.

5

Writing to Effect

Textual Form as Realization in an Integral Community

Michele Chase

How do our textual forms enact an integral perspective, and what advice can be given to those who would like to participate in an evolving integral community through writing and publishing their analyses and research results?

As I ponder this, an upside-down woodpecker with a red cap and stippled black and white feathers hangs just outside, pecking at something in the hard material of which my office window frame is made. The rapid tattoo sound is counterpoint to my musings. I have just gotten off the phone from a conversation with a new student in Holistic Health Education who has been reading *Integral Visions* (2007)—assigned in one of her courses—and is outraged at the lack of substance in Wilber's theory. "This is just common sense that anyone who has been an observer of life and serious about spiritual practice might have come up with," she complains. Meanwhile, other students are turned off by books such as *Integral Spirituality* (2006)—having to wade through diagrams full of bewildering squares and lines and mathematical formulas and to remember lots of names, terms, and acronyms in service of being able to read and carry out research, understand what a complete self-care practice might consist of, or answer vexing questions about what integration in health-care might actually look like. At the same time a professor in the program laments that most authors in *Consciousness and Healing: Integral Approaches to Mind-Body Medicine* appear to consider "integral" simply as a synonym for "integrative," and considers *Integral Health* (Dacher 2006) to be at best a "baby step" to be quickly grown out of. This same colleague and I both examined students' final projects (short thesis) for the MA to determine the degree to which they could demonstrate ability to take an integral perspective—integrative, intuitively integral, integrally informed, or fully AQAL-integral—and along the way, participated in debates about how this might be determined by looking at the papers students have written.

Unless we are doing a lot of scholarly writing ourselves, we tend to focus on the ideas—the content or meaning—and to be largely unaware of how integral a part of meaning-making (and not just meaning-conveying) are authors' choices in genre, structural form, style, persona, diction. And yet just as consciousness and form arise together, so do content and form in written texts. In the integral community writing is central in both knowledge-making and knowledge-sharing. Our writing is at the interesting intersection where consciousness and form meet. In this chapter I will be focusing on texts—not their creation/production but the effects of various textual forms on writers and readers. I will be focusing on *academic writing*, with its conventions, constraints, and possibilities, as a vehicle for transmissions of realizations from an integral perspective, and situated within an integral community. I will be defining it in ways discourse analysts do, and then playing with how we enact an integral perspective through writing, in particular in the Integral Institute's flagship publication, the *Journal of Integral Theory and Practice*.[1] I will often deviate from what would be expected in an academic text in order to suggest that we might match our exciting new insights with innovative textual forms that can enact them. I will be using lots of notes, and in them drawing attention to textual forms I have chosen so that readers will become conscious of their effects. My intention is to artificially tease apart perspective, or realization, from form, as an integral perspective may be expressed to better effect in some forms than in others, even if we just focus on academic writing. Raising these kinds of questions might allow us to formulate a particularly integral style for use within this community. I hope also to lay a foundation for later work in which I plan to discuss how choices in textual form can help us skillfully introduce Integral Theory into disciplinary communities whose members are not yet familiar with it, for example, in the writing of dissertations.

I have been very tempted to use my professional expertise in text analysis (especially of those written in disciplinary discourse communities) to take on Wilber's writing.[2] I notice that he has deeply considered how textual form shapes and constrains what can be thought and known, worked with, and communicated, perhaps in the same way the fact of being embodied shapes and constrains our experience. Besides his large corpus of scholarly writing, he has written *Grace and Grit* (which drew me to read his other books through how he presented himself as a person I could identify with) (Wilber 2001a). He created a novel, *Boomeritis* as an experiment in conveying his ideas in a format that might reach people in a different way or reach different readers (Wilber 2003a). In *One Taste* Wilber (2000b) struggles with having to write in "third-person it-language," and briefly abandons this authorial stance to write from the personal, inside perspective of what the world looks like from each level of consciousness. And sections of his more scholarly books occasionally break into poetic evocations of the grandeur of everything arising in each moment. He clearly understands the role our texts play, not just in transmission of linear thought but in kindling feelings and realizations in deep levels of ourselves.[3] (Dear Readers, I ask that you stop to read each of my footnotes as it arises, for these are going to be integral to the analysis I will present,[4] and also represent a commentary on textual features as they are being used.)[5]

In speaking of the power of gurus, Wilber (2000b) states that "when a person is fairly enlightened, they can transmit—actually transmit—that enlightened awareness through a touch, a look, a gesture, or even through the written word."[6] Whether or not we think of ourselves as transmitting enlightened realization, how do we use the power of language to affect (and use it to good effect) through the textual forms we create and share within the discourse community of scholars developing Integral Theory and in the education of such scholars? How do we reach beyond that to others, to thinkers and students who are not (yet) familiar with this body of work or inspired by it, and even beyond that, to the many who do not necessarily want to participate as scholars but who could use Integral Theory to solve the very real problems they face in business, health, science, and many applied fields?[7]

Strangers in Strange Lands: Applying Insights from Discourse Analysis

An Integral approach is compatible with work in the study of writing from a loosely defined disciplinary grouping of those (in linguistics and applied linguistics, composition and rhetoric, sociology/anthropology, and first and second language teaching) who might call themselves *discourse analysts*. (See Johns 2006 and Hyland 2005 for an overview of this field of study.) Scholars analyzing written discourse have long studied the *processes* through which writers create texts and how readers read them (UL), and also considered *textual forms* (UR) that realize writers' intentions. Contexts—cultural, societal, and gendered, have been considered (LL), as well as the rules and conventions of various *discourse communities* within which texts are produced and function (LR) (see Johns 1997).

Without putting it in those terms, discourse analysts (who are not necessarily associated with literary work—tending to focus on academic and professional writing) have recognized the need to take an all-quadrant perspective and to adopt the various kinds of research methods necessary for getting at each kind of knowledge.[8]

Among discourse analysts there is controversy over whether most important is how texts shape communities or how conventions of communities constrain the kinds of knowledge claims that can be made. There is also disagreement

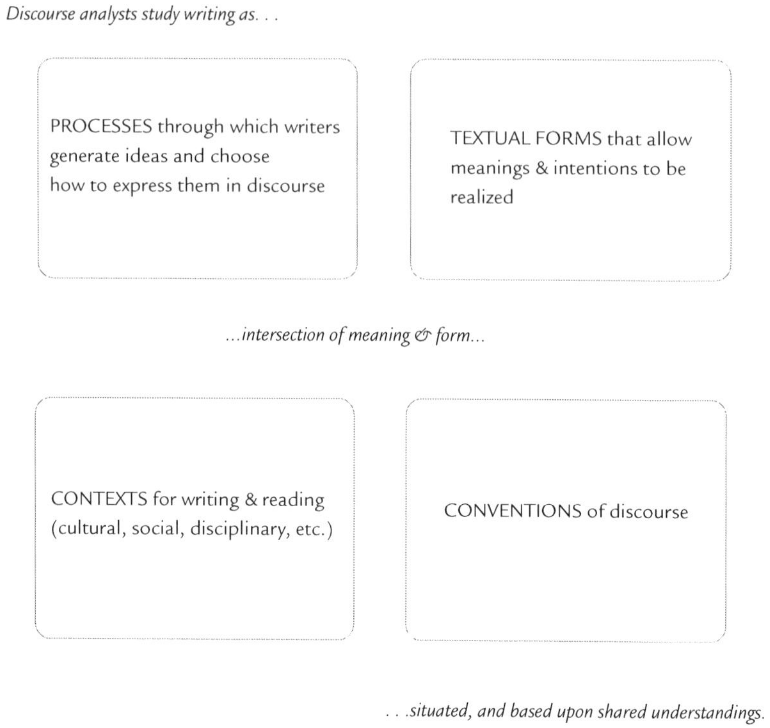

Discourse analysts study writing as. . .

PROCESSES through which writers generate ideas and choose how to express them in discourse

TEXTUAL FORMS that allow meanings & intentions to be realized

...intersection of meaning & form...

CONTEXTS for writing & reading (cultural, social, disciplinary, etc.)

CONVENTIONS of discourse

. . .situated, and based upon shared understandings.

Figure 5.1 Overview of discourse analysis

about the extent to which we can make inferences about discourse communities based on study of their texts, especially from the point of view of outsiders—leading some to make use of interviews with community members and/or to embark upon ethnographic studies (e.g., Swales 1998). Disciplinary discourse communities are seen as cultures that can be studied (Bartholomae 1985, 134), and researchers seek to discover how community membership is created, solidified, maintained through texts.[9] However, most of the prominent voices in this field seem pretty comfortable with a "both/and/all of the above" position (or all-quadrant, as we might say), as Hyland (2005) represents, describing the study of *metadiscourse*, which he defines as "the self-reflective expressions used to negotiate interactional meanings in a text, assisting the writer (or speaker) to express a viewpoint and to engage with readers as members of a particular community" (37).

Much of the excellent work in the field of discourse analysis has been and is being carried out by those who are teaching non-native speakers of English—especially focusing on graduate students who are seeking to enter knowledge communities—which involves being able to read and write texts within subject-disciplinary discourse communities (see Swales 1990; Johns 2002). Those who teach composition to undergraduate first language users of English have also participated in studying texts and contexts so that they may better prepare the students in their charge to write within disciplines (e.g., Bizzell 1982; Faigley and Hansen 1985; McCloskey 1994).[10] Finally, other great analysis has been carried out that looks into writing in the professions (e.g., Bazerman 1981, authors in his 1991 collection; Odell and Goswami's 1985 collection), and this has resulted in more readable technical writing, for example.

While I believe it is extremely useful to investigate the intersection of individual writers with disciplinary conventions and reader expectations, as well as the politics of publication and citation, and all of that, for the purposes of this short chapter I want to focus on the textual forms in *JITP*, at present and going forward, and how these might promote growth of a strong and cohesive integral community. This will require considering how we might define an "Integral insider" and whether or not there is a recognizable canon of work beyond Wilber's (which is surely of interest to those teaching graduate students who are specializing in Integral Theory).[11] Although constraints on the length of this chapter mean that analysis and discussion must be in some sense superficial, I hope by the end to have raised many good questions that may later be taken up and to be able to make some recommendations about how the texts we create and share in a journal such as *JITP* can continue to contribute to creation of Integral Theory as an academic field in its own right.

Lost in the Wilberness

As the initiator of Integral Theory, Wilber's writing[12] has had at least two important aims: first, putting forth his ideas—tracing their intellectual roots, synthesizing, displaying his arguments (and answering his critics)—and second, creating an intellectual insider community that can refine, debate, extend, and apply the theory. The highly successful (and sold out) 2008 Integral Theory Conference, the growing strength of publications such as *JITP*, the existence of a graduate program in Integral Theory, and the original Integral Methodological Pluralism (IMP) research being conducted at the Integral Research Center suggest that a robust discourse community of insiders is in the process of being established, and most of the members have been avid readers of Wilber's work that spans decades as well as being readers and creators of a canon of texts that represent shared knowledge in the community.[13]

But as I have said there's a second group of readers of Wilber's work:

thinkers, researchers, and doers who might use Integral Theory to help them grapple with problems in their own fields, for instance, health, leadership, art, and ecology. To help students and non-insiders with the concepts and terminology involved in Integral Theory, the *Integral Vision* book has been created (Wilber 2007), and this is a great step in making Integral Theory more accessible to a wider public. However, how best can scholars and thinkers in many disciplinary discourse communities be reached—the many who are not yet or will not turn into Wilber's devotees, become members of I-I, or publish within the integral community, and yet who are accustomed to and expect a "scholarly" kind of discourse that follows certain conventions? Or is it too early to think about this? Can we create and publish texts that enact an integral perspective while at the same time being seen as "academic" enough in other disciplinary communities?

A growing community of "Integral insiders" is publishing in the *Journal of Integral Theory and Practice*, and many are also writing on applications of Integral Theory in their own disciplinary publications.[14] I find myself more interested in texts created by these authors than in Wilber's writing for examining how these expert insiders might develop their own conventions that enact the tenets of the theory—for each other—but while also reaching scholars who are not insiders, defined as actively writing in *JITP* or other publications focused on integral perspectives. And at the same time I question whether this is possible (say, in *JITP*) or if these are mutually exclusive ambitions, and reaching outsiders is not, and should not be an aim in these, at least for the present.

It would seem that Wilber agrees that for now the development of Integral Theory requires a protected space. In "On Critics, Integral Institute, My Recent Writing, and Other Matters of Little Consequence: A Shambhala Interview with Ken Wilber," he talks about the small number of second-tier thinkers who really can operate from an integral perspective, in contrast with the much larger number of those at green altitude, who only think they can, and who can be deeply critical (Wilber 2001b).[15] He states that "[y]ou almost have to create a type of sanctuary, or a safe clearing, where integral second-tier research and writing can occur. For that reason Integral Institute is trying to create a space 'where integral theorists can come together, think out loud, and freely speak their minds,' with the hope that soon this circle can be opened to anyone who wants to be involved."[16]

The opening material for the *Journal of Integral Theory and Practice* explicitly states that this official, peer-reviewed journal *for the integral community* welcomes a wide range of scholarly types of articles at many levels of complexity, and emphasizes "the perspectival nature of reality, which emerges as first-, second-, and third-person perspectives interact with each other to generate phenomena. It embraces a post-metaphysical and post-disciplinary perspective. . . " In the Editorial Introduction to Volume Three, the journal's founder and executive editor, Sean Esbjörn-Hargens (2008), tells us that he is dedicating his professional career to establishing Integral Theory as a *legitimate academic field in its own right* (v).[17]

If we are to invoke an "integral community," whose participants share membership in an academic field, we may need to consider what constitutes membership, and especially, what roles written texts play in defining, inviting, and possibly prohibiting membership (at various degrees of involvement).[18] As common sense and numerous studies have shown, written texts are at the heart of any academic discourse community, so it is worth considering how to intentionally and skillfully make use of them to further the agenda(s) of the integral community.[19]

It may be time to consider how the form of what we write enacts the ideas we hold so dear, and yet how we can strategically write for each of the kinds of audience delineated above, whether in *JITP* or not. This might involve teasing apart the conventions of "academic writing" and using them (*or not*) deliberately, for effect. One thing that scholars in discourse analysis have amply demonstrated is that textual forms arise together with disciplinary and institutional contexts (e.g., Berkenkotter and Huckin 1993),[20] and that these need to be learned by novices in each discipline; there is no "given," monolithic, or neutral form of academic writing. And yet, discourse analysts widely agree on certain generic features of academic writing that cross disciplines—summarized by Johns (1997):

- Texts must be explicit (and this includes vocabulary, citations, data analysis, methodology description, and argumentation).
- Topic and argument should be pre-revealed in the introduction (with the caveat that this may vary, depending upon native language, culture, and setting of writers and readers).
- Writers must provide maps and signposts about where they are going—i.e., metadiscourse.
- The language of texts should create a distance between writer and text to give the appearance of objectivity.
- Texts should maintain a "rubber-gloved" quality of voice and character, which means an emotional distance is created toward meaning (which is not touched with naked fingers) (Elbow 1991, 145).
- Writers should take a guarded stance, especially when presenting arguments and results.
- Texts should acknowledge intertextuality—referring to, drawing from, and making use of other texts, without plagiarism. Swales and Feak (1994) claim that citation may be what defines academic writing.

- Texts should display a vision of reality shared by members of the particular discourse community to which the text is addressed (Johns 1997, 58–63).
- Swales (1990) lists six defining features of a discourse community: a broad set of common goals; mechanisms of intercommunication; particular genres of communication; participatory mechanisms that provide information and feedback; a specific lexis of terminology; a threshold level of members with a suitable degree of relevant content and discoursal expertise (24–27).

Given these definitions of academic writing and of discourse communities, which have been substantiated by many years of careful research, we are in a position to ask some interesting questions about how to chart our course in this emerging field of Integral Theory. What forms shall we choose when we write within our own integral community, and how do they enact our perspectives? Scholars within the integral community might consider which conventional notions of generic scholarly writing (e.g., form, citation practices, expert stance, author presence and voice, development of ideas and arguments, etc.) are the best means for knowledge creation within this community and might experiment with alternatives. Such consideration would seem especially crucial to help address charges that Integral Theory (as expressed in existing texts) is "too cognitive" and "not heart language," or does not reach equally those of all cultures, genders, or knowledge-processing styles.[21] Such an examination might also help us grapple with the very real problem of readers and writers and different developmental levels. Do we believe that readers at all developmental levels are effectively reached by the forms of conventional scholarly writing, and which ones in particular best fit a second-tier perspective? And following on that, if the integral community chooses to embrace a wide range of styles and perspectives in its flagship publication (*JITP*) will we be able to expect really good writing in each of the various styles, and how will this be defined and ensured?[22]

Articles in *JITP* up to this point have largely involved applications of the theory to work in various disciplines. "Postdisciplinary" might thus mean *interdisciplinary* as well as *transdisciplinary*, and in an integral community, insiders who are also members of their own academic fields might be able to consciously and skillfully write about Integral Theory, using the language and conventions of their own disciplines for readers who appreciate and welcome differences in how knowledge is created and shared. One option for furthering the agenda of integral knowledge-making as being postdisciplinary would be to welcome each scholar to write for *JITP* using the disciplinary conventions he or she is most familiar with.[23] However, one objection that literature in discourse circles provides evidence for (e.g., Swales 1990; Hyland 2000) is that writers are writing for readers, and those not familiar with such specific disciplinary matters as how texts are constructed, how to understand nuance, mine meaning, follow arguments, and so on, will not find these articles as useful as they would were the journal to have an agreed-upon style guide. Another objection is that we are probably going to be seeing a cadre of specialists in Integral Theory emerge from MA and PhD programs such as the one at JFKU, and these scholars will not always have come to the field already having reached expert status within another academic discipline. For both of these reasons, we might look forward to an eventual Integral Style developing, perhaps in part from the top down, as editorial policy, as well as from the bottom up as authors experiment with textual forms.

The benefits of developing a disciplinary identity for integral are many. One consequence of a robust scholarly Integral Theory community might be that Wilber and other integral writers are more free sometimes to write for a growing group of "integral experts" and do not have to begin each book or article explaining the model, whether to critics who are "outsiders" or to I-I members who are less expert or less involved in knowledge-making and publishing articles. Gradually we will no doubt see articles in *JITP* moving in this direction, with more and more background knowledge about Integral Theory and the body of work often associated with it (e.g., Spiral Dynamics) being assumed.[24] We could also begin to see an additional level of integral texts—and I am referring to the continuum of integrative, to intuitively integral, to integrally informed, to AQAL-integral. Can we expect to see something like "embedded integral," in which the emphasis is not on developing or applying Integral Theory, not as much *about* Integral Theory, but about something else, written from a deeply integral perspective not necessarily focused on or (implicitly or explicitly) *promoting* an integral view?[25] And how long will it be before our writing does not seem like it can always be directly traced back to, be in response to, developing the ideas of, or in conversation with this really large genius figure, Ken Wilber?[26]

I Wanna Be Like Ken

But how cohesive is this community of scholars at present?[27] A very superficial analysis of writing within the integral community (articles published in *JITP*) reveals a group that has been evolving and becoming more cohesive, in large part through the kinds of written texts produced.[28] Up until recently, and perhaps even now, the group's cohesion seems (from my "member-outsider" perspective) to be a result of the powerful presence of our "founder-pundit," whose own texts play such a central role. It seems only natural that the articles published in *JITP* would share certain textual features with Wilber's writing.[29]

Some of the more obvious ones include copious citation, which in his writing I do not see as being used to bolster the ideas but both to give credit where credit is due, and to enact his so strong desire to include as many ideas as possible.[30] Whether or not it is his purpose, the effect of so much citation is also to let readers know that he really has studied as much as a person can in the many relevant fields of scholarship. It gives me an impression (whether it is true or not) that it is almost with reluctance that he has had to develop a theory of everything, after superhuman but unsuccessful attempts to find what he needed (a powerful map for relating and integrating) already in existence.[31]

Other features noticeable to casual scrutiny include abundant diagrams, a strong authorial presence and voice (that ranges from the serious and formal to the playful and informal), as well as ironic humor. Wilber also demonstrates comfort writing in "it-language," as well as "I-language," and acknowledges the presence of readers by invoking "you," though my impression is that he seldom evokes a community of "us" that includes himself (other than when he says "we at Integral Institute. . ."). He also makes up terms (e.g., tetra-mesh) and uses lots of "big words" (sorry for the technical term).

The scope of this chapter is not sufficient to do more than mention features such as these and to suggest that those who are writing and considering publications for *JITP*, for the integral community, take them into account (consciously embracing or consciously rejecting them) as they work toward evolving textual forms through which to realize integral thought. Also of interest might be what level of integral is expected: I notice, for instance, that most articles in *JITP* come from an AQAL perspective somehow, even when they merely nod to aspects of the theory that are not especially relevant for the work they are doing in that article. While quadrants are used by almost all in some way, and would seem to be the most central aspect of an Integral approach, and lines and levels are very frequently evoked and made use of, states and types are less commonly used as central to application of Integral Theory outside of psychology and art, which makes sense. However, aspiring authors take note: AQAL is nodded to in most articles, even if the five aspects of Integral Theory are only listed.[32]

I would also predict that the "eight primordial perspectives," the zones of arising, and associated research methodologies, covered in detail in Wilber's Excerpts posted online in 2002 and his more recent *Integral Spirituality*, which only came out in 2007, will come to be as central as the quadrants in upcoming articles written by expert Integral Theory scholars.[33] My colleague, Sean Esbjörn-Hargens (as editor of *JITP*) told me[34] that in his view, with Volume Three the journal is finally beginning to take the shape he envisaged for it, even though he thinks it will still be awhile before the journal is able to play a more substantial role in raising questions about Wilber's work and that of others in the integral community. For Sean the first few years of publishing

JITP has been about creating a shared theoretical and applied foundation that can more generatively support debate, controversy, and alternative views in the years ahead. Thus, I think we will soon be seeing greater print "conversations" among authors of articles here and between them and authors published elsewhere, especially because Sean and his fellow editors, the reviewers of the articles (including Wilber), and the authors themselves, have been creating a canon of foundational works in these early volumes of *JITP*. I suspect that Sean might be feeling that the work of creating Integral Theory as an academic discipline in its own right has been successfully launched, as we now have theory, a foundation for exploring application, and with Volume Three, a foundation for research (Integral Methodological Pluralism), with exemplars provided. These three aspects can now exist together and inform one another.[35]

The Forms That Carry Realization: Toward an Integral Style

I do not see much development or change in textual form in the three issues, and I would not be alone in claiming that attention to enactment, embodiment, realization—through textual form—is the fourth leg of the table of knowledge-generating and community building. I hope this chapter has suggested options for and consequences of textual choices (especially if you read the notes!), though much more could be done along these lines. I have merely identified possible areas of exploration: genre analysis; looking into authorial stance/persona; diction; structure and format; and metadiscourse features. Someone might want to carry out formal research with a discourse analysis approach, for instance, taking any of the quick and dirty analyses I have carried out (so that I could raise questions rather than draw conclusions) and really doing them. The analysis of textual features should be triangulated by using other methods too, such as interviewing authors and editors, looking at drafts and revisions of articles or having authors compose out loud so that we could get inside their heads. Demographics of I-I members, journal subscribers, downloaders of texts, and authors could be collected, and characteristics of I-I community interaction identified.[36] However, here I have been more interested in promoting thinking by the journal editors and reviewers, as well as by authors. What might an Integral Language or Style be like, and through what textual forms is an Integral approach realized? What kinds of experiments should be encouraged?

If one thing is emphasized more than anything else in the "call for papers" that opens each issue of *JITP*, it's the taking of *multiple perspectives*. I have tried to work out how that is being realized in the published texts. One strategy is simply choice of "person"—first, second, third, singular and plural—and we can see, even in the abstracts for each article, the attempts to balance "I-language," and "it-language," while occasionally writing with a "we" that can assume reader collaboration (or may just be the plural used when more than one author is writing, or even a generic alternative to "I," used when a writer wants to create a bit more distance). As textual experiments continue, it would be worth becoming sensitive to when this is being skillfully done and when the blend of personas comes across as a writer not being able to make up his or her mind or not having a clear sense of audience and relation to it.

Taking multiple perspectives probably means looking at things as they would be perceived by individuals at different developmental levels (though not as an insider perspective but from the outside), coming at a discipline from the perspective of different schools of thought within it (e.g., as in many articles in Volume One), working with psychographs, mapping out how the world looks through the three eyes of perception, and looking at a subject through the lens of different research methodologies (e.g., Luftig 2008). This is all good, and I hope the question of what it actually means to come from multiple perspectives through textual choices will stay before our minds as we write.[37] Another issue to consider is how to bring about realization through questions, paradoxical koan-like writing, poetic language (which is actually very difficult to do skillfully, with the consequences of doing it poorly much more severe than writing in academic style and doing it poorly).[38] Can we write not just *from* second-tier perspectives but in such as a way as to facilitate the development of ability of readers to take second-tier perspectives, and what would that look like?

However, one important perspective has been drastically downplayed, in my view, and that's the perspective of *readers*.[39] We can talk about how textual form realizes theoretical and methodological perspectives, but let us keep in mind that our writing is to be *read*. Earlier I gave an accepted definition of characteristics of academic writing in a generic sense, and it is clear that writing in *JITP* possesses those. However, I would like to raise the question of whether or not the conventions, as pertaining to writer-reader engagement (or distance) are ones we want to accept and expect. Can we publish writing that is "academic" and yet integral?

Even though I am a scholar in my own right, and used to reading academic texts, I felt that many of the articles in the first 3.1 volumes of *JITP* were not really written *for me* to make use of professionally or personally, so much as for Integral Theory building and for community orientation:[40] mapping out applications and overviewing perspectives from the Integral Centers, and creating exemplars of scholarly treatment other than Wilber's, with emphasis on application. Especially with respect to Volumes One, Two, and the first issue in Three, I am not sure I want to read each issue cover to cover,[41] even though I want to *have* them in my collection. Some of the articles would seem interesting mainly to those who are seriously working within a discipline, and much less so to outsiders to those disciplines, though we can also find ones that might be of more general interest, such as Walsh's (2006) on suffering and evil and Pfeiffer's (2007) on significant relationships. The specialist articles are wonderful[42] examples of applying an Integral approach, which might be their central purpose. I do appreciate this, since it is a neat way to handle the problem of just too much to keep up with in Integral Land. Some people might choose to focus their reading, and if I were a scholar in ecology, say, I would feel I might not have to read everything integral in order to feel insider enough to join the conversation about Integral Ecology (as long as I had also read lots of Wilber's work, of course).

However, the place I would start if I wanted to increase the likelihood that articles would be read (by busy people, inundated by information and stimulation, remember!) would be to pay serious attention to how the titles, abstracts, and opening paragraphs can be carefully crafted to draw readers in. I am not so much speaking about being catchy or poetic as simply keeping readers in mind: Why would anyone in the integral community who is not in that discipline want to read that article? If they would not "naturally" be interested, how can authors create such interest, right up front by being explicit about how the work might be more widely relevant?[43]

"Reader considerateness" is also talked about by discourse analysts (e.g., Hyland 2008), and this is realized through strategies such as crafting a structure that guides readers through texts, metadiscourse strategies that have been mentioned here in the notes, skillful citing, and abundance of examples. Those who consider technical writing have defined "readability," as well, and found that certain grammatical features such as using active voice and avoiding nominalizations promote readability (see Williams 1985). As this journal develops, a style guide might be of some use, one that maps out possibilities by giving guidance about characteristics of readers (developmental levels, how much background knowledge to assume, etc.) and how to write effectively for them, about textual forms, and about "good writing." I would suggest that editorial overviews mention not just content but also *how* the texts exemplify aspects of Integral Theory (e.g., taking perspectives), engage readers, and demonstrate academic writing with a particularly integral flavor. Editors will also want to be sensitive to the choice to publish in English, as well as how choices in textual forms and other editorial policies shape

> the voices used by academics when addressing one another rather than outsiders, the voices that define disciplinary boundaries, exclude outsides and authorize contributions as new knowledge . . . the power to use, manipulate, innovate and control particular generic forms valued within a community and which subsequently create particular hierarchical social organization. (Hyland 2000, 168)

In this chapter I have attempted to model (embody) an Integral approach, albeit one that has not been very explicit and yet which assumes readers have a basic knowledge of the theory. I used only one modest diagram, cited little of the canon to develop my points, and did not make much explicit use of Integral Theory.[44] Have I been writing as an integral outsider, or is something else going on? As I suggested earlier, I look forward to a day when this very important conscious knowledge-building, community-orienting stage gives way to a new orientation, to complexify what it means to take an AQAL approach: *embedded integral*. By this I mean the focus shifts from defining and promoting the perspective to living it, writing it, and finding it inextricable from textual form—writing to share thought-life. Scholar-writers write for many purposes, including the ones already alluded to, of creating a solid body of work to lay the foundation for establishment of a discipline, but also to show membership or solidarity with a shared worldview and agenda. Expected textual form is different, depending on the stage of development of the discipline. For instance, more detail might be given in an establishment, or emergent stage, than is necessary or desirable later on, when "maturity" is achieved.

I have raised several questions throughout this chapter, ones that I hope will guide inquiry that might help the integral community move toward discourse maturity:

What forms shall we choose when we write within our own integral community, and how do they *enact* our perspectives (as well as *take* perspectives)? What might an Integral Language or Style be like, and through what textual forms is an Integral approach realized? What kinds of experiments should be encouraged?

If the integral community chooses to embrace a wide range of disciplinary styles, and variations on academic writing in its flagship publication (*JITP*) will we be able to expect really good writing in each of the various styles, and how will this be defined and ensured?

Do we believe that readers at all developmental levels are effectively reached by the forms of conventional academic writing, and which ones in particular best fit a second-tier perspective? Can we write not just from second-tier perspectives but in such a way as to facilitate the development of ability of readers to take second-tier perspectives, and what would that look like?

What is this writing for and who is this writing for?

The subtext for this chapter is what it means to be an "insider" in the community of "knowledge-makers" who are working to develop and promote Integral Theory and help this body of scholarship emerge as an academic discipline in its own right. I am not really sure what role I imagine for myself, but I look forward to a time when one or more works on Integral Theory joins the canon of scholarly works everyone is reading in graduate school, no matter which discipline, in the way Kuhn's *The Structure of Scientific Revolutions* (1970) (for instance) certainly was in bygone days.

In the end, with a motive similar to those of authors of articles in *JITP*, and probably to Wilber's, I have written this chapter as much for the pleasure of being able to integrate two scholarly fields of endeavor, both of which I hold dear. Says M. C. Richards, speaking for me, and perhaps for other authors, as well:

> I am an odd bird in both academic and craft worlds, perhaps because I am a poet, and thus, by calling, busy with seeing the similarities between things ordinarily thought to be different, busy with feeling the relatedness grow through my limbs like a smoke-tree wafting and fusing its images, busy with the innerness of outerness, eating life in its layers like a magic cake made of silica sounds shapes, temperatures and all the things that appear to be separated and stacked together in transparencies of color, and it is perhaps my vocation to swallow it whole. (2007, 7)[45]

Notes

1. *Journal of Integral Theory and Practice* was published for its first two years (2006–07) under the full title: *AQAL: Journal of Integral Theory and Practice* and was often referred to as the "AQAL Journal." Beginning in 2008 with Volume 3 the journal dropped "AQAL" as its title and transformed its subtitle into its offical new title.

2. I would be interested in mapping out textual features, and how they are more or less effective in the context of what kinds of audiences and for what purposes, as well as how his writing might be constrained by the politics of publishing. It may be that there are ways to make the writing of this brilliant thinker more effective, and for a greater variety of audiences, including highly academic ones.

3. I too ponder this and experiment with how our texts help bring about realizations that might be considered "spiritual." I have adapted the notion of the *Three Eyes of Perception* (Wilber 2001c) to my own uses, refined and redefined what they could mean, and renamed them as Eye of Substance (for Eye of Flesh), Eye of Significance (for Eye of Mind), and Eye of Essence (for Eye of Contemplation). I see them as kinds of knowing/viewing organized around parts (substance), patterns (significance), and perspectives (essence) (avoiding entirely the baggage that comes with terms such as flesh/body, and mind). It is another story, and you will be hearing more from me on this! But I suggest that analytical thought and writing is produced with the *Eye of Substance*, while the *Eye of Significance* is a more holistic, integrative, associative perspective, often realized through poetic writing. The *Eye of Essence* works with paradox, creates and appreciates koans—or else keeps silent. In other work I correlate these with the three experience-realms: gross, subtle, and causal.

4. I recognize that I am in effect writing two papers at the same time—the "official" paper and the metatext contained in the notes. I choose to do this as an experiment in textual form, one of many that members of the integral community will no doubt be involved in as this disciplinary specialization develops. I hope it won't be too annoying.

5. Notice here, that by evoking "you" directly, and making a request, I have created an even more "intimate" involvement than is usually the case in scholarly writing, even when first-person or second-person are used. For a chapter that goes all the way with "you," see Friesen's (2006) "integral writing tour," published in *JITP*. In that case the effect is to create a workshop-like event in which readers have a chance to be highly participative (and in fact it's assumed they are wishing to do so), responding to her questions and writing or thinking prompts. There is a conversational style much of the time, with occasional lapses into colorful writing. As a reader, how do you respond to that piece, and this one? Are any of your expectations about "academic writing" being violated? And how do you respond to the "engagement strategy" of asking rhetorical questions?

6. Obligatory Wilber quote?

7. The ability to take various perspectives is, of course, central to Integral Theory, and in written texts one way this comes out is the degree to which the author is explicitly present, resulting in texts that are more or less "author-saturated," as writer/ anthropologist Clifford Geertz (1988) calls it, or "author-evacuated." I have been writing in first person, an authorial stance that in academic writing is more to be found in the humanities and in some "softer" social sciences (as well as in "popular" non-specialist works). (See Becher [1989] for an overview of "academic tribes," and citations elsewhere about disciplinary discourse practices.) I have already given some facts about myself, or implied them, so that you would be able to relate to me as a person, meaning that through writing I am creating a relationship to you, my readers. You are probably picking up on my voice and stance through how I write (deciding if you trust me, respect me, or find me obnoxious, or are willing to accept me as the quirky wise elder I am trying to present myself as) just as you would do were I to speak to you, in that case relating to the tone, pitch, timbre, speaking speed, accent, as much as to the content. In this paragraph I have also evoked "we"—you and I as joint members of a community of knowers. I could probably get away with this in a "conference paper." In a published academic paper—what do you think?

   Authors of articles in *JITP* are experimenting too. See Senzon's (2007) piece on subtle energies, and note mainly "it-language," with occasional evoking of "you," mention of "I," and "us." But just before the conclusion there is an entire paragraph that steps away from the voice and relationship established thus far, and suddenly becomes more "friendly."

8. To reach integral readers this is the place to insert the almost obligatory four-quadrant diagram that is often used to map out kinds or realms of knowledge, the research methods, and kinds of arguments used to arrive at them. I am being playful here: a quick tally of chapters published in the official integral journal (*Journal of Integral Theory and Practice*) as of this writing reveals that in 89 articles only 22 did not have a diagram of the quadrants, and of these, one article was a glossary. In other cases, two articles in the same issue, back to back, were written by the same authors, who may have felt no need to reproduce the same diagrams twice, or chose to present a quadrant diagram in neither piece. Some authors reproduced basic ones from Wilber's work, and then went on to fill in the quadrants with questions and ideas resulting from inquiry into their own disciplinary areas.

The choice to review or not to review basics of Integral Theory before going on to apply and extend it is an interesting one that reflects writers' assumptions about the audience—who they expect to be their readers. The question each author must consider is how much "insider knowledge" can be assumed. I speculate that as time goes on it will be possible to assume more and more familiarity with and deep understanding of Wilber's work such that much more knowledge of Integral Theory can be taken for granted, at least in readers of this journal. This would seem to be essential if the goal is to really move toward developing this body of knowledge, and even for insiders to critique and refine the ideas.

Most authors who did not present a diagram, nevertheless, used or evoked the quadrants in some way. Besides confirming the centrality and power of the quadrants in Integral Theory, my quick analysis suggests that those who would publish in *JITP* would do well to include a diagram based on the quadrants. In fact, even casual readers of this journal will notice the prominence of diagrams of all sorts, which probably reflects the nature of Integral Theory, mirrors Wilber's work, and represents the trend in presentation of academic scholarship in some fields today, especially in presentations (Swales 2004, 26). In this chapter I am assuming an audience that is familiar with Integral Theory.

9. Here I would like to mention a dissonance I am feeling as I begin to get into the specialist knowledge related to textual discourse analysis. It is a surprise to me, but the most difficult part of writing this chapter has turned out to be integrating disciplinary knowledge from the field in which I was trained with Integral Theory, rather than coming to grips with the latter. It should not have been a surprise, given my knowledge that researchers who have studied texts from various disciplinary fields (e.g., Herrington 1983; McCarthy 1987) and describe students' struggles to master the conventions of knowledge creation and promulgation through written texts, have used a metaphor of disciplinary communities as *cultures* with their own languages and conventions of interacting that have to be learned. This leads me to ask how can I, along with others in the integral community, "translate" from one disciplinary culture and language to another, especially given that the integral community is only now emerging and its mores remain to be worked out, and given that many in our "native" disciplinary communities (e.g., medicine) are not yet able to appreciate second-tier views?

And yet trying to write outside my disciplinary discourse community (but not being sure of the social mores in Integral Land) is not the problem so much as knowing what to cite here of work from that other land. It is beyond the scope of this chapter to bring in the nuances of the ideas known to those who are insiders in my field, let alone to cover theories of language, texts, and knowledge-making. I do not plan to mention hermeneutics. I have had to make decisions about what to cite that are very different than those I would make when writing for an insider audience in my field. Strangely, I feel grieved that the scope of this chapter does not allow me to invite all of my friends to the party and introduce them to you.

We have not yet developed a cadre of professionals whose "first (or mother) discipline" is Integral Theory, and the authors of papers published in *JITP* are most often scholars or practitioners in the sciences, social sciences, and humanities who are seeking to apply Integral Theory in their own areas of expertise but here sharing it with members of a community of scholars who are not "natives" in that disciplinary "country" and not familiar with the knowledge base, textual conventions, and modes of communication. This dissonance can lead to very interesting opportunity to debate questions related to what we have in common and how we are different—as well as might there come to be an Integral Language that enacts the "postdisciplinary" nature of integral knowledge. However, there is danger that we should acknowledge in how ideas from our disciplines may be understood (or not) "out of context" and what level of understanding can be expected, given the superficial treatment that they must be given in Integral Land.

I struggled with how much to cite, and why. Of course credit must be given, but surely I do not need to cite so that readers can track down my sources for further reading, as this seems unlikely! I suspect I am citing so that non-specialists can be reassured (by quantity, and perhaps recentness of the work) that I am an expert, qualified to speak in my discipline. As a style note, it would be very helpful were disciplinary specialists to guide us when they cite, by providing comment (metadiscourse) that helps us know about the figures or the work cited. For instance, authors could tell us this is a very prominent person in the field, or the first person to notice something, or a researcher who is considered the authority on a subject.

10. Some (with a strong postmodern bent and a green altitude outlook?) have challenged the use of this work, claiming that to teach the textual conventions of disciplinary discourse communities is to promote hegemonic language use, but these views are not shared by major figures doing work in this field. The same charge could be made about style guides for authors of academic journals.

11. According to Hyland (2005) devices such as the words *clearly, surely, of course,* and so on, are "boosters" that claim certainty. He states that "the balance of hedges and boosters in a text thus indicates to what extent a writer is willing to entertain alternatives and so plays and important role in conveying commitment to text content and respect for readers" (53). I encourage writers and readers of texts in Integral Land to develop sensitivity to these words and our employment of them in our writing, given our emphasis on the importance of perspectives.

12. Style note: one of the great things about Wilber's writing is his playfulness, which he manages while being serious. I aspire to that as well! I did not make up the term *Wilberness*: it is common usage by some students at JFKU.

13. I have carried out a quick analysis of citations to Wilber's work in the first two volumes of *AQAL Journal* to find out which of his works are most often cited and if any pattern emerges. The most often cited is *Sex, Ecology, Spirituality*, closely followed by *Integral Psychology. A Brief History of Everything* and *A Theory of Everything* are frequently cited, along with the collected works. Excerpts A-D are certainly being read, if combined citing of them is any indication. We might note that these are all fairly recent works starting in 1995 and we are all associated with Wilber's phase 4 (AQAL) or phase 5 (post-metaphysical) material. Teachers of graduate students, take note of this list, and also those who would move from being newcomers or novices, who want to increase their participation, as Wave and Wegner (1991), along with others, such as (Johns 2002) have described, is a process serious students must undertake and that involves familiarity with prominent ideas and texts.

14. That considerable use of Wilber's work and Integral Theory as metatheory across many disciplines is already taking place can be seen from note 11 in Esbjörn-Hargens (2006), which contains a long list of publications (348). In his editorial to JITP, Volume 3(1), he states that more than 55 MA theses and PhD dissertations have drawn heavily on Integral Theory. I understand that since that editorial was published in March 2008 the list has doubled. The full list can be found at *www.integralresearchcenter.org/*

source. I hope to be able to analyze this writing one day soon, and to suggest strategies for bringing Integral Theory into the academic communities so many of us might consider our "native lands."

15. I notice that many pieces in *JITP* are nevertheless written as though to people who are not familiar with Integral Theory, which is demonstrated through such things as stating that Integral Theory was originated by "philosopher Ken Wilber" and offering a pronunciation guide to "AQAL." If the writing in *JITP* is actually not for other integral insiders—or at least "members"—but for outsiders who are not familiar with the theory already, and the outsiders also have to be able to take second-tier perspectives, that suggests a rather small audience! An interesting analysis would be to examine the volumes so far and as time goes on to see how this changes over time.

16. So for now, it is closed, or only open a little way?

17. Rather than as a subfield of Psychology, or . . . ? I ask because written texts could be examined as evidence of a shift or breaking away from a parent field, with its conventions of form, relationship, reader and writer behavior, citations, etc. Scholars carrying out *genre analysis* (e.g., Swales 1990, the name one most associates with this subfield) do know something about writing in the social sciences and could compare publication behavior, texts, and the function of texts in different disciplinary communities to see which the integral community publications are currently most like. And we could trace the process of moving from subfield to academic discipline; thereby also creating evidence that we have finally done it.

18. Notice the move I have made by saying "we." I might have chosen to position myself as an outsider who is observing the integral community. With "we" I claim insider status, though with a strange sense of reluctance, for I am with Virginia Woolf (1938) in recognizing the power of being an outsider, and also probably because I am an introverted Five on the Enneagram. And yet, of course, from fields such as anthropology we know the value of being a "participant-observer." I suppose my reluctance to use "we" mainly stems from my inability to keep up with all the writing that is coming from this community. I really do not want to risk "we" because I am not getting to the Integral Naked Web site as much as I would like, reading the blogs, etc. So take this "we" as representing my membership in the we who are very interested in Integral Theory while not being key knowledge-makers, and for the rest, consider me a "member-outsider."

19. Notice what is expressed in this paragraph through use of modal language: "may need to consider," "might involve," "can consider," "would seem," and so on. It's "hedging," meaning avoiding claims that are too strong, which might reflect lack of confidence, cautiousness, recognition of complexity, the politeness of a first-time contributor to the conversation, acknowledgment that many viewpoints are possible, or the diffidence of someone who could be considered a member of the integral community, and yet who is not a member of "the inner circle" (Hyland 2005). And by the way, hedging is fine, even skillful, until it gets sneaky.

20. Some in that field would say texts are "situated within" disciplinary contexts, while also shaping them, but I notice a growing perception that they arise together (e.g., so says the prominent researcher Ken Hyland 2005, 13).

21. Such analytical attention might also involve an acknowledgment of the consequences of the fact that writing within the integral community, published in *JITP*, will be in English, even though my impression is that ever larger numbers of non-native English speakers are becoming members and insiders, and in fact creating such a global

community is an explicit aim. For as scholars in discourse analysis (e.g., Connor and Kaplan 1987; Swales 2004) have pointed out, conventions of argument and style vary by language, with some languages preferring more inductive and less linear, and some more deductive styles than English, and some considering readers responsible for deciphering meaning, in contrast to the case in English, in which writers are responsible for leading readers and helping them decipher meanings (Hinds 1987). Writers in non-English languages sometimes handle proposing innovation, being critical, and how they work with the scholarship of others different from the ways these are done in English. How will these differences affect the ability of those who are less proficient in English to participate in the knowledge-making of this community? In addition to the above, we must consider that the language being English may hinder those non-native speakers who would be concerned about their linguistic capacity to write complex texts, and who may therefore hesitate to seek publication in the journal.

22. An interesting piece of text analysis would be to take papers published in *JITP* and ones written by the same authors but published in their primary disciplinary journals. How would these pieces be similar and different, and what would this tell us? I hope to carry out this project one day soon. I am especially interested in raising questions about differences in the work of those who come to Integral Theory as experts in an academic discipline already versus those whose "first language" is integral, and who turn to look at and work within other disciplines as outsiders to them, "non-natives." I would suggest that the latter go about that work with as much care as would a visitor to another country comment on the mores there.

23. Notice a less formal style: I could have said "the disciplinary conventions with which he or she is most familiar." I might make this choice if this were a conference paper—a written text that moves closer to the style of spoken form (Swales 2004, 197–206). Or it might be a move to establish writing in the integral community as less formal, even when it's "scholarly," in the same way some businesses have a culture that is less formal (and thus seen as innovative, and maybe even radical).

24. Volume One starts out with an introductory piece by Wilber, overviewing Integral Theory in a way that upon first look seems surprisingly basic, if we assume that this is a scholarly journal, for integrally oriented readers who have already read lots of his work, and want a chance to read authors who explore applications and refine the theory. The journal is probably not intended to *introduce* the theory, but Wilber's piece does. However, another way to see Wilber's introduction is as gathering the community together around a carefully articulated statement of what the theory is and is not. I am told by the editor, Sean Esbjörn-Hargens (personal communication), that after articles pass through peer-review Wilber reviews all chapters for content, meaning he takes a look at whether a faithful representation of his view of the theory has been made. Authors are encouraged to take issue with Wilber's view and openly challenge it in the pages of *JITP* but the journal is committed to make sure such critique is accurately aimed. I suspect the need for him to do this will not persist, as this community matures, but for now it would seem especially crucial, given the prevalence of writing in many venues that misrepresents the theory or uses the terms but without containing much substance. In fact, it is not surprising that even within the integral community (defined, let us say, as those who are members of I-I), a continuum of knowledge of the theory exists, ranging from those who have newly discovered it to those who have been working with it for awhile and have read many of Wilber's books. I do appreciate that we can count on the *JITP* for solid Wilber-approved understanding of Integral

Theory, and at least in my mind (and even before I read "Wyatt Earp"), he has amply demonstrated that he welcomes critical engagement with his work and will not be trying to squash ideas he might disagree with or to somehow control what can be said. I also see the wisdom of the decision that early publications in the journal consisted mainly of solicited articles, for while this could inhibit development of new knowledge and many viewpoints once a definite disciplinary community has been established, at this point, where it is just being established, such measures ensure quality and a strong foundation upon which to base future conversation. My understanding is that for the last two years *JITP* has primarily published articles that were not solicited but rather submitted by various scholars and practitioners who were seeking an academic venue to showcase their work.

A really quick flip through the first 3.1 volumes shows evidence that on the whole, writers are assuming that readers know the basics of Integral Theory, and when basics are given (e.g., definition of quadrants or zones or levels) it appears to be more for the purpose of making sure writer and readers are on common ground, before proceeding to applying the ideas. This suggests a cohesive and informed readership, and a strong shared body of knowledge. It will be interesting to see where we go from here. Will there be more controversy or stances that are critical of the theory? How will this be realized in the texts? Since the conference a number of notewothy articles have been published in *JITP*. See for instance the recent debate between Mark Edwards and Steve McIntosh about the role of the Lower-Right quadrant in Integral Theory as well as the critical piece by Rebecca Bailin in 4.2, which points to the conflation of sex and gender in the integral community.

25. Here I have been trying to write such a chapter, at the risk of being dismissed as "intuitively integral," since I am avoiding diagrams and terminology. Does it matter? To me it does, and seems like the distinction between two expatriates who live in a country, and have been profoundly changed by their experiences, by their enlargement of worldview, and both having learned to speak the language. One spends her life writing a really high-quality travel guide to serve others who would like to visit, while the other just lives there happily, occasionally writing letters to friends back home, just to keep in touch and swap experiences. They may be equally conversant with the place, the people, and the conventions.

26. This is not *at all* a criticism (or sour grapes because I have not met the man personally)! I am simply curious about the process.

27. As I have been suggesting, the integral community has many members with different degrees of involvement. Again, I am being playful when I predict that one way you can recognize the real "insiders" in the integral community, is to note who calls him "Ken." Other good signs might include being a founding member, heading an Integral Center, being on the editorial board of *JITP*, and publishing in early volumes of *JITP* (since most of those articles were solicited, according to my colleague, Sean Esbjörn-Hargens, the editor—personal correspondence). But how about writing—must we write like Wilber does?

28. Blogs, transcripts of interviews, the famous Excerpts A-D & G, (hey, what happened to E and F?) and other kinds of texts also play a role in the creation of this community, as might work published in other journals and magazines such as *What Is Enlightenment, Integral leadership Review*, and *Integral Review*, though probably these texts play a different role than *JITP*, and would be textually different and different in how they are produced and in patterns of readership. Some aspiring discourse analyst might take on study of these texts, contexts, and interrelations.

29. Even when it is not conscious, we can hardly avoid writing like those who are founders and "Big Names" within our fields. In my case, I notice many turns of phrase and ways of looking at things that can be traced back to my reading of the large corpus of material written by one of the key figures in discourse analysis, John Swales, who was my mentor and one of the members of my dissertation committee. Discourse analysts have studied the influence of powerful figures and seminal texts on knowledge-creation within disciplinary communities.

30. What are some of the other reasons for citations? These include following a style sheet and disciplinary expectations about how much to cite; being ethical; paying homage; self-aggrandizement (as when one cites him or herself); rewarding (e.g., one's colleagues or students, who may be up for tenure); persuading of the validity of one's arguments, as claims based on expert citations may be more convincing; showing familiarity with the canon of work in a field (which shows that one is an insider); and creating a personal research space (Swales 1990, 6–7).

   I note that self-citing does occur by authors of *JITP*, as does citation of other authors who have published in *JITP*, and even sometimes to chapters that have not yet been published (in the same issue or planned for upcoming ones). This would seem to indicate a close insider group, perhaps one whose members both write for the journal and review chapters that will be published. All of this can be expected at the inception of a new field, but we should be able to expect to see this opening up as time goes on.

31. I do feel a bit concerned about one implication of Wilber's taking on and writing well about matters related to scholarship in several fields. I am not at all bothered when he does it, perhaps because of his copious citation and obvious erudition, but I tend to think that mastery of a scholarly discipline is a huge endeavor. Are we to trust the many journalists writing in fields that are not their area of specialization, as though with some research anyone can be an expert—never mind grappling with the nuances of a field, recognition of controversies and camps and the questions and anomalies within it, and other such things? Or what about the current trend of scientists of a certain ilk pronouncing on religious thought that would seem to be far beyond their field of scholarly expertise? How many disciplines can one really master in their lifetime, even though having mastered one, a scholar is at least familiar with strategies for learning in scholarly realms? In the integral community I see some attempts to write in disciplinary fields in which authors have not received professional training or validation through publication in communities made up of scholars in those fields, and it concerns me. However, I note that copious citation of what I take to be seminal texts offers reassurance that the author is expert in a field, even though as an outsider to that field I cannot be sure if these are texts that insiders in those fields would cite.

32. I wish I had been able to carry out a thorough analysis in this area (the way Fuhs [2008] did of books on leadership), but it might not actually be worth doing, since the conclusion is probably already known. But variations in treatment of all AQAL might be of interest.

33. One other feature of interest to would-be authors and to members of the integral community—especially those involved in educating on Integral Theory—might be the degree to which there is a canon of authors or works other than Wilber's. I took a look at the authors cited by Wilber in his opening chapter in *JITP*. Of those, in the first five issues (which was as far as I got), the ones who had more than one mention, in order, are Beck and Cowan, Kegan, Gebser, Cook-Greuter, and Gilligan, and Gardner.

Surprise! Esbjörn-Hargens, Combs, Hochachka, Graves, M. Murphy, Walsh, Goddard, Habermas, and Parlee also stand out as worth knowing about, and it would be a good idea to know about the Enneagram. I wish I had been able to do a more careful and thorough job on this, but mention it here as one role text analysis can play in hinting at the contours of a discipline. Perhaps someone will take this on, defining an integral canon of texts as a project.

34. "Stride-by, stand in the doorway" conversation, rather than proper "interview," I'm chagrined to say. The convention is to call it "personal communication."

35. Both playfully and seriously I wonder if someday the Ph in PhD might be replaced with In, as in InD and for just that same reasons. I do appreciate the theory and application building work that must be done as integral hits the world, but gradually I would like to see some of us simply conducting ourselves as integral scholars, not necessarily writing about integral, but because of it and through it, as a lens. The In would signal a perspective or methodology, just as Ph does, even when scholars in other fields do not cite texts in philosophy in their dissertations.

36. Lots of fun analyses could be carried out. For instance, it would be interesting to do a study based on texts that compares textual forms with length of time since last academic degree or with some measure of expertise in a discipline. Some have noted the youthfulness of many in the integral community, and if true, what are implications for the integral community and for knowledge creation within it? It's commonly seen that for some time after receiving a PhD, scholars mine their dissertations in publishing chapters, so I wondered if I would see longer citation lists from the younger scholars, but this was not the case. Examining author credentials—who is publishing in *JITP?*—might reveal that within the group are mainly really well-established experts in their fields, or recent graduates of PhD programs, or students, but not as many (like me) who have been around (a boomer) but are not particularly prominent. What might be made of this? (Title the paper "The Geeks and the Geezers.") How are the shape of the discipline and the texts produced within it going to result from the reading and writing preferences of those who make to second tier?

37. I notice that Volumes One and Three, focused on themes, might have more or less appeal, depending on the reader. I did not have time to consider how they might be different in other ways.

38. The difference between ridiculous and merely boring.

39. I hate to conclude with this, for I believe this to be possibly the most fruitful of inquiries to be made.

40. And yet I feel that the notion of "the integral community" seemed like an abstraction, somehow. In looking at chapters, I was not sure who authors thought they were writing for, how much knowledge they thought readers might have, what readers' interests were assumed to be, and so on. I did, however, appreciate a lack of defensiveness that suggests that authors were not anticipating criticism in how they were writing. I share the belief that to develop this academic discipline requires space for taking risks.

41. Discourse analysts have studied reader behavior involving research and scholarly chapters, and studied it in many ingenious ways, and not just by asking questions. They have carefully noted what is being read and not read, and what read with greater attention. Every writer should be aware that people probably are not going to read their piece from beginning to end, and especially if they are not enticed to do so by somehow immediately showing this work to be relevant to their needs and interests.

42. Writers can present an ethos through attitude markers such as evaluative terms (Hyland 2005) that convey surprise, agreement, obligation, frustration, and so on (53). But this is not typical in academic writing. How about in integral academic writing?

43. I tried to do this in my chapter by opening with a question that would be answered throughout the chapter.

44. I am pretty sure I have nodded to all five aspects of AQAL, though, with the exception of states, so let me confess that I am writing this with headphones on, keeping my brain in an inspirational alpha state through Centerpointe's "Quietude."

45. You may have noticed that the beginning of the chapter set the context in a more "literary" way, by evoking a woodpecker, and here at the end I have quoted the beautiful prose of an artist and poet who has inspired many. This is more common in the humanities.

References

Bazerman, C. 1981. What written knowledge does: Three examples of academic discourse. *Philosophy of the Social Sciences* 11: 361–82.

———, and J. Paradis. (Eds.) 1991. *Textual dynamics of the professions: Historical and contemporary studies of writing in professional communities.* Madison: University of Wisconsin Press.

Bartholomae, D. 1985. Inventing the university. In *When a writer can't write: Studies in writer's block and other composing process problems,* ed. M. Rose, 134–65). New York: Guilford Press.

Becher, T. 1981. *Academic tribes and territories.* Buckingham: Open University Press.

Beck, D. E., and C. C. Cowan. 1996. *Spiral dynamics: Mastering values, leadership and change.* Cambridge, MA: Blackwell Publishers.

Berkenkotter, C., and T. N. Huckin. 1993. Rethinking genre from a sociocognitive perspective. *Written Communication* 10: 475–509.

Bizzell, P. 1982. Cognition, convention, and certainty: What we need to know about writing. *PRE/TEXT* 3: 213–41.

Connor, U., and R. B. Kaplan. 1987. *Writing across languages: Analysis of L2 text.* Reading, MA: Addison-Wesley.

Cook-Greuter, S. 1999. *Postautonomous ego development: A study of its nature and measurement.* Unpublished doctoral dissertation, Harvard University.

Dacher, E. S. 2006. *Integral health: The path to human flourishing.* Laguna Beach, CA: Basic Health Publications.

Elbow, P. 1991. Reflections on academic discourse. *College English* 53(2): 135–55.

Esbjörn-Hargens, S. 2008. Editorial Introduction. *Journal of Integral Theory and Practice* 3(1): v–xii.

———. 2006. Integral ecology: An ecology of perspectives. *AQAL: Journal of Integral Theory and Practice* 1(1): 305–78.

Faigley, L., and K. Hansen. 1985. Learning to write in the social sciences. *College Composition and Communication* 136: 140–49.

Friesen, E. 2006. An integral writing tour: Through the four studios of your own awareness. *AQAL: Journal of Integral Theory and Practice* 1(4): 1–49.

Fuhs, C. 2008. Toward a vision of integral leadership: A quadrivial analysis of eight leadership books. *Journal of Integral Theory and Practice* 3(1): 139–62.

Gardner, H. 1993. Frames of mind: The theory of multiple intelligences. New York: Basic Books.

Geertz, C. 1988. *Works and lives: The anthropologist as author.* Stanford: Stanford University Press.

Gebser, J. 1949/1986. *The ever-present origin.* Trans. N. Barstad and A. Mickunas. Athens: Ohio University Press.

Gilligan, C. 1982. In a different voice: Psychological theory and women's development. Cambridge: Harvard University Press.

Graves, C. W. 2002. *Clare W. Graves: Levels of human existence.* Ed. W. R. Lee. Santa Barbara: ECLET Publishing.

Herrington, A. 1985. Writing in academic settings: A study of the contexts for writing in two college engineering courses. *Research in the Teaching of English* 19: 331–59.

Hinds, J. 1987. Reader versus writer responsibility: A new typology. In U. Connor and K. Hyland. 2000. *Disciplinary discourses: Social interactions in academic writing.* New York: Longman.

Hyland, K. 2005. *Metadiscourse.* London: Continuum.

———. 2008. "Small bits of textual material": A discourse analysis of Swales' writing. *English for Specific Purposes Journal* 27(2): 143–60.

Johns, A. M. 1997. *Text, role, and context: Developing academic literacies.* New York: Cambridge University Press.

———. 2002. *Genre in the classroom: Multiple perspectives.* Mahwah, NJ: Lawrence Erlbaum Associates.

———. 2007. Crossing the boundaries of genre studies: Commentaries by experts. *Journal of Second Language Writing* 15(3): 234–49.

Kegan, R. 1982. The evolving self: Problem and process in human development. Cambridge: Harvard University Press.

———. 1998. *In over our heads: The mental demands of modern life* (revised ed.). Cambridge: Harvard University Press.

Kohlberg, L. 1984. *The psychology of moral development.* San Francisco: Harper and Row.

Knorr-Cetina, K. 1981. *The manufacture of knowledge.* Oxford: Pergamon.

Kuhn, T. S. 1970. *The structure of scientific revolutions.* 2nd ed. Chicago: University of Chicago Press.

Lave, J., and E. Wenger. 1991. *Situated learning: Legitimate peripheral participation.* Cambridge: Cambridge University Press.

Loevinger, J. 1987. *Paradigms of personality.* New York: Freeman Publishing.

Luftig, J. 2008. Living for playing: Playing for a living: An integral research study. *Journal of Integral Theory and Practice* 3(1): 61–104.

McCarthy, L. P. 1987. A stranger in strange lands: A college student writing across the curriculum. *Research in the Teaching of English* 21: 233–65.

Myers, G. 1990. Writing biology: Texts in the social construction of scientific knowledge. Madison: University of Wisconsin Press.

Odell, L., and D. Goswami. 1982. *Writing in non-academic settings.* New York: Guilford.

Pfeiffer, R. H. 2007. Breathing together: An AQAL guide for significant relationships. *AQAL: Journal of Integral Theory and Practice* 2(3): 105–21.

Richards, M. C. 1989. *Centering: In pottery, poetry, and the person.* Middletown, CT: Wesleyan University Press.

Schlitz, M., and T. Amorok. (Eds.) 2005. Consciousness and healing: Integral approaches to mind-body medicine. St. Louis: Elsevier.

Senzon, S. A. 2007. Subtle energies viewed from four quadrants. *AQAL: Journal of Integral Theory and Practice* 2(4): 134–46.

Swales, J. M. 1990. *Genre analysis: Academic writing in research settings.* Cambridge: Cambridge University Press.

———. 1998. Other floors, other voices: A textography of a small university building. Mahwah, NJ: Lawrence Erlbaum.

———. 2004. *Research genres: Explorations and applications.* Cambridge: Cambridge University Press.

———, and C. B. Feak. 1994. *Academic writing for graduate students.* Ann Arbor: The University of Michigan Press.

Walsh, R. 2006. Responding to suffering and evil: Integral principles. *AQAL: Journal of Integral Theory and Practice* 1(4): 151–58.

Wilber, K. 1986. Up from Eden: A transpersonal view of human evolution. Boston: Shambhala.

———. 1995. Sex, ecology, spirituality: The spirit of evolution. Boston: Shambhala.

———. 1996. *A brief history of everything.* Boston: Shambhala.

———. 1998. The eye of spirit: An integral vision for a world gone slightly mad. Boston: Shambhala.

———. 2000a. Integral psychology: Consciousness, spirit, psychology, therapy. Boston: Shambhala.

———. 2000b. One taste: The journals of Ken Wilber. Boston: Shambhala.

———. 2000c. A theory of everything: An integral vision for business, politics, science, and spirituality. Boston: Shambhala.

———. 2001a. *Grace and grit.* Boston: Shambhala.

———. 2001b. On critics, Integral Institute, my recent writing, and other matters of little consequence: A Shambhala interview with Ken Wilber; Part III. Retrieved July 1, 2008, from http://wilber.shambhala.com/html/interviews/interview1220_3.cfm.

———. 2001c. Eye to eye: The quest for a new paradigm. Boston: Shambhala.

———. 2002. Announcing the formation of Integral Institute. Retrieved September 22, 2003, from http://wilber.shambhala.com/html/books/formation_int_inst.cfm/.

———. 2003a. Boomeritis: A novel that will set you free. Boston: Shambhala.

———. 2003b. Excerpt A: An integral age at the leading edge. Retrieved July 1, 2008, from http://wilber.shambhala.com/html/books/kosmos/excerptA/intro.cfm.

———. 2003c. Excerpt B: The many ways we touch; Three principles for an integral approach. Retrieved July 1, 2008, from http://wilber.shambhala.com/html/books/kosmos/excerptB/intro.cfm.

———. 2003d. Excerpt C: The ways we are in this together: Intersubjectivity and interobjectivity. Retrieved July 1, 2008, from http://wilber.shambhala.com/html/books/kosmos/excerptC/intro.cfm.

———. 2003e. Excerpt D: The look of a feeling; The importance of post/structuralism. Retrieved July 1, 2008, from http://wilber.shambhala.com/html/books/kosmos/excerptD/excerptD.pdf.

———. 2006. Integral spirituality: A startling new role for religion in the modern and postmodern world. Boston: Integral Books.

———. 2007. The integral vision: A very short introduction to the revolutionary integral approach to life, God, the universe, and everything. Boston: Integral Books.

Williams, J. M. 1985. *Style: Ten lessons in clarity and grace.* Glenview, IL: Scott, Foresman.

Woolf, V. 1938. *Three guineas.* San Diego: Harvest.

## 6

An Integral Understanding
of the Etiology of Depression

Elliott Ingersoll

Depression is a disorder that has increased dramatically in Western societies in the last fifty years. Why do people get depressed? Is it because they lack the motivation to enjoy life? Is it because they have a chemical imbalance? Is it because they inherited a genetic proclivity to the disease? Is it because they have recently suffered a trauma? The answer is more complex than any of these questions imply and this chapter will explore that complexity. Space limitations require me to limit the discussion in this chapter to a sketch of etiology.1

Depression is one of the most overdetermined symptom-sets that mental health clients present with. Recall that the word *overdetermined* means that there are many variables (and combinations of variables) that can contribute to feeling depressed. This is challenging because we do not know what *causes* depression. The news that there is no one thing causing depression is actually good because we know that many variables influence whether or not a person suffers depression and the more we know about these variables, the more help we are to clients. The only model I have found that is able to embrace and coherently lay out these variables is Ken Wilber's Integral model.

In this chapter think of depression as a large territory that is currently being mapped by several mapmakers with different skills and agendas. In true integral fashion, each mapmaker contributes a partial truth to our understanding of why people get depressed and the best way to treat them when they do. When you use Integral Theory to organize your maps and assess your client, you are drawing on the best of all worlds with decreased risk of a category error.[2] In this chapter I cover three terrains of depression mapped via the body (physiological theories of depression), the mind (psychological theories of depression), and the spirit (existential/trans-ego understandings of depression).

When I use the word *depression*, I am referring to any number of or combination of the set of symptoms listed under Major Depressive Disorder in the Diagnostic and Statistical Manual of the American Psychiatric Association (DSM) (APA 2000). I realize that in operationalizing depression this way I immediately incur the wrath of those who prefer narrow, more specific descriptions of depression. Such preferences are usually aimed at diagnostic clarity but the more they narrow and clarify the list of symptoms in the DSM, the farther they depart from the clinical reality of most clients. This said; an integral perspective helps clinicians map the heterogeneous manifestation of symptoms. The symptoms for Major Depressive Disorder proper include:

1. Depressed mood most of the day, nearly every day, indicated by self-report or report of others (in children or teens the mood may be irritable)
2. A diminished pleasure in all or most activities (anhedonia) all day, nearly every day
3. Significant weight loss or weight gain (change of more than 5 percent of body weight in one month)
4. Insomnia or hypersomnia
5. Psychomotor retardation or agitation nearly every day
6. Fatigue or loss of energy nearly every day
7. Feelings of worthlessness or excessive guilt
8. Diminished ability to think or concentrate
9. Recurrent thoughts of death and/or suicidal ideation (APA 2000)

In the DSM clients must have five or more of these in a two-week period. The symptoms for Dysthymic Disorder, thought to be a low-grade depression, are very similar to those listed above. In fact, the symptoms listed above may manifest in many DSM disorders including (but not limited to) Major Depressive Disorder, Dysthymic Disorder, Bipolar I Disorder, Bipolar II Disorder, Cyclothymia, Schizoaffective Disorder, many of the so-called Personality Disorders and are frequently comorbid with Anxiety Disorders. In addition, depressive symptoms can occur after childbirth (postpartum depression), as a side effect of prescription and illicit drugs, in relation to seasonal fluctuations (Seasonal Affective Disorder), and be comorbid with hormonal fluctuations (Premenstrual Dysphoric Disorder). Depression can also be directly related to a medical disorder (such as Multiple Sclerosis, Parkinson's disease, hepatitis, AIDS, and other infectious diseases). Finally depression can be labeled "not-otherwise-specified" (NOS) if a client meets fewer than five of the symptoms for Major Depressive Disorder.

So, why do people get depressed? The answer is it depends and the answer differs depending on the person, situation, and time of life. This is where the categories of DSM and categorical psychiatry in general, depart from allopathic medicine. To pretend that depression is a "disease" like a bacterial infection is confusing psychiatric categories with allopathic medical diseases. The approach of categorical psychiatry used in the DSM has been estimated to be 50 to

100 years behind diagnostic practices in other branches of medicine because psychiatry has failed to find a single correlate for any of the DSM disorders (Charney et al. 2002; First 2006; First and Zimmerman 2006).

The Etiology of Depression

The variables contributing to depression include biological, psychological, and environmental (Goldstein and Rosselli 2003). As I noted above, I will add spiritual variables to this list[3] recognizing that adding such variables implies a transformed psychotherapy to deal with these symptoms whether they reflect states or stages of development.[4] I will elaborate on these and use the Integral model as a framework to understand them as complementary rather than competing maps. We begin by viewing depression through the map of the body.

Physiological Theories of Depression: The Map of the Body

While we know that we cannot account for depression exclusively with physical variables (UR quadrant), we also know it would be foolish to rule them out. We have learned a great deal in the last 25 years about which physical variables are highly correlated with depression. Despite years of research, however, we know little about the pathophysiology[5] of depression or even if there is such a thing. Similarly we know little about the "causative molecular mechanisms of antidepressant therapy leading to clinical benefit" (Zazpe et al. 2007, XX). As long as you remember that there is a complex interplay between physical variables, the mind, and the environment you can avoid the trap of thinking that the physical variables *cause* depression.

A Note on "Chemical Imbalances"

The phrase *chemical imbalance* is what I refer to as "word magic"—attempting to create an illusion of certainty with words where in fact no certainty has been confirmed and/or replicated in scientific models. When some of the early medication for depression [mono amine oxidase inhibitors (MAO Inhibitors) and tricyclic antidepressants] began to show positive results for treating depression, it was quickly learned that one of the first things these drugs do is to increase the levels of a neurotransmitter called norepinephrine (NE). Thus it was assumed that if the drugs correlated with an increase in NE and a decrease of symptoms perhaps the drugs corrected a deficit or an "imbalance" in NE. What we find in reviewing the theories of how antidepressants work is that their mechanism of action is far more complicated than increasing the levels of a given neurotransmitter.

Despite that, the idea that depression was somehow caused by a chemical imbalance took hold, particularly because from the LR quadrant the idea makes it easier to market antidepressant medications. In addition, as Kemker and Khadivi (1995) have pointed out, the chemical imbalance metaphor has been a mainstay of psychiatric training similar to gene expression (which is an equally poor phrase that I will address below). They noted that "regarding chemicals as the cause of mental illness is a growing trend, despite flaws in the logic of this model" (247). These authors note that given the stresses of psychiatric training, it is far easier to describe suffering as chemical rather than undertaking the time-intensive task of understanding the client's psychological and emotional context.

Causation and Correlation

Just because a drug that has chemical properties is correlated with symptom reduction in some, but not all clients,[6] this does not mean that these clients' brain chemistries were "unbalanced" in the first place. The fact that ingesting chemicals (antidepressants) is correlated with symptom reduction in some, but not all clients does not mean the symptoms were *caused by* an imbalance of the same chemicals. It merely means that some alleviation of the symptoms may be accomplished through chemical interventions. This may sound like hair-splitting but it is an important point because there is a great deal of lobbying from pharmaceutical companies and some corners of biological psychiatry to conceptualize mental and emotional disorders as basically allopathic brain disorders.

Having said that though, there *are* numerous physiological changes that correlate with the reduction of, or remission of, depressive symptoms. These correlations appear after several weeks of treatment with antidepressant medications. The physiological theories related to depression describe many of them quite well. The question remains, though: Are these theories of etiology or theories of antidepressant action? Since the mind impacts the brain as the brain impacts the mind we are faced with the proverbial "chicken/egg" problem. The most resourceful way to understand these physiological theories is as partial truths. Only when we weave all the partial truths together (physiological, psychological, environmental, cultural, and spiritual) do we approach a way of thinking about depressive symptoms that honors the complexity of each client.

The Monoamine Theory of Depression

An early physiological theory (Upper-Right quadrant) of why people get depressed grew out of treatment with the first antidepressant medications in the 1950s called MAO inhibitors and tricyclic antidepressants.[7] This theory was called the monoamine hypothesis and its origins are attributed to a biochemist named Albert Zeller from Northwestern University (Snyder 1996). An amine is any compound that is derived from ammonia by replacement of one or more hydrogen atoms with organic compounds. A monoamine is an amine that has a single binding site in its structure. Monoamines include the neurotransmitters dopamine (DA), epinephrine (EP), and norepinephrine (NE). MAO inhibitors and tricyclic antidepressants both increased the levels of norepinephrine (NE) in the synaptic cleft. MAOIs do this by deactivating the enzyme that disables the NE.[8] Tricyclics increase NE by inhibiting its reuptake by transporter molecules.[9] So essentially, because antidepressants helped some (but not all) patients with their depression and because they increased levels of NE, the hypothesis was that depressed people did not have enough NE and thus had a "chemical imbalance." The amine hypothesis was amended to the permissive hypothesis when it was discovered that inhibiting the reuptake of serotonin (5-HT) with Serotonin Reuptake Inhibitors (SSRIs) had therapeutic effects in some but not all patients.

The Downregulation Theory of Antidepressant Action

The monoamine and permissive hypotheses were logical but overly simplistic. Clinicians knew that it could take between two and six weeks for antidepressants to have their full therapeutic effect but, the increases in NE or 5-HT occur within an hour of taking the drug. Thus, the increases of NE or 5-HT could not fully account for the therapeutic effects. What was later discovered was that the increases in NE and 5-HT lead to a decrease in the number and sensitivity of post-synaptic receptors called downregulation. This decrease in the number and sensitivity of the receptors takes approximately two to six weeks to occur. Eureka! Thus was born the downregulation theory of how antidepressants work (UR). This second theory was still a variation on the chemical imbalance theory. It stated that a depressed person takes an antidepressant and quickly increases the levels of NE or 5-HT available in the synaptic cleft. This increase in NE or 5-HT then causes the downregulation (decrease in the number and sensitivity of postsynaptic receptors) and this translates into relief from symptoms of depression in some but not all clients. The downregulation theory still held that some sort of mythic "balance" was achieved through the medications, although no baselines were ever provided to support the theory.

It is important to note the absence of a missing link in both the monoamine and downregulation hypotheses. We began with the question, "Why do people get depressed?" The answers increasingly come to address the mechanism of action for antidepressants, which stops short of explaining how increasing NE and effecting downregulation actually changes mood. The answer is that, at this point, we simply do not know why people get depressed but many practitioners and writers in the field appear reluctant to admit this. With the next theory of antidepressant action, we come one step closer to actually beginning to understand why antidepressants (and other things like exercise and psychotherapy) may improve mood.

Molecular/Cellular Theory of Antidepressant Action

The molecular/cellular theory of antidepressant action (Duman, Heninger, and Nestler 1997) was an exciting development that clearly links depression with the presence of ligands[10] in the central nervous system. The molecular/cellular theory builds on the amine and downregulation theories by describing what happens inside the neurons while increased NE or 5-HT and downregulation of receptors are happening outside. This theory is built in large part on the technologies that allow us to actually learn what is happening inside neurons. In a nutshell, the molecular/cellular theory points out that, after initially ingesting an antidepressant, when the levels of neurotransmitter targeted by the antidepressant increase (norepinephrine or serotonin or both depending on which drug was ingested) there is also an increase *inside* the cell in the levels of cyclic adenosine monophosphate (cyclic AMP).

Cyclic AMP is a molecule important to many biological processes. Inside the neurons of the brain, cyclic AMP governs the production and processing of brain-derived neurotrophic factor, which is a protein that helps the survival of existing neurons as well as encouraging the growth and development of new neurons (referred to as neurogenesis).[11] The following is the key sequence of events in the molecular/cellular theory of how antidepressants act on the body. For the sake of the example we will assume the antidepressant taken is an SSRI.

1. Within an hour of taking the SSRI, the level of serotonin in the synapses increases.
2. At the same time, the levels of cyclic AMP inside of the postsynaptic neuron also increase.
3. Over two to six weeks, the number and sensitivity of the postsynaptic serotonin receptors decreases. While the levels of cyclic AMP inside the postsynaptic cell decrease, they remain *higher* than they were in the pre-medication condition.
4. It is believed that the overall increase in cyclic AMP in the postsynaptic neurons results in more BDNF and thus healthier existing neurons and a greater chance for the growth and development of new neurons.

There is some promising initial research support for this theory. We have known for some time that there is a significant relationship between stress, affective disorders, and BDNF (Licinio and Wong 2002). Exposure to stress, the stress hormone corticosterone (Jacobson and Mork 2006), and social isolation (Scaccianoce et al. 2006) have been shown to *decrease* the expression of BDNF in rats. In addition, both stress and social isolation are correlated with depression in humans. Two research groups (Zanardini et al. 2006; Lee, Kim, Park, and Kim 2007) have recently found lower plasma levels of BDNF in depressed patients when compared to a non-depressed match population. In addition, at least one study has demonstrated that antidepressants reverse BDNF decreases induced by the stress hormone corticosterone (Dwivedi, Risavi, and Pandey 2006).

It is with the molecular/cellular theory that we really start looking at a chain of physiological events that correlates with the presence of depressive symptoms and that is much more realistic than stating that the physiological variables *cause* depression. As early as 2004, researchers had concluded that while deficits in neurogenesis (related to deficits in BDNF) may play a subtle role in depression, these deficits do not *cause* depression (Henn and Vollmayr 2004). As we will see in studying psychological theories of depression, the mind/brain interaction is such that certain psychological experiences in response to environmental stimuli could impact and change the way the brain is working. The brain has a degree of plasticity that is now recognized as far greater than was once believed. This is one of the most exciting directions for clinicians because there are activities such as exercise that begin in the mind as will or motivation which then can actually have an impact on the brain. In the case of exercise, we have studies that conclude that exercise is correlated with a decrease in depressive symptoms (Solomon 2001). The correlation of exercise with reduced depressive symptoms may come about because exercise also increases levels of BDNF (Russo-Neustadt, Beard, and Cotman 1999).

At this point we come full circle in the sense of theory informing clinical practice. We have always known that physical activity could be a useful way to improve mood and decrease anxiety but now we are starting to understand some of the physical mechanisms involved. When a client is told depression is caused by a chemical imbalance, it can reinforce the very external locus of control that contributes to feeling helpless or hopeless (both of which are shown in cognitive research to increase one's vulnerability to depression). On the other hand, if a client is told that exercise can enhance levels of "chemicals" that help brain cells work optimally the locus of control includes some internal variables. Many clients benefit greatly from a six-month regimen of antidepressants but, during that six months, they also make changes in their lives that allow them to maintain gains after titrating off of antidepressants.

The Role of Genetics

If you have learned anything about the role of physiology in developing depressive symptoms, it is that science is always, by definition, incomplete—a work in progress. While many scientists understand this, commercial marketing and the mass media frequently misunderstand it, leaving us with inaccurate phrases such as "chemical imbalance." We see the same problem in trying to isolate the role of genetics (UR; zone 5) in the development of mental and emotional disorders.

The role of gene expression is important in studying any mental or emotional symptoms that constitute a disorder. To start with, the phrase "gene expression," if not word magic, is pretty inaccurate. Genes do not "express" themselves. Genes are simply akin to blueprints or instructions of how to make proteins. This is no small task since the average person has about 24,000 genes with blueprints for making about 50,000 proteins for a multitude of tasks. Genes are found on chromosomes, which are in the nuclei of cells. Every cell's nucleus contains 23 pairs of chromosomes (with the exception of reproductive cells). Most chromosomes are approximately 50 percent deoxyribonucleic acid (DNA) and 50 percent proteins. To "express," the protein sheath must be withdrawn so that messenger ribonucleic acid (mRNA) can "see" the "blueprint" and then initiate a series of events leading to synthesis of that protein.

So what is the point here? The point is that genes do not express, but rather, their instructions can be carried out when the cell, responding to events external to it (and even the body of which it is a part), are configured in such a way that the protein sheath is temporarily withdrawn and the blueprint can be read. This paragraph is critical to making sense of the role genetics play in mental health. The initial hope of researchers was that single genes might be correlated with disorders such as schizophrenia much in the same way as single genes have been identified underlying disorders such as muscular dystrophy or cystic fibrosis. This has not turned out to be the case. We now believe multiple genes contribute to mental disorders and the presence of these genes simply makes one vulnerable to the disorders. The role of the environment (Lower-Left and Lower-Right quadrants) and one's psychological reaction (Upper-Left quadrant) to it comprises the discipline now called epigenetics ("epi" meaning near or around). Thus, epigenetics is the study of events (in the body, mind, and environment) that trigger the withdrawal of protein sheaths around genes and allow their blueprints to be carried out (see Rodenhiser and Menn 2006; Santos et al. 2005; Sharma 2005).

To make matters more complex, the manner in which gene expression occurs is currently being debated. In the 1970s, the idea that genes operate individually became a fundamental belief in the field of genetics. In limited cases (such as those noted above) a particular disease could be tied to a particular gene. This began as the idea that each gene in any organism carries the information it needs to synthesize one (and only one) protein. In July 2007, The United States National Human Genome Research Institute published findings suggesting that rather than genes functioning independently and linking to a single function (such as a predisposition to depression), they operate in complex networks and interact as well as overlap with each other in ways we do not fully understand (Caruso 2007; Bankura 2007).

Psychological Theories of Depression: The Map of the Mind

In exploring what the map of the mind (UL quadrant) has to offer us about the etiology of depression, we will journey into several well-known theories, fascinating research, and learn that in many cultures psychological theories about depression are considered before biological ones. The psychological theories about why people get depressed will take us back to psychoanalysis (zone 1) and through the cognitive revolution (zone 5) in psychology.

Psychodynamic Theories of Depression

In 1917, Sigmund Freud wrote an essay titled "Mourning and Melancholia" (Gay 1989), in which he distinguished grief from melancholic depression. Grief, he said was the result of the loss of a real object.[12] Depression was the result of the loss of a loved object. Frequently, this loved object is a parent or other caregiver who, early in life, abandons the child. Affective states experienced by people suffering from depression have been grouped by Blatt (2004) into two orientations: *anaclitic* (dependent) and *introjective* (self-critical). The anaclitic model of depression is similar to Freud's idea of melancholia. Anaclitic depressive patterns are frequently experienced by people whose relationship with their primary caregiver was disrupted in some way. This evolves into feelings of weakness, helplessness, inadequacy, fears of abandonment, desires to be soothed, difficulty tolerating delay of gratification, and difficulty expressing anger (for fear of driving another loved person away) (PDM Task Force 2006).

Introjective depressive patterns manifest as an experience of "harsh, punitive, unrelenting self-criticism; feelings of inferiority, worthlessness, and guilt; a sense of having failed to live up to expectations and standards; fears of the loss of approval, recognition, and love from important others; and fears of the loss of acceptance of assertive strivings" (PDM Task Force 2006, 111).

Both anaclitic and introjective experiences of depression have been linked to attachment theory. Attachment theory proposes that consistently loving, protective, and nurturing relationships with our parents or caregivers promotes our ability to form healthy relationships with others throughout life. Attachment theory suggests that we develop internal models of self and others from early relationships. If those relationships go reasonably well the models we develop work reasonably well and are the basis for a healthy attachment style. If the relationships are of poor quality (e. g., neglect, abuse) then the models we develop are also of poor quality and underlay an insecure attachment style, making us vulnerable to anaclitic or introjective depression (Reis and Grenyer 2002).

Cognitive-Behavioral Theories of Depression

The earliest behavioral theories of depression were set forth in part to break from the psychodynamic theories that dominated up until the mid-twentieth century. The gist of early behavioral theories was that "the individual who is vulnerable to depression tends to either suppress behaviors that elicit positive responses from others or enact behaviors that elicit negative feedback from others" (Street, Sheeran, and Orbell 1999). These theories gave birth to interpersonal theories of depression (LL quadrant) discussed below. A more straightforward behavioral theory of depression was Lewinsohn, Weinstein, and Shaw's (1969) model that associated depression with lack of social skills and proposed that if the depressed people learned social skills, their depressive symptoms would lessen. The goal of these therapies was to alter behavior so as to increase the probability of positive reinforcement from the environment and decrease the probability of negative feedback or punishment. While such approaches are useful in a small number of cases, the majority of people suffering from psychogenic[13] depression have far more complex causes.

Perhaps the most enduring behavioral paradigm is Seligman's (1975) paradigm of learned helplessness. This began as a behavioral paradigm and was easily adapted to complement what was becoming a cognitive-behavioral approach to understanding depression. The initial work in this area (Overmier and Seligman 1967) was done giving dogs electric shocks in situations where escape was impossible. When the dogs were moved to a shock condition where escape *was* possible, they failed to attempt it. Seligman and Maier (1967) were able to demonstrate that this behavior was caused by the uncontrollability of the original shocks. This became the animal model of the theory that when external events are beyond a person's control, they may lead to depression. This is similar to the earlier behavioral formulations outlined above (that depression is due to a lack of positive reinforcement from the environment as well as perhaps punishment or negative consequences in the environment). Seligman and others always presumed that this would account for some but not all depressive symptoms but the evidence was strong enough to support that claim. The learned helplessness theory was later critiqued and reformulated because of several weaknesses (Abramson, Seligman, and Teasdale 1978). The revisions deal with weaknesses that stem from generalizing from an animal model to human beings.[14]

The sentience or self-awareness of human beings is better accounted for in the revised theory. It differentiates between helplessness that is universal (affecting all people) versus helplessness that is personal (affecting one or a few people). Personal helplessness is correlated with an internal attribution whereas universal helplessness is correlated with an external attribution. The revised theory of learned helplessness also deals with whether or not the helplessness is specific or global. Helplessness that occurs in a broad range of situations is global and helplessness that occurs in a narrow range of situations is specific. If the person perceives the helplessness as global, they are more vulnerable to depression. The time course of helplessness may also vary from person to person, with some lasting minutes and others lasting years. Here the revised theory differentiates between transient and chronic helplessness, with chronic being the more depressogenic of the two.

The reformulated theory of helplessness in depression is as much a theory of attributions. The reformulated theory was summarized as:

1. Depression consists of four classes of deficits: motivational, cognitive, self-esteem, and affective.
2. When highly desired outcomes are believed improbable or highly aversive outcomes are believed probable, and the individual expects that no response in his repertoire will change their likelihood (helplessness), depression results.
3. The generality of the depressive deficits will depend on the globality of the attribution for helplessness, the chronicity of the depression deficits will depend on the stability of the attribution for helplessness, and whether self-esteem is lowered will depend on the internality of the attribution for helplessness.
4. The intensity of the deficits depends on the strength, or certainty, of the expectation of uncontrollability and, in the case of the affective and self-esteem deficits, on the importance of the outcome. (Abramson, Seligman, and Teasdale 1978, 68)

Thus, cognition begins to become part of the theory as attributions requiring some level of sentience are integrated. As Abramson, Seligman, and Teasdale (1978) concluded, "[T]he properties of the attribution predict in what new situations and across what span of time the attribution of helplessness will be likely to recur" (59).

Cognitive Theories of Depression

To the extent that we view attributions as outlined above as types of cognitions, we have moved toward a cognitive theory of depression. As Haaga, Dyck and

Ernst (1991) noted, "[T]here has been widespread agreement that cognitive *therapy* of depression is effective (but) there has been less consensus on the validity of cognitive *theory*" (215). The search for an underlying cognitive theory of depression is noteworthy because it, more than any other theoretical undertaking, has resulted in the different schools of thought being brought together in an integrative or even integral manner.

The psychological theory of depression most studied in recent years is the cognitive vulnerability theory of depression. Simply stated, this theory proposes that "negative cognitive styles confer vulnerability to depression when people confront negative life events" (Alloy, Abramson, and Francis 1999, 128). For our purposes, a negative cognitive style can be defined as "the tendency to explain negative events in stable and global terms" (Joiner et al. 2001, 524). The cognitive vulnerability theory of depression builds on Beck's (1963) earlier theory of depression.

Beck's Cognitive Theory of Depression

Simply stated, Beck's (1963) theory focused on specificity, the cognitive triad of depression, the cognitive distortion bias, automaticity, and schemas. Specificity refers to the idea that depressive cognitions are specific in perceiving final and definite loss. The cognitive triad of depression refers to the idea that depressed people think more negatively about themselves, the future, and the world than people who are not depressed. The cognitive distortion bias is a selective memory for negative things and inability to identify or remember positive things. Automaticity refers to the fact that negative thoughts are experienced as repetitive and uncontrollable. Finally, Beck's idea of schemas is very similar to psychodynamic ideas of the unconscious.

A schema, in Beck's theory, is a cognitive map of sorts, and depression-generating schemas are tacit beliefs that increase the likelihood of negative cognitions.[15] Theories of cognitive maps have a long history dating back to the work of Edward Tolman in the 1930s (see Tolman 1948). Young and colleagues (2003) noted that schemas are cognitive maps reflecting pervasive themes comprised of memories, emotions, thoughts, and bodily sensations that developed during childhood or adolescence. Beck recognized there was a need for further attention to things such as the disruption of early relationships (aka John Bowlby) (Beck 1983), as well as to the environment of depressed people (Beck 1987).

The Cognitive Vulnerability Theory of Depression

The idea that all depression is to some extent significantly associated with increased negative thinking has consistently been supported. While some of the research reviewed above also supported specific subtypes of depression such as the hopelessness subtype, it appears that the negative cognitive style is the cognitive hallmark of people suffering from depression. Therefore, it makes sense for a theory of etiology to target negative cognitive styles directly. Do some people have a vulnerability toward developing a negative cognitive style and thus to developing depression? The answer seems to be Yes.

The construct of cognitive vulnerability and the research supporting it raises a question: What contributes to one's developing the cognitive vulnerability that, in turn, makes one more vulnerable to depression and other disorders? Here, as in the physiologically based theories of depression, we have come full circle back to psychodynamic theories of how trauma and disruption in early relationships can render one more vulnerable to depression. Recall that the anaclitic and introjective theories of depression suggested that neglect or abandonment by caregivers set in motion dynamics that increase the likelihood of a person's suffering from depression. Some of the reasons that people develop cognitive vulnerability to depression sound strikingly similar to the psychodynamic explanations, and it is to this topic that we now turn.

Contributors to Cognitive Vulnerability

We have come a long way from early psychodynamic theories of depression to refutation of those theories by behaviorists, to cognitive therapists' addition of attributions and schemas to learned helplessness. Goldberg (2001) summarized research on vulnerability as defined by openness to experience and neuroticism. These in turn were linked to early childhood adversity. This led other researchers to attempt to more comprehensively assess how parenting and abuse/neglect correlated with cognitive vulnerability. As you can guess, the findings were significant.

Rose and Abramson (1992) suggested that children who experience maltreatment seek the causes in an effort to attach meaning to the experience. The younger a child is, the more the self is a reference point, to the extent that it might be said that development is a journey away from narcissism. Rose and Abramson confirmed this in the sense that because children internalize all events they see themselves as the cause of maltreatment. This internalizing process leads to a negative attributional style which renders one more vulnerable to depression. Then, if negative events are repetitive and occur in relationships with parents or primary caregivers, the events undermine the child's positive sense of self and hope for the future. The persistence of the events and the negative attributional style increase the vulnerability to depression. Ingram (2003) has noted that this combination becomes almost trait-like and serves as a foundation for hopelessness.

Recently a research team attempting to summarize the relationship between vulnerability to depression and parental care (Alloy, Abramson, Smith, Gibb, and Neeren 2006) concluded, "There is reasonably consistent evidence for a link between unipolar depression in offspring and exposure to parenting characterized by low care and high psychological control or overprotection or by the provision of negative inferential feedback" (38). Inferential feedback is basically what the parents infer and communicate to the children about the cause of problems that arise in the children's lives. A second team of researchers (Alloy et al. 2001) supported the hypothesis that if parents had negative ideas about problems in life, children would develop similar negative inferences. These inferences are thought to be part of a negative cognitive style that renders one more vulnerable to depression. Additionally, Alloy et al. found that depressogenic cognitive styles were related to parents' negative cognitive styles and general negative parenting practices (such as lack of emotional warmth).

Interpersonal Theories of Depression

Though we have covered much material on depression, there are still other understandings of how it develops. The interpersonal theory of depression (LL and LR quadrants) has important findings of clinical relevance across the lifespan. While biological and cognitive theories were dominating discourse, researchers were amassing data to support that interpersonal variables could be directly related to depression (Segrin 2000). Probably the most referenced interpersonal model of depression is Coyne's (1976) interactional model. Coyne posited that the interpersonal behavior of people who are depressed tends to increase rejection from others, which of course is also depressogenic. Several researchers have explored and found support for the interpersonal model of depression.

The paralinguistic behaviors (vocal rate, volume, pitch, and length of pauses) of depressed people were rated as less clear (Lewinsohn et al. 1980) than non-depressed people. There is also some evidence that depressed subjects in studies are harder to hear and show different patterns of eye contact (Dow and Craighead 1987) than non-depressed subjects. Not surprisingly, the verbal content of depressed speakers contains more negative statements than non-depressed speakers (see the summary in Segrin 2000). In addition, there are differences in the facial expressions of depressed and non-depressed people with the former being less facially animated than the latter (Schwartz, Fair, Mandel, Salt, and Klerman 1976a; 1976b).

These findings all contributed to the interpersonal theory in that they are partial aspects of interactions with others. By starting with studying these aspects, researchers were able to quantify aspects of social behavior before moving to the more qualitative aspects of interactions such as peer acceptance. Kistner (2006) wrote, "There is no question that low peer acceptance is associated with depression, both elevated depressive symptoms and clinically diagnosed depression" (4). While initially researchers doubted whether one variable predated the other, this was confirmed in research with children. Depression tends to elicit negative responses from peers, and internalization of negative feedback from peers fuels depression (Cole, Jacquez, and Maschman 2001). Even in brief conversations it appears that depressed people are far more likely than non-depressed people to be rejected (Segrin and Abramson 1994). Clearly, the interpersonal researchers integrated what was being discovered by cognitive researchers but then took the next step of integrating cognitive findings into a context of social interactions.

Thus far we see how one set of theories clearly builds on previous ones as well as how we might isolate our client's depression to one or two primary variables. For example, a client may have been abused as a child and developed unhealthy attachment, which created a schema that made her vulnerable to depression. While a psychodynamic theorist might label the depression "anaclitic," and focus on making the difficult childhood an object of awareness through transference analysis, a cognitive therapist may try to make the client's dysfunctional schema an object of awareness by teaching the client how to identify and challenge irrational thoughts. These irrational thoughts, of course, may manifest in interpersonal interactions increasing the probability of rejection from peers and, consequently, exacerbating the depression.

Existential and Spiritual Understandings of Depression

Existential and spiritual variables related to depression are important to consider. While this is important material to include from an integral perspective, the material is less well researched and requires some extrapolation from theory and clinical utility. An important caveat to remember is that we must be clear about how we are operationalizing words such as spirituality.[16]

Existential Understandings of Depression

Existential understanding of depression is related to depressogenic events in a person's existence or more importantly their perception of their existence (Yalom 1980). This sounds like the cognitive theory of depression but an existential theory of depression builds on the cognitive component with certain key concepts. Key concepts include authenticity, responsibility, and freedom to choose. In the late nineteenth century Friedrich Nietzsche proclaimed that modern man's soul had gone stale and all about humanity was the smell of failure. The failure was to live authentically, and this manifests as depression. Nietzsche was fond of paraphrasing the Greek poet Pindar, exclaiming, "You should become him who you are!" (Nietzsche 1974, 219). This idea of "becoming" rather than "being" was central to his existential philosophy. Each person is a work in progress and the existential givens (things such as suffering, illness, injustice, and death) are viewed as the very things necessary to become who we are. As Nietzsche scholar Walter Kaufmann (1974) noted, "[N]ature must be transformed, and man must become like a work of art" (156). It is in saying "yes" to the existential givens and the possibility of transformation that we live an authentic life (Solomon and Higgins 2000).

Part of saying "yes" to life is constantly questioning our own assumptions. Refusing to think beyond our assumptions is what Nietzsche would have described as moral corruption and, this in turn, will inevitably result in unnecessary suffering (Kaufmann 1974). In Nietzsche's (1999) own words, "[M]en of convictions are prisoners" (77). For Nietzsche, life could only be fully lived when one possessed the courage to face it directly without the diversions and distractions of society and those who control society. Engaging diversions was thus a form of sleep and "where sleep is the goal, life lacks meaning" (Nietzsche 1954, 4). The idea, then, is that by facing life we truly become who we are. By running from life's inevitable suffering, we remain unfinished and unhappy and vulnerable to depression.

Recall the different levels of ego identity that have been confirmed by Jane Loevinger and Susann Cook-Greuter.[17] Developmentally, one can use existential therapy at most if not all levels, but the issues treated by existential therapists become far more pronounced for people once they enter the Individualist level of ego identity. Recall that at this level, a person has worked through the ability to live life rationally and focusing on her individual judgments. At the Individualist level, the person is capable of holding multiple perspectives in her mind and realizing that there is no "one right way" of thinking or living. Rather, people very different from herself hold different views and still succeed. This gives rise to an ability to cognitively reflect back on one's self and in so doing, recognize that one's self is, at least partially, constructed in relation to what others and our society tell us we are or should be. To consciously engage life authentically becomes a developmental task at this point. Existential approaches to depression particularly focus on meaning-making as personal meaning (as well as spiritual meaning) have both been correlated with lower rates of depression (Mascaro and Rosen 2006).

Spiritual Issues and Depression

If we hold a broad definition of spirituality, there are several ways that depression can relate to spiritual experiences. Many depressions can grow out of what are referred to in DSM as "Religious or Spiritual Problems (this "V" code is V62.89 in the DSM). One example is what I called the "Job Syndrome" (Ingersoll 2000) in which a person outgrows their understanding of a faith tradition and, lacking support for making new meaning of their tradition, they go into a state of depression. In these cases a person's level of ego identity has frequently outgrown that of her or his spiritual community. In what I call the Job syndrome, a person (like the protagonist of the Jewish poem)[18] wrestles with their concrete understanding of the Divine because their life experience seems to contradict it. Sometimes to resolve the dissonance, as in the case above, a person would feel it easier to assume they had been "wicked" than that their doctrine about the wicked being punished was incorrect.

There are many examples of depressive symptoms related to spiritual issues and we can still use a psychological frame of reference for these. The field trials for the Religious or Spiritual Problem V-code listed other examples where depression may be a problem including loss of faith, conversion to a new faith, intensification of practices, and involvement in cults. This V-code also includes problems that are of a more spiritual nature but that have psychological sequelae. These include near-death experiences, transpersonal experiences, and things like mystical states (Turner, Lukoff, Barnhouse, and Lu 1995). Depression can be one symptom of what is called a spiritual emergency (Grof and Grof 1989). This is when a person is experiencing spiritual growth but for whatever reason, is not prepared to do so.

The majority of studies done are on using spiritual practices as part of treatment (e.g., Baer 2003; Kabat-Zin 2003). Some studies have been done that focus on the role spirituality plays in reducing vulnerability to depression but the results are mixed (Westgate 1996; Young 2005; Nolan 2006; Dein 2006; Zaccariell 2007). Part of the problem seems to be the operational definitions of spirituality. Sometimes the definition is simply one's religious practice, sometimes it is operationalized around spiritual wellness (factors thought to be associated with spiritual health), and other times it is described metaphorically because of its ineffable quality. While studies have found relationships between religion and decreased levels of depression (McClure and Loden 1982; Koenig, Hays, George, and Blazer 1997) there are still multiple variables that may be affecting the outcome of these studies (e. g., spiritual maturity, intrinsic versus extrinsic faith). Until we can agree on operational definitions that reflect cultural and developmental diversity, it will be hard to draw conclusions about the role of spirituality and depression. Figure 6.1 illustrates the variables that may influence depression that I have covered in this chapter.

While this chapter is only an introduction to a complex topic, I hope I have demonstrated the importance of using an Integral framework to understand

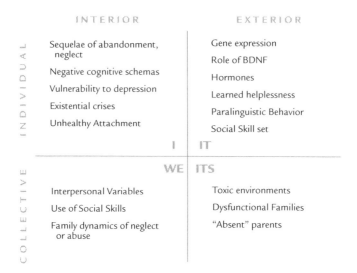

Figure 6.1 Variables related to depression by quadrant

depression from perspectives of body, mind, and spirit. Therapists who have an integral map of depression can record significant symptoms and client variables in the quadrants, as demonstrated in Figure 6.1, identify the "hotspots" or where in each quadrant symptoms arise, and then tailor treatment based on the quadratic understanding of the client's symptoms, the client's developmental level, and the client's type as expressed in any preference for a style of therapy. Given the overdetermined nature of depression, the integral map is the most comprehensive one and is going to serve the client and the therapist through assessment and treatment.

Notes

1. A more in-depth exploration of etiology and treatment is available and the reader can obtain that by e-mailing me at ingersollelliott@gmail.com.
2. Recall that a category error is trying to account for all truths with one perspective. In Integral Theory we say a category error is when someone tries to account for all quadrants (perspectives) with only one or two quadrants or perspectives.
3. Spirituality is operationalized in Ingersoll and Zeitler (2010, ch. 8).
4. Recall that Ken Wilber is the first person to discriminate states of consciousness, which are by definition transitory, and stages of consciousness, which a person has consistent access to barring severe trauma. This difference will be critical when I cover spiritual variables related to depression since spiritual states are temporary and to be treated differently than a symptom that occurs at a spiritual stage.

5. Pathophysiology is the study of the disturbance of biochemical and other physical functions either by disease or other conditions. This is a basic discipline in allopathic medicine and may be inappropriate in studying mental and emotional disorders for reasons discussed in chapter 1.

6. This phrase reflects that studies on medication reflect statistical significance, which always translates into some, but not all clients receiving the medication benefit. The latest data from the FDA database on antidepressant studies puts their efficacy at about 50 percent.

7. MAO inhibitors stands for monoamine oxidase inhibitors. These medications inhibit an enzyme (monoamine oxidase) that in turns breaks down the neurotransmitter norepinephrine (NE) after it is released from the neurons. Inhibiting the breakdown of NE leaves more NE in the synapse to bind to receptors. Tricyclic antidepressants are named for their molecular structure, which resembles three interlocking rings. These drugs work primarily by inhibiting the reuptake of NE again resulting in more NE in the synapse. Both drugs have several other mechanisms of action. For a full description, see Ingersoll and Rak (2006).

8. This discovery that enzymes including MAO disable neurotransmitters was made by Zeller, thus laying what was to become one of the foundation blocks for amine theory.

9. Transporter molecules are proteins that bind to neurotransmitters that have been fired from neurons and take them back into the neuron to be used/fired again. It is akin to recycling the neurotransmitter. Julius Axelrod eventually won a Nobel Prize in 1970 for this research, which he began twenty years earlier.

10. A ligand is a molecule that can bind with a biomolecule to serve a biological purpose. As a class in biology, ligands include neurotransmitters. This use of the term is distinct from its use in metalorganic and inorganic chemistry.

11. It used to be believed that once a person was born, that person had all the neurons they would in life and no new ones would develop. This turned out to be incorrect as several areas of the brain can grow new neurons throughout the lifespan (Jacobs 2004).

12. The word *object* is used in psychodynamic and object relations theories to describe the psychological representation of a person, usually a caregiver or other significant person in the client's life.

13. *Psychogenic* means of psychological origin or etiology.

14. The idea of generalizing from animal models to human beings began with Charles Darwin's idea that "human behavior evolved from the behavioral repertory of our animal ancestors. That idea gave rise to the notion that experimental animals could be used as models to study human behavior" (Kandel op. cit., 40).

15. This idea of cognitive maps derives from the work of Edward Tolman (1948).

16. Wilber (2006) describes spirituality with four different definitions. Briefly they include spirituality as a line of development, as the upper levels of any line of development, as peak experience, as an attitude, and finally, as synonymous with one's religious practice.

17. These levels include Impulsive, Conformist, Expert, Conscientious, Individualist, Autonomous, Ego-Aware, and Unitive.

18. While most readers are familiar with the "Book of Job" in the sacred writings of both Judaism and Christianity, it is technically a poem. See Mitchell (1979).

References

Abramson, L. Y., M. E. P. Seligman, and J. D. Teasdale. 1978. Learned helplessness in humans: Critique and reformulation. *Journal of Abnormal Psychology* 87: 49–74.

Abramson, L. Y., G. I. Metalsky, and L. B. Alloy. 1989. Hopelessness depression: A theory-based subtype of depression. *Psychological Review* 96: 358–72.

Alloy, L. B., L. Y. Abramson, and E. L. Francis. 1999. Do negative cognitive styles confer vulnerability to depression? *Current Directions in Psychological Science* 8: 128–32.

Alloy, L. B., L. Y. Abramson, M. E. Hogan, W. G. Whitehouse, D. T. Rose, M. S. Robinson, R. S. Kim, and J. B. Lapkin. 2000. The Temple-Wisconsin cognitive vulnerability to depression project: Lifetime history of axis-I psychopathology in individuals at high and low cognitive risk for depression. *Journal of Abnormal Psychology* 109: 403–18.

Alloy, L. B., L. Y. Abramson, N. A. Tashman, D. S. Berrebbi, M. E. Hogan, W. G. Whitehouse et al. 2001. Developmental origins of cognitive vulnerability to depression: Parenting, cognitive, and inferential feedback styles of the parents of individuals at high and low cognitive risk for depression. *Cognitive Therapy and Research* 25: 397–423.

American Psychiatric Association. 2000. *Diagnostic and statistical manual of mental disorders,* 4th ed. Text revised. Washington, DC: APA.

Baer, R. A. 2003. Mindfulness training as a clinical intervention: A conceptual and empirical review. *Clinical Psychology: Science and Practice* 10: 125–43.

Bankura, S. 2007. Human Genome: Need to start afresh? *New York Times online.* Retrieved August 21, 2007, from http://www.scienceahead.com/entry/human-genome-need-to-start-afresh/.

Beck, A. T. 1963. Thinking and depression: I: Idiosyncratic content and cognitive distortions. *Archives of General Psychiatry* 10: 561–71.

———. 1983. Cognitive therapy of depression: New perspectives. In *Treatment of depression: Old controversies and new approaches,* ed. P. J. Clayton and J. E. Barrett, 265–84). New York: Raven.

———. 1987. Cognitive models of depression. *Journal of Cognitive Psychotherapy: An International Quarterly* 1: 5–37.

Blatt, S. J. 2004. *Experiences of depression: Theoretical, research and clinical perspectives.* Washington, DC: American Psychological Association.

Bowlby, J. 1977. The making and breaking of affectional bonds: Aetiology and psychopathology in the light of attachment theory. *British Journal of Psychiatry* 120: 201–10.

Caruso, D. 2007. Change to gene theory raises new challenges for biotech. *International Herald Tribune online.* Retrieved August 21, 2007, from http://www.iht.com/bin/print.php?id=6471136.

Charney, D. S., D. H. Barlow, K. Botteron, J. D. Cohen, D. Goldman, R. E. Gur et al. 2002. Neuroscience research agenda to guide development of a pathophysiologically based classification system. In *A research agenda for DSM-V,* ed. D. J. Kupfer, M. B. First, and D. A. Regier, 31–84). Washington, DC: American Psychiatric Association.

Cole, D. A., F. M. Jacquez, and T. L. Maschman. 2001. Social origins of depressive cognitions: A longitudinal study of self-perceived competence in children. *Cognitive Therapy and Research* 25: 377–95.

Coyne, J. C. 1976. Toward an interpersonal description of depression. *Psychiatry* 39: 29–40.

Dein, S. 2006. Religion, spirituality, and depression: Implications for research and treatment. *Primary Care and Community Psychiatry* 11: 67–72.

Dow, M. G., and W. E. Craighead. 1987. Social inadequacy and depression: Overt behavioral and self-evaluation processes. *Journal of Social and Clinical Psychology* 5: 99–113.

Duman, R. S., G. R. Heninger, and E. J. Nestler. 1997. A molecular and cellular theory of depression. *Archives of General Psychiatry* 54: 597–608.

Dwivedi, Y., H. S. Rizavi, and G. N. Pandey. 2006. Antidepressants reverse corticosterone-mediated decrease in brain-derived neurotrophic factor expression: Differential regulation of specific exons by antidepressants and corticosterone. *Neuroscience* 139: 1017–29.

Farmer, A., E. 1996. The genetics of depressive disorders. *International Review of Psychiatry* 8: 369–75.

First, M. B. 2006. Beyond clinical utility: Broadening the DSM-V research appendix to include alternative diagnostic constructs. *American Journal of Psychiatry* 163: 10.

———, and M. Zimmerman. 2006. Including laboratory tests in DSM-V criteria. *American Journal of Psychiatry* 163: 12.

Gay, P. (Ed.) 1989. *The Freud reader.* New York: Norton.

Goldberg, D. 2001. Vulnerability factors for common mental illnesses. *British Journal of Psychiatry* 178S: s69-s71.

Goldstein, B., and F. Rosselli. 2003. Etiological paradigms of depression: The relationship between perceived causes, empowerment, treatment preferences, and stigma. *Journal of Mental Health* 12: 551–63.

Grof, S., and C. Grof. 1989. *Spiritual emergency: When personal transformation becomes a crisis.* Los Angeles: Tarcher.

Haaga, D. A., M. J. Dyck, and D. Ernst. 1991. Empirical status of cognitive theory of depression. *Psychological Bulletin* 110: 215–36.

Henn, F. A., and B. Vollmayr. 2004. Neurogenesis and depression: Etiology or epiphenomenon? *Biological Psychiatry* 56: 146–50.

Ingersoll, R. E. 2000. Gentle like the dawn: A dying woman's healing. *Counseling and Values* 44: 129–34.

Ingersoll, R. E., and C. F. Rak. 2006. *Psychopharmacology for helping professionals: An integral exploration.* Pacific Grove, CA: Brooks Cole.

Ingersoll, R. E., and D. A. Zeitler. 2010. *Integral psychotherapy: Inside out/Outside in.* Albany: State University of New York Press.

Ingram, R. E. 2003. Origins of cognitive vulnerability to depression. *Cognitive Therapy and Research* 27: 77–88.

Jacobs, B. L. 2004. Depression: The brain finally gets into the act. *Current Directions in Psychological Science* 13: 103–106.

Jacobson, J. P., and A. Mork. 2006. Chronic corticosterone decreases brain-derived neurotrophic factor (BDNF) mRNA and protein in the hippocampus, but not in the frontal cortex, of the rat. *Brain Research* 19: 221–25.

Kabat-Zinn, J. 2003. Mindfulness based interventions in context: Past, present, and future. *Clinical Psychology Science and Practice* 10: 144–56.

Kaufmann, W. 1974. *Nietzsche: Philosopher, psychologist, antichrist.* 4th ed. Princeton: Princeton University Press.

Kemker, S. S., and A. Khadivi. 1995. Psychiatric education: Learning by assumption. In *Pseudoscience in biological psychiatry*, ed. C. A. Ross and A. Pam, 241–54. New York: Wiley.

Kistner, J. 2006. Children's peer acceptance, perceived acceptance, and risk for depression. In *The interpersonal, cognitive, and social nature of depression*, ed. T. E. Joiner, J. S. Brown, and J. Kistner, 1–22. Mahwah, NJ: Lawrence Erlbaum Associates.

Koenig, H. G., J. C. Hays, L. K. George, and D. G. Blazer. 1997. Modeling the cross-sectional relationships between religion, physical health, social support, and depressive symptoms. *American Journal of Geriatric Psychiatry* 5: 131–44.

Lee, B. H., H. Kim, S. H. Park, and Y. K. Kim. 2007. Decreased plasma BDNF level in depressive patients. *Journal of Affective Disorders* 101: 239–44.

Lewinsohn, P. M., M. S. Weinstein, and D. A. Shaw. 1969. Depression: A clinical research approach. In *Advances in behavior therapy*, ed. R. D. Rubin and C. M. Franks, 231–40. New York: Academic Press.

Licinio, J., and M. L. Wong. 2002. Brain-derived neurotrophic factor in stress and affective disorders. *Molecular Psychiatry* 7: 519.

Mascarao, N., and D. H. Rosen. 2006. The role of existential meaning as a buffer against stress. *Journal of Humanistic Psychology* 46: 168–90.

McClure, R. F., and M. Loden. 1982. Religious activity, denomination membership and life satisfaction. *Psychology: A Quarterly Journal of Human Behavior* 19: 13–17.

Mitchell, S. 1979. *Into the whirlwind: A translation of the book of Job.* New York: Doubleday.

Nietzsche, F. 1999. *The antichrist.* Trans. H. L. Mencken. Tucson: See Sharp Press.

———. 1974. *The gay science: With a prelude in rhymes and an appendix of songs.* Trans. Walter Kaufmann. New York: Vintage.

———. 1954. *Thus spoke Zarathustra.* Trans. Walter Kaufmann. New York: Vintage.

Nolan, J. A. 2006. *Religious participation effects on mental and physical health.* Unpublished doctoral dissertation: Cornell University.

Overmier, J. B., and M. E. P. Seligman. 1967. Effects of inescapable shock upon subsequent escape and avoidance learning. *Journal of Comparative and Physiological Psychology* 63: 148–56.

PDM Task Force. 2006. *Psychodynamic diagnostic manual (PDM).* Silver Springs, MD: Alliance of Psychoanalytic Organizations.

Reis, S., and B. F. S. Grenyar. 2002. Pathways to anaclitic and introjective depression. *Psychology and Psychotherapy: Research and Practice* 75: 445–59.

Rodenhiser, D., and M. Menn. 2006. Epigenetics and human disease: Translating basic biology into clinical applications. *Canadian Medical Association Journal* 174: 341–48.

Rose, D. T., and L. Y. Abramson. 1992. Developmental predictors of depressive cognitive style: Research and theory. In *Developmental perspectives on depression*, ed. D. Cicchetti and S. L. Toth, 323–50. Rochester: University of Rochester Press.

Russo-Neustadt, A., R. C. Beard, and C. W. Cotman. 1999. Exercise, antidepressant medications, and enhanced brain derived neurotrophic factor expression. *Neuropsychopharmacology* 21: 679–82.

Santos, K. F., T. N. Mazzola, and H. F. Carvalho. 2005. The prima donna of epigenetics: The regulation of gene expression by DNA methylation. *Brazilian Journal of Medical and Biological Research* 38: 1531–41.

Scaccianoce, S., P. Del Bianco, G. Paolone, D. Caprioli, A. M. Modafferi, P. Nencini, and A. Badiani. 2006. Social isolation selectively reduces hippocampal brain-derived neurotrophic factor without altering plasma corticosterone. *Behavior Brain Research* 168: 323–25.

Schwartz, G. W., P. L. Fair, P. Salt, M. R. Mandel, and G. L. Klerman. 1976a. Facial muscle patterning to affective imagery in depressed and non-depressed subjects. *Science* 192: 489–91.

———. 1976b. Facial expression and imagery in depression: An electromyographic study. *Psychosomatic Medicine* 38: 337–47.

Segrin, C. 2000. Social skills deficits associated with depression. *Clinical Psychology Review* 20: 379–403.

Seligman, M. 1975. *Learned helplessness: On depression, development and death.* San Francisco: Freeman.

Seligman, M. E. P., and S. F. Maier. 1967. Failure to escape traumatic shock. *Journal of Experimental Psychology* 74: 1–9.

Sharma, R. P. 2005. Schizophrenia, epigenetics, and ligan-activated nuclear receptors: A framework for chromatin therapeutics. *Schizophrenia Research* 72: 79–90.

Solomon, R. C., and K. M. Higgins. 2000. *What Nietzsche really said.* New York: Schocken.

Street, H., P. Sheeran, and S. Orbell. 1999. Conceptualizing depression: An integration of 27 theories. *Clinical Psychology and Psychotherapy* 6: 175–93.

Tolman, E. C. 1948. Cognitive maps in rats and men. *The Psychological Review* 55: 189–208.

Turner, R., D. Lukoff, R. T. Barnhouse, and F. Lu. 1995. Religious or spiritual problem: A culturally sensitive diagnostic category in the DSM-IV. *The Journal of Nervous and Mental Disease* 183: 435–44.

Westgate, C. E. 1996. Spiritual wellness and depression. *Journal of Counseling and Development* 75: 26–35.

Yalom, I. 1980. *Existential psychotherapy.* New York: Basic.

Young, J. E., J. S. Klosko, and M. E. Weishaar. 2003. *Schema therapy: A practitioner's guide.* New York: Guilford.

Young, J. S. 2005. *Reduction in depression through participation in selected spiritual discipline.* Unpublished Doctoral Dissertation: Oral Roberts University.

Zaccariello, M. J. 2007. *Depression, hopelessness, and spiritual experiences among depressed psychiatric patients.* Unpublished doctoral dissertation: Case Western Reserve University.

Zanardini, R., A. Gazoli, M. Ventriglia, J. Perez, S. Bignotti, P. M. Rossini et al. 2006. Effect of transcranial magnetic stimulation on serum brain-derived neurotrophic factor in drug resistant depressed patients. *Journal of Affective Disorder* 91: 83–86.

Zazpe, A., I. Artaiz, L. Labeaga, M. L. Lucero, and A. Orjales. 2007. Reversal of learned helplessness by selective serotonin reuptake inhibitors in rats is not dependent on 5-HT availability. *Neuropharmacology* 52: 975–84.

part 2

Theoretical Perspectives

## 7

Now You Get It, Now You Don't

Developmental Differences in the Understanding of Integral Theory and Practice

Zachary Stein

Every ultimate fact is only the first of a new series. Every general law only a particular fact of some more general law presently to disclose itself. There is no outside, no inclosing wall, no circumference to us. The theory of today, which haunts the mind and cannot be escaped, will presently be abridged into a word, and the principle that seemed to explain nature will itself be included as one example of a bolder generalization. In the thought of tomorrow there is a power to upheave all thy creed. Step by step we scale this mysterious ladder. Fear not the new generalization. We walk as prophecies of the next age. When science is learned in love, and its powers are wielded by love, they will appear the supplements and continuations of the material evolution.

—R.W. Emerson ("Circles" and "Art")

Introduction: The Problem and the Developmental Maieutic Approach

The wide and diverse community of scholars and practitioners involved with Integral Theory stand in bold contrast to the mainstream academy. In part, this has to do with the *popularity* of the movement, as people from all walks of life are orienting themselves in light of a set of common ideas. But the uniqueness of the integral community also has to due with the *complexity* of the ideas being shared. As popular as this cultural movement is becoming, it is nevertheless not an instance of pop culture. The network of concepts, models, and outlooks that characterize Integral thinkers is not easy to understand because of their dynamism and scope. Yet the real difficulty of understanding these ideas is just beginning to become apparent, as the first efforts are underway to educate and inform the general public via graduate level programs and polished educative media outlets. It is becoming clear—and should be coming as no surprise—that not everyone understands the basic concepts of Integral Theory and practice (ITP) in the same way.[1]

This chapter contains a set of working hypotheses about how to understand the development of reasoning skills in the domain of Integral Theory and Practice. That is, I am taking a first pass at outlining *levels* and *lines* in the development of reasoning about ITP itself. Importantly, the reflections offered here are meant to set the stage for an empirical research project about developmental differences in how individuals understand ITP. Roughly one year ago my colleagues and I at the Developmental Testing Service (DTS) were invited to join an ambitious project, headed up by Sean Esbjörn-Hargens, to research aspects of an MA program in Integral Theory at John F. Kennedy University. This chapter gears into that broad research initiative, offering a first set of speculative rational reconstructions about the development of reasoning in the domain of ITP.

At DTS we have been rationally reconstructing levels and lines in domains from leadership to physics (Dawson-Tunik 2004c; Dawson-Tunik and Stein 2004; 2004a; 2004b; 2006; Dawson and Stein, 2008). We refer to our broad method as *developmental maieutics*. Below I provide an overview of the components of this method, including an introduction to a complex model of human development known as *Dynamic Skill Theory* (Fischer 1980; Fischer and Bidell 2006) and a sophisticated domain general developmental assessments system known as the Lectical™ Assessment System (LAS) (Dawson 2008; Stein and Heikkinen 2008) Briefly, and to foreshadow, developmental maieutics is an approach to the generation of usable knowledge about human development that entails the collaboration of researchers and practitioners and the reconstruction of knowledge domains. Doing the latter involves determining the *horizontal structure* of a domain in terms of the different interrelated sub-domains, themes, and conceptual strands (i.e., determining the different *lines* in the domain). Rationally reconstructing a domain also involves characterizing the *vertical structure* of the domain in terms of the various *learning sequences* that unfold along the clusters of conceptual strands making up the key themes (i.e., determining the different *levels* in the understanding of key ideas).

This is *empirical work*. But in this chapter I am offering *speculative hypotheses*. The goal here is both to frame key issues for empirical investigation and to give a sense of the kind of usable knowledge about the domain of ITP that we will ultimately produce. In doing so the integral community can begin to relate to the key concepts of ITP in a more dynamic and developmental way. Importantly, clarifying the horizontal and vertical structure (the *lines* and *levels*) of a domain can inform building assessments that can be used to generate focused psychographs and inform curriculum development, among other things. But before I introduce our approach and go on to speculate about how development unfolds in the domain of ITP, I want to touch on some broader themes. Habermas (1990), who engages in a method of rational reconstruction comparable to ours, is adamant about the important function of rational reconstructions in critical self-reflective activity. That is, accounts of how reasoning in a domain unfolds can be fed back into the domain itself as a kind of self-reflective quality control mechanism.

When Movements Look in the Mirror: On the Application of Integral Theory to Itself

Around the turn of the last century, Charles S. Peirce—polymath and prodigious integral progenitor—was invited by his dear friend William James to give a series of lectures at Harvard on the philosophical movement they had partnered to spawn, namely, pragmatism. The term *pragmatism* had been coined by Peirce, along with the general philosophical outlook, when they were both burgeoning young scholars. But James had popularized the idea and created a movement, perhaps the last great publicly embraced philosophical movement in America (before integral, that is—and after transcendentalism). But Peirce was not happy about the popularization and felt that his terms and concepts had been "kidnapped," "muddled," and "watered-down." So he did what any good logician and semiotician would do: he used these very terms and concepts to analyze their own popular usage (Peirce 1898; 1903). That is, he employed the principles of pragmatism—"the method of right thinking"—to analyze the popular use of pragmatism. This self-application of the theory convinced Peirce that he needed to set apart two distinct types or levels of pragmatism, one simple the other complex. He coined a new set of terms, pledged allegiance to the more complex brand, dubbing it *pragmatisim,* and left James and his followers with the popular and simpler pragmatism.

Complex philosophical approaches and worldviews can, and do, reach beyond the boundaries of the academy and into the lifeworld. To name a few from the modern West: Emerson's transcendentalism, Darwin's theory of evolution, Marx's communism, Peirce's pragmatism, Freud's psychoanalysis, Sartre's existentialism, Foucault's poststructuralism, Habermas's critical theory, Wilber's integral philosophy. These are rigorous and complex scholarly and scientific efforts that came to be consumed by the public at large. And as the example of Peirce's pragmatism shows, ideas take on a life of their own in the public sphere. Downward assimilations, simplifications, misuses, overgeneralizations, commoditization, and fetishization, are all possible and probable as movements become popular. Thus, these movements tend to branch apart into different streams of discourse. As noted above, Peirce explicitly differentiated different levels of discourse about pragmatism by exercising self-reflective efforts at quality control and clarity.

This last point touches one of my real motives in this chapter. I feel that ITP, as a complex field of endeavors and ideas, is reaching a critical point of self-awareness. Roughly, as Peirce did with his pragmatism, so we should do with our Integral. That is, we should use our basic concepts to analyze our own discourse. There have always been calls for ITP to look at its *shadow*. But a call for ITP to look in the *mirror* transcends and includes this call for shadow work. Critical self-reflection is one key catalyst of growth. And to be fair we should apply *all* the same categories to ourselves that we use to evaluate and understand others. To get to the point: an approach that characterizes the world in developmental terms should be willing to characterize itself that way. If those engaged with ITP are willing to point out the developmental differences between individuals when it comes morality, politics, and religion, etc., then they should be willing to point out developmental difference between individuals when it comes to ITP itself. Of course, it goes without saying, I hope, that the quest for *skillful means* is our motive for seeking conceptual clarity. As Forman and Esbjörn-Hargens (2008) have suggested: "Integral Theory will only thrive insofar as valuable contributions to its criticism, clarification, application, and expansion come from many individuals working within its context . . . [individuals coming] from a committed place to improve Integral Theory by turning Integral Theory in on itself: an act of theoretical-applied self-reflection." This is a key motivation for applying our Integrally informed developmental approach to the domain of ITP.

Method, Metric, Model: Building Usable Knowledge about Human Development

In essence our approach is simple. We have a broad *method* (developmental maieutics) based on a developmental *metric* (The Lectical™ Assessment system) and a developmental *model* (Dynamic Skill Theory). With these tools we aim to tie developmental research and assessment into educational practice, broadly construed. Here I will provide an overview of each aspect of our approach to frame the discussion and hypotheses about the domain of ITP that follow. I will begin with a theoretically oriented introduction to the model and metric.[2] I will then discuss how we put these sophisticated tools to use in the context of practice. This all sets the stage for a discussion of how reasoning skills develop in the domain of ITP.

Structure, Function, and Emergence:
Skill Theory and The Lectical™ Assessment System

Piaget (1977), like Baldwin (1906) before him, maintained that development at all levels is characterized by a continuous function (i.e., equilibration) that gives rise to variations in structure. New structures emerge as a result of unchanging functional activity; equilibration catalyzes restructuring.[3] Following Piaget and Baldwin, Fischer (Fischer and Bidell 2006) suggests an integration of structural and functional explanations that presupposes the ubiquity of self-organization as a property of behavior. This is a *dynamic developmental structuralism* that focuses on the construction of *skills*. The concept of a *skill* is similar to Piaget's *scheme* or Skinner's *operant* (Fischer 1980). It is also similar to Wilber's *holon* insofar as it signifies a generic unit of psychological process at all levels. It is important to remember just how broad this definition of skill is. One can have kinesthetic skills, conceptual skills, reasoning skills, meditative skills, etc. In this chapter we are looking at the development of reasoning skills in the domain of ITP. Importantly, the notion of a skill, like the notion of a holon, also explicitly implies relations between diverse constitutive elements, for instance, biological and sociocultural. If held rightly, it also counteracts the partitioning of cognition and action and behavior and context. But for our purposes here, adopting the notion of skill as basic eliminates the key dichotomy between function and structure.

Skills are mobilized to perform specific functions. Moreover, "the precise way a given skill is organized—its structure—is essential to its proper functioning" (Fischer and Bidell 2006, 322). Thus, each and every skill has both a structure and a function. Because of a general tendency of organisms and behavior toward self-organization, skills are not isolated units, but rather function together in complex structures of inter-participation. An ecosystem or economy should come to mind. Any given skill requires the existence of various others as component parts; these sub-skills function as parts in the skill's structure. And this skill itself is likewise required by others to perform some function as an integral part of their structure. Skill structures are built and rebuilt, honed relative to tasks and context, and vary dynamically over time. Skills support one another, compete for time and attention, and they combine to construct new higher-order emergent skills.

The dynamic construction of new skills is central to learning and development. Given the overview above, it should be clear that skills are built to serve some function and they have a structure built out of and relative to skills already in existence. Importantly, in this context we think of *lines of development* in terms of clusters of interrelated skills. A line of development is made up of a set of skills that all serve a relatively similar function, which makes them develop in relative synchrony. Skill sets with a different function develop in a different way and at a different pace. Yet, and this is key, the same patterns of skill construction characterize developmental processes in all lines. This idea again goes back to Piaget and Baldwin.

If equilibration was the most general function to which Piaget appealed to explain development, *reflective abstraction*[4] was the most general process that he thought accounted for the emergence of new structures (Piaget 1985; 2001). And like most of Piaget's concepts, it is variously defined and elaborated. In several places, Piaget contrasts *reflective abstraction* with *empirical abstraction* (Piaget 2001, 317–22; 1985, 18–19). This is a good way to go. Empirical abstraction consists of a subject's "reading of physical observables" in light of existing schemes (Piaget 1985, 19). This form of abstraction, similar to in some ways to assimilation (see Piaget 2001, 22), makes sense of the senses by a more or less guided act of noticing. Guided by existing schemes, the subject *abstracts* the properties of interest in observables. But this form of abstraction is tied to sensations and actions and limited to the application of existing schemes. Thus, it depends upon the prior accomplishments of reflective abstraction, which consists of, to follow the phrasing above, a subject's reading of their own actions and coordinations.

This process of *seeing important properties of what one is doing* is where new structures come from. In essence, reflective abstraction takes as an object the very acts by which the subject understands the world and this brings new meaning to those acts by grasping them and reconstructing them. To speak loosely, what was once a part of the subject's understanding becomes an object to the subject's understanding. For example, very young children understand objects and people by acting with them physically, arranging and relating to them variously, and generally exploring their properties with sensorimotor schemes. After sufficient experience and activity, these schemes become increasingly interrelated, as the child is compelled to make use of some types at certain times as opposed to others. The degree to which the child notices this patterned variability in their own behavior is the degree to which they have reflectively abstracted more general ways to organize and understand their own actions. Now, there is "bedtime" and "eating," which exist as higher-order integrations of diverse sensorimotor schemes. This restructuring opens up whole new worlds. The child can pretend to eat or sleep when it is not actual time to or adapt new approaches to "hide-and-go-seek" in light of a fixed overarching goal.

Piaget (2001) maintained that this type of process goes all the way up. Specifically (no surprise here), he saw the formalizations of mathematics and logic as the ultimate culmination of this process. And while the elaboration of these formal systems is seemingly endless (e.g., Godel's theorem) they nevertheless signify the *completion* of basic equilibration processes insofar as they exemplify a radical separation of form from content. With this focus on mathematics and logic, Piaget unduly circumscribes the explanatory scope of some of his key concepts, like reflective abstraction. Of course, it could be maintained (see Smith 1993) that Piaget was not interested in explaining things outside the acquisition of "necessary knowledge." But that is beside the point. Regardless, we must look elsewhere if we are out to explain more than the emergence of formal hypothetical-deductive operations.

Several theorists have taken the idea of reflective abstraction (or conceptions inspired thereby) and made it a key mechanism in intellectual development (Campbell and Bickhard 1986; Case 1985; Commons, Trudeau, Stein, Richards, and Krause 1998; Fischer 1980). Looking across all these models, it would appear that the notion of *hierarchal integration* is the modern equivalent of reflective abstraction. A difference of emphasis is clear, but the same basic micro-developmental process is being noticed. Adopting Fischer's (1980) language, this is a process whereby qualitatively new skills emerge via the "intercoordination" or "compounding" of previously existing skills. As in the process of reflective abstraction, skills that were previously employed and focused on independently come to be coordinated and eventually fused into some more complex skill. This results in a hierarchy of increasingly complex skills. While Piaget still breathed, Fischer (1980) outlined the contours of this complexity hierarchy, offering a general model "specifying a universe of possible skill structures [and related] transformation rules" (48) in which the process of *hierarchal integration* took center stage. But unlike Piaget's model, which channels all transformations toward the *telos* of logical and mathematical formalizations, Fischer's model has more pluralistic implications.

So far, our account of Fischer's model has focused on the notions of *skill* and *hierarchical integration*: the former being the most basic *unit,* the latter being the most basic *process*. When combined, we get a model suggesting that human development is best understood in terms of diverse *hierarchies of skills.* As noted above, skills can be analyzed in terms of structure and function. A functional analysis entails specifying the various roles and uses skills have in the overall behavioral economy of the organism. Here, we differentiate skills according to functional role. When taking up a fine-grained level of analysis, skills cluster into domains defined by the specific type of task, but at more general levels of analyses, they cluster into more classical functional categories, for example, intelligence, emotion, interpersonal, etc. (i.e., Wilber's *lines*).

A structural analysis of skills entails locating skills in a "universe of possible skill structures," which is a scale of complexity specified in terms of recursive *hierarchical integrations* (Fischer and Bidell 2006; Fischer 1980). This "common skill scale" (Fischer and Bidell 2006) has been refined in light of decades of research. And techniques of structural analysis have been likewise refined (Stein and Heikkinen 2008). A crucial innovation in this respect was Dawson's work building the Lectical™ Assessment System (the LAS), which refined the developmental analysis of linguistic performances (Dawson-Tunik 2005). Overall, decades of research have yielded a well-specified metric, the LAS, capable of measuring performances across almost the full range of possible skill structures, from *actions* and *representations* through *abstractions* to *principles*.[5]

The terms just listed are known as tiers; they signify major reorganizations of action and thought, that is, the emergence of qualitatively new types of skills. Within the tiers, there are levels of increasing elaboration and complexity of coordination, from single elements, to linear combinations, to multivariate systems. As these systems become increasingly elaborated and numerous, major hierarchical integrations take place, constructing a qualitatively new type of skill that effectively "chunks" a whole system of lower-level skills. Think back to the example explaining reflective abstraction in which various sensorimotor schemes were eventually subsumed under the single representation "bedtime." Major hierarchical integrations of this type mark the transition to a new tier and the beginning of a new series of levels of elaboration. Below is quick tour of the skill scale and the levels measured by the LAS, which begin at the representational tier after the emergence of the semiotic function.[6]

The first tier is *actions*. *Actions* are first exercised independently, but then the various and disparate skilled actions at this level (e.g., reaching, grasping, looking, etc.) become combined and related into systems of actions that are, in a way, the sensorimotor characterization of objects, events, and significant conspecifics. These complex systems of actions are then available to be hierarchically integrated into single *representations*. This is the first major tier shift that has been widely researched (Piaget 1962; Fischer and Jennings 1981).

With the *representation* tier, we find the emergence of the "semiotic function" and the first interanimations of action, emotion, thought, and language. *Representations* are concepts about objects, others, and immediately observable scenes. They are classifications of the properties revealed via actual or possible *actions* on objects. Thus, they catalogue the most concrete types, classes, relations, and possibilities. For example, the *representation* "playtime" synthesizes and invokes a wide range of possible objects, scenes, and emotions. Knowing what "playtime" is means knowing that when it is "playtime," we do this and that and the other (all actual or possible sensorimotor actions). As more *representations* become available, they are combined in increasingly complex coordinations until systems of *representations* become available to be hierarchically integrated to *abstractions*. This is the second major tier shift and gives rise to a whole new array of intellectual and emotional orientations (Fischer, Hand, and Russell 1984; Case 1985; Inhelder and Piaget 1958).

At the *abstractions* tier, we find emergent functions on various fronts, including reflective identity formation and hypothetical-deductive orientations to knowledge. *Abstractions* are concepts that operate upon basic concrete types, classes, relations, and possibilities. That is, they classify and organize *representations* (which in turn classify and organize *actions*). Thus, *abstractions* catalogue general qualities that cut across concrete classes and disclose higher-order ensembles composed of various concrete relations. For example, the *abstraction* "personal integrity" combines and invokes not merely actions, but types of actions (e.g., truth telling, being fair) and not merely certain specific relationships but certain classes of relationships (e.g., good friends, helpful employees), and so on. As more *abstractions* become available, they are combined into increasingly complex coordinations, until systems of *abstractions* become available to be hierarchically integrated into *principles*. This is the third major tier shift and has been studied relatively little (Alexander and Langer 1990; Commons, Richards, and Armon 1984; Fischer and Yan 2002). It is characterizing the structures and functions of skills at this tier that occupy us when we study the "higher stages."

At the "higher stages"—the levels of the third tier (classically considered as second tier by the integral community)—we work to construct worldviews and philosophical frameworks, the consequences of which touch the core of our action orientations. Although empirical evidence is scant, it appears that *principles* guide the reflective self-regulation of entire disciplines and ethical communities and perform unique *discourse-regulative* function (see Sellers 2005). They have a structure that organizes whole systems of abstractions in terms of overarching constructs that are informational dense and dialectically rich (be they linguistic, conceptual, or graphical).

Figure 7.1 displays the core structure of the common metric targeted by the LAS as it lines up with a variety of other developmental assessment systems. This figure is provided only to help acquaint readers with the metric we employ. Given limitations of time and space I cannot go into the details about the validly and utility of the LAS here (for a thorough treatment see: Stein and Hiekkinen 2008; Dawson 2008).

Putting the Model and Metric to Work: Developmental Maieutics

Based on the combined insights and affordances of Fischer's *model* and Dawson's *metric* we have built a general and broad *method* for applying these tools in real world contexts of research and practice. *Developmental maieutics* (Dawson and Stein 2008) involves cycles of research and application using the LAS and its analytical accoutrements as a developmental assessment system and Dynamic Skill Theory as a developmental framework. This method is

Skill levels (Fischer)	GSSS (Commons)	SISS (Kohlberg)	GLSS (Armon)	RJ (Kitchener & King)	SOI (Kegan)	SD (Beck)	Perspective (Cook-Greuter)
14	principled systems	cross-paradigmatic					coral	cosmic
13	principled mappings	paradigmatic	stage 6		stage 6 & 7		global holistic	global/6th person
12	single principles	meta-systemic	stage 5	stage 5	stage 5	interindividual	systemic-integrative	5th person
11	abstract systems	systemic	stage 4	stage 4	stage 4	institutional	relativistic	4th person
10	abstract mappings	formal	stage 3	stage 3	stage 3	interpersonal	individualistic achiever	3rd person
9	single abstractions		stage 2				absolutist	
8	representational systems	concrete		stage 2		imperial	power gods	2nd person
7	representational mappings	primary	stage 1				magical-animistic	
6	single representations	pre-operational		stage 1		impulsive		1st person
5	sensorimotor systems	sentential						
4	sensorimotor mappings	nominal						
3	single sensori-motor actions	sensory-motor						
2	reflexive systems	circular sensory & motor						
1	reflexive mappings	sensory & motor						
0	single reflexes	calculatory						

Figure 7.1 Displaying how the LAS lines up with other systems

the latest in more than a century of efforts at tying developmental theory to practice and reform in education. It implicates a set of perennial themes in this regard.

Concerns about the relationship between education and psychology date to the birth of psychology as a discipline (James 1899). Baldwin (1906) and Piaget (1979) were pioneering developmental approaches guided only by general theoretical interests, that is, they were not out to generate usable knowledge for educators. Piaget (1932; 1965) echoed James in his belief that the psychology of the laboratory could not simply be imported into the classroom. He argued—like Dewey (1929)—about the need for concerted collaborations between educators and researchers for psychology to become a relevant and effective source of knowledge. James, Baldwin, Dewey, and Piaget all envisioned a symbiotic relationship between psychologists and educators. Moving toward this vision of merging research and practice, specifically in the area of human development, is one of the goals of developmental maieutics.

Another goal is the generation of a specific type of usable knowledge about human development: *learning sequences.* A learning sequence (also known as a developmental pathway or learning progression) is an empirically grounded reconstruction of the steps or stages in the acquisition of a concept, skill, or capability. That is, it is a rational reconstruction of how a specific *line* of development unfolds. Well-conceived learning sequences can be used to improve our understanding of human development, craft curricula, inform assessment, and characterize education and learning at all levels in all contexts.

It was Baldwin (1906) who first articulated a speculative vision about the structure and dynamics of human development wherein different types of concepts and skills developed in different ways. In his wake, others have expressed similar ideas. For example, Werner (1948) offered a sophisticated model in which numerous and heterogeneous psychological processes developed in a nonsynchronic fashion, but according to common processes of differentiation and integration. And while most would assume that Piaget thought nothing of the sort, Chapman (1988) demonstrated that Piaget's views regarding *the structure of the whole* are far from clear. Piaget's books are filled with research tracing the distinct developmental trajectories of very specific concepts, such as causality and justice. Again, the image is of different abilities developing along different pathways, each capable of being reconstructed as learning sequence.

More recently, Fischer and his colleagues (Fischer and Biddell 2006) have placed learning sequences at the heart of a wide array of discourses concerning human development. Researchers from various camps have been building learning sequences using different methods based on different theoretical assumptions. All this work has yielded a dynamic picture of cognitive developmental processes where context sensitivity and variability is key (Rappolt-Schichtmann et al. 2007). The acquisition of skills in any domain involves a set of possible learning sequences along which individuals show differentiated, dynamic, and nonsynchronic development trajectories. Recently these various efforts have begun to dovetail, in part as a result of empirical progress and in part as a result of the trajectory of international educational reforms calling for curricula that promote deeper conceptual understanding, especially in the areas of science, critical thinking, social skills, and citizenship (e.g., OECD 2007). It is in this tradition that we understand the construction of the learning sequences that form a fundamental part of the approach we offer.

Our attempts to combine these two themes has generated a broad method for systematically producing usable knowledge about learning sequences via the collaboration of practitioners and researchers with interests in human development. So we have an educationally oriented cognitive developmental perspective in which the promotion of optimal learning involves understanding:

- the developmental pathways through which concepts typically and optimally develop;
- the particular sub-concepts required to construct increasingly adequate understandings at each new developmental level;

- the range of sub-concepts required for an optimal understanding of a given concept;
- effective methods for developing these concepts; and
- accurate and reliable assessments of conceptual development that can be employed by classroom teachers. (Dawson and Stein 2008, 92)

We gain this type of understanding by moving through the steps of an iteratively structured collaborative research endeavor (see Figure 7.2). The approach begins with the establishment of a collaborative relationship with teachers (or practitioners of various types with interests in human development, e.g., coaches, therapists, etc.), with whom we select domains and problems worthy of attention. We then construct a rough sense of the selected domain based on existing knowledge. This entails a hypothetical *horizontal reconstruction* of the domain, which outlines the array of lines or skill sets implicated by the domain. We also generate hypothetical *vertical reconstructions* of the domain, which outline certain *levels* in learning sequences that are of interest. In the next section I presents our hypotheses about the structure of the domain of ITP. We use this rough sense of the levels and lines in the domain to build a set of developmental assessments that gear into relevant parts of the domain. These assessments generate data about the domain that we can use to generate empirically grounded rational reconstructions of the set of learning sequences that comprise the domain.

In Figure 7.2 the method employed to describe the learning sequences is represented in the small sub-spiral to the right of the main figure. The maieutic approach to identifying learning sequences involves submitting interview data to at least two forms of qualitative analysis. First, interview texts are independently analyzed for their developmental level using the LAS. Then we analyze their conceptual content by examining the specific meanings expressed in the performances. The results of these analyses are examined together to make inductive generalizations about trends in conceptual development, that is, learning sequences. Using this method, we have described learning sequences for conceptions of leadership, good education, epistemology, learning, morality, and the self, as well as for critical thinking, decision making, and problem solving (Dawson 2008; Dawson-Tunik and Stein 2004; 2004a; 2004b; 2006).

Based on our findings about the key learning sequences in the domain, we refine learning activities and build better assessments. At this point, our level of understanding about the development in the domain is such that we can design high quality online assessments for general use. We have already done this in the aforementioned domains. These online assessments also allow us to generating focused psychographs for large numbers of individuals across various contexts.

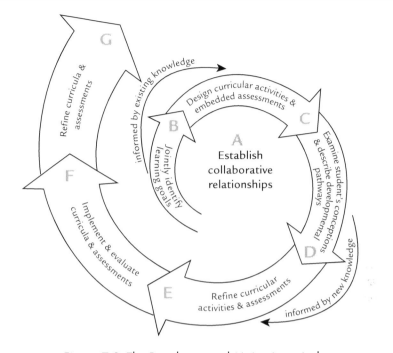

Figure 7.2 The Developmental Maieutics spiral

Rationally Reconstructing the Domain of Integral Theory and Practice

With this brief overview of the approach we take to developmental research, assessment, and application, it should be somewhat clear what we plan to do in the domain of ITP through the development of a new assessment: Lectical Integral Model Assessment (LIMA). The LIMA is one of many assessments constructed by the Developmental Testing Service. DTS specializes in the customized construction and deployment of developmental assessments based around a core psychological technology, the Lectical Assessment System (the LAS). Over the coming years DTS will be working with the LIMA in conjunction with John F. Kennedy University (JFKU) to build knowledge about the domain of Integral Theory and Practice, aiming ultimately at research-based integral designs for optimal educational environments.

The Integral model and its related ideas and practices constitute a unique and powerful domain of knowledge. Currently, a variety of educational initiatives exist aimed at fostering the growth of individuals through this complex arena of theory and practice. Thus, the LIMA has been designed to aid in these educational efforts. It has been built to measure developmental differences in the understanding of Integral Theory and Practice. Thus, it can provide useful insight into the sophistication of student performances, serving as a developmental assessment about the Integral model. In this capacity the LIMA measures student growth, enabling developmentally appropriate teaching and learning. But the LIMA has also been built to increase useable knowledge about the domain itself, enabling the construction of learning sequences for key areas. Studying student learning allows for the understanding of key sequences, confusions, and developmental phases, which can inform curriculum design and pedagogy.

We are looking to collaborate with students, teachers, and educational institutions in the domain of ITP in order to generate usable knowledge about key learning sequences and thus retool practitioners with assessments and information that can inform educative efforts on all fronts.[7] That means we are looking to generate empirically grounded rational reconstructions of the vertical and horizontal structure (i.e., the *levels and lines*) of the domain in order to build assessments that can be used to generate usable knowledge, for example, focused psychographs targeting the key themes of ITP. Both the assessments and the rational reconstructions will be useful for a variety of purposes.

In this section I will lay out some initial hypotheses concerning the general shape of the rational reconstructions we will be researching empirically. These hypotheses are meant to serve several functions. They serve as preliminary and tentative suggestions about what we might find, which help us build our initial assessments. They also serve as examples of the kind of usable knowledge we will produce after we have undertaken the first round of data collection and analysis. Following these speculations I will return to discuss certain practical applications and limitations of this approach.

The Horizontal Structure

Figure 7.3 displays the overarching horizontal structure of ITP as a domain. It is worth noting a few things about this way of conceiving the domain and about this figure. Generally when we approach a domain in order to rationally reconstruct its horizontal structure we aim to explicate at least three degrees of specificity: *sub-domains*, *themes*, and *conceptual strands/learning sequences* (see Dawson and Stein 2004; 2004b; 2008). Even when these divisions are empirically grounded there is nothing fixed or final about this way of slicing up the key dimensions of a domain. The task is fundamentally pragmatic and problem-focused. The idea is to explicate the implicit structural differentiations in a domain of knowledge so that we can build targeted assessments of *relatively* independent clusters of concepts and skills. The question is not about whether this is *the* actual structure of the domain (could such a question ever be answered in domains of knowledge that shift and evolve?). Rather, the question is whether this is a useful way of dividing up the domain for purposes of assessment and pedagogy.

The specific structure sketched in Figure 7.3 is extremely provisional. Future empirical work will flush out the details, particularly where things get most specific. The question of what the key *conceptual strands* and *learning sequences* are is almost entirely an empirical question. We need to bootstrap these dimensions of the domain out of actual performances of understanding by individuals at various levels as they reason about key themes in ITP.

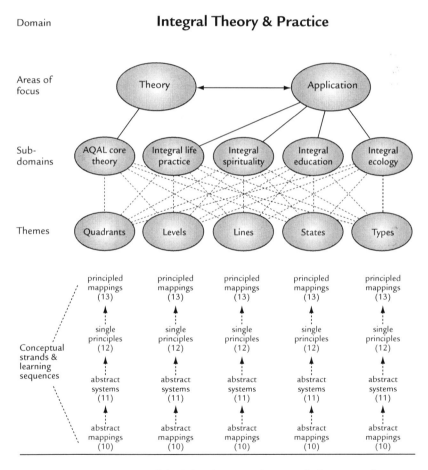

Figure 7.3 A tentative model of the domain of Integral Theory and Practice

The Learning Sequences

Given this general structure we can hone in on sets of specific conceptual strands falling under each theme, which unfold as learning sequences. Table 7.1 presents two hypothetical learning sequences for the themes of *quadrants* and *levels.*

True learning sequences are empirically grounded rational reconstructions tracing the development of key sets of conceptual strands and skills. As explained above, we generate learning sequences by employing a multidimensional methodology to analyze performances of understanding regarding key themes (i.e., interviews, written essays, etc.). This method is one part developmental assessment (using the LAS), one part conceptual coding, and one part inductive reconstructive technique. The learning sequences presented above are based entirely on the third moment of this methodology, that is, they are inductive reconstructions based on my familiarity with the discourse surrounding ITP. Nevertheless, they are accurate enough for our purposes here. They provide a sense of the *range* of possible understandings about these key themes in ITP. Of course, the idea is that for every theme we would describe sequences across the wide range of issues in ITP. Thus, in light of our view of development, the domain is very complex and dynamic with a variety of learning sequences along which individuals can progress at different rates (see figures 7.4, 7.5, and 7.6 below).

It is important to understand that learning sequences are *distilled* out of the complex dynamics of actual developmental processes. They present development in terms of discrete levels and differentiated lines, when in reality lines interweave and development across levels is nonlinear and messy. So, the learning sequences presented above should be understood as *woven* into the broader fabric of reasoning about ITP. Thinking horizontally, it is hard to say where reasoning about the *quadrants* starts and reasoning about *IMP* ends, or where reasoning about *levels* sets in and reasoning about *lines* phases out. Likewise, thinking vertically, the inter-animation of different sequences is a function of level, with new sequences emerging as development unfolds and connections between existing sequences becoming available as more complex capacities come on line, etc. In light of this dynamism, I think it is a mistake to set out looking for *the* actual structure (vertical and horizontal) of the domain. I think we need to proceed in a problem-focused manner (Dawson, Fischer, and Stein 2007), and hone in on the best way to reconstruct the domain for our purposes. What we are looking to do is build assessments that can inform educative efforts on all fronts at all levels. This is particularly true for the MA in Integral Theory at JFKU but extends beyond to any educational context that is using Integral Theory.

Level	Reasoning about the Quadrants	Reasoning about Levels of Development
Principled Mappings	At this level, reasoning about the *quadrants* involves a radical and quasi-transcendental multi-perspectivalism, which is made explicit in terms of a widely applicable post-metaphysical mode of meta-theoretical argumentation. In light of this background, attention is brought to the provisional nature of all methods and models, especially meta-theoretical ones. Integral Theory is broadly construed as a polycentric and evolving network of ideas catalyzed by certain highly normative principles and practices (e.g. IMP, *non-exclusion, enactment enfoldment,* etc.).	At this level, reasoning about *levels* involves the adoption of a post-metaphysical stance toward the task of evaluating people. The provisional, bounded, and multi-perspectival nature of all models and methods is admitted and a set of meta-theoretical principles guides a recursive process of continually refining developmental models and methods in terms of both theory and practice. A broad and explicit philosophical discourse comes to supplement evaluate discussions concerning the notion of "growth to goodness," as the human potentials that characterize the highest levels and the future of civilization are seen as collective constructions for which we are responsible.
Single Principles	At this level, reasoning about the *quadrants* involves an emphasis on their world-disclosing and epistemological significance. They are taken as representing deep-seated aspects of human thought and practice. Explicit appeals are made to various comparable frameworks and the quadrants are thus understood in terms of a broad historical and evolutionary context. Thus Integral Theory is seen as the leading edge of a socio-cultural movement emphasizing comprehensive approaches to pressing problems and the integration of science and religion.	At this level, reasoning about *levels* involves explicit ideas about the limits and affordances of different developmental methods and models, which are framed in terms of arguments about the conditions enabling their valid use (i.e. scoring systems, interview procedures, etc.). The idea of "growth to goodness" is problematized both by concerns over issues of horizontal health and intra-personal variability, and by concerns about the accuracy of different assessment methods. These complexities of method and application temper and complicate speculation on how developmental levels are implicated in a broad range of global problems.
Abstract Systems	At this level, reasoning about the *quadrants* involves a differentiation between their use as simple categories and their use as lenses or perspectives (i.e. *quadriva*). Appeals are made to the theorists, methods, and personal pronouns (I-WE-IT) identified with each quadrant, which begins a focus on the quadrants as *perspectives*. Attention is typically brought to the practical efficacy of applying the quadrants, in personal practice, business, and academia. Creative application is common. Also, the complex ways in which the quadrants frame other core elements of Integral Theory are elaborated; the internal consistency of Integral Theory as a whole is treated as a given.	At this level, reasoning about *levels* involves giving some primacy to the construct of *altitude*, which frames and organizes a variety of developmental models. Persons are understood in terms of their relative development in various *lines*, which are identified with the different developmental models and theorists. The concept of a *center of gravity* supplements this differentiated view and justifies whole person assessments. The relation between levels and other aspects of Integral Theory becomes explicit; the relation between *states* and *levels* complicates the simple notion that spirituality is "at the top." Generally, there are elaborate ideas about how developmental levels are implicated in all kinds of issues (politics, religion, ecology, etc.).
Abstract Mappings	At this level, the *quadrants* are treated as simple categories into which different objects or events can be placed. Classic dichotomies are established in terms of the quadrants: Science is on right, Religion is on the left; Reason on the right, Feeling on the left; Body on the right, Mind on the left, etc. Generally the quadrants are taken as representing the existence of different kinds of *stuff* (i.e. they are read as an ontology). And Integral Theory is taken as a comprehensive map of what there is.	At this level, *developmental levels* are treated like simple stereotypes. Whole persons are classed as being *at* a level, which is typically understood in terms of a single developmental model (e.g. Spiral Dynamics). Development is understood as a kind of simple "growth to goodness", with ignorance at the bottom, science in the middle, and spirituality at the top. Particular levels gain more attention than others and function as more or less entrenched stereotypes, expressing preferences that are not necessarily developmental (e.g. "you are so green").

Table 7.1 Two hypothetical learning sequences for the themes of quadrants and levels

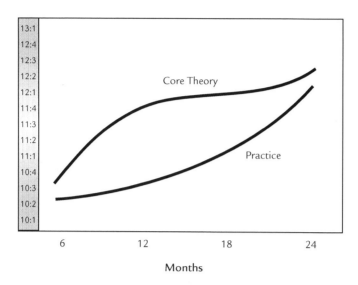

Figure 7.4 Diachronic psychograph focused on areas
of Core Theory and Practice in domain of ITP

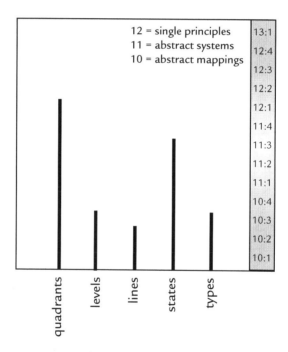

Figure 7.5 Synchronic psychograph focused on a set
of themes in Core Theory

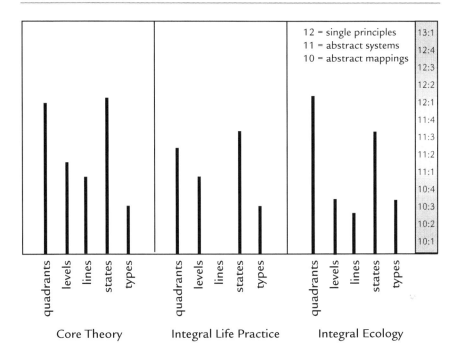

Figure 7.6 Synchronic psychograph focused on set of themes
in both Core Theory and two applied contexts

The Psychographs

The assessments we envision would, roughly speaking, generate a variety of *focused psychographs* (for the types of psychographs that can be generated using this method see Stein and Heikkinen 2008). Figures 7.4, 7.5, and 7.6 give a sense of the kind of psychographs that would ultimately result from this trajectory of research and application.

These psychographs are relatively self-explanatory, but I will note a few things about them before moving on to address larger issues of research, assessment, application, and the future of Integral Education. The diachronic psychograph (Figure 7.4) is admittedly vague. But the point should be clear. Development is dynamic and progress in some learning sequences will outpace progress in others. The implicit hypothesis presented in Figure 7.4 (and Figure 7.6) is that understandings of Core Theory set the pace for the progress of understandings in applied contexts. And the hypothesis implicit in all three figures is that, regardless of the area, development unfolds differentially across different themes, that is, that individuals will be at different levels in their understanding of different conceptual strands in ITP. Both of these hypotheses are amenable to future empirical validation. And I think they will be shown to be more or less correct. In my experience, most individuals involved with ITP are more developed in their understanding of the *quadrants* than they are in their understanding of *levels* and *states*, for example, and they are more developed in their understanding of theoretical issues than issues in applied contexts.

In any case, as sophisticated as these psychographs appear, they are relatively straightforward to generate given the requisite research and the building of appropriate assessments. Comparable psychographs are available now in a variety of domains thanks to efforts at the Developmental Testing Service (go to: www.devtestservice.org). Of course, assessments can be put to use in different ways. As I discussed above, the *Developmental Maieutic* approach is predicated on our beliefs about the necessity of wedding developmental research and assessment with educational interventions and reforms. This leads us to a few reflections about the implications of generating this kind of usable knowledge in the domain of ITP.

Conclusion

> . . . every object rightly seen, unlocks a new faculty of the soul. That which was unconscious truth, becomes, when interpreted and defined, a part of the domain of knowledge—a new weapon in the magazine of power.
>
> .   —R.W. Emerson (Nature)

Let us return briefly to the content of the learning sequences presented above. The types of developmental differences outlined there are clearly significant. There are real differences between individuals who understand the *quadrants* as parts of a new worldview created by a *Wizard,* and individuals who understand the *quadrants* as a provisional explication of certain metatheoretical principles that are a contemporary expression of perennial philosophical themes, or echoes of *the mighty dead* reverberating through a polycentric network of contemporary thought-leaders. Likewise, there are real differences between individuals who understand developmental *levels* as value-laden stereotypes for ranking people, and individuals who understand *levels* as methodologically disclosed and error-prone characterizations of a radically complex space of possibilities and potentials, with nonobvious evaluative and prescriptive import. While we should not dismiss the moments of truth in the lower-level conceptualizations in either learning sequence, we must nevertheless grapple with this *range* of conceptions about the ideas in the domain of ITP.

Moreover, once our assessments get built and refined it will be relativity easy to generate a focused psychograph concerning the distribution of an individual's reasoning capabilities in the domain of ITP. That is, we will know who is developed in their thinking about Integral issues, and who is not. The psychographs presented above are just a taste of the kinds of individualized assessments and concomitant feedback modalities we will be able to generate once research efforts are in full swing.

We will need to be very careful with how we use this knowledge. On the whole, we tend to use developmental assessments irresponsibly (Stein 2008). We use them to categorize and stereotype people and to justify value-based preferences for in-group norms. That is, we do not think in a developed enough way about the meaning of development. A look at the learning sequences presented above suggests that we tend to think about development in Abstract Mappings terms. Now, here my argument is starting to eat its own tail, as the learning sequences are being fed back into the domain for quality control purposes. This aligns with Habermas's (1990) contention that rational reconstructions can serve a *critical* and *constructive* function. When we step back and take a look at what we are doing, we are prone to want to change it for the better.

From where I sit, the implications of all developmental differences should be understood in the context of education. We should tie assessments into our educative efforts at all levels. This means that when we use a developmental assessment to get or give feedback about individual development—or when we are just thinking in developmental terms about an issue or problem—we should frame things in terms of possible and preferable educational interventions. This is the broad vision of the developmental maieutic approach and it is justified methodologically, pragmatically, and ethically. This is the aim and of JFKU's cutting edge and ambitious iTEACH project.[8]

If we admit the provisional and error-prone nature of all developmental assessments then we must never use them merely to categorize individuals. Instead, we should employ developmental assessments to help people learn, all the while keeping one eye on the validity of the assessment itself. Doing this means having some humility about what our assessments can tell us and maintaining a desire to engage in the continual self-correction of our methods and metrics. Theoretically and methodologically we face a *need* for iterative problem-focused and practice-oriented developmental research in which assessments and educational interventions mutually inform one another. If we take up a postmetaphysical view, then we should arrange to use our assessments in situations that allow us to monitor their validity and usefulness. Educational contexts are ideal because they serve as natural experiments. We disclose the interior of the individual with our metric, then we enact a change to try to promote development, see what happens, and are made aware of the limits of our world-disclosing framework. So we retool and try again. There are complex methodological techniques for doing just this, which stem from and can be justified in terms of postmodern psychometric theory (see Fisher 2004; 2005). A postmetaphysical stance toward developmental assessment requires us to remain open to the continual need to improve our metric in light of the contingences encountered in the field.

But there are also ethical and pragmatic reasons for wedding developmental research to educative efforts. As noted above, for more than a century philosophers, psychologists, and educators have been saying that improving the effectiveness of educational endeavors at all levels requires a radical symbiosis of practice, theory, and research. It is hard to disagree when one looks at the ineffectiveness of so much education and the lack of real-world traction that hinders so many developmental theories. If we combine this insight with Wilber's Basic Moral Imperative—that we should work to promote the greatest development (depth) for the largest number of people (span)—then it is hard to see why we would build developmental assessments *just* to rank people (say, for hiring and firing purposes). We should do developmental research and build developmental assessments in order to find better ways to promote development.

In the domain of ITP these efforts are just getting underway. Of course, as this movement looks in the mirror, developmental issues are only one small part of the self-critical self-application of the theory that should be taking place. For example, our measurements of understanding need to be supplemented by measures of action; we can measure the *talk*, but what about the *walk*. Likewise, there are a variety of other dimensions to this endeavor, including organizational dynamics, contemplative practices, and the health of the body, etc. Multiple research efforts need to be underway.

Nevertheless, building knowledge about developmental differences in the understanding of ITP will be particularly important. The most obvious application of this usable knowledge will be in explicitly educational contexts, such the MA program in Integral Theory at JFKU. In this kind of context, where ITP is being specifically taught, the focused psychographs will be invaluable for monitoring student progress (and for students in monitoring their own progress). But we will also be generating knowledge about how the most basic concepts in ITP are learned, which will be invaluable for pedagogical purposes. In particular, reconstructing learning sequences gives us insight into the hierarchical structure of the domain, allowing us to determine which concepts serve as prerequisites for the learning of others. With this knowledge we can build developmentally appropriate curricula. In general, we will be yielding important insights into how to best teach ITP.

Insights into how to best teach ITP clearly bleed over into concerns about how to best execute its broader dissemination. Knowledge about developmental differences in how people grasp and use key concepts in ITP could be used to refine and structure the various media providers and large-scale initiatives aimed at bringing Integral to the general public. For example, gaining a sense about the most typical misconceptions, downward assimilations, and misuses could allow us to cut them off at the pass, with targeted interventions geared into specific aspects of the domain shown to cause common confusion. We will be able to locate the level and line where, for example, it is believed that cultural development and individual development are more or less isomorphic. Then we could counteract this frequent and problematic misconception with information tailored to the array of concepts available at that level, thus building developmentally appropriate tactics for the infusion of ITP into the culture at large.

Finally, issues of education and dissemination aside, the knowledge we will generate about ITP as a domain might help us better deal with the discourse itself, as the task-demands and complexity of trafficking in integral ideas become clear. Generally speaking, there are no shared quality control standards for metatheoretical and interdisciplinary work (Stein 2007). Building standards for work in a field as complex as ITP requires flushing out the different streams of discourse—as Peirce did for pragmatism—and admitting that while we may be using the same words, we are often talking past one another. That is, Integral interlocutors need to be at comparable levels of complexity to be arguing at all; for example, most of Wilber's critics take his ideas at a level or two below where he offers them. The range of possible ways to understand the nature of *levels* is another case in point. Most of the postmodernist critiques are targeting a straw man, because they are talking about *levels* at Abstract Mappings, when any developmentalist worth their salt would talk about levels at Single Principles and beyond.

In any case, it has been my goal here to offer only first approximations and hypotheses about this important area of inquiry. As the broad research initiative unfolds, we will see what this first story is worth. One thing is for sure, however. What Integral Theory and Practice was is not what it will be after these first acts of critical self-reflection.

Notes

I received invaluable help from Dr. Theo Dawson and from Katie Heikkinen. I would also like to thank Sean Esbjörn-Hargens and Mark Forman for their efforts in organizing the conference at which this chapter was originally presented, and Sean for editing this volume.

1. I use ITP to stand for approaches stemming from Wilber's work. But one hypothesis offered below suggests that a certain type of "post-conventionalism" characterizes the

higher levels of reasoning about ITP, i.e., as development unfolds, simple appeals to authority wane, and individuals justify their views in light of a polycentric network of thought-leaders.

2. For a fuller discussion of the differences between models and metrics see Z. Stein and K. Hiekkinen (2009).

3. It is important to note in this context that Piaget's broad vision of multilevel self-organization processes (i.e., equilibration) is comparable to the Wilber's Twenty Tenets.

4. There are various related terms and processes such as *reflecting abstraction* and *meta-reflection*, the introduction of which would unnecessarily complicate our account; this is not a chapter on Piaget. So we are telling a simpler story than Piaget would, but then, aren't we always?

5. Importantly, Fischer, Dawson, and Commons acknowledged that they were honing in on the domain-general *shape of development* (see Dawson-Tunik et al. 2005). This means we can align various skills along a common metric, and yet still admit they are "apples and oranges" with regard to their content. Baldwin first hit upon this, and we traced a line from him through Piaget, Werner, and Kohlberg down to Fischer, where we found an image of multifarious skills, each defined in terms of content and context, any of which can be measured in terms of *a common metric*, e.g., the general properties of the skill's structure. The LAS (Dawson 2008) is an explication of this *common metric* implicit in the various models.

6. For the limits of the LAS in its relation to nonverbal performances, see Stein and Heikkinen (2008).

7. For the next two years (2010–2012) we will be looking for high school and undergraduate classrooms that would like to participate in this research as well as expert integral scholar-practitioners from various domains. If you are interested in taking the LIMA please contact Theo Dawson at theo@devtestservice.org.

8. To learn more about the iTEACH project visit the Integral Research Center (www.integralresearchcenter.org).

References

Alexander, C. N., and E. J. Langer. (Eds.) 1990. *Higher stages of human development: Perspectives on adult growth*. New York: Oxford University Press.

Baldwin, J. M. [1906] 1975. *Thought and things: A study in the development of meaning and thought or genetic logic* (Vol. 1–4). New York: Macmillan.

Campbell, R. L., and M. H. Bickhard. 1986. Knowing levels and developmental stages. *Contributions to Human Development* 16: 146.

Case, R. 1985. *Intellectual development: Birth to adulthood*. New York: Academic Press.

Chapman, M. 1988. *Constructive evolution: Origins and development of Piaget's thought*. New York: Cambridge University Press.

Commons, M. L., and F. A. Richards. 1984. A general model of stage theory. In *Beyond formal operations: Late adolescent and adult cognitive development*, ed. M. L. Commons, F. A. Richards, and C. Armon, 120–41). New York: Praeger.

———. (1984). Applying the general stage model. In *Beyond formal operations: Late adolescent and adult cognitive development*, ed. M. L. Commons, F. A. Richards, and C. Armon, 141–58). New York: Praeger.

Commons, M. L., E. J. Trudeau, S. A. Stein, F. A. Richards, and S. R. Krause. 1998. Hierarchical complexity of tasks shows the existence of developmental stages. *Developmental Review* 18: 237–78.

Commons, M. L., F. A. Richards, and C. Armon. (Eds.) 1984. *Beyond formal operations.* New York: Praeger.

Dawson, T. L. 2001. Layers of structure: A comparison of two approaches to developmental assessment. *Genetic Epistemologist* 29: 1–10.

———. 2002a. New tools, new insights: Kohlberg's moral reasoning stages revisited. *International Journal of Behavioral Development* 26: 154–66.

———. 2002b. A comparison of three developmental stage scoring systems. *Journal of Applied Measurement* 3(2): 146–89.

———. 2003. A stage is a stage is a stage: A direct comparison of two scoring systems. *Journal of Genetic Psychology* 164: 335–64.

———. 2004. Assessing intellectual development: Three approaches, one sequence. *Journal of Adult Development* 11(2): 71–85.

———. 2008. The Lectical™ Assessment System. Retrieved July 15, 2008, from http://www. lectica.info.

———, K. W. Fischer, and Z. Stein. 2006. Reconsidering qualitative and quantitative research approaches: A cognitive developmental perspective. *New Ideas in Psychology* 24: 229–39.

———, and Z. Stein. 2008. Cycles of research and application in science education. *Mind, Brain, and Education* 2(2): 90–103.

———, and Z. Stein. 2004. *National decision-making curriculum: A framework.* Hatfield, MA: Developmental Testing Service, LLC.

———, and Z. Stein. 2006. *Decision-making curriculum. Results of the pre- and post instruction developmental assessments with control group.* Hatfield, MA: Developmental Testing Service, LLC.

Dawson-Tunik, T. L. 2004c. "A good education is . . ." The development of evaluative thought across the life-span. *Genetic, Social, and General Psychology Monographs* 130(1); 4–112.

———, and Z. Stein. 2004a. *Critical thinking seminar pre and post assessment results.* Hatfield, MA: Developmental Testing Service, LLC.

———. 2004b. *National leadership study results.* Hatfield, MA: Developmental Testing Service, LLC.

———, M. L. Commons, M. Wilson, and K. W. Fischer. 2005. The shape of development. *The International Journal of Cognitive Development* 2: 163–96.

Dewey, J. 1929. *Sources of a science of education.* New York: Liveright.

Fischer, K. 1980. A theory of cognitive development: The control and construction of hierarchies of skills. *Psychological Review* 87(6): 477–531.

———. (1983). Illuminating the processes of moral development: A commentary. In A longitudinal study of moral judgment, ed. A. Colby, L. Kohlberg, J. Gibbs, and M. Leibermans. *Monographs of the Society for Research in Child Development* 48: 97–107.

———, and T. Bidell. 2006. Dynamic development of psychological structures in action and thought. In *Handbook of child psychology: Theoretical models of human development* (Vol. 1), ed. W. Damon and R. Lerner, 1–62. New York: Wiley.

Fischer, K.W., H. H. Hand, and S. Russell. 1984. The development of abstractions in adolescence and adulthood. In *Beyond formal operations*, ed. M. Commons, F.A. Richards, and C. Armon, 43–73. New York: Praeger.

Fischer, K. W., and S. Jennings. 1981. The emergence of representation in search: Understanding the hider as an independent agent. *Developmental Review* 1: 18–30.

Fischer, K. W., and B. Kennedy. 1997. Tools for analyzing the many shapes of development: The case of self-in-relationships in Korea. In *Change and development: Issues of theory, method, and application*, ed. E. Amsel and K. A. Renninger, 117–52). Mahwah, NJ: Lawrence Erlbaum.

Fischer, K. W., and Z. Yan. 2002. Darwin's construction of the theory of evolution: Microdevelopment of explanations of species variation and change. In *Microdevelopment*, ed. N. Granott and J. Parziale. Cambridge: Cambridge University Press.

Fisher, W. P. 2004. Meaning and method in the social sciences. *Human Studies* 27: 429–54.

———. 2005. Mathematics, measurement, metaphor, and metaphysics: Implications for method in post-modern science. *Theory and Psychology* 13(6): 753—90.

Forman, M., and S. Esbjörn-Hargens. 2008. The academic emergence of Integral Theory: Reflection on and clarifications of the first biennial Integral Theory Conference. Retrieved December 12, 2008, from www.integralworld.net.

Griffin, S., R. Case, and R. Siegler. 1994. Rightstart: Providing the central conceptual prerequisites for the first formal learning of arithmetic to students at risk for school failure. In *Classroom lessons: Integrating cognitive theory and classroom practice*, 25–49). Cambridge: MIT Press.

Habermas, J. 1990. Reconstruction and interpretation in the social sciences. Trans. Nicholsen. In *Moral consciousness and communicative action*, 21–43). Cambridge: MIT Press.

Inhelder, B., and J. Piaget. 1958. *The growth of logical thinking form childhood to adolescents*. Trans. Parsons and Milgram. New York: Basic Books.

James, W. [1899] 1992. *Talks to teachers*. New York: Library of America.

Organization for Economic Cooperation and Development. 2007. *PISA 2006: Science competencies for tomorrow's world (Vol. 1: Analysis)*. Paris: Organization for Economic Cooperation and Development.

Peirce, C. S. [1898] 1997. *Reasoning and the logical of things: The Cambridge conference lectures of 1898*. Cambridge: Harvard University Press.

———. [1903] 1992. *Pragmatism as the principle and method of right thinking: The 1903 Harvard lectures on pragmatism*. Albany: State University of New York Press.

Piaget, J. [1932] 1997. *The moral judgment of the child*. New York: Free Press.

———. 1962. *Play, dreams, and imitation in childhood* Trans. Gattegno and Hodgson. New York: Norton.

———. 1965. *Science of education and the psychology of the child*. New York: Viking Press.

———. 1977. *The essential Piaget: An interpretive reference guide*. Ed. H. E. Gruber and J. J. Voneche. New York: Basic Books.

———. 1978. *The principles of genetic epistemology*. New York: Basic Books.

———. 1985. *The equilibration of cognitive structures: The central problem of intellectual development*. Trans. T. Brown and K. J. Thampy. Chicago: The University of Chicago Press.

———.[1977] 2001. *Studies in reflecting abstraction* Trans. R. L. Campbell. Philadelphia: Psychology Press.

Rappolt-Schichtmann, G., H. R. Tennenbaum, M. F. Koepke, and K. W. Fischer. 2007. Transient and robust knowledge: contextual support and the dynamics of children's reasoning about density. In *Mind, Brain, and Education* 1(2): 98–108.

Sellars, W. 2005. *Pure pragmatics and possible worlds: The early essays of Wilfrid Sellars*. Atascadero, CA: Ridgeveiw Publishing.

Smith, L. 1993. *Necessary knowledge: Piagetian perspectives on constructivism*. Mahwah, NJ: Lawrence Erlbaum.

Stein, Z. 2007. Modeling the demands of interdisciplinarity: Toward a framework for evaluating interdisciplinary endeavors. *Integral Review* 4: 91–107.

———. 2008. Myth-busting and metric making: Refashioning the discourse about development. Excursus for Integral Leadership Review. *Integral Leadership Review* 8(5).

———, and K. Hiekkinen. 2008. On operationalizing aspects of altitude: An introduction to the Lectical Assessment System for integral researchers. *Journal of Integral Theory and Practice* 3(1): 105–38.

———, and K. Hiekkinen. 2009. Models, metrics, and measurement in developmental psychology. *Integral Review* 5(1): 4–24.

Werner, H. 1948. *Comparative psychology of mental development*. Chicago: Follett.

## 8

The Final Cause of Cosmic Development

Nondual Spirit or the Second Law of Thermodynamics?

Michael E. Zimmerman

Who knows, perhaps *telos*, perhaps Eros, moves the entire Kosmos, and God may indeed be an all-embracing chaotic Attractor, acting, as Whitehead said, throughout the world by gentle persuasion toward love.

—Ken Wilber, *Sex, Ecology, Spirituality*

Evolution . . . is the Universe's devious route to its own negation.

—Stanley N. Salthe, "The Spontaneous
Origin of New Levels in Scalar Hierarchy"

So, we are in a world that, in effect, does not want to be—a world of massive objects that destroy and replace each other incessantly in a perpetual dance of Shiva.

—Stanley N. Salthe, "The Cosmic Bellows"

An important function of Integral Theory is to provide a coherent narrative of cosmic, terrestrial, and human development. Ideally, such a narrative is informed by multiple perspectives, including artistic, spiritual, ethical, scientific, and political. We should assess such narratives in regard to their comprehensiveness, their capacity to orient in a time of confusion, their ability to inspire commitment to a workable future, and their willingness to accept with equanimity the fact that things often do not turn out the way we would prefer. In the past two decades, many useful cosmic narratives have appeared, some more integrative than others.[1] In this chapter, I will examine another cosmic narrative, this one constructed by a remarkably well-informed integral thinker, Stanley N. Salthe, *emeritus* professor of evolutionary biology at City University of New York.

Salthe's views are largely unknown in integral circles, because he has published primarily in technical scientific journals and monographs. I first encountered his voluminous writings five years ago, when researching *Integral Ecology* (2009), a book that I co-authored with Sean Esbjörn-Hargens. Approaching Salthe's work from an integral standpoint, I was struck by the many ways in which his ideas dovetailed with those of Wilber and a number of other integral theories. In addition to having made significant contributions to hierarchy theory, which has much in common with Wilber's discourse about holons and holarchy, Salthe contends that hierarchy can model a developmental trajectory, from the physical to the biological to the mental. Additionally, Salthe adheres to pan-semiotics and possibly pan-experientialism, because he believes that antecedents for human consciousness must already be present at the lowest integrative level, the physical. That Salthe arrived independently at ideas that overlap with such crucial aspects of the AQAL matrix reinforced for me the conceptual value of that matrix.

The centerpiece of Salthe's cosmic myth is the Second Law of Thermodynamics, understood as a universal cosmic attractor that draws all organized form toward dissolution, or entropy. In a startling move, Salthe—along with a number of his contemporaries—adds that the Second Law not only generates entropy, but also gives rise to forms that assist in the entropy-generating process. Indeed, according to Salthe, the Second Law is the final cause of form in the universe! As forms develop and thus become more complex, they acquire other final causes, but forms will always be entrained by the Second Law's behest to dissolve other instances of form—including all possible instances of organized energy. The idea that the Second Law is the final cause of form contrasts with views of a number of other integral thinkers, who suggest that divine Spirit, or cosmic Eros, is the final cause—the primal attractor—of form in the universe. Consider these remarks by Wilber, from the second edition of *Sex, Ecology, Spirituality* (SES):

> Uncreated Spirit, the causal unmanifest, is the nature and condition, the source and support, of this and every moment of evolution. . . .
>
> As the utterly Formless, it does not enter the stream of form at any point. And yet, as Ramana [Maharshi] said, there is a sense in which it is indeed the *summum bonum*, the ultimate Omega Point. . . .
>
> Thus, in the world of Form, the ultimate Omega appears as an ever-receding horizon of fulfillment . . . forever pulling us forward, forever retreating itself. . . . (Wilber 2000, 323, 324)

Despite initial appearances to the contrary, as we shall see, Salthe and Wilber turn out to agree in many respects about the final *causes* at work in cosmic development. In a universe characterized by the polarity of creation and destruction, one form arises and is devoured by the next, in the quest for fulfillment that can never be completely attained in the world of form. Salthe adds that such fulfillment is impossible because increasing specification means decreasing flexibility (S. Salthe, personal communication, June 30, 2008). Both thinkers recognize that the universe is awash in samsara, the ceaseless round of birth and death in the realm of matter and form. Salthe and Wilber also agree that contemplative practices allow for liberation from the ceaseless striving *to be* as well as from the yearning *not to be*, whether those yearnings are entrained by the Second Law or by nondual Spirit. In their forceful cosmic myths, Salthe and Wilber—each in his own way—recommend that while we put forth our best effort to creating a world that limits suffering, we ought not be attached to the fruits of such efforts. As we shall see, however, Salthe and Wilber disagree about certain important matters.

In what follows, I assume that the reader has a working knowledge of Wilber's Integral Theory.[2] I have based my analysis of Salthe's views on only a selective representation of his prodigious publications. His natural philosophy has emphasized scientific perspectives, in part because of his own training, in part because of the expectations of the venues in which he publishes. Nevertheless, as is clear to anyone familiar with his work, Salthe is well informed about art, music, literature, poetry, religion, philosophy, and other domains pertinent to integral theorizing and practice.

The Audience for Salthe's Cosmic Myth

Calling on Aristotle's philosophy, as well as the work of certain nineteenth-century philosophers and scientists, Salthe has revitalized natural philosophy by constructing an integral vision of nature and its development.[3] Influenced by postmodern epistemology, he states that for him nature does not mean an unmediated totality of matter, energy, and form "out there" and thus independent of us. Instead, nature refers to what shows up or is enacted through the models, theories, framings, and experiments generated by *observers*. Developing a scientifically and philosophically informed cosmic myth, which focuses primarily on middle-scale phenomena pertinent and accessible to humans, Salthe proposes both to explain why complex systems (including humans) put on such constant displays of creation and destruction, and to recommend how humankind might resist the pull to continue such displays, which are making the biosphere increasingly unsuitable for human life.

Salthe has made a name for himself in the scientific community not only by his work in hierarchy theory, but also in evolutionary theory, the standard version of which he has strongly criticized as being incapable of explaining the emergence of complex forms (Salthe 2002a). Salthe argues that additional factors—such as the Second Law—must be posited to account for developmental and directional trends in evolution. Given his critique of evolutionary theory, and his interest in renovating natural philosophy, we should not be surprised that he is something of a maverick in the scientific community, much of which remains attached to positivism, reductionism, and—Salthe opines— nihilism. Nevertheless, he describes his own position as a kind of materialism, influenced both by dialectical materialism and by Otto Neurath's vision of the unity of the sciences. Salthe directs his cosmic myth at scientists, who—in his view—do not always appreciate the nihilistic implications of their typically unarticulated natural philosophies. He argues not only that human activity is entrained by an attractor leading us to destroy the conditions for our own survival, but also that science plays a major role in enabling those destructive activities. Scientists who might otherwise balk at "New Age" recommendations, for example, engaging in contemplative practices to resist *consuming the planet*, might be more open to the suggested practices if it were presented in a rhetorically effective way, as in Salthe's scientifically grounded cosmic myth. Now, let us consider some of the chief features of this myth, features that resonate with key points of Integral Theory.

Hierarchies: Scalar and Specification

Drawing upon the work of Paul Weiss and Ludwig von Bertalanffy, Salthe argues that hierarchy theory offers an important way to interpret the interplay among levels in complex systems. (Salthe, n.d., 1983, 2001, 2005c, 1) There are two major kinds of hierarchies, scalar and specification. *Scalar* hierarchies, which represent a synchronic slice of a system, explain how a system maintains homeostasis in the face of perturbations from above and below. To examine a scalar hierarchy, an observer must select a focal level, which would lie in the middle, between a higher and a lower level. Because such levels differ from one another by about an order of magnitude, and because they have different temporal scales and dynamic intensities, events at one level tend not to affect other levels directly. Scalar hierarchy promotes system stability, because the upper scalar level dampens energy flows that might otherwise seriously disrupt or even destroy the level beneath (Salthe 2008, 9). Form is possible only in moderated energy flows (Salthe 2007b, 9). In the scalar triad, the lower level *proposes* (materially causes), while the upper level *disposes* (mediates what happens at the focal level). Possible development at the focal (middle) level, then, is limited by what the upper level will permit (Salthe 2004, 336–37). As an example of a scalar hierarchy, Salthe offers the following: "[Earth [biome [population [organism [cell [macromolecule]]]]], (where [is higher level [lower level]]" (Salthe 2008, 9). To use terms familiar to readers of *SES,* a cell is a holon that stands between the organism and macromolecules.[4]

A *specification* hierarchy may include the same levels present in a scalar hierarchy, but interprets the relation among them either historically, developmentally, or diachronically, rather than synchronically. A specification hierarchy "maps nature's developmental trajectory" (Salthe 2005c, 3), with each new (higher) level marking "a new level of being" (Salthe 2005c, 1). There is no *tabula rasa* in the material world, however. Hence, "Wherever anything begins there are already some forms, propensities, and affordances, however vague" (Salthe 2005c, 12; Salthe 2005b, 135) For instance, human consciousness is a late-stage specification of a propensity present in matter/energy from the very beginning. As we will see later on, Salthe subscribes to pansemiosis and perhaps even to pan-experientialism and hylozoism. He writes that if meaning

> can be successfully generalized from human language into the biology of cells, then nothing stands in the way of generalizing semiosis even further to abiotic dissipative structures, generating a pansemiotics. The motive for this position is ultimately to confront the problem of the origin of life. It is clear that, in a materialist position, nothing is derived from nothing; everything must have a predecessor. (Salthe 2005c, 11)

In a specification hierarchy, levels emerge from one another in such a way that the emergent level (e.g., biology) harnesses or *integrates* the previous level (e.g., chemistry) for its own interests (Salthe 2005c, 3). Specification hierarchies are to be understood as highly complex, top-down, and organizational and integrative systems, which display "intensional complexity," which means that to understand a complex system, one must examine it from several different perspectives (Salthe 2005c, 3). Following Aristotle, Salthe reads different integrative levels as "developmental stages in the ontogeny of the world" (Salthe 2006, 1). By "development," he means *progressive change* (Salthe 2005c, 3). Each level of a specification hierarchy is a *refinement* of the previous one, a refinement that harnesses and regulates the preceding levels. Higher levels *emerge* from and yet remain *dependent* on lower ones.

As an example of a specification hierarchy, Salthe proposes the following: {material world {organic world {biological world {social world {psychological world}}}}}, wherein {} represents a class. The inner terms within the brackets are included within a more encompassing class. As specification hierarchies develop, they move from vague to crisp (Salthe 2008, 5), implying that they acquire ever-greater informational complexity, specificity, and constraints.

As a result, each more upper level opens up new degrees of freedom even as it further constricts lower level degrees of freedom. Upper level forms integrate lower level processes under their emergent rules, *but they do not transcend the lower ones; rather they supplement them.* In this sense the ontology represented is, loosely speaking, "materialist." (Salthe 2008, 10; emphasis mine)

In exploiting some possibilities while simultaneously closing off others, specification hierarchies ramify in a way akin to the branching of a tree (opposed to the concentric tree rings of a scaler hierarchy). Because matter/energy was replete with possibilities right after the Big Bang, the possibility actualized in our universe constitutes only *one* of perhaps a very large number of *possible* developmental trajectories. In attempting to understand cosmic development retrospectively, we must recognize that things could have developed differently. As Charles Peirce would have said, the universe could have acquired habits other than the ones it did. We are not in a position to make specific predictions about future development, although it will continue.

Development Versus Evolution

Salthe distinguishes between development and evolution (Salthe 1993). The former can be defined as "predictable directional change," as in the developmental stages of an embryo (Salthe 2006, 5). A general predictable developmental sequence, one to which Salthe frequently appeals, involves a three-stage process characteristic of all dynamic systems: *immaturity, maturity,* and *senescence.* We can also discern a developmental trend in cosmic history after the Big Bang, even though no one (if anyone could have been there!) could have predicted where such development would head. Mainstream evolutionary theorists, including S. J. Gould, of whom Salthe is critical, indicate that evolution is a contingent and undirected sequence of historical changes. Whatever events have occurred in the history of terrestrial life in particular, according to Gould et al., are the unplanned and unpredictable results of mutations that occasionally confer a competitive reproductive advantage to the organism that has undergone the mutation. Salthe disagrees. Appealing to the idea of "general evolution" animating the work of natural philosophers such as Schelling, Spencer, and Peirce, Salthe conceives of evolution as an intelligible *developmental* process that ultimately

gave rise to humans as a result of working through some principles of change and/or reflecting some sort of finality. [In contrast] Darwinian evolution by natural selection is not a process as such, but mere willy-nilly alterations taking place for no reason at all, driven and mediated by accidents and contingencies. That is to say, it is at base radically historical, and so, *unintelligible in the absence of other principles*. Insofar as natural selection has been demonstrated to occur ... contemporary natural philosophy does not dismiss it, but relegates it to a subordinate role in evolution—the maintenance of adaptation to local conditions ... as suggested by observations in nature. (Salthe 2005c, 4; my emphasis)

The Second Law as the Final Cause of Cosmic Development and Form

What are these other principles that must be posited in order to account for cosmic, terrestrial, and human development? Salthe audaciously proposes that one such principle, the most important of all, is the Second Law of Thermodynamics, an enormously powerful cosmic attractor, which everywhere urges reduction of order to disorder, so as to bring the far-from-equilibrium universe to a state of equilibrium, or entropy. Adapting Aristotle's doctrine of the four "causes" (material, efficient, formal, and final), Salthe conceives of the Second Law as the *final* cause of cosmic development. Although modern science retained only two of Aristotle's four causes, efficient and material cause (form being hidden as "formalism" in models and equations), Salthe maintains that the discovery of complex systems requires the reinstatement of final and formal causes. Unlike an efficient cause, which is a push from the past, a final cause may be understood as an attractor that *influences from the future* (Salthe 2005b, footnote 7).

After the Big Bang, the clumping of matter/energy gave rise to gravitational attraction, the first indication that the universe was far from equilibrium. The Second Law emerges to correct this out-of-balance situation. Positing the Second Law as final cause assumes that the universe is an isolated system.[5] Closed and open systems are also subject to the Second Law, however. Accelerating expansion of the (known) universe has led it ever farther from equilibrium, thus making the Second Law an ever more powerful and impatient attractor, capable of eliciting new forms that can assist in the demolition of other forms, in order to bring about Universal equilibrium, or maximum entropy globally (Salthe 2002b, 6). As open systems subject to the Second Law, life forms are not ends in themselves, but rather are clever means for degrading, simplifying, and disorganizing other forms, especially concentrated, far-from-equilibrium energy gradients. "Order, i.e., organization ... could be viewed as being just a consequence of a system that is not able to reach equilibrium" (Salthe 2003, 6). Complex dynamic forms exist in a state of tension: they both seek to maintain themselves (and they do so by consuming—and thus degrading—other forms), but they are inevitably drawn toward self-dissolution as well. All complex systems, including organisms, move toward senescence. The drive to continue is counterbalanced by the pull toward dissolution and recycling. In Salthe's colorful formulation, the universe is governed by the principle of Shiva, the Hindu Goddess of creation and destruction: "[W]e are in a world that, in effect, does not want to be" (Salthe 2002b, 3).

Before going farther, let us pause to review some pertinent issues about the Second Law. The Three Laws of Thermodynamics, and especially the Second Law, are often regarded as he most basic of all physical laws. Devised by nineteenth-century scientist Rudolf Clausius, the Second Law is based on statistical analyses, according to which in an isolated physical system, a process can take place *only* if it increases the total entropy of the system. That is, organized energy available for work tends to become *entropy*, or disorganized energy unavailable for work. Closed systems can exchange heat but not matter, with their surroundings; open systems (such as organisms) can exchange both heat and matter. Here is a classic example of the Second Law at work in a closed system. If someone opens the windows in a warm house in the dead of winter, heat flows out into surrounding atmosphere, and the house rapidly grows cold. A major source of European nihilism and ennui fashionable at the end of the nineteenth century, the Second Law mandated that the universe was "running down" and would end in "heat death" (i.e., a frozen landscape).

Another nineteenth-century thinker, however, Charles Darwin had theorized that life is not only evolving but also becoming more complex, even though Darwinian principles cannot adequately explain such directional development. Evolving life seems like a river running uphill. For decades, tension existed between physics, the universe is running down, and biology, the universe is winding up. There could be no unity of science, as Neurath opined, until these two trends could be reconciled. In *What Is Life?* (1944), physicist Erwin Shrödinger took on the challenge of explaining how life organizes, sustains, and reproduces itself, despite the Second Law's pull toward entropy. He argued that organisms are open systems that live and reproduce by drawing upon and utilizing useful energy found in the environment. This process is inefficient, however, with typically less than 50 percent of available energy converted to useful work. Organism must pay a high entropy "tax," in the form of dissipated energy, in order to survive. In the 1970s and 1980s, Ilya Prigogine developed the concept of "dissipative structures" to explain how all sorts of far-from-equilibrium, dynamic, open systems (ranging from tornadoes to life forms) arise and maintain themselves by drawing upon available energy.

Dissipative Structures Serve the Second Law

Salthe, along with theorists such as Eric Schneider, the late James Kay, Robert Ulanowicz, and more recently Dorion Sagan, posit that dissipative structures not only follow the Second Law, but also serve it (see Kay and Schneider 1992, 161–72; Schneider and Kay 1994; Schneider and Sagan 2006; Ulanowicz 1986). The *final cause* of all dissipative structures is to use up concentrated energy—including energy that would not otherwise be tapped, such as underground oil exploited by humans—as rapidly as possible, so as to bring such energy into equilibrium, typically in the form of low-grade heat. Salthe maintains that "energy dissipation is the key process in understanding all local events in our universe" (Salthe 2006, 3). As noted earlier, dissipative structures *spontaneously* arise whenever their emergence can turn organized energy into entropy. Given that entropy production is a universal project, life—far from being a highly improbable accident—"would be favored wherever possible" (Salthe 2003, 18; Salthe 2005b, 142).

According to Schneider and Kay, "[I]f there is an energy gradient, then sooner or later a dissipative structure will form in apposition to it, or will discover and degrade it—and the bigger the gradient, the sooner this will happen" (Salthe 2004, 331). For example, the heat concentrated in the subtropical atmosphere *elicits* formation of heat-dissipating hurricanes. Salthe maintains that "because form is capable of initiating orderly convective flows that move energy from gradients toward the [heat] sink more effectively than can haphazard conduction, like diffusion," the evolution of life has been "a finalistic search for untapped energy gradients, seeking ever more finely tessellated and inaccessible ones" (Salthe 2002, 5, 7). Various structures interrupt and delay the otherwise rapid degradation of high quality energy, such as sunshine, by imposing a cascade of hierarchically ordered systems, each of which produces work, between production of energy gradients and their final dissipation as heat (Salthe 2003, 2). The ultimate point of ecosystems and organisms, then, is to generate entropy.

Rapid consumption of energy gradients is inefficient and wasteful, yet greedy consumers (such as organisms) compete for the same resource, so it is *advantageous* to consume as rapidly as possible, rather than to get little or nothing at all. Organisms are relatively poor energy dissipaters, since much energy is used to maintain their own structures. By squandering a considerable portion of relatively high-grade energy in hasty consumption, consumers make its remnants available to other consumers farther down the food chain, to such a point that life forms dissipate energy that might never have been dissipated. Salthe thus maintains: "[N]atural selection . . . tends to support systems that can most effectively produce entropy. In this way, *the Second Law constrains the results of natural selection*" (Salthe 2002b, 12; emphasis added). Turning to ecosystems, Salthe remarks that their evolution, too, has multiplied avenues for entropy production (Salthe 2008, 6). Terrestrial evolution—organismal and ecosystemic—is not only inevitable, but also *meaningful*, in part because it is brought forth by the final cause of the universe, the Second Law.

Pansemiotics: Interpretation and Experience Go All the Way Down

Salthe uses the term *infodynamics* to refer to the fact that dynamic processes are meaningful, because they both generate and interpret information.

> [T]he "meaning" of high quality energy dissipation would be the development and support of some particular complex system.... Semiotically, the world does not merely "exist," but embodies meanings in its productions. Put another way, this thread of thought leads us to final causation. (Salthe 2005b, 134)

Complex dynamic systems do not merely *exhibit* meaning or purpose, they also engage in *interpretation*. Because they must take into account things necessary for their persistence, systems possess semiotic capacity. In explaining infodynamics and biosemiotics, Salthe refers to Von Uexküll's idea of an organism's *Umwelt*, the disclosive domain within which external resources pertinent to the organism manifest themselves as "indications" or "signs" that trigger off pertinent behaviors in the organism.[6] Viewed externally, these signs would make up its niche. Salthe adds, however, that biologists must also take into account the interior, interpretative (semiotic) aspect of the organism, that is, its *experience* (Salthe 2005c, 15; Salthe 2007a, 5). Biosemiotics opens the way for global semiotics, according to which the highest known capacity for constructing and interpreting meaning (human intelligence) is an advanced specification of a vague capacity already present at the physical level (Salthe 2007a, 2). Using Peirce's semiotic vocabulary, Salthe gives an example of such physical level interpretation: "[S]ensing the rate of local entropy production, the northern hemisphere air mass detects a too-slow turbulent dissipation, and in response constructs a slick tornado as its interpretant" (Salthe 2007a, 3). Viewing virtually all the complex systems in nature as *agents*, Salthe contravenes mechanistically oriented scientists, for whom such an idea gets "in the way of dealing with [systems] instrumentally" (Salthe 2007a, 3). Salthe intends for that remark to sting scientists, who tend to think that a third-person, objectifying approach adequately explains the things under investigation. If everything other than humans (and perhaps we are no exception) is inert, unfeeling matter/energy, there is no limit to what we can do to things. What "we" are doing, however, is making the biosphere unfit for human habitation. Therefore, we might add, the objective, mechanistic approach is in a broader than instrumental sense, *wrong*.

Cosmic Nihilism?

Although Salthe sometimes depicts a number of other scientists as nihilists, his own cosmic myth may be read as a nihilistic narrative, according to which developmental history has been entrained by the Second Law. In this narrative, the Second Law tolerates life, but compels it to serve the final end of producing entropy. Life itself becomes meaningless, once one understands what is really going on. Salthe has indicated, however, that his myth is meant in part to be ironic. "My hope," he writes, "is to present (as the mythic implication of science texts) such a horrid picture that folks will ask: 'Is that *really* the implication?'" (Salthe personal communication, June 30, 2008). Through his cosmic myth, then, Salthe wishes to provoke scientists to take a look at what may be behind their worldview, which is typically aligned with the project to control nature. Influenced by Romanticism, Salthe hopes to evoke a heroic response, a great refusal to further cooperation with the Second Law as embodied in capitalism (whose motto is "Grow or die!"), and a struggle against our own natural tendencies.

First-Person Experience and Cultural Interpretations of the Second Law

Salthe's Second Law myth may provide an explanation for the fact that individual human experience is replete with desiring, willing, aggression, yearning, violence, and suffering. German philosopher Martin Heidegger holds that Will is modernity's major metaphysical category, articulated in Fredrick Nietzsche's idea of the Will to Power and embodied in industrial technology.[7] Earlier, the German idealist F. W. J. Schelling asserted that "there is no other being but willing. Willing is primal being . . ."[8] In humans, according to Schelling, this willing takes the form of the incessant yearning for freedom. Schelling's work influenced Arthur Schopenhauer, according to whom all phenomena are manifestations of a blind, striving, relentless cosmic Will that can never attain the satisfaction that it craves. Experienced by humans, Will reveals itself as sexual desire, aggression, and the hankering for survival, all of which inevitably lead to suffering, which Schopenhauer maintained could be alleviated by practices recommended by Buddhism and other spiritual traditions. Sigmund Freud spoke of the ineradicable and competing pull toward work, creation, and eros, on the one hand, and violence, destruction, and death, on the other. In

Civilization and its Discontents, he maintains that people are pulled toward self-destructive activities, so that they can return to a state lacking in tension, that is, death, in which the body turns into inert chemicals. Buddhism maintains that human suffering arises because we are in the grip of the *three poisons*: craving (greed), aversion (hatred), and ignorance (delusion). Addicted to these poisons, we wander aimlessly through countless births and rebirths. In contrast, *nirvana* promises to silence the roaring within us, to extinguish the flames of desire, hatred, and delusions.

Given Salthe's familiarity with Buddhism, he might find the following analysis to be congenial to his viewpoint. From the Second Law perspective, we may view craving as the interior manifestation of the universal imperative to consume energy gradients as rapidly as possible; violence is a manifestation of the yearning to destroy all forms; and ignorance refers not only to blindness in the face of impermanence, but also to delusional strategies (God projects) designed to overcome death. Sexual desire (*eros*) leads to copulation and reproduction, while the death drive (*thanatos*) elicits murder and warfare. For many centuries, commentators from many different traditions have remarked upon the cloud hanging over the heads of human beings, who seem impelled to destroy the things (and people) they love. People are constantly fidgeting, restless, impatient, lacking in satisfaction, full of ambition, obsessed with security and vainglory (or any number of other things). Of course, these energy-squandering behaviors are also wellsprings for human creativity and inventiveness. Without dissatisfaction, people would lack the incentive to create alternatives to the given, yet such dissatisfaction simultaneously leads us to covetousness, jealousy, and hostility. Looking deeply into this condition, while employing different vocabulary to describe it, many—though not all—great religious traditions often conclude that only divine intervention can alleviate the suffering involved in the constant round of creation and destruction.

Like individuals, cultures must find ways to survive "in a world committed to the destruction of all forms" (Salthe 2002b, 11). According to Salthe, cultures survive not only by adhering to supportive traditions, but also "by paying entropy tribute, as by building pyramids and airplanes, and, of course, by then destroying them in wars" (Salthe 2002b, 11). That is, cultures build all sorts of things in line with the imperative to consume organized energy. This imperative also helps to explain why humans so often engage in warfare. Seen from the lowest integrative level (physical), warfare lets entropy "be extracted from cultural artifacts as they get recycled, making way as well for more entropy-taxed construction" (Salthe 2002b, 12). To be sure, other factors are also at work in deciding whether or not to go to war. Salthe remarks that in complex social situations we should regard the Second Law as a continually attracting weak force that never lets up, such that if higher level tendencies tend to cancel each other out, it is right there influencing decisions, So, "Shall we go to war?" On the one hand, "yes," on the other, "no." In this stalemate the vote leans toward "yes." (Salthe, personal communication, July 1, 2008)

Of course, global nuclear war would produce a gargantuan amount of entropy, but immediate annihilation of humankind and so many of its products would prevent future humans from cleverly drawing upon vast energy gradients, including coal, gas, oil, and uranium, to name the ones known to us today. Given how effective humans are at generating entropy—putting the "pedal to the metal" big time—one could even argue that the Second Law has an interest in preserving our species for as long as possible!

The universal sequence of immaturity, maturity, and senescence may also help to explain the historical prevalence of warfare. An immature system greedily consumes as much and as fast as possible; consumption slows down at the mature stage, when systems becomes increasingly burdened with information and set in their ways; in senescence, information overload rigidifies a system and brings it to the point of collapse, at which time its components are recycled. Faced with war, a society must either reenergize itself or perish. Hence, warfare may be "interpreted as a mechanism to prevent ecosocial senescence" (Salthe 2003, 1). Perhaps the drive to avoid senescence helps to explain why old men send young men to war.

Salthe also suggests that global capitalism has in effect been "selected" by the Second Law, because capitalism so effectively enables people to use up vast stores of energy and material. Today's environmental problems do not constitute a deviation from some more "natural" way of life, in which people lived harmoniously with nature. Even if some cultures followed this path, the "winners" have been cultures in which individuals have worked as hard as possible to survive and prosper. Salthe remarks: "[O]ur efforts to sustain ourselves as embodied beings constitute our worship of and service to, the more general and eternal thermodynamic Law, which accepts our sacrifice as it consumes us. If there is a moral implication lurking here, it might just be the work ethic" (Salthe 2005a, 300). The work ethic has spread everywhere, such that the entire surface of the planet is seething with energy harnessed for production, consumption, and destruction.

Final Causes Other Than the Second Law

Critics charge that Salthe's natural philosophy is reductionistic, insofar as it interprets all activity (interior and exterior, cultural and social) in terms of the Second Law, which was originally developed to explain energy-transfer at the physical (molecular) level. Salthe concedes that complex systems exist not only because of the Second Law, but "for various other reasons as well, all of these reasons . . . being consistent with the primary finalism [entropy production]" (Salthe 2002b, 5). A more generally applicable explanation of a phenomenon is preferable because it facilitates comparative studies of interest to a unified view of nature and thus to the unity of the sciences. Moreover, the thermodynamic basis for Salthe's cosmic myth "appears most clearly at the most general (physical) level" (Salthe 2002b, 1; Salthe 2005a, 297). Instead of being a full (all-level) program of understanding, then, Salthe's project seeks to understand

> complex systems from a quite low integrative level, i.e., the material, from the intensional complexity [specification hierarchy] perspective. . . . Info-dynamics need not be in conflict with more specified theories deployed at other levels of integration, provided that they do not abrogate or transcend the constrains imposed at the lower levels. . . . Infodynamics is *necessary but insufficient* for understanding ecosystems [or human societies, MZ]. (Salthe 2003, 19; my emphasis)

In other words, the Second Law remains in play at the highest integrative levels, even though other "final causes" are also at play. Higher levels cannot *transcend* lower ones, but instead are logically *refinements*, *specifications*, or *intensifications* of them. "Evolution probes deeper and deeper into the possibilities chosen, but as it does so, it leaves behind more and more possibilities" (Salthe, personal communication, May 13, 2008). Hence, one may expect to see the final cause (Second Law) operating at *all* levels, even though it is most immediately applicable at the physical level. For instance, in the human world, the existence of a steep gradient—such as prestige or power—*invites* social revolution to dissipate that gradient, after which revolutionaries would build up a new social gradient. Insofar as social revolution is "a more highly specified example of the same principle [Second Law], and not a mere analogy," we can see how focusing "on the most general level has the unifying effect proper to a naturalized myth" (Salthe 2005a, 298).

Of course, if human development is a final cause for social organization, we could argue that revolutions—whether violent or not—have sometimes been inspired by and have also helped to institutionalize universal moral principles, which include all humans (and increasingly sentient nonhumans) in the domain of moral considerability. Most educated people no longer countenance a taken for granted practice that can surely be read in part as elicited by the Second Law, the blood sacrifice of countless people and animals. Although a small percentage of North Americans and Europeans may have "developed" so as to more effectively resist the pull to warfare and heedless consumption, billions of other people remain caught in the tension between the urges to create and to destroy. Capitalism combines these opposing demands in the form of voracious consumption, the increasing tempo of which is stoked by inventing ever more tempting goods. Mandated by the Second Law, production and consumption of goods allows people to plow through steep energy gradients, simplifying and often destroying mature ecosystems in the process.

Other Final Causes

Resisting the charge of reductionism, Salthe concedes that there are other final causes apart from the Second Law. These include the following:

1. *Discourse* can act as a final cause in making observations and drawing conclusions. (For example, the final cause of the importance of natural selection in our current representation of nature is that this 'Nature was constructed by thinkers in a capitalist economic system" [Salthe 2005c, 8].)
2. Final cause is at work in *complex, multiply scaled systems*, when perturbations from higher scale boundary conditions "call for" something from below, by imposing regulatory boundary conditions.
3. A final cause important for ecological systems is the pull of *deep structural attractors*, a notion developed by Peirce as cosmic "habits."

Salthe also maintains that: "Any continuing system needs to rely upon the ability of its components to be assured of the continuing validity of their *future progressive expectations*. These act as final causes" (Salthe 2005b, 134). Put otherwise, "the innermost or highest integrative level of any system has the role of Telos, final cause" (Salthe 2005c, 8). Even more emphatically, Salthe writes:

In a specification hierarchy the observer / discourse (as the innermost subclass) can, in some readings, be taken to be *the final cause of the development of the world*—that is, as the beginning of a series of implications . . . as in: discourse implies (or conceptually subordinates) biology, biology implies chemistry, chemistry implies a physical world. This is a logically based version of the physicist's anthropic principle. (Salthe 2005c, 4; emphasis mine)

Primordial Mind

There are several versions of the anthropic principle, but the most pertinent and controversial one is this.[9] The existence of conscious life forms implies that cosmic history was entrained *from the future* by the requirements needed for the emergence of such life forms, which acted from the future as final causes or attractors, luring the universe to evolve in a certain direction. Salthe notes approvingly that earlier natural philosophers interpreted evolution as an intelligible process that "gave rise to humans as a result of working through some principles of change and/or *reflecting some form of finality*" (Salthe 2005c, 4; italics added). Is it possible that, in Salthe's narrative, there is some cosmic finality at least as powerful as the Second Law?

In "The Cosmic Bellows," Salthe makes another intriguing move. He notes that his inquiry is concerned not with "the ultimate underpinnings of physical reality but only with the material world, i.e., the world of things which beings of our scale deal with more or less directly" (Salthe 2005, 300). Then, he introduces the following specification hierarchy: "{Primordial Mind{inorganic realm {organic realm{biological realm {cognitive realm}}}}}." Salthe reports that he considered using "Logos" instead of primordial Mind, a term (and to some extent a concept) borrowed from Peirce (Salthe 2000, 38). By maintaining that cognition is a final cause for cosmic evolution, and then by adding that cognition itself is a class within the set called primordial Mind, Salthe puts a new spin on his Second Law myth. We may ask: To what extent does this new version resonate with Wilber's notion of divine Eros as the cosmic attractor that stands in the future, influencing prior universal self-organization and development?

Primordial Mind is the outermost and thus most general integrative member of a specification hierarchy, of which human cognition (mentality, mind) is the innermost class. This apparent paradox (mind is included within Mind) may be solved by saying that "thought is a process internal to any classifications that it may construct, including concepts of the mind. . . . Formally, thought processes would be an integrative level contained within the class Mind, or more simply, one aspect of mentality—the system is self-referential" (Salthe 2000, 4) In other words, primordial Mind develops in a way that eventually allows for particular cognitive acts, including the one that constructs the specification hierarchy under consideration. Additionally, cognition itself may be understood as a final cause that has entrained at least one branching evolutionary pathway so as to make possible the development of mind.

We are told that the Second Law does not obtain in primordial Mind, because that Law arose only *after* the Big Bang, which (along with the rest of material nature) is an event that occurs and develops *within* primordial Mind, the most general class of the specification hierarchy in question. "In primordial Mind there was (and/or is) no dissipation. This would imply that the material world had its own origin because, in my view, the essential nature of the material world is friction, delay and dissipation" (Salthe 2000, 4). Cognition is an intensification and enhancement of an extremely vague possibility within primordial Mind, which "refers to pure potentiality—the source of everything else. Peirce took it to be a primal firstness—all possibility" (Salthe 2000, 5). Certain sorts of materialists might be unhappy, but the self-described materialist Salthe assuages them as follows: "[A]ll I am saying here again is that the material world itself had a particular origin, and that *what was before that was not material*—just as organic evolution had an origin . . . and that systems prior to its inception did not evolve" (Salthe 2000, 5; emphasis added). Salthe is confident that sophisticated physicists would not object to this notion of Mind as pure possibility.

Cosmic Mind and Non-dual Spirit

We do not know how or why the Big Bang was initiated, but soon thereafter the Second Law arose to begin its relentless sculpting and refining work, drawing out ever more complex forms needed for entropy production. Yet, if the Second Law entrained the emergence of cognition (self-conscious life) as a specification of primordial Mind, cognition itself exerted *from the future* another entrainment on—another final cause for—that same developmental trajectory. Here is another way of articulating the notion discussed earlier, namely, that the cosmos is pulled not only to self-dissolution, but also to self-enhancement, perhaps especially in the form of self-consciousness. Could the Second Law, then, be viewed as a final cause subordinate to one of the classes (cognition) that it helped to make possible? If so, could we read Salthe's cosmic myth as to a considerable extent consistent with cosmic narratives (such as those formulated by Sri Aurbindo, Swimme and Berry, Wilber, and others) that cosmic history is the story of Spirit not only evolving to become aware of itself within the limits of the material world, but having always already exerted influence on that world sufficient to make such self-recollection possible?

There is not time here to rehearse Wilber's developmental cosmology. Suffice it to say that he holds that formless, non-dual Spirit, not the Second Law, is the major strange attractor for such development. Defining non-dual Spirit seems almost impossible, however, given that human cognition is designed to describe the world of form, not the "causal unmanifest" (Wilber 2000, 323). Nevertheless, Wilber indicates that Spirit is the Omega point that not only lures matter-energy into producing form after the Big Bang, but somehow occasioned the Big Bang itself. Of course, since time arose *with* the universe, one is hard pressed to speak of Spirit as being either before or after the Big Bang, or even as "being" at all. The (post)metaphysical issues involved here are daunting. Nevertheless, Wilber writes: "Thus, in the world of form, the *ultimate Omega* appears as an ever-receding horizon of fulfillment, forever pulling us forward, forever retreating itself" (Wilber 2000, 324; my emphasis).

When presented with Wilber's claim that Spirit is the ultimate lure for form, Salthe stated that his specification hierarchy of primordial Mind "amounts to the same proposition" (Salthe, personal communication, May 13, 2008). But, does it? Salthe and Wilber understand the term *ultimate* differently in this context. According to Salthe, ultimate would mean—at least from the Second Law perspective—the ineradicable pull of the Second Law, which is the most important factor in the second class (physical) within the set enclosed within the primordial Mind hierarchy, and which played a significant role in the emergence of another key formal cause: cognition. The Second Law, however, arose in reaction to the disequilibrium that occurred *within* space/time *after* the Big Bang. In contrast, Spirit is not *in* the universe, but—according to thinkers in many different spiritual traditions—rather provides support and telos for every moment of evolution (Wilber 2000, 323). Yet what Salthe calls primordial Mind also seems incapable of being understood in terms of space/time, matter/energy, and form, although Mind must have vaguely foreshadowed these latter. By speaking of Mind as "pure potentiality," Salthe would seem to move close to the notion of Spirit as pure possibility, as the context of all contexts, with no beginning and no end, forever differentiating itself and beginning anew.

Recently, however, in reply to my inquiry about the relation of primordial Mind as "pure potentiality" to Aristotle's God as "pure actuality," Salthe wrote that—at least in this context—he prefers to invoke not "pure potentiality," but instead "vagueness as the descriptor for Universal Mind" (Salthe, personal communication, July 1, 2008). Development always moves in this way: {vague {less vague {more definite}}}. Mind as vagueness, then, is in some sense "actual," though how its pre-physical actuality relates to post-physical actuality is difficult to define. Many contemporary scientists, however, agree with Salthe that understanding complex dynamic systems requires a logic of vagueness (fuzzy logic is a start, at least), which would counteract science's linear and explicit modeling that conceals as much as it reveals. For Salthe, development involves the ever-greater specification of the vague or merely implicit. Hence, the specification hierarchy model may be understood "as a tree expanding from vagueness into many branches" (Salthe, personal communication, July 1, 2008). Primordial Mind as indeterminate, vague, but enormously fecund source could allow countless universes to emerge, including our own.

Because Wilber defines development somewhat differently, his non-dual Spirit as "ultimate" attractor differs from primordial Mind. Wilber writes:

> Every senior dimension [of a holon] acts as a transformative omega point for its junior dimension, exerting a palpable pull of the *deeper and wider on the shallower and narrower*. . . . Each deeper and wider context in the Kosmos thus exerts an omega pull on the shallower and narrower contexts, and when that particular wider depth is reached, that particular omega pull subsides, with the new depth finding that it now exists in a yet-wider and yet-deeper context of its own, which now exerts an unrelenting omega force to once again transcend, to once again embrace more of the Kosmos with care and consciousness. (Wilber 2000, 319–20)

For Salthe, development involves a deepening but *narrowing*, that is, specification. For Wilber, in contrast, development involves a deepening and *widening*, that is, development achieves greater inclusion, comprehensiveness, and integration. Hence, for example, instead of interpreting the biological domain as a specification of the physical, Wilber holds that the biological brings forth a *new*, emergent capacity. Such a capacity must be consistent with structures of the physical domain, which is more fundamental than the biological, but the biological is more than a *refinement* of the physical. What "emergence" and "novelty" mean in regard to development is, of course, a vexed issue. Despite points of agreement, then, Salthe and Wilber differ in important ways about the relation between earlier and later levels of development.

For Wilber, the ultimate Omega refers to the pull exerted by non-dual Spirit, the infinite context of all contexts, which urges all beings to attain their greatest depth, at which point another yearning for yet greater depth (and inclusiveness) arises, leading to another stage in evolutionary development. Resisting Salthe's notion that the point of the universe is to dissolve itself, Wilber suggests instead that we can interpret the universe as seeking to bring forth beings capable of ever-greater compassion and wisdom. Even if the universe finally winds down or becomes dispersed because of rapid acceleration, attainment of such depth, breadth, and inclusiveness may have been worth the effort. But, such an effort! Wilber does not offer naïve cosmic consolation for the myriad beings subject to birth, suffering, and death over the eons. Indeed, the consequences of Spirit's constant pull resemble in some ways the nihilism in Salthe's cosmic myth.

> Evolution seeks only this Formless *summum bonum*—it wants *only* this ultimate Omega—it rushes forward always and solely in search of *this*—and it will *never* find it, because evolution unfolds in the world of form. . . . And

since [evolution] will *never* find [the timeless], it will *never cease* the search. *Samsara* circles endlessly, and that is always the brutal nightmare hidden in its heart. (Wilber 2000, 324–25)

Salthe agrees that *samsara* is an apt term for describing a pitiless world striving to create form while simultaneously yearning to destroy it (Salthe, personal communication, May 13, 2000). Likewise, Wilber argued in a number of his earlier works that people have long engaged in ambitious though futile "God projects," large and small, designed to make either themselves or their cultures immortal, but typically wreaking destruction at the same time (see Wilber 1980; 1981). Arguably, humans rage against finitude and struggle to become godlike, because they have had a taste of eternal Spirit. Beings find themselves in a highly unsatisfactory condition: somehow arising by virtue of non-dual Spirit, they long to become that Spirit, but temporal beings can never hoist themselves up so high. Ever new forms are drawn up in hope that the *next* one will do the job, but each new form—however remarkable its emergent properties—remains separate from uncreated and formless Spirit. The ceaseless yearning, striving, desiring, clamoring, resisting, hating, fighting—all may be read paradoxically as a deep yearning *not to be*, at least not to be in the realm of form. Wilber's notion that life in the realm of form is a "brutal nightmare" resonates with the view at work in Salthe's cosmic myth of the Second Law.

In Salthe's cosmic myth, the *yearning not to be* is constantly in tension with the *necessity to be:* "We need to 'be' in order to mediate nothingness," that is, to bring about dissolution of some forms by creating countless new ones (Salthe, personal communication, May 13,. 2000). In an expanding universe, global entropy is unattainable, however, a conclusion that makes all the sound and fury involved in cosmic development even more dispiriting.

According to Wilber, we *have to be* because non-dual Spirit has lured us into existence. Once alive, however, we yearn to survive, yet we *do not want to be* conditioned beings wandering in *samsara*. Our desire to become formless Spirit even while having arisen as matter and form, however, cannot be satisfied. "The Formless . . . is indeed an ultimate Omega, an ultimate End, but an end that is never reached *in* the world of form. Forms continue endlessly, ceaselessly, holarchically forever . . ." (Wilber 2000, 324). Even if *this* universe collapses back into itself in the Big Crunch, forms continue endlessly all the way up and down, "in billions and billions of other universes!" (Wilber 2000, 324).[10]

"Why" either primordial Mind or non-dual Spirit allows countless universes, in all their triumph and tragedy, to arise in the first place will perhaps always remain a mystery. Some traditions speak of the world as a cosmic "play" or "sport," lacking in "reasons" that would satisfy our search for justification. All contemplative traditions agree that because humans are enslaved to craving, willing, desiring, aggression, and pride, they should avail themselves of practices aimed at ending such enslavement. Advanced contemplative practitioners typically report transpersonal experiences in which ego, objects, existence, space, and time eventually vanish altogether. From the transformation brought about by exploring absolute Nothingness, one discovers that form and formless, world and Spirit are in mutual embrace. Based on such experience, Wilber recommends following the path described by Mahayana Buddhism: "Abide as Emptiness, embrace all Form: the liberation is in the Emptiness, never finally in the Form (though never apart from it)" (Wilber 2000, 324). Salthe indicates that his own modeling of primordial Mind as creative vagueness stems in part from nondual experiences of his own (Salthe, personal communication, July 1, 2008).

What's the Difference?

Given that both Salthe and Wilber agree that cosmic development involves a constant struggle between the intertwined polarities of creation and destruction, wanting to be and wanting not to be, what *difference* does it make if one person says that the "attractor" generating this struggle is the Second Law, and another person says that the attractor is instead non-dual Spirit? Both are "big picture" ways of making sense of things, not assertions capable of being judged as either true or false. Either position can elicit the same response: resignation on the part of people who conclude that individual effort is pointless in the face of such powerful cosmic forces (or motivation to make the most of things either exploitively or compassionately). As Salthe points out, however, this is our scientific culture's tacit answer to the question of the "meaning of life," even though individual scientists would try to evade such judgment (Salthe, personal communication, November 16, 2007). Both Wilber's and Salthe's positions are frank about the inescapable limitations imposed upon beings in the realm of matter and form. Both narratives are powerful, persuasive, and thought provoking.

Wilber's narrative does offer certain advantages, in my view. First, it provides a far more elaborate, multiperspectival account of physical, biological, and mental development than does Salthe's myth, the scope of the latter being limited because of its scientific audience, although the goals of Salthe's myth are no less ambitious than Wilber's. Wilber's more inclusive narrative can more effectively explain the *limits* of the Second Law's influence on higher developmental levels than can Salthe's. Further, Wilber acknowledges the various destructive aspects of modernity, including capitalism, but simultaneously emphasizes modernity's noble and constructive aspects, such as personal freedom, freedom of inquiry in science, religion, and art, institutionalizing of (relative) liberty in social and political structures, great increases in life span, enormous gains in material wealth, and extraordinary developments in science and technology. By underscoring that modernity has alleviated much suffering while simultaneously opening up many new avenues for satisfaction, Wilber justifies ongoing efforts to promote individual and cultural development, *even within the samsaric world.*

In contrast, Salthe's narrative—despite the influence of aspects of dialectical materialism—sometimes exhibits a romantic antimodernism, which tends to discount the positive developments of modernity. Like Salthe, Wilber is well aware of the dark side of modernity, and also emphasizes the new sorts of pathology accompanying every newly acquired stage of human development. In the case of modernity, such pathology includes an "othering" of nature that threatens the viability of our own species.

Further human developments may be entrained by an as-yet-specified possibility already influencing the present. This possibility might include what Ray Kurzweil (2006) and others refer to as "post-humans" endowed with intelligence, subjectivity, and power unimaginable to us. Drawing on the work of Vladimir Vernadsky and Teilhard de Chardin, Salthe foresees the rise of the noosphere, the developmental stage in which humankind gains total technological domination of the planet. This, of course, would presumably wreak havoc on ecosystems. According to Salthe, however, even a remarkable hypersystem such as the noosphere would end in senescence, as will the Earth's biosphere itself. Kurzweil and his colleagues would reply that the aim of post-humans is to become nonbiological beings capable of abandoning planet Earth. Presumably, Salthe and Wilber would agree that even such extraordinarily advanced post-humans—who strive for immortality and even a measure of divinity—could not succeed in transcending the limits imposed by matter and form. Though admittedly they might creatively work with those limits.

The Role of Contemplative Practice in Overcoming *Samsara*

The narratives composed by Salthe and Wilber are informed in part by their own spiritual explorations, which allow both of them to recommend contemplative practices as a way of limiting entrainments that produce endless craving for what cannot be. Toward the end of "The Cosmic Bellows," Salthe mentions practices that might be useful in disclosing and resisting our cravings, our destructive urges, and our fantasies about achieving immortality. His cosmic myth has already *oriented* us: we are entrained by a powerful attractor that has no interest in our lives, our communities, our values, our histories, except insofar as these somehow contribute to entropy production. Now, he offers some *hope*. At first, speaking mostly with tongue in cheek, he states that resisting capitalism's prime virtue, consumption, would entail honoring practices now depicted as vices: "laziness, procrastination, overcautiousness, and indecision, the last two of which are cousins to complexity . . ." (Salthe 2005a, 311). Going up against a law of nature, however, would require exceptional discipline, rather than laziness. Now, he braves the suggestion that *contemplative practices* would allow us to observe and to accept our passions, without giving in to them (Salthe 2005a, 311). Such practices would be a crucial element in humanity's struggle to free itself from the excesses called forth by the Second Law, which shows up as insatiable desire. As more people attain higher levels of consciousness, and are thus more capable of renouncing the pulls to war and destructive consumption, mature countries may find ways to sustain themselves for a long time, before succumbing to inevitable senescence.

Calling to mind a passage cited by Swimme and Berry, in which a wise man notes that loss and sorrow always accompany even genuine advances, Salthe appeals to those traditions that teach *equanimity* when confronting the irresolvable tension and inescapable suffering that courses through human life (Salthe 2005a, 312–13). Working to create a world that works for everyone, and slowing the overheated engines of capitalism, may be noble goals, but senescence, death, and destruction are inevitable for beings like us.

According to many spiritual traditions, contemplative practices enable one to taste the eternal without the need for high-tech hardware, software, and wetware. Someone awakening from the nightmare of *samsara* is said to dwell in the formless realm, while simultaneously living in the realm of form. Such a view is in some respects consistent with panentheism, according to which Spirit transcends the world while also being present within it. Invoking panentheism has problems of its own, however, including the challenging task of talking about Spirit without using categories belonging to the form world, including existence.

For the awakened, the end of *samsara* brings the dawn of infinite compassion for all who remain attached to matter and form. In nondual Spirit, nothing needs to be attained, because everything is always already complete. Hence, whatever takes place in the realm of matter and form—regression, progression, or stasis—cannot disturb either primordial Mind or non-dual Spirit.[11] Dwelling within such a transformational realization, one can work tirelessly to promote well-being for all, even while recognizing that one's efforts will in most cases be futile.

Notes

1. Among the best are Swimme and Berry (1994) and Wilber (2000).
2. One of the best introductions to Wilber's thought is his book, *A Brief History of Everything* (2000).
3. In *Integral Ecology*, Esbjörn-Hargens and I point out three distinct uses of the word *nature*. In this chapter, I am using "nature" in the context of how Salthe defines and uses it within the context of his own work.
4. By placing Earth at the top of the *scalar* hierarchy, Salthe is not suggesting that there was no Earth prior to the emergence of the preceding scalar levels. The scalar hierarchy is synchronic and spatial, not diachronic, that it, conceives of scalar hierarchies as nested one within the other, without providing a developmental, historical, diachronic account of how such hierarchies arose or relate to one another in terms of complexity. These issues are addressed in the specification hierarchy.
5. See "Thermodynamic System," in which isolated, closed, and open systems are usefully defined. Available at http://en.wikipedia.org/wiki/Thermodynamic_system. Accessed June 25, 2008.
6. See *Integral Ecology* (2009) for an extensive discussion of biosemiotics and *umwelt*.
7. For an overview of this topic, see Zimmerman (1990).
8. F. W. J. Schelling (from his text, *On the Essence of Human Freedom* [1809]), as quoted by Andrew Bowie in "Friedrich Wilhelm Joseph von Schelling," *The Stanford Encyclopedia of Philosophy*. Available at http://plato.stanford.edu/entries/schelling/. Accessed June 28, 2008.
9. For a brief overview of the anthropic principle, see Steve Paulson's interview with Paul Davies on Salon.com: http://www.salon.com/books/feature/2007/07/03/paul_davies/. An excellent physicist, Davies has published many semi-popular books abut the nature of reality, which he regards as saturated with meaning and purpose.
10. Salthe comments that the current condition "depends on the acceleration of the universe remaining more or less the same. If it were to decelerate, then, on my view, the magnitude of gravitation and its dual, the Second Law, would diminish, and the result is a situation so uncanny I cannot imagine it" (Salthe, personal communication, June 30, 2008).
11. I would like to express my deep appreciation to Stanley Salthe for being such a generous and insightful interlocutor about the many topics that he and I have discussed. He also offered several suggestions for improving the present chapter, though of course any remaining problems are my responsibility.

Key to References and Online Sources to Salthe's Essays

Page references are to essays as they were printed out from Salthe's home page (http://www.nbi.dk/~natphil/salthe/) or from his collection of online essays (http://www.harmeny.com/twiki/bin/view/Main/SaltheResearchOnline). At this link, one can find references to Salthe's publications by topic: http://www.nbi.dk/~natphil/salthe/_publ_classified_by_topic.pdf. At this link, one can find many of Salthe's publications online: http://www.harmeny.com/twiki/bin/view/Main/SaltheResearchOnline.

References

Esbjörn-Hargens, S. and M. Zimmerman. 2009. *Integral ecology: Uniting multiple perspectives on the natural world*. Boston: Integral Books.

Kay, J., and E. Schneider. 1992. Thermodynamics and measures of ecosystem integrity. In *Ecological indicators*, ed. D. McKenzie, D Hyatt, and J. McDonald, 159–81. New York: Elsevier.

Kurzweil, R. 2006. *The singularity is near: When humans transcend biology*. New York: Penguin Books.

Salthe, S. N. n.d. Stanley N. Salthe homepage. Retrieved June 20, 2008, from http://www.nbi.dk/~natphil/salthe/.

———. 1985. *Evolving hierarchical systems*. New York: Columbia University Press.

———. 1993. *Development and evolution: Complexity and change in biology*. Cambridge: MIT Press.

———. (2000). A classification of closure concepts. *Annals of the New York Academy of Sciences* 901: 35–41.

———. 2001. Summary of the principles of hierarchy theory. Retrieved June 20, 2008, from http://www.nbi.dk/~natphil/salthe/Summary_of_the_Principles_o.pdf.

———. (2002a). Analysis and critique of the concept of natural selection. Retrieved June 5, 2008, from http://www.nbi.dk/~natphil/salthe/Critique_of_Natural_Select_.pdf.

———. 2002b. Becoming, being, and passing: Our myth from science (the second law and natural selection. Retrieved June 5, 2008, from www.nbi.dk/~natphil/salthe/Becomin_Being_Passing.pdf.

———. 2003. Infodynamics: A developmental framework for ecology/economics. *Conservation Ecology* 7(3): chapter 3.

———. 2004. The spontaneous origin of new levels in scalar hierarchy. *Entropy* 204: 327–43.

———. 2005a. The cosmic bellows: The big bang and the second law. *Cosmos and History: The Journal of Natural and Social Philosophy* 1(2): 295–317.

———. 2005b. Energy and semiotics: The second law and the origin of life. *Cosmos and History: The Journal of Natural and Social Philosophy* 1(1): 128–45.

———. 2005c. The natural philosophy of ecology: A developmental systems approach. *Ecological Complexity* 2: 1–19.

———. 2006. The role of entropy in the philosophy of nature. Retrieved June 20, 2008, from www.harmeny.com/twiki/pub/Main/NaturalPhilosophyPaper2006/Natural_Philosophy06.pdf.

———. 2007a. Meaning in nature: Placing biosemiotics within pansemiotics. In *Biosemiotics: Information, Codes and Signs in Living Systems*, ed. M. Barbieri, 207–17). New York: Nova Science Publishers.

———. 2007b. The natural philosophy of work. *Entropy* 9: 83–99.

———. 2008. Natural philosophy: Developmental systems in the thermodynamic perspective. In *Festschrift In Honor of Saban Teoman Durali*, ed. C. Cakmak. Istanbul: Dergah Yaylinlari.

Schneider, E. D., and J. J. Kay. 1994. Life as a manifestation of the second law of thermodynamics. *Mathematical and Computer Modeling* 19(6–8): 25–48.

—————. 1995. Order from disorder: The thermodynamics of complexity in biology. In *What is life: The next fifty years. Reflections on the future of biology*, ed. M. P. Murphy and L. A. .J. O'Neill, 161–72). New York: Cambridge University Press.

Schneider, E. D., and D. Sagan. 2006. *Into the cool: Energy flow, thermodynamics, and life.* Chicago: University of Chicago Press.

Swimme, B., and T. Berry. 1994. *The universe story: From the primordial flaring forth to the Ecozoic Era—A celebration of the unfolding of the cosmos.* New York: HarperOne.

Ulanowicz, R. E. 1986. *Growth and development: Ecosystem phenomenology.* New York: Springer-Verlag.

Wilber, K. 1980. *The Atman Project.* Wheaton, IL: Quest Books.

—————. 1981. *Up from Eden: A transpersonal view of human evolution.* Garden City, NY: Anchor Press/Doubleday.

—————.2000. *Sex,ecology, spirituality.* 2nd ed. Boston: Shambhala.

—————. 2007. *A brief history of everything.* 2nd ed. Boston: Shambhala.

Zimmerman, M. E. 1990. *Heidegger's confrontation with modernity.* Bloomington: Indiana University Press.

—————. 2008. The singularity: A crucial phases in divine self-actualization? *Cosmos and History: The Journal of Natural and Social Philosophy* 4(1–2): 347–70.

## 9

Frames of AQAL, Integral Critical Theory, and the Emerging Integral Arts

Michael Schwartz

> According to the worldly point of view, artists do not have the ultimate target of reaching enlightenment.... Ordinary artists usually express themselves for communication, fame, or power.... [Because] they do not express themselves with a wisdom point of view, the result is always impermanence and diminishing energy which leads to suffering.... According to the Buddhist point of view, an artist's intention is compassion.... Through the sublime artists' intentions, the outer gross elements are purified into the inner subtle elements and reconnect with wisdom phenomena.... Ultimately, there is liberation through the purification of essenceless art's substance into substanceless essence enlightenment.
>
> —Thinley Norbu

This chapter outlines a philosophically informed and historically mindful integral critical theory of art. Advancing the AQAL model as it has been developed in the writings of Ken Wilber, the first half of the chapter differentiates four distinct framings of the AQAL model, leading to clarification of the ethical charge of an *integral critical theory* (ICT). The second half of the chapter turns this integral-critical lens to matters of art, arguing for and demonstrating the importance of attending carefully to art's artifactual character, leading to a recovery of lessons inherent in early postmodern art that posit a challenge for the emerging integral arts.

Frames of AQAL

AQAL diagrams are, for Bernard Lonergan, *heuristic images* (Lonergan 1992). Such images or diagrams are not in and of themselves conceptual, but provide a foothold from which we enter into a cognitive process of understanding that can flash forth as insight. AQAL, as figure, is the point of departure and ongoing spur for insightful cognitive reflection and comprehension.

How we frame an AQAL diagram, whether we do so consciously or not, orients our cognitive engagement. In what follows I shall distinguish four principal frames of AQAL: (1) philosophical; (2) metatheoretic; (3) integral methodological; and (4) integral critical.

Philosophy

Philosophy has no agreed upon definition. Taken in a speculative and integral key, philosophy is the discursive questioning of and reckoning with the totality of the real and with the mysterious source of this totality. Philosophy, as the "love of wisdom," is the cognitive imitation or anticipation of the direct intuition of what metaphors such as "the one and the many" point to. In Wilber's articulation of this philosophical stream, the orderings of reality are not to be assumed to be pre-given and substantive, but are Kosmic habits gleaned from methodological investigation, the results and procedures of which are always revisable, such a posteriori validity claims fleshing out the transcendental a priori's, minimizing as far as possible one's transcendental presuppositions.[1]

Wilber has called this general approach to philosophy "post-metaphysics." Steve McIntosh (2007), in a related vein, has called it "minimalist metaphysics" (210–16). Lonergan (1992) offers yet another instructive angle, focusing less on metaphysics as result and more on metaphysics as *method* (see chapter 14). The method of metaphysics gathers and orders the epistemic procedures and results of the various human and natural sciences, including the knowledge sedimented in the cultural common sense, generating an *integral heuristic structure. Heuristic* in that it *anticipates* the structure of knowing the totality; *integral* in that the structure points to the order of the anticipated totality. Integral heuristic structure is revisable in light of new procedures of knowing and their resultant knowledge. It is not the totalizing outcome of inquiry, but the anticipation of such results, functioning akin to a Kantian regulative idea of reason.

Integral Methodological Pluralism (IMP) is a concrete instantiation of the integral heuristic structure of an anticipatory metaphysics.[2] It points to the integration of all the current ways of methodological knowing, anticipating knowledge of the totality in its integral unity. Enacting the method of metaphysics in the interrogative mode, philosophical activity is psychoactive; it can lead into genuine ascent, the conceptual activity carried beyond itself: an Erotic path of *Jnana, theoria* flashing forth, wonder breaking through in glimpsing the

Mystery.[3] Philosophical insight can also turn about and inaugurate a descent in an Agapic embracing anew of the manifest world; where in the case of integral studies the AQAL model becomes re-framed as application, the first phases of this activity having principally taken shape as *metatheory*.

Metatheory

Metatheoretical application typically involves the use of Integral Theory and its AQAL model to coordinate preexisting theories within a given domain of inquiry. Whereas the respective theories had been seen to be at odds with one another, they are now shown to harmonize into a higher viewpoint. This approach tends to mine a given discipline, taking note of its various theories and their repositories of knowledge, showing how the AQAL model can integrate what had seemed to be a battleground of perspectives, pointing to ways of integral coherence within an existing discipline.

This metatheoretical frame has tended to downplay specification and enactment of the methodological injunctions proper to the given theories—as this will be the moment stressed within the next wave of application (the IMP framing of Integral Theory). During this metatheoretical phase, no fewer than three habits have emerged that are in tension with the prescriptions of integral philosophy (hazarding possible pathologies in application): (1) privileging those methodologies aligned with or especially complementary to the modern philosophy of the subject; (2) privileging deep structures over surface structures in the manner of universal to particular without sufficient attention to the singularity of the latter; and (3) eschewing concrete historical research, hence the virtual absence of substantive historical reflection as the means of discerning unjust power plays and sociocultural pathologies in the present. I shall address points 2 and 3 later in this chapter. Here I would like to attend to 1.

While the AQAL model points to interiors and exteriors as forms co-arising in unqualifiable Spirit, it is sometimes assumed that interiors ("subjects") are "closer" to Spirit than are exteriors ("objects"). And while in certain practice contexts (as with God in the first-person perspective; or with witnessing pointing out instructions) this is a useful way of speaking, it creates unnecessary problems when used in the context of the AQAL model as metatheory. In light of IMP distinctions of the eight zones, there has been an unwarranted privileging of zone 2 languages and schemas, proper to a Neo-Kantian lineage of thought (one aligned with the transcendental-empirical doublet about which Foucault [1970] spoke in *Les mots et les choses*); and while these methods have a crucial place, their dominance is symptomatically expressed in the use of developmental color codes to speak of the tetra-arising of and interplay among deep and surface structures.

This said, I would like to explore, if somewhat obliquely, this habit of privileging the terms of the philosophy of the subject in the use of the AQAL model
by examining the LL approaches of Emmanuel Levinas on ethics (zone 3) and
of Michel Foucault on discursive analytics (zone 4).

Zone 3: Levinas on I-Thou

Zone 3 in the LL is the inside of the collective interior. The methodological
family that has been emphasized for this zone is *hermeneutics*—the solidarity
of the we-space, the mystery of the dash of the I-Thou that connects us,
through Spirit, in the miracle of mutual resonance. Emmanuel Levinas, one of
the greatest ethical philosophers of the twentieth century,[4] offered a different
interpretation of the dash of the I-Thou. Unlike Buber, Levinas sees this dash
as signaling an irreversible and nonreciprocal mode of relating founded on the
felt-sense of *responsibility* that is prior to and precludes any collective sense of
"we." I-Thou is fundamentally ethical and asymmetrical, the "I" always already
called to responsibility through and for the *face of the Other*. One cannot escape
being called as such; the "I" responsible prior to subjective freedom—the "me"
held *hostage* in an infinite and unending task of *hospitality*.[5]

Whereas Levinas insists on the priority of the asymmetry of the ethical relationship, an integral stance can hold the I-Thou relation as at once symmetrical
and asymmetrical—symmetrical with regard to shared meanings, practices,
and codes in constituting a we-space (roughly, what Levinas calls the *Said*);
and asymmetrical with regard to irreversible responsibility (what Levinas calls
the *Saying*). It is the former, to be sure, that has strong affinities with Hegelian
views of a meta-Subject and hence to philosophies of subjectivity; whereas
Levinas's view of the ethical relation, while by no means eliminating subjectivity, radically reworks its sense, pressing phenomenological analyses beyond
themselves into a relational-ethical mysticism, the subject now, at its core, a
passivity beyond all passivity—a nullity of all nullities always already responsible and responsive—or, said otherwise, a *timeless waiting*, an *infinite patience*.
Levinas's ethical provocations surely deserve a fundamental place in our zone 3
approaches; as they are crucial for anything that we might call *integral ethics*.

Zone 4: Foucault on Discursive Analytics

Zone 4 in the LL is the outside view of the collective interior. Foucault's
discursive analytics is a powerful method proper to this zone.[6] His notion of
the *archive* points not to this or that theme or lineage of ideas, but in analogy
to Heideggerian *Lichtung*, to the ontological space or clearing of a discourse
regime in which such themes and lineage of ideas come forth. This ontological

space or eventing of discourse is not an operation of subjectivity, but aligns with the view that "language speaks us, or speaks through us."

It is important to keep in mind that whereas developmental lines in the UL and the UR unfold in stages, levels correlating between these two quadrants as the individual interior-exterior perspectives of any human occasion, this is not strictly the case with the LL and the LR, where development of social holons does not always unfold in a strict stage-like manner as associated with individual holons, and where the diagrammatic correlations of altitude in each of these zones with those in another quadrant are more statistical and probabilistic, rather than structural and overdetermined. The upshot is that imposing too quickly zone 2 stage distinctions and developmental schemas onto a zone 4 method such as Foucault's discursive analytics can block the fullness and richness of the methodology. Thus, when we speak of an "orange" or a "green" altitude discourse, we are using methods from not one but from two zones, the integration of methods from zones 2 and 4. In other words, the zone 4 deep structure of the archive is not, in the first instance, necessarily spread out in a developmental or stratified manner as we find in zone 2 and its neo-Kantian developmental a priori lines and levels, an essential point in our getting clearer about the tetra-arising of an intelligible world inhabited by self and others.

To get a better sense of what is at stake in zone 4 discursive analytics, let us take up Foucault's own example of the modern discourse of sexuality.

Two guys in their early twenties, both of whom speak English, are hanging out in a bar. At this moment in time, one is resonating at a red altitude in his center of gravity, the other at an amber-orange altitude. They both see an extremely gorgeous, sexy woman. One says to the other (in what David Deida [1997] calls a first stage "macho jerk" moment [xiv]):[7] "Man, would I like to have sex with her!" the other responding in kind: "Yeah man, wow—I'd love to screw her!"

Is there any serious doubt that these guys understand one another?—that they resonate in testosterone-driven desire for the gal? Note that if we use zone 2 strata to clarify mutual resonance, it is difficult to fathom how the guy gravitating at a red altitude could understand the guy gravitating at an amber-orange altitude in an authentic manner—which, I suggest, is in part counterintuitive, and points to the limits of the developmental strata imposed too quickly onto a moment of meaningful interaction. From a zone 2 stance, the amber-orange altitude is said to transcend and embrace the red altitude, so it can in principle grasp the red expression; although as a first-tier altitude it might find itself allergic to the red manner of expressing desire for the gal (as with differences in verbal tone and inflection); while the red wave is said to be underdeveloped and inadequate to totally understand the amber-orange wave, so ought not be able to understand in its fullness the orange utterance—almost as if it was listening to a different language.

Let us then take the example of different languages. There are two other guys, both at an amber-orange altitude, one speaking an obscure Eskimo dialect, the other Tamil; one saying to the other something akin to "I want to screw her" with macho jerk inflections. Is it not obvious that the greater mutual understanding occurs between the first two guys who are at different altitudes? Indeed, Foucault teaches further that the first two guys are not simply speaking English to one another, swimming in the same language, but are also immersed in the same discursive clearing of the modern discourse of sexuality—this clearing, emerging out of empty awareness, out of Awake Intelligence itself, an irreducible condition of common intelligibility, and not, from the start, simply derivative of UL subjectivisms—such being the partial truth of this innovative postmodern methodology.

In speaking as they do, these two guys enact the modern discourse of sexuality, inciting and enhancing their desires for the gal through the performance of "speaking the truth of sex," declaring their desires to be heterosexual, inscribing their essential identities within the newly modern grids of sexual orientation, where such identity performance, in increasing sexual desire, is in functional service to the dictates of *biopower*: for early modernity, to maximize the operational populations of nation states; after World War II, harnessed to drive consumption. The beauty of the integral stance is that we need not adopt a postmodern rejection of the subject, but can in addition take up a zone 2 perspective on these guys' respective altitudes, attuning to frictions between their differing first-tier expressions about sex, the two methods integrating into a higher viewpoint, seeing from the outside the conditions of *mutual resonance-and-dissonance* proper to this interactive human occasion.

The upshot is that the tetra-arising of a world-space is co-conditioned by all four quadrants and their interplay; and need not be construed as centered from the start in, nor warped in the end to, a neo-Kantian developmental schema aligned with the modern philosophy of the subject.

Integral Methodological Pluralism

This brings us more explicitly to the topic of Integral Methodological Pluralism. Whereas metatheoretical analysis was the first principal phase in the application of the AQAL model, and remains an important framework, IMP has more recently emerged as the next phase, its research agenda announced in the 2008 spring and summer issues of the *Journal of Integral Theory and Practice*.

IMP refines the view of the AQAL model, differentiating an inside and outside perspective within each quadrant, distinguishing quadrant analysis from quadrivia analysis, while calling for the enactment of methodological injunctions proper to a given zone. IMP is not just a gathering of prior theories and research results, but is a radically innovative means for newly generating higher and higher viewpoints of integrated knowledge.

In the first issue of *JITP* dedicated to this turn toward IMP as research program, Sean Esbjörn-Hargens (2008) proposes a scaleable approach in the use of IMP, that at minimum one take up at least three methodologies, one each for the first-, second-, and third-person perspectives (20–21). This is a sane and judicious approach—but only if the habit of overprivileging methodologies resonant with the philosophy of the subject is corrected, opening up a truly integral dance of inquiry that harvests all the riches of modern and postmodern methods. (To be sure, the above discussion on Foucault hints as a scaleable IMP approach: the second-person zone 4 method of discursive analytics on the modern discourse of sexuality; the third-person zone 8 method of a systems view of biopower; and the first-person zone 2 method of first-tier waves in psychosexual development.)

Deep and Surface Structures

I want to suggest that there will be another challenge to the balanced enactment of IMP—overcoming the privileging of the language of deep structures. The metatheoretical habit has been to subsume surface structures to deep structures, where the latter can account for the similarities among the former, but does not keep in full sight the actual differences among them, and as such hazards edging into a second-tier variant of what Adorno called "identity thinking."[8] From the point of view of second-tier cognition, deep structures are weak "universals," that is to say, generalizing orientations that subsume surface structures, the latter not only particular expressions of the deep structures, but also singularities in their own right—specific translations, aspects of which cannot be accounted for in the language of deep structures. (Typologies are a more refined form of categorizing translations, but within any given type the given translation remains singular.) From the stance of second-tier cognition, authentic and full-blown IMP analysis is called to be mindful of the dance among universal, particular, and singular (enacting a postdialectical form of scholarship)—and not to ignore the latter as if they were mere epiphenomena. Whereas deep structures can account for identity among the particulars, they cannot in the end (even with the useful inclusion of typologies) account for the differences—*hence, the second-tier status of surface structures as at once particulars and singulars.* Said otherwise, if IMP analysis is to be conducted in a second-tier manner, deep structures, as ascertained via research, are hypotheses, such that the singularity of surface structure can pressure our redefining the deep structures in an ongoing learning process, the model able to update itself reflexively in light of new research.

Being-in-the-World, Being-as-the-World

The tetra-arising of the eight indigenous perspectives discloses an intelligible world-space. Picking up a suggestion from Wilber (2002, part 1), such co-arising is an integral reenvisioning of what Heidegger (1962) called *being in the world*. The eight zones co-emerge and, to follow the Heideggerian line of thought, are *equi-primordial* ("gleichursprünglich") in the clearing of an intelligible world. Each perspective distinctively discloses the occasion; the methodologies proper to each zone distinctively enact reflective knowledge about the occasion; with no zone having an "a priori" priority.

Locating the self-system in the UL, while valuable in the context of an integral psychology or an integral spirituality, in the context of the unfolding of ramified IMP research across the disciplines hazards the replication of a grounding subject-object schema that is at odds with the insights of Heideggerian *Inderweltsein*. Instead, let us say that the self-sense (the inside-feeling of the self-system) precipitates through the integral interplay of the eight zones, and can be imagined as positioned at the intersection of the vertical and horizontal axes of the AQAL grid—all of this proper to a second-tier stance. From a third-tier altitude, we no longer speak so readily of being-in-the-world, but rather of *being-as-the-world*—the self-sense now witnessed as object (I-I); or arising as luminously-and-inherently empty: an egoless ego.

Integral Critical Theory

Using some scaleable version of IMP, attending to deep structures as generalizing orientations and to surface structures as particulars and singulars, taking the eight zones as co-arising in one's being in the world—all are necessary but insufficient conditions for an *integral critical theory*.[9]

Note this often-quoted passage from end of Adorno's *Minima Moralia* (1974):

> The only philosophy which can be responsibly practiced in the face of despair is the attempt to contemplate all things as they would present themselves from the standpoint of redemption. Knowledge has no light but that shed on the world by redemption: all else is reconstruction, mere technique. Perspectives must be fashioned that displace and estrange the world, reveal it to be with its

rifts and crevices as indulgent and distorted as it will appear one day in the messianic light. To gain such perspectives without velleity or violence, entirely from felt contact with its objects—this alone is the task of thought. (247)

Without pretending to do justice to this wonderfully rich text, let us take up our own trajectory in saying that IMP research, however philosophically empowered, is mere technique if not explicitly practiced from the standpoint of redemption: where this redemptive standpoint manifests as the breaking through of the Good in the mode of calling us to enact every greater Kosmic Justice and Care (KJC), such that KJC saturates and intentionally propels our IMP practice fearlessly and without reservation.

It is not enough to profess the Bodhisattva Vow or some noble aim—as this can too easily remain external to one's crafting of a critical practice. Similarly, listing the methods that fall into this or that IMP zone is very helpful and instructive, presenting a tool kit for research; but if this listing only goes so far, it remains instrumental and mere technique. From the standpoint of ICT—here revamping and updating Horkeimer's original distinction between traditional and critical theory from the 1930s—not all theories in a given context of inquiry are equally or expansively *moral*.[10] In addition to the epistemic guidepost of "partial truth," ICT adds the ethical guidepost of the "moral valence" of a given theory and its methodologies, the latter especially pertinent for the nonformal and human sciences.

Wilber's (2007) Basic Moral Intuition (BMI) is a skillful means for reflecting on the redemptive force of our theory choices and IMP-enacted research projects (195–96). So are Cornel West's (1993) four facets of *prophet thought*—(1) *discrimination* through nuanced historical reflection on the present; (2) *connection* to others through unconditional empathy; (3) *tracking hypocrisy* in ourselves and others; and (4) *hope* for a better relative future, keeping our efforts alive (3–6). Especially important for integral critical theory is facet 1, discrimination as the exercising of a nuanced historical sense so to grasp the present in light of the past, disclosing unjust power plays and pathological undercurrents that otherwise go unnoticed.

Integral Historiography

Hence, the important role of an Integral Historiography, adequate discussion of which goes beyond the present chapter. May a few remarks suffice.

There are no fewer than five moments or tropes of an Integral Historiography: (1) *antiquarian*: textured research, attentive to surface structures, that objectifies the past horizon with the present (third-person); (2) *dialogical-nomological*: any value "dialogue" between the two horizons (second-person);

(3) *monumental-exemplary*: aspects of the past are taken back into to the present as exemplary moments and monuments (first-person); (4) *genealogical-symptomatic*: discerning individual and collective dissociations and kinks that engender unnecessary pain and truncated growth at any given tetra-wave of development (shadow diagnosis); (5) *messianic-karmic*: the recollecting of the unnecessary pain and suffering of past sentient beings, the lessons gleaned from the historiographic work to be imbibed and lived so to prevent those past forms of unnecessary pain and suffering from happening again, redeeming—from the messianic point of view of a utopian future—those past lives without ever forgetting their struggles.

Another facet of integral historiography is that of how historical inquiry engages and (re)figures time (where time—as well as space—is disclosed differentially for all four quadrants), reflection upon which includes issues of narrative, emplotment, the relation between history and fiction, and the interplay between Big Picture master-narratives and more thematically focused historical accounts of varying degrees of scale such that the Big Picture adapts and even changes itself in light of ongoing historical research, this more micro research itself illumined and empowered by the Big Picture tale.

Questions of Integral Art

Having gotten somewhat clearer about what an ICT framing of AQAL can look like, we can now take up the topic of art. Up to this point the question that has most preoccupied integral inquiry on art has been the definition and status of "integral art." As a point of departure, let us explore this question.

The early working definition was "integral art is that art made by an integral artist," a posit that contains insights and yet is also pre-critically modernist, stressing the productive primacy of the individual maker (Habermas 1987, 75–82), and can be contrasted instructively with the opening paragraphs of Heidegger's (1971) seminal essay on the work of art, where art and artist are only two terms within a broader hermeneutic circle, the various terms of this circle informing one another, no one term defining another in a linear-causal manner (17–18).

Moreover, this preliminary definition has been at times occasioned by two slippages. (1) The "psychograph" of an artist is all-quadrivia, hence a lens onto the artist's Fullness of Consciousness. Yet in practice such analysis has often slid into the terms of consciousness (with a little "c") as restricted to the UL, focusing on artistic intention, personality anecdotes, and especially zone 2 lines, levels, and states, but almost nothing, say, on class positioning within the overwhelming if background force-field of global economics proper to the LR, the latter equiprimordial to one's being in the world (and which can profoundly qualify an artistic self and condition its artistic enactments). (2) The phrase "integral artist" has at times been confounded with that of "integral human being"—whereas being an integral human being is of a more general status, being an integral artist the more specific role; with the former by no means securing the latter. The issue is how to tell if an artist qua artist is being integral—with an essential approach being: an integrally critical, methodologically ramified examination of his or her art.

Nevertheless, the view that "integral art is that art made by an integral artist" is an important partial truth, especially inspiring for and pertinent with regard to the integral training of artists, increasing the *probability* of an artist making integral art. Here I would posit four moments of such training: (1) Dedication to one's medium of expression, deepening skill in and devotion to the craft. (This needs to be stated up front, given our cultural habits of fetishizing technological innovations and deskilled short cuts.) (2) A ramified and evolving Integral Life Practice (ILP). (3) Communities of integral artists and audiences along with stable institutions for training such artists. (Philip Rustinov-Jacobson is currently exploring such possibilities). (4) Engaging and constructing AQAL models of critical histories of art that: (a) reactivate the morphogenic fields and Kosmic grooves proper to art, leading to greater and greater fullness in inhabiting integrally the various indigenous art-perspectives; and (b) clarify the dignity and disaster of our collective habits of art making and viewing, enabling the historical discernment of the shadowy loci in need of critically renewed practice. In the end, such training will do well to keep in mind Wilber's distinction between post/modern soul artists, imbalanced in their development although having access to and able to express in their work higher stages and/or states, and integral artists, who also have access and can express higher stages and/or states, but who are far more balanced, healthy, and integrated as artistic selves, as this is evidenced in their art.[11]

Art as World-Disclosure

The early definition "integral art is that art made by an integral artist" appeared prior to the clear distinction between artifacts and holons. In this new light the artwork is an artifact; while the makers and users of artworks are sentient holons. What then is distinctive about the artwork, such that its artifactual uniqueness preorients and inflects our perspective-taking and IMP disclosures of art? Here we can only offer a summarily reply to this question.

Drawing upon Heidegger's decisive analyses in his *Kunstwerk* essay (1971), the work of art can be said to open a world within a world (see Luhmann 2003, 1079). The artwork is not a theory or philosophy about the world, although there are hybrid art forms that in part enact and fold within theorizing and philosophizing; rather, art presents patterns of experience proper to a world-space. Again, art's bringing forth of patterns of experience is not the same as a theory about nor cognitive operations that reflect upon the epistemic or moral status of such patterns. While art can enfold within itself the results of such operations, and can mimetically present such activities (as with a scene of philosophers in discussion), art qua art does not enact those operations. Artworks manifest what Deleuze and Guattari (1994) call *percepts* and *affects*—where "affect" means not only this or that emotion, but the affective tone permeating a given world-space, closer to what Heidegger (1962) called a "fundamental mood" that preinterprets and orients being-in-the-world (172).

Mimesis and Drives

Art's opening up of a world within a world is a mode of *mimesis*. In light of Rene Girard's (1996) thesis of mimetic desire, art can be seen as a form of *secondary mimesis* in lieu of the primary mimetic process of human socioacculturation about which Girard speaks with such insight. For Girard, self-in-culture emerges through the triangle of mimetic desire; where one (1) *imitates* (2) another's *desire* for this or that (3) *object*. One the one hand, the imitator is indebted to the other for being transmitted a way of being in the world, where both parties share in a form of life (even if this form of life be preconventional; on the other, the imitator, through a sense of the scarcity of the object, is in unconscious rivalry with the other, engendering basic aggression. Speaking in more integral parlance, communion empowers agency in transmitting the habits of a shared life-world; where the resultant acculturated agency is in conflict with other agents over the desired-goods proper to that world-space. Girard's theory is an attempt to point toward the roots of aggression and human violence in the formation of community, where the force of aggression that results from mimetic acculturation is so strong that it threatens the very existence of the social holon, necessitating the emergence of compensatory cross-cultural mechanisms, such as sacrifice and scapegoating, that align the aggressive energies of the various agents away from each other and towards a common target (the sacrificial object; the scapegoat); discharging the conflictual energies, generating group solidarity. The ritualization of these mechanism is, for Girard, at the heart of the emergence of human culture; and only begins to fall away with the emergence of a true spiritual heart of love of the neighbor (Christ being the mimetic model of such love). Girard's view of mimetic desire accounts for the originary and inevitable tensions that arise in human development between agency and communion, echoing and fleshing out a claim made by Wilber in *Sex, Ecology, Spirituality* (2000, 529).

In light of Girard's theory, art as mimesis to the second power regularly redresses the tensions emergent from first-order processes of mimetic desire (although, as a result of post/modern communications, mass media art is becoming more and more a contributor to first-order mimesis itself, especially in conjunction with advertising's creation of ever new desirable commodities that "one must have," this process reaching down into earlier and earlier stages of development). To give a quick example, the most common content of Paleo-lithic cave paintings are the animals needed for survival. Painted in a manner that expresses a magical form of consciousness, conjuring substitutes felt to be in some manner to be present in the cave, these animal murals redress the mimetic rivalry proper to a world-space constituted by individuals resonating at survival waves within a hunting and gathering mode of production, the murals externalizing and addressing survival fears and unconscious aggressions, these painted magical substitutes present to all members of the human group dwelling in the shelter of the cave. Art here contributes to the reduction of conflictual tensions, not by coordinating aggressions within the collective (proper to other cultural mechanisms), but by supplying imaginative substitutes of the desired object. Of course matters can be much more complex, as with mass media creating endlessly new objects of consumer desire, hence seen from one angle as *exacerbating* the field of aggression. As a more general guideline then let us say that art regularly *works* upon the holonic drives—agency, communion, Eros, Agape—proper to the world-space(s) in which its makers and viewers are embedded.

Aesthetic Experience

As mimetic model, opening and focusing a world within the world, art has the propensity to engender *aesthetic experience*: the gathering, intensifying, and essentializing within perception itself of the lived-sense of this or that world-space, experience shining and shimmering with life-enhancing psychic charge and affect. Although remaining little studied, we can speculate that aesthetic experience in this sense has: (1) developmental strata, Walter Benjamin's (1969) notion of *aura* being a premodern magic-mythic form (217–51); (2) irreducible surface expressions, as with Japanese *mono no aware* (see Parkes 2005); and (3) can have pathological forms, as with the shimmering and superficial sheen of postmodern art and experience proper to the commodity spectacle.[12] Aesthetic experience, where the terms of "aesthetic" in modern and postmodern art writing are wildly varied to be sure, is one of the richest areas of inquiry associated with art, and also one of the trickiest, as the direct experience of the art itself is what is so full, replete, and resonant with such aesthetical styles of being.

Media

The precise ways an artwork (1) opens a world within a world, (2) refigures holonic drives as these find expression in a given world-space, and (3) engenders aesthetic perception are specific to the artifact's *medium*. Media analysis, inseparable from the semiotics of the artifact, is interwoven with the pragmatics of making and using, that, for example, music is heard while a painting is seen, the exploration of these issues pointing to zone 5 reflections on lived-embodiment enacting an environment and on the auto-poetics of the sensorium, exemplary scholars in these veins including the early Nietzsche, Merleau-Ponty, Samuel Todes, Erwin Strauss, and Susan Bordo, to name a few.[13]

The artwork as artifact, in opening a world, does so in a world of sentient beings. We engage in methodological investigation of the world opened by art through the grid of an *integral semiotics*;[14] while we engage in methodological investigation of the world(s) of sentient beings in which the artwork is embedded through the IMP grid of an *integral pragmatics of one's being in the world with art*—the use in tandem of these two grids integrating and healing modern and postmodern oppositions between internal and external art-historical and art-critical methods.[15]

Evaluating Art in Communicative Action

Such would be an outline of an Integral approach to understanding art. But how about evaluating art so understood? What is at stake in matters of artistic taste?

The early modern discourse of good taste (see Minor 2006) is taken up and reworked in Kant's enormously influential third critique (1987), where such judgments are said to be subjectively grounded, beyond rational deliberation, but nevertheless point to the common sense that others ought make this same judgment (sections 1–9). This is not the place to explicate Kant's theory in its complexity and subtlety, only to note that since no later than Kant, evaluating art has come to be construed, in the main, as an individual affair, taste as something personal (if not Kant's explicit view), demonstrations of having good taste, along with their theorizations, often serving (as Christine Battersby [1991, 31–43] has shown) as a badge of social-cultural capital along gender and class lines—issues that are by no means absent from the diverse world-spaces today of interpreting, evaluating, and consuming art: a quick survey of Amazon.com music and DVD reviews of music and film being a case in point.

With the explosion of mass media, and the reception and consumption of art on a scale unprecedented in world history, everyone is positioned as a judge of art. On the one hand there is an empowering democratic impulse to this unfolding; while on the other it has stunted the development of art evaluation on a grand scale, habituating processes of prereflective judgment that are not unrelated to making decisions about commodity preferences as a sign of one's taste.

Let us get clearer then about the status of *judgment*. Aligning with Lonegan's use of the term (see Lonergan 1971, ch. 2, and 1992, ch. 10), judgment is: (1) the affirming or denying of an understanding of what is the case; or (2) a positive or negative evaluation of what is the case. Both modes of judgment have two distinct paths: (A) prereflective, grounded in activation of the inherited cultural common sense proper to a given world-space; or (B) reflective, the terminus in a process of methodological understanding and reflection.

Most commonly, in matters of engaging art, 1 and 2 are conflated and enacted via A. That is, understanding and evaluation are pre-differentiated, enacted via the activation of a pregiven, sedimented stock of judgments. The more mature process is to differentiate 1 and 2 and enact each via B. That is, we first take up a methodological engagement with art, coming to a reflective judgment about the validity of the results of the inquiry (checking our biases during the process of understanding; whether we have asked all the relevant questions in the given context of inquiry; and if we have made use of the available evidence to address those questions); which if sufficiently affirmative, can move into taking up reflection on the value of the work of art so understood, leading to positive, negative, or more nuanced evaluation—with this practice, as it matures, becoming a dance between 1 and 2 enacted via B, the differentiation and integration of is and ought with regard to art.[16]

Okay, then. Let us say that you and I are quite adept in the ICT analysis of film, both of us come to a reflective understanding of *The Matrix Trilogy*, our interpretations are similar, yet we do not agree on the value of the Trilogy. What then? Can we move beyond the all too common sentiment that you have your taste and I have mine?

Here we find the decisive importance of Habermas's scattered remarks on evaluating art in communicative action, that through the procedural giving of reasons, we can reflect together on the value of a given work of art.[17] Departing somewhat from Habermas's view, let us say that the guiding ideal of such deliberations is: how well, and by what means, a given instance of art, symbolically and/or aesthetically enhance, works to transform, and/or heal a self's well-being and participation in the world-spaces of our day. (Please excuse this human-centric and atomistic phrasing; it is a beginning). We deliberate with the intent of learning from one another, ready to change our evaluations, surrendering all demonstrations of individual good taste—good taste, in the ideal speech situation, now to be achieved in the solidarity of mutual resonance. This is a dialogic practice begging to be enacted; a practice that can contribute strongly to moving us out of the narcissistic habits proper to evaluating artworks.

Having engaged in methodological understanding of a work of art and judging that understanding as sufficiently valid, moving onto evaluating that work in light of the Good, and checking this evaluation in discussion with others, one enacts a mode of interaction in public forums that reintegrates the institutionally differentiated (and dissociated) Big Three: Art, Truth, and the Good. The call in the end is to take the lessons learned from the deliberative process, expanding and deepening one's horizons and resources, into one's everyday comportments.

On the Dignity and Disaster of Post/Modern Art

I would like to outline some of the parameters and conditions of the dignity and disaster of post/modern art—a necessary starting point for any ICT of art—and especially so for the flourishing of the integral arts today. Here I summarize ongoing research and teaching, where the pressing parameters and conditions include:

1. the emergence of art as its own value sphere, with this value sphere never becoming integrated into the whole and in part dissociating from the values spheres of everyday life;

2. the emergence of a mass culture facilitated by new technological media of reproduction, the inseparability of this mass culture from industrial and subsequent informational commodity consumption;

3. the consolidating of the hegemony of free markets of art, which first became predominant in seventeenth-century Holland, with the exhibition value of art, which first became prominent with the establishment of the French Salon in the 1730s;

4. the modernist leaning, inherited from Romanticism, to (over)value the I-perspective of the artist and/or the critical audience member, focusing practices of art in the UL;

5. the emergence of the discursive archive of *possessive expressivism* (see below);

6. the performance of this discourse within a competitive field of symbolic capital;

7. symbolic capital itself mediating and veiling monetary exchange value in matters of open market exhibition art;[18]

8. the early and high modernist impetus, by no means having lost its force, of the striving for radical originality,[19] the paradoxical trope of breaking from tradition while requiring tradition to secure legitimacy (see De Man 1983,

142–65)—an artistic manifestation of the post-traditionalism proper to an orange-tinged modernity attempting to create norms out of itself (see Habermas 1981, 3–14; Koselleck, 1984);

9. resulting in the transgression of the audience's horizon of expectation in the shock of the new (see Jauss 1982a, 3–4, and Jauss 1982b, 3-151);

10. art qua art taking up issues of ultimate concern, modeling subtle and causal states with an intent and directness not seen before in the West (Schwartz 2008, 13–15); with all these parameters and conditions constituting

11. the dignity and disaster of post/modern art.

The discursive archive of possessive expressivism requires some additional discussion. It has affinities with three lineages of thought: (1) liberal political discourses of possessive individualism and radical self-ownership; (2) late enlightenment and Romantic discourses of constitutive-expressivism; and (3) early modern recastings of what had been the Renaissance humanist reviving of the praise and blame tropes of ancient *ekphrasis*. This post/modern archive, which manifests in diverse textual, oral, and genre contexts, has as its generative mechanism: that the artist owns, in a strong sense, the product of his or own labor; that this labor is expressivistic (coming from inner depths) and in part constitutes one's being-in-the-world; and that, using some set of criteria, the artistic product is to be or could be praised or blamed, in line with producing or reducing the artist's symbolic capital.

While unparalleled in its creative outpour and brilliance, post/modern exhibition art, on the whole, has been overcharged in the masculine drives of Eros and agency—the Eros of newness and growth over the Agape of embracing existing world-spaces and showing any possibilities of relative harmony and health therein; and with the agency of the artist (or of the viewer-critic) regularly taking precedence over communion, clear communication, and community.

Yves Klein (1928–1962)

To conclude, I shall briefly consider the monochrome project of Frenchman Yves Klein, who was born in 1928 and died in 1962, a prominent soul artist of postwar Europe, whose various artistic enterprises forwarded modernist into incipient postmodernist practice. I shall be using methods from both integral semiotics and integral pragmatics in the manner of an ICT of art.

During his late teens and early twenties, Klein imbibed East Asian philosophies, became a student of the Rosicrucian Fellowship, and traveled to Japan where he studied judo, earning a black belt "fourth dan," later teaching this martial art in Europe, and publishing a book on the discipline.[20] Even more than this training in subtle energies, which led to a number of artistic projects attempting to express subtle states (works often caught in a pre/trans fallacy revealing a magical shadow), Klein was attracted from a very early age to formless mysticiscm, having a series of breakthrough experiences as a young man, his entire artistic trajectory dedicated to directing others to the void. (His first musical composition, for example, is titled Monotone Symphony, one continuous tone—not unlike the background drone of Hindu music.)

Klein's reworking and exploration of the monochrome, invented earlier in the century by the Russian constructivists Kasimir Malevich and Alexander Rochenko, are direct pictorial evocations of the causal state. During the twentieth century, abstract painting, including the monochrome, was articulated in three distinct and intersecting manners: (1) as an expression of the artist's singular interiority; (2) as modeling higher-than-common stages and/or states; and (3) as the manifestation of the pure form, pictorial structures, and/or materiality proper to the medium of painting. In the case of Klein, the second of these interpretive lines prevailed in both his writings and in those of apologist-friends such as Pierre Restany. Among the many variants of the monochrome that Klein created, the most effective are the vertical formats of uniform blue—late modernist Icons of the Void. This hue is extraordinary, a pigment that Klein discovered and patented as International Klein Blue. Contemplating one of these monochromes, a viewer experiences a blue void projected off of the material support of the canvas, an optical zone impossible to determinately locate within the gallery space; a self-luminous field no longer perceived as part of or dependent upon a material surface (Klein spoke of the "immaterial"). Indeed, these monochromes are "pictorial pointing out instructions" with more than superficial resemblances to Tibetan Dzogchen methods such as skygazing; they are serious attempts at directing one toward noticing the immaterial and luminous ground of being. Commenting in 1958 on Malevich's monochromes, Klein said: "Malevich painted a still-life in the style of one of my monochrome pictures. Malevich was actually standing before the infinite—I am in it. You don't represent it or produce it—you are it" (Lehmann n.d.). In addition to the Klein's enactment here of the discourse of possessive expressivism to position his project favorably with the artistic field of symbolic capital proper to advanced painting, he is also demonstrating keen awareness of the difference between the mind's trick of turning a glimpse of causal emptiness into an object (about which contemporary meditation and direct path teachers regularly caution their students) and realizing that, at least within certain Asian Views, one *is* this luminous potent ground that is none other than its display.

Not only did Klein have access to and attempt to express the causal/nondual in his monochromes, he also excavated and reworked background conditions proper to the exhibiting of his art. This is a major facet of his activity, which laid the ground for the expanded sense of the artistic artifact characterized by first phase postmodernism.

In January 1957 Klein's exhibition *Yves Klein: Proposte monocrome, epoca blu* was held at the Galleria Apollinaire in Milan. In the gallery room he displayed 11 monochrome paintings in deep Kleinian blue, all with the same dimensions but with different price tags. Each monochrome was unconventionally mounted on a pole detached from the wall. This series of virtually identical works, displayed object-like without frames, echoes the structure and display of the mass-produced commodity, a recasting of the readymade gestures of Duchamp, who early in the century had taken industrial products and with little or no alteration exhibited them in galleries. The monochromes, in contrast, were individually hand-crafted rather than mechanically produced, an artful parody then of the ubiquitous commodity form and too an update of Duchamp's gesture.

As we have enumerated, in the sphere of modernist exhibition art, symbolic capital had veiled and mediated monetary capital, the prices of the works on exhibition typically not posted on the gallery wall along with the work, but kept to the side. In the 1957 exhibition Klein brings the issue of market value directly into the space of exhibition, not only by the commodity-like serialization of the monochrome, but having boldly foregrounding the prices, assigning different costs to identical works, creating an "irrational" pricing logic, deconstructing the power of exchange value over use value, disturbing the force of an artwork's cost on how that artwork is perceived, attempting to free the spiritual potency of the monochrome from the unconscious dictates of market and commodity forces upon experience. Klein, in short, strove to rework the conditions of reception in the exhibition sphere that had become pathological for the experience of art qua art. Part of this strategy was his placement of the works away from the walls, at first stressing the object-character of the paintings, de-familiarizing reception, in the end keying the projective effect of the monochromes's immaterial field of blue (defeating the canvas's literalness, as Michael Fried would have it). Said otherwise, Klein was attempting to rescue the expansive aesthetic experience of the sublime from the distorted, pathologically inflected aesthetic experience of seductive surface sheen informed by and expressive of LR colonizing processes—this latter aesthetical mode variously articulated in the writings of Benjamin, Adorno, Heidegger, Guy DeBord, Fredric Jameson, Jean Baudrillard, and Benjamin Buchloh.[21]

This is not to say that Klein's innovative interventions into the market forces of art were always questioning of capital's ways. Recall that he patented his blue paint as International Klein Blue. As much as one may want to read this as an ironic move, an artistic parody of the emergent corporative use of brand names, in this instance he seems to have played up, with almost advertising savvy, the branding of his artistic projects in accumulating publicity and symbolic capital.

In sum, Klein not only created late modernist icons of luminous emptiness but in the 1957 exhibition (and in other ventures) expanded the work of art to enfold into its artifactual materials what had been background conditions of exhibiting, redressing pathologies endemic to a dissociated and colonized value-sphere of art. There were, to be sure, ambiguities in his various projects, including flourishes of magical stage consciousness, as well as the patriarchy if not downright misogyny of the Anthropometries (where in one gallery performance he stood to the side in a tuxedo and acted as if he were magically conducting, through the currents of subtle energies, nude women sliding their blue-paint covered bodies over canvases), yet his ventures point us toward something crucial about the arts today: that the conditions of exhibition art are not a given, but rather, as in the hands of advanced artists in the '50s, '60s, and '70s, can become part of the critical work of art itself, expanding what count's as artistic materials, such endeavors often aiming to unearth and heal inherited pathologies that curtail balanced and profound aesthetic experience.

At this juncture, much of the discussion of the integral arts has focused on the health and development of an artist's stages, states, and shadow work; all of which is necessary for the fruition of integral art and artists. But is it sufficient? Klein's impressive if imbalanced artistic projects challenge us to reflect on the taken for granted conditions of making and viewing art and consider folding them into art's critical practice—in integral circles, Alex Grey's *Chapel of Sacred Mirrors* being an effort in this vein. My sense is that unless this takes place, the integral arts, having such promise as gift to the world, will go largely unnoticed and ineffective; that the creative reworking and healing of the conditions of art making and viewing is a *necessary* component for the emerging integral arts to find their way affectively and lovingly into the souls of the many—as this is my ardent prayer.

Notes

1. Wilber has discussed these themes in various contexts; I have been unable, however, to relocate the passage I have in mind that brings them all together with brilliant succinctness.
2. From a guest blog by Zachary Stein, titled "A symbol of our shared trajectory: Philosophical reflections on Integral Methodological Pluralism as regulative ideal". Available at www.kenwilber.com. Accessed March 19, 2009.
3. On the use of the Integral Map in Jnana Yoga, see Palmer (2004, ix–x). See also Lonergan (1971): "On what I have called the primary and fundamental meaning of the name of God, God is not an object. For that meaning is the term of an orientation to transcendent mystery. Such an orientation, while it is the climax of the [cognitive and moral] self-transcending process of raising questions, none the less is not

properly a matter of raising and answering questions. So far from lying within the world mediated by meaning, it is the principle that can draw people out of that world and into the cloud of unknowing" (342).

4. His two main treatises are Levinas (1969) and Levinas (1981). For exemplary commentary, see Gibbs (2000, chs. 1 and 2).

5. Pointing us to Spirit in the second person, Wilber comes close to the Levinasian formulation, albeit with direct reference to Infinite Thouness; whereas Levinas is pointing to how radical Thouness breaks through the face of the Other. See Wilber (2006, 159). Drawing upon both of these pointing out instructions, we can attune to Infinite God(dess) in the second person as such and at the same time to this Infinite Thou breaking through *each and every* perspective, all sentient beings calling the "me" to concrete responsibility and responsiveness (this latter View having affinities with Levinas's discussions of the "third person"),

6. For the initial theoretical elaboration of discursive analytics, see Foucault (1972), and for an exemplary genealogical application, see Foucault (1978).

7. It is unclear whether to categorize Deida's three moments of psychosexual unfolding as more stage-like or as more state-like. Clearly there is temporary state access to the third wave of expanse, as evidenced by his workshops; but whether these stabilize via state-training or in a more stage-like manner, such that the results of the state-training become folded into something such as a developmental self-line, is an open question, pending substantial research-generated evidence.

8. From an integral perspective, Adorno's critique of "identity thinking" is a subtle and nuanced green-dialectical engagement with the (somewhat pathological) habits proper to orange-rational science and research. Such green-dialectical insights are to be transcended and embraced, rather than sidestepped, in the maturation of second-tier research.

    More in line with Adorno's own Lukàcsian understanding, the rise of exchange value over use value that characterizes modern capitalism penetrates the very operations of cognition, the category able to subsume particulars while "suppressing" differences, such differences, as singulars, bespeaking qualitative irreducibles: this process analogous to the ubiquity of capital processes to subsume qualitatively distinct entities through exchange equivalences that in part bypass distinctiveness in use value. In other words, the category's relation to the singular is, for Adorno, the expression of exchange value dominating use value at the level of the *form* (aside from any ideological content) of thought itself. Identity thinking is commodity thinking, the colonization of cognition/psychology proper to the UL by the economics of the LR. While Adorno's argument is analogical, pre-Habermasian, and eschews insights into cognition gleaned from developmental studies, it nevertheless ought to make us pause and rethink any assumption that neo-Kantian developmental schema are unaffected in their unfolding and operations by other factors disclosed in other zones, as with the current hyperflows of financial capital that commodify everything.

9. For a more extensive discussion of integral critical theory, complementary to and in my view empowering the brief remarks presented here, see Matuštík (2007, 227–39).

10. For discussion of Horkeimer's project, see Bernstein (1995, 10).

11. See Wilber's "Foreward" to Philip Rubinov-Jacobson's *Eyes of the Soul* (vol. 3 of the *Art and Spirituality Trilogy*). Available at: http://www.rubinovs-lightning.com/new/books.php. Accessed October 20, 2009.

12. See the comparative aesthetic analyses of Vincent Van Gogh and Andy Warhol in Jameson (1991, 6-12), and see further DeBord (1994).

13. For a related discussion of these art themes, see Schwartz (2007). Note the important remarks by Vanessa Fisher.
14. On integral semiotics, see Wilber (1997, n.12, 314–17), where the quadrant-grid is adapted to coordinate integral methodological analysis of the artistic artifact's: signifieds (UL), semantics (LL), signifiers (UR); and syntax (LR). In the conference version of this chapter, I fleshed out a media-specific integral semiotics of pictorial analysis with reference to some major theorist-methodologists: (1) naming the apparent content (UL; Summers, Wollheim); (2) iconography (LL: Warburg, Panofsky); (3) nonmimetic elements and the image-substance (UR; Schapiro, Marin); and (4) general syntactical order via pictorial space and pictorial light (LR; Riegl, Schöne). Going further, pictures encode models of cognitive *altitude* (most primarily via syntax); and can model *states*. This material on the integral semiotics of pictures— its theory, method, and application—exceeds space limitations for the present volume and will be published as an independent study.
15. On methods proper to the eight zones of an IMP of art, see Rentschler (2008). In order not to dissolve or bypass the artifact's media specificity as artifact, we do well to forward any IMP of art as a *pragmatics of the artifact*. On internal and external art-historical approaches, see Schwartz (2002).
16. Abigail Housen has done extensive research on the developmental waves of responding to art. (Housen's essays are available online at http://www.vue.org/download.html.) I am curious as to how her important research relates to the relation between understanding and evaluating art on the one hand, and on the other to the differences between the enactment of understanding and of evaluation via prereflective or reflective judgments.
17. For discussion, see Ingram (1991, 67–103).
18. On points 6 and 7, see Bourdieu (1993, 1996) and Pollock (1993).
19. On the modernist striving for a "technique of originality," see Shiff (1984).
20. For background on Klein, see Lehmann (n.d.).
21. On the 1957 exhibition, Buchloh (1986), in comparison to the explication presented here, seems to downplay the authenticity of expanded states of causual/nondual consciousness, their intrinsic and relative value, and art's capacity to model and provoke such states (including Kelin's monochromes) (see 48–51). It need be noted that Buchloh's more recent writings, as in his contributions to the two-volume textbook *Art Since 1900* (2005), establish a new standard of excellence in the nuanced social-critical engagement of advanced visual art.

References

Adorno, T. 1974. *Minima moralia: Reflections on damaged life*. Trans. E. F. N. Jephcott. London and New York: Verso.

Battersby, C. 1991. Situating the aesthetic: A feminist defense. In *Thinking art: Beyond traditional aesthetics*, ed. A. Benjamin and P. Osborne. London: Institute of Contemporary Arts.

Benjamin, W. 1969. The work of art in the age of mechanical reproduction. In *Illuminations: Essays and reflections*, ed. H. Arendt. New York: Schocken Books.

Bernstein, J. M. 1995. *Recovering ethical life: Jürgen Habermas and the future of critical theory*. London and New York: Routledge.

Bourdieu, P. 1993. *The field of cultural production: Essays on art and literature*. Ed. R. Johnson. New York: Columbia University Press.

————. 1996. *Rules of art: Genesis and structure of the literary field.* Trans. S. Emanuel. Stanford: Stanford University Press.

Buchloh, B. 1986. Primary colors for the second time: A paradigm of repetition for the neo-avant-garde. 37 (Summer 1986): 36, 48–51.

DeBord, G. 1994. *The society of the spectacle.* Trans. D. Nicholson-Smith. New York: Zone Books.

Deida, D. 1997. *The way of the superior man: A spiritual guide to mastering the challenges of women, work, and sexual desire.* Austin: Plexus.

Deleuze, G., and F. Guattari. 1994. *What is philosophy?* Trans. H. Tomlinson and G. Burchell. New York: Columbia University Press.

De Man, P. (1983). Literary history and literary modernity. In *Blindness and insight: Essays in the rhetoric of contemporary criticism.* 2nd ed. Minneapolis: University of Minnesota Press.

Esbjörn-Hargens, S. 2008. Integral ecological research: Using IMP to examine animal consciousness and sustainability. *Journal of Integral Theory and Practice* 3(1): 20–21.

Foster, H., R. Krauss, Y-A. Bois, and B. Buchloh. 2005. *Art since 1900: Modernism, Antimodernism, postmodernism.* London: Thames and Hudson.

Foucault, M. 1970. *The order of things: An archaeology of the human sciences.* New York: Vintage Books.

————. (1972). *The archaeology of knowledge and the discourse on language.* Trans. A. M. Sheridan Smith. New York: Pantheon.

————. 1978. *The history of sexuality: An introduction* (Vol. 1). Trans. R. Hurely. New York: Vintage Books.

Girard, R. 1996. *The Girard reader.* Ed. J. G. Williams. New York: Crossroad.

Habermas, J. 1981. Modernity and postmodernity. *New German critique* 22: 3–14.

————. (1987). *The philosophical discourse of modernity: Twelve lectures.* Trans. F. Lawrence. Cambridge: MIT Press.

Heidegger, M. 1962. *Being and time.* Trans. J. MacQuarrie and E.Robinson. New York: Harper and Row.

————. 1971. The origin of the work of art. In *Poetry, language, thought,* trans. A. Hofstadter. New York: Harper and Row.

Ingram, D. 1991. Habermas on aesthetics and rationality: Completing the project of enlightenment. *New German Critique* 53: 67–103.

Jameson, F. 1991. *Postmodernism of the cultural logic of late capitalism.* Durham: Duke University Press.

Jauss, H. R. 1982a. Literary history as a challenge to literary theory. In *Toward an aesthetic of reception,* Trans. T. Bahti. Minneapolis: University of Minnesota Press.

————. 1982b. Sketch of a theory and history of aesthetic experience. In *Aesthetic experience and literary hermeneutics.* Trans. M. Shaw. Minneapolis: University of Minnesota Press.

Kant, I. 1987. Analytic of the beautiful. In *Critique of judgment,* trans. W. S. Pluhar. Indianapolis: Hackett.

Koselleck, R. 1984. *Futures past: On the semantic of historical time.* Trans. K. Tribe. Cambridge: MIT Press.

Lehmann, U. n.d. Klein, Yves. In *Oxford art online.* Retrieved August 28, 2008, from www.oxfordartonline.com/subscriber/chapter/grove/art/T046847?q=yves+klein&source=oao_gao&source=oao_t118&source=oao_t234&source=oao_t4&search=quick&hbutton_search.x=32&hbutton_search.y=9&pos=1&start=1#firsthit.

Levinas, E. 1969. *Totality and infinity.* Trans. A. Lingis. Pittsburgh: Duquesne University Press.

———. 1981. *Otherwise than being or beyond essence* Trans. A. Lingis. The Hague: Martinus Nijhoff.

Lonergan, B. 1971. *Method in theology.* Toronto: University of Toronto Press.

———. 1992. Insight. A study of human understanding. In *Collected works of Bernard Lonergan* (vol. 3), ed. F. E. Crowe and R. M. Doran, 31–35). Toronto: University of Toronto Press.

Luhmann, N. 2003. The work of art and the self-reproduction of art. In *Art in theory, 1900–2000: An anthology of changing ideas,* ed. C. Harrison and P. Wood. Malden, MA: Blackwell.

Matuštík, M. B. 2007. Towards an integral critical theory of the present age. *Integral Review* 5: 227–39.

McIntosh, S. 2007. *Integral consciousness and the future of evolution.* St. Paul: Paragon House.

Minor, V. H. 2006. *The death of the Baroque and the birth of good taste.* New York: Cambridge University Press.

Norbu, T. 1981. *Magic Dance: The Display of the Self-Nature of the Five Wisdom Dakinis.* New York: Jewel Publishing House.

Palmer, M. 2004. The invitation of spirit: Editors' introduction. In *The simple feeling of being: Embracing your own true nature.* Boston and London: Shambhala.

Parkes, G. 2005. Japanese aesthetics. In *Stanford Encyclopedia of Philosophy.* Retrieved June 20, 2009, from http://plato.stanford.edu/entries/japanese-aesthetics/#2.

Pollock, G. 1993. *Avant-garde gambits, 1883, 1893: Gender and color of art history.* New York: Thames and Hudson.

Rentschler, M. 2008. Advancing integral art. *Journal of Integral Theory and Practice* 3(3): 128–69.

Schwartz, M. 2002. How "new" is the new art history?: Towards an integral history of art. In *Art history session: Re-thinking art historiography.* Mobile, AL: SECAC.

———. (2007). Occasions of art: Plenary session of the comparative and continental philosophy circle's annual meeting. Seattle, WA: Seattle University, April 13–14, 2007. Available online at http://michaelschwartz.gaia.com/blog/2007/7/occasions_of_art.

———. 2008. Foreword. In *Promethean flames: Rekindling and re-visioning the creative fire.* Bologna: Betty and Books.

Shiff, R. 1984. *Cézanne and the ends of Impressionism: A study of the technique, theory, and critical evaluation of modern art.* Chicago: Chicago University Press.

West, C. 1993. Prophetic thought in postmodern times. In *Beyond Eurocentrism and multiculturalism* (Vol.1). Monroe, ME: Common Courage Press.

Wilber, K. 1997. Integral art and literary theory 2. In *The eye of spirit: An integral vision for a world gone slightly mad.* Boston and London: Shambhala.

———. (2000). *Sex, ecology, spirituality: The spirit of evolution.* 2nd ed. Boston and London: Integral Books.

———. 2002a. Excerpt A: An integral age at the leading edge. Retrieved July 28, 2009, from http://wilber.shambhala.com/html/books/kosmos/excerptA/intro.cfm/.

———. 2006. *Integral spirituality: A startling new role for religion in the modern and postmodern world.* Boston: Integral Books.

———. 2007. *The integral vision.* Boston and London: Integral Books.

## 10

Integral Situational Ethical Pluralism

An Overview of a Second-Tier Ethic for the Twenty-First Century

Randy Martin

The Huddleston Report (1996) concluded, "we cannot survive the 21st century with the ethics of the 20th century." One major conclusion that is highlighted in this report is that we need a "global ethic," and further, it is noted that such an ethic must emerge from a sincere science-religion dialogue. This is an astute and important observation that underscores the need to consider the development/evolution of ourselves, our systems, the world culture, etc., from interior and exterior and individual and collective perspectives. In short, the report is noting that the major concerns facing us in the twenty-first century are at their core ethical concerns, and it also is advocating for a more "integral" approach to addressing these ethical concerns. This general theme also has surfaced in discourses about a variety of more specific contemporary global issues. Meyer and Davis (2003) point out that, in a global economy, the key issues will be ethical, more than financial. Miller (2003) notes that the ecological issues facing the world community are, in fact, moral and ethical issues.[1] Certainly, every culture and society is faced with a wide range of very pressing economic and ecological issues and concerns now and will be into the future, and these issues are becoming ever increasingly intertwined across nations/cultures/societies. To approach these issues in ways that can accommodate both the "global" and "local" aspects that inevitably have to be addressed to create solutions will require a new ethic. The ethics of modernism and postmodernism will not be sufficient to address the ethical issues of the twenty-first century, as they seem to be thus far demonstrating.

Citing Michel Serres, Rossman (2007) notes that in order to skillfully navigate the pressing ethical dilemmas and concerns of the twenty-first century, it will be vital that we wrestle ethics away from the specialists, who break knowledge up into little pieces. He, as have others, recognizes that the solutions to the significant problems facing the global community, the community of all sentient beings, cannot be piecemeal. The ethic of the twenty-first century must be an ethic that can encourage and also provide a mechanism for integration, not dissociation. It must open dialogue across disciplines and domains of study (and domains of existence) and also provide a language for this discourse. It must be an ethic that can promote and open dialogue among cultures/societies, with full recognition of issues relating to differing levels of depth and complexity. In short, the ethic of the twenty-first century must be an Integral Ethic.

In the sections that follow, we will explore an integral vision of an ethic for the new millennium. I will provide an initial sketch of what a global ethic might consist of. While an application of this Integral Ethic is beyond the scope of this chapter, my aim is to initiate a fuller exploration of how principles of Integral Theory such as the Basic Moral Imperative and the postconventional structure of consciousness called *vision-logic* can support a twenty-first century global ethic. But first, it is important that a general definition of ethics be provided.

Defining Ethics

Like all complex concepts ethics has been defined in a number of ways, and of course, there remains ongoing debate over what constitutes the best definition. However, there are a couple standard definitional themes that do seem to surface. One common way of conceptualizing ethics is as the science or scientific study of morality, which of course very much relates to philosophy as an academic discipline. Ethics also is often defined as a system or code of morals and/or standards associated with a particular profession, group, or religion. Finally, some use the term/concept *ethics* to distinguish right or wrong as determined by reason, from right or wrong based on social custom, which is morals.

The relationship between ethics and morals is an important issue, given the definition that I will be adopting in this analysis. Ideally, we would like to be able to characterize the distinctions between ethics and morals, while also capturing their close interrelationships. One way to do so is to think of "good and bad" or "right and wrong" as consisting of both universal and particular elements that operate simultaneously. Habermas (1990) defines morality as being concerned with principles that are inherently universal and which therefore cannot be compromised by particular interests, customs, or local practices. Ethics are more subject to and modifiable by such interests, customs, and practices. So, morals can be viewed as representing the more universal and fundamental principles of good and bad or right and wrong; they are shared core beliefs and values; they relate strongly to human virtues. Ethics, on the other hand, can be conceptualized as the "systems" we develop and apply in trying to manifest these core principles; they are guides to conduct. Ethics also then represent the particulars or more local aspects, which are heavily influenced by cultural and systemic factors. Ethics are, to a great extent, the different "packages" that the universals come in, and they also represent variations and modifications on the central moral themes.

One final definitional point that merits attention is that, from the perspective of this analysis, ethics, at some level and/or in some form, must be an applied endeavor. In addressing what he referred to as "a shift of emphasis in philosophical discussions of ethics, away from purely abstract questions to more practical ones," Jonathan Glover (2001) notes that "this shift of concern, toward 'applied ethics,' has been beneficial. *What is humanly most important has been moved from the margins to the centre*" (5–6; italics not in original). Attributing a strong applied aspect to ethics relates to the distinctions made above, in that morals are the ideas, the concepts, the principles, and ethics are the frameworks within which those concepts or principles are brought to life and realized.

For our purposes, then, we can think of morals as the "theory" or ideas or potentiality of what is right and good and appropriate and ethics as the enactment of, the putting into practice of, that theory or realizing that potential. Put more simply, morals are "knowing" and ethics are the action component, the enacting.[2] As one final caveat, however, it should be kept in mind that in our ruminations about morals and ethics and in our attempts to realize our morals and be ethical, the two concepts are deeply intertwined, and they are virtually impossible to fully separate as they are actually experienced. They are parts of the same deeper process. Thus, at times I will refer to them as ethics/morals.

The Integral View of Ethics/Morality: A Developmental Overview

The integral view of ethics/morals rests on the orienting observation or sturdy conclusion that human moral development goes through at least three broad stages, which are very similar to those conceptualized by both Kohlberg (1969) and Gilligan (1982). Wilber (1995) notes that, while not everyone agrees with the details of either of these specific theories of moral development, there is rather widespread agreement on the three general stages. In support of this conclusion, in addition to Kohlberg and Gilligan, Wilber cites a rather diverse array of developmental theorists, most notably Jean Piaget, Jane Loevinger, Howard Gardner, and Jürgen Habermas.

The three broad, somewhat universally accepted stages of moral development are generally referred to as preconventional, conventional, and postconventional. At birth we are not yet socialized into any "moral system"—

preconventional. We then begin to learn the general moral scheme that is representative of the basic values of our social group/society—conventional. With further growth, the individual *may* come to reflect on her/his society and its rules and thus gain some modest distance from it and thereby realize the capacity to criticize it and even work to reform it—postconventional.

Preconventional (Egocentric)

The preconventional stage is very strongly egocentric, geocentric, biocentric, and narcissistic. At this stage, we are bound to the body's separate feelings and nature's impulses (Wilber 1995, 2006). I feel angry so I will lash out, at whatever target is convenient; I feel hungry so I will eat whatever is there (with no thought to the needs of others). What is right and good is what makes ME feel good. It is truly all about ME; there is no recognition of "convention," norms, or rules, or others generally. This is Gilligan's (1982) "selfishness" stage, where the focus is only on self. This stage is Kohlberg's (1969) first level of moral reasoning, which begins with a very concrete, individual perspective, in which the child avoids breaking rules to avoid punishment, and is ushered out with the early emergence of moral reciprocity, with its focus on the instrumental, pragmatic value of an action (i.e., "you scratch my back and I'll scratch yours").

Conventional (Ethnocentric, Sociocentric)

At the conventional stage, one becomes bound, not to their own feelings and natural impulses, but to one's society, culture, tribe, race. A total lack of recognition of convention is replaced by convention being everything. It is no longer about *me* but now about *we*. Good or right is what "we" believe, do, and/or want. There is a clear and strong recognition of the rules that govern the group. However, the individual is not following the rules because he/she respects the principles that underlie them and feels compelled to follow them, but more simply out of the need for belongingness, to be accepted as part of the group. Others/the group define what is right or good, and I comply because I want and need to be part of the group. At this stage, most any view that is not held by my group or contradicts what my group believes is wrong. This is Gilligan's (1982) "care" stage, in which women feel it is wrong to act in their own interests and come to equate concern for themselves with selfishness. In Kohlberg's (1969) model, this stage (his level 2) is characterized, in its early phase, by an increasing awareness of shared feelings, agreements, and expectations, which take primacy over individual interests. Right is defined in terms of what is expected by people close to one's self and in terms of the stereotypic roles that define being good (e.g., a good brother, mother, teacher). The latter phase of this stage is marked by the shift from defining what is right in terms of local norms or role expectations to defining right in terms of the laws and norms established by the larger social system. It is not so much that the "quality" of reasoning has shifted here, but rather that the "group" to which that reasoning is applied has broadened.

Postconventional (Worldcentric)

We should start by noting that "post"-conventional is not meant to imply postcultural or postsocial. Rather, we can characterize this stage as being post-conformist (e.g., Socrates versus Athens; Martin Luther King versus segregation). When an individual reaches this stage, which may not be all that common actually, they are "operating in the space of universal pluralism." Somewhat ironically perhaps, the focus shifts back to self (as in preconventional), but now one "interacts" with self from a radically different perspective (Wilber 1995). Self is experienced, not as an entity into and of only itself, but as it relates to others' needs and wants. This differs, however, from the immediately preceding stage (i.e., conventional), as the sense of "the other" has greatly expanded and the appreciation for the other has significantly deepened. The "other" now is all humans (and quite possibly also nonhuman sentients). Self is seen, at least to a significant degree, in relation to all others, and the concepts that become central are those that connect self to all others. Self is experienced as and its role is questioned as it relates to core principles and precepts such as justice, equality, humanity, etc. (Wilber 1995). Jane Loevinger (1987) refers to this as a "conscientious self." In Gilligan's (1982) theory, this is the stage of "universal care," where it is recognized that it is just as wrong to ignore one's own interests as it is to ignore the interests of others. This understanding comes through as a concern with connecting with others, but also with the new revelation that connection, or relation, involves two people, and if either one is slighted, it harms the relationship. This is Kohlberg's (1969) level 3, which is characterized by reasoning based on principles, using a "prior to society" perspective (i.e., principled reasoning). Individuals reason based on the principles that underlie rules and norms, they reject uniform application of rules/norms, and they come to value the spirit of the rule over the letter of the rule. This stage evolves from reasoning rooted in ethical fairness principles from which moral laws would be devised, through conceptualizing right as being defined by decisions of conscience, in accord with self-chosen ethical principles appealing to logical comprehensiveness, universality, and consistency. Principles are seen as being abstract and ethical, like the golden rule or Kant's (1785) Categorical Impera-tive, not concrete moral rules such as the Ten Commandments. At the heart of this orientation are universal principles such as justice, reciprocity, equality of human rights, and respect for the dignity of human beings as individuals. This is truly a more fully worldcentric vision. (These kinds of concepts reflect the essence of our interconnectedness with others, and therefore this stage reflects the beginnings of a deeper spiritual experience of self.)

To briefly summarize and juxtapose the three stages: preconventional/ egocentric—I am the world, and I am the sole source of good and right; conventional/conformist—I need others to define me/my world, to define good and right. Good or right is what WE think it is; postconventional/worldcen- tric—the questions of "Who am I?" and "What is good or right?" are answered in regard to others and the broader and deeper world. Across the stages, the definition of right progresses from "it is right because it makes me feel good," to "it is right because my parents say, or my job says, or (later) my society says" to "it is right because of the principle that underlies it." In short, preconventional is all about my interests whereas at conventional my interests are defined by the group and then at postconventional there is an integration of my interests, the group's interests, and interests beyond both.

The Basic Moral Intuition, Vision-logic, and Post-Postconventional Morality

To begin the more specific dialogue about what an Integral Ethic might look and feel like, we need to begin by examining two other fundamental aspects from Integral Theory, the Basic Moral Intuition (BMI) and vision-logic, which will serve as cornerstones for our discussion of an Integral Ethic. In talking about an Integral Ethic, we are basically addressing how the "typical moral stance" would manifest as we move into second-tier consciousness, or in other words, how the BMI might more typically be "unpacked" in the postformal vision-logic stages.

The Basic Moral Intuition

The Basic Moral Intuition (BMI) is the core construct (i.e., a guiding metap- rinciple) in the integral view of morality. According to Wilber (1995, 1996), the BMI, which is present at all stages of human development, is simply to "protect and promote the greatest depth and the greatest span" (613 and 335 respectively). The BMI represents the "actual form" or the "actual structure of spiritual intuition" (Wilber 1996, 335). (When Spirit's intuition is clearly apprehended, it manifests as a desire to extend the depth of I to the span of We, and as an objective state of affairs [It]; it is the desire to connect self, culture, and nature.)

The BMI is present, not only in humans, but in all individual holons.[3] However, the greater the depth of the holon, the more clearly intuited and more broadly extended is the BMI (Wilber 1996). This latter point gets into the ways in which the BMI manifests across the different levels of development/different worldviews. Each stage of development has the same BMI, but each stage also is characterized by different definitions of self, others, and objects/the physical world. Consequently, each stage will manifest a different "typical moral stance" (Wilber 1995); each stage will demonstrate a different modal ethic, as discussed above.

Before we look more closely at the "typical moral stances" that are personified across the different levels, we need to clarify a couple of concepts and then more generally address what all of this has to do with morality, as we would experience it. As generally conceptualized, a holon is a "whole-part," and in fact, there is nothing that is not a holon (upwardly and downwardly forever). So, actually, what we typically refer to as "hierarchy" is really holarchy (i.e., levels of holons). Holarchies have both vertical and horizontal dimensions. The vertical dimension is the number of levels, and the greater the vertical dimension, the greater the depth of the holon. The horizontal dimension relates to number of holons on a given level; the more there are, the "wider" the span. Individual holons exist with other individual holons in holoarchies. Each "junior" individual holon is a "constitutive part or element" of its senior (e.g., whole atoms are parts of whole molecules, which in turn are parts of whole cells . . .) (Wilber 1995).

In order to relate this directly to the BMI, two points need to be clarified concerning the interrelationships among individual holons. The first point relates to the meanings of *fundamental* and *significant*, in regard to junior and senior holons. This differentiation constitutes an essential and foundational distinction. The lower or more junior an individual holon, the more fundamental it is; it is an ingredient or element in many other holons, all those that come above it in the holarchy (e.g., molecules, cells, and organisms all depend on atoms for their existence, so atoms are more fundamental). Higher or more senior holons, in turn, are more significant, because they contain or "signify" many other holons (Wilber 1995). Organisms contain or embrace cells, molecules, atoms, and quarks. Cells, which are less significant but more fundamental, contain or embrace molecules, atoms, and quarks, etc. Depth basically relates to significant, and span relates to fundamental. If the BMI is to promote the greatest depth for the greatest span, then it is vital that this distinction be kept clear. When fundamental is confused with or mistaken for significant, it can cause considerable problems, and this kind of confusion will have important implications for ethical/moral decision making.[4]

This leads to the second point, which is that the destruction of any type of holon results in the destruction of all holons above it and none below it. Wilber (1995) says that this simple rule establishes higher and lower position in any hierarchy (i.e., holarchy). And, again, this would clearly have important implications for ethical and moral decision making. For example, if we are to promote the greatest depth, we would want to promote an environment in which human and other life can flourish. This, for example, would mean that we would most certainly want to address environmental problems such as global warming, which threatens the more fundamental levels of existence but also then in turn threatens more significant holons (i.e., worldwide drought will kill off mass numbers/types of plants, which will impact food sources and oxygen levels for other living creatures farther up the spectrum). Relating this directly to the BMI, in attempting to promote the greatest depth for the greatest span, we must make pragmatic judgments about intrinsic worth or value, about the degree of depth we destroy in the attempt to meet our own and/or others' vital needs. For example, as these moral/ethical judgments pertain to promoting as much depth as possible, it would clearly be immoral (contrary to the BMI) to kill one human to gain for ourselves (or even our family) a million dollars. However, we also are attempting to carry across as much span as possible, so, "What about the decision to kill a thousand people to save a million people?" Or, as Wilber (1995) ponders, what if it came down to killing12 apes or one Al Capone?

One other concept that is relevant here is Eros. Eros is the "secret impulse" of the Kosmos and refers to the "inherent directionality" of evolution toward "increasing depth, increasing intrinsic value, increasing consciousness. In order for evolution to move at all, it must move in those directions—there's no place else for it to go!" (41). This means that, since the universe has an inherent direction, we have an inherent direction, and it would seem then that we may well conceptualize the BMI as the ethic that helps guide that movement, as the Ethic of Eros.

In summary, the BMI is the form and structure that our moral/ethical sensibilities take. It is that which is basically moral in us; it is our capacity to comprehend ethical/moral issues and our capacity to act in response or in regard to those issues. Of course, this capacity will manifest differently across the levels of development. (Also, it should be noted that, as is the case with all aspects of our development and functioning, the BMI can be manifested in both healthy and pathological ways.)

Now that I have generally defined and described the BMI, let us turn back to the more specific expressions of the BMI across the spectrum of consciousness. As Wilber (1995) notes, we all "intuit Spirit" to some extent, and therefore we all, regardless of our level of development, possess the BMI. However, this intuition is unfolded only at that level of consciousness held by each individual. Also, as "Spirit *always* manifests simultaneously in and as the four quadrants, then this spiritual intuition is (and would have to be) unpacked according to how each stage of development cognizes the four quadrants" (614). For the purposes of this analysis, we can focus on three basic stages, egocentric, ethnocentric, and worldcentric. The egocentric moral stance extends depth only, or at least primarily, to self. This stance has a span of one, and it promotes and protects depth only in that span, the span of self; from this level, others typically are seen merely as extensions of self. The view broadens and deepens in the next level, ethnocentric. Here, the span is extended to those who believe as the self does, and their depth is protected and promoted, in the form of what might typically be referred to as a "duty ethic." All those who fall outside of our "group," all those who have the wrong beliefs, are seen as "infidels, who possess no depth, no soul, and thus are not worthy of being protected and promoted (and, indeed, are often sacrificed to the glory of the culture's god)" (Wilber 1995, 613). When we reach the "worldcentric rational stance," the definition of our group is broadened and deepened substantially and ultimately extends to all human beings (and maybe some nonhuman beings as well). The span of self is extended and deepened to include and embrace the connections to other people and even other sentient beings.

One other issue that warrants mention is the fact that, while the BMI may generally reveal itself through a typical, stage-related moral stance, it can still be unpacked differently by different people at the same stage.

> Further, even within a given level of development, the Basic Moral Intuition is just that, an intuition, not an engraved tablet with written instructions. It is given form and shape by the surface structures of the culture in which it finds itself, and—precisely because it is intuition—individuals within a given stage can *legitimately* disagree on precisely what depth is, what span should be included, and what measures should be taken to objectively implement it (I, we, it). (A higher stage would involve a more *authentic* unpacking of the BMI, but that stage would still face its own problems of legitimacy on its own level, and so on.) (Wilber 1995, 614).[5]

Vision-logic/An Integral-Aperspectival View

This section begins from the premise that the most conceptualizations of development generally, and of ethics/moral line more specifically, have typically stopped with rational thinking. Kohlberg's (1969) stage 6 (level 3) and Gilligan's (1982) stage 3 and also the two dominant ethical approaches of the Western world, utilitarianism/consequentialism and deontology, are all ultimately rational; postconventional is not postrational.

Despite this dominant focus on rationality as the apex of development, there is support for the existence of a stage, or stages, beyond the postconventional. Wilber (1995, 1996, 2006) cites a number of such sources from developmental psychology, as well as the works of Gebser and Habermas (see in addition the discussion of the Wilber-Combs Lattice in *Integral Spirituality*, 2006). Also, it should be noted that ultimately Kohlberg (see Kohlberg, Levine, and Hewer 1983; Kohlberg 1984; Kohlberg and Ryncarz 1990) added a stage 7, and Gilligan (1982, 2003) alluded to a stage 4, or a post-postconventional stage. However, most treatments of Kohlberg's and Gilligan's theories either neglect these higher stages altogether, or if they are mentioned, it is most often as an aside or almost in passing, rather than as vital aspects of the theories. (I will delve more deeply into these stages in a later section.) Admittedly more research within moral development needs to be done but there is much developmental research in other contexts (e.g., cognitive, self-identity), which supports the likelihood of higher stages of morality.

Before we get into a discussion of how a postrational/integral ethic might manifest, we need to briefly describe vision-logic as a level(s) of development/consciousness. We are using the concept of vision-logic (teal and turquoise altitude) to refer to what has been portrayed as second-tier or integral consciousness (see Wilber 1995, 2006). In the final stage in first-tier consciousness, pluralistic (green altitude), we come to recognize, and even to honor, multiple perspectives. However, while this stage is postconventional, it is not postrational. Vision-logic is the transformation from pluralism, from a somewhat limited, rational worldcentrism, to a more truly postrational, universal view. "In other words, rationality is global, vision-logic is more global" (Wilber 1995, 259). In discussing vision-logic, Wilber (1995) notes "[W]here rationality gives all possible perspectives, vision-logic adds them up into a totality.... [V]ision-logic is a higher holon that *operates upon* (and thus transcends) its junior holons, such as simple rationality itself. As such, vision-logic can hold in mind contradictions, it can unify opposites, it is dialectical and nonlinear, and it weaves together what otherwise appear to be incompatible notions" (185).

"The capacity to go within and *look at* rationality results in *going beyond* rationality, and the first stage of going-beyond is vision-logic" (Wilber 1995, 258).[6] If one becomes aware of their own rationality, then the nature of that awareness is "bigger than rationality." If we are aware of our rationality then we have, to some extent, transcended the rational worldview. However, it should be noted that, while vision-logic is postrational, it is not yet fully transrational. It "lies on the border between rational and transrational, and partakes of some of the best of both." It is "integral-aperspectival" (Wilber 1998, 132). Integral-aperspectival refers to a level of consciousness that not only recognizes the plurality of perspectives, but also does not privilege any particular perspective, which permits or leads to a more integral view. The stage or structure preceding vision-logic is referred to as "rational-perspectival." At this stage of thinking, one can certainly take different perspectives, but it tends to be more monological in nature/function, privileging a particular perspective and filtering/experiencing the world, and other perspectives, through it. Vision-logic, on the other hand, is "integral-aperspectival." It "adds up all the perspectives *tout ensemble*, and therefore *privileges no perspective as final.*" Vision-logic is the first stage that actually consciously grasps its own holonic nature, thereby finding "its own operation increasingly transparent to itself," which is the fundamental characteristic of the integral-aperspectival mind (Wilber 1995, 187).

There is one other essential point to be made about vision-logic, especially if the goal is to describe the ethic of this stage. The facts that all perspectives are interrelated, that they are relative, and that none is final, in no way means that all perspectives are equal or that none has an advantage over another. "That all perspectives are relative does not prevent some from still being relatively better than others all the time!" (Wilber 1996, 193). Healthy vision-logic fully cognizes the natural aspects of valuation and would not shy away from making such judgments when necessary and appropriate.

One final element of the emerging, second-tier, vision-logic structure relates to what Wilber refers to as "the centaur in vision-logic." The centaur, the mythic half human-half horse, has been used by Wilber (1995), and others, to symbolize body-mind, or biosphere-noosphere, integration. Vision-logic is "the first level where 'human mind' and 'animal body,' ordinarily at odds, are integrated into a single whole" (Wilber 1999a, 181). Consequently, the centaur or vision-logic self is an "integrated personal self" (Wilber 1999a).

In summary, the transformation from pluralism to vision-logic, from first to second tier, is the move beyond rationality into postrational thought. Vision-logic is a "unifying logic" that transcends the proclivity of the rational mind for more cold analytic and divisive reasoning. Also, as unifying logic, it makes possible the (re)integration of "human mind" and "animal body," the unification of culture with nature, the melding of feminine with masculine. Speaking in terms of traditional ethics theory, we might also add that it can bring together the interior focus of deontology with the exterior focus of utilitarianism.

Post-post Conventional Morality: Kohlberg's
Stage 7 and Gilligan's Stage 4

Kohlberg's stage 7 (see Kohlberg, Levine, and Hewer 1983; Kohlberg 1984; Kohlberg and Ryncarz 1990) has been referred to as a "soft" stage. It is oriented toward "metaethical, metaphysical, or religious frameworks," and attempts to answer "limit questions," such as "Why be moral?" (rather than focusing on the question of "how to be moral"). Stage 6 can tell us what is moral and how to be moral, but it cannot tell us why we should act morally. In other words, it can describe "what is just," but cannot answer the question of "why justice makes sense in our world." To construct an answer to this kind of question requires that we get in touch with "theistics" and the "rhythms of nature," that we see our self in "union with a larger self"; it runs beyond the domain of justice and into the domain of "ultimate concerns"[7] (Lapsey 1996, 90). Kohlberg stated that the haunting and daunting question of "Why be moral?" can never be answered if one restricts their inquiry to morality itself. For Kohlberg, stage 7 represents the "quest for an *ultimate* meaning for moral judging and acting" (Carter, cited in Clarke 2000, online source; italics not in original). Rest et al. (1999) state that religious faith becomes Kohlberg's stage 7, but they do not appear to be making reference to the more organized, ethnocentric forms of "faith" that characterize earlier, first-tier development. Rather, they seem to be getting more into the realm of what is often referred to as "Spirit."

Similar to Kohlberg, Gilligan (1982) identified three hierarchical stages of female moral development: selfish, care, and universal care. As noted above, these basically correspond with preconventional (egocentric), conventional (ethnocentric), and postconventional (worldcentric). While most of the work on or about Gilligan restricts the coverage to these three stages, Wilber (2006, 2008) states that Gilligan has actually identified a fourth Integral stage, which she says both males and females can reach, and which "largely integrates male-agency and female-communion."[8] This basically corresponds to vision-logic or the centauric stage in Wilber's Integral Theory, which constitutes the second tier of development and is the doorway to the transpersonal realms (i.e., third tier). It also would appear that this would be somewhat in line with Kohlberg's stage 7, although the issue of the merging of the two gender styles is not necessarily explicitly addressed. Now that we have laid some groundwork, let us move into a more specific discussion of what vision-logic ethics/morality might look like.

Vision-Logic Ethics: Integral Situational Ethical Pluralism

The main questions that still remain are "What is the ethic of vision-logic?", or "How is the BMI expressed in the second tier?" To address these questions, I will frame our discussion around ethics as a line of development in the Lower-Left quadrant. This cultural line compliments the Upper-Left moral line that is based in part on Kohlberg's research. So in addition to the moral line in the UL we can postulate an ethical line in the LL.

The BMI represents our basic moral capabilities and core ability to understand and experience good and bad, but these capabilities are manifested differently as we move up or down the spectrum. For example, the fundamental principle that killing is wrong is manifested and realized differently through various ethical systems, depending on the level of development, and also depending on other kinds of cultural and social systemic factors. At the lower levels of first tier, humans generally may feel little caring or compassion for other sentient creatures and may see killing them simply for sport or enjoyment as legitimate and not something to be questioned. This worldview, however, may be moderated by cultural factors. For instance, if my culture or religion reveres certain animals, we may not accept their killing as legitimate, not even for food when starving, but this sentiment may not extend to other animals. As we move up the spectrum, this view will shift and the sanctity of life is seen differently. We may recognize the necessity of killing another creature for food, but would be appalled by killing as a sport or a means of enjoyment. At the same time, we may recognize as compassionate the act of killing a critically injured and suffering nonhuman animal, but we may not condone euthanasia for humans.

So, it is clear that ethics/morals, like cognition and emotion and other skills and capacities or lines, manifest differently across the spectrum of consciousness. We have variously talked about what ethics/morals may look like at the first-tier levels. Now, the question at hand is what ethics/morals look like when we get to vision-logic; how is the BMI now unpacked or manifested? Vision-logic has been described at several other points in this analysis, but let us again briefly reiterate some of those characteristics to provide immediate context for the discussion of vision-logic ethics. Vision-logic is integral-aperspectival, the first stage that actually consciously grasps its own holonic nature, thereby finding "its own operation increasingly transparent to itself" (Wilber 1995, 187). Another essential aspect is that it recognizes that all perspectives are interrelated, that they are relative, and that none is final, but this is in no way indicative of an acceptance of all perspectives as equal (Wilber 1996). Healthy vision-logic is fully cognizant of and embraces the natural aspects of valuation and would not shy away from making such judgments when called for. We can now examine how these essential characteristics more specifically relate to the ethics/moral line of development.

Asperspectival is beyond perspective, so this is neither a utilitarian nor a deontological ethic. It is not any of the 10 or so versions of consequentialism.

It is not simply ethical hierarchicalism, or ethical realism, or any of the other specific theories of ethics. It is not a prioritizing perspective, not an either/or, not a rational better or worse, but rather it is an "any and/or all of the above" view. When we reach vision-logic ethics, it is recognized that all of these ethical visions or worldviews have value and all, at times, may be right/most applicable/better/best/etc. It is Integral Situational Ethical Pluralism (ISEP).

The vision-logic ethic is deeply compassionate and brutally realistic, at the same instance. It recognizes that there is no dialectic between compassion and reality. The person applying this is fully self aware in the process (monitoring and self-critical); they apply their own ethical system to moral and ethical decision making as it is occurring. However, this certainly does not mean that the vision-logic ethic is perfect in assessing situations and/or in rendering decisions. Perfect implies that there is an absolute right or wrong decision (and only one usually) and that there are absolute and exclusive good or bad outcomes. The vision-logic worldview is not that restrictive or constricted, or unrealistic. There is a deep awareness that right and wrong are not absolutes and may shift with context, time, etc. There is the realization that there may be multiple right and wrong, good and bad solutions to a dilemma. Again, it is ISEP.

ISEP: Obstacles and Pathology

There are two more areas that warrant at least some brief attention before concluding this analysis, the obstacles to moving from first to second tier and pathology and ISEP. Wilber (1995, 1999c) observes that only a relatively small number of highly developed humans actually reach vision-logic. There are numerous obstacles and pitfalls along the journey to second tier and to navigate all of them is no small task. There are many opportunities for our development to be stagnated, derailed, or hijacked. Before we can attain a worldcentric vision and moral awareness, we must rise above natural biocentric impulses, and "egocentric wishes," and "ethnocentric proclivities." To realize our own "highest aspirations" and own "truest self," we have to transcend natural desires, egocentric impulses, and conformist/ethnocentric perspectives. It is only when we are free from the "shallowness of these lesser engagements" that we can transcend the merely rational, feel and express real compassion, and thereby hope to manifest ISEP. As Wilber notes, if it came in a bottle we would all then be paragons of virtue.

As is the case with all levels and all lines, there are healthy and pathological manifestations of ISEP. Wilber (1996, 1999a) has referred to vision-logic as the existential level of development. As such, the primary pathologies relating to this stage are deep-seated existential-type concerns (see 1999a for more detail). The syndrome that seems most applicable for this analysis is existential depression. Existential depression is "a global-diffuse depression of 'life-arrest' in the face of perceived meaninglessness" (Wilber 1999a, 126). It arises when we are confronted with various fundamental issues of existence, or what also have been referred to as ultimate concerns. Four prominent such issues are death, freedom, isolation, and meaninglessness. Death is that great inevitable occurrence, which we cannot avoid and which therefore may render our existence ultimately meaningless. Freedom refers to the absence of external structure, and the necessity for us to create structure in the world. Isolation is realization that, no matter how close we become to others, there is always a gap, and we are therefore ultimately alone. Meaninglessness (or a crisis in meaning) arises out of the other three. If we have to construct our own world, and if in so doing we still remain ultimately alone, and finally we will die anyway, then what meaning does life really have? (Yalom 1980).

In terms of illustrating the impact of a crisis in meaning on ISEP development and decision making, we can refer to the observation made by Ridder (cited in Rossman, 2007) that it is getting "much harder" to be ethical because we are facing so many new, complex, and difficult issues and much tougher choices. The reaction by many to this heightened complexity is to "drop out," both professionally and/or personally, by making irresponsible decisions or by making no decisions at all. There are two common ethical/moral reactions to existential dread or depression. One is to withdraw from life and refuse to even deal with the ethical/moral dilemmas that face us. The other is to lose one's moral compass, to backslide down the spectrum on the ethics/morals line and make decisions based on more egocentric or ethnocentric worldviews, rather than from the worldcentric vision of our current second tier vantage point. The fundamental point is the same for both reactions. If life has no real meaning then it does not matter what I do or even if I do anything. I might as well do whatever I want, as in the final analysis we all end up alone, confused, and ultimately dead.

Once we reach this level of development, we have let go of our grip on meaning as defined by self and also of meaning as defined by the group. We have recognized the limitations of meaning defined by reason, and we also have come to realize that meaning still cannot be purely contextual and that not all visions are equal. We can now see all of the perspectives, recognize that none is privileged, and are capable of making appropriate and necessary valuations among them. However, we also may get lost in the perspectival morass; the awareness of all of these perspectives may serve to highlight even more graphically that none of it really means anything. We let go of the personal realms, only to find that we are even more alone and more confused, and feel more dread over our own mortality. In such a state, it is easy to see how and why one may not even acknowledge the value of ethics/morality. If none of it means anything, then issues of virtue are simple, fabricated moot points. I can do nothing or anything and at the end, it will be exactly the same.

Conclusion

Jacob Bronowski (1968) astutely observed that "almost the most interesting thing about man is that he is like the other animals. . . . But quite the most interesting thing about man is that a small number of crucial differences make him uniquely unlike other animals." It would seem that one of those "crucial differences" is our ability to be so deeply aware of our own functioning, to transcend not just our biological existence, but also our rational existence, while still holding both in consciousness and fully embracing them. Herein, I believe, lies the answer to the "Terror of Tomorrow;" our ability to transform our consciousness is the fount from which a global ethic to help us navigate the twenty-first century can spring.

As we become more and more cognizant of and accepting of levels of development beyond what Western science and philosophy have traditionally recognized and postulated, we also become keenly aware of the inherent complexity and yet simplicity that must characterize these higher domains of consciousness and experience. Integral Theory, along with a number of other more cutting-edge approaches, is continually sketching the maps for this new territory. It would seem that one important developmental territory for us to continue to more fully chart is ethics/morality. Ethics and morality have been essential issues of human development, literally, since we became aware of our own individual and social existence as a species. As our existence becomes ever more complex, as the world becomes smaller and smaller, as our recognition of our interconnections with other humans, nonhumans, and the planet on which we live broadens and deepens, as our technology creates more and more opportunities for both tremendous good and abject destruction, as the developmental center of gravity (hopefully) edges upward, we would be very wise to pay close attention to our ethical and moral development. We began this discussion with a statement from the Huddleston Report (1996), which stated that "we cannot survive the 21st century with the ethics of the 20th century." If we are to endure and thrive as a species and if we are to realize our responsibilities to all sentient beings with whom we share this planet, we will have to find an ethic to guide us.

The fundamental purpose of this work has been to provide a general sketch of what a second-tier ethic might look like, to provide some context for analyzing and understanding that developmental process, and to begin a dialog about such an ethic. There is still much to be done to deepen this dialog and our subsequent understanding of ethics/morality beyond the rational stages of development. Much more theorizing, research, and analysis needs to be done to plumb the depths of the postrational stages, and there are numerous related areas of concern to which the dialog about a Integral Ethic needs to be explicitly extended (e.g., the need for a global ethic). Hopefully, this chapter has helped to move the dialog and understanding a bit farther along.

Notes

1. In the award-winning film documentary *An Inconvenient Truth* (Bender, Davis, and Guggenheim 2006), Al Gore notes that the issue of global warming is really more of an ethical issue than it is an ecological one.
2. This applied aspect also relates directly to the Basic Moral Intuition (BMI), which is discussed in depth later in this work. Of the BMI Wilber (1996) says, "[I]f I intuit Spirit clearly, to *implement* this Spiritual unfolding in as many beings as possible: I intuit Spirit not only as I, and not only as We, but also as a drive to *implement that realization as an Objective State of Affairs (It) in the world* " (335; italics added).
3. Arthur Koestler (1967) introduced the idea of "holon" in his book *The Ghost in the Machine*, and then elaborated on the concept at the Alpbach Symposium in 1968, in a paper titled: "Beyond Atomism and Holism: The Concept of the Holon." Koestler came up with the concept of *holon* as a way to overcome the "dichotomy between parts and wholes and to account for both the self-assertive and the integrative tendencies of an organism" (Koestler 1969, para. 1). Wilber (1995) incorporates the concept of holon as a central component in his Integral model.
4. This distinction can be roughly associated with core differences between utilitarian and deontological views. The utilitarian approach generally focuses primarily, if not exclusively, on span and seems to confuse it with depth. The deontological view is more aware of depth as an important element, but seems to neglect the importance of span.
5. The issue of "pluralism" or "cultural/local specificity" of moral/ethical judgments relates specifically to the viability of AQAL as a model for a global ethic. The conceptualization of the BMI offered in the integral approach would clearly represent the "universal" or core moral/ethical elements, while also accommodating and valuing the "local" aspects, which would be essential for a global ethic.
6. Vision-logic is sometimes presented as spanning three altitudes in Integral Theory (green, teal, and turquoise). In Wilber's more recent writings such as *Integral Spirituality* he tends to confine vision-logic to second-tier consciousness, in which cases it is correlated with teal and turquoise altitude. In either case, sometimes vision-logic is qualified as being "early" or "late."
7. Drawing on the work of Paul Tillich (1957), Robert Emmons (1999) defines "ultimate concerns" as "the multiple personal goals that an individual might possess in striving toward the sacred" (6). Emmons further notes that "contemporary writers have gone to great pains to differentiate spirituality from religion," but that "one common thread that appears to transcend the diverse meanings of spirituality and religion is the notion of *ultimacy*" (6). Bregman and Thierman (1995, as cited in Emmons 1999) have defined Spirituality as how an individual "lives meaningfully with ultimacy, his or her response to the deepest truths of the universe as he or she apprehends them" (95).

8. When asked about the source of Wilber's observation, Gilligan (personal communication, June 10, 2008) responded that she believed the source was likely chapter 6 of *In a Different Voice*, where she does discuss this type of convergence, or, she noted, it could possibly be her book *The Birth of Pleasure: A New Map of Love* (2003), "which doesn't deal directly with moral development or ethics but traces a convergence in men's and women's development through a release of both from (or a resistance to) gender stereotypes that deform human nature."

References

Alter, R. 2007. Idiot compassion. Retrieved May 11, 2008, from http//www.americanthinker.com/2007/06/idiot_compassion.html.

Barad, J. 2007. The understanding and experience of compassion: Aquinas and the Dalai Lama. *Buddhist-Christian Studies* 27: 11–29.

Bender, L. (Producer), L. David (Producer), and D. Guggenheim (Director). 2006. *An inconvenient truth*. United States: Paramount Pictures.

Bregman, L., and S. Thierman. 1995. *First person mortal: Personal narratives of illness, dying, and grief*. New York: Paragon House.

Bronowski, J. 1968. Comment from book jacket. In *Man and aggression*, ed. M. F. A. Montagu. New York: Oxford University Press.

Browne, K. R. 2002. *Biology at work: Rethinking sexual equality*. New Brunswick: Rutgers University Press.

Eisenberg, N. 2002. Empathy-related emotional responses, altruism, and their socialization. In *Visions of compassion: Western scientists and Tibetan Buddhists examine human nature*, ed. R. J. Davidson and A. Harrington, 135, 131–64). London: Oxford University Press.

Gardner, H. 1983. *Frames of mind: The theory of multiple intelligences*. New York: Basic Books.

Gebser, J. 1985/1991. *The ever-present origin*. Trans. N. Barstad and A. Mickumas. Athens: Ohio University Press.

Gibbs, J. C. 2003. *Moral development and reality: Beyond the theories of Kohlberg and Hoffman*. Thousand Oaks, CA: Sage.

———. 2006. Should Kohlberg's cognitive developmental approach be replaced with a more pragmatic approach? Comment on Krebs and Denton. *Psychological Review* 113: 666–71.

Gilligan, C. 1982. *In a different voice: Psychological theory and women's development*. Cambridge: Harvard University Press.

———. 2003. *The birth of pleasure: A new map of love*. New York: Random House.

Clarke, C. 2000. Implications of modern science for a new world view: Social and moral implications. Retrieved May 10, 2008, from http://www.scispirit.com/morality.htm.

Goleman, D. 1994. *Emotional intelligence: Why it can matter more than IQ*. New York: Bantam Books.

Guyer, P. 1998, 2004. Kant, Immanuel. In *Routledge encyclopedia of philosophy*, ed. R. J. Davidson and A. Harrington. London: Routledge. Retrieved February 21, 2008, from http://www.rep.routledge.com/chapter/DB047SECT9.

Habermas, J. 1990. *Moral consciousness and communicative action*. Cambridge: Polity Press.

Huddleston, L. 1996. *Morals, ethics, and common values*. Washington, DC: World Future Society.

Jung, C.G. 1953. The psychology of the unconscious. In *Collected works* (Vol. 7), ed. H. Read, M.Fordham, and G. Adler. Princeton: Princeton University Press.

———. 1959. The archetypes and the collective unconscious. In *Collected works* (Vol. 9), ed. H. Read, M. Fordham, and G. Adler. Princeton: Princeton University Press.

Kagan, S. 1998. *Normative ethics.* Boulder: Westview.

Kant, I. 1785. *Groundwork of the metaphysics of morals.*

Koestler, A. 1967. *The ghost in the machine.* London: Hutchinson.

———. 1969. Some general properties of self-regulating open hierarchic order. Retrieved May 8, 2009, from http://www.panarchy.org/koestler/holon.1969.html.

Kohlberg, L. 1969. *Stages in the development of moral thought and action.* New York: Holt, Rinehart, and Winston.

———. 1984. Psychology of moral development: The nature and validity of moral stages (Vol. 2). New York: HarperCollins.

———, and A. Ryncarz. 1990. Beyond justice reasoning: Moral development and consideration of a seventh stage. In *Higher stages of human development*, ed. C. N. Alexander, and E. G. Langer, 191–207). New York: Oxford University Press.

———, C. Levine, and A. Hewre. 1983. Moral stages: A current formulation and a response to critics. Basel: Karger Publishers.

Lapsey, D. K. 1996. *Moral psychology* (Developmental Psychology Series). Boulder: Westview.

Loevinger, J. 1987. *Paradigms of personality.* New York: Freeman.

Lorenz, K. 1966. *On aggression.* New York: Harcourt, Brace, and World.

Lynch, G., and S. Gerling, S. 1981. Aging and brain plasticity. In *Aging: Biology and behavior*, ed. J. G. March (Series) and J. L. McGaugh and S. B. Kiesler (Vol.), 201–28). New York: Academic Press.

Maddi, S.R. 1980. *Personality theories: A comparative analysis.* 4th ed. Homewood, IL: The Dorsey Press.

Mealey, L. 2000. *Sex differences: Development and evolutionary strategies.* New York: Academic Press.

Meyer, C., and S. Davis. 2003. *It's alive: The coming convergence of information, biology and business.* New York: Crown Business.

Miller, A. 2003. *An introduction to ecololgy, ecoethics and economics.* Lanham, MD: Rowman and Littlefield.

Morris, D. 1967. *The naked ape: A zoologist's study of the human animal.* New York: McGraw-Hill.

Piaget, J. 1932. *The moral judgment of the child.* New York: Harcourt Brace Jovanovich.

———. 1937. *The origins of intelligence in children.* New York: Norton.

Rest, J. R., M. J. Bebau, D. Navarez, and S. J. Thoma. 1999. *Postconventional moral thinking: A neo-Kohlbergian approach.* Mahwah, NJ: Lawrence Erlbaum.

Rogers, C. R. (1959). A theory of therapy, personality and interpersonal relationships, as developed in the client-centered framework. In *Psychology: A study of science* (Vol. 3), ed. S. Koch, 210–11, 184–256). New York: McGraw-Hill.

Rossman, P. 1995/2007. The future of higher education: 2.14—Moral and ethical crisis research? (Vol. II, ch. 14). Retrieved May 8, 2008, from http://ecolecon.missouri.edu/globalresearch/chapters/index.html.

Sullivan, W. M., and W. Kymlicka. (Eds.) 2007. *The globalization of ethics.* New York: Cambridge University Press.

Trasi, N. 1999. *Science of enlightenment. New Delhi*: DK Print World.

Wilber, K. 1995. *Sex, ecology, spirituality: The spirit of evolution.* Boston: Shambhala.

———. 1996. *Brief history of everything.* Boston: Shambhala.

———. 1998. *The marriage of sense and soul.* New York: Random House.

———. 1999a. *Integral psychology.* In *The collected works of Ken Wilber* (Vol. 4). Boston: Shambhala.

———. 1999b. *One taste: The journals of Ken Wilber.* Boston: Shambhala.

———. 1999c. *Transformations of consciousness.* In *The collected works of Ken Wilber* (Vol. 4). Boston: Shambhala.

———. 2000a. *A brief history of everything.* In *The collected works of Ken Wilber* (Vol. 7). Boston: Shambhala.

———. 2000b. *A theory of everything: An integral vision for business, politics, science, and spirituality.* Boston: Shambhala.

———. 2000c. *Waves, streams, states, and self—A summary of my psychological model (or, outline of an integral psychology).* Retrieved May 8, 2009, from http://wilber.shambhala. com/html/books/psych_model/psych_model1.cfm/.

———. 2001. *On critics, Integral Institute , my recent writing, and other matters of little consequence: A Shambhala interview with Ken Wilber.* Part II. Retrieved May 20, 2008, from http://Wilber.shambhala.com/html/interviews/.

———. 2004. Ethics and enlightenment part 1: Compassion in a box. Integral Naked. Retrieved May 20, 2008, http://in.integralinstitute.org/live/view_ethics.aspx#ethics_ and_enlight_part1.

———. 2006. *Integral spirituality: A startling new role for religion in the modern world.* Boston: Integral Books.

———. (2008). Do critics misrepresent my position? Part III. Retrieved May 20, 2008, from http://wilber.shambhala.com/html/misc/critics_03.cfm/.

Yalom, I. D. 1980. *Existential psychotherapy.* New York: Basic Books.

## 11

An Integral Map of Perspective-Taking

Clint Fuhs

By combining past insights into the nature of human perspective-taking with an innovative application of leading-edge concepts in Integral Theory, this chapter offers the most comprehensive description of the territory of perspective-taking. It traces perspectival development through four levels of increasing complexity, shows how different types of perspective-taking enact phenomena in each quadrant-domain, and utilizes an extension of Wilber's Integral Math notation to detail more than 1,700 perspectival expressions emerging as individuals develop through the teal altitude of psychological development.

The capacity for perspective-taking enables humans to understand and experience reality as it is seen and felt by others. By deploying attention through the eyes of another, we can achieve insight into the contours of vast realms of experience beyond our own. Several decades of study implicate this fundamental mechanism of relation as a central facilitative faculty in the cross-domain development of humans. From cognitive to interpersonal and affective to self-sense, development in many domains progresses in accordance with an individual's ability to take perspectives.

This cross-domain prevalence suggests a more fundamental role for perspective-taking in the unfolding of human development. The subject-object dynamic shifting at the core of perspective-taking is recapitulated in the subject-object transformations that occur between macrodevelopmental stage shifts. This recapitulating structure is how development primarily occurs: the subject of one level becomes the object of the subject of the next more-encompassing level. The phylogenetic emergence of new waves of development happens similarly: each new level transcends the previous level by adding novel capacities while including the capacities of earlier levels.

If perspective-taking indeed holds a key role in development, a comprehensive map describing its core structure could prove beneficial to a deeper understanding of the central dynamics at play across development in all domains. While the investigation of perspective-taking has primarily occurred in relation to particular skill domains, an integral map of perspectival unfolding that covers the individual and collective aspects of both the perceptual and conceptual arenas, has yet to be constructed.

The aim of this chapter is to propose such a map, and then use it to describe the contours of the actual territory of perspective-taking available to humans as they develop. The prospect of constructing this map rests squarely on the All-Quadrants and All-Levels (AQAL) components of Ken Wilber's Integral Approach, while also building upon previous work describing perspectival development (see Wilber 1995; 1996; 2000). The description of perspective-taking territory, detailing more than 1,700 very real perspectival expressions, draws on Wilber's pioneering work in the development of a notation system for representing perspectival acts.

While the emergent aspects of this map are not yet research verified, the two chief components of its core structure—the levels of perspective-taking and the domains in which those levels emerge and are expressed—have been investigated extensively. As this chapter unfolds, we will first look at prior work detailing types and levels of perspective-taking, and second, at the notational elements needed to construct perspectival expressions. Finally, the core structural expressions at each level of complexity, along with examples of associated perspectival expressions used to enact phenomena in each quadrant-domain are examined.

The Nature of Perspective-Taking

Definitions and Types of Perspective-Taking

A brief exploration of the several definitions and types of perspective-taking illustrates the need for a integrated map. Before elucidating the core foundational element upon which this map is built, an integration of the partial truths of past approaches delineates the context in which the map rests. It also defines the conceptual range that an integrated definition of perspective-taking must take into account.

A loose categorization of perspective-taking definitions yields three general groupings: (1) those that equate perspective-taking with role-taking, (2) those that relegate perspective-taking to the realm of objects and points of view, and (3) those that place perspective-taking in the realm of making assumptions or inferences about another person's attitudes, thoughts, and feelings. In addition to suggesting what perspective-taking *is*, they also indicate *what* domain perspective-taking attempts to enact: (1) interpersonal, (2) perceptual, and (3) conceptual. Together, these three definitions and three types comprise the first foundational element of an integral perspective-taking map. As we will see, this triadic cartography of perspective-taking highlights how individuals take perspectives on how people experience themselves (first-person perspectives), their and others' relationships (second-person perspectives), and how they view the objective world (third-person perspectives).

The first definition concerns role-taking, an essential social-interpersonal skill, which forms the basis of the first type of perspective-taking. While investigating the connection between role-taking and moral judgments, Robert Selman (1971b), in reference to John Flavell's pioneering work on the development of role-taking in children, equates perspective-taking with role-taking, which he defines as "the ability to understand the interaction between the self and another as seen through the other's eyes" (8). Writing on the same topic in a paper proposing four levels of role-taking, he expands the definition slightly to read: "the ability to view the word (including the self) from another's perspective" (1971a, 1722). A few years later, while describing interpersonal cognition, he gives role-taking a more nuanced description: "the ability to understand self and others as subjects, to react to others as like the self, and to react to the self's behavior from the other's point of view" (Selman and Byrne 1974, 803). The expansion of Selman's definitions toward more inclusive and nuanced articulations points out a key aspect of an integrated definition of perspective-taking.

Equating perspective-taking with role-taking, while partially true, limits the former to only a portion of the developmental territory it truly describes. Additionally, it almost exclusively emphasizes the interpersonal type. Selman explains that in addition to applying to the impersonal domain, Piaget's concepts of egocentrism—present with preoperational thinking—and decentration—a characteristic of concrete operational thinking—also enables perspective-taking in the interpersonal domain (Selman and Byrne 1974, 803). Interpersonal perspective-taking, or that which concerns the perspectives of at least two people, one subject and one object, implicitly elucidates two of the four primary domains utilized in an integrated map. First is the collective domain, or that which concerns two or more individuals, and second, the individual domain, which, while not explicitly mentioned as a type of perspective-taking, is a requisite element for the construction of the interpersonal type. The next class of definitions offers another essential element to an integrated approach to perspective-taking.

Prior to the emergence of simple role-taking capacities, perspective-taking is deployed on a world of objects as seen from various points of view. In an exploration of object construction, Edith Ackerman (1996), defines perspective-taking as the "ability to experience and describe the presentation of an object or display from different vantage points" (27). In a similar object-oriented fashion, Harriet Salatas, writing with Flavell (1976), confines perspective-taking to the developmental capacity to realize that different subjects, in different positions, have different views of the same object (103). While again limiting perspective-taking to an undersized portion of its full territory, this class of definitions offers an important partial truth.

Perspective-taking, in addition to enacting the individual and collective domains, also reveals how different subjects view objective reality. Called perceptual or spatial perspective-taking, this second type enables inferences to be made about visual, auditory, tactile, or other perceptual experiences of both self and other (Marvin et al. 1976, 511). Lawrence Kurdek and Maris Rodgon (1975) follow Ackerman in describing perceptual perspective-taking as the ability to take another person's perceptual viewpoint (643). Other objective phenomena can be added to this, such as behavior, physical characteristics, and sensory data, each of which are enacted via perspective-taking in the third domain of exterior reality.

Moving from the realm of the objective to that of the subjective, the final class of definitions attempts to gain insight into the inner experience of others. Richard Boland and Ramkrishnan Tenkasi's (1995) exploration of perspective-taking in organizations yielded a definition featuring individual's assumptions about the knowledge, beliefs, and motives of others (358). Kurdek and Rodgon (1975) follow a similar thread, defining cognitive perspective-taking as the ability to infer the thoughts, attitudes, and intentions of another person (643). Again with a focus on the subjective experience of others, Robert Marvin and colleagues (1976) see perspective-taking as an inferential rather than perceptual process through which the needs, intentions, opinions, beliefs, emotions, and thinking of others are experienced (511). The shift from objective perception to subjective experience introduces conceptual perspective-taking, the third and final type.

Broadly defined by Marvin (1976) to include the less tangible aspects of another's internal experience, conceptual perspective-taking subsumes the various elements that appear in each of these definitions (511). These include: affective perspective-taking or the ability to assess the emotions, attitudes, and feelings of self and other; and cognitive perspective-taking or the ability to assess the thought, beliefs, knowledge, and intentions of self and others (Marvin et al. 1976, 511; Kurdek and Rodgon 1975, 643). Phenomena accessed via the conceptual type resides in the third and final domain of interior perspective-taking.

An integrated look at the types of perspective-taking delineated by these classifications yields two distinctions—interior/exterior and individual/collective—which intersect in a manner that constitutes the four domains of the All-Quadrants component of Wilber's AQAL model (Wilber 1995). These quadrant-domains are the four dimensions of any occasion enacted via perspective-taking: (1) interior-individual, (2) exterior-individual, (3) interior-collective, and (4) exterior-collective. Fueled by the spirit of unremitting integration, the significant contributions of past researchers are now combined with those resulting from empirical investigation into sequence of perspectival unfolding. Taken together, these two components provide the cornerstones of an integral map of perspective-taking.

Levels of Perspectival Capacity

Over the last three decades, the empirical investigations of several researchers have contributed to our understanding of the structural unfolding of perspective-taking ability. Despite variance in both methods and general understanding of the nature of perspective-taking, the proposed stage models are strikingly similar if compared at the level of core structure rather than surface-level descriptions. As a result, the empirical foundations provided by this work must be included in a integral map of perspective-taking. What follows is a brief description of the stage models of four researchers: Selman and Byrne (1974), investigating role-taking in the context of moral dilemmas; Flavell and colleagues (1968), exploring role-taking in a social problem solving and communication context; Melvin Feffer and Vivian Gourevitch (1960), utilizing a projective storytelling approach; and Susanne Cook-Greuter (1999), postulating levels of perspective-taking as a product of ego development. The comparison of their respective levels is aided by grouping them into four conceptual rather than empirical stages.

Stage 0

At the earliest stage of perspective-taking, children are living an entirely egocentric existence that prevents them from taking a perspective beyond their own. Selman and Byrne (1974), referring to this stage as *egocentric role-taking*, found children unable to distinguish between their true or correct perspective and the personal interpretation by self or other of social action (804). Flavell's (1968) research uncovers a similar initial stage in which children are unable to recognize that another person has choice, which they offer without justification. Susanne Cook-Greuter (1999) recognizes two stages of ego development—*symbiotic* and *impulsive*—which could fall in this Stage 0 grouping. At symbiotic stages, children are unaware of themselves as separate entities, and at the impulsive level, they are limited to a first-person perspective, which provides insight into their own experience but not another person's experience (260). Feffer and Gourevitch (1960) did not describe a stage falling into this grouping.

Stage 1

The next stage of perspective-taking emerges early in development and with it comes the ability to recognize that others have perspectives different from one's own. The *subjective role-taking* stage discovered by Selman and Byrne (1974) features the ability to understand that others have subjectivity and that they have different interpretations or experiences of a social situation because they have access to different information (804). Flavell (1968) discovered children recognize that others have cognitions about themselves and other external objects. Feffer and Gourevitch's (1960) first level, called *simple refocusing*, features an ability to retell a story from another person's perspective with a concomitant inability to coordinate between these perspectives, thereby affecting accuracy (see also Shantz 1975, 29). Cook-Greuter's (1999) *self-protective* (also called *opportunist*) stage features an advancement of the first-person perspective to include the awareness that another person has a perspective but not an understanding of the content of that perspective (261) (see also Cook-Greuter 2002).

Stage 2

The next level of perspectival emergence refines the previous level by adding a reciprocity or coordination of perspectives that are at the same level of complexity. Called *self-reflective role-taking* by Selman and Byrne (1974), this level expands awareness of another person's perspective by adding the ability to recognize that others think and feel differently because they are themselves subjects who have perspectives on the self. This carries with it the ability to reflect on the self from the perspective of another person. Flavell's (1968) research also indicated that children at this stage may change their behavior because they realize their own thoughts and motivations may be the objects of another's perspective-taking (Shantz 1975, 28). The *consistent elaboration* stage, described by Feffer and Gourevitch (1960), shows similar pattern of sequential coordination between the perspectives of self and other (see Enright and Lapsley 1980, 650). Cook-Greuter (2002) describes the next two stages—*rule-oriented* and *conformist*—as featuring a similar reciprocal awareness of second-person perspectives. Whereas the self-protective stage limits the comparisons to simple, external appearances, conformist expands them to include perspectives of interior phenomena (11).

Stage 3

At stage 3, the last empirically recognized level of perspective-taking, a simultaneous, rather than sequential, coordination of perspectives emerges. Selman and Byrne (1974) describe their *mutual role-taking* stage as bringing on line two important abilities: (1) the understanding of the self's view of other and the other's view of self simultaneously, and (2) the emerging ability to differentiate the view of self and other from that of a generalized other or third person (804–805). Flavell describes this stage as an infinite regress where the self understands that another understands that the self knows their strategy. While worded differently than Selman's description, the simultaneity of perspective coordination is the same (Enright and Lapsley 1980, 650). Level 3, called *change of perspective* by Feffer and Gourevitch, also recognizes the simultaneous coordination of perspectives in interpersonal perception (Shantz 1975, 29). Cook-Greuter's next stage, called *self-aware* or *expert*, is characterized in a manner similar to Selman's level 3 insofar as she reports the emergence of a third-person perspective. However, she describes it differently, qualifying the capacity as the act of looking at self and other as an object from a generalized third-person point of view (Cook-Greuter 1999, 262; 2002, 16).

Levels Beyond Stage 3

Deviating from the work of other researchers, an integral map of perspective-taking follows Cook-Greuter's lead in postulating levels beyond the third-person perspective. Common to both is the movement away from empirically derived levels into the realm of the conceptual. While Cook-Greuter's stages of ego development are based on a substantial body of empirical evidence, her treatment of perspective-taking beyond the expert stage thins out noticeably, relying mostly on diagrams over concrete articulations on how perspective-taking unfolds beyond the third-person perspective. Figure 11.1 shows her conceptualizations of perspective-taking through the fifth-person level of complexity.

The previously discussed levels of perspective-taking are indicated as stages 1 through 3/4 in the above diagram. From there, extending through stage 5/6, Cook-Greuter explains higher levels of perspective-taking by expanding these diagrams in a patterned fashion, which adds an additional subject star at every next level. At stage 4 (not shown), she describes a third-person perspective as extending into the recent past and present. At stage 4/5, she details a fourth-person perspective, described as a systems view that allows one to look at the self as changing over time and reacting differently in different contexts, or diagrammatically as able to take as object the third-person conception. At stage 5 (not shown), she shows an expanded fourth-person perspective that takes into account a self embedded in history and multiple cultural contexts, and at stage 5/6, she posits a fifth-person perspective extending into an nth-person perspective, which is not described in text but only understood through the diagram as the ability to take as object the perspectival complexity of the previous level (Cook-Greuter 2002). Cook-Greuter's treatment of perspective-taking is progressive and far-reaching, but, with her primary focus and research

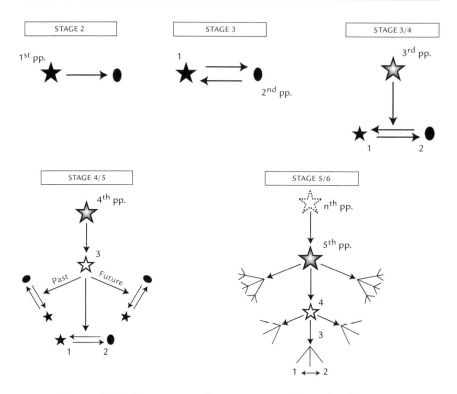

Figure 11.1 Perspective taking at stages of ego development.
Adapted from Cook-Greuter (2002); used with permission

being on ego development, the result is not specific enough to garner a workable understanding of the nature of perspectival structure and unfolding. In
a sense, the limitation of this approach lies in its reliance on illustration to
define perspective-taking. An integral map forgoes diagrams for a better-suited
perspectival notation system. The result, as we will see, is a tenfold increase in
descriptive power.

An Integral Map of Perspective-Taking

An integral map's treatment of levels of perspective-taking aligns with the basic
premise of the research summarized in the previous section while conceptually
extending it in an important way. By replacing diagrammatic and text-based
descriptions with symbolic representations of each level's core structural functioning, three aims are achieved: (1) the emergence of levels is rendered clearly,
(2) domain/level integration is made possible, and (3) a range of verifiable

perspective-taking expressions are produced. In this section, I will combine key elements of the Integral approach with the foundation constructed by past research on types and levels. The result is a map of perspective-taking that integrates quadrant along with the transcend and include structure of developmental unfolding, while offering a refined utilization of Wilber's (2003) Integral Math notation to extend our understanding of perspective-taking.

Quadrants as Domains of Perspective-Taking

The four domains of perspective-taking comprise a pair of critical distinctions made by the quadrants component of the AQAL model. First, we have the distinction between interior and exterior phenomena, and second, the distinction between individual and collective phenomena. Taken together, these distinctions give us the quadrants shown in Figure 11.2.

As the four fundamental dimensions of human experience, the quadrants outline the very real domains that perspective-taking attempts to enact: objective, subjective, interobjective, and intersubjective. Looking through these quadrant domains, perspective-taking subjects enact different objects. In the subjective domain (1p), perspectival objects include individual-interior arisings such as feelings, intentions, emotions, and thinking. In the objective domain (3p), subjects investigate such things as individual behaviors and the physical properties and characteristics of objects. In the intersubjective domain

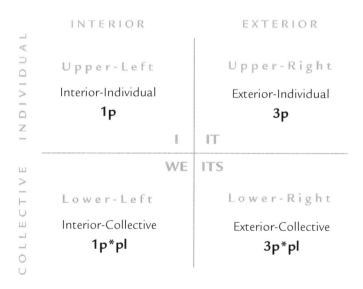

Figure 11.2 The all-quadrants component of the Integral framework

(1p*pl), perspectives can be taken on shared meaning, values, intentions, and other aspects of interiors in resonance between individuals or groups of individuals. Finally, in the interobjective domain (3p*pl), perspectives enact the intersections between individual exteriors in the form of collective behavior, system dynamics, and networks of physical interconnection. Each quadrant is a window that looks onto a distinct dimension of self and other, and it is through perspective-taking that these dimensions are experienced.

The Nature of Levels in Perspective-Taking

Even though the quadrants are the four irreducible domains of every human, full reflexive awareness of them and the perspectival objects they disclose unfolds sequentially as individuals move through levels or stages of development. The spectrum of perspective-taking presented below adheres to the transcend and include nature of development; every level transcends the previous level by adding complexity in structure and form while simultaneously including the capacities earned at previous levels. In regard to perspective-taking this translates in two ways. First, when a new level of perspective-taking ability emerges, the subject retains the ability to take perspectives at earlier levels of complexity. For instance, when the capacity for third-person perspective-taking emerges, the ability to enact first- and second-person complexity perspectives is not lost. Second, as each new level is reached and full awareness of new quadrant-domains is gained, awareness of those domains extends down into the included levels of perspective-taking, altering the range of domains through which those less complex perspectives extend.

To more easily discern the structural complexity of perspectives at each level from the increasing range of available perspectival acts at each level, the former are called *structural expressions* and the latter, *perspectival expressions*. Structural expressions communicate the complexity and core form of perspective-taking at each level. The transcend and include nature of development requires that a further distinction be made between *emergent structural expressions*, which are used to describe the novel complexity added at each new level, and *included structural expressions*, which describe the modified structural expressions from previous levels.

One emergent capacity added at the level of fourth-person perspective-taking substantially modifies both emergent and included structural expressions, and, is therefore worth mentioning at this time. After every quadrant-domain enters full awareness, development likely yields another critical distinction, altering the mode in which each domain is viewed. This distinction, which allows individuals to view each domain from the inside or the outside, renders the four quadrants into eight distinct zones, as shown in Figure 11.3.

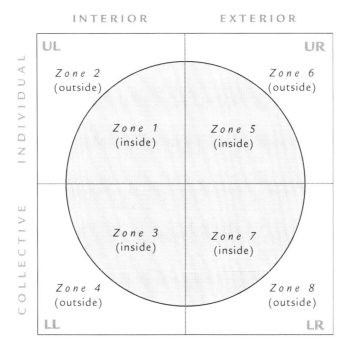

Figure 11.3 The eight zones

The circle dividing the quadrants into zones represents the holonic boundary of an individual holon or whole/part—an entity or occasion that is simultaneously a whole, in that it includes less complex holons, but is also a part of a larger whole (Wilber 2006, 32; see also Wilber 1995). An individual holon has the quadrants as native aspects of its being-in-the-world, and every quadrant domain can be viewed from the inside or the outside. This will be explained in further detail later, but, for now, consider the phenomenological difference between taking perspectives on individual interior phenomena from the inside via an introspective methodology, revealing what an interior *feels* like as compared to investigating it from the outside via a structuralist methodology, revealing what an interior *looks* like (Wilber 2006, 35–40). This additional distinction is mentioned here because it surfaces in the discussion on both the Integral Math notation and the structural and perspectival expressions comprising the spectrum of perspective-taking.

Integral Math Notation System

Integral Math has little or nothing to do with actual mathematics. Sometimes referred to by Wilber (2007) as an Integral Calculus of primordial perspectives, the notation of Integral Math is eminently useful when mapping the territory of perspectival expression. As Wilber is quick to point out, Integral Calculus is simply a map, a set of third-person abstractions but to its credit, this map of third-person symbols explicitly includes first- and second-person realities. This is why he also considers Integral Math a mathematics of sentient beings.

When Wilber first wrote about Integral Math in Excerpt C of the as of yet unpublished Volume 2 of the *Kosmos Trilogy* (2002), he explained its dynamics by mapping out perspectives taken by individuals on specific quadrant aspects of self and other. He used it again in his recent work, *Integral Spirituality* (2006), to describe the typical methodologies used to enact phenomena in the eight zones (40–43). In this chapter, these two aims are combined to map the developmental emergence of perspective-taking in the eight zones. To achieve this, we will need to first define the notation used to construct the structural and perspectival expressions. The notation sets are shown in Figure 11.4 and Figure 11.5. Only the perspectival expressions use the Integral Math notation.

These charts are provided as a general legend for reference purposes. If the meaning of any term is unclear, detailed explanation will accompany the use of expressions in the next section. Finally, we have reached the point where every component needed to describe the developing territory of perspective-taking is in place. An integration of domains and levels with the Integral math notation system provides a method for representing the manner in which humans enact the individual and shared dimensions of reality through

Structural Expressions	
S	A perspective-taking subject
O	A perspectival object
M	A mode or view
MP	A plural mode
P(O)	Plural or "we"object
$(S)_{S1}$ or $(S)_{S2}$ or $(S)_{S3}$	A subject set
$(S \times M)_{S1}$ or $(S \times M)_{S2}$ or $(S \times M)_{S3}$	A subject and mode set
$(M \times O)$	The mode and object set

Figure 11.4 Notation system for structural expressions

Perspectival Expressions	
"x"	Can be read as "of." Signifies the enacting of perspectives
1p, 2p, 3p	A 1st, 2nd, or 3rd person
1p*pl, 2p*pl, 3p*pl	A 1st, 2nd, or 3rd person plural
1p(1p), 2p(1p), 3p(1p)	A 1st, 2nd, or 3rd person's first-person interior
1p(3p), 2p(3p), 3p(3p)	A 1st, 2nd, or 3rd person's third-person exterior
1p*pl(1p*pl), 2p*pl1p*pl), 3p*pl(1p*pl)	A 1st, 2nd, or 3rd person plural's first-person plural or shared interior
1p*pl(3p*pl), 2p*pl(3p*pl), 3p*pl(3p*pl)	A 1st, 2nd, or 3rd person plural's third-person plural or shared exterior
1-p	A 1st-person mode or inside-view
3-p	A 3rd-person mode or outside-view
1-p*pl	A 1st-person plural mode
3-p*pl	A 3rd-person plural mode
1p(1-p), 2p(1-p), 3p(1-p)	A 1st, 2nd, or 3rd person's first-person view
1p(3-p), 2p(3-p), 3p(3-p)	A 1st, 2nd, or 3rd person's third-person view
1p(1-p*pl), 2p(1-p*pl), 3p(1-p*pl)	A 1st, 2nd, or 3rd person first-person plural view
1p(3-p*pl), 2p(3-p*pl), 3p(3-p*pl)	A 1st, 2nd, or 3rd person's third-person plural view
["+"]	Terms in brackets separated by "+" represents a combined view
1/p, 2/p, 3/p, 1/p*pl, 3/p*pl	A "backslash" before a "p" or "p*pl" means the expression is "Stopped" and the process of "knowing" begins. This is used in the perspectival object term

Figure 11.5 Notation system for perspectival expressions

perspective-taking—the only way through which we ever truly come to experience and understand the territory of human experience.

A Spectrum of Developmental Perspectives

Every language system utilizes pronouns, not to refer to actual people but to perspectives that actual people can enact. An "I" doesn't necessarily mean Clint, but any subject who is speaking or enacting a first-person perspective; and this perspective is always situated in relation to other sentient beings, other first, second and third persons. As Wilber (2002) suggests, because of this, pronouns actually embed a universal mathematics of perspectives in their structure. This makes the very notion of using a mathematics of perspectives qualitatively different in aim than that of typical mathematics. Perspectival mathematics, rather than merely representing the objective exterior connections between sentient beings as quantitative variables and abstract operations, also represents the very thing that makes us human, our *sentience*, our individual and shared interiors, mutual resonance, and shared perspectives. The spectrum of developmental perspectives uses this math to show how the connections between sentient beings are expressed and how the capacity to do so unfolds developmentally.

Over the first four levels of complexity alone, these connections span a range of more than 1,700 perspectival expressions between the infrared and teal developmental altitudes associated with development from preconventional to post-postconventional. Developmental altitude, as explained by Wilber (2006), is a content-neutral yardstick used to compare and relate the degree of development present in various developmental lines. Figure 11.6 shows the altitude spectrum set in relation to both the cognitive line and an estimated developmental range of perspective-taking levels.

The good news is that these expressions emerge from only a handful of core structural expressions, and it is both the emergent and included versions of these that are presented at each level. The domains enacted by structural expressions are explained alongside examples of a few perspectival expressions, used as explanatory aids to deepen and make relevant the experience of the very real territory represented in the otherwise abstract expressions.

First-Person Perspective-Taking

Perspective-taking capacity between the infrared and red altitudes is limited to a small range of perspectival expressions enacting phenomena in a limited number of quadrants. Similar in complexity to Selman and Byrne's,

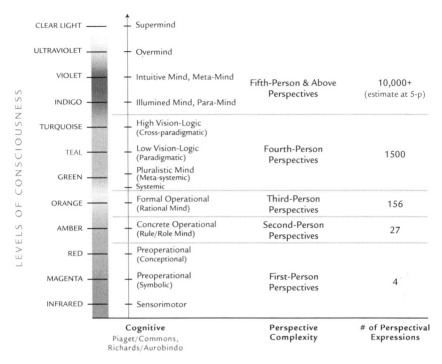

Figure 11.6 Developmental altitude, cognition, and perspective taking

and Flavell's level 0 perspective-taking, emergent first-person perspective-taking is characterized by sensorimotor and preoperational thinking and egocentric ego structures. As seen in Figure 11.7, the structural expression at this initial level is at its most rudimentary, representing a simple object (O) of perceptival enaction.

The awareness of "other" has not emerged at the first-person level. Therefore, in the UL domain, perspective-taking can only enact my interior 1p(1/p) and in the UR domain, my behavior, 1p(3/p), your behavior, 2p(3/p) and that object, 3p(3/p). Research indicates that microdevelopmental emergence of some of the basic second-person perspective-taking capacities for enacting others' perceptual or spatial perspectives emerges later in the range described here as first-person (Flavell et al. 1981). For the sake of macrodevelopmental clarity these perspective-taking abilities have been grouped in the next level of perspectival complexity. Additional investigation into the nature of perspectival emergence may yield a finer-grained map that indicates which perspectival expressions emerge at each altitude. As

First-Person Level	
SE Emergent	(O)
Domains	UL (Partial), UR (Partial)
Total # of PE's	3

Figure 11.7 Perspective taking at first-person

each level of perspectival complexity is described, please keep in mind that the boundaries between these broad levels are not as rigid as this approach renders them.

Second-Person Perspective-Taking

As perspective-taking complexity increases with the late red and early amber altitudes, so does its range and nature of expression. Additionally, two fundamental dynamics concerning the nature of this map are made apparent. First is the hidden term problem, and second, the issue of subject view. Both will be discussed after exploring the territory of the second-person level. Second-person perspective-taking, covered by Selman and Byrne and Flavell's stage 1 and Feffer and Gourevitch's stage 1, is driven by concrete operational cognition and the emerging ethnocentric self-identity, which begins to take into account the existence of other's interiors. As seen in Figure 11.8, the emergent structural expression at this level—(S) x (O)—describes a subject's view or perspective of an object, or for example, my view of your interior. The only included structural expression, carried forward from the first-person level, does not change in form but does now have the ability to enact a larger range of quadrant-domains.

The total number of perspectival expressions expands from 3 to 27 as this new level of complexity is added and awareness of domains increases to include at least a partial view of perspectival objects in all four quadrants. In the UL, the emergent structural expression produces perspectival expressions that include my first-person, 1p(1p), perspective of, say, your emotional state, 2p(1/p). Taken together, this gives the perspectival expression:

$$1p(1p) \times 2p(1/p)$$

My first-person perspective of your interior

Second-Person Level	
SE Emergent	$(S) \times (O)$
SE (1p) Included	(O)
Domains	UL (Partial), UR (Full), LL (Partial), LR (Partial)
# of PE's at (2p)	19
# of PE's at (1p)	8
Total # of PE's	27

Figure 11.8 Perspective taking at second-person

Additionally, awareness of perspective-taking capacity in others allows for this perspectival expression in the UL:

$$2p(1p) \times 1p(1/p)$$
Your first-person perspective of my interior

Inhibited by limitation in accessing the interiors of others, awareness of perspectival expressions at the second-person level includes a third person's view of my interior, $3p(1p) \times 1p(1/p)$, but not of another second or third person's interior. In the partially accessed LL domain, perspectival awareness of shared interiors includes my view of our shared interior, $1p(1p) \times 1p^*pl(1/p^*pl)$, and your view of the same, $2p(1p) \times 1p^*pl(1/p^*pl)$. In the UR, access opens to a full range of perspectival iterations to include my, your, and his or her view of my, your, and his or her exterior. This also includes a first-, second- or third-person's view of an object (a link to Appendix A, which contains a full list of these perspectival expressions is provided at the end of this chapter). Finally, in the LR domain, partial access includes a first- and second-person perspective of our shared exterior or shared behavior. An example of a perspectival expression enacting LR phenomena is:

$$1p(1p) \times 1p^*pl(3/p^*pl)$$
My first person has a perspective of our shared exterior

At the included first-person level, perspective-taking can now enact the expanded domain range afforded by the emergent properties of the second-person level. Thus, entering awareness is the interiors of others, 2p(1/p) and 3p(1/p), the shared interior of our "we," 1p(1/p*pl), and our shared exterior, 1p*pl(3/p*pl).

Hidden Term Problem

At the heart of the hidden term problem is the difference between two concepts: perspectival expressions, which are components of perspectival equations, and the act of taking perspectives. Only the portion of perspectival expressions that begin with 1p(1p), my first person, actually represent perspectives that are taken at a given level. This results from the unavoidable fact that perspective-taking begins with the subject taking the perspective, and that subject is always a first person. If I were to say that George is happy, my first person would be taking a perspective of his interior, 1p(1p) x 3p(1/p). If I was aware that you could take the same perspective of George's interior, I would describe it as your first-person perspective on George's interior, or 2p(1p) x 3p(1/p). This perpectival expression is stated in relation to me—I am a first person talking about you, a second person to my first person. This is a perspectival expression, which can be equated with any other perspectival expression of the same perspectival object to form a perspectival equation:

$$1p(1p) \times 3p(1/p) = 2p(1p) \times 3p(1/p)$$

In one sense, this perspectival equation is a question asking whether my first person's perspective on George's interior is equal to your first person's perspective on George's interior. If we both understand his interior as happy, the equation holds up. An integral map of perspectives shows the range of perspectival expressions that I can equate with my perspective, assuming, that is, the perspectival expression is available in my awareness. The appearance of 2p(1p) x 3p(1/p) in the UL domain at the second-person level does not mean that I can take your perspective of George's interior. Doing so actually increases the complexity of the perspective by adding a term—the hidden term—to the perspectival expression. The act of me taking your perspective of George's interior is really of a third-person level of complexity: 1p(1p) x 2p(1p) x 3p(1/p). If I take the perspectival expression, 2p(1p) x 3p(1/p), as a perspective, a hidden term is implicitly added and the complexity increases. The difference here is subtle but has profound effects at emergent levels of perspective-taking. If I were developed only to a second-person level, I could set two second-person perspectival expressions on either side of an equal sign and investigate if they are the same by asking you to share your perspective on George's interior, but I could not take your perspective on George's interior myself, as I am unable to take a perspective of third-person complexity.

Subject View

Before shifting our focus to the third-person level, the issue of subject view is in need of an explanation similar to the one provided for the hidden term problem. Each time a subject enacts a perspectival object through an act of perspective-taking, it is done through a particular view engaged by the subject. At this point in development, subject view shows up in two forms: a first-person view, which enacts interior objects (UL and LL), and a third-person view, which enacts third-person objects (UR, LR). These views or modes are represented by the terms 1-p and 3-p, respectively. In perspectival expressions they must be stated in relation to the subject taking them: 1p(1-p), my first-person view; 1p(3-p), my third-person view; 2p(1-p), your first-person view; 2p(3-p), your third-person view, and so on. By applying this concept to the perspectival expression previously discussed, we get:

$$1p(1p) \times 1p(1\text{-}p) \times 3p(1/p)$$

My first person has my first-person
view of her third person's interior

$$2p(1p) \times 2p(1\text{-}p) \times 3p(1/p)$$

Your first person has your first-personview of her third person's
interior

The view (1-p) is used in this case because the perspectival object is an interior. The views through which these objects are enacted are not shown in the perspectival expressions at the first-, second-, and third-person levels because individuals do not yet possess full, self-reflexive awareness of their views. It is postulated that this capacity emerges at the fourth-person level when a person can actually choose to view any perspectival object from a first- or third-person view. This is explored in greater detail later. For now, an assumption is made that interior objects are seen through first-person subject views and exterior objects through third-person subject views. This is not to say that perspectival objects determine views, but rather that until views can be operated upon with full awareness the object is enacted through the view associated with the object domain; (1-p) for the UL and LL and (3-p) for the UR and LR.

Third-Person Perspective-Taking

The unfolding of the orange altitude elevates perspective-taking capacity to a third-person level of complexity. In addition to expanding the range of available perspectival expressions, formal operational cognition and an early worldcentric self-identity provide individuals with full access to every quadrant domain and an important addition to the emergent structural expression. At the third-person level, individuals reach the pinnacle of perpectival development as described by Selman and Byrne, and Flavell in their description of level 3 role-taking. The emergent structural expression indicated in Figure 11.9 details the capacity for seeing the self and other interaction from a third-person perspective.

The emergent structural expression reads: One subject's perspective of another subject's perspective of a perspectival object. The subscripts, S1 and S2, differentiate the two subjects whose perspectives are involved. The included structural expressions from the first- and second-person levels are carried forward at the third-person level. While they have not changed in form, they are now involved in generating perspectival expressions in every quadrant-domain across the full iteration of first, second, and third persons.

Third-Person Level	
SE Emergent	$(S)_{S1} \times (S)_{S2} \times (O)$
SE (2p) Included	$(S) \times (O)$
SE (1p) Included	(O)
Domains	UL, UR, LL, LR (All Full)
# of PE's at (3p)	108
# of PE's at (2p)	36
# of PE's at (1p)	12
Total # of PE's	156

Figure 11.9. Perspective taking at third-person

Despite increasing in both range, number, and complexity, perspectival expressions at the third-person level are constructed from the same type of terms used at earlier levels. A few examples from the 108 third-person expressions (there are 156 total when the additional expressions at the first- and second-person levels are included) will make this clear. First, we will look at both my and your perspectives on George's interior as it is understood by Mary.

$$1p(1p) \times 3p(1p) \times 3p(1/p)$$

My first person takes her first-person's perspective of his interior "I think that Mary feels that George is upset."

$$2p(1p) \times 3p(1p) \times 3p(1/p)$$

Your first person view takes her first-person's perspective of his interior "You think that Mary feels that George is frustrated."

These examples of third-person perspectives on someone's interior once again indicate the nature of both the issue of perspectival expressions versus equations and the hidden term problem. If expressions with the same perspectival object are available at a given level of perspective-taking, they can be compared for equality, and, in this case, our views of George are not equal. This check is one component of an investigation of perspectival accuracy. In this third-person example, first we check if our views of Mary's view are accurate. Then, depending on our motivations, we can consider a view from one level of complexity lower. If we are interested in our view of how a particular action that Mary took toward George was motivated by her perspective on his interior, we can stop here. However, if I am investigating if you and I would have acted similarly to Mary, we can compare how my, your, and Mary's view equated with George's view of his own interior. To do so, we look to the following second-person complexity perspectival equations:

$$1p(1p) \times 3p(1/p) = 3p(1p) \times 3p(1/p)$$

My view of George's interior compared to his view of his interior

$$2p(1p) \times 3p(1/p) = 3p(1p) \times 3p(1/p)$$

Your view of George's interior compared to his view of his interior

$$3p(1p) \times 3p(1/p) = 3p(1p) \times 3p(1/p)$$

Mary's view of George's interior compared to his view of his interior

Returning to third-person complexity perspectives, expressions of similar form appear in the other quadrants as well. In the UR, perspectival objects are the exteriors of individuals—their behavior, appearance, and physicality—and are represented as the object terms, $1p(3/p)$, my exterior, $2p(3/p)$, your exterior, and $3p(3/p)$, his exterior or that physical object or "it." In the LL and LR we get first-, second-, and third-person plural shared interiors and exteriors. If I said, "I feel that you feel that we share the deep bond of friendship," we would have the following expression:

$$1p(1p) \times 2p(1p) \times 1p*pl(1/p*pl)$$

My first person's perspective of your first-person's perspective of our shared interior

In a similar fashion, if I am aware of the existence of your view of George's understanding that you and he both have the obligation to pay your taxes by April 15, we would get:

$$2p(1p) \times 3p(1p) \times 2p*pl(3/p*pl)$$

Your first-person's perspective of George's first-person perspective of y'alls shared behavior

The remaining perspectival expressions—spanning first-, second-, and third-person complexities—at the level of third-person perspective-taking are found in Appendix A. As we begin exploring the profound changes brought on by the fourth-person level of perspective-taking, remember that any perspectival expression that does not begin in $1p(1p)$ is not representing a perspective actually taken by you. In the taxpaying example, if I was actually to take a perspective on your view of George's view of y'alls shared exterior, I would place the hidden term in front and find myself squarely in the territory of fourth-person perspective-taking.

Fourth-Person Perspective-Taking

A substantial expansion of the territory of perspective-taking occurs as individual development enters the mid to late worldcentric space from the green to late teal altitudes. Fourth-person perspective-taking moves beyond the realm of empirically validated role-taking into a place described in a limited form by Cook-Greuter. The addition of several emergent elements of complexity, including combined views and awareness of zone-based subject view, distinguishes an Integral Math–based perspectival map as the most comprehensive conceptual outline of human perspective-taking, one that will help define the contours of future research.

The fourth-person level is the first to feature an emergent structural expression that alters the included structural expressions in both form and domain. Explained earlier as an aspect of perspective-taking operating below the level of self-reflexive awareness, subject view or mode appears now as a primary structural element. Put differently, perspective-taking subjects can choose to view perspectival objects from an inside, first-person (1-p) or outside, third-person (3-p) view. As seen in Figure 11.10, this move expands the four quadrant

Fourth-Person Level	
SE Emergent	$(S \times M)_{S1} \times (S \times M)_{S2} \times$ $(S \times M)_{S3} \times (M \times O)$
SE Emergent (Combined View)	$(S \times MP)_{S1} \times [\{(S \times M)_{S2} \times (M \times (P)O)\} +$ $\{(S \times M)_{S3} \times (M \times (P)O)\}]$
SE (3p) Included	$(S \times M)_{S1} \times (S \times M)_{S2} \times (M \times O)$
SE (2p) Included	$(S \times M) \times (M \times O)$
SE (1p) Included	$(M \times O)$
Domains	UL(Z1 + Z2), UR(Z5+Z6), LL(Z3 + Z4), LR(Z7 + Z8)
# of PE's at (4p)	1188
# of PE's at (3p)	216
# of PE's at (2p)	72
# of PE's at (1p)	24
Total # of PE's	1500

Figure 11.10 Perspective taking at fourth-person

domains into the eight zones, referred to as Z1 through Z8, which are now open to perspective-taking at included levels of complexity.

Including a mode (M) component in each structural expression alters them such that each subject (S x M) and object (M x O) set now contain two terms. The first emergent expression—(S x M)$_{S1}$ x (S x M)$_{S2}$ x (S x M)$_{S3}$ x (M x O)—rather complexly reads: A subject through their mode takes a perspective of subject through their mode who has a perspective of a subject through their mode who has a perspective of a perspectival object as seen through a particular mode. The included structural expressions read in a similar fashion with one less subject set for every step down the spectrum. At the included first-person level, objects alone are enacted through an inside or outside mode.

Before explaining the structural expression for combined view, an understanding of mode functioning necessitates a look at a few perspectival expressions. At a second-person level of complexity, I can take a perspective of your interior as you experience it from the inside:

$$1p(1p) \times 1p(1\text{-}p) \times 2p(1\text{-}p) \times 2p(1/p)$$

My first person (1st term) has my first-person or inside view (2nd term) of your interior (4th term) as you experience it from the inside (3rd term)

As I take a perspective on your interior experience, I do so through an inside or Z1 mode that allows me a feeling-insight into how you are experiencing your interior. Alternately, I could take a Z2 perspective of your interior by seeing it from an outside mode as you see it from the outside yourself. If I said, I see your strong valuing of justice as sourced in a postmodern value structure (i.e., green altitude), we would get:

$$1p(1p) \times 1p(3\text{-}p) \times 2p(3\text{-}p) \times 2p(1/p)$$

My first person has my third-person or outside view of your interior as you experience it from the outside

In this example, rather than feeling into your interior as you feel it, I am "seeing" an aspect of your individual feeling awareness as exemplifying green altitude values. A similar dynamic is seen in a more complex fashion at the fourth-person level. Shifting to Zone 3, I could say that I think you think that Mary experiences George and his football buddies shared interiors as overly competitive (the terms and corresponding text descriptions are indicated by the using **bold** to indicate the "x" and using *italics* and <u>underlining</u> to indicate when a variable appears in a different order than simply left to right):

$$1p(1p) \times 1p(1\text{-}p) \times 2p(1p) \times 2p(1\text{-}p) \times 3p(1p) \times 3p(1\text{-}p) \times \underline{3p(1\text{-}p)} \times$$

$$3p^*p/(1p^*p/)$$

My first person **has** my first-person or inside view **of** your first person **who has** your first-person view **of** her first person **who has** her first-person view **of** *their shared interior* **as** <u>he experiences it from the inside</u>

If the first-person views (1-p) were replaced with outside or third-person views (3-p), we could get the same perspectival expression but of a Z4 perspectival object. In this case, the competitive "we" or shared interior is viewed from the outside as if looking in on the we-space rather than from the inside, where the we-space is felt or experienced by its members. The perspectives are of the same object (shared interior or we-space), but they are enacted from different views (first-person or inside and third-person or outside). A perspective of a shared interior or exterior can be taken by anyone regardless of their location in the "we." That is, both a member and a non-member can take an inside or outside view of a "we." While "location" does not affect the ability to take perspective, it does influence the degree of accuracy. Non-members taking an outside view may do so more accurately than members attempting the same, and members taking an inside view will most likely do so with greater accuracy than non-members. The concept of a "we" is at the heart of the emergent structural expression for combined views, the last emergent at the fourth-person level.

Combined View

The structural expression for combined-view perspectives takes on a new form as compared to the structural expressions looked at thus far. In so doing, it simplifies how the structural expression is stated textually while simultaneously capturing the complexity of the most advanced perspectives at the fourth-person level. Combined view expressions describe the perspective that one subject takes on the combined view that two other subjects have on a common perspectival object.

Combined view is more complex than it may first seem. It does not merely describe one subject's view of an object in comparison to another's view of the same, nor does it look exclusively at one subject's view of the other subject's view of the object. Instead, it investigates the shared view that two subjects have on a shared or "we" object. To accurately ascertain this shared or combined view, the perspective-taking subject must implicitly investigate several component perspectives: (1) the individual perspective each subject has of the object, (2) the perspective each subject has on how the other subject views the object, (3) the perspective each subject has on the subject we-space, and (4) finally, the coordination of all of these perspectives to get a sense of how the "we" would describe *their* view of the shared object.

A few examples will illustrate the nature of combined view expression. First, the structural expression—(S x Mp)$_{s1}$ x [{(S x M)$_{s2}$ x (M x (P)O)} + {(S x M)$_{s3}$ x (M x (P)O)}]—which reads: A subject through a plural mode takes a perspective of the mode through which one subject views a plural (or "we") object as it is seen through a mode combined with (indicated by the "+") the mode through which another subject views the plural object as seen through a mode. All of this seeming complexity describes a statement as simple and relatively common as: I think that y'all experience him as angry. One perspectival expression for this perspective is shown below:

1p(1p) x 1p(1-p*pl) x [{2p(1p) x 2p(1-p) x 3p(1-p) x (2p*pl)3p(1/p)} + {2p(1p) x 2p(1-p) x 3p(1-p) x(2p*pl)3p(1/p)}]

My first person 1p(1p) has my first-person plural view 1p(1-p*pl) of both your first person's 2p(1p) [first usage]and your first person's 2p(1p) [second usage] combined (2p*pl) first-person views 2p(1-p) of his interior 3p(1/p) as he experiences it from an inside view 3p(1-p)

Individual interiors and exteriors, as well as shared interiors and exteriors, appear as "we" objects in combined view expressions. These objects can be outside the "we" of the subjects whose combined view is taken—in the previous example, it was the interior of a third person—or, the "we" object can be inside the "we," either one subject's interior or exterior or the shared interior or exterior of the "we" itself. For example, if you thought that she and I saw our shared behavior as collaborative, we would have this expression:

2p(1p) x 2p(1-p*pl) x [{1p(1p) x 1p(3-p) x 1p(3-p) x (1p*pl)1p*pl(3/p*pl)} + {3p(1p) x 3p(3-p) x 3p(3-p) x (1p*pl)1p*pl(3/p*pl)}]

Your first person 2p(1p) has your first-person plural view 2p(1-p*pl) of both my first person's 1p(1p) and her first person's 3p(1p) combined (1p*pl) third-person views 1p(3-p) [first usage] & 3p(3-p) [second usage] of our shared exterior 1p*pl(3/p*pl) as she and I see it from an outside view 1p(3-p) [first usage] and 3p(3-p) [second usage]

As compared to the previous expression, we have changed the object to a shared exterior 1p*pl(3/p*pl) that is viewed from the outside Z8 mode (3-p). In hope of illustrating each variable element contained in all fourth-person combined view perspectival expressions, let me iterate one final component. If you thought that your first-person plural view of us was true not just for each of us involved but also for all third persons anywhere, it would change to a third-person plural view (3-p*pl), and the perspectival expression above would change accordingly.

If each zone's combined view expressions at the fourth-person level are added to the perspectival expressions produced by the included structural expressions at the three previous levels of complexity—which now include the mode (M) component—the complete territory of perspectives for individuals developed to the teal altitude comes in at an even 1,500 perspectival expressions. Interested parties can view each of these in Appendix A. But, before getting lost in hundreds of rows of Integral Math, let us conclude this discussion with a few overdue and important questions. Why is any of this important? What is the point of creating such a map? And, what does all of this tell us about human perspective-taking?

Conclusion

There is absolutely no way of getting around it. This integral map of human perspective-taking is complex. So complex in fact, that it may seem useless. Even though it utilizes two sets of symbolic notations to simplify the vast realm of perspective, which otherwise would have to be described textually, the list of perspectival expressions is long, the notation cryptic, and the learning curve somewhat steep. But, if we step back and consider what this map is truly describing—the entire range of human perspectives from the earliest developmental structures through the near leading-edge of vertical expression—its complexity appears in a different light, possibly as the simplest way to portray a reality that is indeed far more multifarious.

Perspective-taking is the way in which we come to understand the world. Whether it is the world of objects or other sentient beings, we enact their interiors and exteriors through acts of perceptual or conceptual perspective-taking. Perspective-taking is the vehicle that carries our attention through the eyes and minds of others, allowing us to see and understand reality through a view other than our own. Perspective-taking is not only a fundamental emergent capacity, with new levels of complexity earned at each macrodevelopmental step, but also the way in which development expresses itself, with every next level offering a higher perspective on the level before, every new subject taking as object the previous subject. Because perspective-taking is so fundamental to development, the act of creating such a conceptual map possibly has merit on this fact alone, but the importance of this mapmaking is further reinforced in that it also extends into the realm of practice.

It is commonly held that taking perspectives facilitates growth in the cognitive line. The truth of this assertion has yet to be empirically verified, but, along with the desire to cultivate authentic interaction through growth in the interpersonal line—which, incidentally also features perspective-taking—it has served as an impetus to create The Meta-Practice, a perspective-training practice that utilizes the map featured here. Targeting the crucial challenge of cultivating truly authentic interactions with others, The Meta-Practice trains our underexercised and sometimes underdeveloped ability to fluidly and accurately take perspectives in the moment-to-moment flux of relationships. Skillfully moderated interpersonal engagement is combined with precisely guided perspective training, focusing on the specific moments generated between individuals. The purpose of this is to walk people through a range of perspectival expressions from first- through fourth-person levels of complexity. This map informs the perspective work, but does not teach the expressions explicitly. This creates an almost nonexistent barrier to entry, which allows nearly everyone to learn the dynamics of complex perspective-taking, deepen their awareness of the perspectives taken by self and others, and to foster an accuracy of perspective. The Meta Practice aside, even working to understand the perspectival expressions described in this map seems to increase one's ability to recognize them at play in the world.

Beneath questions of its facility in the realm of practice, an inquiry remains: How does this perspective-taking map reconcile with developmental theory? One conclusion seems appropriate: further research guided by the following questions is needed. Is perspective-taking capacity a separate line of development or is it a subset of another line such as cognitive or self-sense? Next, if the macrodevelopmental sequence of perspective-taking proceeds from first-person views to fourth-person views and beyond, how is access to perspectival expression within the macrolevels gained? I suspect the answer will yield multiple microdevelopmental pathways, emerging in a manner similar to what Kurt Fischer and Thomas Bidell (2006) describe in their recent treatment of dynamic structuralism. This research would most likely result in a greatly nuanced map that would help us understand the context dependant nature of emergent access to the territory of perspectival expressions. Finally, because perspective-taking appears as a cross-line phenomenon, how does it relate to Fischer's Skill Theory and the notion of hierarchical complexity being a universal yardstick for cross-line development? Similar to potential conclusions about Skill Theory, does a spectrum of perspective-taking have more to do with what altitude is describing? The need for insight into these and surely many other questions, coupled with the desire to refine perspective training and facilitate perspectival development will guide future development of this map, presented here as a first attempt to describe perspective-taking in specific and comprehensive detail.

Appendix A

Perspectival Expressions from the First- through Fourth-Person Levels

The perspectival expression chart, detailing more than 1700 expressions, is longer than this chapter, and therefore, has not been included in this volume. It can be downloaded at this address: http://www.coreintegral.com/PE-Chart. pdf.

References

Ackermann, E. K. 1996. Perspective-taking and object construction. In *Constuctionism in practice: Designing, thinking, and learning in a digital world*, ed. Y. Kafai and M. Resnick, 25–57). Mahwah, NJ: Lawrence Erlbaum Associates.

Boland, R. J., and R. V. Tenkasi. 1995. Making and perspective taking in communities of knowing. *Organization Science* 6(4): 350–72.

Cook-Greuter, S. 1999. Postautonomous ego development: A study of its nature and measurement. *Dissertation Abstracts International* 60(06): 3000.

———. 2002. A detailed description of the development of nine action logics in the leadership development framework: Adapted from ego development theory. Retrieved February 25, 2007, from http://www.cook-greuter.com.

Enright, R. D., and D. K. Lapsley. 1980. Social role-taking: a review of the constructs, measures, and measurement properties. *Review of Educational Research* 50(4): 647–74.

Feffer, M., and V. Gourevitch. 1960. Cognitive aspects of role-taking in children. *Journal of Personality* 28(4): 383–96.

Fischer, K. W., and T. R. Bidell. 2006. Dynamic development of action, thought, and emotion. In *Theoretical models of human development: Handbook of child psychology*, ed. W. Damon and R. M. Lerner, 313–99). New York: Wiley.

Flavell, J. H., P. T. Botkin, and C. L. Fry Jr. 1968. *The development of role-taking and communication skills in children*. New York: Wiley.

Flavell, J. H., E. R. Flavell, F. L. Green, and S. A. Wilcox. 1981. The development of three spatial perspective-taking rules. *Child Development* 52(1): 356–58.

Kurdek, L. A., and M. M. Rodgon. 1975. Perceptual, cognitive, and affective perspective taking in kindergarten through sixth-grade children. *Developmental Psychology* 11(5): 643–50.

Marvin, R. S., M. T. Greenberg, and D. G. Mossler. 1976. The early development of conceptual perspective taking: Distinguishing among multiple perspectives. *Child Development* 47(2): 511–14.

Salatas, H., and J. H. Flavell. 1976. The development of two components of knowledge. Child *Development* 47(1): 103–109.

Selman, R. L. 1971a. Taking another's perspective: Role taking development in early childhood. *Child Development* 42(6): 1721–34.

———. 1971b. The relation of role taking to the development of moral judgment in children. *Child Development* 42(1): 79–91.

———, and D. F. Byrne. 1974. A structural-developmental analysis of levels of role taking in middle childhood. *Child Development* 45(3): 803–806.

Shantz, C. U. 1975. *The development of social cognition*. Chicago: The University of Chicago Press.

Wilber, K. 1995. *Sex, ecology, spirituality: The spirit of evolution*. Boston: Shambhala.

———. 1996. *A brief history of everything*. Boston: Shambhala.

———. 2000. *Integral psychology: Consciousness, spirit, psychology, therapy*. Boston: Shambhala.

———. 2002. Excerpt C: The ways we are in this together: Intersubjectivity and interobjectivity in the holonic Kosmos. Retrieved March 23, 2007, from http:/wilber. shambhala.com.

———. 2006. *Integral spirituality: A startling new role for religion in the modern and postmodern world*. Boston: Integral Books.

## 12

Second-Tier Gains and Challenges in Ego Development

Susanne Cook-Greuter

Most developmental self theories—if they describe them at all—describe second-tier stages as some sort of idealized place of self-actualization and life competence. It is proposed that life becomes easier, and that problems can now be solved collaboratively in a timely and wise fashion with only the highest principles as inner guides. In general, this reflects a fundamental tendency of theoreticians to envision and describe the levels beyond their own purview in idealized terms.

The data from thousands of sentence completions tests, however, and the feedback from people who have reached those later stages of development, do not seem to confirm this notion. What is generally not seen by most theories is that each later level has its own difficulties, challenges, and attachments. We propose that what does change is the type of issues attended to and one's relationship to difficulties and confusion. Thus, there is a problem between most of the theoretical and idealized descriptions of integral or second-tier stages and the actual lived experience of those measured as inhabiting these more advanced and rarer perspectives.

The characterization and measurement of second-tier ego development has been the focus of my research for the past 25 years. In the following I will share the development from conventional to postconventional meaning-making. I will then focus on the Autonomous (Stage 5) and the Construct-aware (Stage 5/6). They are relatively rare as can be seen on Table 12.1. In ego development theory, both Stage 5 and 5/6 belong to the personal, representational, relative, and ego-mediated realm of experience. I will mention recent observations about these two stages, the developmental gains of each over those that came before as well as some of the stage-specific ego traps and difficulties that each invites. Pascal's (1623–1662) definition of human nature can serve as a leitmotiv for exploring both the strengths of these two levels of ego development as well as their predictable vulnerabilities (Merlot 1962). The insights offered stem mainly from observations of feedback dialogues with participants who have tested at these two high-end ego stages.

Since ego development theory postulates an ego-transcendent or third—tier possibility of human flowering, I will point to the seeming ceiling that separates the relative, vantage point–driven, discursive worldview from a multiperspectival, transcendent, immediate one. I will conclude with an appreciation of the patterns of the whole sequence, and what we might call the evolutionary imperative underlying the drive for individuation and integration.

Data

From its inception in the late 1960s, Loevinger's (1976) ego development theory has been grounded in large sets of empirical data. This is an advantage over other available theories which are variously based on (1) interview-therapy data and theoretical hypotheses (Kegan 1982), (2) integrations of other developmental theories, smaller samples, and/or biographical data (Torbert 1978), or (3) data from a limited age range—usually captive college age students (Graves 1974; Perry 1968). The current set of protocols in our database alone is 6,895 MAPs which translates into nearly to 250,000 sentence completions.[1]

The MAPs range across the whole spectrum of adult development from the Impulsive stage 2 to the Unitive stage 6 (see Table 12.1). The age range is 16–82 with women and men about equally distributed among the stages. To give you a sense of the empirical basis of this research, find below the distribution of MAPs and the percentage distribution separated into a pre-2001 and a post-2001 phase ending in July 2008.[2] Looking at the percentage distribution

Ego Development Theory	Preconventional		Conventional			Postconventional			Ego-transcendent
Stage	2	2/3	3	3/4	4	4/5	5	5/6	6
Distrib. 1980-2000 OLD n=4267	28	304	357	1582	1268	453	195	57	23
Distrib. 2001-6/2008 NEW n=2628	3	14	24	467	1040	602	354	104	20
Distr. by stage Total N=6895	31	318	381	2049	2308	1055	549	161	43
Integral Theoy	1st tier					2nd tier			3rd tier

Table 12.1 Distribution of 6895 SCTi-MAPs across the developmental trajectory

numbers in Table 12.2, one wonders whether we observe an overall shift upward along the developmental trajectory. Such a shift has been eagerly awaited as the need for people with later stage meaning-making capacity has increased in conjunction with the rapidly increasing complexity of our day to day lives as well as the increasing global technical and economic interdependence. We have been on the lookout, therefore, whether we can detect an overall shift in consciousness in the general population.

However, the numbers are misleading. With the publication of my dissertation in 1999, and the founding of the Integral Institute in 2000, we observed a noticeable shift in the circumstances under which people take the MAP. Whereas the earlier sample was representative and consisted of many diverse research projects, professions, educational attainment, and income classes, the latter is no longer representative. It consists of mostly mature professionals in management and executive leadership positions and individuals committed to their own individuation and consciousness evolution. Many of these adults volunteered to take the MAP test. Others took it as part of coaching in response to talent management or organizational change projects. In addition, comparatively fewer research efforts for which we have MAPs were aimed at the conventional tier.

Table 12.2 shows the data of Table 12.1 as percentage distributions. Given the changed subjects pools, we believe that the shift is more a consequence of two different populations tested. It does not signify an overall shift of the level of meaning-making in the general public despite the large numbers of participants. The hope that we are close to a quantum shift in consciousness from first to second tier is not yet warranted in my view. What is a perhaps a hopeful sign is that in general more individuals reach later postconventional

Ego Development Theory	Preconventional		Conventional			Postconventional			Ego-transcendent
Stage	2	2/3	3	3/4	4	4/5	5	5/6	6
OLD %distr. by stage n=4267	0.7	7.1	8.4	37.1	29.7	10.6	4.6	1.3	0.5
NEW %distr. by stage n=2628	0.1	0.6	0.9	17.8	39.6	22.9	13.5	4.0	0.8
% distr. Old and New	0.4	4.6	5.5	29.7	33.5	15.3	8.0	2.3	0.6
Integral Theoy	1st tier					2nd tier			3rd tier

Table 12.2 Percentage distribution of ego stages
for the two samples

stages at earlier ages than they did in the baby boomer generation. Whether these "high potentials" will get the personal, cultural, and structural support to sustain the early advantage remains to be seen. It also needs to be noted that many current subjects are familiar with Integral Theory, Eastern thought traditions, and meditation and thus respond differently than the earlier samples. Many more people now express politically correct notions of equality, remark on world issues, and address spiritual questions at all levels. Whether we take the older 5.9 percent or the current 17.5 percent of respondents at second tier as a starting point, the sheer number of cases has increased and offers new observations and new challenges for the cultural observer and test interpreter.

Postconventional Development

In order to be rated at second tier, the first of two crucial mental shifts has to have occurred. The shifts are characterized by a step-wise deconstruction of the subject/object split fundamental to the modern scientific paradigm. The transition from the conventional to the Individualist/Plural stage 4/5 is the first of these two steps. It represents a differentiation away from the idea of a permanent, independent, separate self-identity at the Conscientious stage and a questioning of its formal operational tenets.

To be rated as early postconventional there needs to be evidence of the following: First, one now realizes that social-cultural conditioning, interpretation, context, and relativity of point of view are constants in meaning-making. We are always participant observers. Although a traditional scientific approach can produce valuable insights (Newtonian physics) into gross level experience, astrophysics and nuclear physics have shown the illusion of true objectivity. In order to grow beyond the socially sanctioned givens, one needs to become aware of one's underlying beliefs, assumptions, and the depth of one's cultural conditioning. Furthermore, the very realization of having been programmed to see the world in certain ways, opens one's eyes to the potential for self-deception. Thus, laying bare one's own inner workings becomes a necessary practice toward more adequate self-knowledge.

Secondly, it is crucial to pay attention to and value multiple, contrasting, even incompatible interpretations and perspectives. Differences are the norm as each person sees reality from a different vantage point, from a different historical, geographic, social, and personal orientation. Thus, arriving at a consensus becomes important to the Individualist/Pluralist. This new capacity for changing perspectives and switching foreground/background can best be illustrated with an optical illusion.

In this first step of deconstruction, one discovers that interpretation is an inevitable aspect of what is perceived. It also represents the move from an "either/or" forced choice characteristic of the rational scientific paradigm to

Figure 12.1 What do you see—an Eskimo or a American Indian Head?

a realization that something can be "both/and" at the same time, depending on one's perspective. Third, product and process, absolute value and relationship, part and whole are equally important in assessing and understanding a situation. So are long-term considerations and unintended consequences of actions.

If relativism is taken to its extreme, it can lead to pervasive cynicisms and nihilism. If there is no stance that is better than any other, we can take whatever position we wish. We do not have to be consistent as our view is as defensible as someone else's. Postmodernism at its worst, or the "mean green meme" as it is also known in integral circles (Wilber 2003), can be seen as an unquestioned take on relativism.

On the personal level, once the firm foundation in a knowable and permanent identity gives way to the relativism at the Individualist/Pluralist stage 4/5, the struggle for a coherent self-story becomes very acute. This is so because one now recognizes the multiple voices of one's own inner tribe, and the many legitimate voices and perspectives of others. Relativism can be experienced in everything. It is often accompanied by confusion about who one is. "If I am not just this, and not just that, and if I am all of these different 'me's at different times and with different people, then who on earth am I? How can I ever figure this out?" Thus, one reaction to this dilemma is to simply rely on and relish one's own immediate experience as it is the only meaningful and assertable reality when nothing else holds. This is the position towards relativity taken by Individualists.

An alternative response to difference in experience and relativism of point of view is to focus on honoring each individual voice. At this level, political correctness is not just a behavior one follows because it is the law—at this level one truly embraces the underlying intention of equality, fairness, and dignity for all. The downside of listening to all voices and consensus seeking is that discussions become endless, and groups can become paralyzed and unable to make decisions. This is the position towards relativity taken by Pluralists.

In summary, this stage has two distinct personal expressions in ego development terms: those we call Individualists deeply cherish their own unique orientation in life and focus on the moment to moment experience. They follow their own drummer despite being aware of cultural expectations and norms.[3] If taken to the extreme, they can become self-centered, even amoral. People we call Pluralists, focus more on the shared, egalitarian values of consensus seeking and community building.[4] Both expressions are reactions to the newly found realization that we all have different and justifiable points of view.

Second-Tier Meaning-Making

It is the next move in development that is generally equated with second-tier understanding, since it is the first to recognize a developmental aspect of meaning making and the inevitability and necessity of making qualitative discernments.

Re-integration, Re-construction at the Autonomous Stage 5

Autonomous adults know about their own history and struggles of becoming. They have a historical perspective and see themselves as links in a generational chain that requires care of future generations. They often express a sense of global citizenship and act upon universal moral principles. They are in a place of re-integration where they can again tell a good, coherent story about themselves and reality. There is rhyme and reason to human meaning making, not just relativism, because there are underlying universal principles and regular dynamic patterns that are discoverable. In the end, individuals do have a choice to make their own meaning as an act of self-affirmation and humanity. In the midst of chaos and uncertainty, they can assert their own understanding and find solace in knowing that they have this choice.

A sense of self-coherence is now coupled with a profound understanding of interdependence and systemic forces at play. "I am whole despite being made up of many parts, and, at the same time, I am a part in many larger nestled wholes." Unlike people at the Conscientious stage 4, however, who see themselves at the helm of their destiny and feel unilaterally in control, Autonomous persons seek self-fulfillment and define their purpose within the constraints of knowing the limits of individual control.

At this stage, a deep trust reemerges that solutions can be found and that difficult conditions can be managed well although requiring far more complex approaches than what was dreamt of at earlier stages. Even seemingly intractable global issues are amenable to solutions. They require the input and collaborative inquiry of global stakeholders, long-term views and planning, as well as ongoing monitoring and dynamic steering that can adjust to changing conditions and new data. Solutions require complex matrices and regular redefinition of where we are (current conditions) and where we are going (altered goals, targets, metrics) as information is gathered and life conditions change. People at the Autonomous stage 5 trust that reality is definable and can be mapped incrementally and more accurately over time.

Unlike at the Conscientious stage 4, where the drive to make the world a better place was based on abstract ideals and turned into external action, with the Autonomous stage ideological and self-blind acting in the world is no longer seen as effective or desirable. Unless the self as the instrument of change is evolving and conscious of its own history, its own limitations and potential biases, the world is not going to change for the better. Thus, self-authorship and purposeful action are now deeply embodied and focused on self-actualization. People at stage 5 tend to report that it is a good and fulfilling place to be because of their sense of choice, strength of insight, and the many coping resources available. They can easily move among multiple points of view and interlaced systems and integrate experience from many sources both external and internal into a coherent self-narrative and meaningful life purpose.

Vulnerabilities of the Autonomous Stage 5

The vulnerability of this stage is its overestimation and overconfidence in what it knows and what it can do. A fundamental and hidden assumption remains that there is one underlying and knowable reality. This reality can be researched and eventually explained and mastered via multiple and sophisticated research methods, concentrated efforts and with global collaboration.

Autonomous individuals will sometimes even use their known faults and biases like a batch of honor. "I have been through it. Because I am a human, all things human are familiar to me." They may share their own suffering with others out of genuine compassion, but they may also do so in a more self-serving fashion to revel in how much self-knowledge they have achieved. The narcissist's motto, "Look at me! Ain't I wonderful?" takes a peculiar tone at this level as it is partially based on real achievements and above-average understanding of human capacity and potential. As part of the human need for self-esteem and coherence, stage 5 persons can often tell a very good story about themselves. Past failures and disappointments can be turned into models of personal insight and victory. While this kind of learning and distilling of experience can be a genuine aspect of a person at second tier, it can also be warped into a form of self-aggrandizement.

Unlike people at earlier stages, Autonomous persons understand that they themselves have evolved over time from earlier to later stage meaning-making and that others may be at different levels of the developmental trajectory than themselves. They are thus conscious of their responsibility to tailor their engagement to others' level of capacity to be most effective. And yet, Stage 5 individuals' chief complaint on protocols and in coaching sessions is often that others just do not get it. If only they were more second tier, or more enlightened or more principled in their actions, then the world would become a better place. They wish that others could think as complexly and know themselves as well as they do. Their egos are bolstered by knowing what they know and by sharing such knowledge with those "needing" to grow in their own view. A passion for transforming others no matter what the circumstance is often a sign of this attachment.

Another complaint one hears often is that their way of interpreting the business reality so outstrips that of the organizational climate and entrenched beliefs that Autonomous leaders often loose their idealism and capacity to hold a larger vision in the day to day struggle and the immediate demands and responsibilities that have to be dealt with.

Let me introduce Blaise Pascal at this juncture as a way to illuminate some of the distinctions between the Autonomous and the next stage of development (see Merlot 1962). Pascal (1623–1662) wrote his philosophical essays about the human condition at the beginning of the French Age of Enlightenment. Reading his *Pensées* (1660) was pivotal in my thinking about later stages. Pascal described the human condition in a way that I believe can help to clarify some of the differences in experience of second-tier development. In answer to the fundamental question, "What then is man's nature?" he wrote: "Man is a nothing compared to infinity, and an infinity compared to nothingness." In broad strokes, Autonomous individuals tend to identify with the latter part of this equation, "I am an infinity compared to nothingness," while the next stage appreciates both sides of the paradox.[6]

The Construct-Aware Stage 5/6

In a move beyond the systemic understanding of the Autonomous stage 5, individuals may gain a perspective from a higher altitude on the rich, complex, and dynamic but stable self-experience of the prior position. They reach a new, more fundamental level of questioning of how humans make sense of things across the globe and regardless of culture. Shared stories about "who we are, where we come from, where we are going, and why we are here" are part of all cultural identities since the earliest records of human presence. There is no known human social group without a language and a common narrative.

In Pascal's terms, the Construct-aware individual now experiences both sides of the paradox. One is both a universe compared to nothingness as well as a nothingness compared to the universe. Once one sees through the very pattern and effort at meaning-making itself by orchestrating ever-greater complexity into coherent narratives, feelings of freedom and feelings of futility and despair often cohabit. Well-integrated persons at this stage experience tension as aliveness and living on the razor's edge as fascinating. However, when one initially realizes the reification game the ego has been playing all along to avoid facing its impermanence and inevitable death, the shock and disillusionment can be profound. And yet, there is also power, joy and liberation in being able to acknowledge the ego's familiar game. One can be free from the incessant demand to be coherent and fit a specific self-image created and often cemented in the interplay of self and others. In the best outcome, one can consciously reinvent oneself as the need arises and experience the constantly shifting self-sense as a delight rather than with concern and confusion.

The transformation from the first milestone in the deconstruction of the permanent self at the Individualist-Pluralist stage on to the second level and further dissolution of the separate self sense can again be illustrated with an Escher image.[5] This time the discovery of the underlying reification process afforded through linguistic representation relativizes one's identity much further than merely recognizing that we have been socialized and culturally programmed.

The Construct-aware person discovers several of the following aspects of all meaning-making through introspection and careful observation of the human cultural scene:

1. that concepts arise as polar opposites or by our defining what something is and what it is not. Thus, light and dark, angel and devil do not mean anything independent of each other. They only make sense as interdependent pairs as they arise together out of the undifferentiated background.

2. that continuing differentiation and naming of parts leads to greater complexity and closer approximations (better maps) but it cannot ever fully represent the original lived, gestalt-like experience of the underlying undivided territory.

3. that, indeed, the best, and most sophisticated maps and theories are always partial and limited.

4. that the language habit with its automatic judgment about what is good and what is bad is a profound challenge and barrier to transformation

beyond the personal realm. As long as we privilege one side of a polar pair, suffering is inevitable.

5. that human beings are storytellers and mapmakers because of our need for a sense of permanence. Mortality is the profoundest threat to our egos.
6. that paradox and ambiguity are unavoidable. Standing in their tension is the most alive place to be: freer and more juicy than any certainty.
7. that radical openness not knowing is a more adequate stance toward life and experience than believing or pretending to know.

How poignant then and real to acknowledge the very futility of one's mapping efforts and, at the same time, to relish the quest for both knowledge and self-existence that anchors this drive. To begin to fully appreciate the irony of the human condition is an aspect of the Construct-aware stage 5/6 capacity and stages beyond.

Some people at Stage 5/6 of ego development come to realize that in the end, trying to fully understand life with our rational minds is a hopeless endeavor. As long as the ego is in operation, it will attempt at making itself and the world permanent. It does so through creating ever more complex maps of what is. Language is ego's greatest ally in this fortification program. The process of naming and labeling experience reliably objectifies and reifies that which is unnamable, in flux, and indivisible, and hence gives a sense of seeming solidity and permanence to the self.

Thus, in order to be rated at this stage several of the following criteria have to be present in a person's self-expression: (1) cognitive complexity, (2) deep insight into the psychological forces and patters of intra-, interpersonal-, and group processes, (3) a focus on the meaning-making process, mind games, and inevitable traps pertaining to the personal, representational realm of meaning-making via storytelling, and (4) an explicit awareness of both the language instinct and the language habit (Cook-Greuter 2000; Pinker 2000).

First, people at the Construct-aware stage 5/6 tend to describe their experience in the most complex matrices and intricate prose. They do so in an attempt to represent the complexity of their experience and reasoning as accurately as possible.

Second, they are often exquisitely tuned in to emotional and interpretive psychological dynamics. They describe their ego's efforts at usurping every thought and feeling for its own benefit or they comment on the interplay and inevitable cross-influences within themselves, with others and at the group consciousness level. One's meaning making is likely shaped not only by history, cultural and personal background, genetic and somatic givens but also by unconscious group processes and subtle energy fields.[7]

A third facet of Construct-aware consciousness is a need to lay bare the mechanics and traps of meaning-making and reasoning in general. Adults at Stage 5/6 can offer sophisticated analyses on the complexities of human mental processing. They critically examine how they know, what they know, and what they cannot know. Regarding their quality of not-knowing, it starts to be an expression and appreciation of the mystery of being. It comes from a knowing of the limits of knowing. They also often become painfully aware of the limits of conscious efforts toward knowing and clarity. They may realize that the more they try to let go of attachments, the more attached they become.

Finally, a fourth criterion indicating functioning at this stage of development, is an explicit awareness and appraisal of the language habit. On the one hand, awareness of how we are embedded in symbolic representations of how language functions in our lives is a salient marker that distinguishes homo sapiens from other higher order mammals. The cultural variety of discursive forms and the uses of language is a crowning achievement of our species. As we evolve, so does our language, and our interpretations of what it means to be a human being.

On the other hand, our reliance on language for orientation can also be experienced as a prison and constraint at this level of comprehension. As we automatically turn every experience into a narrative, the actual experience gets reduced to bits and pieces and "falsified." When experiences are retold repeatedly from memory, the margin of error increases. For example, after years of repeating the story about one's childhood grievances, there may be little resemblance between the actual facts and experience at the time of the original event and one's current story about them as rehashed over the intervening years. The more I realize this, the more I know that what I claim as my identity and suffering is a conglomerate of facts, experiences, memories, interpretations, and inventions, and the more the perceived boundary between reality and fiction disappears.

Construct-Aware Stage 5/6 Vulnerabilities

In the following, I will distinguish between (1) stage-specific forms of suffering that people at the Construct-aware level of individuation themselves express and (2) those difficulties that become evident to the researcher and coach working with people at that level, but which are often not conscious to the client.

(1) From the experience of those who have tested at the Construct-aware level, two concerns are expressed with regularity: loneliness and the fear of going insane.

First, people at this level often say that they feel *lonely.* They realize that they are rarely or never understood in their fullness and complexity by others, often not even by their significant others. They feel their intentions and behavior are time and again misinterpreted by their colleagues and people they interact with. That being alone is an unavoidable predicament at this level of differentiation can be partially explained by the statistical rarity of this type of meaning-making. It is indeed lonely at the top. Sometimes pointing out this reality itself is enough comfort to alleviate some of the immediate stress. Better yet, there are also more active ways we learn to deal with our fundamental aloneness. We can connect with self and others at all levels through our shared humanity. Everyone and every thing can become both our teacher and a focus for our care and compassion. Finding joy and meaning in simply living and experiencing all that transpires in the moment can become connection enough as one realizes that it is the separate self, the ego, that wants to be understood and constantly clamors for acknowledgment.

A second concern expressed by Construct-aware individuals is the fear that they are going crazy. This happens especially with those who have come to see through the needs of the ego and our near-total reliance on language and abstractions for meaning-making on their own reconnoiter, without the benefit of dialogue with others. The extreme conceptual clarity about what they believe they understand, and not being able to share and test their discoveries in a circle of peers, can lead them to doubt their sanity and to fall into despair. Both Nietzsche and Sartre wrote poignantly about what it feels like to be living on the edge between faith and hope and self-doubting dejection. Book titles by Nietzsche such as *The Birth of Tragedy* (1871), *Human, All Too Human* (1878), *Beyond Good and Evil* (1886), and by Sartre such as *Being and Nothingness* (1943), *No Exit* (1944), and *Nausea* (1938) are testaments to that level of disillusion, self-doubt, and existential anxiety that permeates the Construct-aware level of self-scrutiny.

(2) Unlike the Autonomous sense of human greatness as the species at the top of the food chain, and as an individual at an altitude of consciousness achieved by relatively few, the Construct-aware person is more apt to vacillate and feel torn between the power of "I am a universe compared to nothingness" and the feeling of insignificance "I am nothing compared to infinity." They may feel Godlike at one moment, and worm-like at the next.

It is important to distinguish the mature, appreciative experience of this tension from the neurotic identification with either of the poles. The extreme fluctuation between them is sometimes a symptom of mental disorder. At this stage of development, however, we find it more likely to be an expression of a stage-specific ego trap. Well-integrated Stage 5/6 individuals are equally conscious of both poles and multiple positions in between. They have the capacity to tolerate the fundamental experience of polar opposites and they pay attention to all the many ways that existential paradoxes come up in consciousness. More importantly, they notice the ego's temptation to wallow in the tension and to favor one side over the other. Yet they do so with some equanimity and a capacity to hold both views simultaneously without spinning out of control.

When either side of the Pascalian equation gets overemphasized, too different forms of ego-attachment can occur. When feelings of grandiosity—"I am an infinity compared to nothingness"—become the predominant flavor, arrogance of an extraordinary reach can blind the person. When feelings of smallness and unworthiness take over, the individual vigorously hides his light under the bushel instead of stepping into his or her full potential and magnificence. "Who am I to dare to do this or that?" is the general lament. When challenged, the reason given is often "because I am afraid of harming someone, or to stand out and be seen as arrogant." As Marianne Williamson (1992) so eloquently expressed: "Our deepest fear is not that we are inadequate, our deepest fear is that we are powerful beyond measure. It is our light, not our darkness that most frightens us. We ask ourselves, who am I to be brilliant, gorgeous, talented, fabulous? Actually, who are you *not* to be?" (190–91). An overfocus on humility and deprecating the self can thus also be seen as a veiled form of grandiosity especially at this level of psychological differentiation.

Stepping into one's brilliance and risking whatever that may bring with eyes wide open is a natural and healthy expression of one's full humanity. Humility is not absent in this form of self-actualization and offering one's unique gifts. One remains aware of one's foibles and limitations. External dangers and constraints are not ignored, but neither are they used as a hindrance to courageous action and full self-expression and exploration of what is possible.

Confusing cognitive complexity with understanding and ego maturity is a different form of maladjustment we come across at this level more often than at earlier stages. It is on this point that cognitive theories are most distinct from theories of meaning-making. While the former value cognitive complexity as the *sine qua non* indicator of development, the latter see it as a necessary aspect of human functioning, but by no means its most important. This author believes that a sophisticated use of formal operations combined with high IQ is enough to absorb the content of almost any theory, Integral Theory included. What requires later-stage ego development is understanding the spirit behind a developmental theory and translating its tenets into everyday action. Solving specific tasks in specific content areas is not sufficient to show that the tested concepts. are integrated into living and being.

In contrast to the cognitive proponents, Construct-aware meaning-makers are conscious of the distance between their maps and that which they attempt to describe in formal, scientific terms. From a meaning-making perspective one could say that the more abstract a theory and the more certain of its representational adequacy it claims, the farther away from the underlying experience the theory has become. What proponents of cognitive approaches seem often to be missing is a perspective on their perspective as well as ignorance of or blindness of the underlying problem of abstract symbolic representations.

Not surprisingly then, another form of hubris shows up in Construct-aware test protocols when cognitive capacity outstrips respondents' emotional-spiritual maturity. Having studied all of Ken Wilber's books and absorbed the lingo of Integral Theory does not equate with second-tier ego development. On the contrary, cognitive prowess can be a great invitation for the ego to inflate itself and feel entitled to recognition and applause for its extra-ordinariness.

We find that Construct-aware people who are in love with complexity are unable to be ordinary and simple no matter what the context. "Being complex" has become part of their self-identification. Both Autonomous and Construct-aware individuals can become so enamored with systems thinking and complexity, they tend to show their preference by always wanting to elevate others, to transform them to become more complex and developed as well. The shadow of their strength is an inability to appreciate the experience of people at earlier levels than themselves.

This form of privileging is sometimes also conveyed by preferring to congregate exclusively with other special folks. Granted, we all desire to be around others who understand our particular likes, concerns, and preoccupations occasionally, as the need for connection and participation is as basic to human experience as is the need for independence and separation (see Angyal 1965; Bakan 1966).[8] In addition, others who are similar to us also serve a vital function by providing a reality check and ongoing support and challenge. A deep understanding can result from having fully incorporated what it is like to live in others' skins, their hearts, their minds, and in their life circumstances. Wise compassion is one of the great gifts of positive later stage experience. True maturity in the ego development sense allows one to see all experiences and all others as precious and beautiful in their own right while the capacity to make distinctions and act with decisiveness and courage is retained. Helping others is more like being a midwife to their own natural emergence, than an act of transforming them for their own good.

In the coaching context, uncovering the privileging of one of the two sides of the Pascalian paradox often provides a fruitful path to a more balanced and honest self-appraisal.[9]

Other immature expressions found at this stage concern various preoccupations and overattachments. The most striking is a clear privileging of complexity itself. This reveals itself in overly analytical and intricate expressions of one's inner workings. Not just here and there, but tenaciously throughout a person's writing on the test as well as in dialogue. Hyper-complex nestled sentences peppered with diacritic marks, and lots of abstractions are a symptom of this attachment to complexity. Because this hangup is so prevalent and symptomatic for this stage, there is actually a separate scoring category to capture this tendency.

Next, a further common trap of the Construct-aware stage is an attachment to transcendent aspects of experience, turning away from ordinary, everyday concerns and matters. Since extraordinary states and peak moments are more common at this level, and are experienced as a release from ego, one can become greedy for them for their own sake and use them as a batch of specialness. As Trungpa spelled out in *Spiritual Materialism* (1987), the ego is capable of usurping everything, even the sacred, as a way to make itself real, to bolster its image, and to assert its importance. The tendency to circumvent psychological development and individuation in the personal realm in favor of transcendent bliss states is, of course, not just evident at this later stage. I hypothesized earlier (Cook-Greuter 2000), that using higher state experiences as an escape as well as a means to learn about other ways of experiencing reality tends to become more common with increasing ego development because of the growing capacity to watch and witness one's internal processes and because of increasing closeness to ego-transcendent experiences.

Finally, some Construct-aware people show a stage-specific hubris about being special and extraordinary in general. They may feel entitled to the best and exempt themselves from many things that ordinary people are subject to. The sense of grandiosity and superior capabilities leaves them to believe that they can penetrate and discover their own shadows by deep self-examination. Therefore, they feel they do not need others. Instead others definitely need them, the Magician, the Alchemist, the Catalyst, whatever name they prefer to be identified with. They are proud of seeing through things and to model how advanced humans think, feel, and operate in the many territories of awareness open to them. Perhaps the most extreme expression of this attitude I have encountered is from a researcher who suggested twenty years ago that eventually there will be a subspeciation of human beings in which those testing highest on the cognitive complexity scales naturally become the ruling class. While I still recoil from his conclusion, I find that some of the fantastic bionic extensions of human capacity envisioned by futurists—human enhancements, which are already being engineered and implemented—seem less far-fetched. I thus wonder about what it will mean to be a sentient human being in the future and whether my strong reaction to the notion of cyborgs could not partially be a rejection of something unexplored and unaccepted in myself. Who can predict what human beings will evolve into if we take the current assumption of an underlying evolutionary trend seriously and if science and technology continue to evolve at their dizzying pace?

Observing the foibles and attachments of later stages is a good reminder that the ego will and does assert itself wherever it can. Because the ego itself can become aware of its tendency to inflate itself with everything in its orbit, there is a stage in development beyond the Construct-aware stage that I have come to characterize as Ego-aware. It exhibits a conscious struggle, indeed a navel-gazing quality of hyper-vigilance about the ego's shenanigans. At this early point of exploration, I suggest that it is a transition stage between the Construct-aware and the Unitive stage; but perhaps not a necessary step toward ego-transcendence.

To summarize the above, people capable of Autonomous and Construct-aware perspectives have much to contribute to this world, to help, soothe, and to heal. Because of their broader orientation and greater depth of experience they can envision new possibilities and connections, frame and implement more integrative policy, and change the existing structures in positive and life-affirming ways. At the same time, they also have greater power to do harm and to withhold or misuse their gifts. Thus, self-awareness that acknowledges the temptations and the ease with which our egos make even the noblest efforts into a self-trip is a necessary first step toward a healthy embodiment of second tier meaning-making.

There are time-tested ways of balancing and mediating the ego's self-perpetuating drive. We can enlist wise others to give us feedback on our behavior, impact, and blind spots. We can engage mentors farther along on the path to help us cut through our ignorance. We can devote ourselves and surrender to a guru to counteract our self-inflating tendencies. We can be open to teachings from everywhere, especially from the less exalted, mundane everyday world. Simple service to other human beings is powerful connector. Meditation practices to experience all-embracing compassion and to connect with the unfiltered immediate experience of what is can also foster genuine humility and relativize excessive pride in being extraordinary.

This does not mean we should not enjoy and share our gifts and insights. On the contrary: Who are we not to? It just invites a simpler, more seasoned and conscious perspective on life and our place in it. From a Unitive perspective, the described movements and perturbations are just ripples on the surface of the deep ocean of experience. The felt sense of "ego" itself is a natural aspect of individuation within the cultural, language-mediated world in which we function as *homo socius*.

In the end, a telos of human development is to become what Genpo Roshi (2003) would call a fully functioning integrated human being. The Unitive stage in ego-development theory comes perhaps closest to that realization among academically accepted stage theories about mature realization.

I like to conclude with opening up all of the above observations and conjectures about second-tier meaning-making to a direct taste of being. A poem by Laotzu (~sixth century BC) expresses beautifully what human beings can come to realize through the crucible of life and by exploring what it means to live in the relative, language-mediated world. This translation comes from Witter Bynner (1994, 31).

> **Laotzu on Words**
>
> Existence is beyond the power of words To define:
> Terms may be used
> But are none of them absolute.
> In the beginning of heaven and earth there were no words,
> Words came out of the womb of matter;
> And whether a man dispassionately sees to the core of life
> Or passionately sees the surface,
> The core and the surface are essentially the same,
> Words making them seem different
> Only to express appearance.
> If name be needed, wonder names them both:
> From wonder into wonder existence opens.

Notes

1. The test form used is predominantly the SCTi-MAP, or MAP for short. It is a form we developed to respond to the demand for more professionally oriented stems than many of those in use, e.g., Loevinger and Wessler (1970) and Hy and Loevinger (1996).
2. The separation point is an arbitrary one based on clerical ease.
3. Rebellion and nonconformism can look similar and need to be distinguished from postconventional self-exploration and expression. Rebellion is a reaction "against" something one does not like while nonconformism can be an expression of one's unique self , a way of disregarding or oblivious to conventions. In contrast, the postconventionality of the Individualist/Pluralist and later stages is based on

questioning of the underlying conventional assumptions and a free, conscious choice to be different despite pressures to fit the fold.

4. It is the latter only that Spiral Dynamics emphasizes at the exclusion of the equally frequent more individualist expression that results from the same cognitive shift to a more relativistic stance.

5.

6. The full context of Blaise Pascal's original statement from chapter XXII in his *Pensées* is as follows (the translated statement used in the text is in bold): Quelle chimère est-ce donc l'homme? Quel monstre, quel chaos, quel sujet de contradiction, quel prodige! Juge de toutes choses, imbécile ver de terre: dépositaire du vrai, cloaque d'incertitude et d'erreur: gloire et rebut de l'univers . . . Qu'est-ce que l'homme dans la nature? *Un néant à l'égard de l'infini, un tout à l'égard du néant,* un milieu entre rien et tout.

7. Tavistock conferences (http://www.grouprelationsconference.com/) are one way to expose the subtler group dynamics we are subject to. It can be quite unsettling to the ego when one experiences these forces. The group relations conferences thus foster the disillusion from one's belief in individual sovereignty and control.

8. All human life strives to fulfill the human propensity toward both individual differentiation and systematic assimilation (Angyal 1965, 49). At each developmental stage the quality and the balance of these two trends have to be renegotiated.

9. In my experience, it is somewhat easier to invite clients to step more into their full potential than to encourage them to let go of a preexisting sense of superiority and specialness.

References

Angyal, A. 1965. *Neurosis and treatment: A holistic theory.* New York: Viking.

Bakan, D. 1966. *The duality of human experience.* Chicago: Rand McNally.

Bynner, W. 1994. *The way of life, according to Laotzu.* New York: Berkeley.

Cook-Greuter, S. 2000. Mature ego development: A gateway to ego transcendence? *Journal of Adult Development* 7(4): 227–40.

Graves, C. W. 1974. Human nature prepares for a momentous leap. *The Futurist* 8: 72–87.

Kegan, R. 1982. *The evolving self: Problem and process in human development.* Cambridge: Harvard University Press.

Loevinger, J., and R. Wessler. 1970. *Measuring ego development: Construction and use of a sentence completion test.* San Francisco: Jossey-Bass.

Loevinger, J. 1976. *Ego development: Conceptions and theories.* San Francisco: Jossey-Bass.

Mercel, G. R. 2003. *The path of the human being: Zen teachings on the Boddhisattva way.* Boston: Shambhala.

———. 2004. *Big mind—Big heart: Finding your way.* Salt Lake City: Big Mind Publishing.

Merlot, A. 1962. *Précis d'histoire de la littérature française.* Paderborn, Germany: Ferdinand Schoningh.

Nietzsche, F. W. 1886 (1966). *Beyond good and evil.* Trans. W. Kaufmann. New York,: Random House.

Perry, W. G. 1970. *Forms of intellectual and ethical development in the college years.* New York: Holt, Rinehart, and Winston.

Pinker, S. 2000. *The language instinct: How the mind creates language.* New York: Harper Perennial.

Sartre, J. P. 1938 (2007). *Nausea.* Trans. L. Alexander. New York: W. W. Norton.

———. 1943 (1993). *Being and nothingness.* Trans. H. E. Barnes. New York: Simon and Schuster.

———. 1944 (1989). *No exit.* Trans. S. Gilbert. New York: Knopf.

Torbert, W. 1987. *Managing the corporate dream: Restructuring for long-term success.* Homewood, IL: Dow Jones-Irwin.

Trungpa, C. 1987. *Cutting through spiritual materialism.* Boston: Shambhala.

Wilber, K. 2003. *Boomeritis: A novel that will set you free.* Boston: Shambhala.

Williamson, M. 1992. *A return to love : Reflections on the principles of a course in miracles.* New York : Harper Collins.

part 3

Constructive Perspectives

## 13

Rhizomatic Contributions to Integral Ecology in Deleuze and Guattari

Sam Mickey

Ecological theories and practices are relevant not only to the objects of biology, geology, and other physical sciences, but to every facet of reality. Throughout recent decades, the holistic relevance of ecology has become increasingly evident, particularly in light of the increasingly complex character of the current ecological crisis, which weaves together problems of the physical environment with problems of psychological, social, political, and spiritual concern. Furthermore, the holistic relevance of ecology is also evident in articulations of various ecological perspectives that cross the disciplinary boundaries of physical sciences, social sciences, the humanities, and philosophy. These perspectives have spurred the development of numerous ecologically oriented fields (or subfields) of study, including ecological economics, environmental ethics, eco-feminism, political ecology, eco-psychology, deep ecology, eco-criticism (also called eco-poetics), eco-theology, environmental pragmatism, eco-phenomenology, and religion and ecology. Work in these hybridized fields of study takes place between, across, and beyond disciplinary boundaries in efforts to develop viable responses to the complexities of the ecological crisis.

In short, the emergence of the current ecological crisis and of multiple ecological fields of study coincides with the emergence of an integral sense of ecology as an inter- and transdisciplinary engagement. In contrast to the narrow sense of ecology, for which ecology is the study of relationships between organisms and their physical environments, an integral ecology responds to ecological problems holistically, attending to the complexity and multidimensionality of ecological events, in which the natural environment is intimately intertwined with the sociocultural and psychospiritual realities of the Kosmos.[1]

In what follows, I discuss various contributions to Integral Ecology. In particular, I consider how the approaches to Integral Ecology based on the AQAL framework of Ken Wilber's Integral Theory can be enhanced through interaction with the works of the French thinkers Gilles Deleuze (1925–1995) and Félix Guattari (1930–1992). I explore these contributions to Integral Ecology in six sections. First, I differentiate integral approaches to ecology from the reductionism of narrow approaches to ecology. Second, I articulate the relationship between AQAL-based approaches to Integral Ecology and the "ecosophy" expressed in Guattari's work. Third, I describe the intersection of philosophy, science, politics, and spirituality in the untimely postmodernism of Deleuze. Fourth, I discuss the concept of the rhizome articulated in the works co-authored by Deleuze and Guattari. Fifth, I discuss the concept of geophilosophy expressed by Deleuze and Guattari. Finally, I conclude by briefly suggesting some ways that integral approaches to ecology can benefit from dialogical interaction between the AQAL framework and the concepts created by Deleuze and Guattari.

With its attention to multidimensionality and complex interconnected-ness, a Deleuzo-Guattarian approach to ecology could be interpreted as an alternative to the Integral Ecology based on the AQAL framework. However, I argue that, rather than being mutually exclusive alternatives, these different approaches can become mutually enhancing, offering one another important correctives, criticisms, and possibilities for hybrid concepts. Through dialogical interaction, Deleuzo-Guattarian and AQAL-based approaches to ecology can become more creative and effective in facilitating ecological engagements. Deleuzo-Guattarian concepts can work in conjunction with the AQAL model of Integral Ecology to facilitate the creation of maps with which humans, as individuals and members of communities, can understand multiple perspec-tives related to ecology and effectively navigate into increasingly complex and spiritually vibrant engagements with consciousness, culture, nature, and the Kosmos as a whole.

From Reductionism to Integration

Integral approaches to ecology can be contrasted with the reductionism of mechanistic and materialistic approaches to ecology. Whereas ecology in the narrow sense of the word tends toward mechanistic thinking or materialistic reductionism, Integral Ecology tends toward a holistic paradigm that recognizes the intertwining of humans and nature and engages the complex unity of the physical, the mental, and the spiritual. As Robert McIntosh (1986) notes in his history of ecological science, the tension between reductionism and holism appears throughout the entire history of ecology, from the investigations of various proto-ecologists (e.g., Hippocrates, Aristotle, Francis Bacon, Carl Linneaus, and Henry David Thoreau) to explicit articulations of ecology beginning with the works of Ernst Haeckel, who coined the term ecology (*Oekologie*) in 1866 (11–19).

From the perspective of an integral sense of ecology, the narrow sense of ecology is untenable because it fails to cross disciplinary boundaries and address the intertwining of humans and nature in the irreducible complexity of ecological problems. As this complexity increases with processes of globalization, technological development, and the worsening crises in human societies and in the natural environment (e.g., poverty, displacement, pollution, global climate change, and species extinction), an approach to ecology is needed now more than ever that integrates all perspectives of ecological theory and practice.

A call for integration in ecology can be heard in the approach to ecology expressed by Eugene Odum (2000), who proposes a "new ecology"—an "integrative discipline" that is dedicated to holism and opposed to materialistic reductionism (198). With a holistic perspective, "the new ecology links the natural and the social sciences" (198). Furthermore, this new ecology is practical and not merely theoretical, for it seeks "to raise thinking and action" to an integrative engagement with ecosystems (199). Odum also points out that the statements of a holistic approach to ecology "must involve integration of economic and environmental values" (201). Along with theories and practices of physical and social sciences, Odum also considers the importance of including politics and legal issues within the holistic paradigm of integrative ecology.[2]

Odum (2000) provides a short summary of his approach to integrative ecology:

> In summary, going beyond reductionism to holism is now mandated if science and society are to mesh for mutual benefit. To achieve a truly holistic or ecosystematic approach, not only ecology, but other disciplines in the natural, social, and political sciences as well must emerge to new hitherto unrecognized and unresearched levels of thinking and action. (203)

Although Odum's integrative approach to ecology contributes to efforts to overcome reductionism, it still harbors reductionistic elements. "Odum's position," according to Donato Bergandi (2000), "can be defined as crypto-reductionistic" (216). Odum does not engage the spiritual dimensions of ecology; he does not include the humanities within his holistic thinking; and furthermore, he tends to reduce the social, political, economic, and environmental phenomena of ecology to a materialistic calculation of energy flows.

A more integral approach to ecology is expressed by the liberation theologian Leonardo Boff, who used the phrase "integral ecology" before either Wilber or Esbjörn-Hargens. "The quest today," according to Boff (1995), is increasingly for an *integral ecology* that can facilitate a new alliance between societies and nature, which will result in the conservation of the patrimony of the earth, socio-cosmic wellbeing, and the maintenance of conditions that will allow evolution to continue on the course it has now been following for some fifteen thousand million years. (ix)

For Boff, an integral approach implies that ecology is a matter of human society and culture and not only a matter of the natural environment. Ecological complexity is not a merely physical complexity, for "society and culture also belong to the ecological complex. Ecology is, then, the relationship that all bodies, animate and inanimate, natural and cultural, establish and maintain among themselves and with their surroundings" (Boff 1995, ix–x). Integral ecology enacts a "holistic perspective" that gives all questions "ecological consideration," with particular attention to the following "basic question" of ecology: "to what extent do this or that science, technology, institutional or personal activity, ideology or religion help either to support or to fracture the dynamic equilibrium that exists in the overall ecosystem" (x)?

Although Boff's integral ecology is promising, he has not elaborated much on the concept, and thus has not developed a comprehensive map for integral ecology. Although they have limitations, the integral approaches to ecology articulated by Odum and Boff provide a general indication of two important characteristics of Integral Ecology: (1) opposition to reductionism or to any oversimplification of ecological phenomena, and (2) a holistic engagement with the sciences, technologies, institutions, religions, and personal activities that are woven into the irreducible complexity and multidimensionality of ecological phenomena.

Wilber's "Big Three" and Guattari's *Three Ecologies*

The holistic perspective of Integral Ecology is currently being taken up and elaborated by various activists, scholars, educators, and ecologically conscious individuals who are applying Ken Wilber's Integral Theory to ecological issues.[3] In his work on *Sex, Ecology, Spirituality* (*SES*) (2000a), Wilber formulates his Integral Theory in the AQAL Matrix—an "all-quadrant, all-level" model that accounts for physical, mental, and spiritual *levels* of reality from the perspectives of four *quadrants*: subjective, intersubjective, objective, and interobjective perspectives.[4] Sometimes the four quadrants are simply referred to in terms of "The Big Three": subjectivity ("I"), intersubjectivity ("We"), and objectivity (which includes the individual "It" of objectivity and the collective "Its" of interobjectivity) (Wilber 2000a, 149–53). The AQAL Matrix provides a comprehensive framework for varieties of ecological theory and practice. However, this is not to say that Wilber's earlier (i.e., pre-AQAL) works are not relevant to ecology. Indeed, Michael Zimmerman (1994) has shown how Wilber's work as a "transpersonal theorist" in *Up From Eden* (1981) provides a narrative of the evolution of consciousness that is quite relevant to various efforts of radical ecology, including those enacted by proponents of deep ecology, social ecology, ecofeminism, and postmodernism (see 14, 196–217).

The usefulness in applying the AQAL Matrix to ecology is indicated by the fact that the very title of Wilber's magnum opus *SES* refers to ecology. In *SES*, Wilber (2000a) explicitly addresses the relation of AQAL to environmentalism, and he even articulates principles for an integral approach to environmental ethics (543). More recent applications of AQAL to ecological and environmental issues reflect developments that, according to Brad Reynolds (2006), mark a transition to a new stage in Wilber's thinking, a stage following the Wilber-4 of *SES*, a stage that Reynolds and others refer to as Wilber-5 or as Wilber-4/5 (7). This stage includes a more open and generative sense of metaphysics and a more comprehensive orientation to practice and method, which can be seen in Wilber's articulations of Integral Transformative Practice (or Integral Life Practice), Integral Post-Metaphysics (IPM), Integral Operating System (IOS), and Integral Methodological Pluralism (IMP). With these movements toward more generative and comprehensive approaches to Integral Theory and practice, Wilber's framework transcends and includes the holistic tendencies of proto-ecologists and the integral approaches of Odum and Boff.

One of the leading proponents of an AQAL-based approach to Integral Ecology is Sean Esbjörn-Hargens. In 2005, Esbjörn-Hargens (2005a) edited a double issue of *World Futures: The Journal of General Evolution*. The issue contains articles from various authors who focus on the application of the AQAL model to an Integral approach to ecology—an approach that "unites consciousness, culture, and nature in service of sustainability" (1). According to Esbjörn-Hargens (2005a):

Integral Ecology weaves together the myriad approaches to the natural world in an effort to respond as effectively and timely as possible to the complex ecological problems that face ourselves, our communities, and our world in an evolving universe. (1)

In short, Esbjörn-Hargens (2005b) concludes, "Integral Ecology is committed to the complexity and multidimensionality of this world in all its mysterious splendor" (37). Those who use the AQAL framework of Integral Ecology caution against any form of reductionism, and thus they understand "that it is not enough to integrate ecosystems and social systems (e.g., economies, laws, schools) because both of these realities are objective systems" (2005a,

1). Investigations of ecosystems and social systems account for the objective quadrants, but they fail to account for the subjective quadrants (i.e., individual and collective interiority).

For an Integral Ecology, "what is needed is an integration of subjective (e.g., psychology, art, phenomenology), intersubjective (e.g., religion, ethics, philosophy), and objective (e.g., behavior, science, systems analysis) realities" (Esbjörn-Hargens 2005a, 1). In other words, what is needed is an integration of the Big Three into ecological theory and practice. An Integral approach to ecology thus "attempts to integrate the levels of body, mind, and spirit as they appear in the areas of self, culture, and nature" (2005b, 7). It is also important to note that Integral Ecology welcomes a plurality of integral ecologies, which is to say, it promotes "the flourishing of multiple Integral approaches guided by different ultimate premises" (2005b, 37). Such integral approaches to ecology are implicit in the works of Deleuze and Guattari. Although he does not address Deleuzian contributions, Esbjörn-Hargens (2005b) notes that the objective, subjective, and intersubjective dimensions of Integral Ecology correspond with the "three ecologies" articulated by Guattari (37).

In *The Three Ecologies* (*Trois Écologies* [2000]), Guattari—a psychotherapist, activist, and philosopher—proposes a "generalized ecology" that he calls "*ecosophy*," which is an "ethico-political" and "ethico-aesthetic" paradigm that seeks to reinvent human praxis in its relation to three registers of ecological processes: the environment, social relations, and the "existential Territories" of subjectivity (28–37, 52). In his last book, *Chaosmosis* (*Chaomose* [1995]), Guattari says that the basic issue of ecosophy is:

> [H]ow do we change mentalities, how do we reinvent social practices that would give back to humanity—if it ever had it—a sense of responsibility for its own survival, but equally for the future of all life on the planet, for animal and vegetable species, likewise for incorporeal species such as music, the arts, cinema, the relation with time, love and compassion for others, the feeling of fusion at the heart of the cosmos? (119–20)

Ecosophy approaches this basic issue with three ecologies, which correspond with the Big Three of Integral Theory: mental ("I"), social ("We"), environmental ("It/s"). However, Guattari's framework is not as intricate as Wilber's AQAL model. For instance, as Esbjörn-Hargens (2009) observes, the distinction between objective and interobjective perspectives (i.e., individual and collective exteriority) necessitates "four ecologies" instead of the more simplified models of the three ecologies and the Big Three (18). A brief description of each of Guattari's three ecologies can provide a general orientation to some ways in which Guattari's concepts, despite their limitations, contribute to integral approaches to ecology.

Guattari associates his approach to mental ecology with the "ecology of ideas" expressed in the systems thinking of Gregory Bateson (see Guattari 2000, 35). For Guattari (2000), the mental dimension of ecosophy is not restricted to cognition, but includes the active engagement of subjects in their embodiment and in the mysteries of existence: "[M]ental ecosophy will lead us to reinvent the relation of the subject to the body, to phantasm, to the passage of time, to the 'mysteries' of life and death" (35). Subjectivity for Guattari is not a quality of a reified or alienated subject. In other words, it is not a merely egoic or Cartesian subjectivity. Rather, subjectivity emerges through the creative process of "subjectification," which integrates multiple components, vectors, and assemblages of existential engagements (36). To liberate subjectivity from the infantilizing and destructive forces of global capitalism, consumerism, media, and technological progress, Guattari proposes that mental ecology focus on "the promotion of innovatory practices, the expansion of alternative experiences centered around a respect for singularity," and the creation of a "subjectivity that can articulate itself appropriately in relation to the rest of society" (59).

Social ecology addresses the collective dimension of creative processes of subjectification. Some of the important factors of social ecology include the possibility of "sudden mass consciousness-raising," post-Stalinistic opportunities for "transformative assemblages of social struggle," non-capitalist goals implicit in "the technological evolution of the media," and "the reconstitution of labour processes" in support of individual and collective manifestations of "a 'creationist' subjectivity" that overcomes the oppressive and exploitative conditions of contemporary economics (Guattari 2000, 62). Mental and social ecology attend to the irreducible uniqueness and singularity of individual and collective subjectivities. This means that mental and social ecologies must criticize and transform those systems, processes, and institutions that have exploited and oppressed the uniqueness of subjectivity, systems such as globalization, industrialization, colonial and postcolonial regimes, consumerism, capitalism, and patriarchy. Thus, "The question becomes one of how to encourage the organization of individual and collective ventures, and how to direct them towards an ecology of resingularization. . . . It is the whole future of fundamental research and artistic production that is in question here" (65).

Guattari (2000) articulated "a principle specific to environmental ecology: it states that anything is possible—the worst disasters or the most flexible evolutions" (66). Environmental ecology thus makes it possible to engage the processes of chaos, disequilibrium, and destruction in the environment while also facilitating flexible evolutions of the human, natural, and Kosmic systems at work in the environment. Insofar as humans, nature, and the evolving Kosmos can be understood as self-producing systems or autopoietic machines, Guattari mentions that it is possible to "rename environmental ecology *machinic ecology*" (66).[5] Environmental ecology addresses the complex interactions between all autopoietic systems, including interactions of "Cosmic and human praxis," which implies that environmental ecology facilitates "the adoption of ecosophical ethics" and "the invention of a politics focused on the destiny of humanity" (66–67). Moreover, Guattari does not propose a simple unity or undifferentiated homogeneity between humans and nature. Rather, Guattari's three ecologies engender an integration that includes unification and differentiation of human and nonhuman individuals. "Individuals must become both more united and increasingly different" (69).

For Guattari's (2000) ecosophy, "the tangled paths of the tri-ecological vision" contribute to creative efforts to facilitate the emergence of "a nascent subjectivity," "a constantly mutating socius," and "an environment in the process of being reinvented" (67–68). Guattari's ecological vision becomes much more complex when understood in relation to his work with Deleuze. Before describing the concepts articulated in their co-authored works, I briefly describe some of the basic concepts of Deleuze's philosophy.

The Untimely Postmodernism of Deleuze

Deleuze is often described as a postmodern philosopher. His name frequently appears in association with other so-called postmodern philosophers, including French thinkers such as Michel Foucault, Jean-François Lyotard, and Jacques Derrida. Accordingly, Deleuze might be interpreted in terms of Wilber's "green altitude."[6] However, a close reading of Deleuze's works suggests that he includes postmodern themes (e.g., the critique of the modern Enlightenment mentality, an affirmation of difference, and a focus on the liberation of the oppressed and excluded) and moves beyond them, such that his thinking overcomes the constrictive aspects of postmodernity. For instance, Deleuze articulates metaphysical and cosmological theories rather than reducing questions of reality to historical relativism or nihilistic triviality.[7] Furthermore, Deleuze does not negate or break with modernity like so many postmodern thinkers. Rather, he criticizes and transforms modernity, offering reinterpretations of key figures in modern thought (e.g., Leibniz, Spinoza, Hume, and Kant).

Deleuze exhibits what Ronald Bogue calls an "untimely postmodernism," or what could also be called post-postmodernism or perhaps an *integral* postmodernism, which integrates the insights of postmodernism while overcoming its relativism and its negation of modern and premodern ways of knowing and being. Deleuze is "postmodern with a difference, in that his work enriches, enlarges, and ultimately modifies our conception of postmodernity" (see Bogue 2004, 29, 36, 40–41). To further distinguish Deleuze from typical post-modernism, it is important to note that his work is not destructive and does not affiliate itself with deconstruction. Deleuze (2004) speaks to this matter directly in an interview: "As for the method of textual deconstruction, I know what it is . . . but it has nothing to do with my own method" (260). Deleuze's philosophical method is creative and radically interdisciplinary, addressing issues related to science, politics, spirituality, art, and metaphysics. Although a general survey of Deleuze's philosophy is outside the scope of this chapter, I briefly indicate some of the main concepts that appear in his works, with specific attention to his search for an ontology (or metaphysics) that engages creative emergence, complexity, nomadic events, and a Kosmic sense of spirituality.

In a concise summary of Deleuze's ontology, Mark Bonta and John Protevi (2004) point out that Deleuzian ontology affirms emergence and avoids reductionism and positivism, which "deny emergence, insisting that all 'wholes' are mere aggregates" (13). Deleuze's creative ontology affirms the emergence of actual (or "extensive") wholes, which are expressions of "intensive" stratification. Intensive acts "operate far-from equilibrium" and involve multiple modes of becoming, which mesh into "consistencies"—"networks of bodies that preserve the heterogeneity of the members even while enabling systematic emergent behavior"—and these consistencies are manifest in the emergent wholes of "ecosystems and in certain evolutionary phenomena" (Bonta and Protevi, 15). The intensive and extensive unfold from underlying generative structures of reality: "virtual structures." Deleuze calls these structures "singularities" (not unlike the singularities of Guattari's "ecology of resingularization") (Guattari 2000, 65).[8.] Singularities are not simple or homogeneous individuals, but complex multiplicities. Singularity and multiplicity are two ways of expressing the holistic uniqueness or "thisness" (*haecceitas*) that constitutes individuals and collectives (Bonta and Protevi 2004, 16).[9] Furthermore, singularity and multiplicity integrate identity and difference in a concept of the virtual as a creative "difference in itself," from which emergent wholes are generated.[10]

Bonta and Protevi (2004) show how Deleuze's ontology of "the actual/extensive, intensive, and virtual" is closely affiliated with complexity theory, which includes studies of autopoiesis and "the self-organizing capacities of 'open' systems" (16–17). Furthermore, Deleuze (like Guattari) relates these open systems not only to the study of physical and biological events, but also to political events. Deleuze's ontological practices of mapping extensive, intensive, and virtual structures facilitate efforts to wander outside of current political structures and institutions and to facilitate the emergence of new sociocultural wholes. With this political ontology of wandering, singularities must be understood not as isolated and closed monads (as in Leibnizian ontology), but as internally interconnected "nomads" wandering into infinity (see Deleuze 1990, 77, 102, 107, 113). Each nomadic event is, in terms Deleuze (1992) adapts from Alfred North Whitehead, a "nexus of prehensions," which can be described as a wave of feelings vibrating together with every other event in the Kosmos (78). A nomadic event is "a vibration with an infinity of harmonics or submultiples, such as an audible wave" or "a luminous wave" (77).

The nomadic events that constitute emergent wholes are not related only to politics, ontology, and the science of complexity. They are also spiritual. A nomadic event "is the identity of form and void," an identity Deleuze (1990) finds expressed vibrantly in Zen Buddhist practices (e.g., tea ceremonies, koans, archery, flower arranging) (136–37). Deleuze's affinity for Zen is indicative of the Kosmic sense of spirituality implicit in his ontology. Deleuze is very critical of religion and theology, particularly insofar as such systems assimilate spirituality into dualistic oppositions of transcendence and immanence. However, Deleuze's philosophy also resonates with a profoundly spiritual tone, one which echoes Judeo-Christian prophetic and mystical practices as well as various Buddhist practices (including the aforementioned Zen practices, but also Tibetan Buddhist practices of dying).[11]

For Deleuze, spirituality integrates the transcendence of Spirit and the immanence of the Kosmos. Indeed, this integration is the very aim of every act of perception. "The task of perception entails pulverizing the world, but also one of spiritualizing its dust" (Deleuze 1992, 87). The overall point is that we move toward "conscious perceptions" of everything in the Kosmos, microscopic and macroscopic. Deleuze's sense of spirituality thus resonates with the panvitalist and panentheist tones of Spinoza, Bergson, and Whitehead. Peter Hallward, in his work on Deleuze's philosophy of creation, describes Deleuze's philosophical orientation variously in terms of "cosmic vitalism," "cosmic pantheism," "panentheism," and a "*theophanic* conception of things" (Hallward 2006, 4, 9, 13, 161). Deleuze's work bears a soteriological element insofar as it facilitates the liberation of vitality, divinity, and nomadic singularities. Deleuze's work aims "to liberate the singularities" (1990, 141) and "to liberate life from what imprisons it" (1995, 143). Hallward (2006) puts this matter succinctly: "Deleuze's philosophy is redemptive" (56).[12]

With concepts that address emergence, complexity, nomadic events, and a Kosmic sense of spirituality, Deleuze's philosophy can contribute to the holistic theories and practices of integral approaches to ecology. Recent applications of Deleuze's concepts to ecological issues explore the implications of Deleuzean philosophy for rethinking the relations between science and environmental philosophy (Mugerauer 2004), reorienting humans to the complex milieus of space (Lingis 2004), criticizing dominant concepts of environmental harm and regulation (Halsey 2006), and creating novel concepts of ecological spirituality (Higgins 2007). In a cursory glance, it is evident that integral approaches to ecology have much to gain from engaging the philosophy of Deleuze, just as they do from engaging Guattari's ecosophy. Furthermore, integral approaches to ecology also have much to gain from exploring the works that Deleuze and Guattari composed together.

The Rhizome

Deleuze and Guattari (D&G) wrote four books together.[13] Throughout these works, D&G create numerous concepts that engage the complex and multidimensional relationships between the perspectives of science, art, philosophy, and spirituality. Indeed, the very aim of D&G's (1994) philosophical endeavor is to invent new concepts: "[P]hilosophy is the discipline that involves *creating concepts*" (5). Furthermore, D&G (1983) create concepts that facilitate intimate and responsible contact between humans and all beings inhabiting the Kosmos, such that the human is not understood as an imperial force of domination, not "as a king of creation, but rather as the being who is in intimate contact with the profound life of all forms or all types of beings, who is responsible for even the stars and animal life" (4). In other words, Deleuzo-Guattarian concepts facilitate the intertwining of "the human essence" of natural world and "the natural essence" of the human (4). Multiple Deleuzo-Guattarian concepts are relevant to integral approaches to ecology. One such concept is the rhizome.

The concept of the rhizome is expressed in the first chapter (or "plateau") of *A Thousand Plateaus*. Botanically speaking, a rhizome is similar to a tuber or a bulb. It is a horizontal (and frequently subterranean) stem that generates roots and shoots from its interconnected nodes. Some examples of rhizomes include couch grass, ginger, violets, and irises. D&G (1987) extend the strictly botanical meaning of the rhizome so that it refers to a nondualistic system that "connects any point with any other points" and integrates pluralism and monism (21). The nonlinear and nondualistic system of the rhizome stands in contrast to the linear hierarchies of more tree-like ("arborescent") structures, and although the rhizome can include "knots of arborescence," it cannot be reduced to any linear system or any dualism (20). "The rhizome is reducible to neither the One nor the multiple. . . . It has neither beginning nor end, but always a middle (*milieu*) from which it grows and which it overspills" (20). With their concept of the rhizome including pluralism and monism while overspilling them, Deleuze and Guattari "summon principles of inclusion and exclusion associated with borderlines. They eschew expressions built on the polarities of 'either . . . or' and in their own diction replace binary construction with the conjunctive 'and.'" (Conley 2006, 95). Everything can become part of the rhizome, such that the rhizome functions in the place of a fundamental ontological principle. For D&G, even books become rhizomes.[14]

Always overflowing polarities, rhizomatic connections constitute open systems. "Rhizomatic connections form open territories that are not constricted by the enclosing frame of a rigid borderline" (Conley 2006, 95). A rhizome is a milieu that opens and conjoins. This does not mean that rhizomes are opposed to closings or disjunctions. Rather, the openings and conjunctions of the rhizome make it possible to integrate closings, blockages, and impasses: "we can realize that even an impasse is good if it is part of the rhizome" (Deleuze and Guattari 1986, 4). The rhizome overflows boundaries and conjoins oppositions, creating shoots and roots that grow from betwixt and between binaries and dichotomies. In other words, the rhizome is "always in the middle, between things, interbeing, *intermezzo*," such that "the fabric of the rhizome is the conjunction, 'and . . . and . . . and . . . '" (Deleuze and Guattari 1987, 25). Not unlike the principles of Integral Theory and its AQAL model (e.g., holons), the open and conjunctive connections of rhizomes include and overcome binary oppositions, including the opposition between anthropocentric and nonanthropocentric values or practices. As Kerry Whiteside (2002) notes, this overcoming of the anthropocentric/nonanthropocentric dichotomy is a common feature in contemporary French thinking on ecology, which is evident in the works of D&G and in works of other French thinkers (e.g., Michel Serres, Edgar Morin, and Bruno Latour).

Another important aspect of the rhizome is its relation to maps. For D&G, principles of cartography are fundamental to the concept of the rhizome. As with the AQAL framework, the rhizome is a map that is enacted performatively, and is not a merely theoretical or metatheoretical structure. "The map is open and connectable in all of its dimensions; it is detachable, reversible, susceptible to constant modification," such that the rhizome "always has multiple entryways. . . . The map has to do with performance" (Deleuze and Guattari 1987, 12). The rhizomatic map "is entirely oriented toward an experimentation in contact with the real. . . . It fosters connections between fields" and it engenders "the removal of blockages" (12). The connective and open maps of the rhizome promote inter- and transdisciplinary engagements with multiple perspectives of the Kosmos. Such connectivity and openness has led Beth Dempster (2007) to suggest that D&G's rhizome functions as a metaphor for the complex systems engaged by the interactive and relational "no-boundary-thinking" articulated by Wilber (see 95–99, 105–108).[15] The rhizome makes it possible for ecological theory and practice to holistically engage nomadic events, and thus wander outside of the compartmentalizing and alienating boundaries that currently dominate ecology and environmental movements. Accordingly, D&G (1987) associate rhizomatic maps with a rhizomatic science of nomadic events: "Nomadology" (23, 351). Furthermore, the concept of the rhizome makes it possible for philosophy to holistically engage the earth instead of abstracting and dissociating itself from its planetary milieu. This means that the rhizome opens up the possibility of a morality and a philosophy that emerge from their embeddedness on the earth. In other words, the rhizome facilitates a "geology of morals" and a "geophilosophy" (Deleuze and Guattari 1987, 39–74).[16]

Geophilosophy

For D&G (1994), geophilosophy works with the principle that "thinking takes place in the relationship of territory and the earth" (85). Geophilosophical thinking is contrasted with the fragmented and alienated philosophical thinking that posits a mutually exclusive opposition between subject and object. "Subject and object give a poor approximation of thought. Thought is neither a line drawn between subject and object nor a revolving of one around the other" (85). Thought is more holistic than such subject-object dichotomies can express. In other words, thought is rhizomatic.[17] Geophilosophical thought engages complex and interconnected relationships in open systems, weaving together physical, geographical, psychological, sociocultural, and spiritual dimensions of philosophical theory and practice.

Geophilosophy is thoroughly rhizomatic, and thus nondualistic. Accordingly, it does not posit a dualistic opposition between immanence and transcendence, but speaks instead of infinite movements of territory, including movements of territorialization and deterritorialization.[18] These movements engender multiple paths for participatory engagements with the Kosmos. D&G describe these as paths of becoming, which take on infinite modes of expression, such as becoming-animal, becoming-molecular, becoming-cellular, becoming-elementary, becoming-feminine, becoming-cosmic, becoming-intense, and becoming-imperceptible. Ultimately, these generative movements of territorialization and deterritorialization participate in the creation of the world, in which everybody and everything become together, creating a communicating Kosmos.[19]

Territorialization (and reterritorialization) is a way of fixing and reifying events into categories, schemata, institutions, or any other contexts or things (whether subjective or objective, individual or collective). Territorialization is evident when a bird sings a song, when a child whistles to bring order to the chaos of darkness, when strata form in the earth's crust, when religious institutions form in a culture, and when an artist or a scientist expresses a concept. These movements of territorialization are accompanied by movements of deterritorialization, as when a birdsong is mimicked by another bird, when a whistling child gains the courage to explore the darkness, when geological strata transform into new formations and create new mountains, when religious institutions open spaces for spiritual evolution, and when artistic and scientific expressions open new paths of inquiry into the Kosmos. Deterritorialization, as a relative movement, opens events into more complex connections and milieus, and when it becomes an absolute movement, it opens events into the infinite Refrain that composes "the song of the earth," and ultimately, "the song of the universe." For D&G (1994), "everything comes to an end at infinity in the great Refrain" (88).

Territorialization and deterritorialization are always already intertwined, such that the Kosmic openness of absolute deterritorialization engenders new territories, which express more complex interconnections, more creative habits and stratifications, and more intimate contact with the infinite. "Absolute deterritorialization does not take place without reterritorialization," for reterritorialization is needed in order to enact new levels and strata of reality; in other words, reterritorialization makes it possible *"to summon forth a new earth, a new people"* (Deleuze and Guattari 1994, 99–101). In short, the task of geophilosophical thought is to create concepts that facilitate the emergence of a vibrant future for all beings. In other words, geophilosophy aims to enact new forms of absolute and relative contact between the earth, humanity, and the infinity of the great Refrain. "The creation of concepts in itself calls for a future form, for a new earth and people that do not yet exist" (108).

Between D&G and Integral Theory

The movement toward an Integral Approach to ecology is a movement away from reductionism and toward holistic discourses and practices that engage the complex and multidimensional connections between ecological perspectives in order to create a vibrant and sustainable existence for humans, for the natural environment, and for all beings in the unfolding Kosmos. In short, an approach to ecology becomes integral to the extent that it "unites consciousness, culture, and nature in service of sustainability" (Esbjörn-Hargens 2005a, 1). The AQAL-Matrix, Guattari's ecosophy, Deleuze's untimely postmodernism, and the rhizomatic and geophilosophical works of D&G all provide enactive maps that can help individuals and communities overcome the fragmented and binary thinking of reductionism and foster the enactment of more integral forms of ecology.

Through dialogical interaction, Deleuzo-Guattarian concepts and the AQAL framework can become mutually enhancing maps for developing integral theories and practices of ecology. Through dialogue, these maps can become more creative and effective in facilitating engagements with multiple perspectives on ecological issues. These maps can become more creative insofar as dialogue would encourage the creation of novel hybrid concepts. Consider the provocative possibilities of the Kosmic Refrain, The Big Three Ecologies, rhizomatic holons, Integral Methodological Nomadology, becoming-Kosmic, and becoming-Integral. Such hybrid concepts could make these integral maps more flexible and relevant in engaging different perspectives on ecological issues, especially the green altitude perspectives typically associated with postmodern French thinkers (e.g., D&G, Derrida, and Foucault) and environmentalists. This implies that dialogical interaction between Deleuzo-Guattarian concepts and the AQAL framework can facilitate effective interaction between first- and second-tier ways of being/knowing.

Dialogue between Integral Theory and D&G does not only include the creation of hybrid concepts, but also criticisms and correctives. For instance, a rhizomatic perspective can criticize the clear and distinct boundaries of the AQAL map, not to negate or oppose those boundaries, but to show how, when the map engages a territory (i.e., territorialization and deterritorialization), its boundaries appear much more knotty, inextricably entangled in interconnected networks of open systems and nomadic events. The geophilosophy of D&G would function as a corrective to help Integral Theory become more applicable to the irreducible uniqueness and specificity of existential territories. In other words, geophilosophy would help empower individuals and communities to use the AQAL model to trace out their own comprehensive maps, such that each map would enact the Integral framework in a way that is embodied and embedded in a unique milieu of the unfolding Kosmos.

Just as D&G can criticize Integral Theory, the AQAL framework can provide criticisms and correctives of D&G. For instance, proponents of the AQAL framework can criticize the rather destructive tone that, resonating throughout much of French postmodernism, can be heard echoing in the works of D&G. Indeed, the method of analysis proposed in the first work by D&G (1983) is summarized by the slogan, "Destroy, destroy" (311). Integral Theory would thus function as a corrective that emphasizes the constructive efforts of D&G. The AQAL Matrix, whether through criticisms or hybrid concepts, can facilitate a more comprehensive and generative use of Deleuzo-Guattarian concepts, while D&G can facilitate a more flexible and open embodiment of the AQAL Matrix.

Together, the AQAL Matrix and the concepts of D&G can help individuals and communities enact creative transformations that make it possible for humanity to move toward a more ecologically and spiritually vibrant existence. Together, they can foster concepts that are relevant and applicable to the theories and practices of multiple perspectives related to ecology and to the natural environment. Together, they can provide ways for humans to explore maps that facilitate effective navigation into increasingly complex and holistic engagements with other humans, with the natural environment, and with the infinite Refrain of the unfolding Kosmos.

Notes

1. I follow Ken Wilber in spelling Kosmos with a capital K. Deleuze and Guattari spell Kosmos with a "c" (e.g., "cosmos" or "Cosmos"). For consistency, I use "Kosmos" throughout this chapter, except when the word appears in a quotation where it is spelled otherwise. Wilber's spelling enacts a recovery of the Greek sense of the Kosmos as "the patterned Whole of all existence, including the physical, emotional, mental, and spiritual realms." The Kosmos is "not merely the cosmos, or the physical dimension," not merely "matter, lifeless and insentient, but the living Totality of matter, body, mind, soul, and spirit." See Wilber (2000), xi.

2. Odum (2000) suggests that "holistic thinking might help" bring integration to the "divided world," wherein "the scientific and the politico-legal spheres of action" are dissociated from one another (202).

3. Sean Esbjörn-Hargens and Michael Zimmerman explicitly focus on this topic in their book, *Integral Ecology: Uniting Multiple Perspectives on the Natural World* (2009).

4. For an overview of the quadrants see Wilber (2000a, 127–35).

5. By attending to the complexity and openness of autopoietic systems, machinic ecology stands in contrast to the reductionism of mechanistic ecology.

6. For Wilber, the green altitude is one of the levels (or waves) of existence; and more specifically, it is the postconventional wave that is above (i.e., transcends and includes) the scientific/rational wave (orange altitude) and below the wave that marks the emergence of an integral level of existence (teal altitude). The green altitude is the last level of "first-tier thinking," and the teal altitude is the first level of "second-tier thinking." The green altitude is associated with pluralism, relativism, deconstruction, postmodernism, and sensitivity to that which is oppressed and marginalized (i.e., sensitivity to issues in environmentalism, feminism, animal rights, multiculturalism, etc.). Wilber argues that the green altitude brings many gifts (such as the emancipation of the oppressed), but that its pluralistic and deconstructive attitudes are preventing the emergence of an integral wave of existence within our culture. For more explanation, see Wilber (2000, 7–13, 37; 2006).

7. In contrast to much postmodernism, Deleuze did not deny "the possibility of a new metaphysics," but instead "tried to construct one, stating 'I feel myself to be a pure metaphysician.'" See Bonta and Protevi (2004, 12).

8. For Deleuze's articulation of singularities and their relation to the extensive, intensive, and virtual, see Deleuze (1994).

9. The synonymous relation between singularities, virtual structures, and multiplicities is indicative of the wild creation of concepts undertaken by Deleuze, whose thinking and terminology continually evolved throughout his life. Deleuze (1994) sought to undertake "the most insane creation of concepts ever" (xx). The concept of the singularity in the works of Deleuze and Guattari is related to their concept of "haecceity," which can be traced back to the concept of "thisness" (*haecceitas*) in Duns Scotus (see Bogue 1989, 134).

10. Deleuze (1994), 28ff. In terms of the AQAL matrix, Deleuze's schema of extensive, intensive, and virtual could be described as a map of exterior, interior, and holonic, and the poles of singularity and multiplicity could be seen as expressions of the complex unity of individual and collective.

11. For an excellent collection of essays that address the spiritual tones of Deleuze's work, including Deleuze's similarities with Buddhism, prophetic Judaism, and Christian and neo-Platonic mysticism, see Bryden (2001).

12. With elements of untimely postmodernism, holism, mysticism, panentheism, and a soteriology of liberation, one could argue that Deleuze's philosophy is situated in a second-tier way of being/knowing (including and transcending the green meme).

13. Their first two books form a pair: *Anti-Oedipus: Capitalism and Schizophrenia* (1983), and its sequel, *A Thousand Plateaus: Capitalism and Schizophrenia* (1987). In the interim, they focused on Franz Kafka (see Deleuze and Guattari 1986). Their last book was *What Is Philosophy?* (1994).

14. In *A Thousand Plateaus* (1987), Deleuze and Guattari describe how a book evolves with the world and "forms a rhizome with the world" (11). In their work on Kafka, they wrote: "This work is a rhizome" (1986,3).

15. For Wilber's articulation of boundaries and the reality that there is ultimately no boundary, see Wilber (2001).

16. They articulate a "geology of morals" not by focusing exclusively on the matter of the earth, but by mapping the complex strata of the "rhizosphere," which includes the biosphere and noosphere. Deleuze and Guattari elaborate on the geology of morals by articulating a geophilosophy in their book, *What Is Philosophy?* (1994, 85–113).

17. Not only is thought rhizomatic, but so is the body, including the part of the body often associated with thought: the brain. Although the brain is described with the arborescent metaphor of "dendrites," Deleuze and Guattari (1987) claim that the brain is rhizomatic and that "the brain itself is much more a grass than a tree" (15).

18. Territorialization and deterritorialization are key concepts that Delueze and Guattari discuss throughout their books *A Thousand Plateaus* (1987) and *What Is Philosophy?* (1994).

19. For Deleuze and Guattari (1987), "*becoming everybody/everything*" brings the whole Kosmos into play: "Becoming everybody/everything [*tout le monde*] is to world [*faire monde*], to make a world [*faire un monde*]" (280).

References

Bateson, G. 2000. *Steps to an ecology of mind.* Chicago: University of Chicago Press.

Bergandi, D. 2000. Reductionistic holism: An oxymoron or a philosophical chimera of Eugene Odum's systems ecology? In *The philosophy of ecology: From science to synthesis,* ed. D. R. Keller and F. B. Golley, 204–17. Athens: University of Georgia Press.

Boff, L. 1995. Ecology and poverty: Cry of the earth, cry of the poor. *Concilium: International Journal of Theology* 5: ix–xii.

Bogue, R. 2004. *Deleuze's wake: Tributes and tributaries.* Albany: State University of New York Press.

———. 1989. *Deleuze and Guattari.* New York: Routledge.

Bonta, M., and J. Protevi. 2004. *Deleuze and geophilosophy: A guide and glossary.* Edinburgh: Edinburgh University Press.

Bryden, M. (Ed.) 2001. *Deleuze and Religion*. London and New York: Routledge.

Conley, V. A. 2006. Borderlines. In *Deleuze and the contemporary world*, ed. I. Buchanan and A. Parr, 95–107. Edinburgh: Edinburgh University Press.

Deleuze, G. 1990. *The logic of sense*. Trans. C. V. Boundas. New York: Columbia University Press.

———. 1992. *The fold: Leibniz and the Baroque*. Trans. T. Conley. Minneapolis: University of Minnesota Press.

———. 1994. *Difference and repetition*. Trans. P. Patton. New York: Columbia University Press.

———. 1995. *Negotiations, 1972–1990*. Trans. M. Joughin. New York: Columbia University Press.

———. 2004. *Desert islands and other texts 1953–1974*. Trans. M. Taormina. Los Angeles: Semiotext(e).

———, and F. Guattari. 1983. *Anti-Oedipus: Capitalism and schizophrenia*. Trans. R. Hurley, M. Seem, and H. R. Lane. Minneapolis: University of Minnesota Press.

———. 1986. *Kafka: Toward a minor literature*. Trans. D. Polan. Minneapolis: University of Minnesota Press.

———. 1987. *A thousand plateaus: Capitalism and schizophrenia*. Trans. B. Massumi. Minneapolis: University of Minnesota Press.

———. 1994. *What is philosophy?* Trans. H. Tomlinson and G. Burchell. New York: Columbia University Press.

Dempster, B. 2007. Boundarylessness: Introducing a systems heuristic for conceptualizing complexity. In *Nature's edge: Boundary explorations in ecological theory and practice,* ed. C. S. Brown and T. Toadvine, 93–110. Albany: State University of New York Press.

Esbjörn-Hargens, S. 2005a. Guest editor's introduction. *World Futures* 61(1–2): 1–4.

———. 2005b. Integral ecology: The *What, Who,* and *How* of environmental phenomena. *World Futures* 61(1–2): 5–49.

———, and M. E. Zimmerman. 2009. *Integral ecology: Uniting multiple perspectives on the natural world*. Boston: Integral Books.

Guattari, F. 1995. *Chaosmosis: An ethico-aesthetic paradigm*. Trans. P. Bains and J. Pefanis. Bloomington: Indiana University Press.

———. 2000. *The three ecologies*. Trans. I. Pindar and P. Sutton. London: Athlone Press.

Hallward, P. 2006. *Out of this world: Deleuze and the philosophy of creation*. London: Verso.

Halsey, M. 2006. *Deleuze and environmental damage: Violence of the text*. Aldershot: Ashgate Publishing.

Higgins, L. 2007. Toward a Deleuze-Guattarian micropneumatology of spirit-dust. In *Ecospirit: Religions and philosophies for the Earth,* ed. L. Kearns and C. Keller, 252–63. New York: Fordham University Press.

Lingis, A. 2004. The music of space. In *Rethinking nature: Essays in environmental philosophy,* ed. B. V. Foltz and R. Frodeman, 273–88. Bloomington: Indiana University Press.

McIntosh, R. P. 1986. *The background of ecology: Concept and theory*. Cambridge: Cambridge University Press.

Mugerauer, R. 2004. Deleuze and Guattari's return to science as a basis for environmental philosophy. In *Rethinking nature: Essays in environmental philosophy,* ed. B. V. Foltz and R. Frodeman, 180–204. Bloomington: Indiana University Press.

Odum, E. P. 2000. The emergence of ecology as a new integrative discipline. In *The philosophy of ecology: From science to synthesis,* ed. D. R. Keller and F. B. Golley, 194–203. Athens: University of Georgia Press.

Reynolds, B. 2006. *Where's Wilber at? Ken Wilber's integral vision in the new millennium*. St. Paul: Paragon House.

Whiteside, K. H. 2002. *Divided natures: French contributions to political ecology*. Cambridge: The MIT Press.

Wilber, K. 1981. *Up From Eden: A transpersonal view of human evolution*. Wheaton, IL: Quest Books.

———. 2000a. *Sex, ecology, spirituality: The spirit of evolution*. Boston: Shambhala,

———. 2000b. *A theory of everything: An integral vision for business, politics, science, and spirituality*. Boston: Shambhala.

———. 2001. *No boundary: Eastern and Western approaches to personal growth*. Boston: Shambhala.

———. 2006. *Integral spirituality*. Boston: Integral Books.

Zimmerman, M. 1994. *Contesting Earth's future: Radical ecology and postmodernity*. Berkeley: University of California Press.

## 14

Exploring Epistemic Wisdom

Ethical and Practical Implications of Integral Studies and Methodological Pluralism for Collaboration and Knowledge-Building

Tom Murray

Integral studies offers a powerful set of models (or meta-models) for makings sense of our world. It also has implications for how we behave or "are" in the world.[1] As with the story of the monk coming down from his isolated retreat in the mountain cave to interact with people in the village, it could be said that the ultimate application of integral theories and practices is in how people treat each other in the ethical, moral, and practical dilemmas of lived experience. To add a point to this generic claim, we can inquire into the implications of integral studies for the *practice of building* integral theories. Or more generally, what does integral studies imply for how groups of people collaboratively build knowledge, build community, and come to decisions about "what is true" and even "what is right"? What does it *look and feel* like for the members of an organization or community to work together—to dialog, make decisions, coordinate actions, and learn—in an integral (or "second-tier" or postformal) way? In asking these questions we direct the focus of integral inquiry not toward wrestling with academia's grand debates, as Wilber does in much of his theoretical writing, but toward the pragmatic context of collaborative inquiry (still with a scholarly approach). This topic is generating increasing interest in the integral movement. Here are two examples. Forman and Esbjörn-Hargens (this volume) advocate for a commitment to "improve Integral Theory by turning Integral Theory onto itself: an act of theoretical-applied self-reflection" (p. 23) And, in an interview published in *Integral Leadership Review*, Robb Smith, the CEO of Integral Institute, says "We are so good at analyzing . . . at creating a two dimensional analysis . . . from an AQAL perspective. But we are doing a very poor job, in my experience, of getting into the trenches and doing the hard work . . . of figuring out how do we make this stuff work. How do we make it successful for those experiencing real, hard problems? This is what it means to look *as* and not just *at*." (Bellamy 2008; emphasis added).[2]

This topic is complex and wide open—ripe for collaborative inquiry (and "action research"). Many scholars have laid the groundwork and point the way forward in disciplines including organizational and leadership theory, transformational learning, and postformal dialog and decision making. My intention here is to bring attention to some aspects of the topic, as a small contribution to the ongoing inquiry. My point of departure is "methodological pluralism" (MP), the meta-method or approach underlying integral studies that prescribes transcending and including multiple perspectives and methods of inquiry.[3] In this chapter I explore the skills and capacities needed to engage in MP and multiple perspectives. Along the way I elaborate on the related issue of "epistemic indeterminacy," the uncertainties, ambiguities, and paradoxes that arise when people engage in multiperspective taking. The real transformational leverage of MP in collaborative contexts (where "the rubber meets the road") comes where it is cognitively, emotionally, and/or socially challenging to apply it. Applying MP in nontrivial collaborative contexts naturally exposes dissonance and psychosocial vulnerability. Here ethical/moral themes enter and become prominent. I call the set of cognitive/emotional skills and attitudes needed for dealing with these situations (at postformal levels) "epistemic wisdom."[4]

The epistemic wisdom capacities needed to engage in MP (and multiple perspective-taking) are practically the same as the capacities underlying postformal collaborative engagement in general. Thus, by starting off focusing on MP we end up with skills and attitudes that apply broadly to postconventional forms of dialog, decision making, knowledge-building, etc. After elaborating on the components of epistemic wisdom I will briefly mention approaches to supporting these skills through scaffolding, systemic tools, etc. (a subject left for development in other texts). These skills are more generally important for communities interested in reflective transformation, metadisciplinary approaches, or ethically rich knowledge-building practices.

With the recent advent of several journals and institutions focused on integral theories (and other transdisciplinary studies), integral studies becomes even more of a community knowledge-building project, and it becomes ever more important to inquire into how members in integrally informed communities of practice embody integral principles. I believe that integral studies has important implications for society's collective and collaborative endeavors in general, and that knowledge building and decision making can benefit from a deeper articulation of these implications. Integral approaches are being applied in many contexts where communication, decision making, and knowledge-building are central concerns. These contexts include education, organizational development, leadership consulting, and psychotherapy. A deeper understanding of the problems of epistemic indeterminacy and the importance of epistemic wisdom might equip integral practitioners to better help others grow and thrive. Also, integrally oriented communities or organizations are ideal "action-inquiry" testing grounds for highly evolved collaborative principles because of their commitment to maintaining a holistic systemic focus on all elements of body/mind/spirit, interiors/exteriors, and the practical/theoretical.

Methodological Pluralism

Methodological Pluralism (MP) is a foundational principle in integral studies (and in Wilber's Integral Theory).[5] It is an approach or attitude for dealing with diverse claims, models, modes of inquiry, etc. Wilber describes three principles for Integral Methodological Pluralism: *non-exclusion*, *enfoldment*, and *enactment* (Wilber 2005). He captures the essence of MP in the non-exclusion principle that "everybody is right" (to which he adds the caveat "but not equally right"). More precisely, all (legitimate or valid) perspectives have some truth to offer. Perspectives can be thought of as worldviews but are also methods of inquiry—the injunctions, procedures, assumptions, etc. built into a paradigm. Different paradigms bring forth different knowledge and, notes Wilber, practitioners in one paradigm should be very cautious in critiquing truth claims drawn through other paradigms. Every paradigm is like a lens or filter through which reality is viewed, and there is no perspective that is so privileged that it does not have this limitation. In addition, every belief or model springs from a real person or group, and is limited by the numerous (and now well documented) limitations in human reasoning (some of which I will mention later).

The caveat in "everybody is right . . . but not equally right" is that some perspectives are more inclusive than others and thus subsume or contain more or better truths (the enfoldment principle). Also, Wilber maintains that individuals or groups that are more developmentally advanced usually have a stronger or more inclusive grasp on truths (for claims related to the developmental line in which they are developmentally advanced) (the enactment principle).

The validity or usefulness of Integral Theory or the AQAL meta-model is not our concern here. I focus on the spirit (rather than the "letter") of Wilber's IMP, which is the approach or attitude of a "gracious and spacious embrace" that allows something like an Integral Theory to emerge in the first place. Here I eschew debate about the grand claims that scholars make in texts and look toward the everyday interactions of people who are engaged in collaborative efforts at discovering "what is true" and "what is right" for them. This stage may be less illustrious and more mundane, but clashes of belief on this workaday stage are every bit as important and difficult to manage. And, the character of grand-scale theories and worldviews might depend critically on the character of the mundane human interactions that underpin their development.

Product to Process, Ontology to Epistemology, Meta-Model to Paradigm

In fact, this chapter takes the assumption that the nature of a product depends critically on the nature of the process producing it. Wilber's work is experiencing an increasing shift from product to process, that is, from the articulation of meta-models and "orienting generalizations" about "what is" to include an exploration of method itself—*how we (can) know* what is. This turn constitutes an increasing emphasis on epistemology and methodology versus ontology—i.e., on the nature of *knowledge* and how it is *acquired* versus the properties or constituents of *reality*. This as a shift in emphasis, not a change in content, as Integral Theory has always concerne d itself with both the ontological and the epistemological. In recent writings Wilber says, "An integral paradigm is a set of practices, not theories," and "This is a paradigm of paradigms . . . a practice of practices and not a theory of theories" (Wilber 2005). This methodological focus (injunctive, praxis, enactive) serves as the connective tissue between knowledge (epistemology) and reality (ontology).

Perhaps because paradigms are amorphous almost by definition, Wilber does not systematically lay out all of the components of what the Integral paradigm is. Within Wilber's work are several elements of what may constitute an integral (meta) paradigm, including the AQAL model, the eight primordial perspectives, and his "three strands of knowing" (Wilber 2001). But fundamental and prior to all of these is MP, the opening up to and dealing with a sufficient set of perspectives as one engages in inquiry. (As explained below I use the phrase "dealing with" rather than "integrating" or "transcending and including" because sometimes just managing, acknowledging, or opening awareness to perspectives is what is called for.)

Perspectives on Perspectives

Before going farther let us unpack the concept of "perspectives"—the cognitive (or lived) vantage points from which an observation, idea, or thought is posited. Wilber's AQAL model explicitly mentions several types of perspectives. First are the methodological perspectives of the "8 primordial perspectives" or zones (including phenomenology, structuralism, empiricism, ethno-methodology, etc.). These are formal categories for empirically based inference categorized by whether one is looking at the interior or exterior of an individual or collective entity from the inside or outside (Wilber 2006). Related to the enactment and enfoldment principles of MP mentioned above, participants (or groups) can also vary in "where they are coming from" along other dimensions of the AQAL model: their stage (level) along a particular developmental line, and any of the numerous states and types mentioned in the model. In addition to those mentioned in the AQAL model, we can more generally say that every sociocultural or identity group represents a particular perspective.

In addition to the perspective from which an individual or group makes a claim, I will add one more perspective on "perspectives"—that, a multitude of perspectives exists *within* each individual. One can take the perspective of different social roles one holds. For example, one might say, "As your boss I would say . . . while as your friend I would say . . . and as another father I would advise that you . . ." We also harbor different psychic perspectives or voices within us. As in Voice Dialog one can speak from ones' inner critic, vulnerable child, protector, Big Mind, etc.

MP calls us to maintain an awareness of the existence and impact of these various perspectives (internal and external), to deal productively with the them, and, as I will describe in more detail later, to be able to reflect and dialog explicitly *about* multiple perspectives (with what I will call "epistemic wisdom").

Why MP Is Difficult

Up to this point I have advocated for becoming aware of and engaging with multiple perspectives and methods for knowing (using MP) and given some sense of the multitude of sources and characteristics of such perspectives and methods. The injunction to allow for multiple perspectives seems so simple and obvious. It is what we all think we are doing most of the time: considering all of the valid ideas in a situation and trying to integrate (transcend and include) them, while discounting or bracketing ideas that do not seem valid. But, of course, the problem of how people in fact deal with diverse and conflicting sets of ideas, information, models, etc. is deep and wide-reaching, and has serious implications in both knowledge-building and ethics. How people answer tacit questions such as: "Which perspectives and information sources should I consider?" "How confident am I about this?" "How do we proceed when we strongly disagree?" "Do I know enough about this to take action?" "Should I change my mind?" "Can I be transparent about my uncertainty or errors?"—strongly determines the interactive style and ethical character of groups (organizations, institutions, families, etc.).

The fact is that opening to new perspectives is often quite difficult. Let us look more closely at why, because if MP is so important to integral or second-tier ways of being, we cannot support MP if we do not understand why it is problematic in practical situations. The difficulties have to do with both cognitive load (items 1 and 2 below) and emotional load (items 3 and 4), and our resilience (or lack thereof) in the face of these psychological loads.

1. Span complexity

Opening to multiple perspectives increases the complexity of the information people have to deal with. Span complexity is about the sheer number of pieces of information, or the number of inconsistent ideas, people are exposed to. Since each person (or group) has a finite capacity for complexity, one has to compensate when one is exposed to more complexity than one can deal with, often by ignoring some perspective or information source. All of the factors mentioned here apply to the capacities of both individuals and groups. A group may be able to process more complexity than any of its individuals (collective intelligence), but it might also exhibit a lowest common denominator effect (e.g., herd mentality).

2. Hierarchical complexity (depth complexity)

Ideas (concepts, theories, even intuitions) build upon each other, with lower-level ones integrating into single ideas (constructs) at a higher level of complexity or abstraction (Fischer 1980; Commons and Richards 1984). Constructs at each level can be integrated or crystallized at a yet higher level to produce a hierarchy of constructs (ideas). As one lives and learns in each of the domains of life (general task contexts such as mathematics, music, social relationships, and specific contexts like chess, tennis, Greek history, etc.), one gradually builds constructs at successively higher levels of complexity (and abstraction or generalization). One may not be able to assimilate a new perspective because it calls for a level of abstraction or generalization that one has not yet developed.

3. Dissonance

There are both cognitive and emotional elements of why MP is difficult. The term *cognitive dissonance* refers to the feelings of discomfort one experiences in trying to consider incompatible ideas (it can also refer to the discomfort experienced when one is overwhelmed with information or when observations or actions are inconsistent with beliefs). The emotional part of the brain is engaged and often plays a critical role in problem solving, dialog, decision making, and other "cognitive" activities (Damasio 1999; Goleman 1995). In general, the brain finds uncertainty and ambiguity painful.

4. Ego attachment/identity

Finally, many of the perspectives or ideas that people fail to assimilate or accommodate to are rejected or ignored simply because they clash with ideas that one holds dear (consciously or unconsciously). (Attachment is a subtype of the dissonance phenomena above, but important enough to warrant its own category.) This is clearly true in the everyday interactions at home and the workplace, but it is also occurs in formal knowledge-building communities. It is easier to ascertain blind spots and resistance to information in others than in oneself, but one can develop an awareness of the inner sensations of resistance, dissonance, dismissiveness, threat, etc. that signal that one's sense of self or a closely held idea is being challenged.

The Problem of Indeterminacy

The ability to process multiple perspectives is part of an overlapping set of skills and attitudes that I will call "epistemic wisdom." Epistemic wisdom includes the capacity to deal with "epistemic indeterminacy" (EI), which is uncertainty, ambiguity, fuzziness, paradox, and dynamic unpredictability in communication, concepts, and models (Murray 2006).[6]

As humans "tetra-evolve" through the four quadrants comprising the human system (Wilber 2000) cognition and knowledge becomes more complex, culture and society become more complex, institutions and infrastructures become more complex, and our tools and artifacts become more complex. Each of these elements increases in complexity in *response to* the others, in an entangled spiraling dance. Along this journey some knowledge emerges that transcends earlier knowledge, and acts as a more inclusive, robust, accurate, and useful understanding of some corner of the life-world. Yet overall, the ongoing increase in complexity *outstrips* the increase in knowledge and understanding.

Though it may not be true in some local pockets of knowledge, the largest sense, the more we learn the more we see that we *don't* know. People create and become aware of successive layers of cultural, economic, and environmental complexity beyond what can be fully understood, much less predicted or controlled. For example, the decoding of the human genome, rather than solving the mysteries of biology, has opened up vast horizons of unknown territory. Scientists have barely begun to understand the 95 percent of DNA that was once called "junk DNA" because they could not identify its function. Similarly, in cosmology scientists have been forced to postulate "dark energy" and "dark matter" as enormous (and very useful) fudge factors to account for the fact that all of the known matter and energy sources account for only 5 percent of the forces influencing the observed motion of stars and galaxies. These examples show how investigation opens up horizons that, technically, might one day yield to substantial understanding. But hard (inescapable) limits to our knowledge of the world are also coming to light. In physics, principles such as the Uncertainty Principle from quantum mechanics and the "butterfly effect" from chaos theory have made us aware of the limits of human knowledge and control. And, most importantly, through the cognitive and brain sciences we are coming to understand the limits of cognition and reason itself. Research into so-called bounded rationality (Kahneman et al. 1982; Sunstien 2002) is shedding light on cognitive biases and systematic errors found in individuals regardless of occupation, intelligence, or expertise. It may be no surprise to the reader that people's thinking and decision making is often at odds with what would classically be called logical or rational, but research is showing that patterns such as "confirmation bias," "overconfidence," "source amnesia," "distinctiveness effect," and "loss aversion" are ubiquitous and deep-seated, and that no individual or group is immune from them (Meyers 2002; Elster 1999). Discoveries that the bulk of human "thought" happens unconsciously or preconsciously have added more evidence for the fallibility of "pure" reason and logical thought. In addition to flaws in reasoning, scientists are discovering surprising limitations to the accuracy of human memory and perception (Travis and Aronson 2007; Wilson 2002).

Moving from hard-wired or genetic limitations of the mind to the intersubjective realms of experience, scholars are discovering important phenomena in language, meaning sharing, and group behavior. Researchers have discovered that almost every term and concept we communicate with has a fuzzy boundary, such that no precise definition (set of necessary and sufficient conditions) can capture its actual use (Mervis and Rosch 1981; Lakoff and Johnson 1999; also noted in Wittgenstein 1953). Thus, almost any statement or claim will have an indeterminate meaning. George Lakoff shows how abstract concepts in the mind are constituted by multiple, often incompatible, conceptual metaphors (Lakoff and Johnson 1999, 71). For example, "In philosophy, metaphorical pluralism [multiple metaphors for the same concept] is the norm. Our most important abstract philosophical concepts, including time, causation, morality, and the mind, are all conceptualized by multiple metaphors, sometimes as many as two dozen. What each philosophical theory typically does is to chose one of those metaphors as 'right,' as the true literal meaning of the concept" (ibid., 78). So much that what is important to think about does not lend itself to simple black and white (true/false or right/wrong) categorization, yet the mind often forces reality into these boxes, especially when emotions are triggered, in its attempt to efficiently process complex information, create certainty, and take immediate action (Goleman 1995; Damasio 1999, 2003; Matthews et al. 2002). Scholars are also investigating the nature of higher-level thought forms such as mental and formal models and theories, and are showing how they are vulnerable to paradigmatic and sociocultural bias, as well as being limited to the unavoidable imprecision of language (Lakatos 1976; Kuhn 1970).

All of the above phenomena contribute to epistemic indeterminacy (EI). EI can be ameliorated in many situations, but to some degree it is unavoidable and inherent to knowledge, thought, and communication. And, EI is exacerbated and thus needs even more explicit attention in approaches that incorporate MP and multiple perspectives. EI is difficult to deal with for the same reasons MP is difficult to use: span complexity, hierarchical complexity, dissonance, and ego/identification. It is easy to understand how EI shows up in research studies and how it affects people in general. It is more challenging to consider how it affects our own communication and decision-making processes and the certainty with which we hold our own beliefs.

Indeterminacy, MP, and Ethics

EI is strongly implicated in ethical themes and dilemmas. In fact, a major theme of this chapter is that ethical concerns and epistemological concerns are tightly interwoven. This comes out clearly in the work of developmentalists (including Kohlberg, Kegan, Graves, Basseches, and Perry). At a postconventional level of development, ethics becomes as much (or more) about how we go about the communicative *processes* of determining what is right for us as it is about following pre-given social rules. In the complex situations modern citizens and employees find themselves in, determining "what is right" depends on determining "what is true" about the situation (e.g., "Were they manufacturing weapons of mass destruction?"). And determining what is true is fraught with the problems of EI. Conversely, success in determining "what is true" rests on the ethical properties of the truth-finding process.

Philosopher Jürgen Habermas shows that for collaboration to move us in the direction of more adequate (if still tentative) truths it must have certain properties that are fundamentally ethical/moral (Habermas 1993, 1999). These properties include: that sufficient mutual understanding regarding key concepts and assumptions is established; that all important or relevant perspectives are heard; that dissenting opinion is not suppressed; that speech is honest and without hidden agenda; that the power dynamics of the situation are reflected upon; and that participants actively engage in opening up to the sometimes unsettling worldviews of others. Problems in any of these areas can result in systematic bias or distortion in the outcomes of knowledge-building. Thus, *moral* constructs such as freedom, equality, empathy, sincerity, inclusivity, reciprocity, integrity, and mutual regard are deeply entangled with the *knowledge-building* processes of discovering ever more adequate truths. Opening to new perspectives is an inherently vulnerable process. One experiences vulnerability and the accompanying discomfort both in the moments of "not knowing" and in the moments of letting go of (or gaining distance from) beliefs that one is identified with. If MP is to have an impact as a community practice, the extra vulnerability that it produces must be compensated for by an increased ethically driven commitment to creating a "safe container" within the group. In addition to the "softer" elements such as care and empathy, ethical behavior also entails more active elements such as accountability, dedication, or rigor. When any community tries to self-improve by "raising the bar" in terms of any of these elements, it creates (healthy) social pressures that introduce additional levels of vulnerability, which must also be accounted for (as members negotiate how to "hold each other accountable" to the new standards). Epistemic wisdom includes the skills needed to navigate such emotionally/socially challenging situations.

Exploring the Skills and Attitudes of Epistemic Wisdom

Next, I will look more closely at the set of skills and attitudes that comprise what I am calling "epistemic wisdom." These capacities support the knowledge-building approach of MP, first because epistemic wisdom brings one to a *prior* realization of the importance of opening to multiple perspectives, and second because *after* one opens to multiple perspectives these skills are needed to deal with the resulting complexity of ideas. Before looking in more depth at the subskills of epistemic wisdom we will distinguish two general thought modalities.

Convergent and Divergent Modalities

When one looks at how individuals respond to complex situations or multiple perspectives that seem incompatible, one can distinguish two general modalities or movements, one convergent and the other divergent. The convergent process is captured in phrases like "Yes!" "I see!" "Eureka!" In the face of complexity a pattern emerges, a higher whole (holon) forms, and one creates new meaning. One gains understanding, control, and confidence over the information or situation. The divergent process is captured by phrases like "Wow!" "Ugh!" "Yikes!" The experience of allowing for the full novelty, complexity, magnitude, inscrutability, or beauty of a situation can feel pleasant or unpleasant.[7] I propose that, because of the difficulties in assimilating multiple perspectives noted above, we are often too reliant on the convergent process, rushing to conclusions, ascribing too much certainty to models, in an attempt to avoid the sometimes stunning impact and vulnerability of the unknown or unknowable (and see Fischer and Stein 2008 on "dark knowledge"). MP offers an invitation to a vigilant awareness in the balance of both the convergent and divergent modalities in the face of complexity and multiple perspectives. Unlike most treatments of integral approaches, which propose models or practices that are the product of convergent thought, throughout this chapter I invite the reader to also think about the importance and nature of the divergent modality, which gets less attention but is just as important.

From Ontological Humility to Epistemic Wisdom

Below is a list of speech acts that might indicate epistemic wisdom at a basic level. Although these speech acts are mundane, they point to an attitude that is both scarce and important in many contexts.

- I really don't know. But my current best guess is . . .
- I have two seemingly opposing thoughts or impulses going on here . . .
- I was wrong about that. Thanks to your comment I checked it out and . . .
- I felt some frustration and anger upon reading your comment. Let me try to explain. . . .
- What assumptions are we making. . . ?
- Would you be willing to tell me what you think I am saying, as you understand it?
- Both perspectives seem valid to me, but in different ways, as follows . . .
- What is our purpose here? Is our process aligned with it?
- Would some of you like to start a separate discussion about how we can make this dialog more productive?

Fred Kofman, in his book *Conscious Business* (2006), talks about *ontological humility*. Ontological humility is the capacity to say (feel and believe) that "I don't know" or "I was wrong" in situations that might involve vulnerability. Kofman notes that ontological humility is an important element in conscious business (and, by extension, in all collaboration) because it allows individuals and organizations to overcome the limitations of unexamined mental models. Ontological humility is a divergent gesture—"I was wrong," "I don't know," and "what do you think?" allow for the release of unsound beliefs and an opening to new information. Epistemic wisdom goes a step farther to deal directly and proactively with the indeterminacy inherent in knowledge and communication.

Having a deeper understanding of the nature of knowledge allows one to structure dialog, knowledge-building, and decision-making processes in ways that anticipate EI and allow for more flexible and adequate outcomes.[8] For example, a deep understanding of how concepts have indeterminate meanings

may change the character of a dialog; and a deep understanding of the influences of power dynamics in social interaction may change the character of
leadership and decision making.

It has become a common maxim in the integral community to note
that "the map is not the territory." This divergent gesture, acknowledging
that the model or theory (usually AQAL in this case) is not the whole truth,
shows ontological humility. But it often does not go far enough. Applying
a deeper epistemic wisdom would involve being specific about the limitations of the model; exploring the contexts for which the categories of the
model start to break down or become less useful; being explicit about the
underlying assumptions in the model and what cautions those assumptions
point to; mentioning alternative models that are useful where the model is
weak; etc.[9]

Epistemic Wisdom's Component Skills

What I am calling epistemic wisdom includes a rough conglomeration of overlapping and interdependent skills and attitudes—I will not try to give an exact
definition, but these capacities include the abilities to:

- put yourself in someone else's shoes (cognitive empathy and social
  perspective-taking);
- consider multiple perspectives, deal flexibly with uncertainty, ambiguity,
  change, disagreement, and paradox; (dialectical thinking);
- reflect on one's biases, "shadow," tacit intentions, emotional state (social/
  emotional intelligence);
- reflect on one's tacit beliefs, mental models, and monitor problem-solving
  process, the level of certainty of one's inferences (metacognition);
- reflect on and dialog about the quality of communications (meta-dialog);
- consider the big picture, higher-level needs and contexts; focus on the
  needs of the group as a whole; consider the perspective of all stakeholder
  groups (systems thinking);
- understand the nuanced differences in how people create and use fact,
  truth, belief, meaning, etc., and the numerous ways that knowledge is
  validated (epistemological skill).

Elements of the skills of epistemic wisdom have gone by various names in
scholarly research and theory, including: metacognition (Winne 2001); dialectical thinking (Basseches 2005), proprioception of thought (Bohm 1996),
negative capability, reflective judgment (King and Kitchener 1994), cognitive
empathy (Vetlsen 1994), selfdistanciation (Kögler 1992), strategist action logic

(Torbert and Associates 2004), and the metasystematic order of hierarchical complexity (Commons and Richards 1984).

Meta-everything

Epistemic wisdom points to a developmental level in which the individual has a metalevel understanding of mental and communicative processes. As experiences become more diverse and complex, and as life situations become more complex and demanding, the mind is challenged to create ever higher orders of self-organization and meaning. Piaget called the process of cognitive self-organization at successively higher levels "reflective abstraction" (Piaget 1972). Commons uses the term *hierarchical complexity* (1984), and Kegan (1994) employs the related concept of "subject to object " development. Epistemic wisdom involves understanding human processes from a hierarchically more abstract level or metalevel. The list of skills for epistemic wisdom above involves meta-capacities such as:

- meta-cognition (thinking about thinking)
- meta-knowledge (knowledge about the nature and limitations of knowledge)
- meta-learning (learning how to learn, also called triple-loop learning)
- meta-dialog (dialog about how we engage in dialog)
- meta-decision making (making decisions about how we will go about making decisions)
- meta-affect (investigating the feeling of our feelings; somatic awareness of feeling states)
- meta-rationality (making rational decisions about when to employ rational/logical thinking versus intuitive, emotion-based, or other nonrational modalities)
- meta-compassion (reflecting on and caring about how we care for others)
- meta-leadership (supporting leadership in others through leadership)
- meta-transparency (if one cannot be transparent in a situation, one can still be transparent about the fact that one is not transparent, and explain why)

Physicist-philosopher David Bohm suggests that "underneath [humanity's dilemmas] there's something we don't understand about how thought works," and that what is needed is a "very deep" and "very subtle" *awareness of thought itself* (Bohm 1996). We have to go "meta." And the most important area in which to do so is in understanding the overlapping domains of mind (thought/knowledge/communication, etc). As should be evident by now, this is not (only) a philosophical issue, it concerns the sophistication of the commonsense intuitions people bring to bear on a daily basis. The mind is our primary tool for creating our world yet people in general understand so little about it, and so often do not care to try.

Is "Epistemic Wisdom" Too General to be Useful?

This chapter is an exploratory treatment meant to direct attention to some underdiscussed relationships between "being integral," collaborative knowledge-building, ethics, and a skill set called epistemic wisdom. I have introduced epistemic wisdom as a catchall construct that includes a broad set of skills, attitudes and metacapacities listed above. Many of these skills and capacities have a whole research subfield dedicated to their study. Does using a single term to refer to the whole group of capacities enable confusing overgeneralizations that gloss over important differences? Undoubtedly to some degree it does. In addition, epistemic wisdom (like wisdom itself) is so general that it may not be practical to try to measure or assess it, as compared with its more precisely defined constituent skills.

However, these capacities of epistemic wisdom are massively interconnected and interdependent as used in authentic contexts, such that isolating them for theory and clinical study poses its own problems of potential reductionism and practical irrelevance. The sub-skills of epistemic wisdom share a certain "family resemblance" that allows them to be meaningfully grouped. That the construct has some intuitive validity can be argued by noting that if one looks at the list of speech acts above one can hear a coherent "voice"—a vaguely recognizable level of skillfulness and wisdom (which we associate with second-tier development). The same is true for the list of metacapacities listed above. It serves our purposes to use the generic term because (1) it usefully points to a set of skills implied in integral and second-tier thought; and (2) the relationships charted in this chapter between the cognitive, the emotional/social, and the ethical apply to the entire set of skills. Referring to them as a unified though vaguely defined set allows us to point toward an important yet undefined territory of human capacity (alternative terms such as "second-tier capacities" are possible, but that begs the question of what they are).

The sub-skills of epistemic wisdom could also be grouped according to developmental "lines" in Integral Theory. Delineating separate semi-independent lines of development has the advantages and drawbacks mentioned above in theory and practice. My purpose here is to point to the interdependencies and overlaps of these skills rather that their differences. In fact, I agree with theorists who say that differentiating human capacities into separate skills or lines is largely artificial. Kurt Fischer, a leading developmental theorist, claims that skills develop (both genetically/phylogenetically and developmentally/ontogenetically) in response to the demands of real life task situations. He claims that "the skill level that a person displays . . . cannot be considered independently of the context in which that skill is assessed" (Fischer and Farrar 1987, 647). Some primitive human skills such as those dealing with reproduction, eating, and territory, seem to operate fairly independently because the task situations or life-needs they address are relatively independent. But the complex human social contexts of communication, decision making, and knowledge-building have massively overlapping characteristics such that the skills developed to meet these needs should be expected to be equally interdependent and difficult to separate. In *Integral Spirituality* (58), Wilber says, "There are at least a dozen different developmental lines—cognitive, moral, interpersonal, . . . each of the great developmentalists tended to stumble upon onto a particular developmental line or stream to explore in great detail." However, I argue that this seemingly serendipitous fact points in another direction. It shows that human behavior is so complex that it acts as a type of Rorschach Test of scientific theories of mind—if we study human behavior rigorously from the perspective of any of these constructs we observe (enact) a pattern: a pattern that confirms the perspective.

In skillful behavior in authentic contexts such as leading an organization, collaborating on a research project, or engaging in international diplomacy, it is difficult indeed to determine clear lines between emotional intelligence, social intelligence, cognitive intelligence, reflective abstraction, "leadership skill," etc. The rigor of well-defined sub-skills (or levels) is needed to make continued progress in research and theory. However, we do not need to wait for rigorous evidence and models to begin to refer to and support these valuable skills. Very little of the interventions used by educators, leadership consultants, or psychotherapists, can claim extensive and rigorous empirical proof of effectiveness. Rather, numerous alternative approaches claim partial empirical evidence. This (another example of indeterminacy in knowledge building) is primarily because of the complexity of the human condition and the difficulty and expense of research with strong "ecological validity" (i.e., validity in authentic contexts).

Developmental Concerns

Clearly, epistemic wisdom, in its full manifestation, is developmentally advanced (many of its sub-skills align with postformal levels in various developmental theories). Deeply reflective and abstract thought are relatively advanced mental processes that develop slowly in individuals if at all. This might seem to severely limit any goals to support its acquisition or use. However, there are several arguments for supporting and using epistemic wisdom in larger contexts. First, the set of skills and attitudes exist in varying degrees of depth. That is, skills such as "metacognition" and "cognitive empathy" appear weakly at some point and deepen through subsequent levels. The second and third arguments, involving emotional factors and group-level interactions, are given below.

Emotional State versus Developmental Stage

It is easy to imagine a person who thinks and acts from an authority-based conventional level of reasoning in one context, such as in their church community, and thinks and acts from a more systematic, scientific and post-conventional level of reasoning in another context, such as at work. One can also note how a person's intellectual and social/emotional "IQs" can drop dramatically when the brain is "hijacked" by destructive emotions in stressful situations (Goleman 1999; Damasio 1995), and that, at a more subtle level, emotional state may be affecting most rational thought. Similarly, we observe that for ourselves, certain groups of people tend to bring out the best in us, and in their presence our creativity, awareness, and productivity are supported to reach their full potential; while in other groups we are carried in a pattern of lowest-common-denominator downward spiraling that brings out the worst in us and others.

We can draw several conclusions here. First, it is hard to say what the results of a developmental stage assessment (to say nothing about a rough "eyeball" or armchair evaluation) imply for a particular situation without additional information about state and context factors. Second, a person's predominant "developmental level" must be seen as an average (or perhaps ceiling, depending on how it is measured) capacity that exhibits a very wide performance range depending on context. We can envision developmental levels in terms of bell curves by comparing two adjacent developmental levels, rather than imagining two skinny bell curves that barely touch each other, imagine two fat bell curves with significant overlap. This means that the predominant developmental level may not always be a good predictor of a person's capacity to succeed in a given situation (especially in a group context), given the wide variability in performance versus competence. Factors such as culture, emotion intensity, support, etc. may have a significant effect on performance.

Scaffolding, Leadership, and Group Effects

The next point follows directly from the previous one. Individuals with a wide range of developmental levels might still be able to access the basic skills of epistemic wisdom if put in a supportive context. Thus it is reasonable to propose that context, which can set the stage for certain states such as emotional safety and metacognitive scaffolding, can have as much to do with a group's overall performance level as the average assessed developmental level of the individuals.

Supporting Epistemic Wisdom

Having described epistemic wisdom and argued for its importance, I now briefly consider how it can be supported. I will keep my conjectures general and tentative, to serve as pointers to further work.

The Power of Attention/Intention

My first conjecture is that when trying to improve or transform human behavior the first step of bringing attention to a new phenomenon is extremely powerful in and of itself. As has been said, "It is more about asking the right questions than having the answers." In the many examples of metacapacities above, the first step is to focus attention on questions that arise at the meta level. Once human intelligence is focused in a particular direction its adaptive capacities can self-organize toward transformation.

Do not Forget the Ethical/Moral Factors

My second conjecture, argued above, is that in practical situations much of what limits people's performance in areas of epistemic wisdom are contextual and emotional factors such as social vulnerabilities and ego/identity attachments. The skills of epistemic wisdom are developmental, but the basic attitude of openness or curiosity to other perspectives is available to many levels. This can point to the need for individuals to develop emotional/social/ego capacities, but there are also systematic or context implications. The ethical/moral elements of organizational culture, such as mutual regard, trust, forgiveness, appreciation, etc., might have a strong supportive effect.

Focus on Systems-Level Support

As alluded to above, we can approach learning and transformation from two complementary directions. We can work on helping individuals transform through interpersonal interactions including instruction, therapy, coaching, and other direct interventions, and/or we can create *systems* that more indirectly support the desired changes. My third conjecture is that we can get significant mileage by focusing on the systems level—on artifacts/tools, procedures, policies, etc. For instance, what systemic structures might support a culture of appreciation, or greater transparency in decision making, or more consistent checking on the quality of information sources?

To begin to suggest a framework in this area, we can note from above that there are several perspectives from which to approach supporting the skills/attitudes (or any sub-skill) of epistemic wisdom:

Modeling

Leadership can model the use of these skills, and explicitly reflect upon their thought process and reasons for inferences and decisions. This is a good option for when the skill is largely tacit or not understood well enough.

Instruction and coaching

When specific sub-skills are understood well enough to be translated into explicit rather than tacit knowledge, direct instruction, coaching, apprenticeship, etc. are possible.

Social safety and organizational culture

As mentioned above, creating a nonthreatening and collegial environment can have significant effects.

Practices/procedures/models

One can introduce protocols, models, etc. that frame and structure the sub-skills of epistemic wisdom.

Tools and artifacts

Practices, models, cognitive habits, reminders, etc. can be embedded into worksheets, Web sites, performance support tools, etc.

I do not have room in this chapter for more specific suggestions, but refer the reader to other articles in which I suggest practical methods for supporting epistemic wisdom. In Murray (2006a) I explore attitudes for leadership and mentoring, noting suggestions from the literature related to epistemic wisdom such as:

- Framing the models and procedures they promote in reflective and transparent ways;
- Setting and evaluating goals using "multiple bottom lines" that include ethical and systemic concerns;
- Supporting the autonomy and feedback systems that allow for self-organization.

- In Murray (2005) I elaborate on some specific knowledge-building methods related to epistemic wisdom, including:
- Anchoring abstractions with examples;
- Indeterminacy analysis—the analysis of the most important points of uncertainty, ambiguity, or fuzziness in a model or claim;
- "Minimum ontological commitment" and prudence with using integrating models and more focus on component principles;
- Differential analysis—identifying key differentiations, generalizations, and integrations in a model or claim, with an emphasis on reusable differentiations.

In Murray and Ross (2006) we discuss methods and structures for dialog that support epistemic wisdom in groups. And in Murray (2007) and Murray and Benander (2005) we discuss how online communication and decision-support tools can be modified to scaffold the skills of epistemic wisdom, so that the core values and ethical priorities of an organization can be supported in the course of everyday collaborative work.

Conclusion

Second-Tier Communities

In a sense, integral studies and practice, including Wilber's work and the work of many of the leading thinkers drawn to the efforts of the Integral Institute, arises from a need to move beyond the limitations and conundrums of modern and postmodern forms of thought and activity. Frustrated by compartmentalization, tunnel vision, and irrelevance in much of modern thought, those drawn together under the banner of integral studies share a desire for approaches that integrate mind/body/spirit; nature/self/culture; science/morals/art, the true/good/beautiful, knowing/acting/being, etc. This emerging territory is variously called second-tier, integral, post-formal, or post-postmodern within the integral community. I happen to find this narrative compelling and share the general intuition. But the point that I want to make here is that this inner territory of mental and cultural capacity called second tier *cannot* be bound to any particular theory—including Integral Theory. This territory is best characterized by a set of *capacities* (cognitive, emotional/social, etc.) in the same way that "formal operational thought" and "postconventional thought" point to cognitive capacities, not to particular theories, models, or worldviews a person must hold. Our discussion of epistemic wisdom is one attempt to describe that skill set.

Integral Knowledge-Building Communities

The deep and pervasive limitations to reason and knowledge that have come increasingly to light through cognitive science and postmodern critical thought must, or at least should, be a cause for a humbling pause and reflection for those of us engaged in creating or using theories and models of the life-world (indeed, to any engaged in collaborative efforts to find truth, meaning, etc.). Certainty may be a thing of the past, but beyond postmodern critique and deconstruction we must find ways to build knowledge and meaning to answer pressing questions and take action in ways that, as best as we can, take into account the known limitations and indeterminacies of thought and communication.

This chapter makes several main arguments. The first is that factual and theoretical questions of "what is true" and ethical questions of "what is right" are inextricably interdependent. The integral community's aspirations to develop and apply ever-more transcending and including perspectives on the life-world must be accompanied by a deepening attention to the moral/ethical context in which integral models are developed and used. The quality or validity of knowledge and practice depend in part upon the ethical capacity of communities of practice, because moral/ethical problems (such as imbalances of power, denial, irresponsibility, self-absorption, unconscious shadow intentions, etc.) can introduce systematic distortions and omissions in knowledge and purposeful action. These ethical considerations may take the form of social generosities, such as ontological humility, self-distanciation, and reflective listening, as well as more rigorous considerations such as accountability and integrity.

Second, epistemic indeterminacy (uncertainty, ambiguity, paradox, etc.) is omnipresent and increasingly problematic in the (post-post) modern context. It raises its head when we open to multiple perspectives, as the modern context compels us to do. It becomes even more salient as communities evolve into higher developmental territory (e.g., second tier). The set of skills and attitudes I am collectively calling "epistemic wisdom," which can productively address epistemic indeterminacy, involves key moral/ethical capacities.

Third, though these capacities are developmentally advanced in their full bloom, there is every reason to believe that, in their basic forms, they can be supported and strengthened in most communities. Importantly, I have argued that in many authentic contexts, performance that exhibits epistemic wisdom is constrained by state-based (in addition to stage-based) phenomena. Individuals may fail to reflect upon an important perspective because of the feelings of fear, vulnerability, etc. that may come up, or because thinking along those lines threatens ego/identity structures. Groups may fail to exhibit the capacities of epistemic wisdom because the organizational culture does not provide enough psycho/social safety, incentives, or role models to do so. I therefore advocate for systemic approaches that embed participants in environments that actively support and challenge them.

Peter Senge (1990) says that "[a] leader's worth is measured by their contribution to others' mental models" (190). We could add in resonance with other suggestions in Senge's book that a leader's worth is also measured by how well they support others' reflecting on and inquiring *about* their mental models—or more generally, a leader's contribution to others' epistemic wisdom.

Notes

1. I will use "Integral Theory" to refer to Wilber's work, and "integral studies" to refer generally to the emerging body of scholarly work in the integral community. My purpose in this chapter is to make claims about integral studies in general, not to critique or make claims about Wilber's Integral Theory, though I will draw from Integral Theory to make specific points.

2. This is the case for most of the integral community, not because of ignorance or arrogance, but because the field is so new and its scope reaches so far and wide.

3. Wilber has coined the phrase *Integral Methodological Pluralism* (IMP) for his specific meta-methodology. My use of "methodological pluralism" (MP or iMP) refers more generally to an integral approach to the established academic use of "methodological pluralism."

4. The term *cognitive* has narrow and broad meanings. The narrow meaning of cognitive processes is in contrast with affective (emotional) processes. Usually, I will use the more general sense of cognitive, referring to mental processes in general, including emotional and reasoning, conscious and nonconscious processes.

5. From Wilber's (2002) Excerpt C: "The pragmatic correlate of AQAL meta-theory is a set of practices (or meta-paradigms) referred to as Integral Methodological Pluralism, which attempts to honor and include the many important modes of human inquiry already arising in this spacious Kosmos" (1).

6. The words *epistemic* and *epistemology* refer to knowledge: what it is, how it is validated, what its limitations are, how it is created, how it is transferred. Epistemic wisdom could also be called epistemic sophistication, flexibility, fluency, or awareness.

7. The convergent mode is roughly Agape-driven, while the divergent mode is roughly Eros-driven.

8. In comparing the construct of epistemic wisdom with Kofman's ontological humility, I do not mean to imply that Kofman's book does not incorporate many of the elements of epistemic wisdom—it does.

9. In reviewing this chapter Sean Esbjörn-Hargens pointed out, "All too often we mistake our view of the model for the model itself." He emphasized that often when people speak of a model they assume that their interpretation of the model is congruent with the originally intended, most common, or most authoritative interpretation of the model; which in term can stem from treating the model as something that exists "out there" rather than as an interpreted and enacted phenomenon (personal communication, November 15, 2009).

References

Bassesches, M. 1984. *Dialectical thinking and adult development*. Norwood, NJ: Ablex Publishing.

Bohm, D. 1996. *On dialog*. New York: Routledge.

Cohen, P., and T. Gruber. 1985. *Reasoning about uncertainty: A knowledge representation perspective*. Boston: University of Massachusetts.

Commons, M. L., and F. A. Richards. 1984b. A general model of stage theory. In *Beyond formal operations: Late adolescent and adult cognitive development,* ed. M. L. Commons, F. A. Richards, and C. Armon, 120–41. New York: Praeger.

Damasio, A. 1999. *The feeling of what happens: Body and emotion in the making of consciousness*. New York: Harcourt Brace.

Elster, J. 1999. *Alchemies of the mind: Rationality and the emotions*. Cambridge: Cambridge University Press.

Fischer, K. 1980. A theory of cognitive development: The control and construction of hierarchies of skills. *Psychological Review* 87(6): 477–531.

———, and Z. Stein. 2008. Dark knowledge: An era in history and a moment in the learning process. Unpublished draft.

Forman, M. D. and S. Esbjörn-Hargens. 2008. The academic emergence of Integral Theory. Retrieved August 28, 2008, from http://www.integralworld.net/forman-hargens.html.

Goleman, D. 1995. *Emotional intelligence*. New York: Bantam Books.

Habermas, J. 1993. *Justification and application: Remarks on discourse ethics*. Cambridge: MIT Press.

Habermas, J. 1999. *Moral consciousness and communicative Action*. Cambridge: MIT Press.

Kahneman, D., P. Slovic, and A. Tversky. (Eds.) 1982. *Judgment under uncertainty: Heuristics and biases*. Cambridge: Cambridge University Press.

Kegan, R. 1994. *In over our heads: The mental demands of modern life*. Cambridge: Harvard University Press.

King, P. M., and K. S. Kitchener. 1994. *Developing reflective judgment: Understanding and promoting intellectual growth and critical thinking in adolescents and adults*. San Francisco: Jossey-Bass Publishers.

Kofman, F. 2006. *Conscious business: How to build value through values*. Boulder: SoundsTrue.

Kögler, H. H. 1992. *The power of dialog: Critical hermeneutics after Gadamer and Foucault*. Cambridge: MIT Press.

Kuhn, T. S. 1970. *The structure of scientific revolutions,* Chicago: University of Chicago Press.

Lakatos, I. 1976. *Proofs and refutations: The logic of mathematical discovery*. Ed. J. Worrall and E. Zahar. Cambridge: Cambridge University Press.

Lakoff, G., and M. Johnson. 1999. *Philosophy in the flesh: The embodied mind and its challenge to Western thought*. New York: Basic Books/Perseus Books Group.

Mervis, B., and E. Rosch. 1981. Categories of natural objects. *Annual Review of Psychology* 32: 89–115.

Meyers, D. G. 2002. *Intuition: Its powers and perils*. New Haven: Yale University Press.

Murray, T. 2006. Collaborative knowledge building and Integral Theory: On perspectives, uncertainty, and mutual regard. *Integral Review* 2: 210–68.

Piaget, J. 1972. *The principles of genetic epistemology*. Trans. W. Mays. London: Routledge.

Senge, P. M. 1990. *The fifth discipline: The art and practice of the learning organization.* New York: Doubleday.

Sunstein, C. R. 2002. *Risk and reason.* New York: Cambridge University Press.

Travis, C., and E. Aronson. 2007. *Mistakes were made (but not by me): Why we justify foolish beliefs, bad decisions, and hurtful acts.* New York: Harcourt.

Torbert, B. 2004. *Action inquiry: The secret of timely and transforming leadership.* San Francisco: Berrett-Koehle.

Vetlesen, A. J. 1994. *Perception, empathy, and judgment.* University Park: Pennsylvania State University Press.

Wilber, K. 2000a. *Sex, ecology, spirituality.* Boston: Shambhala.

———. 2001. *Eye to eye: The quest for the new paradigm.* Boston: Shambhala.

———. 2005. *Kosmos II: Excerpt B from Volume 2 of the Kosmos Trilogy.* Retrieved August 12, 2008, from wilber.shambhala.com.

———. 2006. *Integral spirituality.* Boston: Integral Books.

Wilson, T. D. 2002. *Strangers to ourselves: Discovering the adaptive unconscious.* Cambridge: Harvard University Press.

Winne, P. H. 2001. *Self-regulated learning viewed from models of information processing. In Self-regulated learning and academic achievement* (2nd ed.), ed. B. J. Zimmerman and D. H. Schunk. Mahwah, NJ: Lawrence Erlbaum.

Wittgenstein, L. 1953. *Philosophical investigations.* New York: Macmillan.

15

Appropriation in Integral Theory

The Case of Sri Aurobindo and the Mother's "Untold" Integral View

Charles I. Flores

Ken Wilber (1999) has called Sri Aurobindo "India's greatest modern philoso-pher-sage" (515) and "one of the great founders of integral spirituality and integral practice." (Wilber 2001, viii). He has been enthusiastically recognized by many in the integral movement as a founding father of their work. And yet, ironically, Aurobindo's Integral Yoga (IY) has been understood and presented by some integralists very partially. This oversimplification unfortunately has tended to fatally distort or omit key aspects of Integral Yoga, which has led them to arrive at various untenable criticisms of its alleged limitations that would need to be "transcended."

This chapter will attempt to address some of the omissions and misun-derstandings thus far perpetuated by many well-intended sympathizers of Integral Yoga one specific case of integral misappropriation. The customarily ignored work and writings of Mira Alfassa, otherwise known as the Mother, Sri Aurobindo's spiritual collaborator and equal, will be presented as an inex-tricable part of the Integral Yoga. I posit that Integral Yoga is not an abstract mental philosophy describing evolution, nor is it a narrow individual-subjec-tive spiritual psychology. It has always been fundamentally a current, living, and holistic spiritual practice with one specific aim, which incorporates both the subjective and the objective, and the individual and the collective. Furthermore, IY has always recognized and honored the value of both yoga and modern science. I will reflect upon how today's integral movement, with its underpinnings in the AQAL model and Spiral Dynamics, is viewed from the perspective of Integral Yoga. I will state a few of the yet unrecognized contributions Integral Yoga can make to Integral understanding and practice, and prospects for future collaboration. Lastly, I call for a larger collaboration between specialists in other fields to put in their voices and make appropriate corrections, without which Integral Theory will arrest in its development.

The Author's Journey with Sri Aurobindo and Wilber

Ken Wilber has been an important figure in my life. In the early 1990s, I discovered transpersonal psychology and came upon his work. It was written in easily readable (if not beautiful) American prose, and spoke with some authority about the various spiritual traditions and how they related to modern Western psychology. He was then a figure that had not published a new book in several years, and his works from the 1980s were fairly difficult to find pre-Internet, even in cosmopolitan New York City. I took much at that time from both *The Atman Project* (1980) and *Up from Eden* (1981). *Spectrum of Consciousness* (1977) and *Transformations of Consciousness* (1986) were influential in my decision to enter a Masters program in psychology.

At about the same time, I came upon Indian sage Sri Aurobindo's work. His writings did not provide instant intellectual satisfaction in the way that Wilber's work did. It was not as easily readable, written in late-nineteenth-century periodic prose form, in which sentences seemed to become entire paragraphs. But even upon the first reading, I intuited that there was a vast vision behind the seemingly cryptic language. It was helpful then that Wilber also seemed to appreciate Sri Aurobindo. Very soon after, I learned of Mira Alfassa, known lovingly by Integral Yogis as "the Mother." I connected with her writings at first, and discovered a consciousness that was just as vast as Sri Aurobindo's, only she seemed to make more effort to simplify her language so that even the school children she taught in the 1950s could understand her, although she knew well that her present and future audience would be comprised mainly of adults. She was not his wife, his consort, or his student; Sri Aurobindo recognized her and announced unequivocally that she was his spiritual equal, and gave her charge of his students' spiritual practices, with his behind her. It was because of her that he could go into seclusion in his room to do yogic work and write from 1926 until his passing. (Heehs 2008, 353–56) Several experiences and months later, my initial interest became yogic practice. While I had met others on that path, no human being proselytized me to join a spiritual or religious club. There were no promises of special experiences, liberation, or enlightenment, though the possibility of the spiritual transformation down to matter here on Earth intrigued me to move forward. The reality behind the writings grew within me, in fact, they were already known to me within, only they were now manifesting consciously in my life. I learned more about various suggested practices of from both Sri Aurobindo and the Mother, and the community of practitioners, which comprise numerous ashrams, centers, schools, study groups worldwide, and a township in India founded by the Alfassa called Auroville.

In 1995, I bought my copy of Wilber's massive tome *Sex, Ecology, Spirituality* on the first day of its release, having preordered it from the now defunct

Samuel Weiser's bookstore in New York—famous for its metaphysical and occult selections. I read the entire book cover to cover in two days. I had very mixed feelings about it. Wilber now added to his earlier work what was later to be called the AQAL model. Taking the notion that everyone is right, but only partially, he now had a way to relate to different fields of knowledge to each other. He could now chart all knowledge in a kind of subject-object/individual-collective Johari's window. Others had had some or many these insights before him, but none before decided to graphically depict Reality in this way. It seemed at one level, "common sense," and I wondered why no one had done this before.

While I was impressed with the breadth of this work, I was left with a strong sense of uneasiness. He now seemed to suggest that it was possible to neatly place all of reality in a strangely flatland depiction that reminded me of the Euclidian coordinate plane geometry I learned in sixth grade in my South Bronx public school. More disturbing to me was that Wilber, from the basis of the "vision-logic" that he claimed emerged from the understanding of this model, could seemingly determine who and what was "partially wrong" in virtually any field. He now adopted strong positions against alleged schools of thought, and from my reading, a new aggressive, and sometimes derisive, polemic against these groups. While it was apparent that he had made some effort to understand the academic positions of certain perspectives through his amateur private study of a number books and correspondences, it seemed very clear to me that he was not an expert in most of these fields, and could not speak with any true authority on most any of them. I believed that one would have to speak with much more humility about other people's life works than to assign broad labels to certain groups such as "eco-feminists" and "flatlanders." This approach was needlessly antagonistic and was sure to provoke anger and backlash from those who probably hardly knew of Ken Wilber.

Sometime after the publication of this book, I learned that Wilber was now taking up the term *integral* as the name for his model. I once again had a mixed reaction to this development. On the one hand, it seemed to be a tip of the hat to Sri Aurobindo, and yet, he was describing something completely different. I had seen Wilber's charts of Sri Aurobindo in which he compared his levels of mind (I believe, incorrectly) to Plotinus, and was reminded of a story I had heard, in which there had been a couple of disciples that had made graphic charts of what Sri Aurobindo called (in a somewhat unfortunate borrowing of Theosophical terminology) "parts and planes of being." According to Ashram lore, a couple of disciples had asked he draw the relationship between these planes, and to humor them, and possibly to amuse himself, he scribbled a crude map on a scrap of paper. As soon as he drew it, he insisted that the depiction he drew should not be taken seriously, that reality could never be plotted in such a mental fashion. A few disciples nonetheless embellished the scribble into colorful graphics, and a later rendition of that map was eventually (and to my mind, sadly) labeled "The Divine Plan."

I knew from both my previous Buddhist training and from this ashram story that all graphic mental depictions of that sort could be momentarily helpful for the mind to imagine higher and wider realities to a point. But they cease to be helpful when these mental constructs are reified (or deified!), veiling that reality in an abstract mental bubble, in which the model is no longer the helper, but the bar. I knew that Buddhists spoke of the paths or yanas as "self-dissolving medicines," rafts to be discarded when their emancipatory usefulness was outlived. Sri Aurobindo and Mother lived this knowledge very well. Wilber wrote of this many times in the past of the "finger pointing to the moon is not the moon," but I feared that he now seemed to be moving toward a new process of mental concrescence, despite himself. The new AQAL model, with developmental streams such as Spiral Dynamics' value meme, would later explain, and later "save" the ancients from (apparently) convincing attacks from today's postmodernists that their own subtle abstractions and cultural biases were mediating their insights (a la Michael Katz, with whom this debate has never been resolved). Indeed, the grand abstraction of Integral Theory and its AQAL model is in many ways surpasses and is more Real than the realizations of the greatest saints and sages of history, because "the Buddha didn't know neuroscience," or more precisely, *none* of them understood how the other three quadrants effected their subjective insights (Wilber 2006, 44–46). So we have been told.

So in some ways my initial allegiance to Wilber's work began to wane in 1995, before Integral Institute, the Integral Naked Web site, and before the turn to mass marketing with promises of "an Integral Experience in Twenty Minutes" for the "Integral Operating System 1.0." But at the same time, I watched with some interest when numbers of younger people began to use the AQAL and Spiral Dynamics value meme models for pragmatic purposes. This model proved to be a useful tool to understand the interdisciplinary fields of knowledge, to use these fields to solve problems of third world and urban development, business, and other fields. My spiritual and theoretical concerns about his model were quite removed from the simple pragmatic utility of the model. These people were less concerned with saving the Great Nest of Being than Saving the World. It was easy for many to grasp, and then use toward addressing local and global problems. Whether Integral Theory actually solves these problems remains to be seen, but there was no doubting that the AQAL model was inspiring some hope of making sense of the world's problems, which have become hypercomplex. These new integralists share many of the same concerns I do, and have found the inspiration to do something about it.

The Integral Theory Conference has been the first communal sharing of the findings of this community, and it is very exciting.

Wilber's Misappropriation of Aurobindo

Today I am still very much concerned with the past and current appropriation of various theories, groups, and individuals into the model of AQAL. This chapter will touch on what I believe to be the misappropriation of Sri Aurobindo's work within the model so far. I have long held some of these views, but I will not document them in detail, since others have done this work for the most part, and I will refer the reader to Hemsell (2004), Kazlev (n.d.), and Vrinte (2002) for more details, if so inclined. My aim in this chapter is not to in any way promote Sri Aurobindo as a spiritual path. I choose Sri Aurobindo because he is the figure that I know the best, but the same set of cautions and reexaminations (within the context of Integral Theory) could and should be done for other towering figures such as Carl Jung, Ramana Maharshi, Jürgen Habermas, Plotinus, or Sakyamuni Buddha.

I strongly believe that each of these and other figures must be allowed to speak in their own voice. Wilber since the start of this integral movement has held his opinions of various fields and various historical figures. He has determined by his own voluminous yet partial knowledge who and what is partly right, and who and what is partly wrong. There is nothing wrong with that, and he is allowed his opinions. I see this case of misappropriation not due to any particular bias against Sri Aurobindo, which he certainly does not hold. As the reader will see in the pages that follow, I believe that in this case, it is simply a result of a lack of scholarship. No one person can do it all *and* do it well. It is probably best for experts in their respective fields who are sympathetic to the model to make the appropriate connections with the model. There is no particular reason that an AQAL model "held lightly" could not do a better job of accurately representing all the fields and figures that it wants to integrate. To the Integral Institute's credit, they have increasingly encouraged and opened up this dialog. I applaud Forman and Esbjörn-Hargens's statement of the purpose of this conference posted on www.IntegralWorld.Net (Forman and Esbjörn-Hargens 2008, this volume). As this integral movement expands to others who take the model, work it, shape it into something that is in their grounded experience and is becomes *theirs,* Wilber's opinions are and will continue to be exposed for their own important yet partial nature. His is an important voice, and yet only one voice in the many. His opinions will be and should be challenged, and it does not matter how he personally reacts to any of it. I have no interest in "Wilber Watching" except where he may add new insights or points of discussion to the collective. "Integral" does not belong to Ken Wilber, or even to Sri Aurobindo, but to all of us in the collective. All of the assumptions within this theoretical model are ultimately up for grabs. Integral's future is largely with the collective. I have far more trust in the collective for discerning the relative veracity of various propositions among each other than in any one or small group of individuals. It is, after all, only a model!

What follows are a few of the facets of Integral Yoga, some the nature and scope of the work of Sri Aurobindo, and other issues that are important to clarify for audiences of Wilber's work and scholar-practitioners of Integral Theory.

Was Sri Aurobindo a "Theorist"?

> Aurobindo's greatest shortcoming is a shortcoming faced by all theorists, namely, the unavailability of the important discoveries made since his time. Aurobindo was most concerned with the transformations of consciousness (Upper Left) and the correlative changes in the material body (Upper Right). Although he had many important insights on the social and political system, he did not seem to grasp the actual interrelations of cultural, societal, intentional, and behavioral, nor did his analysis at any point proceed on the level of intersubjectivity (Lower Left) and interobjectivity (Lower Right). He did not, that is, fully assimilate the differentiations of modernity. But the levels and modes that Aurobindo did cover make his formulations indispensable for any true integral model.
>
> —Ken Wilber, *Integral Psychology*

> . . . but nobody combined both philosophical brilliance and a profoundly enlightened consciousness the way Aurobindo did. His enlightenment informed his philosophy; his philosophy gave substance to his enlightenment; and that combination has been rarely equaled, in this or any time.
>
> —Ken Wilber, *A Greater Psychology*

Sri Aurobindo has long been highly respected by Wilber, and is viewed by him as a founding father of the integral movement. Sri Aurobindo was perhaps the first to use the term *integral* when he wrote in the serial journal *The Arya* essays, which were later to become chapters of the book called *Synthesis of Yoga* in 1914 (Heehs 2008, 282). But as alluded to before, he never had an interest in models, did not like philosophy, and had absolutely no interest in "theory building." By his own account, through the series of yogic developments in his life which became established in him (in what Wilber would call a "stage"), Sri Aurobindo did not write from logic, in which knowledge is built from a rational or even vision-logic line of thinking, but from the insight that he established within him from his practice of Yoga:

> I owed nothing in my philosophy to intellectual abstractions, ratiocination or dialectics; when I have used these means it was simply to explain my philosophy and justify it to the intellect of others. The other source of my philosophy was the knowledge that flowed from above when I sat in meditation, especially from the plane of the Higher Mind when I reached that level; they [the ideas from the Higher Mind] came down in a mighty flood which swelled into a sea of direct Knowledge always translating itself into experience, or they were intuitions starting from experience and leading to other intuitions and a corresponding experience. This source was exceedingly catholic and many-sided and all sorts of ideas came in which might have belonged to conflicting philosophies but they were here reconciled in a large synthetic whole. (Aurobindo 2006, 113)

In another letter to a student, Sri Aurobindo attempted to explain how it is possible for him to live in a state (stage?) that we have been told is ineffable and seemingly otherworldly, and from that place write thousands of words in a form that is understandable to the rational mind. The importance of this letter justifies quoting it at length here:

> I do not think, however, that the statement of supra-intellectual things necessarily involves a making of distinctions in the terms of the intellect. For, fundamentally, it is not an expression of ideas arrived at by speculative thinking. One has to arrive at spiritual knowledge through experience and a consciousness of things which arises directly out of that experience or else underlies or is involved in it. This kind of knowledge, then, is fundamentally a consciousness and not a thought or formulated idea. For instance, my first major experience—radical and overwhelming, though not, as it turned out, final and exhaustive—came after and by the exclusion and silencing of all thought—there was, first, what might be called a spiritually substantial or concrete consciousness of stillness and silence, then the awareness of some sole and supreme Reality in whose presence things existed only as forms but forms not at all substantial or real or concrete; but this was all apparent to a spiritual perception and essential and impersonal sense and there was not the least concept or idea of reality or unreality or any other notion, for all conccpt or idea was hushed or rather entirely absent in the absolute stillness.

These things were known directly through the pure consciousness and not through the mind, so there was no need of concepts or words or names. At the same time this fundamental character of spiritual experience is not absolutely limitative; it can do without thought, but it can do with thought also. Of course, the first idea of the mind would be that the resort to thought brings one back at once to the domain of the intellect—and at first and for a long time it may be so; but it is not my experience that this is unavoidable. It happens so when one tries to make an intellectual statement of what one has experienced; but there is another kind of thought that springs out as if it were a body or form of the experience or of the consciousness involved in it—or of a part of that consciousness—and this does not seem to me to be intellectual in its character. It has another light, another power in it, a sense within the sense. It is very clearly so with those thoughts that come without the need of words to embody them, thoughts that are of the nature of a direct seeing in the consciousness, even a kind of intimate sense or contact formulating itself into a precise expression of its awareness (I hope this is not too mystic or unintelligible); but it might be said that directly the thoughts turn into words they belong to the kingdom of intellect—for words are a coinage of the intellect. But is it so really or inevitably ? It has always seemed to me that words came originally from somewhere else than the thinking mind, although the thinking mind secured hold of them, turned them to its use and coined them freely for its purposes. But even otherwise, is it not possible to use words for the expression of something that is not intellectual? Housman contends that poetry is perfectly poetical only when it is non-intellectual, when it is nonsense. That is too paradoxical, but I suppose what he means is that if it is put to the strict test of the intellect, it appears extravagant because it conveys something that expresses and is real to some other kind of seeing than that which intellectual thought brings to us. Is it not possible that words may spring from, that language may be used to express—at least up to a certain point and in a certain way—the supra-intellectual consciousness which is the essential power of spiritual experience ? This, however, is by the way—when one tries to explain spiritual experience to the intellect itself, then it is a different matter. (Aurobindo 1995, 86–88)

Sri Aurobindo is not a unique figure in his ability to write in this fashion. There have been numerous mystics that have written out of their realizations, and these are often considered inspired revelatory works. But Sri Aurobindo takes pains to explain his vision to others using sophisticated rational arguments so that a modern audience could get something from his exposition. But by his own account, he did not write deductively, but wrote from a downpouring of constant directly inspired experience. While we cannot accept that Sri

Aurobindo's account is the final word on the issue, it does defy any facile notion that Sri Aurobindo should be grouped with lists of scientists, philosophers, and "theorists" such as Whitehead who clearly and overtly hacked and devised their theories using their normal, albeit brilliant, minds. But what I would like Integralists to recognize here is that there is an entire category of mystical writings that point a kind of knowledge that is not arrived at in a mental way, and there is an entire field of study that is *evaluating how it evaluates* these types of accounts. Many do not accept that the accounts of St. Theresa of Avila or Chandrakirti are merely mythic, archetypal, or premodern, but they result from living in a wider and deeper consciousness than our normal human consciousness. To complicate matters in this case, Sri Aurobindo is the unusual case of being a Cambridge scholar and a mystic of the highest caliber in India, thoroughly steeped in modernity. He was not only able discuss yoga in a philosophical form as in *The Life Divine* or *Synthesis of Yoga*, but also in thousands of letters to his students, in his own daily personal *Record of Yoga* between 1914 and 1920, and in a powerful poetic form in his true Magnum Opus, *Savitri*. A 40-year labor which is the longest poem in the English language, and a mantric *tour de force* in the tradition of the Vedas, it was recognized by a nomination for the Nobel Prize for literature in 1950 by Pearl S. Buck and Gabriela Mistral (Heehs 2008, 404).

His mode of deriving knowledge may explain one of the major differences between Integral Theory and Integral Yoga. The AQAL model is one theoretical tool to integralize our understanding of the world from our typical mental mode while in a waking state. We experience things as subjective/objective, individual/collective. It makes sense from this kind of Integral view. Viewed from certain other levels of consciousness, however, the world may not be that way. Our normal waking consciousness may be narrow and false compared to other levels of mentality, and the AQAL model may appear to be a clumsy method of a dissecting mind to create an abstraction of integrality. Sri Aurobindo describes the "Higher Mind" as only the first among numerous levels of mind above the normal "Thinking Mind." Again, given the importance of these distinctions, it is worth quoting Sri Aurobindo at length:

> Our first decisive step out of our human intelligence, our normal mentality, is an ascent into a higher Mind, a mind no longer of mingled light and obscurity or half-light, but a large clarity of the spirit. Its basic substance is a unitarian sense of being with a powerful multiple dynamisation capable of the formation of a multitude of aspects of knowledge, ways of action, forms and significances of becoming, of all of which there is a spontaneous inherent knowledge . . . ; it is a luminous thought-mind, a mind of spirit-born conceptual knowledge. An all-awareness emerging from the original identity, carrying the truths the identity held in itself, conceiving swiftly,

victoriously, multitudinously, formulating and by self-power of the Idea effectually realising its conceptions, is the character of this greater mind of knowledge. This kind of cognition is the last that emerges from the original spiritual identity before the initiation of a separative knowledge, base of the Ignorance; it is therefore the first that meets us when we rise from conceptive and ratiocinative mind, our best-organised knowledge-power of the Ignorance, into the realms of the Spirit: it is, indeed, the spiritual parent of our conceptive mental ideation, and it is natural that this leading power of our mentality should, when it goes beyond itself, pass into its immediate source. (Aurobindo 2005 , 974)

This level of mind just above our typical rationality, with its "multiple dynamisation," would have little need for relatively crude conceptual models to derive each quadrant of knowledge. If we accept that these levels of consciousness are potentials for humanity that have not yet manifested for large numbers of people, then we may imagine that what we mean by "integral" will look very different to us in the future, and that today's AQAL model will be viewed as a quaint tool for an older "thinking" mentality which humanity will have both transcended and included.

Integral Yoga, Sri Aurobindo, and Mira Alfassa—Were They "All Quadrant"?

As Jacobs (2007) has pointed out, Wilber has tended to cast certain major figures into single quadrants, which he has determined was their focus. I would posit that this form of illustrating his points runs the risk of serving a form of integral stereotyping. Rarely is a theorist or author merely concerned with one quadrant; even in cases when an individual focused upon one quadrant, her work connects with the others, even if their work in the other quadrants is not elaborately developed. In the case of Sri Aurobindo and Alfassa, Wilber focuses exclusively in the Upper Left or personal subjective nature of the Integral Yoga, with the addition of Upper Right physical transformation. The charge that mystics are predominately Upper Left is a broad net that he casts upon most mystics, not exclusively Sri Aurobindo. But in this particular case, his overgeneralization is most striking, because Sri Aurobindo's work in the lower social quadrants is highly developed in his writings. In fact, he is considered by many to be the father of the Indian Independence movement before Gandhi, and the main reason he entered a life of Yoga was to help in the struggle for independence (Heehs 2008, 87). To move an entire people toward independence by writing in newspapers and influence the political system, he must have had a very acute understanding of interobjective and intersubjective quadrants even if his theorizing or gnosis does not. Even as his practice took him out of direct political life, his connection to the world was constant. Several of his books, the *Human Cycle, War and Determination*, and the *Ideal of Human Unity*, and the last chapters of the *Life Divine*, are all treatments of the lower quadrants. It is quite surprising that the developmental thesis of the *Human Cycle*, which precedes that of Gebser and Graves, is not even mentioned by Wilber. Sri Aurobindo was by all accounts intimately connected to current events, and both world wars, at times coming out to make public statements, and trying to influence events using occult Yogic means. His yoga not only informed his subjective experience, physical body, and his writings, but the way he related and understood the collective from the exterior and the interior. Likewise, Alfassa ran their Ashram of several hundred sadhaks, and so working with and understanding collective dynamics from both the interior and exterior dimensions were essential. She started a new form of education, known for the last 60 years as "integral education," and now hundreds of such schools exist in the world. Alfassa formed the community of Auroville in 1968 as an experiment for the collective to "serve the Divine" and to learn to achieve the Ideal of Human Unity. This is all very far from a limited subjective-individual focus, and the quadrants are quite well differentiated and explored in Sri Aurobindo's life and writings, albeit not as well packaged as Wilber's AQAL model might have it. But I would argue that the essential distinctions of individual/collective and interior/exterior are present in Aurobindo's work. So while there are important ways the LL and LR lens brings something forward that is not always explicit in Aurobindo such simplistic critiques by Wilber fail to include the ways Aurobindo did interface and even write about cultural and social dynamics. Not to mention such a position dissuades proponents of his work (i.e., Wilberians) from exploring Aurobindo's contribution to these domains. In effect, such posturing encourages the jury to be out before it has a chance to be in.

Another example occurs in *Integral Spirituality*, where Wilber makes the brief claim that Sri Aurobindo was aware of only "4 methodologies, his Integral Yoga exercised 3" (Wilber 2006, 202). However, Wilber does not tell us explicitly which four Sri Aurobindo was aware of or which three he exercised. We are left to guess. So I am not sure how he is counting, or even what he knows of Integral Yoga practices (since nowhere does he expound on them even from an Upper-Left perspective). This is a subject of another article, but I would just suggest here from my study of Integral Life Practice, that there is likely a miscount. In any case, Integral Yoga would not subscribe to a "more zones and methodologies are better and more integral" philosophy. So even though Sri Aurobindo did not use all eight zones of IMP in either a formal or informal fashion that does not diminish his contribution as being less than integral.

At most, one could say that they did not focus on the Upper-Right quadrant, in the narrow sense of the overt use scientific method, at least at the Ashram. They did not build scientific laboratories within the Ashram. But they did place a high value on science. In fact, Sri Aurobindo predicted that the discipline, if it followed its own method with high fidelity and without human prejudice, would find the "occult" or unseen, as it has in physics today. He viewed today's science as related to schools of occult science of the "premodern" past in India. In this statement, he discusses the limitations of science, and he understood it, to use AQAL terms, that the Upper Right cannot in a blatant or subtle "Flatland" way find the deeper spiritual knowledge. As one can see in the following quote, while he was not himself a white lab coat scientist, he was quite aware of modern scientific discoveries of the twentieth century. In a similar fashion I suspect Sri Aurobindo was involved with more zones than Wilber is currently willing or capable of recognizing.

> We see that a seed develops into a tree, we follow the line of the process of production and we utilise it; but we do not discover how a tree can grow out of a seed, how the life and form of the tree come to be implied in the substance or energy of the seed or, if that be rather the fact, how the seed can develop into a tree. We know that genes and chromosomes are the cause of hereditary transmissions, not only of physical but of psychological variations; but we do not discover how psychological characteristics can be contained and transmitted in this inconscient material vehicle. We do not see or know, but it is expounded to us as a cogent account of Nature-process, that a play of electrons, of atoms and their resultant molecules, of cells, glands, chemical secretions and physiological processes manages by their activity on the nerves and brain of a Shakespeare or a Plato to produce or could be perhaps the dynamic occasion for the production of a *Hamlet* or a *Symposium* or a *Republic*; but we fail to discover or appreciate how such material movements could have composed or necessitated the composition of these highest points of thought and literature: the divergence here of the determinants and the determination becomes so wide that we are no longer able to follow the process, much less understand or utilise. (Aurobindo 2005, 312–13)

It is not at all apparent to me that if Sri Aurobindo also had a current understanding of neuroscientific discoveries, this would have substantially changed any of his insights in any fundamental way. Is it the notion that things not yet discovered until after a theorist passes away are always the "theorist's" limitation? It is true that as time-bound creatures, humans are always limited somewhat by what is not yet known? But what is not clear is that a few scientific discoveries necessarily render Sri Aurobindo's and Alfassa's *yogic* insights obsolete; that case has not been made. I would posit that their own yogic discoveries have yet to be even understood and experienced by most, and are far from being surpassed. I realize that Wilber agrees with this.

My point to him and proponents of Integral Theory is that a full familiarity and integral analysis of Sri Aurobindo and other key integral theorists and practitioners will likely reveal a much more complete picture of these individuals and their integral value than what has been initially rendered by Wilber himself. Besides taking a move from the AQAL playbook we would have to acknowledge not just how Aurobindo and other historic figures were limited by what they did not know (scientifically, experientially, culturally, etc.) but that they were simultaneously freed by the burdens of such knowledge, which likely contributed in important ways to the discoveries they did make. In other words, an integral analysis should consider both the dignity and disaster of yesteryear and how a scholar-practitioner both benefited and was limited by their historical context. To only see the limits is quite partial.

On a more practical level, Alfassa strongly encouraged scientific understandings in Auroville, which she called an experiment and a living laboratory. Today in Auroville, science has an essential function in the work of building a city, particularly in appropriate sustainable technologies for the environment (Parker and Vignes 2004). Her spirit was always to embrace new discoveries from any quarters, as she stated in the Auroville Charter:

> Auroville will be the place of an unending education, of constant progress, and a youth that never ages. Auroville wants to be the bridge between the past and the future. Taking advantage of all discoveries from without and from within, Auroville will boldly spring towards future realisations. (Alfassa 1968, 1)

A Call for Integral Collaboration

I believe that those who have been inspired by Ken Wilber's Integral Theory and its AQAL model and those that have found their inspiration from Integral Yoga are moving toward similar aims. Both are very much interested in a kind of transformation of the conditions of life on the planet. In a period in history when the world seems on the brink of disaster, all Integralists are looking for solutions in both science and spirituality. Indeed, all integral people seem to have a penchant for being highly intellectual. Integral Yoga as a spiritual practice does not emphasize humanitarianism, but "serving the Divine," or the larger evolutionary impulse. AQAL is proving to be a useful model to address certain problems, and Integral Transformative Practice, Integral Life Practice, and other kinds of teachings old and new are being used to ground abstract theory into day-to-day behavior and praxis.

Students of Sri Aurobindo have viewed Wilber with some admiration, but also suspicion. The incorrect and partial analysis of Sri Aurobindo that he has made, briefly treated in this chapter, has for some negated his praise. "If Sri Aurobindo is so wonderful, how about at least getting him right?" It was not helpful that in *Sex, Ecology, Spirituality,* Wilber left the impression that Sri Aurobindo was "left behind" in "Wilber-II" and supposedly transcended and included, when many believe that he was never even fully read or understood to begin with. It is fine that Wilber wants to keep track of his own theoretical development with numbers, but these do not correspond with Sri Aurobindo or other figures that inspired him at any particular point. On the other hand, some Integral Yogis do not find Wilber's Integral Theory useful or even relevant to their own practice, so they are indifferent to him and likely have not fully read or understood him.

People who practice Integral Yoga can find many useful practical insights in the work. This can be a challenge to a few Integral Yogis who see Sri Aurobindo's and Mother's work as complete, so there is no need to look elsewhere. I believe this kind of narrowness can exist in any group, a formation of fundamentalism that can beset human beings no matter how wide the teaching. Integral Theory is today being successfully used as a part of an integral (or "Psychic Being"–based) education in the Rainbow Kids Integral Preschool and the Integral Elementary School in La Jolla, California. I think Auroville would welcome the practical application of tools such as AQAL and Spiral Dynamics toward issues there. Sri Aurobindo and Alfassa both passed away decades ago, but Integral Yogis continue to do their work. It is time to move away a little from acrimonious theoretical quibbling that has occasionally appeared, and work harmoniously.

Cornelissen (2005) has called for a "rigorous science of subjective phenomena." While it is no doubt helpful and interesting to study EEGs and brain states that seem to correlate with different states of consciousness, a new kind of scientific study of Left-Hand quadrant phenomena using "yogic" means as science will go a long way to our future understanding of the significance of the levels of consciousness that mystics like Sri Aurobindo described. While the humble beginnings of this kind of research exists (e.g., John Heron's spiritual inquiry, Jorge Ferrer's embodied inquiry), and Wilber suggests the possibility in Integral Theory. I believe that this research will have radical implications for how we view the quadrants. But this research is generally scattered among a few groups; much more collaboration is needed.

Lastly, I hope that Integral explorers will increasingly read the original works of great Integral figures. Secondhand accounts, while initially informative, can also distort and omit. This chapter can only point to the integral richness that exists in the writings, practices, and community or Sri Aurobindo and the Mother. It is up to the reader-practitioner to go further.

References

Alfassa, M. 1968. *The Auroville Charter*. Retrieved June 30, 2008, from http://www.auroville.org/vision/charter.htm.

Aurobindo, S. 1995. *On himself*. Pondicherry, India: Sri Aurobindo Ashram.

———. 2005. The Life Divine. In *The complete works of Sri Aurobindo* (Vol. 22). Pondicherry, India: Sri Aurobindo Ashram.

———. 2006. Autobiographical materials with letters of historical interest and public statements. In *The complete works of Sri Aurobindo* (Vol. 36). Pondicherry, India: Sri Aurobindo Ashram.

Cornelissen, M. 2005. The farther reaches of human identity: An exploration based on the work of Sri Aurobindo. *Psychological Studies* 50(2,3): 226–32.

Dalal, A. S. (Ed.) 2001. *A greater psychology: An introduction to the psychological thought of Sri Aurobindo*. New York: Tarcher.

Heehs, P. 2008. *The lives of Sri Aurobindo*. New York: Columbia University Press.

Kazlev, A. n.d. *Ken Wilber and Sri Aurobindo*. Retrieved June 30, 2008, from http://www.kheper.net/topics/Wilber/Wilber_on_Aurobindo.html.

Hemsell, R. 2003. *Ken Wilber and Sri Aurobindo: A Critical Perspective*. Retrieved June 30, 2008, from http://www.infinityfoundation.com/mandala/i_es/i_es_hemse_wilber.htm.

Jacobs, G. n.d. *Response to Ken Wilber's, "Integral Theory of consciousness."* Retrieved June 30, 2008, from http://www.infinityfoundation.com/mandala/i_es/i_es_jacob_response_frameset.htm.

Forman, M., and S. Esbjörn-Hargens. 2008. The academic emergence of Integral Theory: Reflections on and clarifications of the 1st biennial Integral Theory conference. Retrieved June 30, 2008, from http://www.integralworld.net/forman-hargens.html.

Parker, A. (Producer), and B. Vignes (Director). 2004. *Towards a sustainable future: Auroville 36 years of Research*. [Motion Picture]. Auroville, India: Auroville Centre for Scientific Research.

Salmon, D. n.d. *Overview of Ken Wilber's theory of integral psychology*. Retrieved June 30, 2008, from http://www.infinityfoundation.com/mandala/i_es/i_es_salmo_wilber_frameset.htm.

Vrinte, J. 2002. *The perennial quest for a psychology with a soul: An inquiry into the relevance of Sri Aurobindo's metaphysical yoga in the context of Ken Wilber's integral psychology*. Delhi, India: Motilal Banarsidass Publishers.

Wilber, K. 1999. Integral psychology. In *The Collected Works of Ken Wilber* (Vol. 4). Boston: Shambhala.

———. 2001. Foreword. In *A greater psychology: An introduction to the psychological thought of Sri Aurobindo*, ed. A. S. Dalal. New York: Tarcher.

———. 2006. *Integral spirituality*. Boston: Integral Books.

## 16

Of Elephants and Butterflies

An Integral Metatheory for Organizational Transformation

Mark Edwards

This chapter summarizes my doctoral research to resolve some fundamental issues that I had been grappling with for many years with regard to Ken Wilber's Integral Theory and AQAL framework. These issues revolve around such questions as: What are the basic elements of an integral approach? How do we know which elements to include and which to leave out? How can very different theories actually be integrated within one framework? Why do we see frameworks that are similar to the AQAL model appearing over and over again? I wanted to pursue such questions within a rigorous scientific context and to build up an integral metatheory[1] from the ground up.

The first problem I encountered in this process was to find a method that could assist me in this development project and I quickly found that there were very few suitable methods around. Almost all theory building, and particularly large-scale overarching theory building, is done through the process of traditional scholarship. This basically involves the metatheorist reading through libraries of literature and developing their ideas according to their own personal systems. While remarkable contributions to the history of ideas have been made through this traditional scholarship approach, I wanted a far more systematic and scientifically accountable method for developing my ideas. So in the course of pursuing my research topic I also had to develop a general method for metatheory building, and I will describe this method briefly in this chapter.

The overall plan of what follows will be based on the following: (1) a discussion of the thesis topic, (2) a general method for integral metatheorizing, (3) results of the analysis, (4) a presentation of the integral metatheory for organizational transformation, (5) some implications, and (6) conclusion. In the concluding section I will also speculate on how this metatheoretical research fits within a much broader scheme of integral metastudies. Developing theory here is just one part of the process of knowledge creation and learning and the integral metatheory building research described here can be contextualized within a general scheme for developing integrative knowledge.

The Thesis Topic

The thesis topic I chose for my research was to develop an integral metatheory for organizational transformation. This topic was chosen for several reasons. As outlined above, the thesis aim was to develop a more systematic and scientific approach to integral metatheory building. In so doing, the thesis topic needed to be within a complex field, which had many different disciplines, paradigms, research programs, and theoretical orientations. I also wanted to choose an area that involved radical change and which dealt with the mysterious process of transformation. The field of organizational transformation fitted in with these concerns nicely. Although transformational studies within organizational theory is a relatively recent area of research (having been established only over the last 30 years), there are a great many understandings and explanations for transformation in organizational settings.

I also wanted to choose a topic that was relatively controversial and included many contending theories. Metatheorizing takes an inherently critical approach toward its subject matter and views conflict as a natural outcome of the human process of knowledge development. Wherever a field is characterized by alternative explanations, warring paradigms, and theoretical debates it is probably a highly suitable domain for metatheoretical research.

In a world that is currently facing some crucial global crises, I also wanted to look at an area involving organizations. My natural analytical tendencies are inclined toward psychosocial explanations rather than purely psychological ones, so I wanted to do research at the collective level, or, more correctly, ecological level, rather than at the individual level. Organizations are also crucial to the urgent need for global development in meeting the environmental, social, economic, and political challenges that we currently face. Without widespread and fundamental transformation of organizations we are not likely to be remotely successful in meeting these challenges. Personal transformation, whatever the benefits might be at the level of individual, will not be sufficient for this radical change to occur at any level of community, local or global. This is also why I chose the area of organizational sustainability as an exemplar topic for describing the integral metatheory developed here. Sustainability or generativity, as it might better be described, will be perhaps the most important domain for transformation in the coming decades as we attempt to develop economic and social systems that provide for ecological and intergenerational justice.

Of Elephants and Butterflies

Before moving on to describe the method used in this research I will say a little more about metatheory and what it is. Let me introduce this with an illustrative and oft-used parable.

The story goes that there were six very learned, blind men who had heard about, but never encountered, a fabulous creature called an elephant (Saxe 1963). They wanted to experience firsthand what this amazing beast was and how it might be described. The first learned man approached the elephant, ran his hands over its side and concluded the elephant to be much like "a wall," the second felt a tusk and said, "It's like a spear," the third felt the trunk and decided elephants were "like snakes," the fourth held one leg and exclaimed, "The elephant is like a tree," the fifth chanced upon the ear and said, "This marvel of an elephant is very like a fan," and finally, the sixth seized upon the swinging tail and said, "The elephant is like a rope." And the story goes that these six learned blind men compared their findings and each argued that he had the most insightful understanding of this creature called an elephant.

> And so these men of Indostan
> Disputed loud and long,
> Each in his own opinion
> Exceeding stiff and strong,
> Though each was partly in the right,
> And all were in the wrong! (Saxe 1873, 78)

The moral of the story, and its relevance to my metatheorizing on organizational transformation, lies in the idea that each explanation contains and uncovers some partial truth about the nature of reality, and that together, these partialities have a chance of creating a more integrative and comprehensive picture of that reality. Left to their own devices, however, these partial understandings, while accurate within their own narrow fields, will always be incomplete and even misleading. Metatheorizing is a form of conceptual research that recognizes the validity of each theoretical perspective, while also discovering their limitations through accommodating them within some larger conceptual context.

So we see that metatheory is concerned with "the study of theories, theorists, communities of theorists, as well as the larger intellectual and social context of theories and theorists" (Ritzer 1988, 188). Metatheorizing is the process of developing metatheory or performing metatheoretical research. It is similar to other forms of sense-making in that it attempts to structure and derive meaning from some body of knowledge, information, data, or experience. It is different in that the body of information it draws on, its "data," is other theories (van Gigch and Le Moigne 1989) or "unit theories" as Werner and Berger (1985) call the individual theories that are the focus of study for metatheorists.

George Ritzer (2001) and Paul Colomy (1991) have identified four types of metatheorizing based on their particular aims. Metatheorizing can be used to: (1) become familiar with theories and paradigms for understanding extant theory (Ritzer's M_U); (2) serve as a preparatory exercise to develop middle-range theory (Ritzer's M_P); (3) develop an overarching metatheory for the multiparadigm study of some field (Ritzer's M_O); and (4) evaluate and adjudicate on the conceptual adequacy and scope of other theories (Colomy's M_A).

One of the most important roles that metatheorizing can perform comes from its evaluative capacity. For example, metatheories can be used to identify those orienting concepts that a particular theory utilizes as well as those that it neglects or does not possess. This study is concerned with the pursuit of M_U (metatheorizing for understanding) so that a subsequent M_O (overarching metatheory) can be developed with the additional aim of performing M_A (adjudicating metatheory) forms of metatheorizing.

Conceptual Lenses

In analyzing theories to develop metatheories, it is important to identify the conceptual units by which the new metatheory will be constructed. I call these units "conceptual lenses," "explanatory lenses," and, when they are combined to create large metatheoretical frameworks, "integral lenses."

The notion of a conceptual lens is closely associated with the idea that we explain complex events through reducing that complexity to some sense-making dimension or explanatory factor. The explanatory factors of a theory are its conceptual building blocks, its "endogenous" factors (Klein, Tosi, and Cannella 1999). Together with their interrelationships, conceptual lenses form the "architectonic" of the theory, that is, the conceptual structure that underlies the characteristic form of the theory (Ritzer 2001)

The metaphor of "lens" is frequently used in organizational and management literature as a way of representing the conceptual perspective afforded by a theory, or paradigm, or a definitive conceptual element of a theory or paradigm. Because I wanted to analyze theories at a very fine level of detail it is in this latter sense that "conceptual lens" is to be understood in this research.

The lens metaphor is used here to emphasize that theory has both an active and a receptive relationship to the development of our understandings and to the actual shape of the realities we investigate. In the receptive sense, theory acts as an interpretive filter that structures and makes sense of the data of its subject matter. In the active sense, theory acts as a guide for actively seeking new insights and understandings and for shaping organizational realities. Giddens (1985) has referred to this dual role of theory in society as the "double hermeneutic." Theory not only structures meaning but also informs and shapes its subject matter. The metaphors of "voice" and "tool" could just as well be used to represent this more active involvement of theory in social change.

Figure 16.1 shows the participant researcher (informed by scholarship, culture and scientific techniques) and her conceptual lens(es) as both receptive consumers and active producers of organizational realities. From this understanding, the lenses and voices used to investigate organizational life are constitutive of that life. To paraphrase Deetz (1996, 192), a conceptual lens does not merely interpret organizational objects, it is core to the process of constituting objects.

A theory may contain several of these explanatory lenses in relationship (Wacker 2004). Identifying lenses was central to research carried out here because they form the basic elements from which the integral metatheory for organizational transformations is constructed. In the context of an integral metatheory, these lenses are also referred to as "integral lenses" because (1) Wilber's AQAL framework (which he also calls Integral Theory or the integral approach) is used here as the chief metatheoretical resource for developing lenses, and (2) when brought together into a coherent metatheoretical system, these lenses constitute an integral or comprehensive metatheory for organizational transformation.

A General Method for Integral Metatheory Building

There currently exist very few research methods specifically designed for building metatheoretical frameworks. The most detailed of those described in the literature is metatriangulation (Lewis and Grimes 1999). The general

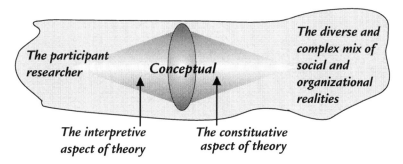

Figure 16.1 Conceptual lens as both interpreting and constituting organizational realities

method described below builds on the comparison of existing approaches and proposes a qualitative method for addressing the weaknesses in existing approaches. This improved method analyzes theories at the level of core themes, describes techniques for identifying lenses both within and across paradigm boundaries and allows for a reflexive and ongoing critical development of its outcomes. Table 16.1 summarizes the connections between metatheory building methods and proposes a qualitative method of conceptual research for metatheory building. The method includes the following phases:

Phase 1: Groundwork

The groundwork phase of metatheory building sets the context and the basic parameters of the study. Groundwork involves defining the topic of interest, providing a rationale for developing metatheory on that topic, setting the boundaries for the study, reviewing relevant academic literature, and describing metatheoretical sources used in the study. Lewis and Grimes (1999) talk here of selecting a topic characterized by expansive and contested research domains with "numerous often conflicting theories" (1999, 678). The topic should be "multifaceted [and] characterised by expansive and contested research domains" (1999, 678).

Phase 2: Procedures and techniques

The procedures and techniques phase outlines the actions taken used to collect and analyze the conceptual "data" for the research. This phase describes how paradigms and theories chosen for the study are sampled. This phase involves identifying and justifying the use of particular sampling procedures and analytical techniques (for example, theme analysis) involved in identifying themes, lenses, or other second-order concepts that are the focus of the study. The range of literature included in the multiparadigm sample is a crucial aspect of the study. Wacker (1998, 368) points out:

> For all stages of theory-building, the role of the literature search in the research procedure is extremely important. . . . Therefore, to assure that all theory-building conditions are filled, an extensive literature search of the academic as well as practitioner articles is required.

Phase 3: Multiparadigm Review

The multiparadigm review helps the researcher to become familiar with the points of connection and distinction between theories. In systematically sifting

General Method for Metatheory Building	Metatriangulation (Lewis & Grimes, 1999)	Multiparadigm Inquiry (Lewis & Kelemen, 2002)	Metatheorising (Ritzer, 2001; Colomy, 1991)	Traditional Theory Building (Wacker, 1998)
Phase 1: Groundwork Rationale: The need for metatheory building study Domain: Specify research domain and scope of review, define key terms Resources: Identify other metatheoretical resources	Groudwork 1 • Define phenomenon of interest • Focus paradigm lenses • Collect metatheoretical sample	**Multiparadigm Review** Conceptual research which identifies connections and differences between various theoretical viewpoints and "alternative lenses"	M_U - **Metatheorising for Understanding** Reviewing the plurality of paradigms, theories and conceptual frameworks	**Domain boundaries** Specify domain, identify research topic, carry out literature review
Phase 2: Procedures and techniques Sampling: procedures for s ampling theories and paradigms Analytical techniques: techniques for identifying lenses				**Term definitions** Define key terms and concepts
Phase 3: Multiparadigm Review Review: Review multiparadigm literature & identify core themes				**Variable definitions** Identify and define core components of the theory, i.e. variables and concepts
Phase 4: Multiparadigm Analysis Lens definitions: Define and refine conceptual lenses Lens relationships: Specify relations between lenses	Data Analysis 1 • Plan paradigm itinerary • Conduct multiparadigm coding • Tabulate and exhibit analyses • Write paradigm accounts • Record/ compare paradigm insights	**Multiparadigm Research** Empirical research carried out from a number of different "paradigm cultures" OR	M_P - **Metatheorising for Preparing New Theory** Developing new theory based on M_U OR	**Variable relationships** Specify relationships between variables
Phase 5: Metatheory Building Build metatheory: Develop metatheoretical system Discuss implications: Develop metaconjectures & propositions	Theory Building 1 • Juxtapose divergent insights • Explore metaconjectures • Develop metaparadigm perspective • Critique the resulting theory • Articulate critical self-reflection	**Metaparadigm Theory Building** Conceptual research that specifies relations between paradigm lenses	M_O - **Metatheorising to Build Overarching Theory** Develop new metatheory based on M_U	**Statement of theory** Formal description of theory
Phase 6: Metatheoretical Conjectures Develop metatheoretical propositions: analyses of extant theories/policies			M_A - **Metatheorising for adjudicating** Adjudicating on the scope & adequacy of other theories.	**Truth claims** Develop hypotheses or "truth claims"
Phase 7: Evaluation Perform evaluation: Evaluate metatheory and any resources used				**Evaluation Phase** Apply criteria for theory evaluation, discuss l imitations & further research

Table 16.1 A general qualitative method for metatheory building (showing comparison of alternative methods)

through theories, models, and frameworks, the researcher can identify the second-order concepts of interest. Lewis and Kelemen (2002, 263) point out that "[m]ultiparadigm reviews first help raise researchers paradigm consciousness to foster greater awareness of insights and blinders enabled by divergent lenses." Theories can be grouped according to paradigm categories to help the process of identifying core themes. However, this serves the purely heuristic function of organizing the identification of themes, and it is important that this process "not reify paradigm distinctions" (Lewis and Kelemen 2002, 263). In the current study the method of text scrutinizing was used to identify themes.

Phase 4: Metatheoretical analysis

This phase involves analyzing the themes extracted during the multiparadigm review so that conceptual lenses can be formulated. Bracketing and bridging techniques can be used to develop lenses that drive from within a particular paradigm or across several paradigms. The analysis may also involve refining lenses according to theory-building criteria such as parsimony, level of abstraction, conservation, and comprehensiveness.

Phase 5: Metatheory Building

The metatheory-building phase develops the conceptual system for the domain or topic that the studying is focusing on. This phase involves identifying the relationship within and between the lenses (or other second-order concepts) identified in the analysis phase. These relationships are then used to assemble lenses together to build the metatheoretical system. As in the current study, exemplar topics may be chosen for describing the new metatheory. Implications of the metatheory are discussed in this phase. These implications can also include "metaconjectures," truth claims and propositions that might be used as a basis for developing or evaluating other middle-range theory and empirical research.

Phase 6: Evaluation

In the evaluation phase, the metatheory is appraised according to (meta)theory building criteria. These can include formal criteria such as generalizability and parsimony and/or postmodern criteria like trustworthiness, reflexivity, credibility, transferability (Guba and Lincoln 1998; Jacques 1992). It is also during this phase that any metatheoretical resources used in the research can also be evaluated

Sampling

Maximum variation was selected as the sampling procedure. Maximum variation is a purposive form of sampling and is appropriate for research that seeks out "important shared patterns that cut across cases and derive their significance from having emerged out of heterogeneity" (Patton 1990, 172). With this type of sampling, "Any common patterns that emerge from great variation are of particular interest" (ibid.).

The chief objective with this form of sampling was to end up with a pool of theories that represented the great diversity of explanatory approaches toward organizational transformation. Two means were employed for maximizing the variety of theories included in the multiparadigm review. The first involved searching through online databases. The second means for maximizing the sample variation involved using previous reviews of organizational change. These reviews identified a great range of theories and paradigms of change and transformation.

From these two means of maximizing the sample of relevant theories, approximately 600 chapters and articles were identified as an initial sample for consideration. These were reduced to around 300 documents by reading abstracts and contents pages to arrive at a set of texts that provided detailed descriptions of theories and models of organizational transformation. This set of articles and books and the theories they described formed the basic sample for the study.

Paradigm Categories

The many theories of transformation were initially sorted into paradigm categories. This process aided the theme analysis and helped to organize the resulting information. Lewis and Kelemen (2002, 260–61) also point out that

> [b]y categorising extant literature within a paradigm framework, reviewers distinguish the selection focus of different lenses. Highlighting paradigm diversity serves to open theoretical choice . . . all lenses are inherently exclusionary and parochial. By clarifying paradigm alternatives, researchers may compare their work to a wider realm of literature, recognise their theoretical predilections, and appreciate insights enabled by opposing viewpoints.

The paradigm categories were particularly useful in appreciating "insights enabled by opposing viewpoints" and in the analysis of relationships between explanatory lenses. Table 16.2 provides the complete list of paradigms of

Paradigm	Theories/Models of Transformation
A. Cultural	collective culture: myth, ritual, worldviewspersonal culture: beliefs, personal values
B. Developmental	action inquiry, spiral dynamics, corporate transformation
C. Evolutionary	population ecology, ecological theory of organisations
D. Functionalist	business process re-engineering, technology and transformation, corporate transformation
E. Interpretive	feminist theory, environmental models, large group interventions
F. Learning	dialogical learning, knowledge levels, double- and triple-loop learning
G. Multiparadigm	theory e/theory o, network organisation, discontinuous change
H. Organisational environment	holonic enterprise theory, inter-organisational theory
I. Paradox/Dialectic	competing values framework, dialectical theories
J. Process	Lewin's field theory, transition cycle, rhizomic model, "n" step models
K. Psychological/ Cognitive	logics of action, reframing theory, information processing, decision-making theories,
L. Spirituality	spirituality and the new sciences, contemplative leadership
M. Systems and New Sciences	soft systems theory, complex adaptive systems, dissipative structures, chaos theory,
N. Teamwork	meso theory, group theory, team-based approach to transformation
O. Transformational leadership	top-down, bottom-up, combined approaches

Table 16.2 Transformational paradigms and representative theories

transformative change, some representative theories and research. The paradigms and their constituent theories and models are presented in alphabetical order. In some cases a theory utilizes themes from more than one paradigm. In these instances the dominant theme has been used to identify the appropriate paradigm for categorization. However, because themes from across paradigms were also collated, these secondary themes were not lost in this categorization process. The grouping of theories into paradigms permitted an orderly analysis and aided in the tracking and collation of the results. The theme analysis itself occurred at the much finer level of detail within each theory.

Identifying Explanatory Themes through Theme Analysis

The basic sample of around 300 articles and books was analyzed to identify the second-order concepts of interest, that is, the fundamental explanatory themes for organizational transformation. This took the form of a thematic analysis technique known as "text scrutinizing" (Luborsky 1994; Ryan and Bernard 2003). The conceptual themes identified in this process provide the basic "data" for the subsequent theory-building phase of the study. Scrutinizing texts for core themes involves looking for textual elements that disclose patterns. These elements include (Ryan and Bernard 2003):

- repetitions: These are "topics that occur and reoccur" (Bogdan and Taylor 1975, 83);
- indigenous categories: The conceptual schemes that authors use to organize their texts;
- metaphors and analogies: Identifying themes through root metaphors and guiding analogies;
- similarities and differences: This involves finding convergences and divergences within the text;
- linguistic connectors: Terms such as "because," "since," "always," and "as a result" often disclose core assumptions, causal inferences, and the basic orientations of the research;
- theory-related material: The thematic content is often disclosed by explicit reference to theory;
- graphical material: Images, diagrams, and other graphical material can indicate core themes;
- structural themes: Themes can be evident in the article titles, headings, and subheadings.

The scrutinizing of the sample of texts identified the basic themes that theorists use in their explanations for organizational transformation. These explanatory themes cover a great range of different orientations toward explaining how, why, what, and when organizational transformation occurs.

Building Explanatory Lenses through Bracketing and Bridging

The large number of explanatory themes included much overlap and conceptual redundancy. They were consolidated and reduced in number through using bracketing and bridging techniques (Lewis and Grimes 1999). Applying these techniques resulted in the amalgamation of themes to form abstract explanatory lenses. These lenses were used as the building blocks for the metatheory building phase of the study.

Bracketing is a qualitative form of thematic analysis used for finding underlying concepts within particular theories and paradigms. Bracketing is essentially a "data reduction" process where researchers "ignore certain aspects of complex phenomena and focus on facets and issues of particular interest" (Lewis and Grimes 1999, 673). Bracketing identifies "the underlying universals" (Gearing 2004, 1433) that a particular theory adopts to research a phenomenon. Bridging looks for connections and transition zones that span paradigms. In other words, the bridging is a form of theme analysis that identifies conceptual lenses from "across paradigms" (Lewis and Grimes, 675). Bridging involves a type of interparadigm scanning that seeks out strong thematic concordances between theories from different paradigms and brings them together to form explanatory lenses.

In summary, the bracketing and bridging techniques are applied to maximize parsimony, minimize conceptual redundancy, and retain uniqueness of each of the explanatory lenses. Bracketing is done within a paradigm and bridging is performed between paradigms.

The methodological phases involved in developing explanatory lenses are shown in Figure 16.2. The figure shows that maximum variation sampling procedure was used to generate a diverse sample of theories. These theories were grouped into paradigms to aid in the analysis and organization of information. From these theories, a large number of themes were found and, through the use of bracketing and bridging techniques, core explanatory lenses identified. The integral metatheory for organizational transformation was developed from these lenses and their relationships.

The Results

The multiparadigm review and analysis resulted in 24 integral lenses being identified for explaining the phenomena of organizational transformation. The relationships between and within each of these lenses was also examined. One simple way of identifying and describing the relationships between lenses is to consider their fundamental morphological patterns, for example, whether they are defined by bipolar or cyclical relationships. These categories can be grouped according to their conceptual shape. The idea is that our explanations are deeply metaphorical and those metaphors can be categorized according to basic visual patterns (Lakoff and Johnson 1999). Looking at these basic patterns, we see that the set of integral lenses can be categorized into the following groups:

1. the holarchical category—these lenses take the form of multilevel holarchies, e.g., the developmental, ecological and governance lenses;
2. the bipolar category—these lenses are defined by complementary dualisms or paradoxes that form binary dimensions, e.g., agency-communion and internal-external lenses;
3. the cyclical category—these lenses are depicted as iterative or phased cycles, e.g., the transition process lens and learning lenses;
4. the relational category—these lenses share a relational form or interactive mode of representation, e.g., the mediation lens and alignment lenses;
5. the standpoint category—these lenses take the form of subjective or

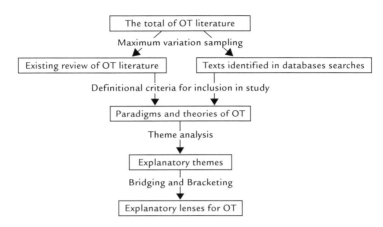

Figure 16.2 Methodological phases for developing explanatory lenses

personal perspectives, e.g., personal perspective lens and the states of consciousness lens;

6. the multiparadigm or multimorphic category—these lenses that can appear in several categories, e.g., the spirituality lens can be expressed as a holarchy, a process, and as a state of consciousness.

Table 16.3 shows the categories that result from grouping lenses according to basic patterns of relationships. Grouping lenses into these categories assists in the investigation how lenses interrelate, and in the following sections some relationships that exist both within and between categories will be briefly explored.

Each of the morphological categories is loosely associated with particular types of questions about change. Holarchical lenses are useful for explaining the structural questions of "what" changes, bipolar lenses for the causal questions of "why" change occurs, cyclical lenses for the process questions of "how" it occurs, relational lenses for the contextual questions of "when" it occurs, standpoint lenses for the personal questions regarding "who" is involved in the change. The multimorphic category contains lenses that can be expressed in a variety of forms and can answer several questions regarding change and transformation.

An Integral Metatheory for Organizational Transformation

The holarchical group of lenses performs a pivotal role in metatheorizing, particularly when such research attempts to bring together so many different

Categories of Conceptual Lenses

Holarchy category: Lenses expressed as holarchical structures, the "what" of transformation

☐ developmental holarchy: transformational levels, stages of discontinuous change

- ecological holarchy: spatial levels multilevel, micro-meso-macro, organisational levels
- governance/organising holarchy: levels of decision-making, power relations, management
- deep structure: the pattern of persistent features that define levels

Bipolar category: Lenses expressed as dualities and polarities, the "why" of transformation

- interior-exterior: contrasting poles of for example subjective-objective
- transformation-translation: radical change-incremental change
- internal-external: the inside and outside of organisational boundaries
- agency-communion: autonomous-relational, task-relationships
- health-pathology: balanced-unbalanced, whole-fragmented

Cyclical process category: Lenses expressed as cyclical processes, the "how" of transformation

- system dynamics: bifurcation points, feedback processes, cyclical dynamics
- learning: single, double, triple loop learning; integral cycle of learning
- transition process: transition cycles, change processes
- inclusive emergence: transcend-and-include cycles
- evolutionary selection: emergence through variation, selection, retention cycles

Relational category: Lenses expressed as relational processes, the "how" of transformation

- mediation: social mediation through artefact-in-use
- alignment: concordance between two structures, processes or entities
- relational exchange: exchanges that occur between two structures or processes

Standpoint category: Lenses expressed as perspectival standpoints, the "who" of transformation

- stakeholder: viewpoints of employees, managers, customers, communities
- states of consciousness: condition of subjective awareness of stakeholders
- personal perspective: first, second and third person perspectives - singular &plural
- decentering: hidden standpoints, hegemonic vs. peripheral viewpoints, local vs. universal concerns

Multimorphic category: Lenses expressed in multiple forms, can consider the "what", "why", "how" and "who" of transformation

- spirituality: a transpersonal level of development, a particular line of development, a process, etc
- organisational streams: domains of organisational life, e.g. people, structures, cultures, systems
- types: non-developmental typologies of key organisational entities

Table 16.3 Categories of Conceptual Lenses
for Organizational Transformation

conceptual orientations to a topic. Using the holon construct as a type of scaffold for including other lenses offers a flexible and nonreductive system for developing conceptually rich theory in complex fields of social activity such as organizational transformation. For this reason, the integral metatheory for transformation is presented within a holonic context. In an article entitled "Holonic Organizational Architectures", Mathews (1996) provides a detailed analysis of the various descriptive levels at which a holonic analysis of change can be presented.

Mathews proposes a model of "three faces" or "three orders of description" that can be applied to any holonic system. First, there is the order of description that pertains to the characteristics of a single, autonomous holon with its "own identity" and "self-activity." This is the *intra-holonic order* of description and its domain is all those qualities that relate to single holons. Second, there is the order of description that refers to relationships between holons, that is, those relational, communicative, and mediating processes and "subsystems" that arise when two holons engage in some shared event. This is the *inter-holonic order* of description. Third, when theorists focus on "holonic systems," that is, on holarchical systems, they are considering a more general *systemic order* of analysis. Although Mathews's approach stops at these three, a more comprehensive model might add a fourth order of analysis. This is the *inter-systemic order,* which applies to relationships between holonic systems. The following is a detailed outline of these four orders of description.

The Intra-holonic Order

In the intra-holonic order the focus is on the dimensional characteristics that pertain to the activity of a single holon. Intra-holonic order does *not* mean within an individual. The prefix *intra-* can refer to any holon, be it an individual, a team, an organization, or a community. What a theorist, model builder, or researcher decides to represent intra-holonically (i.e., within that holon's boundaries) is up to them. For present purposes, this amounts to describing the relationships between lenses as they pertain to one holon. Any number of relevant variables or qualities can be placed onto the holon. As the ecologists Allen and Starr put it, "What a holon shall contain is determined by the observer" (cited in Checkland 1988, 237). The intra-holonic order of description allows theorists to move down into the details of how one holon will behave according to the particular lenses they employ in their analysis. A more complete analysis will, however, always involve the discussion of the inter-, systemic and intersystemic orders.

The Inter-holonic Order

At the inter-holonic order of description the point of focus is the inter-action between holons, for example, the interpersonal, intergroup, and interorganizational relationships that create the social environment of organizational life. The inter-holonic order of analysis is interested in the mediational and communicative processes that flow between holons so that transformation is seen as arising from mutualizing activities between holons rather than from the innate qualities that exist within the individual holon. Describing transformation from the inter-holonic order of interaction, communication, and relationship is associated with the use of the governance holarchy lens. Governance and decision making provide a context for describing inter-holonic relations through expressions of power, authority, influence, and social relationships that inform organizational structures, which are based on function, role, and formal position.

The Systemic Holonic Order

The systemic order of description focuses on the relationship between holons and the holarchy or whole system in which they are embedded. This brings into focus conceptual lenses that deal with systems of relationships (which are more than the sum of their constituent intra- and inter-relationships). Questions concerning transformation move from the intralevel of single holons and interlevel of two holons to the systemic level of the holarchy and its relations with its constituent holons and/or the (holarchic) environment in which it operates. Examples of this order of description include Sarason's (1995) adaption of structuration theory to organizational transformation and Boje's (2002) interorganizational application of holon theory to transorganizational development.

The Intersystemic Order

As noted above, Mathews's model of first-, second-, and third-order characteristics of holonic systems can be amended with a fourth order of description. This is the intersystemic order, which moves beyond the relationships that exist within a holonic system, that is, a holarchy, to also consider multiple systems of holons and holarchies in dynamic environments. At this order of description, holarchic systems can be represented as multilens frameworks that combine lenses from each of the holon categories described in Table 16.3.

Figure 16.3 provides a graphical representation of Mathews's orders of holonic description (plus the newly proposed fourth order) using stylized holons. In each of these orders of application, the holon construct holds together concepts in nonreductive relationship. That is, it provides a window into conceptualizing complexity without reducing that complexity either to some unfathomable whole or to some aggregate of parts. Mathews's model shows the flexibility of the holon construct for dealing with social events at multiple orders of complexity. As he notes, "The principal virtue of holonics systems lies in their flexibility and adaptability" (Matthews 1996, 42) and it is also these qualities that provide holons with the capacity to marry lenses at very different orders of scope (simple and complex systems) and scales of focus (micro and macro levels).

An Integral Metatheory for Organizational Transformation

Mathews's model of holonic orders of description (plus the newly proposed intersystemic order) can be used to present a general summary of the integral metatheory for organizational transformation. This general model for transformation will be represented in a number of diagrams showing each of the 24 integral lenses and their relationships. The first two diagrams show the intra-holonic order where bipolar and cyclical lenses are commonly applied. The third diagram presents the inter-holonic order and the interactive and standpoint lenses that are often utilized at this level of description. The holonic category of lenses is usually described at the systemic order. Finally, in a fourth diagram combinations of holonic and other lenses can be created

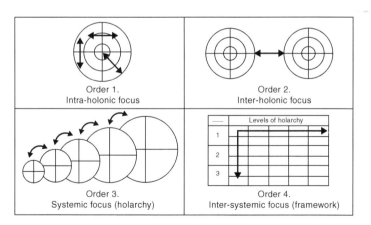

Figure 16.3 Four orders of holonic description

to build conceptual frameworks and typologies. This is the intersystemic order of holonic description. A final figure will presents a number of lenses in combination to show the range of intra-holonic, inter-holonic, systemic (holarchic), and intersystemic orders of description.

Figure 16.4 presents bipolar lenses as well as the multiparadigm lens of developmental streams. The idea here is that any combination of these lenses can be used to develop metatheoretical frameworks at the intra-holonic level. For example, a researcher may be interested in the team-level dynamics (mesolevel of ecological holarchy lens) of transformational change (transformation-translation lens) and want to consider the impact of within-boundary and cross-boundary communications (internal and external lens) and how the team responds through its group culture and collective behavior (interior-exterior lens). The types lens uses combinations of these bipolar lenses to develop categorical models and typologies. Consciousness is an interior quality of the individual holon and so the states of consciousness lens has been shown here within the intra-holonic order of description.

Figure 16.5 presents the cyclical group of lenses within a holarchic framework. The figure shows the systems, transition process, evolutionary, and learning cycle lenses applied to a particular holon—an organization. While this example has applied these cyclical lenses at the intra-holonic level they might just as easily be applied at the inter-holonic level. An example here would be of a researcher investigating how hands-on, reflective, and social learning (learning cycle lens) interact with the crisis, transformation, and integration phases of organizational change (transition process lens) to produce innovations that can be selected and reproduced throughout an organization (evolutionary lens).

The interactive category of lenses is usefully represented at the inter-holonic order of description. The inter-holonic order describes the relationships between lenses as they apply to holons encountering each other in situational contexts

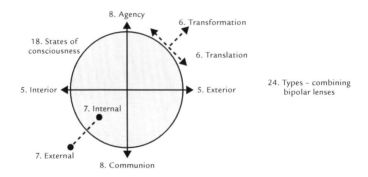

Figure 16.4 Bipolar lenses applied at an intra-holonic order

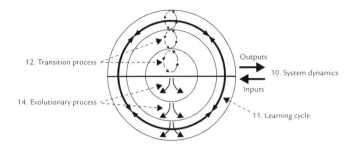

Figure 16.5 Cyclical lenses applied at an
intra-holonic order of description

and environments. Figure 16.6 shows the interactive group of lenses applied to holons as they engage with each other in mediated relationship (social mediation lens), as they makes exchanges at different holonic levels (exchange relations lens), and as they move in and out of alignment with each other (alignment lens). Relationships, interaction, and connection are thematic characteristics of the spirituality lens and, although it has relevance to other orders, the inter-holonic order is an appropriate domain for placing conceptual approaches based on the spirituality lens. The postmodern lens is also relevant to inter-holonic relations in that the postmodern concerns with communication, relationality, and power are all interactive in nature (see Figure 16.6).

Holarchies can be defined by developmental, ecological, or regulatory criteria. The systemic order of description portrays holons in a holarchical context. In the case of the developmental holarchy, the deep structures of each holon are integrated in some way within the deep structures of successive holons. Figure 16.7 shows the three forms of holarchy found in theories of organizational transformation. Also represented here are the lenses of deep structure and

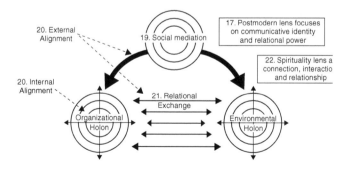

Figure 16.6 Interactive lenses applied at the
inter-holonic order of description

inclusive emergence, which, combined with the developmental lens, form a powerful set of lenses for investigating discontinuous change in organizations. Figure 16.7 also depicts the stream lens within this developmental context. The systemic order of description and representation is also where holarchies can be used as scaffolding systems for combining lenses.

At the intersystemic order multiple systems of lenses can be represented and described. Figure 16.8 shows the relationships between stakeholders (seen through the lens of the ecological holarchy) and the perspectives lens.

The framework describes how the personal perspectives of various stakeholder groups might be studied according to an ecological holarchy of individual owner/CEO, organizational stakeholders (staff, customers, suppliers), community stakeholders (local communities), and global stakeholders (biosphere, next generations). Each level of stakeholder from the "inner circle" of owners and executive management to the community to the intergenerational and environmental circles has their own perspective on, and experience of, transformational endeavors such as sustainable development. An intersystematic inquiry into these perspectives is required for a comprehensive approach to transformation. Each cell in this intersystemic framework can be regarded as a holon and so can be studied via intra-, inter-, and systemic holonic orders of analysis. The full range of bipolar, cyclical, interactive, and standpoint lenses can be subsequently brought into the picture depending on the research questions of interest. The health-pathology lens can be used to consider balanced and unbalanced forms of the contents of these cells.

The diagrams representing intra-, inter-, systemic and intersystemic orders of holonic description are examples only and many of the integral lenses

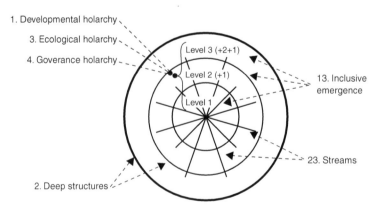

Figure 16.7 Holarchic lenses applied
at the systemic order of description

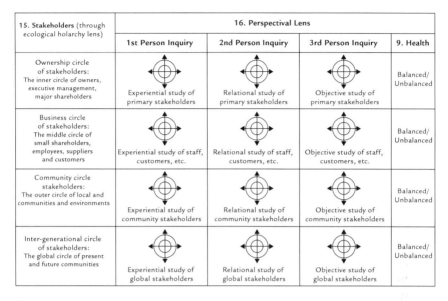

15. **Stakeholders** (through ecological holarchy lens)	16. **Perspectival Lens**			
	1st Person Inquiry	**2nd Person Inquiry**	**3rd Person Inquiry**	**9. Health**
Ownership circle of stakeholders: The inner circle of owners, executive management, major shareholders	Experiential study of primary stakeholders	Relational study of primary stakeholders	Objective study of primary stakeholders	Balanced/ Unbalanced
Business circle of stakeholders: The middle circle of small shareholders, employees, suppliers and customers	Experiential study of staff, customers, etc.	Relational study of staff, customers, etc.	Objective study of staff, customers, etc.	Balanced/ Unbalanced
Community circle stakeholders: The outer circle of local and communities and environments	Experiential study of community stakeholders	Relational study of community stakeholders	Objective study of community stakeholders	Balanced/ Unbalanced
Inter-generational circle of stakeholders: The global circle of present and future communities	Experiential study of global stakeholders	Relational study of global stakeholders	Objective study of global stakeholders	Balanced/ Unbalanced

Figure 16.8 Standpoint lenses applied at the inter-systemic order of analysis

can be applied to several levels of analysis. The diagrams do, however, provide a general picture of the flexibility of the integral metatheory for transformation and some general indications for combining lenses within holonic contexts.

Implications of the Integral Metatheory

The implications of the model will be discussed in terms of (1) AQAL metatheory, (2) the adjudication of other (meta)theories and social policies, and (3) a broader framework of integral metastudies. Let us begin with Wilber's AQAL metatheory.

In summary, this study has found strong evidence to support the metatheory-building aims of Integral Theory and its AQAL framework. All of its major conceptual elements have been found to be present within the theories of organizational transformation reviewed here. In fact, the multiparadigm review and analysis found that all AQAL lenses (including both formal and informal ones) are used by organizational theorists in their theories and models of radical change in organizations. These findings strongly support the application of Integral Theory as a metatheory for organizational studies. There are, however, several weaknesses that have also been identified, and the following recommendations are proposed to address them.

1. All core conceptual elements that formally make up the AQAL framework have still not been satisfactorily identified or defined.

2. Several lenses were identified that are not represented in Integral Theory and their omission means that a major review of the core conceptual elements of Integral Theory is called for.

3. In the application of Integral Theory, particular lenses are always combined in the same way and, while this has benefits for its parsimonious and uniform description and applied use, this inflexibility limits its creative application to the particular needs of the research.

4. Several of the current relationships between AQAL lenses were not supported by the findings of the multiparadigm analysis carried out here. In particular, the relationships between perspective and quadrants and between the interior-exterior and individual-collective lenses should be reviewed to improve the framework's internal consistency. For example, the individual-collective dimension is more accurately represented as a holoarchical lens rather than the current bipolar dimension. The following diagram (Figure 16.9) presents a more integral view of how this lens should be combined with other integral lenses such as interior-exterior.

5. To this point, the development of Integral Theory and its AQAL model has not been based on rigorous research methods of metatheory building and further use of the model could gain from the application of some more rigorous method such as metatriangulation or the more detailed method outlined in this current study.

Moving now to the implications of the adjudicative use of the integral metatheory, it should be clear by now that metatheorizing of this nature is inherently critical in that it can be in both constructive and deconstructive ways to assess all kinds of conceptual frameworks. I have provided an example of this in my article, "Every Today Was a Tomorrow: An Integral Method for Indexing the Social Mediation of Preferred Futures" (Edwards 2007). This article takes a critical stance toward the development of alternative scenarios for future health services. The main argument is that the visions we hold of the future, whether they be of utopias or dystopias, are not simply a matter of personal imagination. We can use integral metatheory to guide our choices about social transformation in general and social policy options in particular.

Finally, a third area of implication for this kind of integral metatheorizing involves a broader conceptualizations of this type of research. I have described a bit more detail on this topic in a recent publication (Edwards 2008) and only sketch the basic overview of this contextualization here.

Figure 16.10 locates integral metatheory building within a much broader context of an integral metastudies. Integral metastudies includes not only

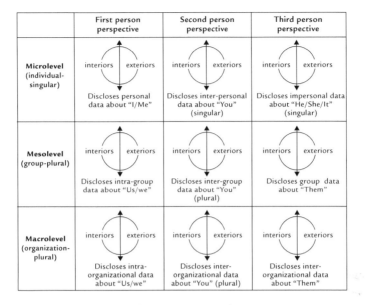

	First person perspective	Second person perspective	Third person perspective
Microlevel (individual-singular)	interiors | exteriors — Discloses personal data about "I/Me"	interiors | exteriors — Discloses inter-personal data about "You" (singular)	interiors | exteriors — Discloses impersonal data about "He/She/It" (singular)
Mesolevel (group-plural)	interiors | exteriors — Discloses intra-group data about "Us/we"	interiors | exteriors — Discloses inter-group data about "You" (plural)	interiors | exteriors — Discloses group data about "Them"
Macrolevel (organization-plural)	interiors | exteriors — Discloses intra-organizational data about "Us/we"	interiors | exteriors — Discloses inter-organizational data about "You" (plural)	interiors | exteriors — Discloses inter-organizational data about "Them"

Figure 16.9 Combing perspectival, interior-exterior,
and ecological holarchy lenses

metatheory building but also metamethodology, method after analysis, and meta-hermeneutics. These four branches constitute a new approach to integrative studies that I call integral metastudies. The process of identifying integral lenses and relationships and building integral frameworks for performing overarching research is one small part of a much broader enterprise that requires an integral approach to building big pictures on methods, data analysis and forms of interpretation. Wilber's IMP is an example of an integral metamethodology and similar work has yet to be done in terms of looking at meta-data analysis and metahermeneutics. This metalevel of scientific work is only just beginning and has rarely been carried out on any systematic basis using rigorous approaches to doing research.

Conclusion

I have presented here a summary of my doctoral research on integral metatheory building within the field of organizational transformation. Although the metatheory presented here has been developed within a rather specific area, I believe that it holds implications for a much broader level of metatheorizing. In fact, I believe that the lenses identified here are of great relevance to the broad range of social science topics. This view is supported by the notion of self-similarity (Abbott 2001) and fractalization (Holbrook

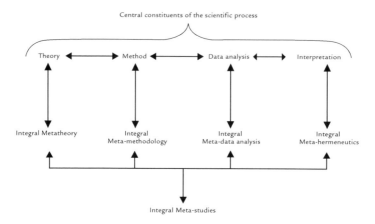

Figure 16.10 The structure of an integral metastudies

2003; Ross 2008) in social science that has recently been put forward as a way of explaining the repeated appearances of the same types of lenses in a great variety of scientific disciplines.

The view presented here is also one of great flexibility and holds immense potential for the creative engagement of researchers in metatheoretical research and metastudies in general. The great variety of lenses that have been identified here cannot be systematically applied to every research question. In this understanding of integral metatheory there is no ready-made combination of lenses that can be instantly applied and there is an inherent need for disciplined imagination and creative insight on the part of the researcher in applying these ideas.

Finally, the approach taken here is one that draws quite distinct limits on integral metatheory building. Integral metatheorizing is fundamentally an integrative approach, a big picture orientation that develops overarching and universalizing concepts. Consequently, it is not a localizing or a particularizing approach that seeks to give voice to every individual instance of experience or activity. Integral metastudies is a postmodern or even post-postmodern activity in that it recognizes multiple forms of pluralism and seeks to integrate them within abstract and generalizing frameworks. As such I regard integral metastudies as a counterpart to the more typical forms of decentering and deconstructing postmodernism which seek to identify and give voice to the personal story, the local history, the grounded experience, and the marginalized instance. These two postmodern activities are fundamentally different and provide critical counterpoints for each other's development. Decentering, pluralist postmodern research is not something I believe is to be integrated within an integral metastudies. Decentering postmodernism and integrative postmodernism are complementary forms of knowledge building. Where integral postmodernism develops abstractions, decentering postmoderism develops grounded stories. Where integral postmodernism creates imaginative generalized frameworks, decentering postmodernism creates particular narratives and personalized accounts of human experience.

This is not a developmental modernism versus postmodernism battle. It is an ongoing complementarity (e.g., Plato and Aristotle). An integral metastudies should not be seen as a rational project of integrating every perspective, concept, paradigm, or cultural tradition within its domain. There must be some things that, by definition, lie outside of its capacities to accommodate and explain. Consequently, an integral metastudies needs a decentering postmodernism that it cannot integrate, that lies outside of its scientific and systematic purview, which continually challenges it and is critical of its generalizations, abstractions, and universalizings. The decentering form of particularizing postmodernism is not something that integral metatheory can locate or neatly categorize somewhere within its general frameworks. Decentering postmodernism will always provide a source of critical insight and substantive opposition to the generalizing goals of an integral metastudies. In the same way that postmodernism often misunderstands integrative approaches as just some form of scientific monism, there is a danger that integral researchers can misrepresent the decentering and localizing concerns of postmodernism as simple relativism.

Table 16.4 shows that integrative and decentering approaches have much to offer each other in their complementary orientations toward social realities.

Integrative postmodernism	Decentering postmodernism
showing connections	showing differences
accommodating many voices	voices are incommensurate
universalising	localising, decentering
generalising	particularising
appreciative/critical	critical/appreciate
abstracting	grounding
tending towards developmentalism	tending towards mediationism

Table 16.4 Some contrasts between integrative
and decentering postmodernism

Where integrative postmodernism focuses on connections, decentering postmodernism focuses on differences. Where integrative postmodernism wants to accommodate many voices, decentering postmodernism wants to show how they are incommensurate and can never be reduced into any general perspective. Where integrated postmodernism seeks universalizing stories, decentering postmodernism seeks localizing stories.

The implications of this distinction between an integral and decentering postmodernism are significant for both parties. I hope that the research outlined in this chapter provides some food for thought not only for the development of a scientific approach to integral metatheorizing but also to a more sophisticated understanding of what might lie within its domain of inquiry and what might lie beyond it.

Note

This chapter is based on and uses material from my book *Organizational Transformation for Sustainability*, published by Routledge in 2010.

1. I use the term *integral* in this chapter to refer to the long tradition of overarching metatheory building exemplified in the work of authors such as Pitrim Sorokin, Haridas Chaudhuri, Ken Wilber, and other theorists and researchers who attempt to develop integrative big picture frameworks.

References

Abbott, A. D. 2001. *Chaos of disciplines*. Chicago: University of Chicago Press.

Bogdan, R., and S. J. Taylor. 1975. *Introduction to qualitative research*. New York: John Wiley.

Checkland, P. 1988. The case for "holon." *Systems Practice* 1(3): 235–38.

Colomy, P. 1991. Metatheorizing in a postpositivist frame. *Sociological Perspectives* 34(3): 269–86.

Edwards, M. G. 2007. Every today was a tomorrow: An integral method for indexing the social mediation of preferred futures. *Futures* 40: 173–89.

———. 2008. Where's the method to our integral madness? An outline of an integral meta-studies. *Journal of Integral Theory and Practice* 3(2): 165–94.

Gearing, R. E. 2004. Bracketing in research: A typology. *Qualitative Health Research* 14(10): 1429–52.

Holbrook, M. B. 2003. Adventures in complexity: An essay on dynamic open complex adaptive systems, butterfly effects, self-organizing order, coevolution, the ecological perspective, fitness landscapes, market spaces, emergent beauty at the edge of chaos, and all that jazz. *Academy of Marketing Science Review* (January): 1.

Klein, K. J., H. Tosi, H., and A. A. Cannella. 1999. Multilevel theory building: Benefits, barriers, and new developments. *Academy of Management Review* 24(2): 243–48.

Lakoff, G., and M. Johnson. 1999. *Philosophy in the flesh: The embodied mind and its challenge to Western thought*. New York: Basic Books.

Lewis, M. W., and A. J. Grimes. 1999. Metatriangulation: Building theory from multiple paradigms. *The Academy of Management Review* 24(4): 672–90.

Lewis, M. W., and M. L. Kelemen. 2002. Multiparadigm inquiry: Exploring organizational pluralism and paradox. *Human Relations* 55(2): 251–75.

Luborsky, M. 1994. Identification and analysis of themes and patterns. In *Qualitative methods in aging research*, ed. J. Gubrium and A. Sanakar. Thousand Oaks, CA: Sage.

Mathews, J. 1996. Holonic organisational architectures. *Human Systems Management* 15(1): 27.

Patton, M. Q. 1990. *Qualitative evaluation and research methods*. London: Sage Publications.

Ritzer, G. 1988. Sociological metatheory: A defense of a subfield by a delineation of its parameters. *Sociological Theory* 6(2): 187–200.

———. 2001. *Explorations in social theory: From metatheorizing to rationalisation*. London: Sage Publications.

Ross, S. N. 2008. Fractal transition steps to fractal stages: The dynamics of evolution II. *World Futures: The Journal of General Evolution* 65(5–7): 361–74.

Ryan, G. W., and H. R. Bernard. 2003. Techniques to identify themes. *Field Methods* 15(1): 85–109.

Saxe, J. G. 1873. *The blind men and the elephant*. New York: Whittlesey House.

van Gigch, J. P., and J. L. Le Moigne. 1989. A paradigmatic approach to the discipline of information systems. *Behavioral Science* 34(2): 128–47.

Wagner, D. G., and J. Berger. 1985. Do sociological theories grow? *American Journal of Sociology* 90(4): 697–728.

## 17

Developmental Action Inquiry

A Distinct Integral Theory That Actually Integrates Developmental Theory, Practice, and Research

William R. Torbert, Reut Livne-Tarandach, David McCallum, Aliki Nicolaides, and Elaine Herdman-Barker

In this chapter, we offer an introduction to our work over the past 40 years of developing the distinctive integral theory, practice, and types of research known as developmental action inquiry (DAI), including the most recent empirical and clinical findings using the psychometric instrument called *Harthill Leadership Development Profile* (LDP).

We will first describe and demonstrate three distinctive features of DAI: (1) its basis in an ontology and epistemology that distinguish among four possible territories of experience; (2) its injunction to interweave first-, second-, and third-person research in the midst of one's practice with others; and (3) its recognition of three different types of research findings (single-, double-, and triple-loop feedback) and their impact on subsequent practices. We will follow this introductory section by describing the LDP, a third-person psychometric, and the ongoing validity-testing research we are performing on it in the fields of our practices. Then we will share some of the more provocative findings from recent research. In this section we focus on the potentials and limitations we observe in the Expert and Strategist action logics. We also introduce a few of the findings from two recently completed doctoral dissertations. (In the context of our "in action" presentation at the conference itself, we interrupted the presentation at several points in order to invite the audience into some first- and second-person research exercises together.)

Theoretically Distinctive Aspects of DAI: The Deep Four

In one of his early books, *Learning from Experience: Toward Consciousness* (1972), Bill Torbert critiqued the positivist, objectivist theory-data model of modernist science and instead named four distinctive territories of experience that humans seek to coordinate and align both in theory and in practice:

1. *the outer world* (as seen and otherwise sensed by a person or measured by an instrument [this includes others' actions seen from the outside— altogether, what modern science calls "the territory"]);
2. *the self-sensing of one's own embodiment*, breathing, moving, perceiving, etc.;
3. *one's own ongoing structures of thinking and feeling* (which in dialogue with others in a scientific community of practice generate what modern science calls "the map"); and
4. *the intentional attention* (which can be distinguished from the other three territories, can experience all three simultaneously, and can be voluntarily cultivated in adulthood, but rarely has been in our culture, up until the recent growth of adult development theories and practices [Kegan 1994; Ouspensky 1949; Torbert 1976, 1987; Trungpa 1970; Wilber 2000).

In the *Power of Balance* (1991), Torbert described how anyone can confirm for him or herself the reality of each of these four territories through thought and attention experiments, somewhat like Descartes' doubting procedure to establish the indubitable fact that we think. To highlight this difference between his "theorizing about trans-theoretical experience" and Ken Wilber's (2000) effort to create a "comprehensive intellectual map of all experience," Torbert sometimes calls these four, mutually orthogonal "territories of experience" the *Deep Four* and Wilber's four-quadrant AQAL model the *Flat Four* (since Wilber's four quadrants in our experience are often held by proponents of Integral Theory as cognitive categories that tend to keep our attention fixated within the single "thinking" territory (as most of you, our readers, likely have been, as you have been reading this). The words for the Deep Four territories of experience are obviously also cognitive categories, but, as the "deep" four, these terms invite us, not just to "think" the categories, but also to experience—now, in each present moment—the pre- and postconceptual realities to which they refer (e.g., the color and texture of the "outside world," the "inner sensing" of our own breathing, moving, and feeling, as well as the kind of "attending" that can "taste" this external text, one's own breathing, one's thinking (about these words now), and one's inquiring into the very source of attention all at once, simultaneously, e.g., now) (see Table 17.1).

Described in these ways, the Deep Four territories of experience constitute what we think of as the first-person field of action inquiry, bounded by the current limits and usually unexamined assumptions of the self's capacity for perception and sense-making (i.e., the specific developmental action-logic through which one currently encounters the world, as will be described below. Given these limits, a more full apprehension, understanding, and engagement of reality requires two additional aspects of all human lives—the second- and third-person fields for first-person work and play.

First-, Second-, and Third-Person Fields of Inquiry

The process of inquiry or research in action is a means of attending to experience of the world, including our dynamic sense-making of that experience, as well as our adaptive engagement. By adaptive engagement, we mean those times when we (the person, team, or organization) are intentionally attempting to assess whether our intentions, plans, actions, and outcomes are aligned with one another and with changing conditions . . . and are responding accordingly. For some, this process is very rare, for others quite regular. An important question is whether and how one tests the validity of the information one is processing in real time. DAI is one of a broader family of recent efforts to begin describing and defining this world of methods for valid inquiry in the midst of action (two others are action science [Argyris et al. 1985]) and Senge's [1990] five disciplines).

The theory, practice, and research methods associated with developmental action inquiry (DAI) all point toward the capacity for individuals, teams or communities of practice, and larger organizations and institutions to conduct interweaving first-person, second-person, and third-person research (studying

Territory	Experience
First	**Outside events:** results of actions, observable phenomena
Second	**Own sensed embodiment and performance:** one's own behavior, skills, patterns of action as sensed from within
Third	**Action Logics:** cognitive/affective structures, models, maps, meaning making style
Fourth	**Intentional attention:** presencing awareness, vision, intuition

Table 17.1 The deep four territories of experience

"myself," studying "ourselves," and studying "them") *in the midst of daily practice* (Chandler and Torbert 2003, Torbert 2000). In contrast to modern science—which offers a model of third-person research "on" "subjects" (who are, ironically treated as objects)—DAI is a model of research on oneself and with others that requires a high voluntary commitment by participants, as well as increasing mutuality and collaboration among them (McGuire, Palus, and Torbert 2007).

A third distinctive feature of DAI is that progress occurs, not just by incremental single-loop hypothesis or market testing, but also by double- and triple-loop learning and change, whereby the very assumptions of one's organization's, team's, or personal action-logic transforms (double-loop learning) or aligns across all four territories for a moment (triple-loop learning). When, during our personal, relational, and collective actions and inquiries, incongruities are found across the four territories of experience (e.g., an unintended result, an ineffective performance, a strategy that feels inconsistent with one's integrity, a lie, etc.), action inquiry gradually generates, in the first-, second-, and third-person human system, the capacity for these three distinct orders of change.

The fourth distinctive feature of DAI (the D in DAI) is the developmental theory used to map the evolution of the action logics through progressive forms of increasing complexity, differentiation, and integrity at the personal, team, organizational, and institutional scales (Torbert 2000a, 2000b). This theory hypothesizes a specific sequence of action-logics (Opportunist, Diplomat, Expert, Achiever, Individualist, Strategist, Alchemist, Ironist, Elder are the names of the personal action-logics) through which any human system can (but may not) transform, as it gradually gains the capacity to monitor all four territories of its activity and to develop greater congruity, integrity, and mutuality among them. Single-loop, incremental learning is practiced increasingly regularly as a person masters the Achiever action-logic. Double-loop, transformational learning is first explicitly recognized at the Individualist action-logic and becomes a touchstone of the Strategist action-logic. Triple-loop inquiry in-moments-of-action is increasingly practiced in everyday life at the Alchemist and Ironist action-logics (Torbert et al. 2004).

Overall, DAI theory and method strike a different balance from Wilber's Integral Theory and its AQAL model. DAI theory and method put primary emphasis on the four attentional and experiential territories of experience we can engage at each moment, rather than on four conceptual fields. DAI puts secondary emphasis on interweaving first-, second-, and third-person and practice, rather than bifurcating attention between the individual and the collective. And DAI puts tertiary emphasis on creating communities of living inquiry with single-, double-, and triple-loop learning at their heart, rather than communities of shared belief.

In attempting to assess empirically who acts regularly at which action-logic and how persons at a given action-logic fare in the rough and tumble world of everyday life, let us look next at the historical evolution from the Loevinger SCT instrument to the Harthill LDP and then at some of the field research using the Harthill LDP.

The Evolution from Loevinger's SCT to the LDP

Loevinger's Sentence Completion Test (SCT) is a language-based instrument, which delineates preconventional, conventional, and postconventional stages of self-development originally designed to address women's issues. An example of this gender focus is evident in a handful of items included in the original test such as "The worst thing about being a woman . . . ," "A good mother," and "For a woman a career is . . . " (Loevinger, Wessler, and Redmore 1970). This test includes 36 open-ended sentences that aim to measure a broad range of content: "moral development, interpersonal relations and conceptual complexity" (Loevinger 1998, 3) and correlate with eight stages of ego development (Loevinger and Wessler 1970, 186–87). Loevinger called her latest stage of ego development "Integrated self-actualizing identity" and suggested, quite peculiarly, that "because this stage is rare in most samples and there are major differences among qualified raters both as to the description of this level and application of the description in specific cases, under most circumstances it is best combined with the (prior) Autonomous stage" (7). She did not imagine, theorize, or research the possibility that integrity may be the fruit of developing a postcognitive, observing, listening attention that registers ongoing transformation across all four territories of experience and all action-logics. Thus, for example, she offers neither theory nor method for scoring this developmental stage.

Working in tandem for many years, Torbert (1987) and Cook-Greuter (1999) set out to modify the SCT in several ways. First, they sought to increase its face validity and usefulness as a work-related, leadership development instrument by creating and validating work-related stems, starting from Molloy (1978) "A good boss . . . " Harthill has continued and extended this work, so that the Harthill LDP now has nine work-related stems, including stems about power, time management, and teams that replace prior stems emphasizing gender or that had the lowest correlations to overall protocol ratings. This is a meaningful and unique contribution because it expands the scope of generalizability of the Harthill LDP test to better map management-oriented topics that are at the heart of developmental action-logic implementations in organizational contexts.

Another unique feature of the Harthill LDP is that the LDP has now twice refocused the Loevinger definitions and scoring manuals for the later action-logics. Cook-Greuter (1999) undertook the first revision. Herdman-Barker and Torbert have undertaken a second revision, aligning the scoring criteria more closely with the Alchemist and Ironist constructs found in Torbert's (1987, 1991, 2004) work and increasing the degree of difficulty of rating an overall profile as showing regular mastery of the Alchemist action-logic. One of the new criteria is whether the sentence completion "treats attention/conscience/consciousness as a process distinct from thinking and acting." For example in a response to the "I am" sentence stem we see nuances of this criterion:

> *"I am, therefore I think"—Descartes got it the wrong way round. Our thoughts and emotions are an inevitable aspect of our being—delightful, painful, exciting, infuriating—but can hide our inner depths from us.*

In the above example we are illustrating how one person differentiates the thinking territory from the more inclusive attention/conscience/consciousness territory.

Another new criterion of an Alchemist sentence completion is whether it conveys "passionate, artistic self-expression, *not* hyper-rational." For example, in the following example of a response to the "I am" sentence completion stem we illustrate what we mean by the passionate and not hyper-rational.

> I am . . . *a riot of differing roles and impulses held together in a loose alliance by something I call me, I am mostly happy and amazed, by any rational analysis my existence is such a staggering improbability that delighted laughter is the only possible response.*

In other words, our scoring criteria for the Alchemist are emerging from a theoretical perspective that treats it as critical to distinguish simultaneous experiential contact with the four territories of experience from sheer cognitive complexity and clever, fashionable, postmodern wordsmithing. We are looking for a weave between cognitive and relational strands and for a unique and glimmering oddness that shines through Alchemists we meet. In addition, based on our coaching, consulting, and workshop contacts with people scored at postconventional action-logics (to be described below), we have raised the number of Alchemist stems and the number of categories those stems must fall into for a total protocol to be scored early Alchemist or full Alchemist. All this, we believe, increases the construct validity of the Alchemist designation when it is used to summarize the center of gravity action-logic represented by a person's LDP.

Over the past twenty years of ongoing research and validity testing of the LDP in field conditions (e.g., executive coaching and organizational change projects), Harthill has shifted the focus from using the measure only for third-person adult development assessment to using it in the context of first- and second-person adult development and transformation as well. In doing so, Harthill reinvented the key names and descriptions of the Harthill LDP to become more descriptive and actionable and less evaluative and abstract than those associated with the Loevinger SCT. Thus, we reconstructed such terms as "from lower to higher stages" to "from earlier to later action-logics." We changed particular "stage" names from Conformist to Diplomat, from Self-aware to Expert, etc. Likewise, we fully rewrote and continue to amend the 20-plus pages of action-logic-related feedback that anyone taking the Harthill LDP today receives as part of the feedback package (along with introducing a 2/300-word commentary written for that particular protocol). All these changes make it feasible and effectual to use the instrument and to offer feedback on people's performance on it in action research situations. These changes seem to us an improvement in accuracy and objectivity. They also make it feasible for us to give individual participants and the institutions involved in the action research useful feedback. This feedback at times generates or supports double-loop, developmentally transformational learning, in addition to testing the external validity of the LDP. We will discuss this in greater detail below. To further establish the value inherent in using Harthill LDP for research and adult development tasks, we explore the reliability and validity of the LDP below.

Reliability Assessment of the LDP

To ensure the validity testing of this instrument, Harthill has invested in reliability assessment, which is an important first step in testing the psychometric value of the LDP, a prerequisite for measurement validity (Schutt 2004). To assess the reliability of the LDP, we conducted three reliability tests. First, we tested the extent to which the set of 36 stems can be aggregated to one score reflecting profile action logic. To do so we tested the *internal consistency* by calculating the Cronbach's alpha score for the 36 stems. Cronbach's alpha values range from zero to one, one indicates perfect internal consistency and zero indicates no internal consistency. In general Cronbach's alpha values higher than .8 are considered satisfactory as indicators of internal consistency (Schutt 2004). Our analysis of the internal consistency of Harthill LDP was built on

891 profiles and generated a Cronbach's alpha of .906, a relatively high value indicating good internal consistency that justifies the aggregation of stems into one score reflecting a single action logic.

Another dimension of reliability testing concerns the assessment of inter-rater reliability. The most recent reliability test between the two authorized Harthill scorers covers 805 profiles, with 13 levels of scoring (from Expert through Alchemist, with three possible levels at each action-logic [e.g., Early Achiever, Achiever, Late Achiever]). The test shows perfect matches for 72 percent of the profiles and agreement within one part-stage in another 22 percent. Hence, there is either perfect agreement or agreement within one part-stage in 94 percent of the cases. There was a difference of more than one action-logic between the two scorers in only one case of 805. Moreover, it is important to note that any difference in the two scores is adjudicated prior to sending respondents their feedback packages.

With regard to the question of whether the six novel business-related stems introduced to this version yield consistent scores, there has not yet been a definitive reliability test between scorers because scoring manuals for each stem are still being constructed. In the interim, however, we can examine whether the new sentence stems are adding to, or subtracting from, the overall reliability of the profile scores. Of course, one of the criteria for eliminating six prior sentence stems was that their scores showed among the lowest correlations with profile scores. The important finding here is that the six new stems show higher correlations with the final protocol ratings than the stems they replaced and, indeed, higher than the average correlations among all the remaining stems. Hence, short of a direct reliability test between the two scorers, the new stems seem to be adding to, not subtracting from, the reliability of total profile scores.

Validity Assessments of the LDP

What follows is a brief discussion of the value of the LDP based on several research studies with participants who were profiled using the LDP and were engaged in the practices of DAI. To further establish the psychometric value of the LDP tool we present key findings concerning *construct validity, criterion validity*, and *external validity* that emerged from the data.

Construct Validity Based on Factor Analysis

Recent efforts to establish measurement validity included a construct validity study of 891 profiles. This study compared a factor analysis among all 36 items in preconventional and conventional protocols (Achiever and earlier; n=830) with a factor analysis of all 36 items in protocols scored as postconventional (Individualist or later; n=61). Not only are the factors in the two sets different from one another, but the structure of the factors is different as well. For the earlier action-logics, stems load on eight factors, mostly each stem on a single factor (only two stems load on two factors). For the postconventional action-logics (Individualist and later), stems loaded on 11 factors, but loadings were not confined to one factor per stem. More than half (52%) of the stems loaded on two factors or more (nine stems loaded on two factors, seven loaded on three factors, and three loaded on four factors). These results illustrate the fundamental difference between the conventional and postconventional action-logics and also echo the adult developmental theoretical foundation on which the Harthill LDP is built. The limited but focused loadings presented by the conventional sample represent a relatively simple mental map, with Aristotelian-ly distinct, independent categories ("nothing can be both A and not-A"), as one would theoretically expect of action-logics up through the conventional. In contrast, more factors along with complex sets of loadings suggest a systems-oriented, inter-independent mental map for postconventionals. Such a movement between personal "independence" and "inter-independence" (McGuire, Palus, and Torbert 2007) occurring in the movement between the conventional and postconventional action-logics is predicted by all the currently-in-ongoing-revision developmental theories (Kegan 1982, 1994; Torbert 1999, 2004; Wilber 2000, 2006).

Criterion and External Validity of the LDP

As readers familiar with validity research on the Loevinger SCT know, there is an extensive body of internal validity research about it (Westenberg et al. 1998), but there is still very little research that shows: (1) whether people measured at different action-logics act differently in their everyday settings according to criterion variables (such as whether they seek feedback, or whether they successfully lead organizational transformation), and how generalizable that result is; or (2) what contexts reliably generate transformation of a person's action-logic. Our action research orientation integrates our own first-person efforts to use the theory to make our own leadership more timely, effective, and transformational and in our second-person teaching, coaching, and consulting efforts to help others become more effective. For these reasons most of our validity assessment efforts have been dedicated to generating and measuring the criterion validity and external validity of the LDP measure. What follows is a brief illustration of how we approach this criterion validity and external validity testing in the action of our research.

Offering feedback and coaching to people who take the measure has permitted one set of criterion validity tests. Developmental theory suggests that people at earlier action-logics are more likely to avoid feedback, especially of a double-loop nature that questions their current action-logic, whereas people at later action-logics will increasingly seek out such feedback and associated transformational opportunities. When we offered a purely voluntary opportunity for feedback on their measured action-logic to 281 adults who had taken the measure, we found that an increasing proportion of each later action-logic in fact chose to receive it. None of those measured Diplomat sought feedback, and only a small minority of those measured Expert did so. A bare majority of those measured Achiever sought feedback, whereas a large majority of those measured as Individualist or later did so. This rank order correlated perfectly with the theoretical prediction and thus confirmed the validity of the LDP in a powerful, new, unobtrusive way (Torbert 1994).

We have also found statistically significant differences that account for an unusually high proportion of the variance between conventional and postconventional CEOs in their success in leading organizational transformation over four-year periods, with the support of consultants (Rooke and Torbert 1998). Of the ten organizations studied, five were led by CEOs at the Strategist action-logic and five by conventional action-logic CEOs (two Achievers, two Experts, and one Diplomat). All five of the postconventional Strategist CEOs generated successful organizational transformation, but only two of the conventional CEOs succeeded. After the initial study was published, we reanalyzed the data, adding the consultants' action-logic scores (three measured as Strategists, one measured at Alchemist). The consultant measured as Alchemist had been the lead consultant in the two cases of conventional CEOs who generated successful organizational transformation, suggesting that (as the theory would predict) Alchemists are more effective at working with action-logic discrepancies than Strategists. The reanalysis showed that the combined action-logic scores of CEO and lead consultant in each case accounted for 59 percent of the variance (according to the Spearman Rank Order test, beyond the .01 level of significance) in whether the organization successfully transformed (Torbert and Associates 2004).

Why and how would leaders' action-logics be so critical to successful organizational transformation, especially given the paradox that their intent is to generate more empowerment, more initiative, and more distributed leadership throughout the organization? A qualitative reanalysis of the ten organization study suggests that later action-logic CEOs and consultants tend to engage increasingly often in an increasing proportion of 27 types of action research (first-, second-, and third-person research x first-, second-, and third-person practice x past, present, and future) (Chandler and Torbert 2003). This increase in, and intensification of, interpersonal and organizational collaborative inquiry (the name for the organizational action-logic analogous to Strategist) increases the likelihood of generating organizational transformation. In short, each later postconventional action-logic person or team engages in a more consistent inquiry process to determine what action is timely now, thus generating more instances of single-, double-, and triple-loop change in conversations, meetings, procedures, and strategies than does conventional action-logic leadership.

In general, what one sees in the transformational focus of the Harthill LDP is typical of developmental transformations from conventional action-logics to postconventional action-logics. First, the third-person, Expert, Empirical Positivist (the name for the scientific approach analogous to the Expert action-logic [Torbert 2000a and b]) scientific base of the original Loevinger SCT instrument is preserved and enhanced. Second, new, postconventional action-logics are conceived, defined, and operationalized through Cook-Greuter's, Herdman-Barker's, Rooke's, and Torbert's work. Third, the third-person measure is reoriented so that it can play a role in a wider field where the effort is to integrate it with practitioners' first- and second-person research and practices in the midst of daily work and life. Thus, the LDP orients toward a relatively-late-action-logic developmental action inquiry paradigm of social science, wherein a psychometric measure is developed as part of an integral system of mutually responsible action and inquiry in the present.

What follows are three illustrations of the implications of DAI in action, supported by the Harthill LDP. The illustrations are based on Herdman-Barker's coaching and consulting practice, and the research of McCallum and Nicolaides. In the illustrations that follow we bring special attention to three unique contributions of DAI in action: first, Herdman-Barker explores the role of fear in catalyzing or inhibiting evolution across the action-logics; second, McCallum attends to the phenomenon of fall-back, a temporary regression from optimal developmental capacity while in action under duress (do late action-logic leaders experience less fall-back than early action-logic leaders?); third, Nicolaides explores how postconventional action-logics relate to and benefit from the experience of ambiguity.

Fear and Transformation in Action: Expert and Strategist Leaders

Triangulating the findings of the LDP with a first-person estimate of one's own action-logic and a second-person action-logic estimate (typically derived from a group analysis of a difficult conversation [Rudolph, Taylor, and Foldy 2008]) supports "seeing behind the curtain"; this process helps us to detect patterns of errors or gaps in perception and, for all concerned, to see "mistakes" in our conceptualizing the world where we have assumed none have occurred. By adding first- and second-person inquiry to the LDP feedback we seek to "round out" the nature of the action-logic—gauging how conceptual complexity relates to in-action behavior; and we seek to bring the individual face to face with his or her reality. Once incongruities or obstacles to action come into personal consciousness, they can be transformed—if this is desired.

Since fear is often understood as a basis of distortions in perception, judgment, and action, we turn attention to its implications for the action-logics, in particular, the Expert and the Strategist.

Expert Action-Logic

Although, as stated above, we have found that persons are more likely to initiate a search for feedback and transformation at later action-logics, we have also found that, when coached by LDP-authorized, postconventional consultants, managers scored as early as the Expert action-logic can move beyond initial resistance and fear of feedback to the notion of transforming beyond their current approach. The quality of reflecting, with positive regard, upon the structure and implicit limitations of one's action-logic frequently ignites a realization of the very presence of a structure, thus validating the LDP's finding. In observing one's tendency to be subject to an event, double-loop insight erupts; for example, the nature of the Expert action-logic becomes visible and felt to the Expert. The fear holding the individual in its grasp is observed as the person feels safe to question his or her assumptions. Moreover, in workshops and coaching sessions, it is often the individuals profiling at this action logic who express heartfelt moments of realization and, it is about these individuals that we hear tales of change, redirection, and hope feeding back from the organization.

For example, Herdman-Barker worked with Michel (not his real name) two years ago, when he profiled at the Expert action-logic and was a Senior Vice President of Operations in the aviation industry. Initially, Michel expressed his resistance, in a workshop, to the LDP. Questioning its validity and reliability, he focused his attention on the technical accuracy of this third-person feedback, effectively distancing *himself* from the inquiry. "*Explain the statistics to me . . . . How do I have more scores in Diplomat but still profile at Expert . . . . I did this in a rush, how does that affect the rating?*" While such questions are helpful, there was an air of dismissal and defense around Michel. Whereas the rest of the group sat forward, intrigued by the framework, drawing on personal experiences, delving into the guts of the theory and engaging in robust inquiry, Michel, consistent with the Expert action-logic, first opposed and then withdrew.

Later, in a one-on-one conversation, it quickly emerged that he believed that it would not further him to go beyond a set way of working; an approach to management that he had held for many years. Eight years before, following an MBA and under the tutelage of a coach and mentor, Michel split away from old limiting habits by adopting a code, of sorts, that focused on personal mastery. It became, he believed, the mainstay of his success. By the time of the workshop, however, Michel was struggling to excel in an environment that required more than individual excellence. Although he was still improving incrementally (through single-loop feedback), he was standing still developmentally (i.e., in terms of double-loop change that could expand his capacity), and that, until this one-on-one conversation, had escaped his notice. The content of his code was irrelevant; its importance lay in its being a structure; an unquestioned and unquestioning way of relating to the world. Michel had stuck, for many years, to what he knew—preferring not to move outside of his comfort zone.

In the process of describing his approach and its limitation Michel began to make visible his assumptions and his fears—he quickly seized the moment: *"I've not changed my thinking in eight years . . . I've not questioned my approach despite new experiences. I've kept to a prototype . . . it didn't dawn on me to notice 'it.'"* Michel's way of organizing himself and his interrelationships moved on during the workshop; his manner of speaking began to invite feedback and he expressed personal vulnerability and doubt. One participant observed *"Most of us expected you to stand miles away from this type of discussion. I felt uncomfortable, at first, when you were so defensive . . . I thought, here we go, Michel's going to block this . . . I could not have predicted your reaction and your support."* Eighteen months later, Michel was acknowledged as one of the more collaborative and supportive leaders in the organization and a strong performer. To an observer, it would be difficult to imagine him otherwise.

Strategist Action-Logic

At first glance, many Strategists who operate in "middle" roles in large organizations and within the shadow of "top" conventional power seem to act very differently and very much like the Strategist CEOs from our earlier study, reported above, who successfully led organizational transformations. The mid-level Strategists often *begin* to seek more imaginative headroom by asking, "What is it that we do not currently envisage or experience?" They also may be less likely than conventional action-logic managers to shy away from the risks of uncertainty and befuddlement. In addition, they possess the capability to notice the system of which they are a part and, akin to comedians, are more able than earlier action-logics to touch the nerve of the organizational body. This, however, often becomes a mixed blessing as the organization develops an allergic reaction to their touch. Thus, when we listened deeply to their reflections and examined their spheres of influence, we observed that they also, in emotionally charged situations, became hamstrung in the midst of action. They displayed a hesitation in translating their insights to action, turning their backs on transformative intervention and quietly yielding to the organizational momentum. Their reactions were, perhaps, based on reason; conventional desires for acknowledgment, inclusion, community, etc. In our assessment, this preference for safety in decision making pointed to a tendency for Strategists to defend their world and to fear exclusion. This is consistent with both McCallum (2008) and Nicolaides' (2008) research described below. Strategists do not always succeed in generating spheres of mutual, creative power. They too may be brought to doing the bidding of fear.

Thus, while in general Experts tend to resist transformational change and Strategists tend to promote transformational change, we see that in certain environments (e.g., a skillful debriefing of the LDP by a coach) Experts will embrace such change, and in certain environments (e.g., a mid-level position in a large, conventional organization) Strategists will cease seeking such change. This illustrates how our first-, second-, and third-person inquiries in action continue to identify and make increasingly explicit, barriers such as fear that hold back the potential for action and transformation.

Fluidity of Development in Action: Exposing Fall-Back

While development is often understood as a process of moving from one stable action-logic to the next more open action-logic that transcends and includes the earlier action-logics, recent research indicates that development is actually a more fluid phenomenon, with more likelihood of falling back to earlier action-logics in action than has previously been imagined. Although theoretically the postconventional action-logics give persons or teams increasing capacity to influence their environment, in fact it appears that developmental capacity seems to fluctuate to some degree based on the context in which a person is situated and on the contingencies that they are facing in the moment. Indeed, using the LDP, observation, journals, and interviews with participants in a Tavistock-style group relations conference, McCallum (2008) has recently found that participants at all action-logics experienced "fall-back" periods during the stressful and ambiguous event, when they acted from earlier action-logics. The difference among the participants was that the later their action-logic, the quicker the recovery of one's center of gravity action-logic. For example, the one Alchemist in the study described being aware of the regression as it was occurring and was able to recover and learn from the fall-back within seconds.

Finding Potential in Ambiguity—Exploring the Later Stage Action-Logics

A final new study (Nicolaides 2008) helps us understand the relative context-dependence of Strategists by comparison to Alchemists. Nicolaides conducted in-depth interviews with nine persons scored at postconventional action-logics about their relationship with ambiguity. Her study included one Individualist, two Strategists, two Late Strategists/Early Alchemists, three Alchemists, and one Ironist. She found that, unlike people at conventional action-logics who tend to try to avoid ambiguity, all of her postconventional sample saw creative potential in ambiguity. But within this broad similarity, she found four distinctive responses to ambiguity: the Individualist *endured* it; the Strategists *tolerated* it; the Alchemists *surrendered* to it; and the Ironist *generated* it. More generally, Nicolaides found that the Individualist and the Strategists worked with ambiguity on particular occasions for particular ends; whereas, in a figure/ground shift, the Alchemists and the Ironist experienced ambiguity as the creative, ongoing element of all experience. This finding is consistent with the change from a primarily cognitive/structural approach to experience to a primarily attentional/spiritual approach in the shift from Strategist to Alchemist.

Conclusion

We hope that we have provided new glimpses into the experiential, action-oriented, and empirical aspects of developmental action inquiry. We also hope we have provided a useful introduction for fellow developmental researchers and practitioners to the evolution of the Harthill LDP, as well as to the many new first- and second-person ways of ongoingly testing the validity of this measure while using it to support transforming leaders and transforming cultures. How to develop communities of inquiry in real time that offer and digest single-, double-, and triple-loop learning can become a primary question for the social sciences and social arts over the next several centuries.

References

Argyris, C., R. Putnam, and D. Smith. 1985. *Action science.* San Francisco: Jossey-Bass.

Chandler, D., and W. Torbert. 2003. Transforming inquiry and action: By interweaving 27 flavors of action research. *Journal of Action Research* 1: 133–52.

Cook-Greuter, S. 1999. *Postautonomous ego development: A study of its nature and measurement.* Unpublished doctoral dissertation. Cambridge: Harvard Graduate School of Education.

Erikson, E. 1959. Identity and the life cycle. *Psychological Issues* I(1).

Fisher, D., and W. Torbert. 1991. Transforming managerial practice: Beyond the achiever stage. In *Research in organization change and development*, ed. R. Woodman and W. Pasmore, 143–73. Greenwich, CT: JAI Press.

———. 1995. *Personal and organizational transformations.* London: McGraw-Hill.

Foster, P., and W. Torbert. 2005. Leading through positive deviance: A developmental action learning perspective on institutional change. In *Positive psychology in business ethics and corporate responsibility*, ed. R. Giacalone, C. Jurkiewitz, and C. Dunn, 123–42). Greenwich, CT: Information Age Publishing.

Hauser, S. 1976. Loevinger's model and measure of ego development: A critical review. *Psychological Bulletin* 83: 928–55.

Hy, L., and J. Loevinger. 1996. *Measuring ego development*. Mahwah, NJ: Lawrence Erlbaum.

Kegan, R. 1994. *In over our heads*. Cambridge: Harvard University Press.

Loevinger, J. 1998. History of the Sentence Completion Test (SCT) for ego development. In *Technical foundations for measuring ego development: The Washington University Sentence Completion Test*, ed. J. Loevinger. Mahwah, NJ: Lawrence Erlbaum.

———, and R. Wessler. 1970. *Measuring ego development: 1. Construction and use of a sentence completion test*. San Francisco: Jossey-Bass.

Loevinger, J., R. Wessler, and C. Redmore. 1970. *Measuring ego development: 2. Scoring manual for women and girls*. San Francisco: Jossey-Bass.

McCallum, D. 2008. *Exploring the implications of a hidden diversity in group relations conference training: A developmental perspective*. Unpublished doctoral dissertation. New York: Columbia University, Teachers College.

McCauley, C., W. Drath, C. Palus, P. O'Connor, and B. Baker. 2006. The use of constructive-developmental theory to advance the understanding of leadership. *The Leadership Quarterly* 17: 634–53.

McGuire, J., C. Palus, and W. Torbert. 2007. Toward interdependent organizing and researching. In *Handbook of collaborative management research*, ed. A. Shani et al., 123–42). Thousand Oaks, CA: Sage.

Merron, K., D. Fisher, and W. Torbert. 1987. Meaning-making and management action. *Group and Organizational Studies* 12: 274–86.

Molloy, E. 1978. *Toward a new paradigm for the study of the person at work: An empirical extension of Loevinger's theory of ego development*. Unpublished doctoral dissertation. University of Dublin, Ireland.

Nicolaides, A. 2008. *Learning their way through ambiguity: Explorations of how nine developmentally mature adults make sense of ambiguity*. Unpublished doctoral dissertation. New York: Columbia University Teachers College.

Ouspensky, P. 1949. *In search of the miraculous*. New York: Harcourt, Brace, and World.

Reason, P., and H. Bradbury. 2007. *The SAGE handbook of action research: Participatory inquiry and practice*. London: Sage Publications.

Rooke, D., and W. Torbert. 1998. Organizational transformation as a function of CEOs' developmental stage. *Organization Development Journal* 16: 11–28.

Rudolph, J., S. Taylor, and E. Foldy. 2008. In *Handbook of Action Research*, ed. P. Reason and H. Bradbury. London: Sage.

Scharmer, O. 2007. *Theory U: Leading from the future as it emerges*. Cambridge MA: The Society for Oganizational Learning.

Schumacher, E. 1974. *A guide for the perplexed*. London: Jonathan Cape.

Senge, P., O. Scharmer, J. Jaworski, and B. Flowers. 2004. *Presence: Human purpose and the field of the future*. Cambridge MA: The Society for Organizational Learning.

Schutt, R. K. 2004. *Investigating the social world, the process and practice of research*. 4th ed. London: Pine Forge Press.

Shani, A., S. Mohrman, W. Pasmore, B. Stymne, and N. Adler. 2007. *Handbook of collaborative management research*. Los Angeles: Sage.

Torbert, W. 1972. *Learning from experience: Toward consciousness.* New York: Columbia University Press.

———. 1976. *Creating a community of inquiry.* London: Wiley Interscience.

———. 1987. *Managing the corporate dream.* Homewood, IL: Dow Jones-Irwin.

———. 1989. Leading organizational transformation. In *Research in organizational change and development,* ed. R. Woodman and W. Pasmore, 83–116). Greenwich, CT: Jai Press.

———. 1991. *The power of balance: Transforming self, society, and scientific inquiry.* Thousand Oaks, CA: Sage.

———. 1994. Cultivating post-formal development: higher stages and contrasting interventions. In *Transcendence and mature thought in adulthood,* ed. M. Miller and S. Cook-Greuter, 181–203). Lanham, MD: Rowman and Littlefield.

———. 2000a. A developmental approach to social science: A model for analyzing Charles Alexander's scientific contributions. *Journal of Adult Development* 7: 255–67.

———. 2000b. Transforming social science: Integrating quantitative, qualitative, and action research. In *Transforming social inquiry, transforming social action,* ed. F. Sherman and W. Torbert, 67–92). Boston: Kluwer Academic Publishers.

———, and D. Fisher. 1992. Autobiographical awareness as a catalyst for managerial and organizational development. *Management Education and Development* 23: 184–98.

———, and Associates. 2004. *Action inquiry: The secret of timely and transforming leadership.* San Francisco: Berrett-Koehler.

Trungpa, C. 1970. *Meditation in action.* Boston: Shambhala.

Westenberg, M., P. Jonckheer, P. Treffers, and M. Drewes. 1998. *Personality development: Theoretical, empirical, and clinical investigations of Loevinger's conception of ego development.* Mahwah, NJ: Lawrence Erlbaum.

Wilber, K. 2000. *A theory of everything.* Boston: Shambhala.

AFTERWORD

The Dawn of an Integral Age

Ken Wilber

A volume like this is essential to the ongoing development of Integral Theory as a distinct academic discipline with real-world import. It provides a context for the debate, clarification, exploration, and critical analysis needed for the health and growth of a new field. While my own writings have contributed much to the development and articulation of Integral Theory, I am thrilled to see so many qualified voices (as presented in this volume) joining the conversation. Each of you reading this book is part of this conversation and your involvement in the development and application of Integral Theory is invaluable. The next decade is going to be an exciting one for Integral Theory as it continues to build inroads into different professional and academic contexts signaling the arrival of a more inclusive world.

It does indeed look like we are moving from an age of what sociologist Jeffrey Alexander called *microanalysis* to what he called *An Integral Age*. The former denies big pictures (except its own), focuses on individual narratives and meaning-making, and believes all knowledge is just a social construction, a fashion like clothes or songs. The Integral Age believes that "everybody is right" if you have a big enough picture, and thus spends its time on elucidating and outlining those bigger, more comprehensive, systemic, and integral pictures. The Integral Age thus "transcends and includes" the results of the age of microanalysis, having intentionally included those results in its bigger pictures.

This also means that we are moving from attempted solutions to the world's problems that are piecemeal and fragmented to solutions that are more comprehensive and inclusive, and thus actually effective. "Everybody's right" means that every major approach to a particular problem or issue has some degree of truth to it, and what is required is including them all in a truly integral fashion. What you have seen in the previous pages of this book are examples of exactly that: larger, more comprehensive, and truly integral maps, frameworks, theories, and practices across dozens and dozens of major issues, showing how such integral methods go a long way toward not only solving the major problems in the particular field, but knitting together and uniting the various branches of the field itself, often for the first time in history.

This Integral Age is arriving none too soon. In fact, it seems exactly timed to help solve the world's major issues—from ecological to economic to cultural—because all of these, for the first time in history, have just recently become global in scope, and can only be addressed with equally global approaches. Take perhaps the three outstanding world problems at this time: environmental, economic, and cultural. For the first time in history, ecological issues have spread from local ecospheres and now threaten the entire biosphere itself. Nothing less than worldcentric or global methodologies are even capable of grasping the nature and extent of these issues, let alone solving them.

Likewise with economic problems. The world has recently faced a global economic meltdown, and only truly global, systemic, or worldcentric economic theories and practices will be able to address these issues. Such a worldcentric economic theory would take into account the interior beliefs and values of individuals and cultures as well as their exterior actions and behaviors (which alone are included in today's flatland economics).

Similarly with culture and the worldwide culture wars, which are behind everything from terrorism to traditional wars, all increasing in their frequency and intensity. What is required to even understand the genesis of these culture wars is a global framework that is comprehensive enough to include all of the major cultural worldviews—including their growth and their development. Only an Integral framework can come anywhere close to such a task.

But that is exactly what the Integral approach has done, in all of those areas—from environmental to economic to cultural, to mention just a few. A truly Integral Methodological Pluralism has been able to map everything from forms of local knowledge to universal values and systems, and do so in a multicultural fashion not objected to by rational holders of the various cultures themselves.

This Integral framework is what has indeed led to the beginnings of an Integral Age. In all of human history, there have been perhaps only five major epochs: archaic, magic (egocentric), mythic (traditional), rational (modern), and pluralistic (postmodern). The Integral Age looks to be the sixth major epoch to evolve in human evolution, and the results of its appearance do indeed appear to be epochal. Not only can many problems be solved that previously seemed intractable, but the knowledge fields themselves can be brought together in a coherent and systemic way, shining a brighter light on the nature, function, and extent of human knowledge itself.

Moreover, this Integral framework includes not only "horizontal" states and structures but "vertical" states and structures, too, thus including not only normal human growth and evolution but the higher and even highest states and structures of human development—and thus including items such as spiritual enlightenment and awakening. Because one of the first things that becomes obvious in looking over a complete or comprehensive view of human being-in-the-world, is that there are at least two different types of "spiritual" or "religious" engagement, one of which is traditional, exoteric, or dogmatic (and involves beliefs about the ego and its immortality), the other of which is transpersonal, esoteric, or superconscious (and involves the transcendence of the ego in timeless eternity). This gives us a tremendously enriched cartography of spiritual states and stages, and allows a much finer understanding of exactly what it is that people are doing when they say they are involved in "religious" behavior. These two meanings could not be more different, and understanding them alone makes an integral view worth its admission price.

But that is just the beginning of the rich results that are headed our way in the coming Integral Age. The first Integral Theory Conference was held in 2008, and the contents of this volume are the results of some of the best presentations delivered there—and a rich collection it is indeed! This event was truly historic—an international gathering of nearly 500 integral scholar-practitioners from more than 50 different disciplines. Now JFKU and I-I are preparing for the next conference ITC 2010, which will build on the momentum of ITC 2008 and continue to showcase the amazing integral work being done around the globe. Such a showing is a real testament to the need and success of Integral approaches in our complex world. I am very encouraged at the variety of integral applications that are emerging around the world—this conference and the resulting volume in your hands being a wonderful sampling of that work. But such an extraordinary variety is just the tip of the iceberg headed our way, as every single aspect of our work, play, education, medicine, economics, and self-understanding becomes profoundly transformed and changed in numerous significant ways. This volume is simply one selection of many of these changes. Sit back and know that many, many more are on the way. I encourage you to take an active role in contributing to and developing Integral Theory for the emerging Integral Age. May you put this book down dog-eared and filled with margin notes and feel renewed and inspired in your own integral commitments to foster a better global community.

Contributors

Michele Chase, PhD, John F. Kennedy University: directs the Master's Program in Holistic Health Education at John F. Kennedy University. Her PhD in English opens many possibilities for applying her knowledge of language and communicative contexts to the field of health promotion and in this integrally informed program. She is currently working on a publication in which she looks at health-related words, metaphors, and meanings. Michele says, "I am a poet who went searching for wholeness and found health."

Susanne Cook-Greuter, EdD, Cook-Greuter and Associates LLC: is internationally known as the leading expert in ego development theory and measurement. She does ongoing research and development on the Sentence Completion Test called MAP. Susanne leads trainings for coaches and consultants in the Leadership Maturity Framework and offers a certification track for MAP-scorers. She collaborates with other integral consultancies in bringing a developmental perspective and an integral approach to business into corporations and executive teams worldwide. More information is available at www.cook-greuter.com.

Mark Edwards, PhD, University of Western Australia: holds a Masters degree in developmental psychology and a PhD in organization theory. He currently teaches business ethics and organizational change at the Business School, University of Western Australia, and has recently developed a course on metatheoretical studies for the John F. Kennedy University in California. His academic publications have been in the areas of organizational change, futures studies, leadership, management, and integral metatheory. Before his academic career, Mark worked with people with disabilities for more than 20 years.

Sean Esbjörn-Hargens, PhD, John F. Kennedy University: is an associate professor and founding chair of the Department of Integral Theory. He is founding director of the Integral Research Center, founding executive editor of the *Journal of Integral Theory and Practice,* and he is co-founder/co-organizer of the biennial Integral Theory Conference. Sean is a leading scholar-practitioner in Integral Theory with articles appearing in numerous academic journals. He is the co-editor of *The Simple Feeling of Being* and *Integral Education*. He is co-author of *Integral Ecology*. He is as an Integral Coach and consultant through Rhizome Designs (www.rhizomedesigns.org). He lives in Northern California among redwoods with his wife and two daughters.

Vanessa D. Fisher, Independent Scholar: is a published writer and poet currently residing in Vancouver, BC, Canada. Vanessa's writing has been published in both mainstream magazines and academic journals. Vanessa presented at the First Biennial Integral Theory Conference in August 2008 and received an award for her scholarship in the field of feminist aesthetics. She is also currently co-editing the first anthology dedicated to applying Integral Theory to the field of sex, gender, and sexuality research.

Charles I. Flores, PhD, John F. Kennedy University: is adjunct professor at JFK University, and has taught for the Sri Aurobindo Ashram at the University of Tomorrow, and other universities. He is also an associate managing editor of the *International Journal of Transpersonal Studies*. He has been Coordinator of Auroville International USA. A practicing National Certified Counselor in mental health and Master Addiction Counselor, he has worked on issues of diversity, social activism, and integral psychology for fifteen years. His recent scholarly work focuses on Evolutionary Spiritual Activism.

Mark D. Forman, PhD, John F. Kennedy University: is an assistant professor in the Integral Studies Department at JFK University, as well as co-founder and co-lead organizer of the Integral Theory Conference. Mark is a clinical psychologist and is author of *A Guide to Integral Psychotherapy: Complexity, Integration, and Spirituality in Practice* (2010, SUNY Press). Mark is currently in private practice in Northern California, and has been a student of Advaita Vedanta and non-dual Kashmir Shaivism for the past 18 years.

Clint Fuhs, Doctoral Candidate, Fielding Graduate University: is the founder and CEO of Core Integral, Inc. and adjunct faculty for John F. Kennedy University and Fielding Graduate University Integral Studies programs. Clint is a senior student of Ken Wilber, former operations and curriculum manager for Integral Institute, Inc. and Integral Life, Inc., and he is completing his doctoral studies on the development of human perspective-taking capacity at Fielding.

Elaine Herdman-Barker, Independent Consultant: is a Senior Advisor to Harthill, UK, a faculty member of De Baak Management Centre in the Netherlands and an independent consultant. Building on years as senior scorer of the *Harthill Leadership Development Profile*, as an executive coach, lecturer, and research associate of Bill Torbert and David Rooke, she is developing the Leadership Development Framework to help identify and support high potential leaders across action logics.

Elliott Ingersoll, PhD, Cleveland State University: is a psychologist, licensed clinical counselor, and life coach in private practice in Ohio. He is Professor of Counseling at Cleveland State University, a trainer in the Integral Psychotherapy program and co-director of the Integral Psychology Center. He is the among the first SCTi-MAP scorers certified in the United States by ego development expert Dr. Susanne Cook-Greuter. Elliott also performs original FreeThought Folk Music across Northeast Ohio musing about Gods, Goddesses, evolution, and cookies.

Reut Livne-Tarandach, Doctoral Candidate, Boston College: earned her MSc in Organizational Studies from the Technion, Israeli Institute of Technology. She is currently a PhD candidate in the organization studies department of the Carroll School of Management at Boston College. Her primary research interests are creativity, learning, and organizational change. Her dissertation work is devoted to the intersection of organizational change and creativity where she explored how creative episodes are utilized by change agent groups to ignite, invigorate, and revive change vitality. She has published in numerous academic journals.

Randy Martin, PhD, Indiana University of Pennsylvania: is a professor of Criminology at Indiana University of Pennsylvania. He has been involved with Integral Institute since its inception and has been intimately involved in the development and delivery of II's collaborative graduate programs. He has worked extensively in applying the Integral model in criminology and has published several articles in that area.

David McCallum, SJ, EdD Le Moyne College: is a professor of Leadership in the Management Division at Le Moyne College in Syracuse, N.Y. His research and practice focuses on the intersections of adult development, leadership, and spiritual growth. He gives retreats, facilitates leadership development, and is serving as assistant to the president for strategic development. Currently, he is helping found a program for "Contemplative Leadership in Action" in New York.

Sam Mickey, Doctoral Candidate, California Institute of Integral Studies: is an adjunct professor in the Theology and Religious Studies department at the

University of San Francisco, and an adjunct professor in the Engaged Humanities program at Pacifica Graduate Institute. He teaches a variety of classes related to ethical and spiritual perspectives on ecology. He is also the Web content manager and newsletter editor for the Forum on Religion and Ecology (http://yale.edu/religionandecology). Sam is a PhD candidate on the Integral Ecology track in the Philosophy, Cosmology, and Consciousness program at the California Institute of Integral Studies.

Tom Murray, EdD, Independent Scholar: has been consulting, researching, publishing, and leading workshops in the areas including integral philosophy, applied ethics, cognitive tools, online communities, adaptive learning environments, and knowledge engineering since 1985. He is an associate editor at *Integral Review* journal, has held positions as visiting/adjunct faculty member at the University of Massachusetts and Hampshire College. He is currently working as an independent scholar and consultant at Perspegrity Solutions. See www.tommurray.us, www.perspegrity.org.

Aliki Nicolaides, EdD, Columbia University Teachers College: Dr. Aliki Nicolaides is an assistant professor at the University of Georgia, Athens in the department of Lifelong Learning, Administration, and Policy. Dr. Nicolaides joins the faculty at UGA to grow and develop the program in adult learning, adult development. She serves as Adjunct Assistant Professor in the program of adult learning and leadership, at Teachers College Columbia University where she teaches graduate courses in Strategic Learning, Adult Development for Leadership, and Self Awareness in Action through Developmental Action Inquiry.

Karen O'Brien, PhD, University of Oslo: is a professor in the Department of Sociology and Human Geography at the University of Oslo, Norway, and chair of the Global Environmental Change and Human Security (GECHS) project. She was a lead author of the adaptation chapter in the IPCC Fourth Assessment Report, and has written and edited numerous books on the human dimensions of environmental change. Her current research uses an integral framework for understanding adaptation to climate change.

Michael Schwartz, PhD, Augusta State University: received his PhD in art history from Columbia University and is currently professor of History and Philosophy of Art at Augusta State University, GA. He is co-founder of the Comparative and Continental Philosophy Circle (www.comcontphilosophy. org); co-editor of *The Gift of Logos: Essays in Continental Philosophy* (2010); and Aesthetic Editor at Integral Life (www.integrallife.com).

Theresa Silow, PhD, John F. Kennedy University: directs the Somatic Psychology Program at JFK University. She received her PhD in Somatic Studies from The Ohio State University. Her dissertation research focused on the function and meaning of sensation—particularly as it contributes to the experience of "self" and "no-self." She currently participates in a UCSF conducted and NIH funded research project that seeks to develop a comprehensive measure of body awareness. Theresa explores the body as the experiential matrix for psychological organization and spiritual awakening.

Zachary Stein, Doctoral Candidate, Harvard Graduate School of Education: received his BA in Philosophy from Hampshire College and an EdM in Mind, Brain, and Education from Harvard University's Graduate School of Education. Zak has received many awards at Harvard including an Intellectual Contribution Award and a Faculty Tribute Fellowship. He has numerous academic publications, presentations, and editorships. He has been senior Analyst at the Developmental Testing Service since 2004, where he has worked to deploy metatheoretical models and developmental assessments in real world contexts. His central areas of research involve philosophy, developmental psychology, and psychometrics.

William R. Torbert, PhD, Boston College: is a Professor Emeritus of Leadership at Boston College who has authored many books and articles, including *The Power of Balance*: *Transforming Self, Society and Scientific Inquiry* (1991) and *Action Inquiry: The Secret of Timely, Transforming Leadership* (2004). Winner in 2008 of the Organization Behavior Teaching and Management Society's Distinguished Educator Award, and in 2010 of the Western Avademy of Management Outstanding Scholar Award, he currently partners with Harthill Consulting UK, serves on the board of Trillium Asset Management, and offers by-invitation Alchemists Workshops.

Roger Walsh, MD, PhD, University of California, Irvine: is professor of Psychiatry, Philosophy, and Anthropology, as well as adjunct professor of Religious Studies. His publications include the books *Paths Beyond Ego*, *Essential Spirituality: The Seven Central Practices*, *The World of Shamanism*, and *Higher Wisdom: Eminent Elders Explore The Continuing Impact of Psychedelics*. His research and writings have received more than two dozen national and international awards and honors, while his teaching has received one national and six university awards. In addition to his academic work he has been a student, researcher, and teacher of contemplative practices for three decades.

Ken Wilber, Independent Scholar: at age 56, Ken became the first philosopher-psychologist to have his collected works published while still alive. With two dozen books translated into some 30 foreign languages, he is the most widely translated academic writer in the United States. Ken is the internationally acknowledged originator of modern Integral Theory, the founder of Integral Institute, and co-founder of Integral Life.

Michael E. Zimmerman, PhD, University of Colorado, Boulder: is professor of Philosophy at the University of Colorado, Boulder. Author of four books, as well as many articles and book chapters, Zimmerman's research areas include environmental philosophy, Heidegger, Nietzsche, posthumanism, and Integral Theory. In 2009, Zimmerman and Sean Esbjörn-Hargens published *Integral Ecology: Uniting Multiple Perspectives on the Natural World*.

Index

Made in the USA
San Bernardino, CA
08 November 2016